# Lepanto 1571

# Lepanto 1571

## The Madonna's Victory

Nic Fields

Pen & Sword
**MARITIME**

First published in Great Britain in 2020
and republished in this format in 2023 by
Pen & Sword Maritime
An imprint of
Pen & Sword Books Ltd
Yorkshire – Philadelphia

ISBN 978 1 39900 286 8

A CIP catalogue record for this book is available from the British Library

Typeset by Mac Style
Printed in the UK by CPI Group (UK) Ltd, Croydon, CR0 4YY.

MIX
Paper | Supporting
responsible forestry
FSC
www.fsc.org    FSC® C013604

Pen & Sword Books Limited incorporates the imprints of Atlas,
Archaeology, Aviation, Discovery, Family History, Fiction, History,
Maritime, Military, Military Classics, Politics, Select, Transport,
True Crime, Air World, Frontline Publishing, Leo Cooper,
Remember When, Seaforth Publishing, The Praetorian Press,
Wharncliffe Local History, Wharncliffe Transport, Wharncliffe True
Crime, White Owl and After the Battle.

For a complete list of Pen & Sword titles please contact

PEN & SWORD BOOKS LIMITED
47 Church Street, Barnsley, South Yorkshire, S70 2AS, England
E-mail: enquiries@pen-and-sword.co.uk
Website: www.pen-and-sword.co.uk
or
PEN AND SWORD BOOKS
1950 Lawrence Rd, Havertown, PA 19083, USA
E-mail: Uspen-and-sword@casematepublishers.com
Website: www.penandswordbooks.com

# Contents

For Matt,

*Mission accomplie, mon pote.*
*Merci bien.*

# List of Plates

1. Portrait of the Ottoman sultan Selīm II (r. 1566–74). Selīm died just three years after the capture of Cyprus and the battle of Lepanto, fracturing his skull by slipping in his bath – ironically, while drunk on wine. An unlikely candidate to the Ottoman throne, he was to succeed through the intrigues of his mother, Süleymān's favourite wife, the supremely beautiful Hürrem Sultan, known in the west as Roxelane. Although he was in favour of continuing his father's aggressive policy of territorial expansion, Selīm left the running of most military and naval matters to his advisers, particularly his grand vizier Sokollu Mehmed Paşa. It was Sokollu Mehmed who was responsible for a peace treaty (1568) with the Holy Roman Emperor, Maximilian II, and a treaty of capitulations (1569) with Charles IX of France. (*Belli değil / Wikimedia Commons / Public Domain*)

2. Bronze statue of Miguel de Cervantes by the Mallorcan sculptor Jaume Mir Ramis (1915–2012), Cultural Park of Cervantes, Old Port, Naupaktos. Put up in 2000, the inscription on the statue's plinth (written in Spanish and Greek) reads: *Miguel de Cervantes Saavedra / 1547–1616 / Spanish soldier / genius of letters / honoured by humanity / heroically wounded at the battle of Lepanto 1571*. He was only twenty-four years of age when he lived the dramatic experience of Lepanto. In our own day his fame rests rather on his wit, whose ridicule gave the final blow to the mediaeval courtliness, rather than the bravery he displayed on that fateful day. Amongst other wounds, he lost in this battle the use of his left arm; his right hand was destined to gain him another kind of immortality. His fame was destined to outshine even that of the Christian commanders at Lepanto. (*Dimkoa / CC0 / Public Domain*)

3. Martinengo Bastion (left) and San Luca Bastion (right), northwest corner of Famagusta (Gazimağusa), viewed from the south. The

Venetian walls of Famagusta average a height of fifteen metres, thickness of eight metres, and are studded with fifteen bastions and pierced by five gateways. The Venetians had gradually raised them atop the existing Lusignan mediaeval fortifications between 1489 and 1540, according to the latest western European precepts of engineering and ballistics. Its low profile and massive construction was built slightly higher than the opposing counterscarp to present a small target to cannon fire while its arrow shape was designed to prevent areas of shelter at its base and protect the ditch and bastions on either side. The Martinengo Bastion was the work of Giovanni Girolamo Sanmicheli, nephew of the famous fortification architect, Michele Sanmicheli of Verona. He arrived in Famagusta in 1550 to oversee the improvement of its fortifications. After approximately nine years of construction the bastion was completed. (*Gerhard Haubold/Wikimedia Commons/CC-BY-SA-2.5*)

4. Table altarpiece of Pius V by the Venetian artist Bartolemeo Litterini (1669–1748), Capella di San Pio V, La basilica dei Santi Giovanni e Paolo, Venice. For those of you familiar with Chesterton's poem 'Lepanto', Pius V will always be the pope who "called the kings of Christendom for swords about the Cross" (stanza 1, line 10). A fitting tribute, for Pius V was the prime mover in the founding of the Holy League, an alliance of Catholic nations, republics and city states against the Ottoman empire. The pope is said to have burst into tears when news of the victory at Lepanto reached him: it is attested in his canonisation that he miraculously knew when the battle was won, he himself being in Rome at the time. He was to pass away seven months later, and the league he had worked tirelessly to form would follow suit not long afterwards. Pius V was beatified on 1 May 1672, and canonised on 22 May 1712. (*Didier Descouens/Wikimedia Commons/CC-BY-SA-4.0*)

5. Milanese half-armour (Wien, Kunsthistorisches Museum, inv. A 1048/49) belonging to Don Juan de Austria. Meticulously handcrafted and made-to-measure, this panoply is of polished steel and iron, gilded and etched with figurative and floral patterns. The panoply consists of bullet-proof breast and back plates complete with a gorget and helmet. The latter is a heavy steel morion cabasset,

with its distinctive comb and sweeping sides that come to a point front and back. Don Juan also wore a pouldron, vambrace, cubitière, and gauntlet to protect his sword arm; he would receive a wound in a thigh when boarding the Ottoman flagship, the *Sultana*. (*Vert/ Wikimedia Commons/CC0-1.0/Public Domain*)

6. Detail of the head, monument to Don Juan de Austria on Zieroldsplatz, Regensburg, Bavaria. This is a copy of the monumental sculpture (originally gilded) erected in Messina, Sicily, on the initiative of the local senate in 1572 to honour the victor of Lepanto. The copy was erected in Regensburg, Don Juan's birthplace, in 1978, the fourth centenary of his death. Don Juan, the natural son of Charles V, proved to Christendom at Lepanto that the Ottomans were not invincible upon the tide-less seas of the Mediterranean. On that fateful day, it was by the prestige of his royal name and his zeal that he was able him to impose a temporary unity of purpose on the quarrelling and jealous commanders of the Holy League and to form the several national contingents into an effective fighting fleet. (*Dr Bernd Gross/ Wikimedia Commons/CC-BY-SA-3.0*)

7. In 1971, to commemorate the 400th anniversary of Lepanto, a full-sized replica of *La Real*, the Spanish galley and flagship of Don Juan de Austria, was built and displayed in the Museu Marítim de Barcelona, where it can be viewed today. *La Real* was sixty metres in length with a beam of 6.2 metres at her widest point, was equipped with two masts, and weighed 237 tons when empty. With seventy oars (thirty-five banks), *La Real* was powered by the bone and muscle of 420 oarsmen at Lepanto and, in addition, her fighting complement centred around no less than 400 élite harquebusiers. She also carried an impressive bow battery of five guns – a *cañón*, which was flanked by two *media culebrinas* and two *sacres*. Fighting elements aside, *La Real* seems to have resembled Cleopatra's pleasure barge in the splendour of her appointments, as the stern interior was adorned with gilded and brightly painted sculptures, woodcarvings and bas-reliefs. (*Richard Mortel/Wikimedia Commons/CC-BY-SA-2.0*)

8. Wrought iron *pierrier* (Musée militaire vaudois, Morges). With their swivel mount, this type of naval piece could be pointed easily in any direction, and being a breech loader could be quickly reloaded

using spare chambers. These were mug-shaped devices filled with gunpowder and projectiles (solid shot or scattershot). With its high rate of fire – several chambers could be prepared in advance – the *pierrier* was horribly effective at close range, making it the weapon of choice on warships during boarding actions. However, it did have one disadvantage: it leaked and lost powder around the chamber. (*Hmaag/Wikimedia Commons/CC-BY-SA-3.0*)

9. Two bronze 5.5-pounder *sacres* (Madrid, Museo Naval), recovered from the wreck of the Spanish galleon *San Diego*, which was sunk off Fortune Island, the Philippines, on 14 December 1600. The barrel of a saker was approximately 2.9 metres long, had a calibre of 8.26 centimetres, and weighted approximately 860 kilograms. It was named after the Saker Falcon (*Falco cherrug*), a raptor native to the open grasslands of Eurasia. As a rule, on a Spanish galley at Lepanto, the inner flanking pieces of the bow battery would have been a pair of *sacres*. The Spanish *sacre*, Venetian *sacro* and Ottoman *sayka topu*, while roughly equivalent to each other, were equivalent not to the English saker but to the English demi-culverin. (*Dorieo/Wikimedia Commons/CC-BY-SA-4.0*)

10. Half-figure portrait of Sebastiano Veniero (or Venier) at Lepanto (Wien, Kunsthistorisches Museum, inv. GG_32), oil on canvas by the Venetian artist Jacopo Robusti, better known as Tintoretto (†1594), dated to 1578. At the time of the sitting, Veniero was the 86th doge of Venice (r. 1577–8), but at Lepanto he had been *capitano generale da mar* of the Venetian fleet. In this portrait the grizzled warrior – he was already seventy-five-years-old at Lepanto – stares at us from beneath a thicket of white eyebrows with a look of suppressed fury. As well as the baton of his office, the irascible Veniero wears the mantle of crimson silk with which the Republic of Venice invested its generals and admirals. The battle, in which he fought wearing carpet slippers and wielding a crossbow, is illustrated in the background of the portrait. (*Biddatenbank/Wikimedia Commons/Public Domain*)

11. Pen and black ink drawing (London, British Museum, inv. Pp, 1.19) of a seated janissary by Gentile Bellini (†1507), one of the earliest illustrations of a member of this élite corps, dated to 1480 when the Venetian artist was in Constantinople. The previous year Bellini had

been despatched to the Ottoman capital by the Republic of Venice to paint the portrait of the autocrat of Constantinople, Mehmed II *Fatih*: the result is the renowned oil painting that now hangs in the National Gallery in London. Bellini returned piled high with gifts and honours, including the title of *bey*, 'lord'. Bellini's janissary wears an inner and outer kaftan, and the characteristic sleeve-cap, or *zarcola*, of white felt. He is armed with a composite recurve bow and a *kılıç*. (*Hohum/Wikimedia Commons/Public Domain*) western Turkey. We are looking out across the Aegean Sea towards Greece and over the Ionian Sea where the boot of Italy and the eastern coastline of Sicily are just visible. In the centre of the image is the Gulf of Corinth with the funnelled-shaped Gulf of Patras beyond and the Ionian islands of Kephalonia, Ithaka and Zakynthos (It. Zante) nestled at its entrance: in this sheet of water was fought the battle of Lepanto. (*Image courtesy of the Earth Science and Remote Scanning Unit, NASA Johnson Space Center*)

15. The town and port of Naupaktos, the Gulf of Corinth, and the Panachaiko massif in the Peloponnesos, viewed from the Venetian fortress. At the time of Lepanto the town and fortress were held by the Ottomans, and had been since 1499. Naupaktos would be recaptured by the Venetians in 1687 to be handed back in 1699 to the Ottomans, who would lose the place for good during the Greek war of independence. Situated just within the entrance to the Gulf of Corinth, it was the best anchorage on the northern coast of the gulf. It was in the safe waters of the harbour, protected by the guns of the fortress above, that the Ottoman fleet anchored on the eve of Lepanto. (*Conudrum / Wikimedia Commons / Public Domain*)

16. Polychrome panel (Bilbao, Museo Vasco) from a coffered ceiling, Casa-Torre de Arana, Bilbao. Part of a scene depicting a 16th-century naval battle, we can see two galleys about to come to grips. On the prow of the galley to the left, a harquebusier discharges his harquebus at a soldier armed with half-pike and shield. He appears to be wearing a helmet too. Spanish and Italian armour and weapons (Toledo and Milan standing out as manufacturing centres of excellence), particularly firearms, had much to do with the Christian success at Lepanto. Even a harquebusier could be equipped with a plate corselet and morion, though this would have been munition quality armour, known in England as *almain rivet*. This mass produced armour was often heavier and made of lower quality metal than fine armour for commanders. (© *Esther Carré*)

17. Spanish rapier (Bilbao, Museo Maritimo Ria de Bilbao, inv. 0242), with characteristic complex, sweeping hilt, second half 16th century. Spanish rapiers, *espadas roperas de lazo*, had a relatively long and slender double-edged blade of 2.5 centimetres or less in

width, were rarely less than 104 centimetres in length, and ended in a sharply pointed tip. Rapiers were unmistakably designed for point-play. Toledo was known as one of the foremost centres for the manufacturing of arms and armour in Europe, and a fine Toledan steel blade was a valuable weapon indeed. The finely made rapier did not pass inspection until it could bend in a half-circle and survive a full-force impact with a steel helmet. (© *Esther Carré*)

18. Half plate armour (Bilbao, Museo Maritimo Ria de Bilbao), consisting of a heavy corselet complete with gorget, pouldrons, vambraces, cubitières, gauntlets and short tassets, as well as a morion cabasset. Infantry armour such as this example could be 'russetted' or enamelled black to prevent rusting, though that worn by Spanish officers are often said to have been lavishly decorated and subjected to blueing, silvering and gilding. (© *Esther Carré*)

19. *The Battle of Lepanto of 1571*, oil on canvas (Greenwich, National Maritime Museum, inv. BHC0261) by an unknown near-contemporary artist. Some of the galleys are labelled, including that of Gianandrea Doria (IL GIO.ANDREA.DORIA), the commander of the Genoese contingent, and the flagship of the Genoese Negroni family (LA CAPITANA DENEGRNI). In the right foreground is the flagship of the Christian renegade Uluç Ali, inscribed OCHIALLRE.DALGIERIFUGE.DALLABATTA. GLIA (Ochiali, King of Algiers flies from the battle). Flags on the Christian side include: the Lion of Venice, the red Saint George cross of Genoa, the gold and silver standards of the Papal States, and a standard of Christ on the Cross alongside the Habsburg double-headed eagle on *La Real* of Don Juan de Austria. The *Sultana* of Müezzinzāde Ali Paşa flies a flag with three crescents. The galley of Murād Re'īs flies a horizontal three-striped ensign with a single crescent on the central bar directly above the stern of Uluç Ali's. (*Madame Grinderche/Wikimedia Commons/Public Domain*)

20. *The Allegory of the Battle of Lepanto* (c. 1572), oil on canvass (Venezia, Gallerie dell'Accademia) by Paolo Veronese (1528–88). The lower half of the painting shows the events of the naval battle. In the top half, above a curtain of cloud, a female personification of Venice is presented to the Blessed Virgin Mary, with Saint Roch de

Montpellier (dressed as a pilgrim), Saint Peter (with keys), Santa Giustina di Padova (with the sword of her martyrdom), San Marco (with lion), and a group of angels (one of which is hurling flaming arrows at the Ottoman fleet) implore the Virgin to grant victory to the Christian fleet. After San Marco, Santa Giustina is a second patroness of Venice, her feast day being 7 October, while the tomb of Saint Roch is in Venice. As a whole, the painting represents the Christian victory as divine intervention. (*Eugene a/Wikimedia Commons/Public Domain*)

# Abbreviations

| | |
|---|---|
| Ar. | Arabic |
| bk(s). | book(s) |
| *c.* | circa |
| cap. | *capitulus* (chapter) |
| cf. | *confer* (compare) |
| ch. | chapter |
| cod. | codex |
| col(l). | column(s) |
| Cz. | Czech |
| ed(s). | editor(s), edited (by) |
| f(f). | *folio/foliis* (and following) |
| *fl.* | *floruit* (flourished) |
| fol(s). | folio(s) |
| Fr. | French |
| fr(s). | fragment(s) |
| Ger. | German |
| Gr. | Greek |
| ibid. | *ibidem* (in the same work) |
| It. | Italian |
| L | Latin |
| l(l). | line(s) |
| leg. | *legajo* (dossier) |
| MS(S) | manuscript(s) |
| n. | note |
| NIV | New International Version |
| no. | number |
| OF | Old Frankish |
| op. cit. | *opere citato* (in the work cited) |
| p(p). | page(s) |

| | |
|---|---|
| pl. | plural |
| r. | recto |
| rev. | revised (by) |
| rev. edn. | revised edition |
| s.a. | *sub anno* |
| sec. | section |
| sg. | singular |
| sic | *sic erat scriptum* (thus it was written) |
| Sp. | Spanish |
| Tk. | Turkish |
| trans(s). | translator(s) |
| v. | verso |
| viz. | *videlicet* (that is to say) |
| vol(s). | volume(s) |
| † | died |

# A note on Turkish words and transliteration

I have chosen to use the modern Turkish orthography of words such as *ağa* and *paşa*, even though these have entered the English language as agha and pasha. I humbly beg non-specialist readers and those unfamiliar with the Turkish language for forgiveness but feel that this choice, which is indeed confined to a few words, makes for a more consistent typescript.

All letters have one and only one sound, a factor which makes the language easy to read and pronounce. No letters are silent. There are no genders and no articles. Vowels have their short continental value as in French, Italian or German. The following is a quick guide to pronunciation:

*c* like *j* in *jolly*: e.g. *cami* (mosque) = *jahmy*
*ç* like *ch* in *chess*: e.g. *çeşme* (fountain) = *cheshme*
*g* is always hard as in *give*, never soft as in *gem*
*ğ* is almost silent; it tends to lengthen the preceding vowel
*i, İ* like *i* in *interest*
*ı, I* like *e* in *women*
*ö* as in German, similar to French *eu* in *bleu*
*s* is always unvoiced as in *sit*, never like *z*
*ş* like *sh* in *shambles*: e.g. *çeşme* = *cheshme*
*ü* as in German, similar to the French *u* in *tu*

In effect, modern Turkish is the language of the Ottoman period purged of the vocabulary and idioms that it had acquired from Arabic and Persian.

# Lepanto Prelude

In the heart of the island standeth NICOSIA, sometime the regall and late metropoliticall cityie thereof and in the East end thereof Famagusta, sometime called TAMARTA, a famous, rich citie, the chiefe and onely port of that most pleasant island.

Richard Knolles, *The generall historie of the Turkes*, vol. 1, p. 263

In his *Histoire des voyages de Scarmentado*, 'History of the Travels of Scarmentado', published in 1756 but set in the years 1615 to 1620, Voltaire's young hero and narrator, born in Crete and sent aged fifteen to Rome by his parents, sets out on a Grand Tour of Europe in search of truth, but instead finds only violence caused by religious and political discord. In Paris he is invited to dine on a morsel of roasted flesh hacked from the fallen favourite of Louis XIII (r. 1610–43); in London he notes that a number of "pious Catholics, for the good of the church" had recently tried to blow up "the king, the royal family and the whole Parliament" (the Gunpowder Plot). Next, Scarmentado visits The Hague, where he sees a venerable old man being led out for public execution. It is Johan van Oldenbarnevelt (1547–1619), chief minister of the Dutch Republic for forty years. Puzzled, the narrator enquires of a bystander if the old man is guilty of treason:

> "He has done much worse," replied a preacher in a black cloak, "he believed that men may be saved by good works as well as by faith. You must be sensible", adds he, "that there must be severe laws to suppress such scandalous and horrid blasphemies."

Disgusted, our hero moves on to Seville, where he is imprisoned for six weeks and fined by the Inquisition for a careless word overheard while forty sinners are burnt at the stake for heresy. He counts himself lucky to escape to the relative peace and harmony of the Ottoman empire.[1]

Bigotry and empathy are strange bedfellows at the best of times, and we can see the extent to which a biting satirist could vilify the importation into ancient Rome of alien culture and custom, especially those of the Hellenised east:

> For years now Syrian
> Orontes has poured its shit into our native Tiber –
> Its lingo and manners, its flutes, its outlandish harps
> With their traverse strings, its native tambourines,
> And the whores who hang out round the racecourse.
>
> Umbricius, in Juvenal *Satura* 3.62–5

A loyal Roman citizen, Umbricius can no longer endure the city of his birth and thus is leaving Rome for a better life in the countryside. For the benefit of the audience, he speaks his mind in an extended monologue, listing all the reasons why he has been driven from Rome.

Racial intolerance is an insidious thread that runs throughout human history. In this the British empire was no better (or worse) than that of Rome, which after all perpetuated many conquests equal in brutality to those of Rome. Like the Roman empire long before, it was large, highly successful, and it suppressed the identities of the peoples it conquered. There is no moral equivalence implied by comparison with the Roman empire.

On the other hand, it was usual to think in terms of invasion and colonisation as the sole begetters of change, more usually characterised as 'progress'. Take, for instance, FitzRoy Richard Somerset, 4th Baron Raglan (1885–1964), soldier, author, amateur anthropologist and great-grandson of the one-armed veteran of Waterloo, who could say without fear of contradiction at the time "that savages never invent or discover anything?"[2] Then again, he said the same of Muslims.[3] Or, again, the forthright views of Cecil John Rhodes (1853–1902), the British imperialist and industrialist who founded Rhodesia (Zimbabwe) with the help of the Maxim machinegun:

In the struggle for existence the White race had unquestionably come out on top … And as He is manifestly fashioning the English-speaking race as the chosen instrument by which He will bring in a state of society based on Justice, Liberty and Peace, He must obviously wish me to do what I can to give as much scope and power to that race as possible.[4]

Later, as the prime minister and virtual dictator of the Cape Colony (1890–6), the 'Colonial Colossus' would speak of British dominion of the 'Dark Continent' from the Cape to Cairo and build the Cape to Cairo railway.[5]

Empires naturally create a culture of pride and pomp, and foster the rhetoric of racial superiority. Perikles, Virgil, and Kipling all talked and wrote of the grandeur of imperial domain. Perikles could showcase his Parthenon from the extracted tribute of empire; Virgil's eternal epic promotes the imperial destiny of Rome as captor and civiliser; the Ottoman sultan, as caliph, sincerely thought Europe should submit to the will of Allah; and Queen Victoria could proudly boast that the sun never set on British shores.

According to an old Spanish proverb, "History is a common meadow in which everyone can make hay".[6] It has also long been a battleground for the perpetuation of nationalist myths and political attempts to reshape the past. The battle of Lepanto would quickly become an important item of national and religious propaganda, a perennial reminder of the force of Catholic unity and the heroism of the individual Christian participants. Celebrated in much of Catholic Europe at the time, it was commemorated by Italian imperialists and Spanish nationalists in the 20th century, and adopted, more recently still, in debates about the 'clash of civilisations'.

On 20 May 1939, General Francisco Franco (1892–1975) attended the solemn *Te Deum* service held at the church of Santa Bárbara to celebrate the triumph of the Nationalists in the Spanish Civil War (hailed as *la cruzada*). Surrounded by the sacred symbols of Spain's Catholic past, he presented his 'sword of victory' to Cardinal Isidro Gomá, archbishop of Toledo and primate of Spain (in office 1933–40), under the blue damask embroidered banner bearing the image of Christ Crucified that Pius V had blessed and had been presented to Don Juan de Austria. Franco believed his destiny was to become the equal of the omnipotent Philip II of Spain. He also sought somehow to reincarnate the mediaevál military hero Rodrigo Díaz de Vivar (1043–99), variously known as *el Campeador* or El Cid. Predictably, hanging near the battle banner of Don Juan was the battle banner of El Cid. Conceivably Franco fancied himself as the spirit of El Cid once more made flesh. Miguel de Cervantes of *Don Quixote* fame – much more on him presently – would muse that, although "there can be no doubt that he [El Cid] existed, and certainly none about Bernardo del Carpio, but I think it exceedingly doubtful they ever performed the deeds people say they did".[7]

It is not exactly new, obviously, but a tyrant does not need to traffic in hard facts or supply supporting substantiation. He expects his beliefs and desires to be enough. One of Franco's strongest beliefs of Spanish traditionaists was that Catholic Spain was a nation that had saved Christendom from the threat of expansionist Islam at the time of El Cid and liberals, 'reds' and separatists, now allotted the rôle of contemporary infidels, in the days of General Franco. Paradoxically, El Caudillo, as Franco dubbed himself, had relied on Moorish mercenaries to launch his *cruzada* against the heirs of *La Reconquista*, a paradox not lost on the Republicans, who lambasted Franco for bringing Moors back to Spain. It was ugly, and it was about to get still uglier. Was it not Churchill who praised Franco as a "gallant Christian gentleman"?[8] And was it not H.G. Wells who corrected him: "murderous little Christian gentleman"? In this particular matter, perhaps Franco was the equal of Philip II.

Even today people like falling back on national myths of greatness, an almost insane nostalgia for a lost empire, as if the old empire really was a wonderful thing, as if it brought nothing but civilisation to the rest of the 'uncivilised' world. We live in a time in which the dark past lies heavy on a dangerous present. But we need to be careful; empire, along with colonialism and slavery, are national evils. Equally, it does not mean we have to subscribe to the 'great man' theory of history – the outdated theory that claims events are moulded not by ordinary folk, social movements and economic processes, but by key individuals who stamp their will on the world through force of personality.

This has a depressing present-day ring to it. Yet any total, all consuming creed will first separate 'us' from 'them', and then separate 'them' from the rest of the human family. A new generation of politicians, political parties and media personalities openly talk the language of race war, sucking their rhetorical purpose from xenophobia and Islamophobia, but for the most part, in their pursuit of vandalistic end-times ethnonationalism they eschewed the culture of violence associated with genuine racist populism. On the whole, they tend to be men who adhere to the aforementioned view that history is made by great men and are enough of a narcissist to count themselves among them. What is more, in their pursuit of an imagined national greatness the present can not be interpreted without immediately searching for parallels in history. Yet such are the times in which we live.

## To the gates of Vienna

It is fair to say that at a stretch the 'golden age' of the efforts and achievements of the Ottoman Turks was from the fall of the Byzantine capital of Constantinople – Istanbul as it is now – in 1453 to their second (failed) siege of the Holy Roman capital of Vienna in 1683. Just one and a half decades before an Ottoman army had successfully prosecuted the siege of Candia (Herakleion) on the island of Crete between 1667 and 1669. Against Vienna itself the Ottomans earned praise from European observers for the efficacy and proficient engineering of their siege works.[9] Their second siege of Vienna may have been unsuccessful, but in the Mediterranean Ottoman galleys still posed a serious threat, and their Barbary allies could be relied upon to give support when naval conflict broke out.[10]

Even so, the 16th century was certainly the best of this 'golden age', though one could argue that only under the celebrated Süleymān I *Kānūnı* (r. 1520–66), the Lawgiver to his subjects,[11] or the Magnificent as this brilliant and ambitious sovereign was known in Christendom, was this true. For Süleymān lived up to the official image of the ideal sultan as a head of state, namely that of a warrior who personally led his troops into battle.[12] An only son, he had become sultan when he was twenty-six years of age, and was to die, on active service, as an old warrior of seventy-two. In a letter sent to the Habsburg ruler Ferdinand I, the king of Bohemia and Hungary (r. 1526–64) and Holy Roman Emperor (r. 1556–64), on

27 November 1562, Süleymān introduced himself, hyperbolically, as "I, Lord of the Orient from the land of Tsin [China] to the extremity of Africa...". The empire he ruled did not in fact reach as far as China, or even to the Atlantic coast of North Africa. Nevertheless, other Muslim powers could not match the power of the Ottoman sultan, controlling as he did an empire stretching from Yemen at the mouth of the Red Sea almost to the Straits of Gibraltar. Süleymān during his long reign had taken the field at the head of an army on thirteen military expeditions,[13] and added Aden, Algiers, Baghdad, Budapest and Rhodes to his already vast domains.

All this said, we have to be cautious not to give too much weight to the off cited 'long and protracted decline' of the Ottoman empire and its armed forces, which remained surprisingly effective through the early 18th century, even though usually the sultans no longer led their troops to battle. It was with such forces that the Ottomans not only nearly captured the capital of the Holy Roman Empire in 1683, but also defeated Peter the Great, Tsar of Russia (r. 1682–1725), in 1711, defeated the Venetians and recaptured the Morea (Peloponnesos) in 1715–17, and both retook Belgrade from Austria and scored victories against both Austria and Russia in the war of 1736–9, but this is not really the topic of this present book. For our journey takes us to the Mediterranean at a time when it was viewed as the frontline in what was a long, shifting struggle between rival colonialisms, Christian and Muslim.

## Two Tribes Go to War

Two decades or so ago, it would have been unimaginable for us to be talking about a current conflict between Christianity and Islam. Yet here we are, revisiting the plot of the Christian-Muslim tragedy, the past harrying the present. Apparently, or so it seems, the best stories are the ones that manage to explain a complicated cosmos in a clear, compelling way. All the questions have easily digestible answers, and all these bite-sized answers are black and white. Today we witness the rise of Christian fundamentalism in the United States of America armed with high ambitions and unscrupulous aims to 'restore the natural order'. At the same time, Muslim conservative circles in the Republic of Turkey have done a *volte-face* by turning back with pride towards the Ottoman past. Though the Ottoman defeat at Lepanto has yet to make an appearance in schoolbooks, the Turkish navy (Tk. *Türk Donanması*) does celebrate as its own day the anniversary of the Ottoman victory at Préveza. On the other hand, those Turks who still honour the memory of Kemâl Mustafā Atatürk and his deeds summarily dismiss the Ottoman empire from a position of Olympian distain as backward and inferior, and those who yearn for its revival as out of touch with reality. These are just a couple of the many bad fruits of 9/11.

In some ways, these opposing sides are acting as one would expect socio-political factions to act in a national debate, seizing the best rhetorical arguments at their disposal and running with them. On that note, it has been argued that Selīm II (r. 1566–74), Süleymān's sottish son and successor, preferred wine bottles to winning battles. And not just any wine bottles, so the rumour continues. For the sultan had a profound passion for the heady wines of Cyprus, but whether or not this was symptomatic of the Ottoman designs on Cyprus, a Venetian outpost since 1489 floating in the middle of enemy territory, we can probably ignore this tale as a case of Christian 'fake news'. After all, not only did the island's harbours and bays provide safe havens for Christian corsairs and pirates, but the island was also within striking distance of the Anatolian coast. Every time the Ottomans went on campaign, troops and ships had to be left behind against a potential attack launched from the island. With regard to the Porte's geo-strategic goals, Cyprus was a thorn in the empire's flesh.

On a more personal level, it is probable that Selīm II felt the genuine need for an Ottoman victory over Christian forces to redeem his father's failure at the siege of Malta in 1565. The new sultan wanted also, like his father, to go down in history as one who had added fresh territories to the Ottoman empire's already vast dominions. Others, however, took a more disparaging view.

In Christian sources the sultan, who skulks in his seraglio, often appears as a tyrannical, cunning, unwarlike and dissolute character; he was universally known as 'Selim the Sot' for his rather un-Islamic drinking habits. The Englishman Richard Knolles (†1610), who wrote the first book written in English (as opposed to Latin) on the subject

of the political and military aspects of the Ottoman empire, describes
Selīm as, unlike his father, "wholly given to wantonness and excess; so
that he never went to Wars himself, but performed them altogether by his
Lieutenants".[14] Throughout his massive masterpiece – a bestselling and
much reprinted book – it is evident that Knolles wanted to acquaint his
Christian readers with their mortal enemy, the enemy of their faith: in his
introduction 'To the Christian Reader', the author invariably paints the
Ottomans as 'infidels', 'heretics', 'princes of darkness', and not just an
enemy to the country they attack and invariably occupy but a "common
enemy of Christianity".[15] Similarly, the Venetian *bailo*, or ambassador, to
Constantinople,[16] Andrea Badoer, has left us a rather unflattering pen
portrait of the new sultan, confirming for his bosses back home Selīm's
nastiest indulgences:

> The Sultan Selim is fifty-three years of age, small in size and weak
> of health. This is due to his intemperance, with women as with
> wine, drinking great quantities of the latter. He is very ugly indeed,
> with all his limbs out of proportion, according to everyone more a
> monster than a man. His face is burnt and ruined, from too much
> wine and the spirit [*rakı*, perhaps] he drinks to digest... Not only
> is he ignorant about arts, but also can barely recognise written
> characters. He is uncouth in his speech, unversed in state affairs
> and lazy, leaving all the great weight of government to the grand
> vizier [viz. Sokollu Mehmed Paşa]. He is miserly, sordid, lecherous,
> unrestrained and reckless in all the decisions he makes ... What he
> enjoys doing most is drinking and eating, something he does for
> days on end: I am told that His Majesty sometimes spends two or
> three days constantly at the table.[17]

This character assassination is probably pure invention, as it magnifies
Selīm into a poster boy for avarice and alcoholism, though we cannot
know for sure. As Sir Henry Wotton (1568–1639), England's witty
and cynical ambassador to Venice, memorably described international
diplomacy in 1604: "An ambassador is an honest man sent to lie abroad
for the good of his country".[18] True or not, this particular diplomatic
report from their man in Constantinople must have been sweet music to

the collective ears of the Venetian authorities, for it draws an eye-popping cartoon of an evil infidel autocrat for them to point to as a fitting example of what is currently wrong with the Sublime Porte.

Though it is true Selīm delegated most government business to Sokollu Mehmed Paşa, in his defence it should be understood that his father had never bothered to tutor him properly in the art of statecraft for the simple reason Selīm, as the third son, was destined to be honourably strangled, not become sultan. In the Ottoman Turkish tradition, there was not a law regulating the matter of inheritance. According to this, when a ruler was deceased, each of his descendants had the right to claim for the throne since the crown would be granted by God. Thus, civil war was justifiable and the outcome of the war was accepted since it was considered the will of God. However, since the days of Mehmed II *Fatih* (r. 1444–6, 1451–81) the cruel law of fratricide had prevailed, whereby a new sultan, on his succession, put to death all his brothers to avoid the possibility of dispute or civil war; the loss of a prince or two was less to be deplored than that of a province, and indeed the Ottoman empire was noticeably free of internal strife. Although such competition was not missing from Selīm's youth, by 1559 all of his brothers – and thus all possible rivals for the throne – were dead: Mehmed died in 1544, Mustafā and Mehmed Bāyezīd were executed in 1553 and 1559, respectively. On the death of Selīm II in 1574, his son Murād III would consign five younger brothers to be strangled by deaf-mutes with a silken bow-string, the most honourable form of death. On his death in 1595, his son Mehmed III did the same to no less than nineteen of his brothers and half-brothers.

If the plain truth be told, Selīm II was far from being slothful, uneducated and coarse, for he was a skilled archer, an accomplished poet and a discerning patron of the arts, worthwhile talents expected of an Ottoman sultan. Indeed, in Ottoman history he is rightly remembered as *Sari* Selīm, 'Selīm the Sallow'; due to his yellowish complexion or perhaps to the blond hair inherited from his mother Hürrem Sultan.[19] Ottoman sources also promote a more nuanced view of the sultan's statecraft. With *Sari* Selīm it was not simply a situation of rule and ruin.

Still, nothing in the world is so unpleasant, so disconcerting, so utterly abhorred, as the plain truth. Precisely. "A lie can travel halfway round the world while the truth is putting on its shoes", is a quote habitually attributed to Mark Twain.[20] In our world of social media, let us make that all the way round the world while the truth is still searching for its socks. For a lie sufficiently repeated comes to be credited by its very mutterer. And meanwhile, the calumny has sped from tongue to tongue, from text to text, gathering matter as it goes. The truth, we submit, is a deal less simple.

Though not a patch on his fighting father, who had reminded him that, for the Prophet, wine was "the mother of all vices",[21] and allegedly had one of his drinking pals executed, throughout his reign Selīm maintained a pro-*status quo* position and avoided direct conflict with the Sublime Porte's two *main* rivals, the Habsburgs and the Safavids. Venice, on the other hand, was an entirely different matter. As a matter of fact, the sultan had previous designs regarding Cyprus. While he was still the crown prince (his brothers were already liquidated), he commissioned spies to obtain intelligence on topographical details, fortifications, and garrisons of the island from members of its Orthodox community during a revolt of discontented Greek Cypriots in 1562. In Selīm's eyes, it would appear, Cyprus had to be Ottoman, by treaty or by force.

The Venetians had only a shaky legal title to Cyprus. In 1191 the Christian island had been seized by the Anglo-Norman crusader king Richard Cœur de Lion (whose betrothed, Berengaria of Navarre had been insulted by the Byzantine prince Isaakos Doukas Komnenos, the self-proclaimed emperor of the island). This was the opening event of his short crusade, hardly a blow against the infidel. Richard sold the island a few months later for 100,000 *bezants* to the Knights Templar; in May 1192 the Order passed Cyprus on to Guy de Lusignan (r. 1192–4), erstwhile sovereign of the Kingdom of Jerusalem (r. 1186–92). It continued in this French family till the death of Jean II de Chypre in 1458. Jean left two children, a legitimate daughter, Charlotte (Gk. Καϱλόττα), and her brother Jacques *le bâtard*, the son of Jean by his mistress Mariette de Patras. Charlotte de Lusignan married, first, Jean de Coimbra (†1457), and, secondly, Louis de Genève (†1482). He was crowned in the cathedral of Nicosia on 7 October 1459 as the king of Cyprus, Jerusalem and Armenia. Jacques, with the aid of a band of Egyptian Mamlūks conquered the kingdom and drove Charlotte and Louis out of it.

Although united by a common Catholic faith, the Genoese and the Venetians had little more than contempt for one another. The always fierce, occasionally bloody, competition between Genoa and Venice for the valuable Levantine trade routes ensured the two would forever remain rivals. And so it was that the Genoese, who had a trading post at Famagusta, took the part of Charlotte: the Venetians supported the side of Jacques. Marco Cornaro, a Venetian settled in Cyprus, assisted Jacques with money to conquer the island, and gave him his niece, Caterina Cornaro, in marriage, with a handsome dowry. She had previously been declared the daughter of the Republic of San Marco and duly crowned as queen. Jacques by this act became the son-in-law of the Republic. The marriage took place in 1473, and a child was born in the same year, which was regarded as king of Cyprus under the name of Jacques III de Chypre. Father and infant son died mysteriously within a year of each other – of Venetian poison, it was rumoured – leaving Caterina to reign precariously in her own right. That was until the Venetians persuaded her to abdicate in 1489; she was given a sop in the town and hinterland of Asolo in the Vento, where she continued to keep a court of some splendour until her death in 1510.

Cyprus was still, however, under the suzerainty of the Mamlūk sultans of Egypt, and Venice had to pay an annual tribute to them, which was devoted to Mecca and Medina. With the Ottoman conquest of Egypt, the tribute continued to be paid to Constantinople.

Aside from the regular Venetian tribute, by Selīm's day this of course was all in the distant past. But most recently, by letting the galleys of the Knights Hospitaller take shelter in Cypriot ports after their raids against Muslim shipping, the Venetians had been giving needless provocation to the Sublime Porte.[22] We shall say much more about the Hospitallers in due course.


## A seaport in Cyprus

The Ottoman invasion of Cyprus came after four decades of peace with Venice, as Selīm II broke, despite Sokollu Mehmed Paşa robustly advising the contrary, with his father's policy. It is mainly for this reason that Selīm has had, to put it mildly, a bad press from contemporary

Christian commentators. Take for example the neo-Latin poem *Victoria Naupactiaca*, written in 1572 by Giovanni Baptista Arcucci, a jurist and theologian of Naples:

> The Venetian fathers possessed it [viz. Cyprus] for many years, but when Süleymān came to the end of his life and stopped breathing the sweet air, the more brutal Selīm took control of both the state and the sceptre; soon he wishes to extend the confines of his kingdom, and he breaks the treaties that his valiant father had once struck with the courageous Venetians, swearing they would never be dishonoured.[23]

The Ottomans commenced their hostilities by landing a large force on 2 July 1570. This was on the island's southern shore at Salines, the port of Larnaka, famous for the (second) tomb of Lazarus of Bethany, 'the friend of Christ' who was raised from the dead four days after his burial,[24] fled Iudaea and was appointed the first bishop of Kition (Larnaka). The defenders of Cyprus were outnumbered – by about seven-to-one by all reckoning – but then again, the defenders of Malta five years earlier had faced stiffer odds. Being stretched thin everywhere, the Venetians had pulled their available forces into Nicosia, the capital of the island, and the key seaport of Famagusta.

Nicosia was attacked first, falling in spite of a gallant resistance to a massive assault on 9 September, and by the end of the month the Ottomans had overran the whole island bar Famagusta. Situated on the east coast, the walled seaport of Famagusta held out against the Ottomans for ten and a half months in one of the celebrated sieges of the age. Before the Ottoman army showed up under the ramparts of Famagusta, the Venetian *patrizio*, patrician, Marc'Antonio Bragadin, *capitano generale* of the city, received an epistle from Lala Kara Mustafā Paşa, Ottoman land commander, demanding surrender. It was accompanied by the head of the *lugotenente generale del regno*, Niccolò Dandolo, on a platter; the Venetian governor of Cyprus had proved to be a man of small resource and less courage, irresolute, without energy, and too proud to accept advice and counsel from his inferiors. Not so Bragadin, who in reply wrote:

I have seen your letter. I have also received the head of the lieutenant general of the kingdom, and I tell you herewith that even if you have easily taken the city of Nicosia, with your own blood you will have to purchase this city, which with God's help will give you so much to do you will always regret having encamped here.[25]

Full of confidence after their recent successes, the Ottomans held their fleet ready to counter a possible relief, and established lines of circumvallation around Famagusta, digging zigzag trenches to approach the land walls, raising earthen forts at various intervals to serve as gunnery positions so as to harass the defenders, and opening up mining operations so as to undermine the defences. Mustafā Paşa was hoping the seaport would fall quickly. In this he was to be disappointed.

Jacques Le Saige (†1549), a Flemish silk merchant of Douai who had visited Famagusta back in 1518, then made the following observations concerning the city:

Sunday, August 28, the night of the beheading of S. John (the Baptist), we anchored our vessel in the harbour of Famagosse. We were greatly astonished to see so strong a city. For vessels cannot come nigh by reason of the rocks, and the walls too are terribly thick, and there are fosses lined with masonry along the town. Hence you may gather that one might attack it from without yet be unable to injure that city ... The walls of Famagosse are all freshly repaired, and there is a very grand boulevard. In brief it is an impregnable city if it had a sufficient garrison. But there are only 800 soldiers in the pay of the Venetians, for they have the whole land of Cyprus under them.[26]

Fortification was an expensive business – the 16th century built fortresses as earlier centuries had built cathedrals. In 1570 Famagusta (called *Famagosto* by the Venetians) was still a good post, with a front covered in part by the sea, but its fortifications had not been completely brought up to date like those of Nicosia. Between 1567 and 1568 the renowned military architect Giulio Savorgnan had completely rebuilt the city walls in the shape of a star, providing Nicosia with a 4.5-metre-thick circuit studded with eleven state-of-the-art bastions and pierced by just three heavily fortified gateways. Even so, Savorgnan considered the work of little use since Nicosia could not be relieved from the sea and stood in a valley surrounded by hills. Still, Niccolò Dandolo was confident that the city's state-of-the-art fortifications would more than compensate for any deficiency, be it a matter of topography or men and matériel, the latter deriving from his men's inexperience and lack of harquebuses.

There again, however, the siege of the capital was a comparatively short affair of seven weeks (22 July to 9 September 1570), whereas that of Famagusta (as we have noted) was to be a very lengthy affair (15 September 1570 to 1 August 1571). The seaport, the last foothold of the Venetians in the island, was gallantly defended against fearful odds by the Bragadin, ably supported by Astorre Baglione di Perugia, and the Venetian patricians, Lorenzo Tiepolo, Antonio Querini, and Luigi Martinengo. Every advantage had been taken to secure Famagusta against the foe; but months of fighting, watching, and fasting had exhausted the garrison, and their stores of ammunition and provisions were almost finished. Famagusta finally fell to a combination of mining operations and six major assaults, which cost the Ottomans some 52,000 men, including the eldest son of Mustafā Paşa. Contemporary sources estimate between 140,000 and 170,000 iron cannonballs were shot off during the seventy-five day siege.[27]

There had been one relief attempt, however, and a successful one at that. Assembling a force of four large merchantmen loaded with 1,600 fighting men plus stores and munitions for the beleaguered garrison and an escort of thirteen galleys, Marc'Antonio Quirini, *capitano del Golfo* the preceding year, set sail from Candia on 16 January 1571. Because of their different sailing abilities, the merchantmen and the galleys proceeded autonomously, carrying out an apparently predetermined rendezvous off Famagusta seven days later. At this point Quirini displayed sound tactical judgement. He sent the four merchantmen in toward the harbour first, followed at a considerable distance astern by the galleys. This presented the seven Ottoman galleys of the blockading force with Hobson's choice. They could let the supply vessels through uncontested – an obviously unaccepted course of action – or they could expose themselves to a flank attack by Quirini's galleys in attempting to stop them. Three of them were sunk outright, almost certainly by the bow guns of Quirini's galleys, and the rest forced up against the beach under cover of the Ottoman land forces. This gave Quirini a free hand. He was able to capture a sizeable prize; a large oared transport, known as a *maona*, loaded with munitions and a crew of 300, and to destroy the remaining four Ottoman galleys on the beach while his four supply ships unloaded. Mission accomplished, the combined force left Famagusta on 16 February and was back in Candia five days later. To save face (and his head) Ali Paşa, the naval commander, exaggerated the size of Quirini's force in his report to Constantinople, saying it had comprised of twenty-two galleys, and sought to excuse his defeat on the grounds that he "had no reserves of rowers and was short of bread".[28]

In the ceremonial of war, the Ottomans still followed the traditions of their ancestors. A supreme field commander, *serasker*, with the untrammelled power of life and death and entrusted with the sacred war banner, could not be countermanded except by the sultan himself.[29] Not that the *serasker* was a completely free agent, for failure would bring disgrace, dismissal or even death. When news of failure in the field reached Constantinople heads could roll – literally. The Ottoman sultan was not inclined to forgive those who had failed. In the Ottoman tradition the sultan would share success, as in this current campaign for Cyprus, but would disclaim responsibility for any failure and act accordingly.

At Famagusta the victor, Mustafā Paşa – by all accounts a nasty piece of work already notorious for his double dealing – reneged on his promises of clemency, namely that the garrison would be expelled and the people spared. Without question he was irked at having been so valiantly defied by the tiny garrison of 8,100 native Venetian foot, Italian mercenaries and Cypriot militia, Greek or Frankish by race,[30] and at a cost too. On 15 August 1571, the Feast of the Assumption, the noble companions of Marc'Antonio Bragadin were butchered on the spot and their heads lined up for display in the main square of the seaport. Bragadin himself was mutilated; first his ears and nose were cut off, then he was forced to hump sacks of earth and stone as a captured slave. Ten days later, after having been tied to a chair and hoisted to a galley yardarm, where he was exposed to the taunts of the Ottoman seamen, he was flayed alive in public. The body was then quartered, and the parts displayed in various locations of Famagusta. His skin was pickled, stuffed with straw, clad in the owner's crimson robes of office and carried through Famagusta on the back of an ox. Then it was hoisted to a galley's main yard and borne triumphantly around Cyprus before being despatched to Constantinople as a gift for the sultan.[31] News of Bragadin's gruesome torture and execution would not reach the Christian fleet until 4 October, three days before the battle of Lepanto.

Two centuries earlier Birgitta of Sweden (†1373), mystic and saint, had bravely stood in the main square of Famagusta and told the abusive citizens of said city how the Lord Jesus Christ had come to her in a vision and warned of a macabre destiny when he had said:

> "Wherefore, O people of Cyprus? I now announce to you that if you will not correct yourself and amend your life, than I shall so destroy your generation and progeny in the kingdom of Cyprus that I shall spare neither rich nor poor. Indeed, I shall so destroy this same generation of yours that in a short time, your memory will thus slip away from the hearts of human beings as if you had never been born in this world. Afterward, however, it is my pleasure to plant new plants in this kingdom of Cyprus that will carry out my precepts and will love me with all their heart".[32]

And so Birgitta predicted that one day Famagusta would go the way of Sodom and Gomorrah because of the wicked sins of its citizens and the royal court. When all is said and done, humanity, with slight external differences, is identical in all ages. The blatant breach of faith of Mustafā Paşa is not without parallels in ancient, mediaeval and contemporary history; a political crime, perhaps necessary, but for which there is neither extenuation nor excuse. But still, let it be remembered that the Muslims in the 16th century were no more or less cruel than the western Europeans, and were, at the risk of being labelled 'politically correct' by those in certain quarters, far more civilised. This is not to paint a picture of the Ottoman empire as some oasis of unvarying justice and blissful tolerance – imperialism is imperialism, no matter its ethno-religious shade – but it must be said that the Ottomans were a lot more tolerant of Judaism and Christianity than the Christians were of Judaism and Islam.

Religious rigidity and bigotry aside, flaying, impalement, endless casual brutalities on both sides were commonplace: all were done for a purpose, for a theatrically sadistic gesture acted as a sop to their own side and served to frighten or infuriate the enemy. All empires and autocracies fuel anger against the 'others' – people said to be dangerous outsiders and employ cruelty to spread fear. They sometimes succeeded in both respects, but usually only invited tit-for-tat retaliation. It is said that Mustafā Paşa had learned that fifty Muslim pilgrims whom the Venetians had incarcerated had now been executed. While it was the time of the Renaissance in Europe, a period of splendour in all the arts and sciences, it was still one of the cruelest of ages, and rough and ready cruelty was the principal means adopted to ensure success; sheer terror was seen as the weapon of the successful leader. The Renaissance was thus a time of strongly contrasted light and shade, in which the most refined civilisation existed side by side with evidence of an intolerance and brutality that we should not be shocked by.

Then, as in similar situations today, lessons remained unlearned: notably that extreme cruelty and violence breed extreme cruelty and violence in return.

Then again, Cyprus had always been viewed as a relatively secure island, with Famagusta serving as the base for merchants from not only Venice, but those from Genoa, Barcelona, Ancona, Narbonne, Messina, Montpellier, Marseilles, and elsewhere too; its ruined Gothic churches still testify to the wealth its merchants accumulated. In fact, Famagusta had served as the centre of eastern Mediterranean trade for virtually three centuries. Europe wanted goods being delivered from the Levant – cloves, cinnamon, and nutmeg as well as commodities such as wheat, cotton and silk. Famagusta, with its natural harbour on the east coast, the island's deepest, was the ideal location for this trade as it was centrally located between Asia, Africa, and Europe. At the same time, pilgrims were travelling in the opposite direction to the Holy Land. Aside from its location, the island possessed a profitable production of cotton and sugar, and the wines were famous. It is not surprising, therefore, to find that the reaction of Christendom was unprecedented, though a considerable and well-appointed fleet was only commissioned after a delay of many months, due to incessant bickering among the allies.

The anti-Ottoman Holy League of western navies would consist of Habsburg Spain (including the Kingdom of Naples and the Kingdom of Sicily), the Papal States, the Republic of Venice, the Knights Hospitaller, the Republic of Genoa (firmly under Spanish control), and the duchy of Savoy. It was finally agreed that Don Juan de Austria (1547–78) should be leader of a war council made up of Venetian, Spanish and papal commanders, with the pope – because he was the 'Ruler of the World' – as supreme arbiter. It is worth remembering that this Christian alliance was an uneasy one that would probably never have coalesced at all except for the Ottoman invasion of Cyprus. Moreover, despite Lepanto, the Ottoman threat to Christendom was one which was to continue until the late 17th century.

*Part I*

# The Players

*Chapter 1*

# The Veteran

"It seems clear to me," replied Don Quixote, "that thou art not well versed in the matter of adventures ..."

Miguel de Cervantes, *Don Quixote*, part 1, ch. 8, p. 58 Grossman

It has often been said that there is perhaps no law written more conspicuously in the teachings of history than that nations who are ruled by priests drawing their authority from supernatural sanctions are, just in the measure that they are so ruled, incapable of true national progress. The free, healthy current of secular life and thought is, in the very nature of things, incompatible with priestly rule. The argument continues, saying that be the creed what it may, Islam, Judaism, Christianity, or fetishism, a priestly caste claiming authority in temporal affairs by virtue of extra-temporal sanctions is inevitably the enemy of that spirit of criticism, of that influx of new ideas, of that growth of secular thought, of human and rational authority, which are the elementary conditions of national development.

That all being said, the prevailing impressions of Castilian Catholic culture in the Anglo-speaking world are dominated by two conflicting images: the vengeful Inquisition, known officially as the Holy Office of the Inquisition, and the tall, pencil-thin Don Quixote. The former was an institution that stood for the forces of tyranny, cruelty, and greed – for intellectual rather than moral darkness. But it is the latter choleric character and his cerebral creator that concerns us at this juncture, products of the lively intellectual world of 16th century Spain, in this respect deservedly called *los Siglo de Oro*, the Golden Age of Spain. In actual fact, Miguel de Cervantes Saavedra (1547–1616) wrote one of the few books of the 16th century that are still readable in the 21st century.[1] Here should be included another Castilian classic, *La verdadera historia de la conquista de la Nueva España*, 'True History of the Conquest of New Spain', by the conquistador Bernal Díaz del Castillo (1495–1584), perhaps the most honest writer on the conquests in the great land masses of the Americas in the service of their sovereign ruler Charles V. It must be said, however, Bernal Díaz, who served as a common soldier under Cortés, and styled himself the 'mouthpiece of *los conquistadores*', does lack the humour and satire of Cervantes.

Satirists are supposed to comfort the afflicted and afflict the comfortable. This statement certainly runs true with regards to Don Quixote's maker Miguel de Cervantes Saavedra, a disabled war veteran, a Castilian *hidalgo*, a great poet, a fertile novelist, and a good Catholic. In *Viaje del Parnaso* (1614), 'Journey to Parnassus', a festive mythological poem full of autobiographical references, the old novelist and playwright was to quip "Thy left hand shattered lost the active power / It once possessed, for the glory of the right!"[2] Who could argue with the superlative Spanish writer? Was it not his right hand that wrote one of the cornerstones of western literature, the wonderfully complex and beguiling *El ingenioso hidalgo don Quijote de la Mancha* (1605, 1615)? Cervantes' gaunt, aged and crazy knight-errant, the self-styled Don Quixote de la Mancha, and his mule-straddling squire, Sancho Panza, frozen in winter, burning in summer, charging around the high plains of La Mancha encountering *moriscos*, merchants, mendicants, picaroons and ex-slaves, characters of low social rank, without honour or marginal and surviving from day to day by being resourceful, have entertained academics and critics alike.

## A story for all ages

No other word encapsulates a useless but well-meaning quest in quite the same way as the term Quixotic, and the phrase 'tilting at windmills' to describe a fight against imaginary enemies has slipped into common parlance. But in his tale of a mad, aged fabulist who stops at nothing to revive the so-called age of chivalry, Cervantes also gave us the phrases 'bigger fish to fry' and 'the proof of the pudding is in the eating'.[3] Even if you have never read his crazily wonderful *Don Quixote*, you probably use phrases from it all the time. Cervantes the man of arms and Cervantes the man of letters have occasion to express themselves again and again in his major *opus*.

A story of a fifty-something gentleman in anachronistic armour and as bony as his poor aging horse, Rocinante, Don Quixote regards himself as God's knight. He is driven by a mad plan: to revive a long-eclipsed era (one, in fact, that never existed) of knights-errant, who sally forth into a world of beautiful princesses and fearsome giants helping the weak, righting wrongs (no matter that the victim of these wrongs is only ever himself), and dispensing justice to those who would otherwise never know it. It is a plan which seizes him after avidly consuming chivalric romances that crammed his bookshelves, chivalric romances to which he attributes the veracity of history.[4] History, after all, is less the science of retrieving the past than the exercise of a complex hermeneutic or method of interpretation. Its ultimate quest is not simply to determine 'what happened' but to understand how what happened continues to shape human experience.

Like the Bible, Cervantes' fantastic story, and particularly its central character, has appeared to each succeeding age as symbols of the human condition, which that age interprets in terms of its own leading preoccupations. Indeed, Don Quixote, a ridiculous buffoon with a madly fierce twinkle in his eyes who blunders into fights and loses but never for one moment doubts his cause, has become an international figure whose story has enriched the literature of other cultures and a variety of artistic forms. In the time of Cervantes, God was ever-present to the people of Spain. So for the biblically minded, Cervantes narrates a vulgar adventure which, in a very real sense, is the inverse of that of Saul, the son of Kish, a wealthy Benjamite landowner, who went forth to seek his father's strayed asses and found a kingdom.[5]

Yet it is the story of Cervantes' useless left arm, a war wound, that is equally extraordinary, and goes right back to the Ottoman conquest of Constantinople. This dramatic event was to mark the consolidation of Ottoman rule in Greece and the Balkans, which had begun when the Ottoman Turks first crossed from Asia to Europe one-hundred-and-one years earlier, in 1352.

After the conquest of the Byzantine metropolis, the Ottomans quickly realised the importance of a blue water navy. More importantly, the navy was needed to connect the Levant and the Ottoman empire's more distant provinces. Thus, the calm blue harbour of the Golden Horn gave birth to an Ottoman navy so feared and respected that it bequeathed the word 'arsenal' (an Arabic word, actually) to the English language. However, the Knights of the Hospital of Saint John of Jerusalem (also known as Knights Hospitaller), currently stationed on Rhodes, were a constant obstacle to Ottoman designs in the eastern Mediterranean. Since the loss of Constantinople the Knights Hospitaller held the dominant Christian position in the Levant, and their buccaneering and intercepting of Ottoman ships laden with merchandise, pilgrims and communiqués led the Sublime Porte (as the Ottoman court was often known) to determine upon their removal. We shall come to these *dramatis personae* later in the book.

But what did this all mean for the author of the timeless *Don Quixote*? It meant life as a sea soldier filled with the romantic notions of one faith, one king and one empire. It also meant Cervantes could either be remembered by commentators in a series of easily skipped footnotes, or he could end up having a sizable volume to himself. It is clear from his literary output which option he preferred. However, a much earlier event nearly ended the author's life before he ever dreamt of putting pen to paper. This was the battle of Lepanto, which took place on Sunday, 7 October 1571.

Histories of civilisation and ideas concentrate on tiny groups – thinkers, artists, politicians; they can be easily studied. Most people are rarely heard of – minorities and workers, soldiers and peasants, slaves and the *hoi polloi*. Popular revolutions bring them briefly on history's stage; then they are ignored as if swept aside. Historians should personally commit to Cervantes' model of historical objectivity. According to this, as put into the mouth of Don Quixote:

> "[H]istorians must and ought to be exact, truthful, and absolutely free of passions, for neither interest, fear, rancor, nor affection should make them deviate from the path of truth, whose mother is history, the rival of time, respository of great deeds, witness to the past, example and adviser to the present, and forewarning to the the future".[6]

These are the words, not personal political preferences, which should guide historians. There again, without doubt Cervantes' participation in the battle of Lepanto would have gone unnoticed had he not later written *Don Quixote*. In fact, what other common soldier is remembered from that fateful day? Historical truth, as Cervantes understood it, could only be attained through personal experience. Thus, truth with regards to war was to be found not in abstract speculation, but in the smell of gunpowder and blood. Francesco Balbi di Correggio (1505–89), an Italian of unknown origins who served as a common harquebusier with the Spanish contingent defending Senglea during the siege of Malta in 1565, opens his war journal with the following sonnet: "The true history of war is best written / When he who wields the sword takes up the pen".[7] Yet writing a history from the perspective of the common man is easier said than done, though with Don Quixote and Sancho Panza riding together the novel runs smoothly and rapidly, for the mad knight was able to discourse about the ways and events of this world from the perspective of the common man.

## Creative beginnings

But let us consider first who Cervantes was. He was born in the ancient Castilian town of Alcalá de Henares, near Madrid, to parents of *hidalgo* blood, whose position in the world had fallen. As a result, by the time Cervantes was born in 1547,[8] most probably on the Feast Day of Saint Michael and All Angels (Sp. *San Miguel*), his father, Rodrigo de Cervantes (b. 1509), was a *médico cirujano* of little means who often had to wander from village to village in search of work or to shun creditors. It is believed Rodrigo had suffered from acute deafness since his infancy. Unable to become a physician because of his deafness, he thus chose to be a surgeon, which, in 16th century Spain, held about the same status as being a barber or a butcher, who also required sharp implements to practise their respective trades. In other words, Rodrigo probably did not enjoy a high social status. His licence allowed him to bleed, repair broken limbs with splints, and apply compresses under the supervision of a physician. University-trained physicians were seen as the caretakers of medical knowledge who were privy to the inner workings of the human body. They alone could rightly interpret the body's signs using the knowledge of Galenic and Hippokratic theories, prognosticate, and treat accordingly. Barber surgeons, on the other hand, could only treat conditions pertaining to the external surface of the body.

Even so, despite his father's lowly occupation, it appears that Miguel received a decent education in Córdoba or Seville and perhaps in Salamanca courtesy of the Jesuits: in the short story *El coloquio de los perros* (1613), 'The Conversation of the Dogs', Cervantes defends Jesuit education, saying his education was a model one. It is fairly certain that he was a pupil of Juan López de Hoyos, an Erasmist intellectual and the rector of the city high school, Estudio de la Villa, Madrid, in 1568. Hoyos referred to Cervantes as his beloved pupil, and were it not for a twist of fate the following year, he would certainly have remained one of his students.

Having gotten into some trouble for drawing a sword at court, he had had to flee his homeland of Spain as an outlaw. Or so the story goes. In Madrid on 15 September 1569 agents of the king issued a royal warrant ordering the arrest of a student named Miguel de Cervantes for wounding a master mason, Antonio de Segura, in a duel.[9] By all accounts the fracas took place within forbidden territory, namely under the colonnade of the royal palace, and was the end result of an intrigue with a lady of high birth. The common sentence for anyone drawing a weapon near a royal personage or within the precincts of the royal palace was lopping off the offender's right hand at the wrist in public and condemnation to ten years' exile.

Although the names and dates match, there is a question about how and why a son of a humble barber surgeon would have been in such a situation. There again, situations always change. Cervantes, later as an author, wrote of a similar incident no less than three times: *La gitanilla*, 'The Gypsy Girl', where a young man and his friend kill two rivals in a duel and flee to Italy; *El amante liberal*, 'The Generous Lover', where the heroine tells how a suitor of hers wounds her brother in a duel, then flees to Italy; and in Cervantes' posthumous work, *Los trabajos de Persiles y Sigismunda* (1617), 'The Labours of Persiles and Sigismunda', a novel in which two characters travel from Spain to Italy. One tale involves a soldier named Saavedra, which was the family name that Cervantes later assumed, and all three fugitives choose Italy as their place of refuge. This might indicate Cervantes was writing about his younger self, and that he indeed had to flee Madrid to escape the king's justice.

Understandably, the historical facts concerning the reasons why Cervantes left Spain for Italy are uncertain. Anyhow, Italy (largely under Spanish Habsburg domination at the time) was the obvious choice for a Spaniard fleeing abroad and so in December 1569, Cervantes turned up in Rome, a city where the pope and not Philip II held sway, and gained employment as chamberlain in the household of a prelate-diplomat in the Vatican, Monsignor Giulio Acquaviva d'Aragóna (1546–74).[10] He was to discover that one was not acceptable in the household of a nobleman unless one could produce evidence of what was then called purity of blood, that is, no Jewish or other non-Christian ancestry. There is a satirical reference to this requirement in the aforementioned *El coloquio de los perros*, where one of the dogs remarks:

> The lords of earth are very different from the lord of Heaven. The former, before they take a servant, must investigate his pedigree, test his abilities, note his appearance, and even pry into his wardrobe; whereas when it comes to entering God's service the poorest is the richest and the humblest is the highest born, providing only he be disposed to serve Him with a pure heart, in which case he is at once entered in His book of wages ...[11]

In the 16th century, a chamberlain in a noble or royal household was usually a kind of head *valet de chambre*. It was an honourable post. Though he followed the cardinal (Acquaviva received his red hat from Pius V on 9 June 1570) to Palermo, Milan, Florence, Venice, Parma and Ferrara, he did not stay long in his service as he decided to sign up with a Spanish unit going to war against the Ottoman empire. It appears Cervantes enlisted in August or September 1570 at the Spanish military depôt in Rome.

## The good soldier Cervantes

Rank-and-file soldiers leave little trace in the records of the period and what does survive as evidence of their actions and motives is scant and unevenly spread in space and time. With Cervantes, however, we are somewhat lucky. Those enlisted in military service came from backgrounds quite different from Cervantes, who had studied in high school and served in the Vatican. Most enlisted men were a strange brew of poor farm boys fleeing starvation, street thugs from the urban slums, disinherited sons of destitute noblemen, impecunious students who had run dry of funds and curious poets who were on a quest to see what life was really like. We can only wonder why Cervantes enlisted in the Spanish army, since he had enjoyed life in Rome. Although his experience in the Vatican may have been less then exciting. If it was excitement he was after, then he was not long in finding it.

Posted as a foot soldier to Naples, where he joined *Tercio Nuevo de la Mar de Nápoles*, 'New Tercio of the Sea of Naples', currently under the command of *maesre de campo* Miguel de Moncada (hence its alternative name of *Tercio de Moncada*),[12] Cervantes joined the fleet of the Holy League at its rendezvous, the Sicilian seaport of Messina, on 2 September 1571. The Christian fleet set sail on 16 September and on 7 October Cervantes found himself at the battle of Lepanto among the ranks of the 200 soldiers serving on the Spanish galley *La Marchesa*. Cervantes had been taken ill shortly before the battle began, and on that fateful morning he emerged on deck delirious with malarial fever and feeling nauseate.

The testimony of his *compadres* is noteworthy. Cervantes appeared on the poop before the battle began, and, in response to the captain of his company, *capitán* Don Diego de Urbina,[13] and concerned comrades who advised him to take cover because he was sick and in no condition to fight, he exclaimed:

Señores, up to now I have served as a good soldier. I shall not do less on this occasion, even though I am weak and full of fever. It is better that I should fight in the service of God and the king and die for them, than keep under cover.[14]

Picture Cervantes, then a young soldier of twenty-four, stricken with fever and standing before his *capitán*. If the captain wanted his company to obey his orders he had to set an example, since, in the words of the Spanish nobleman Francisco Gómez de Quevedo (†1645), "It is more efficient to command by example than by order; the soldier prefers to keep his eye on his captain's back, rather than to have the captain's eye on his back. What is ordered is heard, [but] what is seen is imitated."[15] We gather that Cervantes' *capitán* was such an officer.

In the violent mêlée that followed the same eyewitness adds Cervantes "fought like a valiant soldier against the aforementioned Turks in the aforementioned battle, by the launch berth, as his captain ordered him to do".[16] Obviously set on fighting the Muslim foe, and it was there that Cervantes was hit twice in the chest and once in the left hand by harquebus bullets. For our valiant young Spaniard, Lepanto was brutal as it was brief. Luckily, his body armour would have taken most of the impact of the shots to the chest. However, it was the third wound that had the most enduring effect because he lost the use of his left arm for the rest of his life and garnered him the nickname *el manco de Lepanto*, 'the one-handed soldier of Lepanto'. Nowadays of course we would call him a disabled war veteran. His heroic service that day got him several letters of commendation; one being from Don Juan de Austria himself. Unfortunately, these treasured letters were on his person when he was later captured by Barbary corsairs and taken in chains to Algiers.

The heavy bullets fired by the muzzle loaded handguns called harquebus – "leaden messengers", Shakespeare poetically called them, "that ride upon the violent speed of fire"[17] – easily fractured bones and burst internal organs. Though an arrow, for instance, has an impressive penetrative ability, this is largely the product of its superior shape. Whereas the arrow penetrates because of the concentration of its kinetic energy behind a narrow cutting edge, a hot harquebus bullet smashes through by brute force and ignorance. It carries dirt, grit, gunpowder and bits of cloth inside the body too, almost guaranteeing inflammation, suppuration, then sepsis and, ultimately, death. And not only that: because a lead ball often flattens on impact, causing terrible, gaping wounds, hits on limbs usually require amputation.

Without anaesthesia or effective painkillers – opium, henbane, mandrake, and of course the ubiquitous strong spirits being the only offerings – the surgeon's speed was the only remedy for pain.

When early in his military career, decades of which were spent fighting in the Habsburg-Valois squabbles in Italy, Blaise de Monluc (1501–77) was shot during the siege of Forca di Penne in Abruzzo, the French surgeons wanted to cut off his arm in order to save his life. However, a captive surgeon advised Monluc that he should risk death and refuse amputation, for he was still very young and it would be better for him to die than live for decades more without an arm. Looking back, Monluc thanked God that he heeded the captive surgeon's advice and refused to have his arm cut off.[18] Not so for Monluc's younger contemporary, the Huguenot captain François de La Noüe (1531–91), seigneur de La Noüe-Briord. At the siege of Fontenay-le-Comte in the Vendée in 1570, his left arm was shattered beyond repair by a bullet and afterwards amputated; a mechanic of La Rochelle made him an artificial iron arm (hence his sobriquet *Bras-de-fer*) with a hook for holding his reins. Amputation in the field was a rough and ready procedure, though there was more to it than simply hacking away at the smashed limb:

> You shall have in readiness a good strong form and a steady, and set the patient at the very end of it. Then shall there bestride the form, behind him a man that is able to hold him fast by both his arms. Which done, if the leg be to be taken off beneath the knee, let there be also another strong man appointed to bestride the leg that is to be taken off, and he must hold fast the member above the place where the incision is to be made, very steadily without shaking, he that doth so hold should have a large hand and a good grip, whose hand may the better stay the bleeding ... In like manner there must be another skilful man that hath good experience and knowledge to hold the leg below, for the member must not be held too high, for staying and choking of the saw, neither must he hold down his hand too low for fear of fracturing the bones in the time it is a-sawing off. And he that doth cut off the member must be sure to have a sharp saw, a very good caitlin [a long, narrow, double-edged, sharp-pointed, straight knife], and an incision knife, and then boldly with a steady and quick hand cut the flesh round about to the bones without staying ... then set your saw as near the sound flesh as easily you may, not touching it, and with a light hand speedily saw it off.[19]

So wrote William Clowes the elder (†1604),[20] an army surgeon who went in 1563 with the ill-fated army commanded by Ambrose Dudley, 3rd Earl of Warwick, to Le Havre in support of the French Huguenots.

The following year the ragged survivors of Warwick's army returned to England, but Clowes remained in Portsmouth and served in the Queen's navy for a number of years. With years of experience in the navy behind him, he was expert in treating the injuries and wounds which befall men on active service. In 1585 he was commanded by Elizabeth I to accompany Sir Robert Dudley, 1st Earl of Leicester (1532–88), to the Low Countries. After this expedition Clowes returned to London, only to serve in the fleet which defeated the Spanish Armada. His book contains detailed case-histories of a wide variety of battlefield wounded, chiefly among the men he treated in the Netherlands campaign. Priding himself as a 'true artist', our English surgeon concludes his amputation discourse by observing that the surgeon must have a good eye, a strong arm, and a stout heart. We can take for granted that a strong stomach was also required.

No amputation for Cervantes however – despite a number of later paintings and prints that depict him as one-armed – so he did not have to join that growing band of amputee veterans found in Spain begging for a livelihood. Without a doubt, compared to numerous others that day, our future author got off extremely lightly. Packed on deck, a hundred or so of his *tercio* comrades were also wounded, but another forty of them were speedily cut down by a hail of lead, including *capitán* Diego de Urbina. And remember, these casualty figures are for a company of just 200 soldiers. These men were, to borrow words of our English playwright once more, said through the agency of the cruel but charismatic Sir John Falstaff, "food for powder, food for powder".[21]

The more usual fate of soldiers with gunshot wounds was revealed by Don Luis de Requeséns y Zúñiga (he also fought at Lepanto), *capitán general* of *Ejército de Flandes*, Army of Flanders, as it was known to its contemporaries and to posterity. In 1575 he wrote that many of his soldiers had been wounded and that "most of the wounds came from pikes or blows, and they will soon heal, although there are also many with gunshot wounds (*arcabuzazos*), and they will die".[22] In the words of *el manco de Lepanto*, said through the agency of his spare and foolish knight, Don Quixote:

"[W]hen the prows of two galleys collide in the middle of the wide sea, for when they lock and grapple, the soldier is left with no more than two feet of plank on the ram of the ship; despite this, seeing that he has in front of him as many ministers of death threatening him as there are artillery cannons aimed at him from the other side, only a lance's throw away, and seeing that at the first misstep he will visit the deep bosom of Neptune, despite this, with an intrepid heart, carried by the honour that urges him on, he makes himself the target of all their volleys and attempts to cross that narrow passage to the enemy vessel. And the most astounding thing is that no sooner does one man fall, not to rise again until the world comes to an end, then another takes his place, and if he too falls into the sea that waits like an enemy, there is another, and another who follows him, and their deaths come one after the other, without pause: no greater valour and daring can be found in all the perils of war".[23]

Paradoxically, Cervantes is not primarily remembered for being a soldier, yet the autobiographical overtones of this passage are striking, for our author, wielding the pen as a sword, vividly recaptures the adrenalin-fuelled tensions of the battle for the reader. Something of the shock and confusion of the fierce struggle Cervantes must have experienced that day is also captured in the chaotic style of Luis Cabrera de Córdoba (1559–1623), a near-contemporary historian of Philip II:

Never was a more confused battle seen, the galleys being joined one with another or two or three with another, however their luck would have it, grappled by the prows, gunwales, sterns, or prow to stern; if so it turned out. The aspect was terrifying because of the wild cries of the Turks, the shots, the fire, the smoke, the laments of the dying. Turned to blood, the sea was the grave of dying bodies tossed by the waves, upset and foaming from the shock of galleys and the horrible blows of the artillery, pikes, spears, swords, fires, hail-like clouds of arrows that converted the masts, yards and hulls into veritable hedgehogs and porcupines. Frightful was the confusion, fear, hope, furore, stubbornness, grit, courage, rage, fury; the pitiful dying of friends, the encouraging; wounding, killing, capturing, burning; the throwing into the water of heads, arms, legs, torsos, miserable men: some already dead, some about to give up the ghost, some gravely wounded and receiving the *coup de grâce*, some swimming to the galleys to save their lives at the cost of their freedom, grabbing oars, rudders, cables, asking with pitiful voices for mercy ..., only to have their hands cut off without pity ...[24]

War is a grim business out on the sea. In this merciless environment, not only do men fear losing their footing almost as much as a wounding blow, but the panic that there is nowhere to run when things turn out for the worse stalks men like a black shadow. Cervantes understood this – how soldiers (and seamen) actually performed in a sea battle involved a complex matrix of physical and psychological factors, and Cervantes' personal account goes some way to recreate and evoke the physical and psychological realities of war at sea – with its triple risk of steel, fire, and water – as experienced by Spanish common soldiers. It was such selfless sacrifices by these men on this dark day of horrors that enabled the forces of Catholic Europe to decisively defeat the Ottoman Turks and stall the Muslim advance westwards.

In the case of Cervantes however, the euphoria of victory would not last long. Not often enough do we think of Cervantes' life as a soldier when evaluating his plays and novels, but a soldier he was. When the battle was over he was found standing at his post, a sword in his right hand, his left hand and chest bleeding from deep gunshot wounds. Some six years later as a captive in Algiers (more of which below), he remembered this moment with deep satisfaction in a verse epistle addressed to Philip's secretary, Mateo Vázquez:

> At this sweet moment I, unlucky, stood
>     With one hand buckled firmly to my blade,
>     The other dripping downward streams of blood;
> With my breast a cruel thrust had made
>     A deep and gapping wound, and my left hand
>     Was bruised and shattered, past all human aid;
> Yet was the delicious joy and grand

> That thrilled my soul, to see the faithless foe
> Crushed by the valour of the Christian band,
> I hardly knew if I were hurt or no,
> Although my anguish, cutting and unkind,
> At times with mortal swooning laid me low.[25]

When writing much later in his life of these terrible battle wounds, he has this to say to his readers of his didactic poem, *Viaje del Parnaso*:

> If my wounds do not shine in the eyes of those who see them, they are, at least, esteemed by those who know where they were acquired; it seems better for a soldier to be dead in combat than safe in flight, and I believe this so firmly that even if I could achieve the impossible now, I would rather have taken part in that prodigious battle than to be free of wounds, and not to have been there.[26]

On the day after the battle, Don Juan visited the sick and wounded men of his victorious armada. It is likely that he saw and spoke to Cervantes or at least heard some account of his bravery, for it appears that an increase in his pay was authorised on that very day.[27]

After being hospitalised for six months in Messina, the creator of *Don Quixote* continued to serve the Spanish crown with his good right arm. Leaving hospital on 24 April 1572, Cervantes resumed active military duty, joining the company of *capitán* Manuel Ponce de León, of *el tercio* of Don Miguel de Moncada, *el Tercio Nuevo de la Mar de Napoles*. In the following years, Cervantes participated in the disastrous campaigns of Navarino (1572),[28] La Goleta (1574), and Tunis (1574) against the Ottoman Turks, where the Spaniards were drastically defeated. After the three wounds received at Lepanto, three campaigns against the Ottomans, and four years in military service, Cervantes decided to return to Spain, which he had left as a fugitive. Promoted to *soldado aventajado*, élite soldier, he obtained two letters of recommendation from duque de Sessa and Don Juan de Austria recommending to Philip II that Miguel de Cervantes be given command of one of the new infantry companies being formed in Spain for service in Italy.[29]

## Barbary bound

During the first week of September 1575, *soldado aventajado* Miguel embarked at Naples, on the galley *El Sol*, with his younger brother Rodrigo (b. 1550), a soldier like him who had also fought at Lepanto. *El Sol* was one of the four vessels making up a Spanish flotilla that set sail for Barcelona, with Cervantes on board, under the command of Sancho de Leiva, the renowned commander of many fleets under Philip II. A few days later, a storm scattered the Spanish galleys. While three of them finally reached port safely, the last one, *El Sol*, would not make it. *El Sol* was probably swept toward Corsica by a violent mistral or strong west wind that turned into a storm, perhaps as described in a passage from *La Galatea* (1585), the first novel published by Cervantes on his return to Spain after he had given up the life of a soldier. For in it he says:

> And so the ship, driven by its fury, began to run with such speed over the stormy sea, that in the two days that the mistral lasted, we sped by all the islands on that course without being able to take shelter on any.[30]

On 26 September 1575, in sight of the Catalan coast, *El Sol* was attacked by Barbary corsairs, and its surviving crew were all hauled off as captives to Algiers. A new chapter in Cervantes' life was about to begin.

The head of the three corsair galiots was an Albanian renegade, Arnaut Mamí, a corsair as famous as he was cruel – he acted on the principle that it is better to be feared than loved, if one must choose; his lieutenant, of Greek origin, was called Dalí Mamí. During the fierce resistance aboard *El Sol*, which lasted for several hours, many Spaniards had perished – including the galley commander, Pedro Gaspar de Villena. The results of this combat are summarised by the narrator of *La Galatea*, Cervantes himself:

> After we had fought for sixteen hours, and after the captain and nearly all the crew of the ship had perished, at the end of nine assaults, the Turks furiously boarded the ship.[31]

The shattered survivors were transported, bound hand and foot, to the Algerian galiots. Suddenly, the rest of Leiva's squadron appeared on the horizon, chasing the corsairs, who escaped in haste with their human booty. The prestigious signatures on the letters of recommendation found on Cervantes led the corsairs to believe that he was an important personage, worthy of a king's ransom. While his brother Rodrigo was designated as part of the booty reserved for *beylerbeyi* Ramadàn Paşa, the Corsican renegade who ruled Algiers between 1574 and 1577, Miguel fell into the hands of Dalí Mamí, nicknamed *el Cojo*, the Cripple, who demanded as the price of ransom the exorbitant sum of 500 *escudos de oro*, an amount the poor Cervantes family could not pay. As for Rodrigo, he would be liberated on 24 August 1577 at the cost of sixty *escudos*: the money had been granted to his mother, Doña Leonor de Cortinas, by royal decree on 6 December 1576.[32] Rodrigo would make a career of soldiering, reaching the rank of *alférez* and dying a soldier's death in Flanders at the battle of Nieuwpoort on 2 July 1600.

Miguel de Cervantes, on the other hand, was to remain a Barbary slave for five years of gruelling captivity in one of the *baños*, prisons, of Algiers, the capital of corsair activity *par excellence* in the Mediterranean. *Baños* were large enclosures surrounded by small rooms which served as dormitories.[33] Fra' Diego de Haedo, a captive in Algiers between 1578 and 1581 and acquainted with his fellow Spaniard Cervantes, describes these dormitories as "dark, damp, stinking rooms".[34] Some of the *baños* had two storeys and could hold up to 300 captives. The captives were divided by nationality, and each one had a *major-domo* who was exempt from work and distributed alms sent from their home country. According to Fra' Diego, for sustenance captives were "given only water and two little loaves of bran or barley bread".[35]

Cervantes was not idle in captivity, for he made four unsuccessful escape attempts (1576, 1577, 1578, and 1579), in which he barely avoided death. Fra' Diego, after mentioning that on those four occasions Cervantes found himself in imminent danger of execution by implement, hooking, or burning alive, concludes with these words:

> One could write a separate history ... of the captivity and exploits of Miguel de Cervantes. Hassan Pasha king of Algiers used to say that if he could keep that maimed Spaniard under guard, his Christian slaves, his ships, and even his whole city would be safe; so much did he fear the scheming of Miguel de Cervantes ...[36]

Hassan Pasha (known to Cervantes as Azán Agá) was Uluç Hasan Paşa, a Venetian renegade who had been appointed *beylerbeyi* of Algiers in the late spring of 1577, and would hold the post on three occasions (1577–80, 1582–5, 1586–7), and for a short while also that of Tripoli (1585–6) before being appointed *kapudan-ı deryā*, grand admiral of the Ottoman navy. It is possible of course that Hasan's exasperation with the maimed Spaniard is an exaggeration on the part of the good monk, but there are indications that Cervantes had been scheming to organise a general uprising of the Christian slaves in Algiers.

Although demographic reports for the Barbary Coast are often suspiciously exaggerated in Christian reports, sources suggest that slaves comprised up to twenty or twenty-five per cent of the total population in Algiers during the 16th century.[37] In comparison, although the result of Lepanto flooded slave markets, galley slaves in the European ports of Naples and Venice typically comprised roughly four per cent of the total urban population.[38] In the light of this, we can understand why Uluç Hasan felt the need to load Cervantes with irons and lock him up in the royal *baños*, where he was to remain for some five months. We shall cross paths with Uluç Hasan once again later.

Eventually Cervantes was rescued by the Order of the Holy Trinity, a religious order well represented in Spain, which specialised in ransoming Christians who had fallen into Muslim hands. The Trinitarians had received from Leonor de Cortinas the sum of 300 *escudos* for the ransom of her son Miguel, "who is thirty-three years of age, crippled in his left hand, and who has a blond beard".[39] The somewhat substantial shortfall in the ransom demand was made up by the ransomer monks. On the morning of 19 September 1580 Miguel de Cervantes was to attain his liberty, which, in the words of Don Quixote, "is one of the most precious gifts heaven gave to men; the treasures under the earth and beneath the sea cannot compare to it".[40]

## PTSD

Even if you have not read the novel, you will be all too familiar with Don Quixote's encounter with windmills. As our hero and his sidekick are riding across the Campo de Montiel, the knight errant calls to his squire's attention thirty or more giants with whom he proposes to fight. Sancho Panza immediately recognises the giants as windmills and is quick to warn his master not to attack them. But Don Quixote's head is too full of encounters between giants and knights to heed Sancho's warning. As you will remember, he thrusts his lance into one of the turning sails of a windmill and is overthrown. This is one of the abundant examples of Don Quixote's misinterpretations of reality. Sensible Sancho has no problem of interpretation. Only Don Quixote could make so ridiculous a mistake as to believe the windmills to be giants.

Cervantes greatly amused his contemporaries with his narration of crazy adventures like that just reviewed. But such adventures were contrived to reveal a gamut of misinterpretations of reality arising from the manifestation of madness unable to discriminate fact from fiction to the realisation that even the supposedly sane sometimes find such discrimination beyond their powers. Cervantes inhabits his vast novel so pervasively that we need to see that it has three unique personalities: the knight, the squire, and the author himself. It is plausible that the non-conformist Don Quixote shows us the underside of reality but whether he mirrors the author's own condition is another question.

Cervantes returned to Spain, but events had moved on and his past services as a sea soldier were now forgotten; Lepanto had proved a barren victory and Don Juan de Austria was dead. He saw nothing before him but to do what he had done ten years previously, though not, we may rightly assume, with the same wild-eyed eagerness: he once more re-enlisted in the ranks of *los tercios*. But Cervantes was now growing weary of the hard, ill-paid and brutal life of a soldier, and after fighting under Fernando Álvarez de Toledo y Pimentel (1507–82), Gran Duque de Alba, in the campaign to annex the neighbouring kingdom of Portugal (1580–2), he threw aside his pike for the pen. He would thus become the most battered of eminent writers.

The positive result of this was that on his return to Madrid Cervantes included his traumatic experiences in his comical masterpiece, notably the interpolated novella known as *La historia del cautivo*, 'The Captive's Tale',[41] which read at your leisure, as well as two plays set in Algiers, *El trato de Argel* (1582), 'Life in Algiers',[42] in which our author's memories of slavery are freshest, and *Los baños de Argel* (1615), 'The Prisons of Algiers'. Cervantes cannot be counted among the ranks of "unscarr'd braggarts of war", to borrow the fitting words of one of his equally erudite contemporaries.[43] The French nobleman Pierre de Bourdeilles (†1614), abbé et seigneur de Brantôme and a contemporary of Cervantes, mentions a Spanish common soldier who showed him half a dozen scars he had, explaining at which battle he received each. Each one had its own story and memory, like a verse in an epic poem. The scars thus served the veteran as bodily memoirs, or a bodily 'palace of memory', which could immediately be transformed into an oral life story.[44] If truth be told, as one traverses the corpus of Cervantes' works, the phantoms of his capture and subsequent captivity in Algiers reappear in countless fictions, from *El trato de Argel* and *La Galatea* to *La historia del cautivo* and *Los baños de Argel*. Indeed, the last reference to his capture occurs in his last tale, *Los trabajos de Persiles y Sigismunda*, a novel the writer finished on his deathbed.

Violence, slavery, and imprisonment were the staples of Cervantes' life, an endless struggle to stay alive and shake free the chains of captivity (a factor that should not be underestimated in Cervantes' thought). Students of 17th-century literature will know that no story of high adventure was complete without 'captivity among the Moors', the stock asset of the romancer. Yet for Cervantes 'captivity among the Moors' was an actuality not an anecdote. Traumatic truth, then, was increasingly diffused and mixed with fiction in his literary production.

When the captive Aurelio, at the opening of *El trato de Argel*, describes his current existence as "*¡Oh purgatorio en la vida* [purgatory of life]" and "*infierno puesto en el mundo* [a hell put on earth]",[45] the nod to the work of Dante Alighieri, a scholastic of a stripe all his own, is clear, but the difference for the young Cervantes is that those condemned to either place do so, not because of their own sinfulness or wrongdoing but by reason of a capricious coincidence in their life or from the working of an inexplicably adverse fate. Worse for him was the fact that the wanton evil of others caused so many innocent people to be pushed to the brink.

Stated simply, seen from today's vantage point, the primary takeaway from the author's enslavement is that the gravity of the crisis described in his texts carries all the symptoms of post-traumatic stress disorder (PTSD). This is a medical condition which has been recognised as commonly affecting persons who have been exposed to severe violence. Recovery can be a prolonged and difficult process. Cervantes' *œuvres complètes* are a valuable window through which we may understand the horrors of slavery.

As for his right hand, his biggest weapon as a writer, Cervantes proudly declares in the prologue to the *Novelas ejemplares*, published eight years after the first part of *Don Quixote*, that "he would sacrifice it too if the stories should offend against virtuous ideals". Looking back on the occasion of Lepanto from the safe vantage point of the 1613 prologue to *Novelas ejemplares*, Cervantes describes the battle with over brimming pride as "the most memorable and lofty occasion that past centuries have beheld, or that future centuries may hope to see". Two years later these terms of praise were repeated nearly verbatim in the prologue to the second part of *Don Quixote*, where the pride remains untarnished, even after thirty-four difficult years.

Miguel de Cervantes died on Saint George's Day, Saturday 23 April, 1616, ten days before his great contemporary and spiritual kinsman, William Shakespeare,[46] writers whose texts explore the human condition. To the pious minded, heaven received at one stroke two illustrious literary souls. Coming from very different cultures and backgrounds, Shakespeare was a poet and dramatist who elevated English theatre to universal status, whilst Cervantes, who achieved neither fortune nor fame with his plays, left behind a novel Fyodor Dostoyevsky called "the ultimate and most sublime work of human thinking".[47] True, for *Don Quixote* is a spiritual journey through one man's life and, to borrow the words of Havelock Ellis, "before he wrote of life he had spent his best years in learning the lesson of life".[48] Both erudite writers describe the transit from old world magic and religion, to the new world of human rationality. Yet while Shakespeare may have brought over thirty-eight stories to life on stage, we know for a fact that Cervantes actually lived them. Violence, slavery, imprisonment, and penury had been the staples of his colourful existence; it is safe to say that Cervantes had the more eventual, albeit traumatic, life.

The modernist poet and literary critic T.S. Eliot once boldly declared:

Dante and Shakespeare divide the modern world between them; there is no third ... Shakespeare gives the greater width of human passion; Dante the greatest attitude and greatest depth. They complement each other.[49]

Precisely, and no literary critic would ever deny the greatness of these two literary minds and their toning talents, which still enchant us. Yet Eliot failed to mention the obvious 'third': the Spanish master Miguel de Cervantes Saavedra. Courtesy of Cervantes' ingenuity with words we are witnesses to richly diverse dramas about humans, about hopes and motality and dreams. Of course, anyone who chooses may quarrel with this argument.

## Re-internment

Nigh on four centuries after his death a multidisciplinary team of researchers, including forensic anthropologists, archaeologists and historians, discovered the bones of Miguel de Cervantes. It was recorded that he and his wife, Catalina de Salazar y Palacios (she was to live until 1625, nine years after her husband's death), were interned in Madrid's Convento de las Monjas Trinitarias Dexcalzas, the very order of monks that had rescued him from the yoke of captivity in Algiers, just as he requested. However, his coffin was subsequently lost in 1668 when the convent's modest church was demolished to make room for the current baroque church. Deploying infrared cameras, three-dimensional scanners and ground-penetrating radar, a team of nearly thirty researchers were able to locate the fragmented bones of the literary giant among the mortal remains of fifteen bodies consigned to a niche in a forgotten crypt beneath the building.

As for proving which bones definitively belonged to the author, the investigators did have some clues. Cervantes died at age sixty-nine and had written three years previously that he had only "half a dozen" teeth, "in bad condition and very badly placed": like many another artist, Cervantes left us a self-portrait, in this case in his famous prologue to the *Novelas ejemplares* (1613). Also, as we well know, he had battle wounds: three harquebus shots, two in the chest and one in his left hand. And so it was that on Thursday, 11 June 2015, the bone fragments of Miguel de Cervantes were given full honours at a reburial ceremony at the Convento de las Monjas Trinitarias Dexcalzas.

*Chapter 2*

# The Corsair

'Strangers, who are you? From where do you come sailing over the watery / ways? Is it on some business, or are you recklessly roving / as pirates do, when they sail on the salt sea and venture / their lives as they wander, bringing evil to alien people?'

*Odyssey* 3.71–4 Lattimore

So, whilst litterateurs savour Cervantes and laud his work, the big part the state-sponsored corsair Hayreddin Barbarossa had to play in bringing bookish glory to Cervantes' busy but virtuous right hand has to be considered. For this purpose, it is necessary to go back a little and consider some earlier developments. Perhaps Cervantes' story – and hence the story of Lepanto – began in 1505.

## Mare nostrum

It is true to say that politically the Mediterranean basin was anything but calm during the 16th century, even if it ever had been. It was, quite literally, a sea of troubles. On the waters of the Adriatic, the Aegean, and the Tyrrhenian, piracy was once more on the rise.

In 1505, Ferdinand II of Aragón was triumphant after years of warfare in Italy, having not only recovered the Kingdom of Naples from the French but also added it to his dominions after nine years of grinding warfare. We shall return to this conflict later. Between 1508 and 1510, the efficient Spaniards, set loose from the war in Italy, busied themselves in North Africa. Here they conquered the inaccessible el Peñón de Vélez de la Gomera (1508),[1] a corsair nest mostly supported by the Moroccan sultans, Orán (1509), Bougie, and Tripoli (1510), where they methodically built *presidios*, fortresses, an attempt to neutralise the North African corsairs. Led by the legendary Italian war veteran Pedro Navarro

(†1528) – a former picaroon turned engineer and artillerist, known in his bad old days as *Roncal el Salteador*,[2] Roncal the Highwayman – an army of 10,000 men sacked these seaside towns, distributing the booty among themselves and selling the Muslim inhabitants into slavery.

Spain's endeavours along the North African littoral were obviously spurred by more than the passion to convert the Muslims to Christianity and to control the frontiers of Islam. True, Cardinal Francesco Jiménez de Cisneros (1436–1517), promoter of these so-called crusades in North Africa, on entering Orán ordered the establishment of two churches for the Catholics, two monasteries for missionaries, and the appointment of an Inquisitor. Yet the spirit of adventure and the bait of riches lying ahead on the African continent had as much influence on the 16th-century Spaniards as the preoccupation with eternal salvation. Possessing the coasts of the Maghrib, moreover, helped to bridle Muslim piracy, the great resource of the Maghribi ports. In Tangier and Bône, in Orán, Algiers, Bougie, Bizerte, and Tunis, to cite only a few important havens, Muslim corsairs armed galiots and galleys which they launched against Christian shipping – the longstanding control of the Mediterranean by Italian and Catalan merchants was turning into a distant memory.

The back-story: the Barbary corsairs at first sight seem very different from the highly organised Knights Hospitaller, as we shall discover later in this book. Yet the corsairs too were warriors who had travelled far to earn their reputation. A number were the descendants of Greeks, renegades who had themselves renounced the Christian faith; others were of Calabrian, Corsican, Sardinian, Albanian, Jewish, Genoese, Venetian, even Hungarian origin, again Christians who changed their religion, *farsi turco*, and became renegades or, as contemporaries would say, *turco de profesión*. Most of these renegades were ironically Habsburg subjects. They were not, or not all, roving psychopaths dedicated solely to their own profit and amusement. They included skilled navigators, notably Pìrì Re'ìs, whose detailed maps of the Mediterranean and the world beyond furnished the Ottoman court with precise information in the age of discovery. But the most famous corsair was Barbarossa, so called in Christendom because of his red beard. In truth, he was not one but two corsairs, Oruç, and his younger brother Khizr.[3] Around these men there developed a whole series of stories, and it is not always clear what is fact and what is fable.

The story of the two Barbarossa brothers is an instance, for it does seem these two horrors of men had done terrible things during their careers as corsairs. The eldest acquired a thoroughly bloodthirsty reputation as the sort of man who would bite out a victim's windpipe like a mad mastiff, while Khizr, who would acquire an even more fearsome reputation than Oruç – it is told that when he once became irritated with seven captured captains he had them sliced up with sharp knives – dyed his own beard red to emphasise his succession to the elder, red-bearded, Barbarossa. If the truth be told, the Barbarossa brothers were tenacious, menacing, solipsistic adventurers who enjoyed a reputation for violence and brutality the bare idea of which created universal terror. After all, men who took and held power by the threat of extreme violence could not afford to appear passive or indecisive.

The brothers, it is strange to say, were born in the village of Palaiókipos on Lésvos (Tk. *Midilli*) in the days of Mehmed II *Fatih*.[4] Their father was Yusuf Ya'kub Ağa, the son of a converted Ottoman *sipahi* of Christian Albanian descent (he was from Yenice-i Vardar, present day Yiannitsá, northern Greece), their mother an Orthodox Christian Greek, named Katerina, a widow of an Orthodox Greek priest. Ya'kub had volunteered to take part in the Ottoman conquest of Lésvos in 1562, currently ruled by the Genoese duke, Niccolò Giustiniani. Subsequently, Ya'kub settled, married Katerina, and raised four sons, Ishaq, Oruç, Khizr and Ilyas. Ya'kup comfortably established himself as a potter; he traded in his ceramics all round the Aegean, as far north as Constantinople itself, and often took Oruç and Khizr along with him. It was on these journeys that the Barbarossa brothers acquired their skill as seamen.

On one such journey, around the year 1490, Oruç collected timber from the shores of Anatolia (what we now call Turkey), only to find his vessel pursued by *Santa Maria della Concezione*, a Hospitaller galley out of Rhodes. Oruç was captured and sent to toil as a galley slave, though after a couple of years he was ransomed, which was not unusual; nonetheless, a story of heroic escape began to be told. He happily returned to the sea, spending time in the waters between Spain and the Maghrib in the company of Khizr; it is claimed that they helped ferry Jewish and Muslim refugees out of southern Spain in 1492 , the year that witnessed the triumphant entry into Granada of Isabella of Castile and her consort husband, Ferdinand II of Aragón.

## Career change

The brothers' first fighting vessel was a light galley, crewed by about a hundred volunteers, all in search of booty and glory, and around 1502 their base became Djerba off the Tunisian coast. In antiquity this offshore haven had been known as the Isle of the Lotus-Eaters,[5] and long a nest of thieving pirates and the scene of conflict between Christian invaders and Muslim defenders. They built ties to the court in Tunis, operating as licensed privateers of the Hafsid caliphs, the Sunni Muslim dynasty of Berber descent who had ruled *Ifrīqya* (western Libya, Tunisia, eastern Algeria) since 1229. In 1504, they set sail for Elba, whose deep coves favoured corsairs, and swooped on two ships which proved to be sailing in the service of pope Julius II, as well as a Spanish ship carrying 300 soldiers and sixty Aragonese noblemen to Naples. They easily took the papal vessels, enormously enhancing their reputation as heroes in Tunis and as fearsome enemies in Rome.

By 1506 the enterprising brothers possessed eight ships, but their successes had earned them so much fame that the Ottoman sultan Selīm I *Yavuz* would later bestowed on them the honorific title 'the outstanding of the Faith', *khayr-ad-din*, or, in Ottoman Turkish, 'Hayreddin'. A war of attrition was being fought between Muslim corsairs and their Christian foes; these were not just Genoese and Catalan sailors (whether merchants or corsairs) but the Portuguese and the Spaniards, who insistently intruded themselves into coastal forts along the Mediterranean and Atlantic shores of Morocco. Despite their successes at Melilla and Orán, the best the Spaniards could achieve at Algiers was the capture of some isolated rocks guarding the port, which were fortified with cannon in 1510 but were no substitute for control of the city itself.

Depending on which side you were on, the brothers were either the blood-thirstiest pirates afloat on the Mediterranean, or they were privateers in the same way Francis Drake or Walter Raleigh were for the English monarch, mariners as callous as the lawless high seas they sailed on. The categories are blurred. Privateers interrupted a rival's trade, raided its shores, sank his naval shipping in a form of pre-bout sparring permitted by the rules of war, and borne with because of the horrendous cost of ending it by war itself. For the Ottomans, the brothers were legitimate admirals of the fleet with orders to attack the Knights

Hospitaller as well as the Spanish Habsburg domains. Collectively they became known as the 'Barbarossa brothers' – so named by Italian contemporaries, from their red beards – they are generally regarded as being the two founding fathers of the corsairs of the Barbary. The term 'Barbarie' was not used in the North African Arabic or Ottoman Turkish languages, but to 16th-century English writers it referred to the Ottoman regencies of Tripoli, Tunisia and Algeria, and the kingdom of Morocco. The Barbary states constituted distinct geopolitical entities; fortified ports, in fact, dotted along the coastal area of North Africa, with Algiers the wealthiest and the most frightening symbol of them.

Englishmen like Drake or Raleigh also did not follow government objectives and also did not declare cargoes and prizes. They became, save in name, pirates pure and simple, as likely to attack the shipping of a neutral power, like Portugal (before its annexation by Philip II in 1580) or Denmark, as that of the common foe Spain. At least the Barbary corsairs preserved a steadily ideological policy. They preyed neither on one another nor on vessels belonging to their nominal overlord and occasional employer, the Ottoman sultan, who would employ them as his eyes and ears, the probing point of his sword. At the other end of the Mediterranean they gave the sultan a cost-free naval presence when he needed it, and one which he could repudiate whenever it suited his diplomacy. In fact, their attacks on Christian coasts and shipping were checked neither by truces nor peace treaties between the two faiths.

Distinguishing *piracy* and *pirates* from *privateering* and *privateers*, or *corsairs*, the French historian Fernand Braudel advances the following:

> Privateering is legitimate war, authorized either by a formal declaration of war or by letters of marque, passports, commissions, or instructions. Strange though it now appears to us, privateering had its own laws, rules, living customs and traditions.[6]

In fact, though piracy was endemic in the 16th century, the terms *pirate* and *piracy* were not in use at that time, being first used in the 17th century. Still, pirates could be capable allies on occasion, and apart from warfare, the pirate had a most useful place in the economy of the Mediterranean; he was the general slave merchant.

## Master of Algiers

In a strange quirk of history, the brothers managed, with the help of Ottoman janissaries, to establish themselves in Algiers, killing its ruler, Sālim al-Tūmī. Various traditions recount the murder in striking ways: the emir was stabbed, strangled with his own turban, or asphyxiated in the royal steam bath by Oruç himself, stories that dramatised the cruelty of the elder Barbarossa brother and expanded his notorious fame throughout the Mediterranean.

Much like the Knights Hospitaller, the city would develop into a major thorn in the side of European maritime activities. Algiers was the largest and most populous port on the Barbary Coast between Tangier (then controlled by the Portuguese) and Tunis, but it was never a significant corsair base before the Barbarossa brothers took control of it in 1516. A 16th-century Spanish writer described Algiers as "a big city, well-populated, and surrounded by vast walls". Another Spaniard, Jean León, recorded that the walls were strongly built using stone salvaged from the ruins of the small Roman town of Icosium, which had stood on the site. The following year Oruç defeated a Spanish Habsburg force sent to capture the city, but he then relinquished control of his emirate and offered it to the Ottoman sultan Selīm I *Yavuz* (r. 1512–20), the Grim, who had just conquered Egypt. The sultan expected the obedience of Oruç, particularly in matters of foreign policy; an annual financial tribute to Constantinople or Istanbul – both names were used; and to be provided with ships and men for his fleets when they were demanded. Otherwise Oruç was given a surprisingly free hand to govern his territory as he saw fit. This sacrifice of his autonomy in return for Ottoman military support was well judged. In 1517, while Khizr raided the coasts of southern Italy, Oruç inflicted a costly defeat on a Spanish Habsburg force that landed west of Algiers.

Oruç then led a small army out of Algiers and headed into the hinterland, intending to secure control of the region to thwart any further Spanish landings. He seized Médéa to the south, and then moved west to Miliana, before marching northwest to capture the Spanish-held port of Ténès; Khizr supported his brother by assaulting this port from the sea. Assured of Ottoman support, but without waiting for reinforcements to actually arrive, Oruç then marched inland on Tlemcen. Since 1512

Tlemcen had been a vassal state of Habsburg Spain; Oruç defeated its Zayyanid puppet ruler and captured the town. Early in 1518 the Spanish responded, predictably, by sending an army to recapture Tlemcen; during the siege that followed Oruç was killed,[7] and the town was recaptured by the Spanish.

Khizr promptly stepped into his elder brother's shoes, but faced with the growing power of the Spanish, he understood that if he was going to survive he needed a powerful patron. In 1519 he fully submitted to Selīm I *Yavuz* in exchange for the title of *beylerbeyi*, or provincial governor (literally 'lord of lords'), a rank superior to *bey*, governor (literally 'lord') but lower than a *paşa*, which was the sole title bestowed by the sultan that carried any rank and precedence. For the rest of his career Khizr, now the only 'Barbarossa', juggled his personal interests as a privateering commander with the duties of an Ottoman *beylerbeyi*. Privateering was not only a lucrative weapon of war but was also deeply embedded in Barbary culture. So it was that, from well-fortified Algiers, Khizr singled out and preyed upon the Mediterranean fleet of Charles V, the Habsburg emperor whose aggressive Catholicism had up to now manifested itself in the subjugation of South America, war with the Protestants, the Inquisition and the removal of any last vestiges of Islam in Spain.

It is Hayreddin (as we shall call him) who now demands our attention. Physically and in action, Hayreddin was the stuff that adventure stories are made of. He had been able to attract the most audacious bands of seamen of his day into his service, as well as making alliances with the maritime city states along the coast of North Africa (Tunis, Tripoli, and Salé) who provided him with a safe refuge for his ships when he wanted to escape from the Christians who were hunting him. Using booty he had been able to capture to organise a trading market, he had rapidly expanded his fleet of Barbary corsairs, manned by ruffians of all sorts – Algerian Muslims, Berbers, Turks, exiled *moriscos*, and many Christian renegades – making it both fast and frightening. He was soon the *primus inter pares* among the freelance Muslim corsairs drawn to the Barbary Coast.

Each Barbary state began as a Berber fiefdom, but as the 16th century got into its stride all of them, apart from the Moroccan sultanate, eventually succumbed to Ottoman control. In 1520 Hayreddin had been forced out of Algiers, this time not by the Spaniards directly, but by the combination of local allies. After the recent defeat of Oruç in the region, local rulers were against Hayreddin and he was having a hard time to find worthwhile allies in the region. The rulers of Tunis and Tlemcen were eager to extirpate the corsair chief from the region since they considered him a more serious threat than the Spanish.

Hayreddin had the one supreme merit of never knowing when he was beaten. He possessed patience too, the most important of the virtues. Driven from Algiers, the disposed ruler was to bide his time for five years before he re-conquered Algiers and eliminated his hostile neighbours. However, his hold over Algiers was still contested and unless he eliminated the threat from el Peñón de Argel – the Spanish *presidio* buried deep in the harbour of Algiers – he would not consolidate his rule in the city. In May 1529 Hayreddin launched a definitive assault on el Peñón de Argel and captured it after a twenty-day bombardment – the artillery, by the way, was French. Hayreddin had the fortress demolished and built a breakwater linking the islet to the shore in order to build a safe harbour for his growing corsair fleet. Now the complete master of Algiers, his power increased immediately.

## Grand Admiral

Hayreddin received official recognition as *beylerbeyi* of Algiers, though he liked to call himself *kapudan paşa*, Captain General. Previously Selīm I had sent him an Ottoman standard, cannon and other war munitions, but in 1533 Selīm's son and successor, Süleymān *Kānūnı*, invited him to court in Constantinople. Upon his arrival, the corsair chief enjoyed a grand ceremony and an audience by the sultan to whom he offered his gifts: "twenty-one male slaves, two *tavashis*, silver artefacts such as decanters and mugs, coloured clothes, a crown of coral, two clocks, and velvet, satin, woollen, and brocade clothes to the Sultan on 12 Cemziyelevvel 940 (29 November 1533)".[8] In return, Hayreddin and his captains were given robes of honour and salaries from the sultan; in other words, they became official servants of the Ottoman state for service to the sultan superseded all other allegiances.

More significantly, Süleymān officially made Hayreddin *kapudan-ı deryā*, grand admiral of the Ottoman navy,[9] an office he would retain until his death; the Ottoman navy had recently suffered a series of serious defeats at the hands of the veteran Genoese admiral, Andrea Doria, greatest among contemporary Christian mariners. The sultan also placed at his disposal a sizable body of janissaries. With such resources to hand, Hayreddin was able to capture Tunis the following year. The other importance of course was the fact these janissaries gave Hayreddin an élite military body alien to the local population and loyal to him, not a small advantage given the unreliability of his local allies, tribesmen in the main who addressed their loyalty to their tribes rather than to an alien government.

Leaving Algiers for Constantinople, Hayreddin became the most powerful and richest man of the Ottoman court. In the following years, the Ottoman fleet commanded by him devastated the Italian coasts, abducting a great number of captives. On several occasions the agents of Charles V attempted to entice the corsair into the Habsburg camp. In the course of the secret negotiations conducted by Andrea Doria, the experienced Genoese *condottiere* of the sea who habitually served the emperor as high admiral, and Fernando Gonzaga, the viceroy of the Three-Tongued island of Sicily (viz. Sikelian-Greek-Latin), for the release of Spanish captives, Charles offered to recognise Hayreddin as king of Algiers and Tunis if he broke his alliance with Süleymān.[10] But the feared Barbarossa was not to be turned, and he went on to dominate the Mediterranean Sea after his decisive victory over a large Holy League fleet – twenty-seven papal galleys, ten Knights Hospitaller galleys, forty-nine Genoese and Spanish galleys, as many as fifty-five Venetian galleys – near Préveza (Gk. Πρέβεζα) on 28 September 1538.

Part of the Turkish War of 1537–40, this was a battle the Christians should have surely won. They found the unsuspecting enemy fleet anchored off Préveza, an Ottoman-held port on the north-western coast of Greece. Not only did they catch Hayreddin completely by surprise, but also their attack came at a time when his fleet was in a very poor shape. Shortly before, it had been struck by a severe storm in which over thirty galleys had been lost and many others badly damaged. To make matters worse, an epidemic had then killed over two-thirds of the Ottoman fighting force and galley slaves while the fleet lay in port undergoing repairs after the storm. These disasters left the Ottoman fleet half as large as the Holy League fleet and vastly inferior in fighting ability. So sure were the Christian commanders of overcoming the enemy that they even dispatched a vessel before the battle began bearing news of victory to the pope; the battle was decisive, but not in the fashion which they anticipated. As it turned out, Hayreddin turned the tables on the Christians and trounced their fleet, causing the Holy League to collapse. Little wonder, therefore, his name brought unholy terror to those who heard it, as well as honoured respect. The popular imagination was converting him gradually into an almost legendary figure.

Hayreddin, however, was more than just an unusually successful corsair chief; he was a powerful international actor in the region. He had captured Charles' territory, attacked his urban centres, safely transported Hispano-Muslim and Hispanic Jewish refugees from post-*Reconquista* Spain, and went on to attack Ostia at the mouth of the Tiber causing the church bells of Rome to toll unceasingly in fear and consternation. The audacity of his menacing methods is best illustrated by his raid on Fondi on the night of 8/9 August 1534, when Hayreddin swooped down on that Italian town simply, or so it is alleged, to seize Giulia Gonzaga – a young widow since 1528 and reputedly the most beautiful woman in Italy – for the sultan's harem: the fair duchess of Traetto (present-day Minturno, Lazio) hardly escaped from the corsair's clutches in her nightgown.[11]

Hayreddin's dominance of the Mediterranean eventually led to several developments: better shipping designs to avoid capture and the search for alternative routes to South Asia and Indonesia. More importantly, it led to the forming of alliances between the Catholic European states and princes in the 16th century, which resulted in the battle of Lepanto in 1571, their first major naval victory against the Ottoman Turks.

Most everyone knows that the battle of Actium was the last great sea battle of antiquity. It was fought on 2 September 31 BC, off Cape Aktion at the entrance to the Ambrakian gulf. Most everybody knows too that the battle of Lepanto was the largest sea battle fought in the Mediterranean since Actium. In spite of this common knowledge, however, it is not commonly known that the victory at Lepanto had taken thirty-three years in the making. Yet revenge did not taste as sweet as envisaged. This was because the architect of the trouncing of the earlier Holy League alliance at the naval battle of Préveza, fought in very same waters as Actium, had long departed this life.

Hayreddin had ended his days in comfortable ease, having built himself a magnificent palace overlooking the Dardanelles, established seminaries, and written five hand-written volumes of his memoirs, which went under the grandiose title of *Gazavat-ı Hayreddin Paşa*, 'Conquests of Hayreddin Paşa'. For the querulous European allies of Préveza, the setback sowed mutual distrust that would linger for decades. Once the red menace of the Mediterranean, Hayreddin was to pass away peacefully in Constantinople on 5 August 1546 at the ripe old age of eighty years.

Though their lord had departed this world, his disciples, colloquially known as 'the school of Barbarossa', continued to bully the Mediterranean basin. Operating from Algiers, the Barbary corsairs sailed all over the Mediterranean, and even sallied into the Atlantic Ocean, in search of human bounty. In the meantime, the Ottoman Turks advanced from the eastern Mediterranean, capturing Tripoli from the Knights Hospitaller in 1551 and the island of Djerba in 1560.

## Chapter 3

# The Emperor

"I speak Spanish to God, Italian to women, French to men, and
German to my horse".

Witticism attributed to Charles V
(Francophone by birth, polyglot of necessity)

In 1519, the grandson of Catholic monarchs Ferdinand II of Aragón
(r. 1479–1516), called *el Católico*, and Isabella of Castile (r. 1474–
1504), Carlos I, king of Spain (r. 1516–56), had metamorphosed into
Charles V, the emperor of the Holy Roman Empire (r. 1519–56, †1558)
– under him Spain and the Holy Roman Empire had become dynastically
one power. The heir of Ferdinand and Isabella was their son Juan, who
seemed destined to reign over the Spanish portion of that great peninsula
which was now united for the first time. He, however, suddenly died,
and his posthumous child died also as soon as it was born. Their first
daughter and eldest child, Isabella, currently married to the king of
Portugal, Manuel I, now became the heir, and it seemed as if the entire
peninsula would be subject to a single ruler. She, however, died, and her
son Miguel da Paz after her. The inheritance now passed to Juana, called
*la Loca*, the third child and second daughter of Ferdinand and Isabella,
who had been married to Philipp I von Österreich *der Schöne*, son of
Maximilian von Österreich, the future Holy Roman Emperor.[1] An heir
had been born to them on the day of Saint Matthias, 24 February 1500,
in Ghent, then the second largest city in Europe after Paris. He was the
Habsburg prince Charles de Ghent, as he was then known, a weakly
child who was destined to reign over half Europe under the name of
Charles V, a monarch whose titles would read like the roll of some mighty
drum. It was the consequence of such a series of accidents that such vast
dominions were united under a single crown. Yet, at the end of his long
reign, he was to willingly give up his power and saw to it no member of
the House of Habsburg would hold such vast territories again.

The Habsburgs took their name from their point of origin – a small castle known as *Habichtsburg*, Hawk's Fort, close to the town of Brugg, in the area of today's Switzerland known as the Aargau. For many decades the full extent of their limited possessions could be seen from the tower of the *Habichtsburg*. They emerged from the mass of minor nobility when Rudolf von Habsburg (†1291) was elected King of the Romans in 1273, as a compromise candidate. In his *Divina Commedia* Dante finds Rudolf sitting outside the gates of purgatory with his contemporaries, collectively known as the Negligent Rulers, and berates him thus:

> He who is seated highest, with the look / of one too lax in what he undertook – / whose mouth, although the rest sing, does not move / was Emperor Rudolf, one who could have healed / the wounds that were the death of Italy, / so that another, later, must restore her.[2]

Nine years later, he awarded the border duchies of Austria and Styria to his sons, and these eventually became the basis of the Habsburg family patrimony. As we can see, the Habsburg were an energetically Catholic, Spanish-German dynasty originally springing from a Swiss castle, flourishing on Austrian soil and moving, through a series of stunningly-engineered marriages, into the position it was enjoying by the late fifteen-twenties – one of the most dominant forces in Europe.

## Empire in the Sun

From his Habsburg paternal grandfather, Maximilian von Österreich, Charles V had received the ancestral Habsburg lands in central Europe. From his Burgundian paternal grandmother, Mary of Burgundy, Charles inherited a highly volatile mixture of duchies, counties, and lordships in the Low Countries and the Franche-Comté of Burgundy.[3] From his Castilian maternal grandmother, Isabella, Charles received Castilla y León and its outposts in North Africa, the Caribbean, and Central America; from his Aragonese maternal grandfather, Ferdinand *el Católico*, he inherited Aragón, Naples, Sicily, and Sardinia. Charles himself added several more provinces in the Low Countries, some by treaty and others by conquest; he annexed the duchy of Lombardy in Italy when its native dynasty died out; and he led the army that acquired Tunis in North Africa

– fond of flowers, particularly carnations, after capturing Tunis he sent back to Europe the first root of the Indian pink. Little wonder, therefore, it was the huge shapeless empire of Charles V on which it was said that *el imperio en el que nunca se pone el sol*, 'the sun never sets'.[4]

Without a doubt, it was an empire upon which the sun never set. On 20 October 1535, just after the acquisition of Tunis and Peru, the port city of Messina in Sicily had warmly welcomed Charles V with the felicitous phrase coined by the Roman poet Virgil for the possessions of the emperor Augustus, fifteen centuries before: *A solis ortu usque ad occasum*, "From the rising to the setting of the sun",[5] inspired by the Biblical passage "From the rising of the sun to the place where it sets, the name of the LORD is to be praised."[6] At the time of Miguel de Cervantes' birth in 1547, Spain, led by Charles V, was rich, powerful, and rightly feared by other nations. Yet the emperor was essentially a simple and good man. His favourite reading was romances of full-blown chivalry, which Cervantes was later to laugh out of existence, and he liked to think of himself as a knight errant, chosen by God to defend Catholic Europe against its chief enemies – the acquisitive Lutheran princes to the north, the ever present Ottoman threat to the east. Yet, least we forget, greed, violence and religion have shaped much of imperial Europe, and the empire that Charles ruled over was certainly no exception.

## Impresario of War

The emperor king Charles had inherited a geographically scattered succession of duchies, principalities, kingdoms and states whose only element of union, beyond hereditary rights, was cohesion of beliefs on the part of most of his subjects. There was no common tongue, no central capital,[7] no body of laws, and no coinage in general use. Charles' bewildering jigsaw of possessions were separated and cut off by enemy states that often declared war to consolidate their position in the face of his excessive power. Under these circumstances, Charles' life would be burdened by struggles with the Lutherans in the Low Countries, conflicts with Catholic France, and the war with the Ottoman Turks, which took place on two fronts simultaneously: along the Danube basin, the natural invasion path into Europe from the east, and around the entire Mediterranean Sea.

For a man with no military leanings, it is somewhat ironic that Charles' life would be dominated by war.[8] He fought his first battle in 1535 at Tunis when he confronted Islam in person, overcoming the fleet and forces of Hayreddin, the lord of Algiers and grand admiral of the Ottoman fleet. Charles' Tunisian campaign is immortalised in a series of vast tapestries now in the Kunsthistorisches Museum in Vienna.[9] The emperor had his court painter/war artist, Jan Cornelisz Vermeyen (1500–59), with him on this particular North African adventure, and the Flemish artist had shared the whole expedition from start to finish. He was thus able to put on canvas the unfolding events of the siege, and what he reproduced in oils eventually became (through a set of tapestry cartoons) the magnificent series of twelve large tapestries. These wall hangings pay homage to the emperor's authority, his bravery, and his abilities as a general, and celebrate him as the defender of the Christian world against the 'Infidel Turks'.

As one can imagine, for this martial achievement Charles V was publicly acclaimed as the 'Destroyer of the Turks'. It had been towards the end of June 1535 when a combined Spanish, Papal, Genoese and Maltese fleet of seventy-four (other sources say eighty-two) galleys had swooped upon Tunis. After taking the key stronghold of La Goleta (Fr. La Goulette, Ar. *Halq al Wadi*), the expeditionary force marched towards its main objective, Tunis. The troops of Hayreddin were routed, the victorious emperor triumphantly entered the city on 21 July, and thanks to Charles' victory, the former Hafsid caliph of Tunis, Muley al-Hasan (r. 1526–42), was restored to his throne. La Goleta was reduced to a minor stronghold in order to be able to defend it with fewer soldiers. Charles capped his victory by taking also Bône (Annaba) and Bizerte before returning home via Sicily and Italy in what was one uninterrupted triumphal progress. One of the highlights was held in Rome on Easter Monday, 17 April 1536, when the emperor made an important political speech in the presence of the pope, Paul III (r. 1534–49). It is not surprising that much of Charles' energy would be devoted to preventing Ottoman expansion westward into the Mediterranean and eastern Europe.

But the Ottoman Turks were not the sole threat. Ruler of a broader realm than Charlemagne's, Charles V faced the opposition of France, of the German Protestants, and often that of the pope. He thus carried on a persistent fight to hold together in his Holy Roman Empire the people of Germany, the Low Countries, Italy, and Spain. Without a doubt, for one man this was a heavy burden to bear.

Charles V, wracked by gout and exhausted by his herculean labours,[10] abdicated his crown and retired to the Hieronymite monastery of Yuste in 1556. At his death two years later, though his imperial title, as well as the crowns of Bohemia and Hungary,[11] passed to his brother, the Spanish-born, clever and modest Ferdinand de Austria (†1564), not to his son Philip II, the king of Spain, who still controlled, along with the Low Countries, Milan, Malta, Sicily, Naples, and the island fortress of La Goleta in the bay of Tunis.[12] But Charles V set no ordinary standards for his son to emulate. A successful soldier and statesman, an experienced traveller fluent in five languages, a master of regal gesture and apposite phrase, a born leader of men: he set a hard standard to follow.

## Chapter 4

# The King

Rather than suffer the slightest thing to prejudice the true religion and service of God I would lose all my State. I would lose my life a hundred times over if I could, for I am not and will not be a ruler of heretics.

Philip II to Pius IV, 1564

In the late-17th century an English savant, Henry Neville (1620–94), considered all the governments of Europe in his discourse between an English gentleman, a noble Venetian, and the latter's physician. In what was an important republican tract, Neville observed that empires, since ancient times, were brought down by becoming enmeshed in 'ceremonious follies'.[1] In the previous century the mighty Catholic king of Spain, Philip II (r. 1556–98) – Felipe II to the Spanish of course, the Philip of 1588 and all that – had ruled his vast seaborne empire by writing detailed and elaborate letters, and had seldom emerged from a small suite of rooms in the huge monastic palace he had built in the mountains north west of Madrid, San Lorenzo del Escorial. He consequently saw little of his domains, instead experiencing the empire primarily as a series of communications that landed on his desk each day.

Securely shut away in the comforting seclusion of his secret rooms in the Escorial, Philip ruled, or hoped to rule, a world of almost infinite complexity. Geographically his empire was the largest, and most widely dispersed, any monarch in history had yet controlled: in Europe, despite the division of his father's territory into a Spanish and an Austrian portion, there was Spain and Portugal, Sicily, Naples and Milan, and sizeable slices of the Low Countries (viz. Flanders, Brabant) and France (viz. Franche-Comté); and overseas the Spanish and from 1580 onwards, the Portuguese dominions in the Americas, Africa, India and the Far East. In Philip's lifetime, Spain's maritime empire would swell, peak, but was as yet to collapse.

## Continuum of majesty

Under Philip II, Spain's success story would continue apace. For after 1580 he governed one-fifth of the land mass of western Europe and one-quarter of its population. In the meantime, Spain's armies were triumphant. Its Merino wool was the finest in Europe. Its universities flourished. The conquistadors' unquenchable thirst for *plata* meant silver and gold poured into the imperial treasury across the Atlantic from the Americas. Right on the other side of the world the Philippine archipelago was named after Philip. And for two years in his youth his marriage to the Catholic queen Mary Tudor (r. 1553–8)[2] had also made him titular king of England, though his power as such was hedged about by many restrictions, imposed upon him by a suspicious and hostile parliament.[3] Only the Spanish possessions overseas had come to him purely by conquest; those in Europe had fallen into his hands by tricks of inheritance, through the tangled branches of royal family trees. So, though the Habsburgs had acquired some territories by conquest, all the major gains came through a tenacious policy of 'matrimonial imperialism' – or, more accurately, of incest: intermarriage over several generations among a few dynasties in order to achieve and consolidate expansion. In the words of a humanist couplet that first became popular in the 15th century, *Bella gerant alii; tu, felix Austria, nube*, "Let others make war; you, happy Habsburgs, marry."[4]

Certainly, when you think of monarchy, you might think of an inbred Habsburg – the family's distinctive jaw, how generations of rulers were crippled by a variety of diseases due to their tendency to marry within the immediate family. The Habsburgs were a dynasty that brought suffering, and eventual ruin, on themselves through inbreeding. Such practice was of course common among all European royalty, but the Habsburgs had the worst possible luck with it. A few unfortunate family traits were bottled up and intensified. As generations of family members intermarried, the Habsburgs became prone to epilepsy, gout, dropsy, and depression. The most prominent sign of their familial connection was the aforementioned Habsburg jaw, a lower jaw that jutted out from the face.

Philip himself had been married within the family four times: first, to the heiress of Portugal, María Manuela, his double first cousin; second, to the queen of England, Mary Tudor, his first cousin once removed;

third, to a daughter of France, Elisabeth de Valois, who was descended from their mutual ancestor Alfonso VII of Castilla y León; and fourth, to a daughter of Austria, Anna de Austria, his niece. As a result, Philip had been simultaneously the cousin, uncle and brother-in-law of the Holy Roman Emperor, Rudolph II (r. 1576–1612), and had not seen any of his brides before the ceremonies started. All of them had died, three of them as a result of childbirth.[5]

One way and another he could prove the king of Spain was related to almost everyone with royal blood, and could lay some kind of a claim to every throne. For example, Philip had employed a team of genealogists to prove that he had a hereditary right to the English throne and they claimed to have proved it through the family of John of Gaunt.[6] To be quite certain, he officially announced that Mary Stuart (queen of Scots, r. 1542–67, †1587)), facing death on the axe man's block, had bequeathed it to him. Sometimes he had supported a shaky claim with the threat of the much feared Spanish *tercios*, as with the Union of the Crowns forced on the Portuguese by him in 1580. There were other claimants, but none could match Philip's power.[7]

But it was not only a geopolitical empire; it was also a religious entity, and that was what made it so complex. Philip was *Rex Catholicissimus*, His Most Catholic Majesty.[8] He believed (wrongly, as it turned out) he was appointed by God to defend the truth and purity of his faith against infidels and heretics. The pope was God's Vice-regent, as Earthly Vicar of Christ: Philip, in his own eyes, was Champion of Almighty God, the equal of the pope in God's designs. In this sense, his boundaries were vague. There were people all over Europe, caught in the ebb and flow of Reformation and Counter-Reformation, whose loyalties were divided between their country and their church. In almost all of Philip's Catholic domains, the rank heretics that men called Protestants had been smoked out and exterminated, or pushed far under ground, by the Inquisition.[9] The only exception was the Low Countries, which Philip had inherited from his father, and its discontented people, who Philip regarded as his own subjects. All through his reign they had been in revolt, partly against the shame of foreign rule and partly to protect their Protestant creed (with explicit opposition to Catholicism). In order to chastise them, he had to keep an immensely expensive army there, the largest in Europe too, and it had never succeeded in putting the insurgent Dutch down. But he was not only concerned with his own domains. It was his personal duty, divinely imposed as he believed, to punish Protestants everywhere and rescue Catholics who lived under Protestant rule. The core issues – nuances about the best way to achieve everlasting life through Jesus Christ – hardly seemed to justify mass slaughter, but they led to an unimagined brutality in the name of God.

## In the name of God

Of course, Philip was far from being alone in this lack of pity; it was an era when churches, especially the Spanish Church, disregarded the virtues of charity and mercy. The Spanish concept of majesty stressed the exalted nature of kingship where the monarch was specially selected by God to rule, in charge of his own destiny and that of his subjects. The God that Philip served was all-powerful, all-knowing and unforgiving. He could and did take part by miracles in men's affairs. Yet paradoxically He depended on His servants to do His will. He demanded worship absolutely exactly in the forms the Catholic Church proclaimed, and not in any other. He also demanded the most cruel and terrible punishments men could devise for anyone who deviated in the least degree. Especially, He demanded this service from the man to whom He had given the highest earthly power: Philip II of Spain. It was truly an awful burden for a man to carry.

It was also a burden for a human empire. Saddled with that primitive belief, the Spanish Habsburg empire was doomed to fall to pieces, and during Philip's long reign the cracks had begun. In an age when reports and orders were carried by horsemen and sailing ships, the empire was too big for any kind of central control – and far too big for the beady eyed, clerkly bureaucratic control he tried to impose on it. In his final paper of advice to his son and successor, the future Philip III (r. 1598–1621), the king himself blamed many of the problems he had faced on "the distance that separates one state from another", and in the course of his reign he repeatedly complained about delays in the transmission of important information.[10] So did his ministers – indeed, one of them joked that "if we have to wait for death, let us hope that it comes from Spain, for then it would never arrive."[11] Nevertheless, though much criticised, Spanish communications in the 16th century were on a whole a match for anyone's. When the ambassador of the Republic of Venice (which prided itself on the speed and efficiency of its communications network) hurried to the royal palace to inform Philip II of the great victory of Lepanto, he found that the king had already received the news from one of his own couriers.[12]

Here was the situation. Prevented from making significant improvements by the divine nature of his rule and no doubt his own nature too, the dour king hated to delegate an atom of his power: among the heaps of papers momentous questions waited his decisions while the master of tedium struggled with trivialities. In 1553 the duque de Alba, viceroy of Naples after the death of Don Pedro Álvarez de Toledo y Zúñiga, who had already established himself as an impressive – and was to become a notorious – military commander,[13] wrote, not without some resentment, that "Kings are born to do their will, and we, their vassals and servants, are born to do their will likewise."[14] It was in the same vein that in 1584 Antoine Perrenot de Granvelle (1517–86), then Philip's senior advisor, complained bitterly:

> I see in all matters these delays, so pernicious and in so many ways prejudicial to our own affairs, including the most important ones, which become lost to view with so much delay. And the reason is that His Majesty wants to do and see everything, without trusting anyone else, busying himself with so many petty details that he has no time left to resolve what matters most.[15]

It was all too true. For unlike some of his contemporary monarchs, who waged their wars in person,[16] Philip directed the affairs of his great empire from his file encumbered study, sitting for hours, alone, stylus in hand. We think of Philip as dark and brooding, and so he was – to the degree that it is surprising to remember that he was blue-eyed and fair-haired. But the lasting image, especially to those of English blood, is the pen portrait by G.K. Chesterton:

> King Philip's in his closet with the Fleece about his neck
> (Don John of Austria is armed upon the deck.)

The walls are hung with velvet that is black and soft as sin,
And little dwarfs creep out of it and little dwarfs creep in.
He holds a crystal vial that has colours like the moon,
He touches, and it tingles, and he trembles very soon,
And his face is a fungus of a leprous white and grey
Like plants in the high houses that are shuttered from the day,
And death is in the phial and the end of noble work ...[17]

Put bluntly, Philip was a painfully suspicious ruler who was obsessed with personally micromanaging every nitty-gritty detail of his entire empire. A flood of dispatches arrived for him everyday from viceroys, generals, judges and ambassadors all over the world. His industry was unremitting; the king alone would decide. To quote a couple of examples: in 1580, during the invasion of Portugal, the king informed his field commander that "I want you to let me know every day what is going on"; while eight years later, during the Armada campaign, the king instructed his agents that "now is the time to advise me of everything minute by minute."[18] Little wonder, therefore, the empire was choking to death on paper coded in bureaucratese.

In the 16th century (as in the 21st century) there was only so much that one man could absorb, digest and act upon in a given period of time. Early modern Europe's first superpower grew persistently slower towards the end of the 16th century; imperial overreach, over reliance on colonial treasure, myopic policy making and micromanaging operations all inhibited development. Faced with a blizzard of problems, many Spanish were led to believe that *se va todo a fondo*, 'the ship is going down'. The miracle was that the ship stayed afloat for as long as it did.

It was bankrupt too. Vast treasures flowed into it from the Americas – the silver mines of Peru and Mexico, the gold mines of Colombia and the emerald fields of Venezuela – but nobody understood that continually creating new money only led to inflation. Philip had mortgaged all the empire's revenues for years ahead, mainly to foreign bankers. He always hoped some windfall would pay off his spiralling debts; but the Genoese bankers, who handled most of Spain's external credit until 1670, knew Philip would never be solvent again, and Philip began to find he could not even borrow.[19] Trite though it might seem, the designs of God needed money – an awful lot of it.

Reading Philip's correspondence in the 21st century and judging him by 21st-century standards – which of course has the inherent unfairness of history, written, as it is, with the benefit of hindsight – he was barbarous in his own way, using his religious faith and convictions to justify state-sponsored brutalities, which included torture, branding, execution, unprovoked massacre, and a slave system that consumed thousands of Amerindian and African lives. Indeed, you would have to say he was bigoted, dogmatic, self-righteous, illogical, ruthless and hopelessly confused. In that regard, you would be correct.

It was in this atmosphere of *desengaño*, of national disillusionment, that Cervantes wrote his *Don Quixote*. Here, among many other parables, was the parable of an imperial nation which had set out on its holy crusade only to learn that it was tilting at windmills. In the end was the *desengaño*, for ultimately the reality would always break in on the illusion. Cervantes' life – from 1547 to 1616 – spanned the two ages of imperial triumph and imperial retreat, and the events of the last decade of Philip's reign had suddenly brought home to more thoughtful Spaniards the harsh truth about their native land – its poverty in the midst of riches, its power that had shown itself impotent.

## God's chosen instrument

In September 1587, Don Álvaro de Bazán, the marqués de Santa Cruz and a battle-tested veteran of Lepanto (where we shall meet him again standing on the fighting platform of a galley), pointed out the folly of sailing against England in mid-winter, and inquired about a fallback strategy. Now Don Álvaro, born in 1526, had gone to sea at an early age, in 1544 fighting his first naval engagement against a French corsair squadron. An expert in Atlantic as well as Mediterranean warfare, Don Álvaro had participated in every major expedition against the Ottomans, including Malta and el Peñón de Vélez de la Gomera, a Spanish rock and tied islet off the north coast of Morocco. Given command of the Neapolitan Spanish squadron, in short time he had made it a model of efficiency and, in 1569, Philip II in reward for his outstanding services at sea elevated him to marqués de Santa Cruz. He commanded the Spanish fleet during the invasion of Portugal in 1580, and two years later – 1582

– won a brilliant naval battle against a combined French and (unofficial) English fleet off Punta Delgada, in the Azores, thereby clinching Philip's conquest of Portugal.[20] Earlier attempts to the Azores, a crucial outpost for shipping to and from the New World, had failed. A superb administrator, as well as a gifted tactician, Santa Cruz had been chosen to lead the Armada being assembled to invade England the following year – the great sea fighter had actually proposed such an invasion as long ago as August 1583 following his aforementioned victory off Punta Delgado.

Santa Cruz had his own ideas regarding the invasion of England. He recommended that the enterprise should be conducted entirely from Spain with a great army carried in the fleet, sailing as one unit to the shores of England.[21] He, who had witnessed a somewhat poor performance by the English seamen in action with the French fleet in the engagement off Punta Delgado, was confident that the Armada could push its way to England against the resistance of the English ships. The army could be landed in Cornwall or Devon, which would neither necessitate the hazardous voyage up the Channel, nor involve all the complications of carrying out a junction with Alessandro Farnese, duca di Parma e Piacenza (r. 1586–92), in Flanders.

Now, let us return to where we began this section, namely, to the genuine operational concerns of Santa Cruz, a man whose prestige was enormous. In spite of all that and more, the king replied serenely to the marqués falling back, as was his habit, on messianic imperialism:

> We are fully aware of the risk that is incurred by sending a major fleet
> in winter through the Channel without a safe harbour, but ... *since
> it is all for His cause, God will send good weather* (emphasis mine).[22]

It was a scanty substitute for strategy, and it may serve to remind us that Philip was not a fighting warrior but a deeply religious man who put his trust in God and his own unending devotion to administration. Clearly Philip happily embraced the notion that his English venture was divinely guided, that his rôle was that of a universal crusader-cum-chief-clerk who carried the true faith with him. Generally regarded as the foremost fighting seaman in Spanish history, it was perhaps providential for England that Santa Cruz died on 9 February 1588.

Philip might today be considered a religious fanatic, always quite convinced that, whatever he chose to do, it was the will of God that he should succeed. In other words, for Philip who saw himself as *rex et sacerdos*, the religious principle always prevailed over the political calculation. But also, Philip was appallingly sincere. As a finished product of his time and place, he could have believed in the rightness of his mission and viewed the liquidation, by means of steel and faggot, of nonconformists as actually bringing them salvation. What is more, he saw it as not only his duty but also his route to personal salvation to win back lost ground for Catholicism in Europe. Conceivably, the king was some kind of unwitting god, forcibly exiled to Earth, his memory of his own divinity erased by jealous members of his former pantheon. We may not seem to have much respect or affection for the two things that Philip loved and cherished above all else on earth; namely Holy Spain and the true Apostolic Church as embodied by the *Sancta romana ecclesia*.

What we need to remind ourselves of here is the fact that the relationship between the Habsburg ruler and his subjects was not conditioned by a local sense of belonging or citizenship; it was rather a moral duty towards the monarch, expressed in religious terms that connected the subject to the dynasty. Running an empire that stretched from the Americas to the Philippines, from Flanders to Sicily, from Portugal to Milan, it was natural that the Habsburg understanding of assimilation was religious; the Roman Catholic identity was the only thing that could link people born in a number of different places to a common monarch. Religion was the glue which held the sprawling Habsburg empire together. The element of providential mentality cannot be overlooked or denied, and some scholars would go so far as to argue that the Spanish monarchy was founded upon the providence of God, which not only legitimated Spanish imperialism (especially in the New World) but also gave the monarchy a historical rôle: uniting Christendom under a universal sovereignty, extirpating heresy and defeating the Infidels. But to argue so is to indulge in the second guessing that is so simple long after the event. Besides, the Ottomans and their satellites, Philip's 'infidels', were not going to be overpowered that easily, even with God's help.

## Disaster at Djerba

At Djerba the Ottoman fleet was commanded by the *kapudan-ı deryā* Piyale Paşa, a talented young grand admiral of Balkan Christian ancestry, and it has been claimed that his order to hoist sail and run down the Christian fleet during the early morning light "ranks among the great snap decisions in naval history".[23] By breaking one of the most basic tenets of galley warfare, attacking without lowering his sails and yards – normally an imperative since one of the massive lateen yards, brought down by gunfire, could hazard the vessel – Piyale Paşa would pull off a signal victory. The Ottomans bore down with incredible speed on the panic-stricken Christians, whose only instinct was to flee *sauve qui peut*.

The outcome was inevitable. Only eight Christian galleys managed to escape the destruction that followed at Djerba, and in two of these both Gianandrea Doria, the grand nephew of the great Andrea Doria, and Juan de la Creda y Silva, duque de Medina Celi and Spanish viceroy of Sicily, reached safety. The Sicilian and papal fleets took years to recover from the defeat (the Ottomans had seized all five of the papal galleys), while Cosimo I de' Medici, II Duca di Firenze (r. 1537–69) and I Granducato di Toscana (r. 1569–74), had sent four of his newly acquired galleys to join the Djerba expedition, only to lose two in the ensuing disaster, *La Toscana* and *La Elbigina*. Maritime skill was something not to be acquired overnight, as the Florentine duke had learnt at his expense.

For Spain, on the other hand, the débâcle of Djerba was a good deal worse, ending as it did with the loss of forty-two ships. As damaging as the loss of ships was the loss of life among the Spanish and Neapolitan officer class and among skilled seamen and artisans (coopers, boatswains,[24] marines) – about 600 of Spain's best maritime men. The Ottomans then put 14,000 troops ashore, and the fight for the island lasted eighty days, Don Alvaro de Sande and his men yielding only when Djerba's brackish water supply had given out. Perhaps Philip recalled, as he contemplated this costly reverse, the advice of his father, Charles V, concerning war at sea: "Fleets at sea are as uncertain as the waves that bear them."[25] The emperor knew firsthand the terrors of the sea. Charles, when a young man and still the king of Spain, once made a vow to go on pilgrimage to Santiago de Compostela. It was like this: on Monday, 7 September 1517, Carlos I set sail from Middelburg in Zeeland for Spain. The ship's captain was Jan Cornelis from Zierikzee, the very man who in 1506 had brought Carlos' father Philipp I *der Schöne* to Spain. Five days into the sea voyage, a violent storm blew up when the ship was crossing the Bay of Biscay. The storm lasted fourteen hours and it was noted on 12 September that "because of the tempest the king swore a vow that he would make a pilgrimage to Santiago in Galicia".[26]

The victory boosted the confidence of the Ottomans and offered them a vision of the future. They had good reason to feel that they were on the verge of a breakthrough. Ships could be replaced, but to rebuild a significant pool of experienced naval personnel took years. Even though the débâcle at Djerba orchestrated the start of a galley construction programme in the Mediterranean shipyards of the Spanish Habsburg domains, with Philip II expressing his views openly that "Spain needs a very strong fleet not only defend itself, but also strike her enemies in their own lands",[27] it would be some time before the Spanish could again tackle the Ottomans at sea. For this reason, when the Ottoman host descended on Malta in 1565, the viceroy of Sicily and *capitán general de la Mar Mediterraneo y Adriático*, Don García Álvarez de Toledo Osorio (1514–77), did all within his powers to safeguard the meagre resources he had at his disposal, biding his time until it was deemed safe to despatch a relief force to the island. Thus, on the night of 5 July, four companies of *Tercio Viejo de Sicilia* sent by the viceroy quietly slipped past the Ottomans to reach the harbour forts, in the defence of which these 600 veterans would play an essential part. According to Don García, although the number of the galleys participating in the operation was more than fifty, the whole operation was executed so silently and carefully and not even an oar was lost during the landing (*sin perder un remo*).[28] In fact, Philip II had instructed Don García that his priority had to be the preservation of the galleys; if lost, Malta could be retaken at some point later.[29] The anxious king was to write to Gianandrea Doria in 1570, the year prior to Lepanto, warning him if any misfortune should come to his galleys "you know what damages might occur to all Christendom. Be very careful where you place them."[30]

The Ottoman invasion (and subsequent conquest) of Cyprus in 1570, the most distant of the Venetian outposts, heightened the crisis in the Mediterranean. The confrontations between Charles V and Süleymān and then between Philip II and Selīm II, Süleymān's successor at the Sublime Porte, fuelled by the privateering conducted by Barbary corsairs, culminated in the battle of Lepanto, in which (as we have seen) the Spanish soldier Miguel de Cervantes fought heroically against the Ottoman Turks.


## Anno 1588

Habsburg Spain, the backbone of western Christendom, was to play the major part in the decisive and unexpected victory of Lepanto over the 'Infidel Turks' in the Mediterranean in 1571, allowing it to scale down its galley fleet there to around twenty vessels, supported by smaller squadrons operating from Genoa, Naples, and Sicily. The Spanish Habsburg galley force – *La Armada de las galeras de España* – in the Mediterranean was composed of four separate fleets. The first one, of course, was the Spanish fleet, the second was the private fleet of the Doria family of Genoa, the third was the fleet of the Kingdom of Naples, and the fourth was the fleet of the Kingdom of Sicily. In addition to these fleets, galleys of the Knights Hospitaller and the Order of Saint Stephen supported Habsburg operations by corsair activities against the Ottomans. When a major naval campaign was decided upon, the fleets came together under the command of the *capitán general de la Mar Mediterraneo y Adriático*, who represented the king of Spain and could give orders in the name of the king (*representando nuestra Persona*, in the words of Philip himself). This was the official position that Don Juan de Austria had held at Lepanto. Yet it was not until after the death of Don Juan that Philip decided it was time to deal with the 'heretic English'. To that end, therefore, the king launched *la Armada Felicisma* – the 'Most Fortunate' fleet – under the command of a land-lubber. The course of history sometimes turns on the luckiest of events (or unluckiest, depending on the results).

One of the many remarkable things about the Armada was that its commander-in-chief, the *capitán general del Mar Océano*, Captain General of the Ocean Sea, had scarcely ever been to sea and did not want to go. Surely Don Juan would have been a much better and braver match on the high seas for the Tudor navy under the aging high admiral of England, Lord Charles Howard of Effingham (with that venerable sea dog Sir Francis Drake as his second-in-command), than the many-syllabled VII duque de Medina Sidonia, Don Alonso Pérez de Guzmán y de Zúñiga-Sotomayor *el Bueno* (1550–1615). He was a grandee of Spain and a man of considerable administrative experience (he virtually ruled the southern province of Andalusia, perhaps the wealthiest part of the country) but who had never pretended to be a warrior aristocrat, let alone a good soldier, nor ever wanted to be; and much less a sailor. He had of course been bred to arms, as all Spanish nobles were, the art of warfare being a normal stage in a man's life as opposed to a closed profession, but he never attempted to conceal the fact that arms were the last things he cared about. As a matter of fact, his reaction to the order appointing him *capitán general del Mar Océano* was to write to the king's secretary, Don Juan de Idiáquez, begging to be relieved of his command because, among other things, of his propensity to seasickness. Whatever he may have thought about himself, the king clearly regarded him as the right man for the job, and refused to listen to his objections.[31]

Ironically two years previously, it was the same duque, then serving in the capacity of the official in charge of protecting the Indies trade, who had informed the king that, in his opinion, Elizabethan aggression overseas would be more cheaply and more effectively countered by mounting a major seaborne attack on England, the pirates' base,[32] than by strengthening the fleets and fortresses of Spanish America. It was not, of course, the duque's intention that, when his advice was accepted, he should be charged with leading the attack in person. More active with his pen than with his sword, the honest duque would soon put to paper his argument to his superior in San Lorenzo del Escorial. But he would find his royal audience less than receptive.

It is a well-known fact that accidents can play a considerable rôle in both history and the lives of individuals.[33] We can certainly see that with the events of 1588, for another great irony had taken place three decades previously. In September 1555 Philip, then king consort of England, appeared before the Privy Council to point out that:

> Since England's chief defence depends upon its navy being always in good order to serve for the defence of the kingdom against all invasion it is right that the ships should not only be fit for sea, but instantly available.[34]

Accordingly, a new generation of ships were added to the Tudor royal navy – the majority of which took part in the running sea fights up the Channel in July and August 1588, such as the 900-ton, 64-gun *Elizabeth*

*Jonas*, laid down in 1558 as the *Philip* but renamed after the accession of Philip's sister-in-law, the Protestant monarch Elizabeth I, later that year, and in service until 1618. It was the hardiness of these ships and the seamanship of their commanders, and not their guns, which was the deciding factor during the three general engagements on 31 July (Start Point), 2 (Portland Bill), 3 (Isle of Wight), and 4 August (Owen Banks).[35]

Yet a sea battle on an extended scale was no part of the Spanish plan. If one were forced upon them, they would have chosen, with their galleons and galleasses and well disciplined veteran soldiers, to have engaged closely, as Don Juan had done to good effect at Lepanto. Because the Spaniards tended to regard boarding and physical capture as the ultimate naval tactic they concentrated on short-range, ship-smashing artillery – the 'cannon type' (whole cannon and demi-cannon) and the 'perrier type' (cannon-perrier) – with which they hoped to cripple an enemy to a standstill before coming alongside to grapple and deliver the *coup de grâce* with hot shot and cold steel. So for the Spanish the winning trick was to be won on the enemy's deck, to see said deck a dreadful shambles. On the other hand, Elizabethan naval gunnery tactics were a matter of hit and run and accordingly required a ship (and its company) that could manoeuvre with deftness. In a lengthy epistle containing his instructions to Medina Sidonia as he preparing to depart, Philip II had displayed some tactical insight:

> There is little to say with regard to the mode of fighting and the handling of the Armada on the day of battle ... [but] it must be borne in mind that the enemy's object will be to fight at long distance, in consequence of his advantage in artillery, and the large number of artificial fires with which he will be furnished. The aim of our men, on the contrary, must be to bring him to close quarters and grapple with him, and you will have to be very careful to have this carried out ... The enemy employs his artillery to deliver his fire low and sink his opponent's ships; and you will have to take such precautions as you consider necessary in this respect.[36]

Whereas the Spaniards were going for boarding and entering, the English opted for cannonading. Closing would have been foolish.[37] As *capitán* Antonio de Vanegas, the gunnery officer aboard the Spanish flagship

*São Martinho*, which was in the thick of the Channel fights, recounts, "The enemy ... did well because of the extreme nimbleness and the great smoke that came from their artillery."[38] The Lepanto veterans considered that, in comparison, the cannonading they experienced in the Channel was twenty-times more furious.[39]

We have wandered a decade or so ahead of our story, however, for the Armada did not sail from Lisbon until 30 May 1588. As far as our story is concerned, many Spanish veterans of Lepanto were aboard the vessels of the Armada and serving in its strong military contingent. Drawn from the trained garrisons of Naples and Sicily, and replaced by raw recruits from Spain, these were steadfast battle-hardened soldiers who boasted with justification that in the century now drawing to a close they had never lost a fight (about which more later). They too must have shared the hope of bringing back the days of English satellitism when their king, His Most Catholic Majesty Philip II, had been briefly married to Mary Tudor, queen of England. That collective hope proved to be considerably brittle, for what had originally been planned as an overnight triumph turned instead into a watery nightmare for these battle-tested veterans of naval combat.

As is well known, after its run in with the English fleet, the shot-wracked Spanish fleet limped around Scotland towards ultimate disaster on the rock-fanged Irish coast. The treacherous waters around Ireland had their first taste of Spanish timber on 4 September 1588, when the 27-gun *Castillo Negro* (750 tons) vanished without trace off Donegal. It was during that month that many of the veterans of 1571 ended up as washed-up corpses along the shoreline of the Irish Atlantic coast when the Almighty blew to destruction the remnants of the Catholic king's Armada, or having scrambled to safety, half-drowned and weak through hunger and thirst, only to be butchered on shore by the hostile locals. Ireland, that sodden green rock pounded by the long rollers and the fierce sou'-westerlies of the black heaving Atlantic, was then a little-known place on the very edge of Europe, where feuding cattle herders lived in a wild and wet wilderness. Professional soldiers know that death is a likely event, but in this instance those who escaped drowning seem to have hoped for succour from the Irish who, they knew, were Catholics like themselves. But they seldom received it.

To this day no one knows for certain how many ships were wrecked off the western coast of Ireland or, in many cases, where. Altogether sixty-three ships out of 122 were lost from the Armada, the fate of thirty-five being unknown. Only two were lost through accident during the Channel sea fights, the 46-gun *Nuestra Señora del Rosario* (1,150 tons and a crew of 359), the flagship (*capitana*) of the squadron of Andalusia and perhaps the best-gunned ship in the whole Armada, which was taken in action, and the 25-gun *San Salvadore* (953 tons, Spanish measure), a galleon belonging to the squadron of Guipúzcoa, which was set adrift after her magazine caught fire. A number were wrecked off the coasts of the Netherlands, France, England and Scotland but the majority off Ireland.

Lest we forget, however, by the spring of 1590 Philip II had a powerful fleet once again, which included twelve formidable new vessels, Spanish galleons of 500, 600 and 800 *toneladas* (tonnes), four ships of each tonnage, a series later known as the Twelve Apostles because each one was named after one of Christ's disciples. In general, Spanish galleons were magnificent if cumbersome engines of war, displacing from 250 to 1,000 tonnes (275.6 to 1,102.3 tons) apiece and carrying up to fifty guns. They were literally floating fortresses, with high forecastles and sterns (now discarded by the English, who favoured the 'race-built' design) crowded with soldiers in times of battle. The galleons did sport some powerful guns, but the Spanish were still wedded to the close-and-grapple form of naval warfare. One can safely say that by 1650 the galleon had faded out of use as better, sleeker warships were being built and rated according to the number of guns carried on hoard.

The Museo Naval in Madrid has a splendid gallery devoted to the Christian victory of Lepanto; there is only a small display devoted to the 'unsuccessful expedition against England'. The Armada sailed from Lisbon gloriously decked out, splendidly confident – fated for destruction in the Atlantic waters around Britain and Ireland. Lepanto was the largest galley battle of the early modern period and also the last major clash involving the Mediterranean's nimble but fragile warships. It also ranks as one of the bloodiest single days in military history, with an estimated 40,000 combatants killed. Given the patriotic or celebratory nature of national histories, we should not be surprised by the fact that some individuals, some events, and some campaigns are better treated than others, as more glorious, inspiring, or to employ the terminology of militant jingoism, as 'worth remembering'.

## Chapter 5

# Spanish Steel

And he sees across the land a straggling road in Spain...
G.K. Chesterton, 'Lepanto', *Poems*

With the taking of Tripoli, *la fortuna di Cesare*, that is to say, the
same incredible series of events that had helped Charles V
every time his numerous and powerful enemies seemed to have
the upper hand, had triumphed once again. If one believes that monarchs
may sometimes stamp their character on the ages in which they lived and
ruled, then Titian's equestrian portrait of Charles V says it all. Painted
to commemorate the battle of Mühlberg in 1547, the emperor's decisive
victory over the German Protestants, Titian represents the jutting-jawed
Charles clad *cap-à-pied* and astride a spirited Spanish horse caparisoned
in scarlet, giving his subject the air of a gallant Christian knight about
to enter battle confident in his stout lance and strong right arm. Charles
was an excellent horseman; the Spaniards said that by becoming emperor
they had lost their best cavalry officer. This was the emperor's favourite
portrait, and he took it with him to the remoteness of Yuste when he
abdicated nine years later (it now hangs in the Museo del Prado, Madrid).
Charles was often called Caesar. It reflected the Spanish tendency,
commonplace in the early modern centuries, to compare Spain's imperial
achievement to those of the Greeks and the Romans, be the focus on
military logistics, governmental vision, or moral justification. More to
the point, as the Holy Roman Emperor, Charles was *the* Caesar of the day.

Definitely no friend of the Spanish, the Christian king Louis XII of
France (r. 1498–1515) had entitled himself the 'Second Caesar' and chosen
the porcupine as his royal device, coupled with the motto COMINVS ET
EMINVS, 'from far and near'. Symbolically, with its ability to wound
far and near, the aggressive, invincible and warlike porcupine resembled
the mass of pikemen twenty to thirty deep, *el tercio español*, 'the Spanish
third', which was the key innovation of 16th-century warfare.

### 'War in the Spanish style'

For reasons which are far from clear, the Spanish had, in the closing years of the 15th century, adopted the use of individual gunpowder weapons to an extent unmatched by any other nation, excluding possibly their neighbours in the Iberian peninsula, the Portuguese. By the turn of the 16th century the harquebus was well on its way to replacing the crossbow in Spanish service. Gonzalo Fernández de Córdoba (1453–1515), justly known to his contemporaries as *El gran capitán*, the military genius against whom all others would ultimately be measured, decisively defeated the French in battle just outside the small town of Cerignola in southern Italy on 28 April 1503.

Up to this point in time the Kingdom of Naples had been snarled and quarrelled over by France and Spain, both having menaced its independence, both having disseminated spurious claims which do not concern us. What does concern us, however, is the significant political result of the battle which was the addition of the Kingdom of Naples to the crown of Spain – in fact, Naples rejoined Sicily and Sardinia as an Aragonese possession, and was brought, like them, under the government of viceroys and the jurisdiction of the Council of Aragón. Already a grizzled veteran of the *La Reconquista* wars (1481–92), Fernández de Córdoba was the right-hand man of his exact contemporary Ferdinand in the latter's stunningly successful dynastic metamorphosis from prince of Aragón and titular king of Sicily to joint ruler of a united Spain, all of southern Italy, and the principal military power in Europe. The highly efficient armies forged during *La Reconquista* wars, whose details belong elsewhere, were thoroughly reorganised into a standing army under full royal control. It was from this that the 16th-century Spanish army sprang, the formidable army that was to fight in the eight Italian wars (1494 to 1559) against France.

The Italian wars were the dawn of a new military era and the slow demise of an old one. This was the period of rapid military development: over a seven-decade period came the rise of handheld firearms and mobile cannon. Neither were strangers at the beginning of the wars, but by the end gunpowder weapons, having become more numerous and reliable, were clearly on the way to dominance on the European battlefield. However, the traditional pike and lance still had their place. The initial wars were a curious turning point – a bridge connecting the old with the new – a struggle in which Miguel de Cervantes might well have politely smiled at the decline of feudalism and welcome in a new era; as he did, subsequently, in *Don Quixote*.

During his Italian campaigns of 1495–7 and 1501–04, in which both France and Spain strove to conquer the Kingdom of Naples, Fernández de Córdoba was to show himself a commander of outstanding ability, quick to learn the lessons taught him by the enemy and apply them to his own troops. As a result, just as these years saw the creation of a professional diplomatic service that would serve Spain well for many decades to come, so also they saw the creation of a fully professional army, whose skill and *esprit de corps* were to win Spain its great victories of the 16th century and the first-half of the 17th century. This brings us to the other significant result of the battle, namely the tactical one.

At Cerignola it was the battle-hardened Spanish harquebusiers firing from the protection of pikemen firmly planted behind a palisaded ditch and rampart, which shattered the opposition's assault led by Swiss pikemen, the most famous of European foot soldiers at that time – using their traditional, well-tested tactic based on a swift and well-timed head down attack in three deep blocks (*haufen*, 'heaps') of pikemen in échelon – and French *gens d'armes*, the best heavily equipped cavalry then available on the European battlefield. It had been believed by the French high command that the combination of Swiss mountaineers and French chivalry would decide the battle – as they always had – that day. How mistaken it was. The day had been won, according to the disgruntled Fabrizio Colonna (†1520), the celebrated Roman *condottiere*, by "a little ditch, and a parapet of earth, and the arquebus".[1] Social snobbery on the part of a pure shock specialist, perhaps, but Spanish small arms – lock, stock and barrel – had stopped in their tracks the massive assault by the Swiss pikemen and the gallant charge of the French *gens d'armes*. It is also noteworthy that the death of Louis d'Armagnac, duc de Nemours, the French commander, was due to harquebus fire, his armour being sieved by no less than three leaden bullets fired by anonymous harquebusiers.

The following year, Fernández de Córdoba systematically drove the French from their remaining garrisons in the Kingdom of Naples. It would not be an exaggeration to say that Gonzalo Fernández de Córdoba may be the most commonly known name in the military history of Spain. However, although other, later Spanish commanders conquered on a continental scale, it was from *El gran capitán* that they learned their trade and from whom they drew inspiration. Thus, though *El gran capitán* died in 1515, the military 'school' that he had developed survived him and, on the tactical level, the Spanish mastery of handheld firearms continued to mature.

Clearly, Fernández de Córdoba preferred to position his harquebusiers behind barricades, which not only offered a degree of protection but also increased accuracy. On 27 April 1522 Spanish harquebusiers, standing four ranks deep and immediately behind a rampart, decimated the Swiss in French pay at Bicocca, a mannor park some six kilometres north of Milan. This was the first unequivocal defeat of the Swiss pike blocks in open battle. Their total losses were more than 3,000 dead. As Francesco Guicciardini (1483–1540), a contemporary Florentine historian, courtier, and diplomat, was to observe about that day:

> They [viz. the Swiss mercenaries] went back to their mountains diminished in numbers, but more diminished in audacity; for it is certain that the losses which they had suffered at Bicocca so affected them in coming years that they no longer displayed their wonted vigour (*non dimostrorno il solito vigore*).[2]

In spite of Bicocca marking the end of Swiss dominance among the infantry of the Italian wars, it was one of the first engagements which established the decisive rôle of handheld firearms on the battlefield. Yet the French failed to take heed. Blaise de Monluc remarks that in 1523, when he was a young ensign in the company of Monsieur de la Clotte, he had only six harquebusiers with him, and they were all deserters from the Spanish army.[3]

War was changing with or without the French aboard, and the growing supremacy of handheld firearms would be demonstrated once again. On 24 February 1525, Spanish harquebusiers operating independently and in relatively open terrain helped to bring about the defeat of the French army of François I at Pavia, in Lombardy. The French *gens d'armes* were unhorsed and slaughtered by point-blank harquebus fire or by a stiletto slipped through the visor, and their king hauled off into captivity to sign the humiliating Treaty of Madrid.[4] Guillaume II Gouffier, seigneur de Bonnivet, *amiral de France*, who was to fall at Pavia, said of his opponents:

> I can only say the 5,000 Spaniards seem to be 5,000 men-at-arms, and 5,000 light cavalry, and 5,000 infantrymen, and 5,000 sappers – and 5,000 devils supporting them.[5]

Further, and fuller, information comes from the pen of Pierre de Bourdeilles, abbé et seigneur de Brantôme, who writes:

> Fifteen hundred (Spanish) harquebusiers, the ablest, the most experienced, the cleverest, above all the most agile and devoted, were selected by the marquis de Pescani [Fernando Francesco d'Ávalos, V marqués de Pescara], instructed by him on new lines, and practiced for a long time. They scattered by squads over the battlefield, turning, leaping from one place to another with great speed, and thus escaped the cavalry charge. By this new method of fighting, unusual, astonishing, cruel and unworthy, these harquebusiers greatly hampered the operations of the French cavalry [viz. *gens d'armes*], who were completely lost. For they, joined together and in mass, were brought to earth by these brave and able harquebusiers.[6]

A decisive episode of the Italian wars, the outcome of Pavia cemented Spanish Habsburg ascendancy in Italy.[7] On the personal level, for Charles V (he was then in Spain) the battle (it was also his twenty-fifth birthday) was the first military victory of his long reign, and he would later laud the martial abilities of his soldiers, commenting that "the fate of my battles was decided by the fuses of my Spanish harquebusiers".[8] As we shall see later on, the shipboard harquebusiers of the Spanish *tercios* would play a major part in the Christian victory at Lepanto.

The pike, however, though ceasing to be the paramount weapon, remained as essential to infantry organisation as the firearm. Indeed, as the only trustworthy weapon for wet weather, and as a weapon for ultimate action at all times, it continued to be the more indispensable of the two. His experience in the Kingdom of Naples encouraged Fernández de Córdoba to organise *coronelías* (also called *colunelas* or columns), new field commands inspired by the old laws of the Roman military order, that is to say the Roman legions. He ordered that each *capitanía* should consist of 500 men: 200 pikemen, 200 sword-and-buckler men, and a hundred harquebusiers. Ten mixed companies, plus another two of pikemen alone, formed a *coronelía* commanded by a *coronel* (hence 'colonel' in English), with a total of 6,000 men. This would also have two attached cavalry squadrons, one with 300 men-at-arms and the other with 300 horsemen. Two *coronelías* made up an army, led by a *capitán general*. However, two points should be understood. First, the numbers given above, as always is the case with such matters, were only theoretical and were unlikely to be achieved in practice due to recruiting problems, desertion, disease and death during campaigns. Second, this organisation was not inflexible; the *capitanías* could be concentrated or could operate separately, according to the requirements of particular operations. From being the major unit, the *coronelía* of Fernández de Córdoba's day became just one of three making up a *tercio*, the first large permanent infantry unit, both administrative and tactical, each bearing a territorial title.

## Sword-and-buckler

Colloquially known as sword-and-buckler men, the Spanish knew them as *rodeleros*, shield bearers, or *espadachines*, swordsmen. They often wore steel helmets and corselets. The *rodela*, 'buckler',[9] was a small circular shield, at least *dos palmos* in diameter,[10] but no more, and most often made of steel and consisted of a face, a central boss (a bowl-shaped protrusion allowing room for the hand) and a handle. The face was often circular, but could be square or shaped to create one or more hook-like protrusions at its rim for catching and deflecting an oncoming blade. It was commonly curved to redirect blows and the rim was occasionally sharpened to allow cutting. The boss could be rounded for crushing blows. Held one-handed in a fist grip (as opposed to worn on the arm), bucklers were used to punch and parry upward the thrust of a pike, thereby allowing the Spaniard to dodge under the five-metre pole and close in for the kill with his sword.

The versatility of the sword and buckler as a method of fighting can be said to lay in its simplicity. As a two-weapon combination, it is simultaneously defensive and offensive. The buckler offered some protection against missile weapons and was convenient for facing heavier weapons such as pole arms and axes. Yet its small size made it agile and quick. Combined with a good shearing sword designed more for cutting blows or a lighter tapering cut-and-thrust blade, which allowed for greater use of agile thrusting and quick slices, it could deflect attacks, strike blows of its own, and yet still allow the user's own sword to cut around in any direction. Another advantage of metal bucklers was that unlike wooden shields the point of an opponent's weapon would not get stuck in the face of the buckler, nor would the edge of a blade damage the rim.

The halberd, a shafted weapon two-metres long serving both for thrusting and striking because it carried a hatchet blade as well as a spike at its business end, was not adopted by the Spaniards. They judged, correctly, that the arming of infantry with sword and buckler gave them greater mobility and flexibility. Mixed among the pikemen, sword-and-buckler men waited for an opportunity to strike when opposing pike blocks locked together. The lightly armed sword-and-buckler men moved through the ranks swiftly, penetrating the enemy pike formation for the kill. These soldiers used their metal bucklers to lift the pikes of the enemy formation and approach the men wielding the pikes.

Machiavelli writes of how at the battles of Barletta (1503) and Ravenna (1512) the Spanish sword-and-buckler men dealt with the Swiss, renowned for their competence at handling pikes *en masse*. These rather enigmatic mountaineers had adopted a 5.5-metre-long pike manufactured from ash, walnut, or some other 'noble' wood. The lower one-third (from the butt-end of the shaft) was thicker, to ensure that it would not warp or break over the course of time. The steel point came in several shapes, the most usual being a four-faced diamond section. This is what Machiavelli had to say:

When they engaged the fight, the Swiss pressed so hard upon the enemy with their pikes that they soon opened their ranks; but the Spaniards, under the cover of their bucklers, nimbly rushed in with their swords and fought them so furiously that they slaughtered the Swiss and gained a complete victory. Everyone knows what numbers of Swiss infantry were similarly cut to pieces at the battle of Ravenna; for once the Spanish infantry closed with the Swiss, they made such good use of their swords that not one of the enemy would have been left alive if a body of French cavalry had not come up to rescue them; thereupon, however, the Spaniards drew up close together and made a handsome retreat with little or no loss.[11]

Once on the battlefield, the Swiss had a habit of kneeling down to pray and then kissing the ground as a sign of humility; but that was as far as their humility went. After a battle had opened, they were fierce and pitiless fighters, believing the key to victory was to advance ferociously, regardless of cost, regardless of obstacles, relying on their ferocity and speed to do the business. The Swiss spared no-one, not even themselves. Violent, nasty and businesslike, they had a habit of hanging the first man to panic in an unlucky crisis, and it was not unknown for them – so long as they were paid in advance – to literally fight to the last man in time of defeat. Panic and discipline are ill bedfellows.

And what of the aftermath of battle? The Swiss were men who were known to murder their prisoners without hesitation or remorse – especially from among the *Landsknechte*, whom they loathed as impostors: when the two sides met in battle it was known as *schlechten krieg*, 'bad war'. Had they felt a need to justify their cruel acts, they might very well have said that their victims knew the risks and the rules of the game and would as quickly have done the same to them.

### 'Push of Pikes'

Especially in its early forms, the 'push of pikes', as it was nonchalantly known, was a rare show of organised savagery practised *en masse*. When two pike blocks collided, the pikemen viciously prodded and poked with their long weapons, trying to open gaps in the opposing formation, creating a murderous tangle of vibrating pike-staves jutting back and forth in a wild rhythm, bashing against each other, while their steel tips searched for a path through the guard and the armour of their targets, attempting to stab at each other's faces, throats and thighs. As this happened, soldiers brandishing all sorts of *arme corte* (two-handed swords, halberds, swords and bucklers, etc., etc.) took advantage of every opening to try to push their way through the layers of the wall of pike-heads to reach those who were brandishing them. Those in the rear ranks of the two pike blocks who were unable to use their own arms literally pushed their comrades ahead for support and momentum and stepped in their place as these fell – hampered by 5.5-metre pikes, it must in practice have been more difficult than in the ancient Roman army that was the model for close-order tactics.

If the mêlée continued and neither of the two sides yielded, the pressure mounted, shafts often broke, or were cut, or left to fall because they were unusable. The border between the two formations became less and less defined, with groups of men fiercely fighting with anything available in the mayhem of pike-staves, stepping on the bodies of the dead and wounded. It does seem unlikely that such a confrontation could have lasted many minutes before one side or the other faltered, but it must have been a hideous ordeal while it lasted. As a *Landsknecht* (that is, one of the mercenaries as a rule from the Rhine Basin, Alsace, Baden Wurttemberg, Vorarlberg and Austrian Tyrol, all of them young, strong and eager, and who fought *à la suisse*)[12] ballad about the battle of Pavia (24 February 1525) recounts, "in blood we had to go, in blood we had to go, up to, up to the tops of our shoes. Merciful God, look at the misery!"[13] This was the fateful day fellow Germans fought each other to near extinction in a fratricidal bloodbath.[14] It must have been a gory scene – the streams of blood were not a literary convention – with men with heads split open, men with limbs cut off, disembowelled men, men crushed to a pulp, men torn asunder by harquebus balls, maddened men trapped with no way to turn. Within minutes, too, the air would have turned fetid with rank odours: sweat; blood; urine; faeces. Blood would have seeped into the ground until it could take no more and then flooded upwards.

Despite this however, the recruiting sergeants of the 16th-century mercenary world – poverty, greed, boredom, unemployment or underemployment – were never short of volunteers, whether they lived long enough to make it all worth it.

Thus a 16th-century woodcut by Erhard Schön (†1542) shows a *Landsknecht* and his female companion with an eight-line ditty accompanying each character. The *Landsknecht*, a former cobbler, explains that he will abandon shoemaking for soldiering to gain what he can, since being a cobbler rewards him little, though "in many wars I have won / Great wealth and manifold honours / Who then knows whom fortune favours?" She replies that, "Perhaps so much may be my winning [from pillage] / Much more than ever I could whilst spinning."[15] In his commentary on the elegant proverb *Dulce bellum inexpertis*,[16] the Dutch humanist and theologian Desiderius Erasmus (1469–1536) condemns the greed and petty violence of common soldiers:

> Those are called soldiers, who rush off of their own accord to the fight in the hope of a small profit, and fight on either side, like gladiators, though they may be brothers against brothers, and both belong to the jurisdiction of the same prince.[17]

Erasmus' alarm at the fraticidal combat of mercenary armies speaks for his commitment to the cause of Christian pacifism in the early modern period.

Because they were good at their work, it is worth saying a word or two on the *Landsknechte*. It was these stalwart pikemen who were now the sturdy, unshakable, non-prisoner-taking exterminators on early modern Europe's red fields of battle. This was reflected in their garish garments: a diverse array of large, floppy, wide-brimmed hats topped with peacock or ostrich feathers, doublets and shirts with billowing, slashed sleeves with the material beneath pulled through, tight-fitting, multi-stripped hoses with different hues on each leg, tight or voluminous breeches, called *hosenteufel*, devil's breeches,[18] and outrageous codpieces stuffed with straw. Hose could be cut short, leaving the lower leg bare, sometimes including the buttock. Freakishly dressed like this the *Landsknecht* not only stuck out and displayed a careless disposition, but his flamboyant way of dressing also indicated he was in breech of societal customs. The sumptuary laws which kept, for instance, the English from wearing apparel above their social station, and even specified what kind of fabrics people of different classes could parade in public, clearly did not apply to the foppish *Landsknechte*.[19] When other imperial troops complained about the flamboyant outfits of the *Landsknechte*, their creator

Maximilian von Österreich (later the Holy Roman Emperor Maximilian I) famously replied: "Give them a little happiness and pride in their lives, which are so full of danger."[20] Though the recruits had to provide their own clothing, weapons and armour, for a man of modest social origins, military life afforded both uncommon riches and unusual opportunities for the public display of wealth. What you wore, and how you wore it, was a matter of deep significance.

*Landsknechte* carried idiosyncratic side arms: a unique dagger with a thin, stiletto-like blade and a short double-edged broadsword, called *katzbalger*, or 'cat skinner', with distinctive figure-of-eight or S-shaped quillons. They regarded their multi-coloured swaggering units as independent corporations and as a rule even elected their own junior officers (*voerder*, *gemeene weyfel*, and *fourier*), administered justice, and agreed their terms and conditions of employment without interference from any state. Priding themselves on their toughness, smartness, and a capacity for violence, they used their corporate solidarity to drive up pay rates and to impose what now might be termed in the labour market as restrictive practices.

Before battle the *Landsknechte* would pray or recite a hymn, then throw dust over one shoulder for luck. A brief speech from the unit commander, *Obrist*, '… We want, as God wills, to do our duty today and get rich…", then the closed-packed square rolled forward to the sound of fife and drum – something new at the time – the drum banging out five beats, giving rise to their menacing mantra: *Hut – Dich – Baur Ich Komm!*, 'Look – Out – Here I Come!'[21] By contrast, Spanish infantry typically fought in silence, broken only by their traditional war cry, which broke out just before they went into close-quarter combat, *¡Santiago y cierra, España!*, "Saint James and attack, Spain!"[22]

## 'Spanish Thirds'

The Spanish *tercio* was to be the nemesis of the classic Swiss/*Landsknechte* pike block. The increased reputation that infantry acquired was due mainly to the Swiss and their conscious imitators the *Landsknechte* – contemporary Italian commentators often fail to distinguish between them – but its increased versatility was due mainly to the Spaniards who, unlike the Swiss and the *Landsknechte*, did not regard firearms as an auxiliary to the pike. Bringing together shock and shot infantry, the pikemen of *los tercios españoles* were supported by detachments of harquebusiers, who could indeed 'defend from afar'. The precursor of the musket, the harquebus was fairly cheap to produce and made a great deal of noise, making it the perfect mate for the then-king of the infantry weapons, the steel-tipped ashen pike. From the four corners of a *tercio*, the harquebusiers would let loose a volley, and then retreat into the centre of the pike formation to reload. Until weapons technology made it redundant, *el tercio* was a most effective and versatile infantry formation. It needed no ditches or palisades; it could stand its ground, advance or retreat; and it could offer a wall of fire on all four sides.

The *tercios* were created in the early fifteen-thirties by amalgamating existing *coronelía* in threes. The original *tercios* were the three of the army of Italy – *Tercio de Lombardia*, *de Nápoles*, and *de Sicilia* – as officially recognised by Charles V in the 1536 Ordinance of Genoa, later known as *los tercios viejos*. It may be this tactical development which gave rise to the name *tercio*, but it is likelier that it came from their resemblance to one of the three massive, homogenous units, or 'battles' (from which we derive the modern word 'battalion'), of mediaeval armies: main body, vanguard, rearguard, which had been usually so manoeuvred as to serve as shock absorber, flanking diversion and support.

Only in Spain's armies was there an organisation regularly based on self-contained units. Thus, in a *tercio* company, of which there were ten, each *compañia* had a nominal strength of 300 men. The company was organised (in theory, of course) as follows: *capitán* – captain, *alférez* – ensign (second-in-command and responsible for the company standard, the symbol of the unit's honour), *abanderado* – standard-bearer, *sargento* – sergeant (in charge of discipline, drilling and deployment), *capellán* – chaplain, *furriel* – quartermaster, *tambor* – drummer – and *pifano* – fifer (signal givers as well as morale raisers),[23] *barbero* – barber surgeon,[24] *cabos de escuadra* – several corporals (one for each squadron),[25] 150 *piqueros* – pikemen, one hundred *arcabuceros* – harquebusiers (later, musketeers), and forty *rodeleros* – sword-and-buckler men, whom Niccolò Machiavelli, writing in the second decade of the 16th century, so much admired.

In theory, therefore, a *tercio* was 3,000 strong; in fact, their average strength was only about 1,500 men, with a tendency to become smaller as time went on. As with all tables of military organisation throughout military history, armies in the field almost always fell short of their paper strength and attrition reduced them further. Also, with the *tercios* there were various, gradual changes to their internal organisation over time. In 1567, for instance, the duque de Alba added thirty musketeers to his *tercios*. For the record, the *tercios* that went to Flanders in 1567 were: *Tercio Viejo de Nápoles*, 3,200 men; *Tercio Viejo de Lombardia*, 2,200; *Tercio de Sardinia*, 1,600; and *Tercio Viejo de Sicilia*, 1,600 – giving Alba a total of 8,600 men instead of the theoretical 12,000. Suffice it to say that these were privileged formations.

Although he profited from long-established Spanish martial traditions and usages, Alba must be considered the creator of the Army of Flanders. As one of Europe's most experienced soldiers, he was uniquely qualified to forge this army and impose his personal imprint upon its organisation. Born in 1507, Fernando Álvarez de Toledo y Pimentel, El Gran Duque de Alba, had been raised almost from the cradle to be a professional soldier in both theory and practice. He saw his first battle at age six, had reportedly memorised (presumably in the original Latin) Vegetius' *De Re Militari* by age thirteen, and participated in most of the major campaigns of Charles V in Spain, North Africa, Italy, France, the Low Countries and the Holy Roman Empire.

The motif of strong defence was applied both to military architecture and to strong formations like *el tercio*, which were vulnerable only to a concentrated cannonade. Gerat Barry (fl. 1624–42), a Catholic Irish captain in Spanish service, fully recognised that:

> [T]he armed [viz. armoured] pike(man) is the strength of the batell [battle formation, viz. *tercio*], so without question, is the shot [viz. the harquebusier] the furie of the field: but the one without the other is weakened, the better halfe of their strength.[26]

A large, deep infantry formation such as a *tercio* was comparable to a moving fortress, with walls of pikemen instead of stone and with outlying bodies of shot in place of bastions.

Similarly, the great military thinker the Austrian Habsburg fighting general Raimondo Montecuccoli (1609–80) would describe the pikemen *en masse* as the "castles of the battlefield".[27] His treatise is remarkable as an analysis of the lessons of recent wars as a basis for a prognosis for the future – quite different from the scholastic recapitulation of classical antiquity penned by his fellow Italian Niccolò Machiavelli.

Initially the pikes used by the Spanish were shorter than those of the Swiss and the *Landsknechte*, but by the mid-16th century the Spanish pike had to be around twenty-seven Castilian *palmos* (5.5 metres) in length, and never less than twenty-five *palmos* (5 metres). This gave the pike a weight of some 3.5 kilograms. In battle, pikes were normally carried vertically at the right shoulder until the time came for the charge into contact, when in the first three ranks they were lowered. The metal point came in various shapes, the most usual being a four-faced diamond section, and was called *moharra*, from the verb meaning to dip something into sauce (viz. 'dunking'). Period commentators describe two postures for pikemen fighting against pikemen: with the pike at thigh height, which was more comfortable but which lacked impact, or with the pike held at shoulder height (favoured by the Swiss), which was more fatiguing but which lent greater weight to the thrust.

The pikeman's body armour, at least for the first couple of ranks (viz. *coseletes*), included a heavy corselet (back-and-breast-plate), gorget, pouldrons, vambraces, tassets (steel plates protecting the throat, shoulders, arms, and upper thighs respectively), and gauntlets, though much of this armour could quickly disappear in the field – even without the helmet, all this could weigh up to a staggering eighteen kilograms. His headpiece was an open-faced burgonet – a steel helmet covering parts of the face and cheeks, well-stuffed for comfort – or he might wear a morion of Spanish or Italian origin. In popular imagination the 'combed morion' has become a symbol of the Spanish soldier and *conquistador*, but in fact it was widely used in many European armies, and was most typically produced in Italy. The comb, which became more prominent from about 1530, served both to reinforce the structure of the helmet and to deflect blows. Men usually wore a head cloth or a cap under their helmets.

When Montecuccoli first went soldiering during the Thirty Years' War (he had fought at Breitenfeld in 1631 as a cavalry officer in army of Graaf van Tilly) the steadfast Spanish were still the most formidable infantry in Europe, feared for their proven competence in a wide range of military theatres. As mentioned before, in the previous century the Spanish had succeeded the pious *Landsknechte*, who in their turn had succeeded the fanatical Swiss. It was the Swiss who had first demonstrated the potential of the pike in their struggle against an expansionist Burgundy in the fourteen-seventies, an epoch when the chivalric cult of the emblazoned individual heavy horseman, or man-at-arms, the fully-equipped fighting man of the day, still had its focus. It was at the battles of Morat (22 June 1476) and Nancy (5 January 1477) that the men-at-arms of Charles *le Téméraire* (r. 1467–77), unable to break up the blocks of the Swiss and to penetrate into the forest of their pikes, were thoroughly humiliated. This event was a European sensation; infantry had earned its place in the military organisation of the period.

The pike block ultimately died out around 1700 when refinements in cannon and the use of flintlock weapons meant that pike formations became exposed to gunfire – the flintlock produced a spark by striking a flint wedge against a spring-loaded steel pan cover. Coupled with this development was that of the bayonet, which united the advantage of missile and shock weapons in the hands of the individual foot soldier. Still, let us not forget the fact that the pike's longevity and battlefield success illustrate how the simplest weapon system can be decisive if wielded with intelligence.

## Waged men of war

Spain was, at this time, the mightiest nation in the world – colonised the Americas, linked to Portugal and the Portuguese possessions in Asia, lord of the Spanish Netherlands. It had the riches of Mexico and Peru, most of Italy was an ally, a powerful navy, the finest infantry in Europe. It was the endeavours of the latter that had made Spain the dominant military power of Europe, primarily because they were the only real 'regulars' west of the Ottoman empire – 'regular', that is to say, in the sense that they alone were permanently employed, since Spain was permanently at war.[28] Its soldiers fought in Spain itself, Orán and Tripoli, Italy, Ireland,[29] France, and the Americas. However, Spain's footprint was largest in the

Low Countries where a large contingent of confident and disciplined Spanish infantry were permanently deployed,[30] and would be so for decades, fighting a fruitless forever-war.

With its practically non-stop record of wars from Granada through Naples, Algiers, Lepanto and the Armada to the fighting that petered out in the Low Countries in 1609,[31] *los tercios* were the most efficient military force the Spanish Habsburg crown could deploy. They had beaten the Dutch, the French, the Portuguese, and others on the battlefields of half a continent, and feared no foe. This was only to end when they met their nemesis of defeat at Rocroi in 1643. The repute had rested on the early adoption of new arms and tactics: it collapsed now on failure to meet the new tactics of the enemy.

The Welsh professional soldier and military theorist Sir Roger Williams (†1595) describes how Spanish commanders valued experienced soldiers over raw ones (*besonios* in Spanish):

> What makes the Spaniards discipline to be so famous as it is? Their good order ... Their order is, where the warres are present, to supplie their Regiments [viz. *tercios*] being in Action; with the Garrisons out of his Dominions & Provinces: before they dislodge, *besonios* supply their places, raw men, as wee tearme them. By these meanes hee traines his *besonios*, & furnisheth his Armie with trained souldiers: yet though these Garrison men be wel trained Souldiers, God knowes they are but raw men for a long time, in respect of the men of Action: then iudge you, what difference there is betwixt expert Soldiers & raw.[32]

Williams may have been a prolific writer but he was no 'paper' soldier. He had gained extensive combat experience serving in the Army of Flanders, the centre of professionalism (viz. expertise, standards, and longevity in service) in the Spanish Habsburg army of the day, between 1574 and 1578, and against the Spanish thereafter. He knew firsthand how the Spanish took particular care over the training and integration of newly raised men, using their garrisons in Italy as a training ground. These soldiers were transferred to more active theatres of war, such as the Low Countries, once they had been trained and were replaced with a new batch of recruits. Clearly the Spanish were acutely aware of the simple truth that inadequately trained and conditioned soldiers were more likely to become casualties of war than were experienced and hardened ones. Such a system allowed them to achieve some level of competence and cohesion before they entered the bloody maw of battle. For one who has experienced modern soldiering such a system is logical, but in the 16th century not to send newly-recruited men directly in to the maelstrom of combat, as the Spanish did, was *avant-garde*.

This is why every army worth its salt has cherished grizzled veterans with long years of seasoning under their belts. Some of the Spanish soldiers Williams had met had been on active service for thirty years, and they were commanded by officers who had spent many years in action before rising to senior rank. Still, despite their obvious professionalism, it appears no two soldiers looked exactly alike, and although new recruits wore cheaper clothes, many veterans were attired like society dandies. In the words of one of the Spanish professionals, writing slightly later in 1610:

> There has never been a regulation for dress and weapons in the Spanish infantry because that would remove the spirit and fire which is necessary in a soldier. It is the finery, the plumes and the bright colours which give spirit and strength to a soldier so he can with furious resolution overcome any difficulty or accomplish any valorous exploit.[33]

Prints of the period certainly show the extravagant dress of Spanish soldiers. Incidentally, because a good number of them were Catalan whose language was incomprehensible to the Castilian troops, they were given the nickname *papagayos*, 'parrots'.[34] In any case, Catalan or Castilian, these soldiers of the Spanish crown looked like a colourful carnival. Unlike their 21st-century successors, each soldier decked himself out as he wanted, or could afford. One could put on any helmet or hat one wanted, and stick in as many plumes, feathers and ribbons one desired.

More than any other 'nationality', the solid, disciplined and well trained Spanish soldiers were persistently deployed to defend Spanish and imperial interests in the most remote corners of the Spanish Habsburg domains, from Hungary in the north to Africa in the south. No one perhaps put it better than the eminent Spanish historian and statesman Claudio Sánchez-Albornoz y Menduiña (1893–1984):

> They fought over the Andes and in the Alpine foothills, on the plains of the Po and on the Mexican plateau; beside the Tiber against the Pope, and beside the Mapocho against Arauco; on the banks of the River Plate and the Danube, the Elbe and the Tagus, the Orinoco and the Escalda; at Pavia and Cuzco, in the Alpujarras and in the Amazon jungles, in Tunisia and in Amberes, in the Gulf of Lepanto and off the English coast, at Navarino and Terceira, in La Goleta and La Habana, in Algeria and in the Philippines, in Lombardy and in Naples; at all four points of the compass in France, from Provence to Brittany, from the banks of the Bidassoa to the banks of the Marne and from Rousillon to Normandy; in the Low Countries, in Portugal, in Africa and in Ireland ...[35]

Written like a magic spell. But true to the last word; a colourful narrative of the mobility and campaigns experienced by the hard-bitten Spanish soldiers who traversed the Spanish empire in the 16th century, crisscrossing four continents as they did so.

*Chapter 6*

# The Bastard

A bastard had to learn to notice things, to read the truth that people hid behind their eyes.

Jon Snow, *A Game of Thrones*, ch. 5, Jon I

In his short life Don Juan de Austria would turn out to be an ambitious schemer whose favourite plan was to land a Spanish expeditionary force in Scotland, where he would march south across the border and liberate Mary queen of Scots from her confinement, and, who knows, perhaps marry the widow renowned as such a beauty and in her name displace Elizabeth Tudor on the throne of England, who – to use the expression of a writer of the time – was "a greater enemy to Rome than the Turk".[1] Don Juan was at least a desirable husband, indeed the most eligible bachelor in Europe: extremely handsome, young and dashing, a great favourite with the ladies (he fathered a number of bastards), and, of course, the soon-to-be hero of Lepanto. However, that was not to be. His saturnine half-brother, Philip II of Spain, seems to have been jealous of his energetic enterprises and discouraged them before they could be put into effect.

## Growing up in Spain

Don Juan de Austria was born in the Danubian fortress city of Regensburg, Upper Palatinate, Bavaria, on 24 February 1547. He was the illegitimate son of Holy Roman Emperor Charles V (a widower since 1539) and Barbara Blomberg (1527–97), a singer and the daughter of a widow of an officer. Though the son of a Flemish-born father and a German-born mother, the infant Juan was sent to Spain where he essentially was to grow up Spanish; he was given the name Gerónimo, the Spanish for 'sacred', and put in the care of foster parents of humble birth, living at a village near Madrid. At the age of seven, he was transferred to the household of Doña Magdalena da Ulloa, the young wife of Charles' trusted friend, the soldier courtier Don Luis de Quijada, and brought up in their country house near Valladolid, still in ignorance of his true parentage. The little bastard boy had been successfully disposed of, out of sight and conveniently forgotten. Or so it seemed at the time.

Charles V passed away in 1558, and a codicil in his last will recognised Juan as his son and entrusted him to the care of Charles' successor, his legitimate son Philip II of Spain. Though Philip acknowledged Juan and brought him to court, he never awarded him the designation of Highness. His Excellency, however, would be known as Don Juan de Austria, the Spanish king allowing his half-brother to use the dynastic title *Austria* as a surname, which thus ranked behind the legitimate members of the royal family but ahead of the ranks of the Spanish nobility. Moreover, Philip had Juan educated alongside the Infante Don Carlos (1545–68), the mentally unstable heir apparent who made everyone around him uncomfortable,[2] and his nephew Alessandro Farnese (1545–92). Alessandro's mother was Margaret de Austria, the bastard daughter of Charles V by Johanna Maria van der Gheynst, the daughter of a Flemish tapestry weaver. His father was Ottavio Farnese, duca di Parma e Piacenza (r. 1547–86).

Philip II intended Juan to enter the clergy and pursue an ecclesiastical career, as had been stipulated in their father's will. But, to the good fortune of Spain, Juan made it clear he wanted to become a soldier, a wish to which Philip finally acceded. In contrast to his half-brother, the younger, energetic Juan clearly burned with ambition, dreaming of high adventure and military glory. To this end, when the Knights Hospitaller were enduring their heroic siege on Malta in 1565, Don Juan left Barcelona to join the fleet which Philip's viceroy in Sicily, Don García Álvarez de Toledo Osorio, was dispatching to their rescue. Don García had commanded his first war galley at the age of nineteen. Now loaded with years and crippled with rheumatism, he held the high office of *capitán general de la Mar Mediterraneo y Adriático*.[3]

In 1566 the king made Don Juan a Knight of the Order of the Golden Fleece,[4] Spain's most exclusive order of chivalry, of which Philip himself was grand master. Two years later, upon turning twenty-one, Don Juan was given command of a powerful squadron of thirty-three galleys to fight the Barbary corsairs, proving that he had an evident gift for this kind of warfare.

## Moor-slayer

In 1569 Don Juan fought against the rebellious *moriscos* in the Kingdom of Granada, who had risen in revolt on Christmas Eve the previous year. Back in 1502, following the conquest of the Islamic kingdom of Granada and the final defeat of the Moors ten years before, official state policy had decreed that Muslims did not exist in Spain. For Spanish ultra-conservatives that event marked both the culmination of the long crusade begun by Visigoth warlords back in the 8th century and the beginning of of Spain's civilisation. The nation that was the sword arm of the pope could not allow any heretical minorities within its frontiers, and so Spain's Islamic population had been given their historically fatal choice: baptism or banishment. These 'converted' Hispano-Muslims, which formed around four per cent of the kingdom's population, were called *moriscos* by the Christian Spanish.[5] In many cases the conversion was superficial and previous customs, language and costumes were retained. Indeed, many were actively disloyal and, as a consequence, were to take up arms to resist a series of royal decrees that curtailed their cultural and economic activities. Unable to take Granada immediately due to inclement weather and bad timing, the rebellious *moriscos* retreated into the mountains to wage a guerrilla war.

The revolt, already displaying all the brutality of a religious conflict, was destined to become more brutal as the year wore on, many atrocities being perpetuated by both sides. For readers of Miguel de Cervantes, the fate of the townfolk of Galera in Granada is of interest in that the whole population of some 2,500 was systematically slaughtered during an operation conducted house-by-house, the town was then razed and salt was sown amongst its ashes. When this occurred Cervantes was twenty-one, but fifty years later the same horrific image is used in *Viaje del Parnaso*, wherein the god Apollo has the Muses sprinkle salt over the battlefield so that from the blood of the slain – the inferior poets – offspring poetasters will not rise.[6] Don Juan, who had personally supervised the suppression of Galera, ultimately defeated the rebels by unleashing overwhelming firepower on their strongholds, after which he oversaw the collective expulsion of approximately 80,000 *moriscos* from the Kingdom of Granada to other parts of the Crown of Castilla y León, making no distinction between the small number of the rebels and the majority who had remained loyal to the crown. Nearly 15,000 died in the process; others were enslaved under the pretext that, although baptised, they had abandoned Christ for Muhammad. The *moriscos* would not trouble Catholic Spain ever again.

The revolt in the Kingdom of Granada had not been without its effect on Don Juan. His ruthlessness against the *moriscos* soon won him the command of the unruly Holy League fleet destined to fight at Lepanto, the historic battle for which he is still remembered, and the same soldiers and officers who ruthlessly suppressed the rebels were to fight there too under his command.

Ever since they had taken Constantinople in 1453, the Ottoman Turks had dominated the eastern half of Europe and had conquered Greece and the territories known today as Rumania and Bulgaria; the importance of the former lay in the fact that it was to serve as the breadbasket of Constantinople. They had been equally successful on the waters of the Mediterranean Sea, the *Akdeniz* or White Sea, as they knew it, and their invasion and conquest of Cyprus in 1570 was to force the Catholic powers of Europe to put aside their differences in the face of this common threat to the western Mediterranean. Pius V, currently filling the throne of Saint Peter, called for an alliance to combat the approaching Ottomans.

### The Making of a Hero

Don Juan de Austria possessed a quality that his half-brother the king of Spain lacked: charm and diplomacy. In a war that depended on quarrelsome allies, pumped up with their own sense of self-importance, Don Juan was the past master of the tactful gesture. Despite the necessity to concentrate their combined energies to fight the common foe, there was still enough energy among the principal officers to carry out private feuds without which no Holy League campaign would have been complete. Apparently the veteran Spanish commander and viceroy of Sicily, Don García Álvarez de Toledo Osorio, had written to Don Juan of the problems he would face in handling his subordinate officers, all older men from different nations, jealous and suspicious of one another, every man of them intent on demonstrating his own sagacity, shrewdness and skill, and each insistent on his own ideas of strategy with the sole aim of winning every possible advantage for his own nation. The commander had suggested that Don Juan talk to each one privately so as to sound out his opinions. "Then Your Excellency will have time to reflect on these different opinions and, when you call all your advisers together in council at last, you will have taken your own decision and should not tolerate any opposition or disputes."[7]

With a personal experience in Mediterranean warfare which went back over thirty years, Don García Álvarez de Toledo Osorio, IV marqués de Villafranca, knew precisely what he was talking about. He was a man of high family and of great sagacity and experience. He had filled some of the highest posts in the government, and, as the reader may remember, was viceroy of Sicily at the time when Malta was besieged by the Ottomans. Hard-headed men in high places might have private reservations about entrusting the fate of Christendom to a royal bastard aged twenty-four and known for his rashness, but to old Don García young Don Juan – as he saw it – was made of the right stuff, someone who in council would rise above pettiness and envy, who, when the crunch came, would lead without flinching. Following his sound advice and having weighed carefully the separate opinions of his officers, Don Juan reached his decision. Against the urgings of caution from some of them – most especially Gianandrea Doria, the proud, subtle Genoese admiral, and the *comendador mayor de Castilla* Don Luis de Requeséns y Zúñiga, who was serving as the *lugarteniente general de la Mar*, Deputy general of the Sea – his plan of action was to seek out the Ottoman fleet and destroy it. Besides, both Doria and Luis de Requeséns were politically tied to the duque de Alba, the current commander of the Spanish Army of Flanders, and thus not in favour of a sustained Spanish commitment in the Mediterranean.

As presently we shall see, due to dissent among the allies, the Christian victory was not followed up as it should have been, but it roused Don Juan's military ambitions further. He knew that, being illegitimate, he would never achieve a place among the ruling families of Europe, and he began to entertain ideas of winning a kingdom for himself. He thought of erecting first a principality in Albania and the area of Greece south of Lepanto known as the Morea, then occupied by the Ottomans, and from there move north up the Adriatic and establish himself in today's Bosnia. This plan was nullified by the Venetians, who withdrew from the Christian alliance and made a treaty with the Ottoman sultan. Don Juan then led an amphibious expedition in October 1573 to take Tunis, a port city on the Barbary Coast that he hoped to hold as ruler, but it was again speedily lost. He sought assistance from his half brother, the solemn recluse Philip, but the king, while happy to utilise Don Juan's military leadership, refused to support his attempts to win a kingdom for himself. Ever suspicious and perverse, Philip by and large viewed his commanders with distrust, and often interfered to change their plans of campaign. All the more unfortunately for them, their master was a man whose intelligence was clouded by webs of deception and dogma.

## Post-heroics

In 1576, following the death of Don Luis de Requeséns y Zúñiga, Philip appointed his affable and romantic half-brother governor-general of the Spanish Netherlands (also known as the Provinces) with the thankless and endless task of trying to suppress the rebels of the heavily fortified coastal provinces of Holland and Zeeland.[8] These provinces, the most northerly of the old Burgundian possessions, formed a natural redoubt, surrounded by the sea, rivers and low-lying land that could be flooded. In the words of one caustic English traveller, Holland and Zeeland constituted "The great bog of Europe".[9]

And this 'great bog' had long been a hotbed of red rebellion against Spanish Habsburg rule, and although the religious divisions among them were great, they were at one in their hatred of Habsburg Spain. William the Silent (correctly 'the Wily', 1533–84), prince of Orange, had become their recognised leader, and was elected *stadholder*, or provincial captain in charge of the urban militias or *schutters* (sg. *schutterij*),[10] so when Don Juan took up his appointment, he found the Provinces united in opposition. The Dutch rebels embraced republicanism, albeit republicanism of a very unique sort that most today would not recognise. The values of Dutch republicanism rested on the myth of Batavian freedom – Batavia being the Roman name for what was now the Netherlands – and combined a utopian vision of biblical Iudaea with that of Periklean Athens to claim that liberty, stability, virtue and prosperity were best guaranteed by a consultative government of wealthy, educated men with time to dedicate themselves to the public good.

Don Juan negotiated without success for months, trying to satisfy the Provinces' demands for a measure of self-rule, including employment of Netherlanders in government service, but was eventually forced to sign a treaty meeting many of their demands on 12 February 1577. On 1 May that same year, he made his official entry into Brussels but soon found that he was governor-general only in name and that the persistent William the Silent exercised real authority. In July, Don Juan moved south to the citadel of Namur, in the Catholic section of the Provinces, where he hoped to gain more support. The prompt response of William the Silent was to enter Brussels himself and exercise his authority openly there. But though confidence-inspiring, William's nickname does not give a true picture of the man: his use of language to animate his followers, or mislead his opponents or to hide his own thoughts was masterly. Nor was he a puritan – though by the age of forty, having been once a Lutheran and twice a Catholic, he was taking the sacrament in the Calvinist manner with his hat on. That was no more than a wily gesture, meant to reassure the Calvinist militants who served as the backbone of his little army.

The situation came to a head with the arrival of large numbers of soldiers from Spain, under the command of Alessandro Farnese di Parma. Philip trusted to his renowned *tercios* to make the Dutch rebels pray the same way he did. They had the answer that Protestantism deserved. Still, it was his new commander who would prove to be the more effective antidote against this heresy. Alessandro Farnese, unlike his predecessors, would demonstrate that he was intent on prosecuting the conflict vigorously, and Philip was supporting this policy. Preferring campaign to the company of his wife, the Portuguese Infanta María (they had not met until two days before the nuptials), and the dull domestic life in the princedom of Parma (his correspondence of this period is filled with complaints of enforced idleness), he was to win the reputation as the greatest general of the age (at Lepanto he had served with distinction aboard the Genoese flagship).[11] Both a discreet diplomat and a skilful strategist, he was responsible for developing the Flanders school of warfare (he was to succeed Don Juan as governor-general), namely the careful, methodical approach to warfare that became a central feature of the Spanish military system well into the 17th century, traditionally known as the age of Spain's 'decline'.

With these reinforcements, Don Juan attacked the Provinces' army on 31 January 1578 at Gembloux, thirty kilometres south of Brussels. The Provincial army – preponderantly foreign and not Protestant enthusiasts, English, Scottish, German and Danish foot, German and Huguenot horse – under Antony de Goignies, an undistinguished veteran who had served in the wars of Charles V, fought bravely enough, but the skill and daring of Alessandro Farnese led to a decisive victory for the Spanish forces. Early modern European armies included soldiers from many areas and countries, with units in one army sometimes fighting their own countrymen in another. In fact, most of these soldiers were quite without religion, serving whatever paymaster would promise the highest wages in hard cash, perquisites, and plunder. Those who did have religion simply put their trust in the Almighty without concerning themselves with such tricky questions as the true nature of the Eucharist. The Spanish army was likewise of a mongrel nature; only a small portion of this polyglot army was actually Spanish, the rest being Italians, Burgundians from the Franche-Comté and Luxembourg, Catholic English, Catholic Scottish, Irish, Germans, and Walloons.[12] The army may have been Spanish in the sense that it was the army of the king of Spain and he was their paymaster, but it was its very heterogeneity that made this army so difficult to control when not in battle.[13]

Don Juan's victory at Gembloux regained the southern portion of the Netherlands for the Spanish Habsburg crown. In one sense, the Netherlands was the religious cockpit of Europe where Catholic and Protestant powers fought by proxy. Indeed, to keep the Provinces' cause alive after Gembloux, Elizabeth I of England toyed with direct intervention, but as an alternative decided to finance a mercenary force commanded by a radical Calvinist, Johann Casimir von Pfalz-Simmern (1543–92).[14] While most of the duke's troops would be his own Germans and Swiss, it was suggested that English volunteers should join him.

Shortage of money and material supplies, including clothing and munitions, meant that Don Juan was unable to follow up his victory, and he spent the summer appealing in vain to his penurious half-brother in Spain; for, like other monarchs, the king was very sensitive in the purse. The crux was always money; money with which to wage war, money which simply was not there unless the war itself could be made to provide it. The idea was, of course, that the enemy should do all the paying. But the scheme depended altogether too much on the collaboration of the enemy: and the Dutch rebels were no collaborators.

Meanwhile Spain's soldiers, lacking the luxury of a commissariat, not to mention their pay, robbed left and right, living on the land in which they were, paying for nothing, and invariably leaving utter desolation and destitution as their calling card. Many were no strangers to theft, and when faced with a choice between violating orders or starvation, most if not all took the former course. Apart from victuals, the chattels of the civilians were considered fair game and the soldiers helped themselves to portable property as well. Four years earlier, in 1574, a Utrecht chronicler had grimly written that the soldiers in Spanish service were "robbing and plundering as if the peasants were enemies".[15]

There is an an apposite Chinese adage that succinctly sums up the freeloading, brutal relationship between civilian and soldier: "good iron is not beaten into nails, and good men are not made into soldiers". The military forces of the 16th century were not remarkable for the excellence of their discipline. With death from disease, exposure and outright starvation stalking the common soldier, he was encouraged to live by scavenge and sack. It was the opinion of Miguel de Cervantes, a hero at Lepanto, which he puts in the mouth of his hero on paper, Don Quixote, that the work of a soldier was the most wretched to be had:

"[F]or he depends on his miserable pay, which comes late or never, or whatever he can steal with his own hands at great risk to his life and conscience. Sometimes he is so naked that a slashed and torn doublet is both uniform and shirt, and in the middle of winter, in an empty field, the breath from his mouth is his only protection against the inclemencies of heaven, and since that breath comes from an empty place, I consider it certain that it must come out cold, contradicting the laws of nature. But wait for the night to fall, when he can make up for all these discomforts in the bed that awaits him, which will never sin by being too narrow unless he makes it so, for he can measure out as many feet of earth as he desires, and toss and turn to his heart's content without fear of wrinkling the sheets."[16]

As Cervantes himself recognised, the lot of the poor soldier was bound up with tramps, gypsies, beggars, vagrants, brigands, and highwaymen (most Renaissancce soldiers were commoners). Of course the representation of a soldier's suffering is not common; it is more usual to hear about his depredations upon civilians, on women. Take Erasmus for instance, who laments on "the sins of all our sinful soldiers":

Their mercenary outlook incites them to commit every outrage, as they set out for war intent on plunder and return to plunder more, sometimes more ruthless towards their own people than towards the enemy; they cart their whores with them, they get drunk in camp, play dice, forswear themselves, quarrel, fight; in fact, they are only attracted by the freedom it confers to commit crimes and play the hope of booty.[17]

No matter what the subject he is writing about, and he was one of the most prolific writers in history, soldiers are constant fodder for Erasmus, who has absolutely nothing good to say about them. Erasmus, however, was not a lone voice in this respect; for humanist commentators, soldiering was not considered an occupation, but rather a means of escaping 'honest work'; that is, the abandoning of one's appointed station in life in search of maintaining oneself in war. As a German saying of the time makes clear, *Der Lentz nimbt Knecht an*, 'Laziness recruits Landsknecht'.[18] Yet the issue of slothfulness aside, the cruelty of war is inevitable, as is the harshness that it inculcates in those whom Christian princes hire to fight on their behalf. To ask that soldiers on campaign, as Erasmus does, to abandon their habits of violence and disorder is to struggle against an evil that will admit no remedy.

Armies were expected by their governments to be largely self-financing and self-sufficient, following the principle of *bellum se ipsum alte*, 'the war will feed itself'. This obviously meant that they were literally forced to live off the land – by extracting sustenance, shelter, sex, swag, and other sastisfactions from the local inhabitants – by force if necessary.

Even the Spanish Army of Flanders, in most respects the best professional outfit in Europe, consisted of half-starved, half-clothed, under-equipped, and unpaid soldiers, some of whom were in fact rogues, vagabonds and convicts. No small wonder, therefore, they busied themselves carrying away everything they could turn into ready money. The truth of the matter is simply put: early modern European armies still comprised mercenaries who fought only as long as they were paid.

One disadvantage of contract troops was that money not only had to be found up front to employ them, but a continuing stream of liquid cash was also essential to retain their services. This was always going to be difficult for cash-strapped governments. This was true not only of the *Landsknechte*,[19] but also of *los tercios*. Soldiers mainly from Germany, Lombardy and Sicily fought brilliantly in Italy, France and Flanders in spite of appalling conditions. The danger however of non-payment of wages could (and did) trigger campaign-weakening mutinies.[20] During the Thirty Years' War (1618–48), a gruesome multi-front affair in which the Army of Flanders was to play a part and the *tercio*, until it went down forever on the field of Rocroi (18–19 May 1643), was to prove still viable despite the tactical improvements introduced by the Dutch and the Swedes. There was a saying that "[e]very [Spanish] soldier needs three peasants: one to give up his lodgings, one to provide his wife, and one to take his place in Hell".[21] Habsburg propaganda would have the Spaniards of the time believe that the king's policy of military suppression of Protestantism was being successfully conducted throughout his domains. Yet in Flanders the soldiers of *los tercios* were under pressure: they were far from home, embedded within a hostile population, and badly fed, driven close to mutiny by lack of pay. Living conditions for the Spanish infantry 'trailing a pike in Flanders' could be appalling. Many did die in that flat, waterlogged country, landowners – occupiers, at least – of a grave some *siete palmos* in length.

## End Times

Worn out with fatigue and with the travails of his office, Don Juan's health gave way under an attack of fever; death surprised him suddenly on

Sunday, 1 October 1578 at the early age of thirty-one and broke the too-short thread of his designs. Six years later, on 10 July 1584, his opponent William the Silent,[22] the core of anti-Spanish, anti-Catholic resistance, would be assassinated in Delft by an agent of Philip – the first man ever to kill a head of state with a handgun – a heinous act that prompted the Dutch to offer sovereignty to Elizabeth of England. She was reluctant to accept anything from the rebels; nonetheless English hawks in her court won the day and pushed England into the Dutch rebellion so as to help the fight against their common Catholic enemy.

With the signing of the Treaty of Nonsuch, guaranteeing English military support to the Dutch rebels, a bantam field army of 7,400 men (8,000 Englishmen were already serving in the Provinces unofficially, alongside a motley crew of Scots,[23] Germans and Danish) was despatched in 1585 under Sir Robert Dudley, 1st Earl of Leicester, whom the Dutch accepted as their political and military leader. It was not a happy arrangement. The Dutch enterprise became another of Elizabeth's shoestring operations. The unpaid English troops failed to defend the Dutch, while Leicester conspired with Calvinist militants to seize greater authority. The failure of his attempted *coup d'état* in 1587 decisively shifted the Dutch towards republican government. It was a suitable beginning of a relationship that would strain diplomats for years. All the same, England's involvement with the Dutch rebellion formally had begun nearly two decades of war with Spain.[24]

Don Juan de Austria was first buried at Namur, but a year later his remains were taken to Spain and re-interned in the Escorial, where he lies to this day. In his *El trato de Argel* Cervantes would mourn the premature death of his one-time commander-in-chief Don Juan with the following lines: "*quiso el hado/cortar el hilo de su dulce vida* (destiny wished to cut the thread of his sweet life)".[25] The striking portrait of him by Titian shows a young man who embodied the virtues of the age. A true prince of his times, his premature passing was a serious blow to Habsburg Spain. Like Charles Martel (†741) and Jan III Sobieski of Poland (r. 1674–96), Don Juan is remembered today for a single battle – but a battle that was a decisive victory against an enemy threatening the whole of Christian Europe. Lepanto had shown that the mighty Ottoman empire could be defeated, and Don Juan de Austria rightly earned his place in military history.

*Chapter 7*

# La Serenissima

Once did She hold the gorgeous East in fee; / And was the safeguard
of the West; the worth / Of Venice did not fall below her birth, /
Venice, the eldest Child of Liberty.

> William Wordsworth, 'On the Extinction of the
> Venetian Republic', *Poems, in Two Volumes*[1]

The affairs of Venice now claim our attention. Throughout the
16th century the Mediterranean was dominated by the Ottoman
Turks, Habsburg Spain and Venice. All were imperial powers.
Only one, however, was named after a mere city. *La Serenissima*, the
Most Serene Republic of Venice, the most effective military power in
15th-century Italy, became a second-rate military power in 16th-century
Europe, capable of defending its independence but acquiring its further
moments of military glory only in its ability to mobilise for and check
the onslaught of the Ottoman empire. When the League of Cambrai had
been formed by the powers of Europe in 1508, it was with the avowed
object of crushing Venice, and of checking the Republic's ambition to be
as powerful by land as it had been by sea. The league had succeeded but
too well; and Venice, humbled and weakened, never regained its former
position, or took rank again as a state entitled to unquestioning respect
and consideration. The loss of external power brought with it, as it often
does, the canker of internal corruption. The state was governed by a city;
the city was governed by a small party among the citizens. Extravagance
and luxury increased with gigantic strides.

Nevertheless, for all its domestic faults, Venice was a city like no other.
While the sovereignty of Philip II of Spain was expressed in strictly
religious terms, the legitimacy of the Venetian government did not derive
from God's mandate. A republic with a well-ordered system of civil
magistracies, it imbued its inhabitants with a sense of civic identity so

much so that one contemporary saying went *non est vivere extra Venetiis*. Not only a political ideology shared by an exclusive political élite but also a myth communicated to the populace by means of art, architecture, literature, history, and most importantly civic rituals.

This was the 'myth of Venice', a mythic vision of Venice as a sovereign and free city with a perfected social hierarchy and contented classes, which made the Venetians believe that they lived in an exceptional place; a divinely ordained centre of religious, civic and commercial life, governed by a balanced constitution in the Aristotelian sense, one that harmonised the monarchy, aristocracy, and republican liberty. It was not a republic like most people would understand today. The head of state was an elected leader, the doge, the most fettered ruler in Italy. Beneath him and his six councillors, *minor consiglio*, were the body of ministers, *collegio*, which formed the executive, and the largely autonomous collegiate body the Council of Ten, *consiglio dei dieci*. Often maligned, *consiglio dei dieci* was the most powerful executive organ in the Venetian republican system and deliberated in secret, convened when the Senate could not reach a decision. The council in fact consisted of seventeen members; ten councillors, the doge, and his six councillors. Inevitably advanced in years – it was rare for doges to be elected before the age at which most popes were already dead – the doge served for life, but the other sixteen members, while inaugurated at different times of the year, only had one year appointments. All sixteen of them were chosen from the Senate, which consisted of 200 mainly men of advanced age, *vecchi*. Below that was the Great Council, *maggior consiglio*, which effectively contained the ruling caste, the patricians.

Despite its obvious narrow nature, and the Serene Republic may be regarded as a gerontocracy,[2] contemporary Europeans widely admired Venice's collegiate government for its stability, and this too was jealously guarded by the patrician families who constituted the state. In 1560, of approximately 150,000 inhabitants, roughly 2,500 adult patricians – those whose houses were inscribed in *il Libro d'Oro*, the Golden Book – were eligible to govern the state. These *primi di la terra*, 'the first ones of the city', as Venetians called them, could expect to hold high office as long as they were able, willing, and acceptable to their peers. Despite this, however, all those born in Venice belonged to a privileged community;

they were members of the Most Serene Republic of Venice, a polity that was protected by San Marco and autonomous from other powers in the world. In short, they were proud Venetians.

## Floating Republic

The great naval encounter of Lepanto, in the sparkling sapphire waters at the entrance to the Gulf of Patras, has long been regarded as one of the decisive sea battles in history, but modern commentators have been hard pressed to explain why: "the most spectacular military event in the Mediterranean during the entire 16th century",[3] according to the French historian Fernand Braudel, whose magisterial study of the Mediterranean world in the age of Philip II of Spain culminated in an account of the battle. That may be the case, and we will pick up this theme at a later point, but the Ottoman Turks had revealed in the months before the battle that they aspired to win the Adriatic, and had accompanied their sea raids with land raids from Ottoman Bosnia towards the Venetian possessions at the head of the Adriatic. These raids were not simply motivated by empire building or the wish to spread Islamic rule. As will become clear, the Ottomans were also goaded by Slav Christian pirates and bandits in northern Dalmatia. We should not forget that based on the theory of *mare clausum*, the Venetians considered the Adriatic their own, needing, for instance, Istria for its stone and Dalmatia for its timber. The dominion over the Adriatic was a foundation on which the prosperity and existence of *la Serenissima* rested. "First and last, Venice depended on the Adriatic",[4] wrote Frederic Chapin Lane, simply and accurately summarizing the intimate connection between Venice and the Adriatic. All ships that sailed in this *Golfo di Venezia* had to obey Venetian laws. No foreign armed ship was allowed while the merchant ships sailed with a passport and followed an established course from and to their original destination. Naturally this claim brought Venice the responsibility of protecting merchant vessels.

As Jan Glete makes clear, "Warfare at sea is essentially a contest about the maritime lines of communication."[5] The Venetians had a foothold ashore, on the Italian mainland and the Dalmatian littoral, but their island republic looked out to sea. The Venetian sea empire, *impero da mar*, comprised a series of clusters of islands and ports ending in two widely spaced and weighty pendants, Crete and Cyprus, Venice's latest acquisition (1489). Acquired partly by conquest, partly by inheritance, purchase and gift, it reflected, in its long-drawn-out inconsequentiality, a dialogue between ship and shore that had been going on for centuries as Venetian merchant and war fleets sailed out and back between the lagoon and the Levant.

The logical result of this exchange was twofold. First, it catered for Venice's need for many ports of call (given the galley's scant space for provisions), a few strategic bases, and recruiting areas whence to *intraterzare*, or top up, galley crews. Second, it was symbiotic, as the coastal and island populations' (mostly non-Venetian) desire for, or willingness to put up with, Venetian protection. In reality, this *impero da mar* was a continuous chain of Venetian service stations that stretched from the northern reaches of the Adriatic past the strategic island of Corfu, which guarded the entrance to the Adriatic, to Famagusta, the jump-off point for voyages to Beirut and Alexandria. For the Venetians these two Levantine ports were depositories for Venetian cargo as well as profitable markets for the goods that arrived via horse, mule, and camel from India, Persia, and China. And their greatest customer was the Ottoman empire.

Despite the knowledge of the inability of Venice to act alone in the 16th century, the island republic was still a naval power not to be taken lightly. In 1538 the Republic joined the Holy League formed by the pope, Paul III, and the Holy Roman Emperor, Charles V, to confront the Ottomans and keep them in check. The Venetians were to furnish fifty-five galleys, and in return were to receive back the possessions which they had owned in Constantinople following division of the territorial spoils of the Fourth Crusade. Charles V was to be proclaimed Emperor of the East, and a suitable dominion was to be allotted to the pope. All these spoils, of course, were subject to a conquest of Constantinople in the aftermath of a victory at sea.

The strange conduct of Andrea Doria, who commanded the Holy League fleet at Préveza, blasted all these hopes and irretrievably ruined the Christian cause. It is widely speculated that his lack of zeal was due to his unwillingness to risk his own ships (he personally owned a substantial number of the Genoese-Spanish contingent) and his long standing enmity towards Venice. The result of his indecision, or incapacity (or hideous treachery even), spelt disgrace and disaster to the Christians, and secured to the Ottomans the naval supremacy in the eastern Mediterranean.[6]

## Gilded galleys

As we touched upon above, Venetian history is very closely bound to the sea: Venice rose from the sea, and its wealth and power came from the sea, which was indeed the primary cause of the prominent political and economic standing *la Serenissima* achieved throughout the Mediterranean world. The Venetians' ability to support a sizeable navy allowed them to build a colonial empire dotted with bases and ports of considerable strategic importance. It is important to remember the frequency with which Venetian war galleys – the backbone of the navy – needed to restock with victuals and fresh water, given the limited storage on board. In the first year of the War of Cyprus (1570–3) Venice was able to equip 140 galleys; though some were destroyed or damaged by the weather, the following year there were 110 ships flying the winged-lion of San Marco at Lepanto.[7] At a later point we will recollect the key rôle played by the Venetian fleet at Lepanto, but it is worth underlining at this point that this naval strength was nevertheless insufficient to prevent the loss of Cyprus to the Ottoman Turks, and therefore of Venice's most important Mediterranean base.

Though both employed the *levantina*, Venetian galleys were slower under sail and suffered more damage in storms than their Ottoman counterpart – with the increased importance of cannon, the bow of the galley was so heavily loaded with artillery that when the ship was sailing before the wind her forecastle was buried in the waves – yet at the end of the 16th century the Venetians still had the deserved reputation of building the finest galleys made. It was during this century that the Venetians employed methods of large-scale production in building their war fleet, and did so at the Arsenale di Venezia.

The Arsenale was already well established in the early 14th century (the mediaeval Arsenale was erected in 1104), when Dante heard in its dark depths the echoes of Hell itself:

As in the arsenal of the Venetians,
all winter long a stew of sticky pitch
boils up to patch their sick and tattered ships
that cannot sail (instead of voyaging,
some build new keels, some tow and tar the ribs
of hulls worn out by too much journeying;
some hammer at the prow, some at the stern,
and some make oars, and some braid ropes and cords;
one mends the jib, another, the mainsail);
so, not by fire but by the art of God,
below there boiled a thick and tarry mass
that covered all the banks with clamminess.[8]

Its name comes from the Arabic *Dar al Sina'a*, dockyard, and the concept clearly owed as much to Islamic inspiration as to the Byzantine model on which the Arsenale was supposed to be based. It was first conceived simply as a dockyard, but by Dante's day it increasingly took on the functions of a veritable factory for producing shipping.

Thus, in our period of study the Arsenale was not only a dockyard; it was a pre-industrial age version of a mass assembly line where everything from fitting the hull and planks to launching the finished vessel was done in a simple, unified process. Venetian vessels now had the frame-first system, which differed from the Graeco-Roman system in that the ribs or framework were constructed before the planking was applied, the ancients having made a planked hull to which they then attached the ribs. This modern system was not only faster but used much less wood. First the framework was built by the ship carpenters. Then the planking was fastened into place and the cabins and superstructure built.

Reserved for the galley commander and his staff, the cabin, or *carosse*, was at the stern and all fighting orders were imparted from the *spalliera* or the platform found just in front of the *carosse*. Stretching across the whole width of the back section of the galley, the *spalliera* was the galley's brain, its nerve centre, and a vital post from which to direct battle. It should be noted that the stern cabin was gorgeously decorated with gilded and brightly painted sculpture and bas-reliefs. Finally, when the galley was called into service, her seams were filled with tow and pitch, the hull covered with tar or grease, the galley launched, the deck fixings fastened in place, the rigging and mooring provided, the oars and arms given out to the crew.

In this final phase of production all the departments of the Arsenale were involved. Therefore, it also contained warehouses where galleys could be outfitted with cannon, as well as firearms and such for their complement of sea soldiers. There were even facilities to assemble rigging and mooring too, and large magazines of weapons-grade gunpowder. In a city where fortifications were otherwise completely absent, the Arsenale was the only location surrounded by a high fortress-like wall.

In most European states the 17th century was the age of creation upon a large scale of permanent war fleets with ships of the special design required for combat. For Venice the need of a large permanent navy came earlier, between 1470 and 1540. The vessels needed of course were not ships of the line of fifty guns or more, but galleys of maximum speed. Therefore the Arsenale, unlike the later shipyards of the oceanic naval powers, confronted problems peculiar to the building and outfitting of oared fighting ships.

At its peak of efficiency the Arsenale could, in an orderly fashion, fit out, arm and provision a newly built gallery with standardised parts on a production line basis unseen anywhere else until the Industrial Revolution. Such was the awesome fame of the Arsenale that news of its destruction by fire and explosion on the night of 13–14 September 1569 was said to have encouraged the Ottomans to invade, and ultimately seize Cyprus. Despite this disaster, however, when the Ottoman design to attack Cyprus became known, the Senate on 28 January 1570 ordered that thirty galleys be put into order by the middle of February, thirty more by the end of that month, and forty more by the middle of March.[9] Assuming the galleys were ready waiting on the docks, all they needed were oars, cordage, anchors, sails, masts, spars, deck furnishings, and those arms ready and sorted in the warehouses assigned to them, the whole fleet of one hundred galleys was to be sent out of the Arsenale fully equipped for war inside of fifty days. And so it came to pass; the fleet left Venice at the beginning of April. This rapid launching of the Venetian war fleet was a feat of organisation no other power could match.

The Venetian war galley, the *galea sottile*, possessed a serious artillery advantage over its fellow nautical powers. Although each vessel's armament varied, the heavy 50-pounder centreline bow gun (It. *canone de la corsia*) always went to battle with a vast accompaniment. Usually, this arrangement at the time of Lepanto included two 12-pounder and two 6-pounder guns. In the stern, the galley sometimes armed two 3-pounder guns. Along the sides, they bore between six and thirty-six mounted 1-pounder swivel guns.[10] These smaller weapons along the sides allowed Venice to circumvent boarding and entering tactics. Although the contending Spanish and Ottoman forces possessed many soldiers and oarsmen to man their galleys, *la Serenissima* simply did not. By arming its galleys with significantly more ordnance, Venice seemingly found a "better way to skin the tactical cat" despite its deficiency in manpower.[11]

It goes without saying, of course, that when naval encounters were but land battles transferred to ships, the essential armament of a galley was her crew. Venetian oarsmen, *galeotti*, which accounted for seventy-five to eighty per cent of the men embarked on a galley, were usually *buonevoglie* (sg. *buonavoglia*) or volunteers from the lower orders (rowing skills were encouraged through races and regattas in Venice), lured by the tantalising recruitment bounty of twenty-five *ducati* in addition to a yearly pay of roughly twelve, comparable to that of an unskilled labourer, and supplemented by assurances of food and clothing. Sometimes the bounty was doubled or even tripled, a considerable incentive for individuals coming from the lower strata of society.

The bounty, however, was intended to cover each oarsman's future expenses. Every galley had an account book recording not only the earnings and expenses of each *galeotto*, but also details of his illnesses, dismissal, desertion or death. From the volunteer's original credit were deducted the cost of clothing, medicines, extra rations, any money he might owe to other members of the crew, and so on. Very soon the original credit nearly always became a debit, and as a result the free oarsman rapidly found that he was bound to the oar as an indentured labourer until his debt was paid. Once this debt was paid he was free to leave the service, during which period he was treated no better than a slave but not shackled and was armed when the galley was hard pressed in action.

Apparently, *buonevoglie* were sometimes cajoled into service by underhand methods not too dissimilar to press ganging. Though we have no direct evidence for this happening in Venice, we do have an account written by *capitano* Pantero Pantera, a commander of the papal galley *Santa Lucia*, who describes one such method:

> [A]dopted by the rulers [viceroys] of the Two Sicilies [Kingdom of Sicily and Kingdom of Naples], who opened gaming houses staffed with skilful touts, who lent money to lure young gamblers. Naturally these lost their money, and engaged themselves as *buonevoglie* in acquittal of what they believed to be debts of honour.[12]

For some unfortunate souls, no matter how long they rowed, their debt never seemed to be paid off.

On the other hand, all *galeotti*, including convicts (on the eve of Lepanto Venice had twelve galleys entirely crewed by convicts), prisoners of war and slaves, each carried somewhere on the vessel a few wares to trade. At each port of call they went ashore to hold a miniature fair.[13] Additionally, Venetian free oarsmen were trained to fight – they wore light helmets and metal-lined *corrazzini* flexible body armour – and loot acquired in battle could potentially nullify their debts and provide profits. Overall, life at the oar could easily shift for or against an oarsman's favour, and few were willing to gamble on an oarsman's life. Especially considering the logistical needs of feeding and equipping a vessel almost entirely powered by muscle, traditional galleys proved to be "veritable money and food sponges".[14] Aside from oarsmen, in a time of crisis or war, these vessels also required troops to board enemy vessels or to deflect an attack.

Venetian galleys carried a minimum complement of sixty fighting men, *scapoli*.[15] Throughout the 16th century, Venice recruited soldiers from its scattered holdings as well as its *terraferma*,[16] or Italian mainland, populace – the writ of Venice reached as far west as Bergamo besides the green waters of the rushing Adda where the winged lion of San Marco brushed against the viper of Milan. Venice also employed Protestant infantry like the Swiss Grisons, for the patricians were not squeamish over such trifles: the people, as they put it themselves, were Venetians first and Christian afterwards, an attitude that naturally provoked the anger of various popes, who periodically took it upon themselves to place the Republic under an interdict.

Still, the inherent weakness in the defence of the Venetian empire was that its extended flanks had to be protected, each from a different threat. The Spanish Habsburgs to the west, the Austrian Habsburgs to the north and east, and the Papal States to the south were all potentially hostile powers surrounding *la Serenissima* in Italy. Venice had once lost control of the *terraferma* briefly after the crushing defeat of Agnadello in 1509,[17] but soon recovered it. Beyond the Adriatic, risk of war with the Ottoman empire, the source of much of its lucrative trade, was a permanent risk. Like many contemporary powers, it depended on mercenary companies, especially 'foreign' Italian troops. When war erupted, numerous contracted captains accepted Venetian pay, but not as many reported for duty. Additionally, by mid-century, the growing presence of the Spanish Habsburgs in Italy and a waning relationship with the papacy removed many previous sources of troops. Throughout its Levantine holdings, Venice also competed with Ottoman recruiters, important for the recruitment of light-armed horsemen such as *stradioti* (Gk. στρατιώτες/*stratiōtes*), who were practically brigands complete with a mixture of Greek and Turkish attire, liable to plunder indiscriminately if they were not closely watched. These were originally survivors of Skanderbeg's struggles with the Ottomans in Albania,[18] but later recruited from Greeks and Croats as well.

### Lagoon militia

To augment these difficulties, *la Serenissima* attempted to devise a militia or *ordinanza* units, the blueprint for such calling for a military reserve of 20,000 men to defend the *terraferma* and a naval one of 10,000. The chief attraction for signing up of course was the right to carry arms. Still, this scheme, admirable as it was, more or less resulted in administrative confusion and the recruitment of soldiers of questionable value. Most recruits were aged between seventeen and twenty-four, and trained only five Sundays a year. In practice, the standard of the militia proved to be of dubious military value. Abysmally equipped and lacking training, they were unable to confront professional forces, and their reluctance to serve away from their immediate locality further restricted their usefulness. The Veneto was not a good source of supply for troops as it was on the whole settled and prosperous enough to make soldiering unattractive. Erasmus would have approved.

In Venice the basic infantryman's monthly pay remained unchanged from 1509 to 1599 at three *ducati*; by comparison, in the mid-century, unskilled workers in the Arsenale di Venezia received eight to ten *soldi* per diem, a *soldo* being worth half a *ducato*. Yet the government calculated this pay not by the month but by the 'month': for it suited the convenience of the government to spread the 'month' and thus hand out pay less frequently. Angelo Beolco's Italian peasant soldier, Ruzante, when asked if he would serve again, replied:

> "How do I know? If they paid up, and didn't stretch a month to a hundred days, I might think of going back."[19]

This is a fine specimen of wit from the pen of the Paduan actor and playwright Angelo Beolco (†1542), bright, quickly delivered, pungent, and to the point. Though exaggerated for comic effect, this merely distorts common knowledge.

In peacetime, Venice gave out monthly pay every forty-five days, or eight times a year, up to 1589, when ten pays became the norm on *terraferma*. Overseas, where the cost of living was higher, ten pays were occasionally given as a temporary measure to attract new drafts; it became the norm only from 1573. In wartime, or during precautionary mobilisations, the Venetian rate was ten pays a year until 1570, when the calendar month was adopted. Venice was at peace between 1540 and 1570.

In this respect, Venice shared a problem common to all states: the obtaining of recruits sufficiently motivated to be determined soldiers. Shakespeare's Boult, in *Pericles*, spoke from common, not merely English knowledge:

> "What would you have me do? Go to the wars, would you, where a man may serve seven years for the loss of a leg, and have not money enough in the end to buy him a wooden one?"[20]

The authoritative art of Shakespeare is firmly rooted in his amazingly vivid and powerful evocation and expression of lots of different choices. Many of them are, of course, political choices, about such matters as gender identity and human relationships, about forms of power and government, about how wealth should be distributed. Anyway, the response to the recruiters' drums was so disappointing in quantity and dubious in quality that it was by no means only Venice that lifted the sentences of men banished for crimes of violence in return for their enlistment.

The widely experienced military engineer and *general d'altegliaria*, Giulio Savorgnan del Friuli (1510–95), summed up in 1572 his impression of the men employed by Venice by asking why Italians enlisted. "To escape" – he answered himself – "from being craftsmen, working in a shop; to avoid a criminal sentence; to see new things; to pursue honour (but these last are very few). The rest join in the hope of having enough to live on and a bit over for shoes and some other trifle to make life supportable."[21] He might have added that the eloquence of the recruiters' drums in the previous two years had been aided by the desperation caused by disastrous harvests; some eighty per cent of those who joined up in 1571 had to be completely equipped by the Venetian government.

### The Guns of San Marco

Venice had the reputation, which seems to have been deserved, of being in the forefront of the development of artillery. It was thought by contemporaries to have been the first state to use artillery effectively on a large scale – against the Genoese in the War of Chioggia (1377–81), so named after a small town at the southern end of the Venetian lagoon.[22] Indeed, one important feature of this war, the fourth bloody conflict between the two hereditary maritime rivals, is that the Venetians made extensive use of gunpowder, using cannon mounted on the forecastles of their ships. The Genoese commander, Pietro Doria, died when a Venetian cannonball hit a siege tower that collapsed on top of him. Venetian government interest was stimulated not only by the potential of guns in sea warfare, but also by its extended defence commitments in the east.

Gunpowder weapons redressed the imbalances Venice faced concerning the tremendous military might of the Ottoman empire and Habsburg Spain. Whereas previous naval mêlées were akin to land battles, gunpowder ordnance made short, decisive engagements possible. Venice, traditionally long on cash and short of manpower, quickly identified the advantages these weapons provided and embraced nascent gunpowder technology at sea by the late 15th century.

During the 16th and 17th centuries, Venetian ordnance was considered by experts of all western nations as the best of the Mediterranean[23] and, at the European regional level, the second best after Germany only because the humidity of the Lagoon did not permit the perfect drying of the *forme* or moulds. Although Venice had within its borders various copper mines, this strategic metal was nearly always bought from German merchants. The copper from Tyrol and from the northern Hungarian mines, the same mines that Gábor Ágoston informs us the Ottomans tried to conquer, was of the best quality available on the international market.[24] Copper of inferior characteristic from the Venetian mines of Agordo was used only in emergency when better material was not readily at hand, while tin was invariably delivered from the mines of Cornwall, England.

With interchangeability between ship and shore in mind, Venice progressively stepped up the production of rust-free bronze artillery at the expense of iron guns, which were, in any case, more difficult to cast with the same degree of accuracy. While some iron artillery was cast in Brescia and in private foundries in Venice itself for sale (subject always to licence) to individuals, boat owners or foreign arms dealers, bronze artillery was made in the Arsenale or the nearby Tana, and from July 1526 all government work in bronze had to be concentrated within the Arsenale itself in the interest of security and the close supervision of materials – though the law accepted that in exceptional circumstances weapons could be made in the Tana.[25]

*Chapter 8*

# The Hospitallers

In Malta, the Wars of Religion reached their climax. If both sides believed that they saw Paradise in the bright sky above them, they had a close and very intimate knowledge of Hell.

Ernle Bradford, *The Great Siege, Malta 1565*

O ne of the most peculiar organisations in the world today is the Order of Malta. The Order is at once a lay religious order of the Holy Mother Church, an aid body that runs soup kitchens, homeless shelters, health clinics, hospitals and ambulance services in 120 countries,[1] and a sovereign entity that issues its own coins, stamps, vehicle registration plates and passports, and enjoys United Nations observer status and diplomatic relations with 104 countries, though few of the key ones, such as the United States, Russia, France, Germany and the United Kingdom, for example. Yet, believe it or not, it has no country to call its own.

## Mediaeval Origins

The tiny southern Italian sea town of Amalfi left a lasting imprint further east, in Fātimid territory no less. Around 1023 merchants of the Duchy of Amalfi (It. *Ducato di Amalfi*) obtained from 'Alī az-Zāhir, the seventh caliph of the Fātimids (r. 1021–36), the authorisation to rebuild a combination church, convent and hospital dedicated to Saint John the Baptist in Muslim Jerusalem, with the understanding that the hospital would admit pilgrims of *all* religions and races.[2]

Jerusalem was a city which offered little commercial advantage beyond the trade in increasingly improbable relics. Still, an obsession with the Holy Land was one of the marks of the age, and as agents of the abbey of Montecassino, the merchants of Amalfi made it possible for the Benedictine monks to provide care for poor, sick (bar lepers) or injured pilgrims, regardless of their nationality, faith and gender,[3] who in growing numbers set out from Europe – often by way of the ports of southern Italy – for the Holy Land. In the wake of the success of the First Crusade, the first rector, Gérard d'Amalfi (later Blessed Gérard), founded the charitable brotherhood of the Hospital of Saint John, or Hospitallers, into a strictly constituted religious body subjected to the jurisdiction of the Patriarch of Jerusalem.

The monastic Hospitaller order was formally named and recognised on 15 February 1113 in a papal bull, *Pie postulatio voluntatis*, issued by Paschal II (r. 1099–1118), thereby establishing its sovereign status by proclaiming it was independent of both lay and other religious authorities. Since crusading was, to say the least, violent by nature, the Hospitallers were soon to acquire a military bent as they strove to defend pilgrims and conquered territory from the 'infidel' Muslim. Raymond du Puy, who succeeded Gérard in 1121/1123, adopted a new rule and constitution which was of a more open, Augustinian nature, with its emphasis on personal responsibility for salvation and good works, compared with the relatively cloistered Benedictine rule. The new office of Constable of the Hospitallers was created and by 1126 the military development of the Hospitallers had begun. Raymond thus assumed the title of Master and reorganised the Hospitallers on a military basis in accordance with western European feudal principles, but without renouncing its original philanthropic rôle, at least outwardly.[4] The Hospitallers took a further step in the militarization process on 20 February 1131, when Innocent II (r. 1130–43) issued his circular letter *Quam amabilis Deo*, which formally assigned them the duty of defending the faith:

> The Sick are being administered a thousand kinds of services of charity. Those who are harmed by manifold constraints and dangers are getting back their old vigour, and in order to enable them to visit the places, which were sanctified by the life of our Lord Jesus Christ on earth, the brethren of this house [are] always prepared to risk their life for their brothers [pilgrims] from the attacks of the infidels on their way to and fro ... These are the people who God uses to cleanse the Oriental Church from the dirt of the infidels and to fight the enemies of the Christian name.[5]

Nevertheless, it is hard to exaggerate the importance of the care of the sick in shaping the character of the Hospitallers and in distinguishing it from their rivals, the Knights Templar.

The rules of the Hospitallers were amended to include the defence of the Holy Land and that the members wear the sign of the cross on their cloaks. With the Knights Templar, they became the most important representatives of the crusader ideology, wielding their swords against the rival Muslim faith in the heart of the Holy Land. This also explains the fervour with which feudal Europe supported them financially and morally. Thus, from its small beginnings, this hospice developed into the monastic-chivalric Order of Knights of the Hospital of Saint John of Jerusalem (Latin: *Ordo Fratrum Hospitalis Sancti Ioannis Hierosolymitani*), also known as Knights Hospitaller or Hospitallers for short, and its fighting monks later defended Rhodes and Malta from the Ottoman Turks.

A continuous line stretches from the 11th century to the Sovereign Military Order of Malta, now currently based in Rome from where it continues its humanitarian tasks in most parts of today's world under several different names and jurisdictions.

A legend reports that Amalfitans were within Jerusalem when it was besieged by the armies of the First Crusade in 1099. Ordered by the Muslims to throw rocks at the crusading rabble outside the walls, they were forced to comply; miraculously, the rocks were transformed in midair into bread rolls, and fed the famished Christian army. The truth was, of course, that the Amalfitans flourished when they avoided taking sides in conflicts between Christians and Muslims.

## A Military Rôle

In the Military Orders,[6] the Latin princes of Outremer found soldiers of high quality who helped to offset the numerical weakness of the feudal host and their inability to hire sufficient mercenaries. As a result, the Military Orders gradually assumed the rôle of the standing army of the Kingdom of Jerusalem, and the secular barons soon lost the complete control of military operations and policy in the Holy Land. Without their military assistance, whose worth in a fight went far beyond their numbers, the crusader states would have perished far sooner.

The greatest Latin army that was ever assembled in the Holy Land, that which was decisively defeated on 4 July 1187 by Salāh al-Dīn (Saladin) bin Ayyūbī, sultan of Egypt (r. 1169–93), near the twin peaks of Qurūn Hattīn (elev. 326m) northwest of Tiberias,[7] included around 1,200 mounted knights of which half were Templars and Hospitallers. After the battle, in which the True Cross, the instrument of the Passion, was irretrievably lost, all 200 of the Templars and Hospitallers taken prisoner were bound hand and foot and beheaded by order of Salāh al-Dīn; the lay nobility were spared.[8] In his monumental universal history Ibn al-Athīr (1160–1233) remarks in his account of the massacre of the prisoners: "These men were singled out to be killed only because they fought more fiercely than all the [other] Franks."[9] As recorded by the Persian scholar 'Imād al-Dīn al-Isfāhanī (1125–1201), who was present at the battle, Salāh al-Dīn himself said of the Hospitallers and Templars:

I will purify the earth of these two filthy races (*jins*). For their custom has no use and they will certainly not desist from aggression and they will not serve in captivity. They are the most wicked of all the infidels.[10]

When we consider the fact that Salāh al-Dīn was considered both in the east and the west a praiseworthy, principled man we may have good reason to doubt these words, but 'Imād al-Dīn al-Isfāhanī was a close adviser and a good friend of the sultan. Moreover, recent research has suggested that the Persian's work on the conquest of Jerusalem was written in the sultan's lifetime and that part of it was actually read out to him in 1192.[11]

In 1191, after Salāh al-Dīn had liberated Jerusalem, the Hospitallers moved their headquarters first to Margat and then, in 1197, to Acre in Palestine. Bitter rivalry arose between them and the Knights Templar, ending in hostilities in which the latter got the upper hand. Clinging to Acre, the Hospitallers were driven out in 1291, along with the Teutonic Order and the Knights Templar, by the Mamlūks after a terrible siege. The Mamlūks were a military caste in Egypt, which had developed from the ranks of slave soldiers who had been sold to the Egyptian sultan by the Mongols in 1238. These were mostly enslaved Turkic peoples, Egyptian Copts, Circassians, Abkhazians and Georgians. A dozen years later, however, one of their leaders, Izz al-Din Aybak (r. 1250–7), revolted and seized power, thereby ousting the dynasty of Salāh al-Dīn. With the Hospitallers decimated and with their master Jean de Villiers (r. 1285–94) gravely wounded, they retired to the Lusignan stronghold of Cyprus, where they already had some possessions. Henri II de Lusignan (r. 1285–1306, 1310–24), who had witnessed the fall of Acre (28 May 1291), assigned them as a headquarters the coastal town of Limassol. Seven crusades had come and gone with nothing in the end to show for the substantial waste of life and lucre.

### Homeless

Restricted and unappreciated, the Hospitallers fled from Cyprus to Rhodes in 1306. A Genoese adventurer (some say pirate), Vignolo dei Vignoli, who had obtained lease of the islands of Kos and Leros from the Byzantine emperor Andronikos II Palaiologos (r. 1282–1328), had come to Cyprus and suggested to the master, Fra' Foulques de Villaret (r. 1305–19, †1327), that he and the Hospitallers should conquer the Dodecanese in its entirety; once conquered, the archipelago of twelve islands would be divided between them, with dei Vignoli retaining one-third for himself. Fra' Foulques de Villaret quickly obtained the pope's blessing for the enterprise and the conquest of the island was finally achieved in 1309 with the capture of the city of Rhodes.

Having conquered Rhodes, the Knights Hospitaller built a fleet in order to protect the island's trade routes, which were vital for its survival. They remained committed to the ideal of a holy war against Islam, and they could draw on their estates scattered across all of Europe, from which they drew rents, to pay for the upkeep of perhaps half-a-dozen well-equipped war galleys. Engaging actively in bloody-handed piracy was another source of income and the Hospitallers actively encouraged the taking of Muslim ships by force; one-tenth of all prisoners brought to Rhodes was the perquisite of the Order, who also had the right to buy the rest if it so wished.

In France meanwhile, their bitter rivals the Knights Templar had become a state within a state, and that was their downfall. At daybreak on Friday, 15 October 1310, hundreds of Templars were arrested on the orders of Philippe IV *le Bel* (r. 1285–1314). Whether or not the fact the French king was heavily in debt with their bank, in a blaze of scandalous publicity, the Templars were accused and condemned on charges of blasphemy, idolatry, and heresy by Clement V (r. 1305–14), Philippe's creature residing in Avignon. In 1312, with the brutal dissolution of the Templars as a viable organisation, the Knights Hospitaller became even more powerful, acquiring a large slice of the extensive endowments of their rival order – the rest went to Philippe *le Bel*. In a memorandum written in 1305 Jacques de Molay, the twenty-third and last grand master of the Templars (r. 1298–1312, †1314), asserted that "the Hospitallers were founded to care for the sick, and beyond that they bear arms ... whereas the Templars were founded specifically for military service."[12] The Templars, in other words, were single minded. The Hospitallers were ambivalent. Moreover, unlike the Templars, the Hospitallers had realised, as early as 1300, that their former rôle of mounted knights fighting in the Holy Land was a thing of the past. From their seizure of Rhodes they became predominately sea soldiers, taking up their new rôle with all their old get-up-and-go and grit: it is but emblematic that henceforth we never hear of the Hospitallers fighting as mounted knights. In brief, the Templars had one over-riding goal. The Hospitallers had several.

With the loss of the Holy Land the fierce struggle between Christian and Muslim now continued in the eastern Mediterranean. The Knights Hospitaller took part in most of the military enterprises. In 1334 they formed an alliance with the Holy See, France, Venice and Cyprus. Ten years later the allies captured and held Smyrna until it was besieged and taken by the Turkic conqueror Timur in 1402.[13] In 1365, with Venice and Cyprus as allies, the Hospitallers took Alexandria in a surprise attack, destroyed the Egyptian fleet, burnt the city, and promptly left. In the battle of Nikopolis in Bulgaria (25 September 1396), in which the Ottoman sultan, *Yıldırım* Bāyezīd, wiped out the flower of a multinational army of French, Germans, English, Scottish, Flemish, Savoyards, Lombards and Hungarians, an army of a new crusade led by Sigismund de Luxembourg, king of Hungary and Croatia (r. 1387–1437). The sultan ordered the killing in cold blood (it is said) of more than 10,000 Christian prisoners after the battle. The commander of the Knights Hospitaller present at this Christian débâcle was Fra' Philibert de Naillac, who just managed to escape with his life back to Rhodes: the following January he was proclaimed master of the Order (r. 1397–1421).

For two centuries the Knights Hospitaller successfully defied any Muslim attempt to take Rhodes: the Ottoman Turks in 1313; the Mamlūk sultan of Egypt in 1444; Mehmed II *Fatih* in 1480. At last, in June 1522 Süleymān I *Kanuni*, having recently captured Belgrade, the gateway to central Europe, turned his victorious army, which is said to have numbered some 100,000 men, against Rhodes. The Knights Hospitaller mustered only 650, with the addition of 200 Genoese sailors, fifty Venetians, 400 Cretans, 600 of the local Greek inhabitants, and 4,000 mercenaries. The former tutor of Charles V and now pope, Adrian VI (r. 1522–3), vainly implored the princes of Christendom to come to their aid.

Arriving on Rhodes on 26 June, at first the Ottoman fleet blockaded the harbours. The land forces then secured the heights above Rhodes (the ancient acropolis) and thence the artillery pounded the fortifications and the infantry attacked in wave after wave. For several months the besieged repelled the Ottoman Turks – expecting the siege, the defenders had measured the distance to all the points where the besiegers might attack – and repaired the breaches in the walls, but their numbers daily diminished. In December the Ottomans, whose losses to date numbered some 50,000 dead, made another and final breach in the walls. The Hospitallers capitulated on honourable terms and at dawn on 1 January 1523, the grand master of the Order, Fra' Philippe Villiers de L'Isle-Adam (r. 1521–34) and the surviving brethren embarked on their ships and left the island forever.

## A New Home (again)

Having lost Rhodes and now homeless, the Knights Hospitaller were determined to renew the fight against the Muslims. Fortunately, Charles V, Holy Roman Emperor and ruler of the lands of the Crown of Aragón, which included Sicily, had a ready answer. He granted the Knights Hospitaller a magnificent charter in March 1530 (Act of Donation of Malta), in which he pointed out that they had 'wandered for several years' and sought a 'fixed residence'; he was ready to dispose in their favour of several dependencies of the Kingdom of Sicily: Tripoli along with the bare and windswept archipelago of Malta, which had been under the dominion of the Crown of Aragón since 1284 and the Hospitallers would rule until 1798 when Napoléon Bonaparte made them homeless once again.

Thus did the Order of Knights of the Hospital of Saint John of Jerusalem become known as the Order of Malta. In deference to its origins in the Holy City, it was known as the Hierosolymitan Order of Malta well into the 20th century. Adopting a new name was simple enough; developing the harsh and deforested land of the archipelago would be more difficult. More importantly, politically speaking, L'Isle-Adam had insisted they could not take Malta over as a feudatory to the Crown of Aragón, as that was contrary to the fundamental idea of the Order – its impartiality in its relations with *all* the powers of Christendom. The sole condition of service, therefore, was only nominal: all that was required in recognition of Sicilian sovereignty was a gift of a gerfalcon to the viceroy of Sicily each All Saints' Day (this annual rent was immortalised in *The Maltese Falcon*, a 1941 film noir starring Humphrey Bogart). The Medici pope, Clement VII (r. 1523–34), who was a knight of the Order and had formerly been prior of Capua, sanctioned this act with a papal bull of 7 May 1530, and the Order established itself on Malta later in the year. And then there was Tripoli of course.

Ferdinand *el Católico* had installed a Spanish garrison in Tripoli following its capture on 15 July 1510,[14] though it was proving difficult to hold the town against the Berbers who pressed in from each landward side. For Charles, holding vulnerable Tripoli was what mattered; it was lost on 15 August 1551, after which it became obvious that holding the small stony patches of Malta and Gozo (316 km²) was no less important, standing plump in the straits between Europe and North Africa, between the Christian and the Muslim worlds. Undeniably, for the Order Tripoli had proved a liability and its loss was something of a relief, enabling the Hospitallers to concentrate their energies and resources on strengthening Malta.

Strategically, Malta occupies an enviable position in the centre of the Mediterranean. Its geographical nearness to the Muslim world was an advantage to a certain extent and the galleys of the Order reaped rich harvests of prizes at sea. But that was only possible due to the strict control exercised by the navy of the Order on the seas round Malta; the Hospitallers insisted on the right of search on all ships sailing in all directions of the Mediterranean, an unpopular practice at the best of times. Friendly harbours situated at most a few hundred kilometres from Malta ensured refuge in dangerous situations. On the other hand, the strategic value of the position of Malta would have been of little benefit if the island had not been endowed with deep, natural harbours. In due course, these would be defended by well-built, state-of-the-art fortifications.

## Socio-ethnic Makeup

Relics of the crusades, the Knights Hospitaller still fought in plate armour and (in theory) only against Muslims. The Order was divided into three ranks: knights (*milites*), chaplains (*cappelani*), and sergeants-at-arms (*servientes armorum*) or serving brethren (religious men but not priests) who served the knights either at war or in the hospital.

The knights were usually the younger sons of great families; they were expected to prove an impeccably aristocratic descent. It was essentially this class in whose hands authority resided, very few exceptions being made for the other two classes. The knights therefore occupied all the major administrative and military offices, such as those of master, bailiffs, preceptors, and so on.

The chaplains were not noblemen, but they were not sons of serfs or those who engaged in base trades either. They did not bear arms, as is forbidden by canon law. They were the priests of the Order and their duties were limited to performing religious rites. Within this class there were three ranks: clerics, chaplains and priors (who should not be confused with preceptors). The clerics assisted at religious services. Each commandery had its own chaplain, many of whom were assigned to the Order's headquarters, though some accompanied its navy or army on military campaigns. Eligibility to the highest rank, prior, was conditional on serving for at least one year and being at least twenty-six-years of age. Every preceptory had a prior whose authority extended over all the chaplains in his domain.

The family origins of the sergeant-at-arms need only be respectable. They assisted the knights in warfare, administration, and in tending the sick, poor and needy. They only held the lower commissions in the command of the army.

The civil dress of the Order was black with a white cross of eight points (representing the eight beatitudes that Jesus pronounced in his Sermon on the Mount) sewn on the left breast (later known as the Maltese Cross), black and white being the colours of the Augustinians, whose rule the Hospitallers chiefly followed. The members of the Order were bound by religious ritual and in addition to the normal monastic vows of poverty, chastity, and obedience to their lawful superiors, they also took a unique fourth vow to be *the serf and slave of our lords the sick*. They also pledged devotion to the Holy Mother Church and dedicated themselves to fight against Islam. They were not supposed to drink after supper, and had to be silent at meals and in bed. They were not to sleep in the dark. All had to maintain a war horse, and none but dignitaries and the sick were allowed to ride a mule. In short, they were ascetic monks who were also professional warriors.

Depending on their origin, each knight was allotted to one of the seven (later eight) tongues or *langues* in the order, which, in order of precedence, were those of Provence, Auvergne, France, Aragón (in 1462 subdivided into Aragón and Castile), Italy, England (with Scotland and Ireland), and Germany. These *langues* constituted the basis for the communal life and military organisation of the Knights Hospitaller. Each tongue maintained its own *auberge*, or inn, and each tongue was responsible for the defence of its own allotted section of the city walls. Every tongue was headed by a *pilier*, or pillar, who belonged to the highest rank of officials, each being entrusted with specific duties within the machinery of government. At least four of them had to be in residence at any one time in the seat of the Order and no one could be absent from the seat of the Order without the permission of the Council.

Each *langue* was divided into various priories or grand priories and these into bailiwicks, which in turn were divided into commanderies (revenue yielding territories) to which several knights were attached under the authority of the commanders. They were all ruled over by a master, which changed to grand master (*magnus magister*) during the fourteen-thirties, who was voted into office by the knights themselves, and then confirmed by the pope. The grand master always came from the first class of knights and had to be noble. He was elected for life and was the administrative and military head of the Order, usually ruling in consultation with his Council.

During our period of study, the Order lost forever one of its *langues*, that of England. Henry VIII of England, soon after the fall of Rhodes, had shown himself unfriendly to the interests of the Order, but had been pleased by the visit of Grand Master Fra' Philippe Villiers de L'Isle-Adam in February 1528. But the Tudor monarch's subsequent dealings with the papacy and the monasteries inevitably involved the Hospitallers, who had large holdings both in England and Ireland. The Grand Priory of the Order was in the Clerkenwell Priory, just beyond the confines of the London Wall, and the grand prior, Sir William Weston, held a seat in the House of Lords. Henry wrote a letter in 1538 to the grand master, the Aragonese Juan d'Homedes y Coscon (r. 1536–53), wherein conditions were laid down for the maintenance of the Order in England. The two main stipulations where that Englishmen admitted into the Order must take an oath of allegiance to the English Crown, and that no member in England must in any way recognise the jurisdiction or authority of the papacy.

Henry was well aware the Hospitallers could never consent to such terms as these, which were the negation of the fundamental principle of the international neutrality of the Order. Naturally the king's demands were refused, and the tongue of England perished. Many of the Knight Hospitallers fled to Malta; others were executed for refusing obedience to the Act of Supremacy of 1534. Clerkenwell Priory was acquired by the king to be used for the storage of his hunting-nets. Its great bell tower was later blown up with gunpowder by Edward Seymour, 1st Duke of Somerset and Lord Protector of England (1547–9) during the minority of Edward VI, to provide building materials for his Thames side palace, Somerset Place.

With the accession of Henry's Catholic daughter Mary Tudor, in 1553, negotiations were at once opened with the Order for the restoration of the tongue of England, and during her reign it was restored once again, though its properties and lands were not returned.[15] But Elizabeth, in the first year of her reign, suppressed the Hospitallers for good and all. Nevertheless, the Order proudly kept up the fiction of it existence thereafter.

## Ranking officials

There were a further seven, later eight, high offices below that of grand master: grand commander (second in rank to the grand master), marshal (responsible for the logistics of the army and navy), hospitaller (responsible for the treatment of the sick and social welfare), admiral (in command of the fleet, except when the grand master was present), draper (attended to the dress of the members of the Order and responsible for garment manufacture and storage), turcopolier (commander of the *Turcopoli*, a body of mounted archers),[16] grand treasurer (the account of the Order's finances) and, from 1462 onwards, grand chancellor (in charge of the grand master's secretariat). They were the leaders of the tongues and were elected by the grand master irrespective of their nationality. From 1320 onwards, however, each office was assigned to a specific tongue: the grand commander (*pilier* of the tongue of Provence), the marshal (*pilier* of the tongue of Auvergne), the hospitaller (*pilier* of the tongue of France), the admiral (*pilier* of the tongue of Italy),[17] the draper (*pilier* of the tongue of Aragón), the turcopolier (*pilier* of the tongue of England)[18] – a survival from the Holy Land days – the grand treasurer (*pilier* of the tongue of Germany), and the grand chancellor (*pilier* of the tongue of Castile and Portugal).

## Collective Bodies

The Chapter General (*capitulum generalis*) exercised extreme authority and all offices of the Order were entitled to participate. It had control over all the actions of the administrative and military bodies of the state. Its decisions were law. In the beginning it met every five years, and occasionally every three, later every ten or even fifteen years. An extraordinary Chapter General was convened on the death of the grand master.

The council (*capitulum* or *conventus*) assisted and advised the grand master, as well as taking decisions on important issues. It was always based at the headquarters of the Order. During the first two centuries of the Order's existence, members of the council were elected by the Chapter General or chosen by the grand master from the class of knights, regardless of the tongue to which they belonged. In 1320 the Chapter

General decided the council should henceforth comprise the leaders of the tongues, the bailiffs.

The original 12th-century statutes of the Order had been written in Provençal. In 1357 these had been translated into Latin, which was the *lingua franca* of Europe. In 1410 a Chapter General was held in Aix in southern France rather than Rhodes, the then seat of the Order. It had been convened to carry out reforms, to remove fraud, restore the authority of the grand master and attempt to ensure the brethren obeyed the statutes of the Order. The revised statutes were also drawn up in Latin, and in 1567 Italian finally became the official language of the Order.

## Local Administration

The Order was a highly bureaucratic organisation with vast and wealthy estates throughout Europe, from Portugal to Denmark, Hungary and Bohemia and from England as far as Cyprus. There was a centralised system of administration over the domains in Europe, ultimate authority being vested in the Chapter General, the grand master and his council. There were two local administrative units: the *commandery*, or preceptory, which were gathered into provinces called *priories* by the Hospitallers.

The commandery was the first and basic administrative unit of the Hospitallers' state with authority over an indeterminate number of neighbouring settlements and estates. A commander (*comendator* or *praeceptor*, so named from his duty of receiving and training novices) governed it, who was a knight of the first class with at least three year's service in the Order. The commanderies crucial to defence were known as castles and the castellan (*castellanus*) had to have served for a minimum of five years. Some knights or sergeants were aides to the commander and a chaplain was charged with serving the community's religious needs.

The holder of a commandery was appointed by the prior of the province and was obliged to pay a specific annual tax to the head of the priory.

A priory, such as France or Auvergne, consisted of a variable number of commanderies. The prior was proposed by the grand master and appointed by the Chapter General. At the time the Order occupied the Dodecanese, the offices of grand preceptory and grand prior were introduced.

Since the primary purpose of European estates was to support the fighting men initially in Rhodes, then in Malta, every priory kept detailed records of rents, incomes and properties, the entire system being directed by the grand master and his household. In order to maintain strong and continued ties between the distant provinces and the central administration, the prior was obliged to go to the seat of the Order and give an account of his work whenever the grand master commanded.

The prior, assisted by a provincial council, appointed the commanders. He also collected the rents and incomes from the commanderies and despatched these to the Order's headquarters. He made periodic tours of inspection of his province and controlled its administration and economic affairs.

## To the Sea

The entry into the Order as a novitiate knight was preceded by production of proofs of nobility, the examination of which gave rise to an inquest. After this inquest, a nobleman was admitted into the Knights Hospitaller as a Knight of Majority, entering the novitiate at an age of between sixteen and twenty. After a twelve-month novitiate, the knights took simple vows, performed their *carovanes* (a reminiscence of the Order's days in the Holy Land), cruises of at least six months on Malta's galleys against the Muslim 'infidel', and could take solemn vows at the age of twenty-one. The average knight spent years in Malta serving on the numerous congregations that administered the Knights Hospitaller, and above all – if he could afford the expense involved – seeking the command of a war galley.

Galleys, after all, were the chosen instruments of the Knights Hospitaller, the professional soldiers of the Holy Mother Church, who used them in their defence of the True Faith manned with crusading knights (*crusading* seems the proper term, since the maritime enterprises involved had religious as well as other purposes, and usually had hearty support from Rome). The Abbé de Vertot, an 18th-century historian of the Knights Hospitaller, referred to its members as "a militia composed of the noblest blood of the Christian world".[19] They thought of themselves as, and in some circles were reputed to be, an élite of Christendom.

Normally there were twenty to twenty-five knights per galley, and thirty on the *capitana*, complemented by a few score of soldiers and a comparable number of seamen. These latter hailed generally from Malta, Corsica, Sardinia, Sicily or Calabria.

It was in this capacity that the Knights Hospitaller preyed on Ottoman traders (and others besides) as part of the ongoing *corso*, or *guerre de course*, between Muslim and Christian nations. The *corso* was considered legalised piracy (for the Venetians, the Hospitallers were merely 'corsairs parading crosses'), whose primary purpose was to seize the enemy's seaborne cargo, which included that of a human nature, which was then ransomed to fill the coffers of the Hospitallers' treasury. The alternative to ransom was life as a galley slave, which tended in any event to be short. At any rate, it was the grand master who received one-tenth of the profits of all the loot from the *corso*. Everybody on board, except the slaves, had a right to a share of the profits. This share obviously varied according to the relative posts of responsibility on board.[20]

As was discussed earlier with regards to Venetian galleys, during the 16th century the method of rowing *a sensile* was replaced by a new way of handling the oars known as *a scaloccio*. Just to remind ourselves, rowing *a sensile* involved three oarsmen sitting on the same bench each pulling their own individual oar, while rowing *a scaloccio* required three or more oarsmen sitting on the same bench and pulling a single large oar together. On a Hospitaller galley a *ciurma* normally counted no less than two hundred men, and would include Muslim slaves, *buonevoglie* and convicts. With regards to the latter, it was usual for convicts from nearby countries, such as Sicily and Naples, to be sent to row in the Order's galleys, the convicting country thus getting rid of its criminals and the Order getting gratis a source of the oarsmen for its galleys. Even so, from the Order's perspective the *corso* was a steady source for the procurement of slaves, who were the motor force of its galleys, and of provisions and munitions including lumber, iron, nails and lead, not to mention guns and all sorts of victuals.

The *corso* season lasted from 1 July to 31 December and 1 January to 30 June.[21] Although shipping almost vanished during the winter months, yet there was always the chance of some fat prize being encountered. The Order felt that its galleys sailing in winter reduced the number of young bloods prowling the streets of Malta looking for trouble.[22] As we can easily imagine, many Hospitallers, scions of the European Catholic nobility confined to living in such a restricted space, were punctilious on matters touching their honour. The smallest slight on a knight's honour, real or imaginary, invariably led to a duel even though strictures were in place prohibiting members of the Order from indulging in such. On 2 April 1568, for instance, Grand Master Jean Parisot de la Valette (r. 1557–68) decreed that no member of the Order, regardless of rank, could keep pistols in his possession. Those who failed to obey that law lost two years' seniority.[23] Another law passed a month later, on 8 May, decreed that no member of the Order or his servants could carry arms by day or by night except the customary sword and dagger.[24] All the same, it was to be expected that the martial swagger of these young noblemen warriors very often led them to duel.

Still, there was more to the Knights Hospitaller and its navy than the profitable game of *guerre de course*. In the amphibious war against the Sublime Porte and its Barbary allies the Hospitallers participated in a number of naval battles. The Order despatched the carrack *Sant' Anna della Capella* (launched in 1522) and three galleys to support the Spanish Habsburg conquest of Tunis (1535),[25] the firepower of the *Sant' Anna* contributing significantly in the assault on the *presidio* of La Goleta which controlled the entry into the bay. The *Sant' Anna* had fifty great guns, classed as culverins and reinforced cannon, which were distributed evenly on the two main gun decks, and carried a greater number of smaller-calibre guns on the remaining four decks and at her stem and stern,[26] and could stand her own against a whole flotilla of smaller ships.[27] The Genoese admiral Andrea Doria, a sailor who knew his ships, had nothing but praise for the *Santa' Anna* and saw in her great possibilities as a weapon of war.[28]

The galleys of the Order were always ready to make a common cause with anybody who was fighting the Muslims. They thus participated in the battle of Préveza (1538), and joined with the Spanish every time they attacked the North African coast, such as the Algiers expedition (1541) and the battle of Djerba (1560), all notable defeats for the Christian forces. As we shall see, three of the Order's galleys were present at Lepanto.

Though the knights may in some cases have donned a complete harness of full steel plate, as they predominantly fought on foot they would be more likely to wear half-armour or brigantine, over which was worn a *côte d'armes*, a loose scarlet *sopravesta* – a tabard type garment – emblazoned with a flat-ended white cross. They carried various hand weapons, useful in naval warfare, such as halberds, half pikes, two handed swords and so forth, and axes and one or more of a variety of heavy bludgeoning weapons; and it was, indeed, these which they frequently found more useful for ship boarding. For in battle, be it on land or at sea, there were few opportunities for the exercise of skilled swordsmanship, since great strength, stamina and spirited determination were attributes more likely to gain the victory in what was usually a chaotic mêlée. Finally, to judge by near contemporary prints many of them bore oval bucklers, scarlet with the flat-ended white cross, a buckler being a handy supplement to an axe and its like in combat.

Though the Knights Hospitaller would only provide three galleys for the engagement at Lepanto,[29] the intrepid knights, sergeant-at-arms and sailors that manned them were by far the most experienced in naval warfare, which after all was their stock-in-trade. Most, if not all, fighting members of the Order were trained as warriors from birth, and adding this to the traditional religious monastic vows of chastity, poverty and obedience made them formidable fighters, reckoned among the toughest in Christendom. Moreover, the actual fighting capacity of the three galleys and their crews, forged as it was in the perpetual state of warfare with the 'enemy' (i.e. the Muslims) where boarding and hand-to-hand fighting decides the issue, was second to none. Additionally, the Order was renowned for producing adept naval commanders, knights of vast seagoing experience who had grown old in that service. It was for this reason probably that Don Juan de Austria had a veteran Hospitaller, Fra' Gil d'Andrada, as his ship captain aboard *La Real*.

Among the several Hospitallers who served as papal galley commanders was the Gascon Fra' Mathurin d'Aux de Lescaut (1528–81), *dit* Romegas from the name of one of his family's estates, a masterly seamen and one of the Hospitallers greatest naval commanders, whose galley raiding exploits against the Ottomans were legendary.[30] The eighteen-year-old Romegas had enrolled in the Order on 16 December 1547. Four days later, he took the habit of a Knight. After this, Romegas had to undertake the statuary two year apprenticeship completing at least four *carovanes* of six months each.[31] His love of the sea and chase probably dates to this time. From then on Romegas spent nearly all his life on the galleys of the Order. He was totally committed to the defence of the *Sancta romana ecclesia*, fighting with unbound zeal Muslims and Protestants alike, maintaining a fearsome reputation for seamanship, audacity, and demonic violence. As Fernand Braudel points out, the boldest western corsairs were the Knights of Malta, led, from around 1560, by Romegas.[32]

Romegas happened to be one of the lucky survivors of the unexpected hurricane that capsized the four galleys in the Grand Harbour of Malta on the evening of 23 September 1555. He, along with the monkey he kept on board his galley as a pet, was rescued the following morning. Romegas had spent the whole night clinging to the keel with his head in an air pocket of the overturned galley. This nightmarish incident did not leave him unscathed however; from then on his hands shook uncontrollably, so much so that he could hardly bring a glass to his lips without spilling half its contents: it is possible that Romegas suffered from PTSD, induced by his close brush with a watery death. Presumably his hands were steady when he gripped a sword.

One of Romegas' greatest naval exploits was the capture of a large and heavily-armed Ottoman galleon off Alexandria on 14 June 1564. Owner of the ship was Kustir Ağa, the chief eunuch of the sultan's seraglio, and the *Sultana*, as she was so named, was carrying freight worth 800,000 *ducati* – a cargo of luxuries on their way to Constantinople. Romegas' seven galleys engaged the galleon and a sharp and costly fight ensued, since 200 janissaries had been placed on board to give the ship special protection. After the *Sultana* was taken, Romegas found several persons of interest on board, including the governor of Cairo, the governor of Alexandria, and, perhaps the biggest catch, the former wet-nurse of Mihrimah Sultan, Süleymān's most powerful and only daughter.

The event led Süleymān to mobilise the great armada that went against Malta the following year. Richard Knolles, in his *Generall historie of the Turkes* published several decades later, claims to quote the sultan's justification for attacking Malta. Süleymān supposedly described the Knights Hospitaller to his courtiers in the following manner:

Crossed Pyrats, which vaunt themselves to be the Bulwark of Christendom … You your selves daily hear the pitiful complaints of our Subjects and Merchants, whom those Maltæses, I say not Souldiers, but Pyrats, if they but look into those Seas, spoil and make prize of, whose injuries or revenge, all Laws both of God and Man require.[33]

The result was an epic siege in which the Ottomans were totally humiliated. Though it is highly debatable that this defeat was a turning point in Mediterranean history, for it certainly did not destroy or even much damage Ottoman naval or military might. Nor did it change the course of Ottoman expansion. It was, however, the last great feat of arms by the Order, and as Voltaire would say with some justification, "*Rien n'est plus connu que ce siège*".[34]

Romegas, this Gascon corsair hardened by many a sea battle, was invited by Pius V to serve aboard the flagship of Marc'Antonio Colonna with the rank of superintendent of the papal galleys. In fact, the pope had written directly to Romegas on 1 June 1570 informing him of his alliance with Spain and Venice against the Ottomans and to *order* him to leave all other matters which he might have in hand and hasten to join the papal forces.[35]

Other Hospitallers were scattered throughout the Christian fleet that day, sometimes as galley captains but in many cases simply as volunteers, such as Fra' Pagno Doria (brother of Gianandrea Doria) and Fra' Luigi Mazzinghi.[36] What is more, the Hospitaller contingent at Lepanto brought powerful religious symbolism, connecting the Holy League fleet to the crusaders of the Holy Land as well as the Hospitaller defenders of Rhodes (1522), Tripoli (1551), and Malta (1565). The three galleys of the Order would have stood out as they were painted vermillion red above the water level and white below.[37] In addition, the *Santa Maria della Vittoria*, the *capitana* of Malta, carried the idiosyncratic banner of the Order from a flagpole rigged just in front of the stern cabin.

*Chapter 9*

# His Holiness

A Borgia prince lived in that house there. / He murdered his brother on the Tiber
    Desmond O'Grady '10 Piazza Campitelli', *The Wandering Celt*

U ntil the Italian unification in 1870, the pope continued to rule as a sovereign prince over a large slice of central Italy, the Papal States, which still survive as a faint echo in Europe's Heavenly City, the *Città del Vaticano*, an independent sovereign state of 44.11 hectares (109 acres) defended by the Tiber and Castel Sant'Angelo, surrounded by Italy and supported by the world. Here rules – as absolute monarch – the pope: bishop of Rome, successor of Saint Peter, who Jesus handpicked for leadership, *Pontifex Maximus* (a title borrowed from Roman antiquity), the leader of Roman Catholicism. This august figure keeps, among many other things, the keys to the Kingdom. He claims nothing less than this: he is the Vicar of Jesus Christ the Saviour and resides in the earthly outpost of Heaven. Its size does not match its history.

It is so easy for the 21st century, with its jaded physique and sophisticated brain, and the magnificent perspective of half a thousand years, to conceive of the pope as an uninteresting, far-away, semi-diplomatic species of clergyman, nourishing pretensions of utter insignificance. It will be well to remember that once upon a time the pope was a power, who saw nothing figurative, metaphorical, or extravagant in the exordium 'Know yourself to be the Ruler of the World, the Father of princes and of kings, and the Earthly Vicar of Jesus Christ our Saviour', who was not by any means a negligible quantity in the world's affairs, and who literally had the unquestioned right of making or unmaking princes and kings or even emperors. In the view of that obsessive conspiracy theorist William Tyndale, a pope could reduce kings and emperors "to shadows, vain names and things idle, having nothing to do in the world but when our Holy Father needeth their help".[1] In another place the English scholar amplifies his argument, declaring that if "all the kings christened" united against pope and prelates, "they might haply, by the secret practice of them, be put out of their own seats".[2] Tyndale himself would be convicted of heresy in Vilvoorde (Filford), Spanish Netherlands, and on 6 October 1536 he was executed by garrotting, after which his body was burnt at the stake. His dying prayer was that the eyes of Henry VIII of England would be opened.

## Dissent and Division

The common wisdom is that 'Rome fell', boom. Invaded and sacked by 'barbarians', papal Rome became barbaric. Grass grew in the Forum. Wolves howled. *Roma caput mundi*, Rome conquered the world, but now could not even police its own streets. Vicious family tribes (the Orsini, the Frangipani, the Colonna) mutilated their foes, raped nuns, and robbed monks, turning the Eternal City for months together into shambles. The papacy itself had a dreadful reputation, notably among religious sectors that were deeply critical of those apparently ineradicable twins papal corruption and political incompetence and so in favour of reform; charges of simony, abuse, influence peddling, lax morals and ostentatious wealth were everyday occurrences. This mood was reinforced by the Great Schism and thereafter the desire for reform grew stronger as time passed.

Pope fought anti-pope: in 1378 began the Great Schism between the papacy and a line of rival anti-popes. The sheep of Christ's flock were sorely neglected, while the shepherds fired anathemas at each other; the rival popes were widely accused of 'rending the garments of Christ'. It had all happened before – many times before – usually as an ethnic quarrel over whether the Italians (viz. Romans) or the French should control the Holy Mother Church.

This particular confusion of authorities was put an end to by the Council of Constance (1414–18), which in 1417 deposed the three existing popes and elected Oddo Colonna, who took the name of Martin V (r. 1417–31) – though rival claimants lingered on in obscurity even for a decade after that.[3] It was eight years previously, in 1409, when these three 'authentic' popes had emerged (one in the Vatican, two others in Avignon),[4] along with riot and rebellion, fighting it out for ultimate power at God's business address on Earth. One faction vowed to eat their children rather than surrender, and all this pristine horror in the name of the Holy Mother Church. Martin V was the best pope of his age, but from his election a new period began; the popes became more than ever absorbed in purely temporal interests, and the papal court reached a depth of abasement unequalled by that of any princely court in Italy. In terms of the 16th century a concerted attack on the authority of the papacy was set in motion by a German Augustinian friar by the name of Martin Luther (1483–1546). Although his Ninety-Five Theses of 1517 were for the most part a vigorous critique of the practice of indulgences, they equally marked a rejection of the pope's authority.[5]

In a mid 16th-century woodcut, the German painter and woodcut artist Matthias Gerung (†1570) depicts the turbaned Turks (as the Ottomans were then called) and their demonic minions slaughtering defenceless Christians (men, women and children) and destroying their churches, a stock image of the 'infidel' Muslim. In the same woodcut, however, just over the next hill, the pope and his own demonic minions (a couple of them dressed as either Swis *reisläufer* or *Landsknechte*) are tormenting Christ's flock with faggot and steel.[6] In fact, this is a stock image of the Reformation, 'Turks and Papists' grouped in the same frame, and Gerung created several satirical pieces that criticised the Catholic Church and the Holy See.

## The Rise of the Bastard

Italy as we know it today was created through the 19th-century wars of unification. On the other hand, in our period of study Italy was but a cultural and geographical expression, the Italian peninsula being divided into a patchwork quilt of numerous sovereign city states and petty princedoms. The five principal states of Italy were Milan, Florence, Venice, the Papal States and the Kingdom of Naples. Jammed as they were in the dangling length of the peninsula there were tensions, which made war an ever-present reality. "Peace and war, war and peace / These two rule the world today", wrote an anonymous versifier in the course of the thirty-six year wars of Italy.[7] Besides, as we shall discover in due course, many of the Italians participating in the 1571 campaign were Neapolitans, Sicilians and Milanese, all subjects of the king of Spain.

In this political arena of competing sovereignties, the strength of virtually every powerful pope was measured in family members, including sons – invariably bastards of course, as their vows did not permit the popes to marry – who were rapidly advanced to the rank of cardinal, often before they reached the age of eighteen. Alexander VI (r. 1492–1503), born Rodrigo Borgia, and his illegitimate sons Giovanni and Cesare spring immediately to mind.[8] In the year following his election, Alexander VI made Juan *capitano generale* of the papal armies, while Cesare (then sixteen) was elevated to the rank of cardinal. However, the pattern was true with less infamous popes; Alexander himself was the nephew of Alfonso Borgia (Sp. Alfons de Borja), who became pope under the name Callistus III (r. 1455–8). Rodrigo was advanced through the church hierarchy by means of his influence, being named a cardinal the year following Alfonso's election. Little wonder that there was less and less fear of moral condemnation from the Holy Mother Church. The pope's authority was increasingly martial, not moral.

Take for instance the conquest and colonisation of the Americas by the Iberian imperial powers. Under the terms of the Treaty of Tordesillas, drawn up by Alexander VI in 1494, Spain enjoyed exclusive rights, along with Portugal, to trade in the western hemisphere, and Spain was to seize vast amounts of gold, silver, and other treasure from the Americas. Thus, for example, the New World produced 50,000 tonnes (55,115.6 tons) of silver between 1540 and 1700, doubling the existing stock in Europe. The Treaty of Tordesillas still plays a rôle in international relations, with Argentina citing it as a foundation for its claim to the Falkland Islands/ Las Malvinas. Alexander also granted the right to Ferdinand II of Aragón and Isabella of Castile to collect the tithes in the territories they colonised in the 'Indies', as America was still called in the papal bull of 1501.

Closer to home on the political front, Alexander VI strove to maintain a balance in the Italian peninsula, which was divided principally into four major powers: the duchy of Milan and the Republic of Venice in the north, the Papal States in the centre, and the Kingdom of Naples in the south. Two great European powers, Castilla-Aragón and Valois France, both of which coveted the Kingdom of Naples and the duchy of Milan, posed an external threat. The papacy carried with it considerable income, and so papal armies tended to rely more heavily on *condottieri* and mercenary bands than even other Italian city states; for his wars in Romagna Cesare Borgia was not adverse to allowing Swiss, Germans, Gascons and Italians to serve in the same unit.[9] The Gascons, for instance, were men of fiery disposition and irregular habits, while the Swiss lived by their motto *kein geld, kein Schweiz*, and they liked, when practicable, to be paid in advance.[10] Still, despite Gascon strong-mindedness and Swiss pecuniary attitudes,[11] the military efficacy of Cesare and his armies became legendary, though his diplomacy was apparently as effective as the force of arms, if not more so. Together, Alexander VI and Cesare, now *capitano generale* following the assassination of Giovanni,[12] used the military and fiscal power of the papacy to carve out a hereditary Borgia princedom in central Italy independent of the papacy – unsuccessfully, as it happened, but certainly not for lack of trying. The duca di Valentino was made famous by Machiavelli in *il Principe*.[13]

The archipelago of Italian city states, whether princely courts or prosperous republics, could be seen as both the graduate school of humanist learning and the dangerous seat of Catholicism, the peninsula of the graceful courtier of Baldassare Castiglione (1478–1529) and of the evil '*Machiavel*'. Italy brought with it the promise of the new humanism and the dangers of the old Catholicism, the intrigues of Machiavellian policy, or courtly manners, and the glories of art.

Castiglione was the papal nuncio to the court of Charles V in Spain, although for most of the period during which he was drafting and revising his work (1508–28) he was a courtier and diplomat at the courts of Urbino, his native Mantua, and Rome. *Il Libro del Cortegiano*, 'The Book of the Courtier', expresses the author's opinion that society by now ought to have grown out of warfare, except against the infidel, and it describes the social and learned graces whereby time could be passed fruitfully and delightfully in peace while not neglecting training the body against the eventuality of war. Yet despite being the most widely read – in the Italian, in subsequent translation and a host of later plagiaries – lifestyle book, it was a diverse publication, less peaceful in its posture, which caught the attention of aristocratic audiences.

The first published large-scale and systematic treatment of warfare, complete with tactical diagrams, was of course Machiavelli's *Arte della guerra* of 1522. The book takes the form of a dialogue between the Florentine gentleman Cosimo Rucellai (†1519) and the papal *capitano generale* Fabrizio Colonna (†1520) set under the shade trees in the Orti Oricellari, the walled gardens of the Rucellai family. The friends who met there from 1517 to 1520 included a group of Cosimo's intimates: Zanobi Buondelmonti, the man (along with Cosimo himself) addressed in the proem to Machiavelli's *Discorsi*, as well as Luigi Alamanni, Batista della Palla, and Lorenzo di Filippo Strozzi, to whom *Arte della guerra* is dedicated. Machiavelli's evocation of a conversation that develops from its dramatic setting under the shade trees in the garden exemplifies the commonwealth of humane letters of the Italian Renaissance. After all, the author himself had witnessed war but not handled a weapon: just as no battle was fought by the book, no army was composed by it.

## Power and Piety

As we have just witnessed with the Borgias, the pope came to play an increasingly unique rôle in Italian politics, as both head of the Church and as a secular prince, controlling a wide swathe of territory across the middle of Italy, the Papal States.

Take, for example, that most dedicated and indefatigable adversary of Alexander VI, the della Rovere pope Julius II (r. 1503–13), who went even further down the secular path by wielding both the sword and the crosier. Unlike Cesare Borgia, who shed his cardinal's robes and hat before making a career as a soldier, Julius II strapped his war panoply over his priestly vestments to lead papal armies against enemies of the Church.

Riding a fiery steed, *il papa terribile* (in Italian, not 'terrible' but 'awe-inspiring') swept all before him; his volcanic spirit set the stage of the early modern papacy. More than a theologian, he was also a philosopher, plotter, patron of literature and art, and empire builder. He was a man after the heart of the age, a great captain, an acute politician, a mixture of the fox and the lion, ready to don armour and shed the blood of those petty lords who stood in his way (he pursued his conquests in the Romagna in person). He was also the first pope to establish a war chest, in an innermost room of Castel Sant'Angelo; it was quickly emptied by his successors. He also instituted the Pontifical Swiss Guard or *Cohors Helvetica* (22 January 1506). Swiss only, the della Rovere pope needed a select body of men to whom he could entrust his personal safety, a private guard completely loyal and resistant to the plots and machinations of European monarchs and nobles.

Full of enterprise and energy, more fitted to be a great prince than a great priest, Julius II behaved very much like a secular ruler in the ways he sought to secure the interests of the papacy. In 1506 the pope planned and executed a military campaign to retake lands lost from the Papal States, including their second most important city after Rome, Bologna. These petty tyrannies were originally fiefs of the Holy See and held by its vicars, who, however, had long since repudiated the pontifical authority, refused the payment of their annual dues and feudal tributes into the chancery of their lord paramount. For while the popes were absent from Rome during the Great Schism, powerful neighbouring families had established their own authority over the now lost papal holdings. Worse still, in some instances, such as Bologna, these tyrannies had even gone so far as to bear arms against the Church. From time to time these strong men and petty tyrants sallied forth with armed *condottieri* to replenish their stores from the pillage of towns and villages. The region was ravished from end to end by their excesses. As a consequence of his warlike endeavours, Julius II was able to unify various fragments of the Papal States, a union which would last for more than three-and-a-half centuries until this papal monarchy came to a dramatic end during the pontificate of Pius IX, in 1870.

In order to stabilise and secure the Papal States, Julius II was willing to use or block foreign powers, as seemed expedient at any given time, especially since he faced a formidable Italian foe in Venice. Italy had already been divided into three with the Valois in the north and Aragonese in the south. Between the two there was room for only one and that should be the papacy. Quick to profit from the collapse of Cesare Borgia's dominion in the Romagna, the Venetians had swooped in and snapped up the papal dependencies of Faenza and Rimini, thereby raising the ire of the warlike pontiff. Julius II had not manoeuvred his entire life to obtain the tiara of Saint Peter only to see his possessions filched by a nation of upstart fishermen. Apparently he said one day to the Venetian ambassador in Rome, "I will make Venice into a fishing village." "And we", replied the ambassador, "will reduce you again to the status of a petty priest if you are not sensible."[14] The duty of the ambassador was of course to magnify the importance of the Republic of Venice, but *il papa terribile* was not to be browbeaten.

The outcome of all these jealousies and haughtiness was that a league (France, Spain, the Holy Roman Empire, the Papal States, Florence, and the neighbouring princes of Mantua and Ferrara) was formed against Venice at Cambrai on 10 December 1508, the object of which was the destruction of Venice and the partition of its possessions. The League of Cambrai is a serious blot on the heroic reputation of Julius II. He consented to invite the great powers of Europe as invaders into Italy in order that he might recover a few towns of no great importance. Venice was only saved by the quarrels and mutual jealousies of the anti-Venetian allies, and by the sluggishness of the Holy Roman Emperor Maximilian I (r. 1508–19), a man notorious for promising aid and never following through.[15] Then again, after the crushing victory of the French over the Venetians at Agnadello (14 May 1509), Julius II got the jitters about Valois power in the fertile and richly citied plains of Lombardy and created a Holy League against the French. Switching sides and joining Venice, the pope also managed to persuade Spain and the Holy Roman Emperor to enter this new coalition. Henry VIII joined in too. The pope's Holy League was fated to suffer a heavy defeat at Marignano (13–14 September 1515) – on this occasion Maximilian I had taken the path of neutrality – though Julius II had already died and met his maker two years beforehand. Perhaps fitting enough, the monstrous Moses of Michelangelo in San Pietro ad Vincula marks the unfinished tomb of *il papa terribile*.

## To Kill a Queen

When William Shakespeare was but six years old, a wealthy Catholic, John Felton, was hanged, drawn, and quartered for fixing a copy of a papal bull on the gates of the palace of the bishop of London and for asserting "that the queen ... ought not to be the queen of England".[16] Many English

Catholics, especially in the north of the kingdom, considered Elizabeth's claim to power illegitimate, since her parents' marriage had not been sanctioned according to Catholic law. In their view, Elizabeth's younger cousin, Mary queen of Scots, had a more legitimate claim to the English crown (she was the paternal granddaughter of Margaret Tudor and a devout Catholic). Accordingly, she became the focus for the machinations of the Catholic powers of Europe and for the dangerous conspiracies of Catholic extremists at home. Mary herself was foolhardy enough to lend her name to sinister designs against Elizabeth on her behalf.

James V of Scotland (r. 1513–42), had married a French Catholic noble, Mary de Guise (1515–60), and after James' death she ruled the kingdom as regent on behalf of their six-day-old daughter, Mary Stuart. Stepping ashore at Leith, which had suffered an English siege only the year before, she arrived from France in the haar-veiled early morning of 19 August 1561. The widowed teenager – vivacious, tall, red haired, an unearthly beauty – was the anointed ruler of Scotland and despite her French upbringing had come home. The drama of Mary's brief but bloody reign and its ruthless denouement at the hands of a close relative has lent it a disproportionate significance in Scotland's history. Unhappily for Mary, all Scots were not Catholics.

In post-Reformation Scotland – led spiritually by the relentless John Knox – Mary Stuart was reviled for her Catholic faith and for her sexual allure at a time when princesses were considered mere chattels and chess pieces to be paraded across the kingdoms of Europe to seal treaties and unite empires. She was suspected of complicity in the murder of her second (English) husband, then accused of adultery with the man who soon became her third, and at whose side she waged war on many of her own people. In his virulent *A Detection of the Douings of Marie, Queen of Scots* published shortly after Mary's abdication, the Protestant George Buchanan (1506–82) denounced her "unnaturalness, hatred, barbarous fierceness [and] outrageous cruelty".[17] By contrast, the Catholic bishop John Lesley (1527–96), one of her most steadfast friends, made Mary the pious and long-suffering heroine of his *A Defence of the Honor of Marie, Queene of Scotland*, published in 1569. Here, Mary could not be further from Buchanan's "poisoning witch ... with greedy eyes".[18] Instead of a bloodthirsty and lascivious wife, she is a "most careful, tender mother with all" whose "godly and virtuous life past, do far repel and drive away all suspicion".[19] Both Buchanan and Leslie used narratives about Mary Stuart to support arguments about the legitimacy of female rule and about the desirability of a Catholic monarchy.

And so it came about that Mary was forced to sign her crown away at the castle on Lochleven, where she allegedly gave birth to stillborn twins, and whence she escaped, disguised as a laundress. The small army she subsequently rallied went down to a defeat at Langside (13 May 1568), and three days later she crossed the Solway and set foot in England. Her short stay in Scotland saw the collapse of the Scottish church and the temporary eclipse of the Scottish monarchy. For most of the remainder of the century Scotland became a political football for England and France, with warring pro-English and pro-French factions struggling for control at the Scottish court.

The exiled queen, detained by her cousin in a series of draughty castles with little opportunity for exercise, entertainment or extramural activity, gradually allowed intrigue and conspiracy to become her principal pastimes.

The mastermind behind these conspiracies against Elizabeth, it was widely believed, was the pope in Rome. His special agents were the Jesuits – who would be officially banned from entering the kingdom, on pain of death, in 1585 – sworn to obey him in everything; his hidden legions in England were the thousands of 'church papists' who outwardly conformed to Protestantism and yet harboured allegiance to the Holy Roman Church in their hearts. Though a man of God, the pope was not chary to so-called principled violence directed against an anointed monarch.

The papal bull that cost John Felton his life was that issued on 25 February 1570 by Pius V excommunicating Elizabeth as a heretic – he had testily declared her a "vassal of iniquity" – thereby releasing her subjects from any obligation they might have sworn to her. Indeed, they were solemnly enjoined to disobey.[20] This was a drastic step, as Felton clearly knew. Pius V did not like Elizabeth, and like many Catholics, he believed she was illegitimate, and thus had no right to the throne of England. A decade later, his successor Gregory XIII suggested that killing Elizabeth would not be a mortal sin. On the contrary, as the papal secretary of state,

Cardinal Tolomeo Gallio, declared on his master's behalf, "there is no doubt that whoever sends her out of the world with the pious intention of doing God's service, not only does not sin but gains merit."[21] He was writing to the Welsh courtier and spy William Parry, who had become a double agent. Having gone over to the Catholic side, Parry was planning to kill Elizabeth with his dagger in her private gardens or, failing that, to shoot her at Saint James'. Parry had previously written to Pius V offering to assassinate the queen, and for which service the pope granted him a plenary indulgence. In his confession, written in his own hand before Sir Francis Walsingham (1532–90), Parry implicated the Jesuits, English recusants and seminaries, and the pope himself. For his troubles he was hanged, drawn, and quartered on 2 March 1585.

In December of 1583 only the vigilance of her ministers saved Elizabeth from Francis Throgmorton's plot to assassinate her and put Mary Stuart on the Tudor throne: and Don Bernardino de Mendoza, the Spanish ambassador (and spy), caught red-handed as an accessory, was expelled from the kingdom (he was to resurface as Philip's ambassador in Paris). The plot showed that Spain posed a real threat to Elizabeth's rule (Mendoza had Philip's full support). The assassination of William the Silent (which everyone knew had been carried out at Philip's behest) the following year – 1584 – obviously heightened the fear of another attempt on the life of Elizabeth. As the queen's principal secretary and spymaster, Walsingham started to look more closely at Mary, who would be the beneficiary of any successful plot against Elizabeth and return England 'into the thralldome of Popish tyrannie'. Least we forget, Walsingham was zealously committed to the Protestant cause and wished to persecute *all* Catholics in England.

It is thanks to Walsingham that Elizabethan England boasted a highly efficient secret service, and the evidence the spymaster needed to connect Mary with a plot to kill the English queen was provided when Sir Anthony Babington (1561–86), a member of the Catholic gentry and onetime courtier to Mary, was arrested after he communicated with her in 1586 concerning a planned uprising by English Catholics supported by a seaborne invasion of the kingdom by Spanish-paid troops. Babington also wrote that he and a few others would support the local rising and invasion by murdering the 'tyrant'. Babington's missive, as well as Mary's reply to it, in which she wrote that she supported both the hostile invasion of England by a liberating Catholic army and the overthrow of Elizabeth, fell into Walsingham's hands as it was fated to do since he secretly controlled all communications to and from Mary by means of double agents. In September 1586 Babington and most of the conspirators were hanged, drawn, and quartered. Mary would go to her death the following year in what would become known as the Babington Plot. Her death, at first rejected by Elizabeth, was finally ensured by a campaign of misinformation, including a warning of imminent invasion of England by Spain and reports of plans for Mary's rescue and Elizabeth's assassination. Walsingham cleverly crafted these false stories to goad the queen to order her cousin's execution.

And so it was, after the best part of nineteen years being held, without charge or trial, in detention in England – it is only in the imagination of a novelist or a filmmaker that the two queens ever met – Mary Stuart was executed for treason at Fotheringhay Castle on 8 February 1587, her long, graceful white neck suffering three strokes of the headman's axe in front of 300 witnesses. By order of the Privy Council, all her possessions were burned. A year later, the Catholic Philip II of Spain launched his great Armada, perhaps – to some degree – urged on by Mary's unlawful execution. She was, after all, an anointed monarch, having been crowned queen of Scots at nine months of age, queen of France for a short period, and even had her eye on the English throne, and that cemented her downfall.

But Mary's beheading was controversial, inadvertent, and botched, and Elizabeth could not relax her guard. For Mary Stuart was not only an anointed monarch, she was also the mother of James VI of Scotland, the cousin of Henri duc de Guise, leader of the French Catholic League, and sister-in-law of both Henri III and Philip II (through his third wife Elisabeth de Valois, who had also been Mary's playmate). The latter's agents were everywhere, capitalising to the utmost the illegal execution of Mary Stuart, and using it to justify their king's maturing designs to extirpate the tyrannous 'English Jezebel'.


## The Pious Plotter

As a strong advocate of the Counter-Reformation and the canon of the Council of Trent, the temporal concerns of Pius V were twofold:

reforming the Holy Mother Church by combating the heretics, and establishing the Holy League for a crusade to defend Christianity against the Ottoman Turks. His ambition concerning the latter was to be fulfilled with the victory of Lepanto. Rather than defeating the Ottomans with superior arms, it was the pope's marshalling of divine assistance and the religiosity of the Holy League's pious commanders and soldiers that won the battle, or so promoted Pius' hagiographers.

It may be of interest to know that Antonio Ghislieri, as he was then, was born of a noble but recently impoverished family from Bosco, near Alessandria, in the duchy of Milan (now Bosco Marengo, Piedmont). Paul Ghislieri, his father, was a muleteer who shipped grain across the Alps, while young Antonio earned a living as shepherd. At age fourteen he joined the Dominican order, taking the name of Michele, and was ordained a priest in 1528 at the age of twenty-four, bishop, cardinal and grand inquisitor by the age of fifty-eight, and finally supreme pontiff at the age of sixty-one. He strived to emulate the authentic spirit of Saint Dominic by fasting, doing penance, by meditating and praying for long hours during the night; in a word, he was a truly pious man of the unworldly ascetic type, who strove to abide by those seven virtues as enunciated by Gregory I (r. AD 590–604) at the commencement of his papacy: chastity, temperance, charity, diligence, patience, kindness and humility. He wore a hair shirt beneath the simple white habit of a Dominican friar, was often seen in bare feet, and observed the fasts and other austerities of the Dominican rule. His normal fare apparently consisted of eggs and wild chicory or some other wild herb all without seasoning.

In 1556 Paul IV (r. 1555–9) made the inquisitor for Lombardy, as Father Ghislieri was at the time, bishop of Nepi and Sutri near Rome. This promotion was quickly followed by the dignity of a cardinal's hat, choosing as his titular church the Dominican basilica of Santa Maria sopra Minerva. On the accession of Pius IV (r. 1559–65) Cardinal Alessandrio (Ghislieri) was confirmed in the office of inquisitor general, the position to which he had been appointed by the previous pope.

Though profoundly learned, he still had traces about him of the awkward, angular simplicity of a poor but pious man, convinced that the particular brand of religion in which he happened to have been brought up in must be right and all the others wrong. When he exchanged his scarlet and ermine attire for the plain white robe of Christ's Vicar, he kept his customary hair shirt. One of his first acts as pope was to dismiss the papal court jester and no pope after had one. All in all, the new pope's habits and tastes were of the simpler kind, in an age of singular luxury.

Elizabeth Tudor, on the other hand, is one of, if not the, most celebrated monarchs in English history. On 7 January 1566 in London where Elizabeth held her throne by what was as yet a precarious tenure, two comets with large and bloody tails were to be seen, following the midday sun. Believe it or not, this was the very day of Cardinal Alessandrio's election to the Throne of Saint Peter over the heads of better placed cardinals of good families and great influence.

A firm advocate of strict orthodoxy (in 1543 he had refuted the 'errors' of the Lutherans in a masterly thesis dealing with many points of 'false' doctrine), Pius V revitalised the Inquisition, expelled the Jews from the Papal States (they had been welcomed there by Alexander VI), ordered the extermination of the Huguenots, conspired to dethrone Elizabeth of England, encouraged Philip II of Spain to crush the Protestants in the Low Countries, and of course he played the key rôle in the formation of the Holy League against Islam.

## The Holy League of Pius V

Ever since the fall of Constantinople it had been said from time to time (and was now being said again) that, as the successors of Constantinus and the Byzantine emperors, the Ottoman sultans claimed Italy as their rightful possession. *La Curia romana* was well aware of the alleged Ottoman ambition. After all, was it not what Mehmed II *Fatih* would have done, had he not died suddenly? He already considered himself *Kayser-i Rum*, Caesar, after taking Constantinople and he further desired to capture Rome in order to unify and revitalise the old empire. Anyone living in Italy in those days felt almost physically menaced by the Ottoman Turks, who were openly boasting once again of turning Saint Peter's one day very soon into a mosque. When he was a cardinal, Pius V had once lost his baggage to a corsair. His nephew Paolo Ghislieri had been a slave in Algiers until the pope ransomed him. Nepotism matters in high places, but this particular pope, as we shall learn all in good time, was cut from a coarser cloth. The young man turned out to be too luxurious and immoral to make a success of his promotion as captain in the papal guard: his uncle gave him ten days to get out of Rome.

Though Pius V had long cherished the idea of rekindling a crusading spirit against the Ottomans, when he first mooted the notion there had been little enthusiasm because of the rivalries, jealousies, difficulties and division that existed among the Christian nations. The Cyprus crisis changed the mood and Philip II immediately agreed to the formation of a Christian alliance to combat the Ottomans. But negotiations took their time. The wine and the words may have flowed freely, but the would-be allies of the Holy League had brought to the negotiating table their old animosities and their current jealousies. There were conflicting strategies too. For Venice, the alliance was a device to save Cyprus. For Spain, on the other hand, it was a means to recover lost possessions along the North African littoral. The outcome of all these shenanigans was to be six months of bitter wrangling and haggling before terms could be agreed, particularly between the Spanish and the Venetians.

Thus matters stood, and in the Sala del Concistoro on 25 May 1571, through the tireless efforts of the iron-willed pope, Spain and Venice, the major sea powers in the western Mediterranean, and others solemnly agreed to combine their fleets in the common cause. This was a manifest triumph by Pius V, considering Philip II had a marked dislike for the Venetians since they were almost the only Italians the king could not control.

According to the terms of the treaty signed that day, which was of course written in Latin, the triple alliance was to be maintained *in perpetuum*, offensive as well as defensive, directed against the Ottoman Turks and against the Muslims in Algiers, Tunis, and Tripoli. The forces to be used in the coming expedition, at sea and by land, were to consist of 200 galleys (*triremes*), one hundred transports (*onerariae naves*), 50,000 Italian, German, and Spanish infantry, and 4,500 light horse (*equites levis armaturae*) plus an adequate number of cannon (*tormenta bellied*), munitions, "and the other necessary things". The potential cost of this armament was calculated by the duque de Sessa, one of Spain's foremost naval commanders, who arrived at the total for the campaign of 2,700,000 *escudos*, which, divided in the simple ratio of Spain three, Venice two, and the Papal States one, as stipulated in the treaty, would cost Spain about 1.6 and Venice 1.1 million *escudos*.[22] This substantial outlay for the Holy League fleet would be defrayed, and plunder, if any, shared in the same proportions. The spoils of battle, of course, would be proportionally shared too; business, even when the Mother Church was involved, was always business. Every year in March or in April at the latest these forces were to be assembled, ready for action "in eastern waters (*maria in orientem*)". Every autumn the envoys of the high contracting parties were to gather in Rome to decide upon the expedition for the following spring.[23]

*Chapter 10*

# The Porte

The Ottoman empire whose sick body was not supported by a mild and regular diet, but by a powerful treatment, which continually exhausted it.

Charles–Louis de Secondat, baron de Montesquieu,
*Les Lettres Persanes* (1721), no. 19

It can justifiably be said that the Ottoman Turk has generally been cast as the villain in our story. European awareness of the Ottoman empire far predates the 16th century, and certain dramatic events such as the fall of Constantinople (29 May 1453), God's own city, and the Ottoman amphibious landing in the southern Italian peninsula, which culminated in the sacking of Otranto (11 August 1480), could hardly be ignored.[1] But, until the fall of Belgrade (29 August 1521), followed by Rhodes (22 December 1522), the Ottomans remained a remote and somewhat academic concern for most of Europe. Yet, in stark contrast to "diseased and divided" Europe (the evocative words of G.K. Chesterton), the Ottoman empire was remarkably healthy and united in the 15th and 16th centuries. Couple this with the fact that the Ottoman armed forces were far superior to those of any single European realm, even if Christendom as a whole was far more powerful. Here lay the reason for Ottoman success: its empire was a united power and Christendom a group of separate, squabbling states.

## The Decline Paradigm

We are certainly looking far beyond the paradigm of the so–called 'sick man of Europe'. Then again, often the battles between Christian Europe and the Ottoman empire that took place around this time are viewed as a kind of cataclysmic clash of civilisations and creeds old and new –

of two great monolithic civilisations butting up hard against each other. In sober fact, of course, there was nothing binary or monolithic about the Mediterranean world during our period of study. Christendom itself was deeply conflicted with Catholics against Protestants and the reformed church itself divided between Lutherans and Calvinist, a more uncompromising breed of Protestants. Further, there was very bad blood between Latin Christians and the Eastern Church.

In contrast, the Ottoman side was much less prone to division: the Ottoman empire, with its epicentre in Constantinople, was a big tent and could accommodate all kinds of people. To borrow the words of Karen Barkey, the Ottoman sultans presided over an empire of difference, "a marvel of flexible control over diversity".[2] As a result, the period saw the customary disgraceful dissension among the Christian powers, with Christian countries sometimes making deals with the Ottomans to spite their enemies within Christendom. And hence the Ottoman empire continued to expand westward and across North Africa.

Let one example suffice. France, *la belle France*, would be represented at Lepanto by the Knights Hospitaller, so many of whom were Frenchmen, but not as the nation itself. The great period of the *fleur-de-lis* had passed away with the end of the crusader kingdoms. Now the king of France, *Rex Christianissimus*, could support no venture in league with the Habsburgs, whose dominions surrounded him and thus stood in the way of his kingdom's territorial expansion. It mattered little that France and Spain were Catholic nations. Their monarchical rivalry trumped any shared sense of religion. Worse, the French king was quite willing to cut deals with the Ottoman sultan in order to turn Barbary corsairs against Genoese and Spaniards and away from Frenchmen (unless they were Knights of Malta, where Frenchmen of the old school continued to flourish and infuriate, owing allegiance directly to their Grand Master and to the Vicar of Christ). France had become the most important ally of the Ottoman empire against Spain, a common European enemy. So the French king (given the title *pādiṣāh*, presumably because he was a firm Ottoman ally), from the line of Valois, Charles IX (r. 1560–74) would send a cold, brief and negative reply when requested to join the Holy League, pleading exhaustion from having to fight the Huguenots. "The shadow of the Valois is yawning at the Mass", in Chesterton's biting words.[3] Still, poetry would have been the last thing on the young king's troubled mind as he swung like a pendulum from the influences of one courtly faction to the other.[4] He may have occupied the throne of France, but the kingdom was managed by his power-hungry mother, Caterina de' Medici (1519–89), perhaps best known for supposedly killing Jeanne d'Albret (1528–72) with a pair of perfumed gloves. So the result of French *realpolitik* was that France would sit this one out. Their absence is yet another proof of how disunited the Catholics were.

## Turning Turkish

The dynasty of Osmān (r. 1290–1326), of whose name Ottoman is a westernised corruption, rose to power upon the verges of the reduced Byzantine empire at the turn of the 14th century; originally one of the small confederations of nomadic Turkish horse tribes in northeast Anatolia (Bithynia) where they formed a *gāzī*, or frontier state of Islam, pledged to conquer lands for the Faith. The Ottomans therefore had behind them a long tradition of Islamic culture, even if they were hostile to its heirs. The Yeşil Cami, the Green Mosque, in Bursa, the ancient capital of Bithynia and the Ottoman capital from 1326, the year it was taken by Orhan *Gāzī* (r. 1326–59), the son and successor of Osmān, after a ten-year siege, until 1413, and the Üç Şerefeli Camii at Adrianople (Edirne), which was their next capital, shows clearly the sophistication and beauty of Ottoman architecture before it was exposed to the influences of Byzantine Constantinople.

The Osmānlı, 'the followers of Osmān', Turks were good and faithful Muslims, but they also had a specific Turkic heritage *in addition* to Islam that suffused the empire which they went on to create. It had been the 10th century before the Turkmen tribes had begun to accept Islam, and had done so in practice rather than theology. The Ottoman empire was not a Turkish empire, far from it: a big territorial entity in southeastern Europe and western Asia, and as such more diverse in terms of human and human geography as modern nation states. And even though it was an Islamic state in the classical sense, unlike their Christian counterparts, Islamic states by and large did not impose uniformity of belief on the inhabitants of the territories they ruled over.

'To become Turk' and 'to turn Turk' (Ger. *Türke werden/zum Türken werden*, It. *farsi Turco*, Fr. *se faire turc*, Cz. *poturčiti se*) are the phrases most frequently used by early modern Christian Europeans when talking about the conversion of a fellow Christian or Jew to Islam.[5] As will be discussed shortly, many of the top-flight Barbary corsairs had European origins, Christian renegades being treated virtually as equals by the Muslim authorities and could enter the army or the higher posts in government.[6] A celebrated example is that of the Englishman of Kent, John Ward (†1622); also known as Jack Ward, who voluntarily converted to Islam and assumed the name Yusuf Re'īs. Operating out of Tunis, where he lived in the style of an oriental potentate, he actively committed acts of piracy in the western Mediterranean against Christian and non-Christian shipping for nearly two decades. Ward's exploits eventually became the subject of a play *A Christian Turn'd Turk* (1612) written by the Jacobean dramatist Robert Daborne (†1628). Despite offering James I a reported 30,000 gold crowns for a General Pardon to return home – we know the king really disliked piracy – Ward died of the plague in Tunis.[7] As well as enjoying a lost-lasting career in a number of ballads, books, films and television mini-series, various Turkish newspapers and websites popularised a hypothesis that Captain Jack Ward of Kent could be the inspiration for the Hollywood pirate Jack Sparrow.[8]

In contrast, a *turc fait chrétien*, 'Turk made Christian', was a Muslim convert. For the French to be *fort comme un turc*, 'strong as a Turk', was to be extremely robust. Even a century after the second siege of Vienna the word 'Turk' still had negative connotations, even though the Ottoman threat had since faded. People called their dogs 'Turk', churches still had *Turckenglocken*, 'Turkish bells', where people had gathered to pray for deliverance from the Ottomans. Words such as *türkenzen*, 'to act like a barbarian', or *turkeln*, 'to stagger drunkenly', were still in currency among German-speaking Christians.

The term 'Turk' was used by early modern Europeans to refer to almost any Muslim and was often used interchangeably with the term 'Moor'. Nowadays, on the other hand, historians do not use the word 'Turk' on the grounds that Ottomans considered a 'Turk' as a rustic fool, and were hence grossly insulted to be called a 'Turk'. Thus, literate circles in Constantinople would not identify themselves as Turks, and often, in phrases such as 'Turkish mischief makers' or 'senseless Turks', used the word as a term of abuse. True enough: if no Ottoman would have self-identified as a 'Turk' until the late 19th century, still at the same time they gloried in their Turkish ancestry and origins. Ultimately, it was a Turkic identity that provided the ideology for Kemāl Mustafā Atatürk's new nation, the Republic of Turkey.

## Princely Purdah

The harem was much misunderstood by the Christians, who conceived of it only as a furnace of lust, in which sultans indulged their wildest passions, and the women gratified each other's desires. In fact its origins arose from Islam's preoccupation with female purity, which meant that women were to be separated from all men except their husbands and young sons. The world of women was forbidden (Ar. *haram*) to all other males. In the hands of the Ottomans this system of seclusion became a political and social institution as well.

Naturally, the imperial harem was designed for the sexual gratification of the sultan. At some moments the rooms – some 300 of them, almost all surprisingly small – of The Harem of the Grand Seraglio contained nearly 2,000 women and girls in various stages of training. It is however noticeable that those who attracted the attentions of the ruler and bore children were scarcely ever Turkish. By male descent the later sultans were no doubt derived from Osmān but the percentage of actual Turkish blood in their veins was negligible.

We have already made mention of the law of fratricide, whereby a new sultan, on his succession, put to death all his brothers to avoid the possibility of dispute or civil war. Gradually, however, in the 17th century this pitiless practice changed to the confinement of the cadets of the dynasty within the Topkapı Sarayı, where in the Fourth Court were a series of pavilions known as *kafes*, the Cage. On too many occasions a bemused or inexperienced prince had to be released from the *kafes* to assume the throne of a dead brother, destined to become little more than a mere cipher in the hands of his ministers. This grotesque emasculation of the line meant that power was often a prize to be squabbled over by the valide sultan (the mother of the sultan), the Chief Black Eunuch, *kızlar ağası* – the Ottomans having inherited the Byzantine practice of employing eunuchs – the grand vizier and the janissaries.

## Slaves of the Sultan

What made the Ottoman army in our period of study unusual for its time and quite distinct from fully-mobilized European armies, which tended to be composed mainly of last-minute conscripts filling in the ranks around a small core of permanent imperial or princely units, was that it was much better practised than any of its potential opponents at accomplishing an effective fusion of forces leading to a successful team effort. Indeed, during the 16th century, reflecting in part changes in tactics and armaments, and in part the growing number of state-sponsored and -maintained military forces, military provision became the nearly exclusive preserve of two groups: the seasonally-mobilized, provincial cavalry supported by *timar* land grants, and the sultan's permanent, standing, salaried, armed forces (both infantry and cavalry, but predominantly infantry) called the *kapıkulu* (literary, 'servitors of the [palace] gate', or household troops).

It should be understood that in the Ottoman empire slave status was not incompatible with economic, political, and military power. In this respect, the Islamic model of slavery was much closer to the Graeco-Roman system than the Atlantic one, designed, as it was, to obtain cheap and expendable labour to cultivate massive plantations, which so much dominates our conception of slavery today. In the Ottoman empire, female as well as male slaves often wielded considerable authority and even economic independence within the scope of their masters' households.

One example will suffice to illustrate this point, namely that of Johannes Wild (†1619). Wild had been taken captive by Ottoman soldiers in 1604, at the age of nineteen, while serving as a *Landsknecht* with the Habsburg forces campaigning in Hungary. He was enslaved and sold several times before he ended up in Cairo where his master eventually manumitted him in 1609. Even before his manumission, so Wild tells his readers:

> I … could indeed earn money while I was with this [i.e. his seventh] master for he had to administer many villages and several hundred

Arabic peasants under him. From those I had to collect the tithe
and rent ... My master gave me four fields to cultivate. The profits
I derived from them were to be mine. I was to either work the fields
myself or lease them to some peasants. When I was at [my master's]
house and had nothing to do for him I engaged in trade.[9]

After manumission, the proceeds which Wild had thus derived from
agriculture and trade enabled him to travel to Constantinople from
whence he eventually returned to his native Nürnberg.

Nevertheless, Wild was, of course, a slave and as such had little power
to determine his own fate or even protect and control his own body in an
environment in which corporal punishment for perceived misbehaviour
was the norm and in which female slaves, in particular but not exclusively,
could freely be used for their masters' sexual gratification.

Indeed, Wild experienced rough times. Throughout his memoirs he
bitterly complains about his sixth master who, he claims, treated him
very badly. While this rather poor relationship may have had a lot to
do with the young German's quarrelsome nature and bad temper, the
ways in which the two slave owners treated him may also be related to
their different statuses within Ottoman society. Wild's sixth master was
a merchant and thus a member of the re'aya (literally the 'flock'), which
encompassed the empire's 'ordinary' subjects – peasants, artisans, and
merchants of any faith – who paid taxes to the Ottoman state. His seventh
master, however, as a local commander of the janissaries, was a member
of the Ottoman military-administrative élite.[10] In granting Wild such
authority and economic freedom, this master's treatment of his slave,
therefore, was probably more strongly influenced by the system of kul
household slavery epitomised by the sultan's household: the sultan's
kullar were slaves who had received a palace education, and thus could
be accepted into the privileged status of the sultan's official high ranking
state servants.

## The Timariots

The primary purpose of the tīmār system was the maintenance of
the provincial cavalry forces and the provincial administration of the

Ottoman empire. Under this system, cavalrymen and provincial officials were allocated a prebend in return for military service. Such grants were known as *dirliks* (literally 'livelihood') and *tīmārs* (variously translated as 'care, attention' and 'horse grooming') after the name of the smallest of such grants which would have been sufficient to support a single cavalryman, or *timarlı sipāhi*, and his horse. The recipients of such grants are generally referred to as timariots.

Although often described as quasi-feudal, a *tīmār* grant was not a fief which bestowed ownership of the land on the timariot, but simply an entitlement to the revenue from taxes and fines from a given locality. The value of such grants, and thus the size of the locality, were determined by the *tīmār* holder's rank, with the largest category of grants, a *has*, generally reserved for provincial governors. In the process, the sultan devolved some of his authority on the *tīmār* holders and their deputies (Tk. *kahya*, *kethüda*) who were charged with collecting taxes and fines from the local population, overseeing their economic activities, and exercising powers of police. In this way, they served as local representatives of the Ottoman state. They did not, however, dispense justice. The *tīmārs* of a certain district, or *sancak*, would come under the control of a *sancak bey*, and *sancaks* were grouped together to form a province, or *beylerbeik*, under a *beylerbeyi*. With the exception of a few hereditary *sancaks*, the sultan appointed district and provincial governors, and the same was true for most *tīmār* holders.

The *tīmār* system was possible for two reasons. For one, the vast majority of land was *miri*, that is to say, belonging to the sultan. Second, the sultan's subjects owed their allegiance to him only, prompting Machiavelli to comment, "The entire monarchy of the Turk is governed by one lord, the others are his servants",[11] a sweeping statement, perhaps, but one containing a lot of truth. Thanks to the *tīmār* system, the sultan could plan a military campaign with a precise idea of the number of *sipāhis*, the rank-and-file of the cavalry, at his disposal.[12]

## The 'Terrible Turk'

The enduring western view of the signature characteristics of Ottoman military identity was constructed out of a seemingly endless series of

European defeats against the superior Ottomans. That identity included armies composed of vast numbers of soldiers, chained cannon, and monster bombards, relentless janissaries, and swarms of reckless irregulars. It was an identity that rekindled olden European memories of limitless Persian and Mongol hordes. It became the material from which nightmares were born and generations of European children learned to pray for delivery from the 'Terrible Turk'.

In reality, the Ottomans were the dominant power in the Balkans during the later mediaeval and early modern periods. Their campaigning armies tended to be varied and colourful, mustering locally recruited troops as well as men from Anatolia. These were the 'lands of *Rūm*', broadly signifying the former Byzantine territories where the Ottoman venture began, the core regions of *Osmānlı* civilisation. On the whole, the Ottoman army was an important institution of the Ottoman state and one that in many respects, from the recruitment to the timely payment of soldiers' wages to monitoring the political influence of its officer corps, required a considerable amount of time and effort from the state leadership, regardless of whether the Sublime Porte was at peace or war. Ever since, centuries before, the Ottoman Turks had started raiding out of their tiny principality in northern Anatolia and gone on to besiege and capture Constantinople, they had been a people organised for war. The government and even the judges followed the army on the march. The *dīvān-ı hümāyūn* might well meet and confer on horseback. Ministers doubled as commanders in the field, and the sultan himself was both monarch and commander-in-chief. War had become the Ottoman way of life. The Ottoman army was an unequivocally Islamic army, which officially was motivated by faith in Islam, and waged a general holy war (*jihād*) on the infidels and the heretics, non-Sunni. This exclusivist ideology did not allow much room for admitting in large numbers the many non-Muslim subjects of the empire to the army.

It is worth pausing at this point to observe that, in the Ottoman empire, religion *was* nationalism. Whereas the cultural identity of early modern Europeans was becoming very much a matter almost exclusively of nationhood, that of Muslims had at least as much to do with their faith. What appears to Europeans at the time to be religious fanaticism was viewed there as something very close to patriotism. Even so, Ottoman society favoured a live-and-let-live policy. As a result, the sultans allowed the various religious communities to run their own affairs, provided this did not lead to unrest. Moreover, during the 16th century, Ottoman society made itself (for practical reasons) increasingly open to renegades or, to use the modern terminology, 'defectors', 'apostates' and 'traitors' from neighbouring states in Europe.

## Apostate Admirals

Two of the most celebrated renegades were Uluç Ali Re'īs from Calabria, who escaped unscathed from the disaster at Lepanto, and Ciğalzade Yusuf Sinān Paşa, formerly Scipione Cicala, a Genoese patrician captured at sea during the Djerba expedition with his father, visconte Vincenzo Cicala, who was a galley entrepreneur for Philip II. Some of his brothers and nephews were Jesuits. His brother Carlo was a founder of the military Order of the Star, a company of knights in Messina (where the brothers had been born), ostensibly established to aid the struggle against the Ottomans. Carlo also served as a spy for the Habsburgs but eventually defected to Constantinople, and eventually became *beylerbeylik* of the Aegean island of Naxos for the sultan. Scipione became a corsair captain and rose to become *kapudan-ı deryā*, grand admiral of the Ottoman navy, in 1591, which he held for four years, an office he would hold for a second time in 1598. In 1594 he appeared off Syracuse and burned many villages, before moving on to overwhelm Reggio Calabria, which he sacked for two days.

Scipione clearly kept his memories and familial ties intact, without forgetting his native tongue, and completely foregoing his initial faith. He also continued communicating with his kin in the Christian world. In September 1598, in exchange for a truce, he persuaded the viceroy of Sicily to allow him to visit his aged mother in Messina and other relatives (including some knights) in the port; seventy Moslem galleys fired salutes in the harbour in the honour of the aged Signora Lucrezia and the grand admiral lavishly entertained his relatives on board his flagship.[13] Leaving Sicily in peace, as he promised, he looted Malta on his way home, but was driven off by the knights and the militia.[14] Scipione was eventually made grand vizier, which he held for just forty days between 27 October to 5 December 1596, and married first one (1573) and another great-granddaughter of Süleymān I *Kānūnı* (1576).[15] In 1604 he assumed command of the empire's eastern marches, where a new conflict between the Ottomans and the Persian 'heretics' had broken out the preceding year. His campaign of 1605 against the Safavid rival was unsuccessful, and he died in the course of a retreat in December of that year.

However, the one renegade that concerns our story is the famous Algerian corsair Uluç Ali Re'īs (later Kiliç Ali Paşa) – clever, cruel and scabby-headed, known by the Spaniards as Euchalí or Uchalí – who, from the status of a poor Calabrian fisherman had scrambled to great heights in the service of the Sublime Porte. Uluç Ali was the last of the school of Barbarossa.

Originally Giovanni Dionigi Galeni, he was born in a village called Le Castella in Calabria, the tip of Italy's boot, into a family of fishermen, reputedly becoming a Dominican friar. He had been taken captive by Ali Ahmed, one of the corsair captains of Barbarossa, on 29 April 1536 when he was about seventeen years of age. After his enslavement, he was initially made to serve as a rower on a North African galley, in which capacity he participated in the battle of Préveza in 1538. Since Islam implies brotherhood, no Muslim could hold another as a slave. Galeni formerly repeated the verbal formula which transferred his allegiance to Allah, so though he tugged at the same oar as before, from that moment on he did so as a volunteer. Now known as Uluç Ali, he rose in the community of corsairs to become a successful galley captain in his own right. In 1548 he became attached to the famous Turgut Re'īs, known as the 'Drawn Sword of Islam', although the circumstances and nature of this attachment remain unclear. Turgut is probably better known as Dragut in European sources.

Born of Greek parents in 1485, Turgut Re'īs had begun his naval career in the Aegean as a *levend* (Ar. *lawend*), an ambiguous term which Ottomans applied to naval irregulars as well as corsairs, to gradually shift his basis of operation further west to the Maghrib and his theatre of activity towards the Habsburg waters of the western Mediterranean. Even though he was one of the most talented corsairs of his generation, Turgut never made it to the top in the Ottoman naval establishment. In spite of his seafaring skills, his career had its ups and downs. In 1540 he had been surprised and captured by Gianandrea Doria, the nephew of the great Genoese admiral, and had served three years shackled to a bench of a Genoese galley. One of the last acts of Barbarossa had been to ransom his lieutenant in the port of Genoa, in 1543, for 3,000 *escudos*, an arrangement the Genoese afterwards sorely regretted.[16]

Turgut and his ships time and again joined the Ottoman fleet as naval irregulars, but he did not receive a direct appointment until after his successful participation in the conquest of Tunis in 1551. In that year, both Turgut Re'īs and Uluç Ali became *sancakbeyis*. Uluç Ali continued to participate in Ottoman naval operations as part of Turgut's retinue before he was made captain of an Ottoman galley in 1556. Together, the two men served in the battle of Djerba in 1560, a disastrous setback for the Spanish navy, and the siege of Malta in 1565, where the overlords of the island repelled the Ottoman besiegers after prolonged and intense fighting that inflicted devastating losses on both sides. While the eighty-year-old Turgut was fatally wounded by a splinter of rock during the latter engagement – the tough old corsair was to linger on the verge of consciousness for five days – Uluç Ali, who had been given responsibility for the defence of the Ottoman Aegean after Djerba, succeeded his erstwhile patron to the *beylerbeylik* of Algiers.[17]

Miguel de Cervantes, in *Don Quixote*, mentions Uluç Ali under the name of "*Uchalí Fartax* – in the Turkish language it means 'the Renegade with Scabies' – which is, in fact, what he was".[18] He also describes briefly his rise to the regency of Algiers:

And this man with scabies rowed in the galleys as a slave of the Great Lord for fourteen years, and when he was past the age of thirty-four he became a renegade because of his fury at a Turk who slapped him while he was rowing: in order to take his revenge, he abandoned his faith; his valour was so great that, without using the vile and devious means that most of the Great Turk's favourites employ in order to succeed, he became king of Algiers and then admiral of the sea, which is the third position in that empire. He came from Calabria, and morally he was a good man who treated his captives very humanely; he had three thousand of them, and after his death they were divided, according to the terms of his will, between the Great Turk, who is heir of everyone who dies and shares in the inheritance with the dead man's children, and his renegades.[19]

It was in this position that Uluç Ali made significant contributions to strengthening the Ottoman claim to suzerainty over the Maghrib against the Spanish. In October 1569, for instance, he turned on Muley Ahmad, the Hafsid caliph of Tunis, who had been restored to his throne by Spain. Marching overland with an army of some 5,000, he quickly sent the caliph and his forces fleeing and made himself ruler of Tunis. Muley Ahmad found refuge in the Spanish *presidio* of La Goleta in the bay of Tunis.

Uluç Ali Re'īs was to further distinguish himself during the naval campaigns of 1571 which culminated in the battle of Lepanto. Despite the Ottoman defeat, and in recognition of his excellent record, he received the honorific epithet *kılıç* (sword) and was appointed *kapudan-ı deryā*, Captain of the Sea, to oversee the rebuilding of the destroyed Ottoman navy. In the aftermath, Kılıç Ali Paşa, as he was now known officially, participated in a number of further campaigns, crucially supporting the re-conquest of La Goleta and the fortress town of Tunis from the king of Spain's forces in 1574. Although he repeatedly lobbied the Porte for a renewal of naval campaigns in the western Mediterranean throughout the fifteen-eighties, the ongoing war with Safavid Persia prevented the sultan and his fellow viziers from lending their support to the undertakings suggested by the grand admiral.

We may perhaps be forgiven for speculating that no career illustrates what one could provocatively call the 'Ottoman dream' better than that of Andrea Celeste who, according to Venice's *bailo* in Constantinople, Giovanni Moro, 'was born in … [Venice] in poor fortune' but died as Uluç Hasan Paşa in one of the most prestigious military administrative offices of the Ottoman empire, the admiralty (Tk. *kapudanlık*).

Celeste was eighteen or nineteen years old when he, too, had been captured and enslaved by Algerian corsairs under the command of Turgut Re'īs in 1563. By then, the young Venetian had already gained seafaring experience as a scrivener (*scrivanello*) in a Ragusan merchant ship named *Fabiana*. Although the details of the next few years are hazy, it seems that Celeste, while still a slave, embraced Islam, possibly at his owner's instigation, and henceforth became known as Hasan. On his initial master's death, Hasan passed first to Turgut Re'īs and, after Turgut's death during the siege of Malta in 1565, to the aforementioned Uluç Ali Re'īs, who was appointed *beylerbeyi* of Algiers in the same year. Quickly gaining the favour of Uluç Ali, Hasan rose quickly in his master's service to become his *kahya* or major-domo, managing his vast household full of renegades like himself.

In 1577, Uluç Hasan Paşa (or Hasan Veneziano as he was known by the Europeans) entered the sultan's service directly when he was designated *sancakbeyi*, or district governor, of Selanik (Thessaloniki). He never assumed this post, however, instead lobbying for his appointment as *beylerbeyi* of Algiers. His wish was granted in the same year and he held this position until 1580. His subsequent career at the Porte remained deeply connected to North Africa and the naval milieu. In 1582, the Venetian-born renegade resumed the governorship of Algiers, and one of his slaves was Miguel de Cervantes who made a lively portrait of his master and his wife Zahara, the daughter of Hacı Murād Re'īs and the widow of the Saadi sultan of Morocco,[20] in *Don Quixote*, named Azán Agá, Agi Morato, and Zoraida by the author.[21] From Algeria Uluç Hasan was transferred to Tripoli in 1587. The following year, the sultan called him to Constantinople to assume the high office of *kapudan-ı deryā*, which his former master Kılıç Ali Paşa had held from autumn 1571 until his death in 1587, even though the two men had fallen out in 1585 and never reconciled. Like Kılıç Ali Paşa, Uluç Hasan held the *kapudanlık* until his abrupt death in 1591 at the age of forty-seven or thereabouts.

The careers of these two grand admirals delineate the upper limits of what individual renegades might achieve in the sultan's service. As much as the offices and honours which they both attained, the fact that both died of natural causes is a testament to their success in the Ottoman political arena.

A glance at the naval forces arrayed in the 16th-century Mediterranean reveals that the coming of the Ottomans had created a new order, reminiscent, if anything, of the early days of Islam. Now that a Muslim empire was once again seeking to expand its power by land and sea in all directions, navies under Muslim command gained control of the waters of the eastern Mediterranean and challenged Christian navies in the western Mediterranean by means of their proxies, the rulers of the Barbary Coast, many of whom were renegades. It was an extraordinary transformation. After centuries in which Muslim navies had exercised tentative control of waters close to the Islamic states – Mamlūk fleets off

Egypt and Syria, Moroccan ships in the far west, Turkish emirs within the Aegean – Muslim sea power had expanded outwards on a massive scale. Constantinople became the command centre of an enormous fleet, in great contrast to the Byzantine era, when naval power had increasingly fallen into the hands of the Genoese and Venetians. Skilled admirals became expert in the art of war at sea.

## The Latest Hardware

The Ottomans showed remarkable success in assimilating gunpowder technology into their army, as we shall discover with the janissaries, and their navy. They were fortunate to have abundant ore deposits (copper, iron, and lead) needed for cannon casting, and raw materials (saltpetre, sulphur, charcoal, and fuel wood) necessary for powder manufacturing. The only metal they lacked was tin, which they managed to obtain from import, mainly from England.[22] Chemical analysis of extant Ottoman cannon barrels and production data suggests that Ottoman founders cast bronze cannon whose alloy contained 8.6 to 11.3 per cent tin and 89.5 to 91.4 per cent copper, an alloy very similar to that suggested by Vannoccio Biringuccio in his posthumously published *De la pirotechnica* (1540) and used by European founders in the 16th century.[23]

The quality of Ottoman cannon in terms of casting and design is still a controversial topic. According to both contemporary observers of the Ottoman empire and modern scholars, Ottoman cannon clearly lagged behind the European designs by clinging to older, gigantic stone-firing bombards of poor-quality metal composition. For instance, during the siege of Famagusta the Ottoman besiegers deployed a couple of giant 180-pounder basilisks, cast pieces of the culverin type. However, some modern researchers are revising the commonly-held conviction that views the Ottomans as being cultural and technological conservatives and unable or unwilling to keep pace with western military technology. According to more recent findings, Ottoman military engineers managed to produce cannon with up-to-date designs in line with their European counterparts until the beginning of 18th century. Thus, Gábor Ágoston's study of the Ottoman weapons industry in the 16th and 17th centuries has done much to disperse the older legends of Ottoman dependence on Christian-European expertise and advisers, particularly in matters of military technology, at least before the 18th century.

The impressive series of siege victories against the modern fortresses of Hungary (based on the latest Italian designs) during the second half of the 16th century also proved the level of Ottoman artillery technology and its field application to be on par with Europe. Additionally, most of the technologically-related problems that affected the Ottoman artillery system were common problems also affecting its archenemies, Habsburg Spain and Venice. That all being said, Venetian standards were such that most of the 115 Ottoman guns captured as trophies of war at Lepanto were not only sent home to be melted down as technically deficient, but had a certain amount of good metal added in the furnace "because the material is of such poor quality".[24]

## Chapter 11

# Invincible Infantry

Verily, Allah loves those who fight in His Cause in rows [ranks] as if they were a solid structure.

Qur'ān, Sūrah 61, āyah 4

As remarkable, if less flamboyant than the household cavalry, called *kapıkulu süvarileri ocağı*, the *sipāhis* of the Porte, were the professional infantry, the famous (or infamous) fierce janissaries (Tk. *yeniçeri*, 'new troops') of Islam, first established either under Orhan *Gāzī* (r. 1326–59), the son of the legendary founder of the Ottoman dynasty, or his son Murād I (r. 1359–89): the first definite mention of the janissaries only occurs after Orhan's death, yet Turkish historical tradition is positive in attributing their origin to him. Whichever Ottoman sultan was responsible, the creation of the janissaries is generally attributed by historians to the need of the sultan to have a personal army as a counterweight to the followers of the lords of the frontiers (viz. the periphery), who were not always ready to submit unquestioningly to the will of the sultan (viz. the central authority).[1]

The janissaries were perhaps unique among Muslim military elites in that they fought exclusively on foot. Be this as it may, one thing is certain: for many in Christendom the mere name was sufficient to inspire terror. For two hundred years the janissary *ocak* (literary 'hearth') or corps had been the key to the Ottomans' extraordinary success in war. Yet in the late 14th century they were still nothing but a small unit of household guards, called *kapıkulu*, slaves of the Porte, closely attached to the sultan's person, and not more than a thousand strong. Bertrandon de la Broquière (†1459), a Burgundian spy who visited the court of Murād II (r. 1421–44, 1446–51) in 1433, speaks of them in one place as about 3,000 in strength, but in another passages he says that these *jehainicères*, who are the only infantry of value in the sultan's army, may be as many as 10,000.[2] In a similar vein, a French knight of the Knights Hospitaller who visited the court of Süleymān I, Fra' Antoine Geuffroy (†1556), made the observation that "[a]s for foot soldiers, [the Ottomans] have none apart from the janissaries, at least none that are worth anything …'.[3] Clearly their precise number is problematic and cannot be easily ascertained. Even if we stick to the more realistic figure of 3,000 for their number under Murād II, then under Mehmed II within a short span of two years the janissaries had apparently increased to 5,000.[4]

## Source

Initially, these regiments of pride, discipline and fanaticism were made up of prisoners of war, *pencyek*. This Persian term (Ar. *khums*) refers to the fifth part of the booty gathered during the raids and the battles against the infidels – the part which, according to Islamic law, belongs to the sovereign. From the late-14th century onwards, however, nearly all janissaries would have shared a common origin.[5] They were Christian children, aged between seven and ten, taken from the villages of the newly acquired Balkan and western Anatolian territories, *devşirme* (literary 'collection'), made infamous as the 'boy levy' in Christian-European writings, and brought up in Islam, vowing to celibacy, absolute loyalty and obedience. Obviously the curriculum included the study of the Qur'ān and the Hadīth, but, not surprisingly, the emphasis was also on the arts of war and especially archery skills. But the religious dimension of the military education of the recruit was crucial. His identification with his new faith of Islam complemented superb skills in the arts of war.

It is fair to assume that conversion of these recruits was often less than fully voluntary, although the 'compensations' offered by the careers which the boys would subsequently have embarked on may have acted as powerful incentives. As a result, after ten years of training under spartan conditions, the new soldiers were drafted into the corps of janissaries. In return the sultan provided a career, a status and a salary for life. Some documents date the start of the *devşirme* system to the reign of Murād I when the newly-established Ottoman state sought to enlarge its territories. Others, on the other hand, place it in the period after the battle fought outside the small town of Çubuk on a high plain to the northeast of Ankara (28 July 1402) – the same plain where Pompeius Magnus overthrew the power of Mithridates VI Eupator. It was here that Bāyezīd I *Yıldırım* lost his empire and his parched Ottoman army suffered a severe setback and was in urgent need of consolidation.[6]

As many historians have pointed out, the *devşirme* directly contravenes Shari'a law, which clearly forbids the enslavement of non-Muslim subjects (Tk. *zimmis*, Ar. *dhimmī*) of a Muslim ruler. In this context, the conundrum of how the institution might be squared with Islamic law is less important than the fact that it was apparently never seriously challenged on legal grounds.[7] Moreover, the new religion which they embraced was not simply any form of Islam; it was specifically the Ottoman Sunni variety which had begun to more clearly delineate itself from other forms of Islam over the course of the 16th century, notably the Shi`ism made dominant in Iran by the Safavid dynasty.

## Slaves Salaried in Silver

Free from everyday distractions, the janissaries were able to devote themselves single-mindedly to the state and its sovereign, on whom they were entirely dependent for pay (*'ulūfe*), which was paid in cash four times a year in solemn ceremonies in the second yard of the Topkapı Sarayı. Foreign ambassadors were invited to these ceremonial meetings, as they were perfect occasions to show off the power of the Ottoman state. On top of their regular wages, the janissaries received the basic necessities of life, such as a yearly clothing allowance and subsidies for bread and meat. Further, there was a cash bonus (*bakhşiş*) on the accession of new sultans, and extraordinary grants were also expected during the campaigns, as an incitement or a reward. To neglect these traditional grants was a serious risk for the sultan. Selim II experienced the consequences when he refused to give the *bakhşiş* to the janissaries at the beginning of his reign.

The sultan thus acquired a body of first-class soldiery who were strong supporters of his absolutism. In this respect they were the better-known military arm of a much larger body, the *kapıkulari* or slave institution, which filled every civil post from palace cook to grand vizier: to be a *kul*, or slave, of the sultan was a privilege and an opportunity. An alternative to the erratic Ottoman Turkish levies, these professional soldiers were the sultan's most powerful single weapon; their very name was feared from the banks of the Euphrates to the gates of Vienna.

Cut off in childhood from their families, discouraged from marrying,[8] not allowed – and indeed, without any skills – to engage in trade, their lives were made up of fighting in war time and the preservation of order in peace time; the corps was headed by the *ağa çırağı* of the janissaries who was also the chief of police in Constantinople and sat with the ministers, judges and men of religion at the *dīvān-i hümāyūn*, the imperial council. They were given uniforms, a long caftan over a short coat, full trousers, and heavy boots or sandals. Some were trained as horsemen, but most became infantry, allocated to one of the *ortas*,[9] the first permanent infantry regiments in all of Europe and founded at least a century before any other example. Each *orta* had its own insignia, sometimes a plant or flower, which was painted on the doors of its *oda*, barracks in which it was lodged, and embroidered on the white silk regimental banners and on the round tents in which each *boluk*, or squad, of soldiers lived on campaign. Within a few weeks of admission, most young janissaries had rubbed gunpowder into their arms or face and had tattooed themselves with that same insignia as an outward and visible sign of belonging to an honourable military caste. Interestingly enough, the most revered object for the entire janissary corps was the sacred soup cauldron, *kazan-ı şerif*. Certainly, one pervasive element in the building of a group identity and sense of belonging was food, feasting and the soldiers' everyday mess arrangements. Similarly, the soup cauldrons of each *orta* were more sacred than their respective standards or flags; indeed, each and every one of them was the very altar of authority in their respective units. Needless to say, the élan and cohesion within each regiment was very strong.

The janissary *ortas* became something of a great family with the sultan playing the rôle of father. At the heart of the main janissary barracks was a huge drill ground called *Et Meydanı*, 'the place of the meat' (not to be confused with the *At Meydanı*, 'the place of the horse', the old Hippodrome). The sultan took the training of the janissaries very seriously. Each week, they paraded there in full equipment to practise the prescribed battlefield manoeuvres. Rushes, sudden mass attacks, sword play and archery became second nature, but they also trained with the long barrelled harquebus – under Murād II they had begun to use *tüfek*, handguns – more powerful than lighter weapons used in western armies. Many janissaries were trained as sharpshooters: with the powerful powder charge and much greater range and killing power of their weapons; considerably more accurate than European firearms, they were a devastating weapon.

## Corporate Identity

We talk of the janissary 'corps' as if it were a single, uniform entity. Certainly every individual was taught to be conscious of the honour of his detachment and of the order as a whole, but in reality the strength of the janissaries (and their weakness) was that they were 'bands of brothers', of between ten and fifteen men. You trusted your brother-in-arms, tattooed like you with the emblem of your *orta*. That came first; then loyalty to the *ocak* and its officers; ultimately there was loyalty to more distant figures, like the commander, *ağā çırağı*, of the janissaries and the sultan himself. But although janissaries would fight with extraordinary courage, they were also intractable if given orders of which they did not approve. They did not give blind, slavish obedience, as every wise janissary officer knew. They were the warriors of the sultan, but also the inspired soldiers of Allah, their zeal and fervour encouraged by the Bektaşi dervish preachers who were attached to every *orta*. They had to be won over and cajoled by their commanders, like wild and mettlesome horses: use some stick but also the titbits of honours, rewards and plunder. But ultimately each janissary fought and died as a warrior, *gāzī*, of the True Faith.

Exactly how many janissaries were stationed throughout the empire fluctuated over time. The janissary payroll muster rolls, *mevācib defteri*, were often illegally enlarged, with corrupt officials living off the proceeds. Treasury balance sheets show that the number of janissaries fluctuated between 7,000 and 9,400 from the fourteen-eighties through the late fifteen-twenties. In 1569 they numbered 11,535. Their number quickly doubled to 23,359 by 1592, then increased to 39,282 in 1609, and surpassed 50,000 by the mid-17th century.[10] It should be noted that registration in the muster rolls of the janissaries guaranteed both the monthly salary and the daily rations, or their monetary equivalent. As such, this represented the single greatest privilege of the corps, by which all profited, up to and including the grand vizier. Naturally the janissary pay system was open to abuse, the rolls susceptible to inflation by names of the long dead, of deserters, and even fictitious janissaries, the ensuing income lining the pockets of officers and civil administrative officials alike – much the same problem as that facing the armies of Habsburg Spain and Elizabethan England where it was usual to draw pay and allowances for large numbers of men who were no more than names in a muster roll.

The diplomatic representative of the Habsburg ruler Ferdinand I, the king of Bohemia and Hungary (r. 1526–64) and Holy Roman Emperor (r. 1556–64), to Süleyman I *Kānūnī* between 1554 and 1562, Ogier Ghiselin de Busbecq, first saw the famous janissaries in Ottoman-occupied Buda. Their drab appearance came as a surprise to him, and it is worthwhile to quote a lengthy paragraph from one of his letters that illustrates this:

When they are at full strength, the sultan possesses 12,000 of them, scattered throughout his empire... They wear robes reaching to their ankles, and on their heads a covering consisting of the sleeve of a cloak (for this is the account which they give of its origin), part of which contains the head, while the rest hangs down behind and flaps against the neck. On their foreheads rises an oblong silver cone, gilded and studded with stones of no great value.[11]

He continues his in-depth discourse:

Really, if I had not been told they were janissaries, I could well have believed they were a kind of Turkish monk or the members of some kind of sacred association; yet these were the famous janissaries who carry such terror wherever they go.[12]

Obviously the Ottoman government understood the importance of uniforms in order to promote élan, raise morale and discipline, and for the practical application of differentiating friend and foe. These uniforms were simple but serviceable and sturdy.

Most artists, Ottoman or western, depicted the janissaries as dressed in standard, sometimes brightly coloured, uniforms. Janissary officers certainly wore long robes, with bright brocades and fancy fur trimmings, but the ordinary soldiers' uniforms were the drab wools and felts that Busbecq describes at firsthand:

> Almost all wore uniforms of the same shape and colour, so that you could recognise them as the slaves or household of the same master. There was nothing very striking in their attire, which had no slits or eyelet-holes.[13]

But, as is often the case, appearances can prove deceiving. If their clothes were plain, their famous headgear, with the broad, soft white flap which served to keep the sun off a soldier's neck, were decorated with plumes and crests, "and here they let their fancy run riot, particularly the veterans who brought up the rear. The plumes which they inserted in their frontlets give the appearance of a moving forest."[14] Yet every plume, every badge or decoration, was in fact a mark of honour or long service, or, most prized of all, a distinction granted for bravery. The tall janissary cap was their badge of privilege, and Busbecq obviously saw battle-hardened veterans who had proved their prowess in battle.

## Drums and Guns

Did these men live up to their fearsome reputation? They were better equipped, better supported and better fed than their future opponents. The janissaries and *sipāhis* of the Porte were trained professionals, expert players in the game of war, but what distinguished them was how and why they fought. In the Ottoman ranks, among the janissaries (and *sipāhis* of the Porte), matters were different from the armies that would confront them. Serving and living together for long periods, fiercely loyal to the emblems and badges of their *ortas*, strong and hardy fighters, nevertheless they fought as individual warriors. The tales told around the janissary soup cauldrons were of heroes, past and present. In their barracks in Constantinople old soldiers stayed close to their units, and became a living memory for great deeds of the past. Officers seeking to rouse their men would evoke that history. Each unit went into battle incited by the music of the *mehter takımı*, the military band which, like the pipers of the Highland clansmen, stirred the bellicose spirit of men facing death. Huge kettledrums boomed and thundered, while smaller drums crashed and rattled out an insistent faster rhythm, and over all the steady clash of cymbals announced a charge.

The *charge* was what they talked about in barracks, and what they had practised on the drill ground. Each man chanted the battle cry in unison, a single roar rising from thousands of throats growing louder and louder as they closed with the enemy. As they audaciously rushed forward, firearms were laid aside; bows slung for the last stages of the assault; each man, a *kılıç* – whose blade had a pronounced curve at the distal third, that is, the farthest third from the base of the blade – or a fearsome janissary *yatağan* – a slightly curved one-edged short sword that could lop off a head with a flick of the wrist – in hand, fixed his gaze upon a foe as he dashed the last few metres into the enemy line. In those moments each janissary was an individual bent on killing those he faced. Once launched, his charge could not be recalled: either it succeeded or it was driven back. Christian commanders noted that the janissaries would advance into an inferno of fire, climbing over their own dead, and would instantly exploit any flaw or weakness in the defence. They seemed to know no fear. If the first assault failed, a second and a third would follow. Either way, those in the enemy ranks knew what they were in for.

We have very limited information about janissary combat formations and how they actually fought other than what was known as the *tabur cengi* formation. Generally, they positioned artillery at the centre, and often a screen of Azabs covered their front with *sipāhis* of the Porte positioned behind them or on the flanks. We also know that the janissaries preferred several rows of deep formations and achieved a continuous barrage of fire by rotating rows forward. They were able to maintain this formation even against heavy enemy fire because of their discipline, courage, and training. Occasionally, some *ortas* were positioned within linear trenches during defensive battles, but in the open, taking cover against incoming fire or breaking from the lines were always seen as cowardly acts. To keep this from happening, junior officers and elderly soldiers were tasked to keep the lines intact and in combat their duties were focussed on this important task.

The janissaries' firepower, especially in the early 16th century, often proved fatal for their adversaries. These élite troops could fire their weapons in a kneeling or standing position without the need for additional support or rest. All this is corroborated by Süleymān's chancellor Mustafā Çelebi Celālzade (†1567) in his account of the decisive battle fought on the endless Hungarian plain near the town of Mohács on 29 August – the day of the decollation of John the Baptist – 1526. Here he claims that "four thousand janissaries (under the command of the *beylerbeyi* of Rumeli) were deployed in nine consecutive rows according to the rules of imperial battles [led by the sultan]", behind the chained guns (viz. the Ottoman version of the Hungarian *wagenburg*, which they called *tabur*), small field pieces known as *darbzens* (also called *zarbzen*, *darbuzan*, and *zarbuzan*), and that these "gunners [*tüfekendaz*] were firing their guns [*tüfek*] row by row".[15]

Despite the fact that Ottoman artillery is usually associated with monster siege pieces, the sultan's armies made extensive use of an artillery piece called the *zarbzen*. Weighing only 125 pounds (one *kantar*), a pair of barrels could thus be loaded on a packhorse and easily carried in whatever direction the army might decide to take. Used in coordination with the janissaries, it was these guns that were to prove a great tactical asset, real battle-winning weapons. The basic mechanism of the *tabur* was simple but very difficult to apply. Before the start of the battle war wagons (150 of them at Mohács) were chained together and cannon were placed within. Several janissary units armed with heavy harquebuses were also positioned with the gunners, and the remaining janissaries – several rows deep – remained within the formation.[16]

A double-page miniature of the battle from 1561 depicts janissary harquebusiers firing in two rows: soldiers in the first row are in a kneeling position reloading their weapons, while those standing behind them in the second row are firing their matchlock harquebuses at the advancing Hungarians. Behind them stand officers in tall caps armed with composite recurve bows. The janissaries are depicted as being behind a line of guns, chained together, a well-known arrangement from earlier and later battles.[17] Although painted some three decades after the battle, the miniature is very realistic in its depiction of the janissaries' rotating ranks, though the painter is able to show only two of them whereas, as aforementioned by the contemporary Çelebi Celālzade, there were nine consecutive ranks in this battle. Altogether these testimonies show that the janissaries were fighting in three or nine consecutive ranks, and that they were firing and then reloading in a well-trained manner. Obviously in battle the janissaries placed a premium on firepower, much like the Parachute Regiment in the Falklands/Malvinas War with far more than the statutory complement of general purpose machine guns per section (squad in American parlance), beefed up with anti-tank weapons for use against enemy trenches.

The janissary style of war had evolved over two centuries, changing with the enemies and battles that they had to fight. In the 14th century, they had been the solid, disciplined heart of the Ottoman battleline, fighting behind a screen of excitable, expendable irregular auxiliaries, or a line of wagons, drawing in the enemy on to their composite recurve bows (later harquebuses too), spears, swords and such other arms as the individuals fancied to wield. In battle they could halt the charge of armoured knights with their measured volleys of pine-shafted arrows and leaden shot, and then rush forward, ululating and bellowing their battle cries, to shatter an enemy in disarray. To the janissary, the *yatağan* fitted his temperament perfectly. It was a close quarter weapon and the janissary was never one to engage in distant fire fights, but rather he sought every opportunity to personally engage his foe in battle. Savage hand-to-hand fighting was at the heart of the Ottoman art of war.

Lazarus von Schwendi (†1583), one of the better known German military thinkers (he wrote *Kriegsdiskurs*) of the 16th century and an eyewitness observer of Ottoman military practice, was *Feldoberst in Oberungarn*, captain-general of Upper Hungary, from 1565 until 1568. A soldier of proficiency in war and possessed of experience in the Hungarian theatre of operations, Schwendi was to note the effective tactics and deadly firepower of the janissaries. He is emphatic that the Christian forces should not allow the Ottomans to lure them to within reach of the *wagenburg*, the mobile fortification in the centre of the Ottoman line of battle. He comments, too, on the extraordinary marksmanship of the janissaries: "There are about 12,000 harquebusiers with long harquebuses, which they manage excellently."[18] As a keen observer of the military establishment of the janissary corps, founded as it was on the principle of hierarchical subordination, discipline, and social obligation, he repeatedly urged the introduction of a similar system.

Similarly, Busbecq was often impressed by the organisation and discipline of the janissaries. In one of his letters, he notes their skill in using firearms "which they have acquired by long practice in warfare and continual exercise".[19] The Irish military writer Gerat Barry, who has served "in his Catholike Majesties service a monghste the Spaniard, Italian and Irish ... in the lowe countries and Germany, as a Souldior, Princioner Aventajado, Alferis, Ajudalte, and Captaine",[20] wrote of the value of regular weapon training:

> Let him [the common soldier] practice him selfe in eache sort of Weapon, to imitate as neere as possible the *Ianisaros* Turcos [janissaries], who were moste experte in armes trough theyre continuall exercise.[21]

On the other hand Barnabe Rich (1542–1617), an English contemporary of Barry's who had seen the wars in the Low Countries too, considers a common soldier can be well trained and made "fit for the wars" in a month. If he cannot master his weapons and learn to march in that time, he never will.[22] There again, our janissary was no common soldier and Barnabe Rich had probably never met one.

With the right conditions, on the right day, the janissaries could outmatch any western troops. In the wrong circumstances, with a commander they did not trust, they could easily deteriorate into a rabble. Even so, the defeated army could quickly recover its spirit and sense of conviction and counterattack, with devastating consequences for an overconfident enemy. For anyone who fought in the east, these were risks they faced daily. These were foes more dangerous, swifter and more lethal than any European enemy. To face a howling tide of janissaries racing towards you, to watch the heads and limbs of your companions spin off the sharp edge of a janissary *yatağan* required exceptional courage.

The celebrated Ottoman traveller and writer Evliya Çelebi makes explicit reference to the usefulness of the corps of drummers as a means for lifting the flagging spirits both of battle-wary and (later on) battle-weary warriors.[23] In addition, it is known that the Ottomans used their military band, *mehter takımı*, among other purposes, to coordinate and communicate with the units in action. For instance, writing about a battle in 1521 in Damascus, Matrakçı Nasūh mentions that the janissaries in the *wagenburg* fired their weapons after the drums played.[24] The use of visible signs could be dangerous, as they may have been simply misunderstood in the excitement of battle or obscured by rain, mist, dust or smoke. Of course it was possible for the men to distinguish only a few sounds without the danger of confusion. Still, the Ottomans set great store by the use of such devices to induce a state of psychological readiness for battle and in the 18th century the janissary *mehter* band would serve as a model for European armies who sought to introduce similar practices.[25]

Meanwhile back on the plain of Mohács, standing securely behind the chained artillery, the janissary harquebusiers and *archers* (see below) were to decimate and disperse the clumsy, suicidal surge of the Hungarians with their volleys.[26] Although the Hungarian infantry of some 10,000 men in the middle and the left wing fought bravely, they, too, were unable to break the obstacles erected in front of the cannon and janissaries and were slaughtered by the volleys of the latter. According to one Christian source, the Hungarians "were now fighting not on open ground but only ten paces from the guns, which filled the air with smoke and scared the horses ... The rapid fire and the cannonballs whistling above the heads of those of us next to the king (Louis) aroused great fear in everyone."[27] It appears that the Hungarians were not even aware the Ottomans had artillery until it opened fire on them. The young Hungarian king was killed, as was most of his court. Three bishops left the field of the slain alive.

Ottoman firepower superiority that day was pronounced more with regard to the artillery than hand firearms. The Ottomans had 150 to 200 pieces of ordnance and some larger cannon (*top*),[28] 4,060 handguns, and 3,000,000 projectiles. The number of handguns brought to the campaign indicates that only about half of the janissaries carried firearms. The rest of the janissaries and the *sipāhis* of the Porte used the 5,200 composite recurve bows and 1,400,000 arrows, listed in the campaign inventory.[29]

The big advantage of early firearms such as the handguns and harquebuses was that they required far less training. Making a skilful archer was a lifetime's undertaking: making a decent harquebusier was a matter of a few weeks of intensive instruction. In 1444, during the campaign of Varna, the Burgundian chronicler Jehan de Wavrin (†1474) notes in his account that the janissaries "are renegade Christians and slaves, all archers and all wearing white hats".[30]

## Man the Measure

Technology must match man: man is the measure. The story of the formidable Ottoman bow is a classic example. Obviously archery was still a highly valued battlefield skill in the Ottoman empire, and this formidable skill was not easily acquired, the archers practising constantly. While resident in Constantinople Busbecq took up the Ottoman bow, a weapon, he writes, with which the Turks are "extraordinary skilful". The Flemish diplomat continues at some length:

> They begin to shoot at eight or even seven years of age and practise continuously for ten or twelve years. The result is that their arms become exceedingly strong, and they become so expert that no objective is too small for them to hit. The bows which they use are considerably stouter than ours, and, being shorter, easier to handle; they are not made of a single piece of wood but of sinew and ox horns fastened with glue and flax. A Turk after long practice can easily draw the string of even the stoutest bow right back to his ear; yet any one, however strong, who was unaccustomed to this kind of bow, could not draw it sufficiently far to release a coin fixed between the bow and the string in the angle where the latter is attached to the notch ... They wear on the thumb of the right hand rings of bone on which the string rests when they pull it, while the arrow is held in check by the knuckle of the joint of the left thumb, which is extended – a very different method from ours.[31]

Here Busbecq is clearly describing the Turkish use of the composite recurve bow. Composite means that it was made of more than one material: a wooden core backed by sinews and bellied with horn glued on in layers. The bow was held together with a natural, water soluble fish or bone glue and then waterproofed by lacquering. The thumb ring was normally made of horn but could also be made out of bone or ivory.

Recurve means that when the bow was unstrung, it curved in the opposite direction from when it was strung. In other words, the act of stringing the bow made the lamination of sinew the back of the stave (to resist stretching) and horn the belly (to resist compression). The composite construction gave it extra strength, and the recurve gave it extra power. This meant that greater latent power could be stored in the bow than could be stored by bending a straight stick. More powerful even than the famed English longbow (and even many types of bullet), a well-made composite recurve bow could shoot an arrow through an iron breastplate or fifteen millimetres of wood at close range, say fifty to one hundred metres. The janissaries carried their arrows and bows, ready for use at a moment's notice, in a combination case that hung from their waist belt.

With its strongly double-curved silhouette, most archery experts agree that with the Ottoman composite recurve bow this weapon reached the epitome of its form and effectiveness. For strength and fire power, beauty of design and accuracy, plus the expert application of ancient craftsman's knowledge, Ottoman bows were the commanding weapon on the battlefields of western Asia until the use of firearms became prevalent in the 19th century. For the highest quality bow, glue that was made either from the tendons or a combination of the ears or hide of cattle and skin from the roof of the mouth of a Danube sturgeon, had to be cooked. The most common wood used as the core of the bow was maple because of its ability to accept the glue. An excellent bowyer knew exactly where and when to find the best trees to use to obtain this particular wood. Horn that was appropriate for the bow had to be smooth and free of any imperfections, while the pieces for the top and bottom of the bow had to be near identical as was possible.

Without a doubt, tradition is not always irrational; the retention of the highly effective composite recurve bow by Ottoman armies – used with devastating effect on the hosts of Peter Alexeyevich of Russia as late as the four-day battle of Stănileşti (18–21 July 1711) – is an excellent case in point. It is noteworthy, however, that the basic accoutrements of the Ottoman bow – the glues, sinew, horn, and wood used in its construction, as well as the thumb ring, arrows, and quiver – had remained basically unchanged over the millennia.[32]

The original Turks had been steppe nomads who fought from horseback, using composite recurve bows as their primary shock weapon. That was the one form of fighter western armies never could handle well. Their composite recurve bows were wonders of nomad hi-tech weapon design. Sleek and graceful, accurate and powerful, this was no AK47, for it took a skilled bowyer a full year to make, starting in the autumn and finishing the following summer, gluing together with patience slender plates of horn and slivers of sinew to various types of wood for the perfect combination of give and resistance. Though it looked like a toy compared to the English longbow, the finished bow was a masterful combination of carefully selected natural products and human ingenuity, and it could fire twice as fast and penetrate body armour at greater distances.

A steppe archer mounted on one of those sturdy small horses raised in the Eurasian steppe lands was a fighting machine so superior to the typical western man-at-arms that most of the clashes between the two kinds of horse warrior turned into massacres, with the mercurial horse archer picking off the heavier armed opponent at will. Masters of battlefield mobility, one of their favourite battlefield moves was to herd the enemy into separate groups the way steppe nomads had been doing with their flocks and herds for centuries. Mission accomplished, it was now time for the killing.

To return once more to Mohács: the battle, which put an end to the independent kingdom of Hungary,[33] is a reminder that even a relatively 'modern' army was vulnerable to an opponent with numerical and firepower superiority.[34] As for firepower: the Ottoman cannon did little damage, for their shots landed beyond the attacking Hungarians (likely due to the uneven terrain and the resulting elevation of the gun barrels). Rather, it was the iron discipline, the insurmountable obstacle, and the murderous volleys of the janissaries that figured decisively in the Ottoman victory. As Gábor Ágoston notes, "most European and Ottoman sources on Mohács attributed the Ottomans' success in the battle to the janissaries' firepower and not to the cannon, in sharp contrast to later historians who usually claim that it was the Ottoman artillery that decided the fate of the Hungarians."[35] All available contemporary evidence and recent scholarly work suggest that the firing technique used by the janissaries during this battle was a form of volley fire and that it proved to be decisive. However, as Ágoston also points out, we "should also be careful not to overstate the importance of the janissaries' volleys and consider the destructiveness of archers, whose arrows could cause more damage among the enemy than musket fire".[36] Moreover, if it rained, the harquebusier may as well have gone home.

Since the harquebuses were muzzle-loading and smoothbore weapons firing roughly spherical lead shots, it is difficult to calculate their range and rate of fire. The period in which they were used most preceded by several decades the first real efforts to systematize the calibre of arms and the firing procedure and to calculate their effect. According to modern-day tests, under optimum conditions a veteran harquebusier could carry out the laborious process of reloading and firing in about thirty seconds, and though its maximum range was much longer, a shot fired by a harquebus retained an acceptable combination of penetration capacity and accuracy at a distance of under thirty metres.[37]

## Our Man in Constantinople

Ogier Ghiselin de Busbecq, the acknowledged natural son of George Ghiselin II, seigneur de Busbecq, was born in western Flanders in 1522 at his father's château close to the French frontier. He was his father's favourite child, and though he was legitimised by Charles V in 1549, the stigma of his illegitimate birth made his social position ambivalent. Busbecq escaped its constraints largely by his drive and forceful intellect. This erudite Flemish writer, zoologist, botanist, numismatist, antiquarian, and diplomat served three generations of Habsburg monarchs on many minor missions, so he was a natural choice as a Habsburg imperial emissary to the court of Süleymān I (*Soleiman* in the English translation). It was also a hardship post: his predecessors had been terrorised, imprisoned and threatened with a worse fate.

Busbecq's *Turcicae epistolae* was an instant European bestseller. His first letter appeared in the original Latin in 1581, and the first edition of all four letters appeared in Paris in 1589, prior to his death in 1592. Latin was of course Europe's only international literary language, but over the course of time many other editions appeared, and the *epistolae* were translated into French, German, Dutch and Spanish, and, notably in English. Often other writers simply took Busbecq's astute observations and paraded them as their own knowledge. Three hundred years after his stay in Constantinople, his work was still in use as an accurate and contemporary source, and it remains in print to this day. There is an earthy freshness to Busbecq's *epistolae*, all written to Nicholas Michault, a fellow imperial diplomat from Hungary and a close friend from his student days in Venice, where he was a pupil of Johannes Baptista Egnatius, the friend and correspondent of Erasmus, the renowned scholar of the age and the leading moderate of the Reformation, although he never joined the Protestants.

Busbecq seems to have made few changes to his original drafts when they were published but he was plainly impatient with those in Christendom mistaking the nature of the Ottomans; Busbecq emphasised what his fellow Christians should learn from them. Busbecq's letters present a man of invincible curiosity who, kept under effective house arrest, filled his courtyards and stables with a menagerie, which he studied and observed. Busbecq was greedy for sensation, keen to see this new and exotic eastern world. He wrote ruefully to Michault, who had asked about what he saw in the great city:

> I do not generally do so unless I have dispatches from the Emperor for presentation to the Sultan, or instructions to protest against the ravages and malpractices of the Turkish garrisons. These occasions occur only twice or three times a year. If I wished from time to time to take a ride through the city with my custodian, permission would probably not be refused ... What I enjoy is the country and the fields, not the city – especially a city which is almost falling to pieces, and of whose former glory nothing remains except its splendid position. Constantinople, once the rival of Rome, is now laid low in wretched slavery.[38]

Busbecq observed minutely, whether it was antiquities, flowers and plants, scenery or human beings. His letters, in all their many editions, were unadorned by engravings and devoid of censorious comment.

Classicists also owe him a great debt of favour too; it was Busbecq who discovered an almost complete copy of the *Res Gestae Divi Augusti*,

'The achievements of the divine Augustus', in the temple of Rome and Augustus at Angora (Ancyra), a town in Galatia, the modern Ankara. On this matter he writes:

> At Angora we saw a very fine inscription, a copy of the tablets upon which Augustus drew up a succinct account of his public acts. I had it copied out by my people as far as it was legible. It is graven on the marble walls of a building, which was probably the ancient residence of the governor, now ruined and roofless. One half of it is upon the right, as one enters, the other on the left. The upper paragraphs are almost intact; in the middle difficulties begin owing to gaps; the lowest portion has been mutilated by blows of clubs and axes as to be illegible. This is a serious loss to literature and much to be deplored by the learned, especially as it is generally agreed that the city was consecrated to Augustus as a common gift from the province of Asia.[39]

Busbecq's letters are a treasure trove of early modern travel literature, reflecting the writer's rich literary talent, classical education, love for discovering and collecting antiquities, and remarkable power of observation.

## Food and Power

Appearances can be deceptive: the janissaries were technically possessions of their sultan, but had accumulated traditional rights, which they guarded jealously, much like a guild. True, each janissary fought for his faith, assured like any *gāzī* who fell in battle that he would be translated directly to heaven. He fought for the sultan, whom he served as his slave. But greater than his loyalty to the sultan was his loyalty to his comrades, and members of the same barrack room had the greatest claim of all by an oath sworn on a tray holding salt, a copy of the Qur'ān, the book which contains their sacred mysteries, and a sword. Many of the janissary mutinies that occurred started as pay disputes, when they interpreted government measures as unjustly transgressing on their acquired rights.

As mentioned before, even more revered than the standards of their *ortas* were the huge copper soup cauldrons, *kazans*, of which each barrack room had two or three, in which their daily ration of soup, *pilav* – boiled cracked wheat and butter – and mutton was cooked and around which they sat and socialised in the evenings. If one of these hallowed emblems of their corporate life were ever lost in battle all the officers of the barrack room were dismissed with ignominy and never again accepted into the same *orta*, if they were reaccepted into the army at all. On the other hand, when the janissaries mutinied, they ceremoniously kicked over and upset their huge and heavy cauldrons to signify that they no longer accepted the sultan's rations and renounced their obedience to him. This was known as *kazan kaldırma*, 'toppling of the soup cauldron'. Even the sultans most known for their generally forceful manner were sometimes subject to troop rebellions over pay or general conditions, and the janissaries were no exception. This happened in 1446 at Buçuk Tepe when, although the exact sequence of events is somewhat unclear, the dissatisfaction of the janissaries over their wages led to the removal of the young Mehmed II from the throne, and the postponement of his definitive succession until his father's death in 1451.

Likewise, in the short interregnum between the death of Mehmed II and the accession of Bāyezīd II (r. 1481–1512), the janissaries rioted and plundered parts of the capital, and it was the janissaries who forced the abdication of Bāyezīd in favour of Selīm I (r. 1512–20). Broken in spirit, the old sultan died two months later; it was rumoured he had been poisoned by his son Selīm. Maybe the best known case involves the problems that Selīm had with the janissaries during and after the successful campaign against the Safavids and the battle of Çaldīran in 1514. The janissaries first mutinied on the way to Çaldīran, and a few months later after the victory there refused to spend the winter in Karabakh, too far away from their base, with a view to a new campaign. The reason for the two mutinies was that the janissaries had experienced a very long march under difficult weather conditions, harsh terrains, and lack of provisions. This was all aggravated by the scorched-earth tactics of the Safavids and their avoiding battle until the Ottoman army was exhausted and led to Çaldīran, which presumably was thought to be a battleground advantageous to the Safavids (their cavalry was to be blown away by the entrenched Ottoman cannon and handgun-armed janissaries). Despite being nicknamed *Yavuz*, the Grim, and being notorious for his violent disposition, Selīm was forced to in the first case to placate the mutineers and talk them in to continuing the march, and in the second to accede to their demands, retreat to Ottoman territory, and cancel the following year's campaign.[40]

Superb on the field of battle, the janissaries were often irresponsible and quarrelsome in times of peace. Fra' Diego de Haedo, writing at the end of the 16th century, had this to say about their arrogance and special status:

> If anyone not a janissary were to strike a janissary or even push him merely to get him out of the way or lay hand on his chest or arm, the penalty is to have the hand cut off; to kill a janissary means for the offender to be burned alive, or impaled, or hooked, or to have his bones smashed with a mace, as we have seen done so any times ...[41]

It goes without saying that the inhabitants of Algiers where our Benedictine monk had witnessed such goings-on (he was a captive there between 1578 and 1581 and knew Miguel de Cervantes), tried to steer clear of such privileged and brutal men. Equally so, as an armed group stationed in Constantinople, the central troops *par excellence*, the janissaries were as powerful a force in the internal politics of the empire as they were on the battlefield. At first a source of strength to the Sublime Porte as being the only well-organised and disciplined troops in the empire, the janissaries would one day become its bane. The relationship between the sovereign and his *kullar*, we submit, was never as simple and predefined as that between master and slave.[42]

The symbolism of cooking and eating was deeply ingrained in their customs and, as mentioned before, the Ottoman name for the corps of janissaries was *ocak*, meaning the communal hearth of an encampment, while its officers were given titles, like that of the *orta* commander, *çorbacıbaşı* or chief of the soup. This reflected Turkish nomadic tradition, where a tribal leader had been responsible for providing his men with their one meal of the day. Just as the sultan was known by his janissaries as 'the father who feeds us', certainly one of the most bizarre aspects of the janissaries was the naming of titles for its officers. Most of the junior and middle-ranking janissary officer titles were intimately related with kitchen terminology. Apart from the aforementioned *çorbacıbaşı*, there was the quartermaster, *aşçıbaşı* or chief cook, and the lieutenant, *odabaşı* or chief of chamber (viz. barracks). This was not because janissary officers spent more time supervising the ration supply than leading in war, but rather to the revered status of regimental cauldrons.

In Anatolia, a cauldron was a symbol of hospitality according to the Bektaşi tradition, a Sufi dervish order (Tk. *Bektaşi Tarīkatı*) with which the janissaries had close connections, and with the abolition of janissaries, the order was banned throughout the Ottoman empire. In the *tekkes*, convents of the Bektaşi dervishes,[43] the soup in the cauldron was continuously served to both the guests and the needy. Besides being a symbol of hospitality, the cauldron was seen as a medium to convey messages, displaying power in various forms. Hence, as we have discussed, the cauldron becomes a symbolic object beyond being a functional piece of kitchenware.

*Part II*

# The Pieces

*Chapter 12*

# The Galleys

Everyone knows that the navigation of sail ships is completely different from that of galleys.

Andrea Doria to Philip II, Genoa, 19 June 1560.[1]

The galley had a long history. Primarily a Mediterranean oared fighting ship, galleys fought in all the maritime wars of the great Mediterranean powers – Athens, the Hellenistic kingdoms, Carthage, and Rome – and mediaeval maritime warfare would witness the arrival of Muslim galleys, and those of Venice, and Genoa. In time, the Ottomans too would rely on galleys as their principal fighting ship. Driven by one bank of oars per side, employing as many as five men at each, these sleek vessels were fast and manoeuvrable, the epitome of efficient muscle power.

Galleys were fragile, of limited range, and expensive to operate. Nonetheless they were the dominant force in Mediterranean naval warfare because within the Mediterranean environment they had decided advantages to offset their obvious weaknesses. The main advantages of the galley in naval war were dash speed, manoeuvrability, and a certain degree of independence of wind. These advantages were conferred by an 'engine' consisting of a large crew of oarsmen who powered the low, slender vessel, with their oars acting as its 'legs'. During the actual fighting the oars gave it the ability to respond to the fluctuating needs of battle or, if need be, to make a hasty retreat.

## Oar Power

The early modern *galea sottile* (literally 'slender galley') was basically a slender oared vessel, low in the water, with a very shallow draught and large lateen (triangular) sails. Galleys carried up to three masts, but only as a form of auxiliary propulsion. Compared with the square-rigged sailing ships of the 16th century the galley's rig was very simple. One to three vertical masts were fitted with long yards, often consisting of two overlapping spars lashed together, each of them carrying a lateen sail on the long yard (a triangular sail set at an angle of 45° to the mast with the highest part aft of the mast),[2] which propelled the galley in good winds. The masts were the mainmast, which was large and stout, with the possible addition of the foremast (It. *trinchetto*), and the mizzen (It. *mezzana*).

Efficiency as a sailing vessel was the prime determination of a galley's strategic radius of action. Yet oared fighting ships were notoriously bad performers under sail. Their unavoidably narrow beam and shallow draft left them without the rigidity needed to carry a heavy press of canvas. Their low freeboard and projecting oars meant they could not heel very far before shipping water aboard. Their lack of keel area made them leewardly and inefficient on a beam reach or when bearing to windward, the only points of sailing where their large lateen sails were particularly effective. The lateen sails had to be set on the side opposed to the wind (lee side), and if the galley wanted to go about or tack (turn through the wind) the yards had to be reversed. Something in the order of twelve nautical miles per hour with a stiff following breeze and a fairly flat sea probably represented about the most that a galley could achieve.[3]

Thus the oar remained the *raison d'être* of the galley: it was under oars that it fought. Rowers were essential for acceleration, manoeuvrability, and propelling the vessel in calm conditions. A man pulling an oar generates only one-eighth horsepower of energy. Then two hundred or more oarsmen were needed. The chief difficulty here was one of keeping this large crew fed and watered. So a captain had to provide food and especially water, but his light vessel had little storage capacity, a capacity that was also crammed with ammunition, weapons, extra suits of sails, spare oars, and all the other gear of the galley, not to mention his officers, sailors, fighting men and of course oarsmen.

## Logistical and Practical Limitations

Mediterranean naval warfare, as has been admirably pointed out by John Francis Guilmartin, was amphibious in nature, and the strategic, tactical and logistical assumptions that governed it were radically different from those that governed the conflicts fought by fleets of broadside sailing ships in the *mar oceano*.[4]

While sailing ships depended on winds, galleys, given their logistical and practical limitations, depended on coasts and harbours. Being unable to navigate for more than a few days without stopping to take on water and food, oared warships could not command the sea or enforce blockades in the Mahanian sense,[5] as ably argued by Guilmartin, though it should be stressed that the Mahanian concept of the 'command of the seas' would only become a practical naval strategy in the course of the long years of wars after 1650.

As well as their logistical limitations, galleys were not able to withstand heavy seas or adverse winds, and could not, therefore, put to sea in the winter, setting out in principle, if not often in practice, at the vernal equinox, and returning to port in October or early November when campaigning with galleys in the Mediterranean was perilous. Galleys needed a relatively low freeboard to accommodate the oars, limiting their seaworthiness even in summer storms. When stormy weather was brewing, commanders of galleys had good reason to encourage their oarsmen to bend their oars so as to swiftly seek safe haven in the nearest port. The Mediterranean is a cruel sea. Here, the winds, rather than the tides, rule supreme. And what monsters: the Vendavel, the Mistral, the Bora, the Meltemi, the Sirocco, the Levanter, often heralding their arrival with screeching like a banshee. Thus, the beginning of October 1571 was rather late in the season for galleys to be out and about.

On the other hand, what galleys could do was to control the coastline and, above all, the harbours and their facilities. As one of the poems composed in Latin to commemorate the Christian victory at Lepanto puts it: "A commander conquers with oars, and with oars he rules the waves."[6] Typical duties of galley fleets were shipping troops and supplies to where they were needed, preventing the enemy from doing the same and, in concert with the land armies, covering the maritime side of their advances and operations. In short, armed with up to five guns at the bow, one of which could be a 50-pounder, the main siege weapon of the era, due to its ability to use oars and position itself into a favourable firing position, galleys proved to be excellent tools for support of land operations, either by firing precise salvos at shore fortifications or at enemy troops. Additionally, their manoeuvrability made galleys well suited for the landing of assault parties.

When the Ottoman navy engaged in an action, for instance, it was typically an amphibious assault on a coastal or insular fortress, rather than a battle in the open sea, whereby its oared fleets were employed as vehicles for amphibious operations. Almost all Ottoman naval victories, from the conquest of Mytilene in 1462 to the capture of Chania in 1645, were of this sort. Moreover, these campaigns were characterised by the need for a speedy passage and disembarkation. This need for urgency was to ensure an operation had the best possible chance of success. Direct confrontations between squadrons or even large fleets of galleys were considered neither necessary nor worthwhile. Battles were at best costly and dangerous affairs, and their uncertain outcomes would have no decisive effect on the progress of the war at sea or on land.

To these limitations we should add the fact that until the introduction of gunpowder technology in the second-half of the 15th century, *boarding* (putting ships in contact) and *entering* (swarming onto an enemy deck) remained the only viable tactic to overcome an opponent. Therefore, the offensive potential of the galleys and the other smaller oared vessels, *galeotte*, *fusta*, *brigantino* and *fregata* (in descending order), consisted mostly in the number of the combatants they could put afloat. This made the *galea grossa* – literally the great galley, a military version of the large *galea da mercato* – the central element of galley fleets, and limited their effectiveness against both big round ships like the carracks (which often proved to be virtually invulnerable to the attacks of galleys) and coastal fortified strongholds. This state of affairs was radically changed by the appearance and relatively-quick spread of effective centreline bow artillery capable of smashing hulls (and walls, if disembarked), which drastically increased the offensive capabilities of the galley, making it a much more effective predator.

Galley fleets, with their ravenous need for provisions, could not remain at sea for more than a few days. A consequence of this need to take on food and water at frequent intervals was that galley fleets could not operate safely if they were far from their own shores or if the sea lanes were insecure. This factor, combined with the short campaigning season, limited their range. For this reason, the Ottoman fleet could not dominate the western Mediterranean without a base for the winter and a supply of provisions. This was possible only briefly when, in cooperation with the king of France, the Ottoman fleet under Barbarossa, in 1543–4, was able to over-winter in Toulon and thus aided the French in their military operations against the Habsburgs at the same time (even though direct military cooperation was rare, the Porte and France considered each other useful for counterbalancing their common enemy, the Habsburgs). For the same reason, Christian galley fleets could not gain command of the eastern Mediterranean. Even after the great victory at Lepanto, the fleet of the Holy League had no choice but to return to its home bases before the onset of winter.

All this said, galleys did have some positive operational advantages in the Mediterranean. They offered both flexibility and dependability of movement – being capable of great precision of navigation in skirting maritime obstacles, and at times of turning both weather and topography to advantage, of which something will have to be said later. They were particularly favoured by Mediterranean powers for inshore and amphibious operations in the narrow, rocky and island-strewn, or shallow waters of the Aegean, Adriatic, and Tyrrhenian seas. Variable currents, coupled with the intermittent winds, squalls, and calms that characterize even the summer Mediterranean, involved serious handicaps for sailing vessels. Sighting an enemy, the commander of a galley could change course with minimum regard for wind and weather. He could quickly take good tactical position, choosing either to engage or, in the face of overwhelming strength, to seek some port or river refuge, regardless of the wind. In short, oar-driven craft were well adapted to dealing with some of the peculiar characteristics of naval warfare in the Mediterranean climate and geography. In the Mediterranean, where weather was predictable, tides minimal, and ports common, galleys reigned.

## Galley Construction

By the middle of the 16th century the galley was one of the most complex pieces of technology in existence. Every item on the vessel had a name; every rope had a purpose and timing and discipline were the essence of every manoeuvre. The *raison d'être* of the galley was to enable its fighting element to board and enter an enemy vessel.

In the Mediterranean, where the shipbuilding tradition was older, it was also more complex, and the creation of specialised types of ships was there carried further during the mediaeval period than it was in the seas of northern Europe. From the time of the Phoenicians, Mediterranean ships had been divided into long ships and round ships. Long ships were equipped with oars, round ships depended entirely on sails, the former being low and narrow, the latter high and wide. In general, this distinction was the same as that between warships and merchantmen, though it should be mentioned that the Venetians built two types of galley, light galleys, *galee sottili*, for war and great galleys, *galee grosse*, to carry costly commodities (silk, spices, bullion, and other fabled luxuries of the east) on great trading voyages. This being said, the mediaeval longship was the war galley, which would dominate Mediterranean naval warfare from its inception to the 17th century.

The Mediterranean war galley was carvel built, that is, with the planks butting up against each other edge to edge rather than by the fastening together of heavy, overlapping planking, which was then reinforced by ribs, as in the clinker built vessels of the northern seas. Carvel built technology, because of its stronger framework of ribs and clamps produced a sturdier hull, which in turn facilitated greater length and breadth. Its design was dominated by the desire to give it the speed needed to outmanoeuvre an opponent, and this purpose determined both the proportions of the hull and the arrangement of the superstructure.

Proper seasoning of timber required only that cuts in the forests produce substantial surpluses of properly assorted timber over a number of years. A stockpile would then naturally develop, which needed only to be properly stored. Vessels built with unseasoned timber, whether sailing ships or galleys, were bound to require much maintenance and generally to be short-lived. Built into a vessel, green timber dried unevenly – some pieces warped, some of those above the waterline also shrank, fittings worked loose, and seams opened up. No amount of care could keep such a craft seaworthy for long. Shipwrights had known from time immemorial that only seasoned timber should be built into seagoing craft. The constructors of galleys were well aware that the use of unseasoned timber was bound to shorten the useful life of a galley. For that reason, for example, the Venetians habitually seasoned their timber for as much as ten years before they put it to use.

Here it should be understood that each Mediterranean power of the 16th century had its own galley-building philosophy, developed according to its strategic and economic needs. Besides, different building skills meant that no two galleys were alike, the judgement and ability of individual master builders playing a crucial part in the construction of each vessel. There were, however, two basic types of galleys: the *ponentina*, employed by Genoa, Savoy, Tuscany, the Papal States, Malta, Spain and its Italian dependencies, and the *levantina*, used by Venice and the Ottoman empire. The states of the Barbary Coast normally built vessels of the first type, although adapted to the requirements of the hit-and-run warfare practised by Barbary corsairs. Another difference was the fact that the *ponentina* relied more on slave labour. Ottoman and Venetian galleys drew less water than *ponentina*, being swifter under oars. On the other hand, when it came to sailing the *levantina* did not perform so well as their western cousins, the latter having larger sails.

Builders of oar-powered warships faced two related imperatives: constructing a vessel that was fast in short bursts and manoeuvrable in crowded formations. Nevertheless, a standard type of galley never existed in practice, and this is not the right place to attempt a categorisation of the various classes and sub-classes, but it ought to be noted that, with the exception of the Venetian galley (which displayed many characteristics typical of the Ottoman type) the type of galley referred to in this book is the western variety of *galea sottile*. Excluding the iron tipped spur (5–6 metres), or *sperone*, protruding from the bow, the rowing frame and the other platforms built on it, the hull of a galley was about forty-one metres long and five to six metres wide. The length/width ratio of a galley varied according to its size, from the 8:1 of an average *sottile* up to the 6:1 of the larger versions. Another fundamental design feature was the fact that the hull of a galley was built as low as possible in order to maximise the mechanical advantage enjoyed by the oarsmen.

A Venetian *galea sottile* designed by Pre Theodoro around 1550 had a depth amidships of only five Venetian feet (*piede*) or 1.74 metres.[7] The standard papal galley described by Bartolomeo Crescentio at the end of the 16th century had a height of 7.25 Neapolitan *palmi* or 1.98 metres to the gunwale.[8] There is a priceless treatise that goes by the name *Architectura navalis*, which was written by the Bavarian mathematician, engineer and architect Joseph Furttenbach *der Ältere* (1591–1667). As a young man he had spent a number of years in Italy (1607/08 to 1620), especially in Milan, Florence and Genoa, and it was at the latter place where he learned of *l'arte di costruire navigli*. It is on the basis of his observations and direct experience with regards to the Genoese way of shipbuilding that Furttenbach provides a detailed account of the construction and operation of a Genoese galley at the beginning of the 17th century. Accordingly, the overall length of a galley was 180 Genovese *palmi* or 44.64 metres,[9] with a deck beam of 5.6 metres, hull depth of 2.3 metres, and a draught of 1.6 metres. Five types of wood were used in its construction: oak, elm, fir, beech, and walnut.[10]

## Oar Mechanics

The oar mechanics of galleys had little in common with the rowing we are familiar with nowadays. It would hardly be a paradox to say that the only common factor is the use of an oar. Galley rowing was linked to a notion of time rather than distance. Time in a galley was regulated by small, half-hour sandglasses or *ampoulettes*. Because the human engine is not very powerful and tires quickly, a galley might row one or two *ampoulettes* or more if the relay system was adopted, such as 'quarter' rowing. Here the oarsmen were divided into two teams working in relay, the aft quarter and the forward quarter. Depending on the voyage, each quarter would row for two to three *ampoulettes*, that is to say an hour or an hour and a half rowing in turns. This was the best way of rowing in calm seas and over long distances when there was no requirement to row 'with all hands'. It was also by and away the most economical way of rowing because it spared the rowers; the work period of the oarsmen never exceeded an hour and a half in each shift and was equalled by the rest and recuperation period.

Another even greater difference was in the rowing technique itself. In both rowing modes, as will be seen, the oarsmen made use of the weight of their bodies, rising from their bench and then dropping back on to the same bench, applying the maximum weight possible to the oar. Because of the close confines of the rowing bench, this operation was carried out with arms continually outstretched. This position – arms constantly as straight as a plank – necessarily restricted breathing, and hence the ability to recuperate during a prolonged period of effort. With hands welded to the handhold battens, the oarsmen formed one body with the oars, rowing with a monotonous backwards and forwards motion and laboured breathing. The fate of the vessel and its crew was at all times dependent upon the strength and also the skill of these men.

Projecting beyond the gunwale, the outrigger to mount the tholes was already a familiar piece of galley paraphernalia, and had been since at least the classical period.[11] As on modern racing shells, the outrigger was used to increase the leverage of the oarsmen without the disadvantage of having to increase the size of the amidships (i.e. in the middle of the ship) beam at the waterline. The oarsmen were grouped together in twos, threes and fours and were positioned on the same level bench. This reduced the top hamper and really made the galley a low-freeboard vessel. This arrangement did improve things, but because each man had an oar – a very ancient practice – the benches had to be slanted obliquely towards the poop so that their inboard ends were further aft than their outboard ends. This slanting of the benches made it possible to have all the oars parallel without interfering with one another. An oar measured at least ten metres and was twelve centimetres in diameter. Only about a third of the oar was inboard, but the deck end was weighted with lead so that the whole oar would be balanced near the thole pin and the oarsman relieved of its weight. Grips were attached to the handle for the benefit of the oarsmen. In front of the benches were low steps on which the oarsmen mounted to put their oars into the water and on which they could brace as they fell back with a bump and threw their weight on the oar. For obvious reason the oarsmen covered their benches with rags or makeshift cushions stuffed with straw or dry leaves. This system was known as *alla zenzile* (or *alla sensile*) rowing, literary 'in simple fashion', which had been developed in the Mediterranean from the 10th century onwards and was very popular with the Venetians.

Nevertheless, an arrangement of this type had its limits. Vettor Fausto (b. 1480), humanist naval architect, was one of a growing number of

Venetian scholars (he was a professor of Ancient Greek at the Scuola Grande di San Marco) at the beginning of the 16th century to examine ancient military texts in order to assist in the defence of Venetian territory against their erstwhile Ottoman enemies. In 1517 Fausto was the first to translate the Aristotelian *Mechanica* into Latin,[12] a short treatise dealing with the application of general mathematical principles to the specific subject of mechanics. What is more, Fausto had carefully examined Greek and Roman texts concerning naval warfare with oared ships, as well as speaking with Venetian shipbuilders and ship masters, and mariners from many other ports that came to the floating city on the Adriatic.

It is plausible to infer that Fausto was either inspired by the ancient works to re-imagine how a galley could be improved, or used the ancient texts to support his ideas. To be more specific, Problem 4 of *Mechanica* asks:

Q: Why do the rowers in the middle of the ship contribute the most to its movement? A: The oar acts as a lever with the thole-pin (i.e. oarlock) as the fulcrum, the moving weight (the rower) is on the inside of the ship, and the moved weight (the sea) is on the outside. Since the ship is widest at the middle, more of the oar is on the inside, so the movement of the oar against the thole-pin causes the pin (and therefore the ship) to move forward the greatest distance.[13]

I would like to point out that all of the oars of a Greek trireme were of roughly equal length and arranged to form a straight line outside the ship, so the oars at amidships were longer inboard than the ones at the narrower bow and stern.[14] The 'lever law' here assumes that the paddle entering the sea is fixed, so the fulcrum (thole-pin) moves forward, pushing the ship forward. The question we ask ourselves, did Fausto attempt to directly apply Aristotelian mechanics to Venetian naval architecture?

Though they were all pulled on a one-level system of oars, Venetian galley types had adopted the classical names of biremes, triremes and quadriremes according to the number of oarsmen per *bench* and not *bank* of oars. Thus, before 1540 the backbone of the Venetian navy was the *triremi alla zenzile* of twenty-four benches of three oarsmen per bench (so seventy-two a side, 144 all told), each pulling his own individual oar.

Though three men to a bench pulling individual oars seems to have represented some kind of optimum with regards to propulsion efficiency, Fausto came to the conclusion that the *triremi alla zenzile* could be greatly improved by employing additional oarsman. To this end, therefore, on 18 August 1525, according to the eyewitness Marin Sanudo (usually Italianised as Marino Sanuto), the Venetian senator and diarist, Fausto presented to the Senate his model of a quinquereme, a five-oarsman-per-bench galley, which he argued would be more effective than the *triremi alla zenzile*.

On 29 April 1529 Fausto completed and launched a full-sized quinquereme, but the subsequent sea trials were not conclusive. Though it won a race against a *triremi alla zenzile*, it was harder to manoeuvre. An entry in *I diarii* of Sanudo, dated 23 May 1529, tells how this galley proceeded up the Grand Canal "as far as the Palazzo Foscari, where she was turned about, but with the greatest possible trouble, as she was twenty-eight paces (some 47.55 metres) long, and more than three paces (some 5.5 metres) wide".[15] What is more, with more than three oarsmen to each bench, the outside positions were difficult to maintain and because the oars were very close together clashes were inevitable. This meant that oars were used up at an alarming rate. The concept was not immediately accepted by the Senate, but over the course of several decades the Arsenale di Venezia, the sprawling dockyard to the east of the main square of San Marco, built a number of quinqueremes, which continued to be in service for the next forty years. Indeed, a Fausto quinquereme was originally the flagship of Marc'Antonio Colonna (†1584), the pro-Spanish papal admiral who we shall meet anon at Lepanto, before it was struck by lightning and burned in October 1570 (a year before the battle).[16]

Another system was then tried, although derived from the previous one. The idea was to make all the men on one bench pull a single oar together, but one which was longer and stronger. This was called *a scaloccio* ('ladder style') rowing, which undeniably made life a little easier for the outside oarsmen without obstructing the cycle of the man at the end of the oar. He – called the *pianero* or lead oarsman – led his group and set the stroke. The transition from *remi piccoli*, small oars, to *remi grandi*, large oars, was slow and lasted beyond the end of the century, mainly because there were those who were still not convinced of the suitability of the system. Nevertheless, the introduction of one large oar pulled by many men placed the whole problem of propulsion on a new basis, for as many additional men might be placed on the same bench to pull a single oar as the width of the galley permitted.

The significance of this is that, with three men to an oar and the oar itself being longer and heavier, the stroke rate is reduced, while the arc of any stroke taken from a seated position would be much shorter. A slightly longer stroke might have been achieved with the three-man oars if the man at the end of the oar took the stroke by standing up and sitting down, or even by taking a step forward and then backward. With any more than three men to an oar, all the men would have had to take such a stroke. The overall result would be a significant reduction in the maximum speed attainable compared to galleys with only one-man oars, even though the spreading of the load among more oarsmen would allow an acceptable cruising speed to be maintained despite the increased size of the vessels.

An ancient Greek oarsman aboard a trireme has been calculated to apply 90 to 110 watts (0.12–0.15 horsepower) of actual power to his oar over an extended period.[17] Thus, during the period under consideration, when galleys increased in size, the number of oarsmen had to be increased disproportionably. By the mid-fifteen-sixties the *ciurma* of Spanish galleys, still of twenty-four banks but slightly larger than before, had increased in size from 144 to an optimum of 160.[18] By 1571 this figure had further increased to 174 and the galleys of Spain and its dependencies had their *ciurma* reinforced to no less than 200 for the Lepanto campaign.[19] Even if the extra men helped but little in pulling the oar, they might be useful in battle, provided they were free men of course. This increase mirrored an increase in the total complement of galleys, an increase that was particularly sharp aboard *lanterne*, which might have as many as seven men to an oar. A *galea de lanterna* was so named for its multiple large and elaborately decorated stern lanterns (usually three) displayed to mark it as a selected galley heavily armed and manned to serve as a tactical focal point in battle. Though outside our period of study, it is worth noting that in the late 17th century the galley of a commander, a *capitana* could sometimes have as many as eight men to an oar. It goes without saying that the best galleys were those with the highest number of the most skilled and experienced oarsmen.

We need to make mention of the human factor too. It is now known beyond doubt that there were occasions when chained convicts and slaves rowed *alla zenzile*, a duty which was once reserved for free men. However, because both feet were chained, the rowing technique had to be adapted to the situation, so short, fast strokes were necessary. Some galley commanders were always to prefer this style of propulsion.

The new *a scaloccio* mode of rowing made the 'tuning' of the oar crew easier because a single man, the *pianero*, feathered the oar and set the pace, giving his comrades no alternative but to match the stroke rate. The *pianero* was the man who manned the inboard end of the oar, near the gangway. He was also the man who worked much harder than those nearer the hull side or thole. This factor was certainly quite important, because the new mode of rowing also required the oarsmen who were convicts or slaves to be shackled differently, by one foot only. In Venice, we should add, the use of slaves was strongly contested, officially for ethical reasons, but then finally introduced in 1545. Volunteer oarsmen from mainland territories were initially used in order to fill gaps owing to recruitment difficulties. Still, because of the discomfort encountered by these new recruits, landlubbers unused to a life at sea and unskilled as rowers, the new system of rowing was supposed to resolve this particular problem.

Because it was difficult to row properly with the old system without a lot of experienced men – *alla zenzile* rowing was a real skill – in *a scaloccio* rowing only the *pianero* was involved in setting the stroke – all that the others had to do was to pull. In other words, the shift to rowing *a scaloccio* reduced the need for experienced oarsmen. For this reason, galley fleets which depended mainly upon forced labour for rowing, such as that of Spain and the Knights Hospitaller, welcomed the new change. As Jean Marteilhe de Bergerac says of his own bench:

There are six convicts to each oar, the strongest and most vigorous always being strokesman [viz. the *pianero*], who has the hardest work. He is of the first class, the next the second class, and so on till the sixth class. This last is usually the weakest and feeblest slave on the bench.[20]

Though Marteilhe was enslaved in 1701, material conditions on the galleys hardly changed. Clearly pulling a galley oar demanded coordination and dexterity, qualities at least as important as physical force. Most important of all, perhaps, was a sense of rhythm and the ability to work with precision as part of a team. For that reason, handling the oars demanded experience and application. The oarsmen needed to prepare their bodies and toughen up the inside of their hands to get a good grasp on the oar.

The number of thwarts on each side varied considerably, but usually did not exceed twenty-four. During the first half of the 16th century the oarsmen of a *galea sottile* usually rowed *a terzarolo*: that is, sitting three to a bench and pulling individual oars of different lengths. The number of rowing benches was usually higher (up to thirty-six) in the case of the significantly larger *galea bastarda*, which in some cases reached fifty-five metres in length, seven across. The *bastarda* combined elements of the *galea sottile* and the *galea grossa*, which meant *galee bastarde* were supposed to be more seaworthy than *sottili*.[21]

The price revolution and the resulting rise in the salaries of the free oarsmen prompted the adoption of the more flexible *a scaloccio* rowing system (with five men or even more sitting on the same bench and pulling a single large oar). Despite a noticeable decrease in rowing efficiency compared with *a terzarolo* style, this reduced the need for trained free oarsmen and allowed the construction of larger and more heavily equipped and manned vessels. The number of men crammed onto the long, narrow deck of a *galea* to face the fortunes of war (and the often far more destructive fortunes of the hungry sea) could vary considerably. It could depend on purely contingent reasons, the tactical rôle and technical characteristics of the craft or the articles of the *condotta* stipulated by its commander.

The rowing gang of an average *a terzarolo* galley could amount to about 140 to 150 men. Renaissance *galee* were usually rowed by a combination of free salaried oarsmen (*buonevoglie*), convicted *forzati* and slaves. The proportions of these categories on the rowing benches of the galleys of a naval power changed according to the fleet's strategic function and, above all, the sources of manpower it could count on. Venice, for instance, preferred to use *buonevoglie* and, thanks to its *impero da mar*, was able to pursue this policy well into the 16th century. France, Spain and

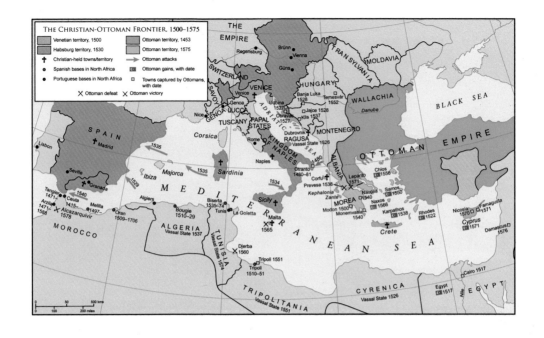

THE CHRISTIAN-OTTOMAN FRONTIER, 1500–1575

- Venetian territory, 1500
- Habsburg territory, 1530
- † Christian-held towns/territory
- ⊙ Spanish bases in North Africa
- ● Portuguese bases in North Africa
- Ottoman territory, 1453
- Ottoman territory, 1575
- → Ottoman attacks
- ☪ Ottoman gains, with date
- ☐ Towns captured by Ottomans, with date
- ✕ Ottoman defeat  ✕ Ottoman victory

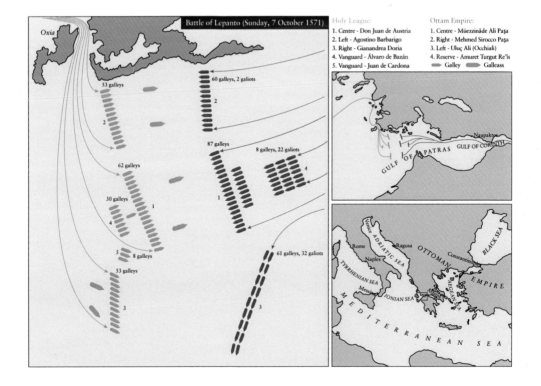

Battle of Lepanto (Sunday, 7 October 1571)

Holy League:
1. Centre - Don Juan de Austria
2. Left - Agostino Barbarigo
3. Right - Gianandrea Doria
4. Vanguard - Álvaro de Bazán
5. Vanguard - Juan de Cardona

Ottam Empire:
1. Centre - Müezzinâde Ali Paşa
2. Right - Mehmed Sirocco Paşa
3. Left - Uluç Ali (Occhiali)
4. Reserve - Amuret Turgut Re'îs

▭ Galley    ▭ Galleass

1. Portrait of the Ottoman sultan Selīm II (r. 1566–74). Selīm died just three years after the capture of Cyprus and the battle of Lepanto, fracturing his skull by slipping in his bath – ironically, while drunk on wine. (*Belli değil / Wikimedia Commons / Public Domain*)

2. Bronze statue of Miguel de Cervantes by the Mallorcan sculptor Jaume Mir Ramis (1915–2012), Cultural Park of Cervantes, Old Port, Naupaktos. (*Dimkoa / CC0 / Public Domain*)

3. Martinengo Bastion (left) and San Luca Bastion (right), northwest corner of Famagusta (Gazimağusa), viewed from the south. (*Gerhard Haubold / Wikimedia Commons / CC-BY-SA-2.5*)

4. Table altarpiece of Pius V by the Venetian artist Bartolemeo Litterini (1669–1748), Capella di San Pio V, La basilica dei Santi Giovanni e Paolo, Venice. (*Didier Descouens/Wikimedia Commons/CC-BY-SA-4.0*)

5. Milanese half armour (Wien, Kunsthistorisches Museum, inv. A 1048/49) belonging to Don Juan de Austria. Meticulously handcrafted and made-to-measure, this panoply is of polished steel and iron, gilded and etched with figurative and floral patterns. (*Vert/ Wikimedia Commons/CC0-1.0/Public Domain*)

6. Detail of the head, monument to Don Juan de Austria on Zieroldsplatz, Regensburg, Bavaria. This is a copy of the monumental sculpture (originally gilded) erected in Messina, Sicily, on the initiative of the local senate in 1572 to honour the victor of Lepanto. (*Dr Bernd Gross/ Wikimedia Commons/CC-BY-SA-3.0*)

7. In 1971, to commemorate the 400th anniversary of Lepanto, a full-sized replica of *La Real*, the Spanish galley and flagship of Don Juan de Austria, was built and displayed in the Museu Marítim de Barcelona, where it can be viewed today. (*Richard Mortel/Wikimedia Commons/CC-BY-SA-2.0*)

*Above:* 8. Wrought iron *pierrier* (Musée militaire vaudois, Morges). With their swivel mount, this type of naval piece could be pointed easily in any direction, and being a breech loader could be quickly reloaded using spare chambers. (*Hmaag/Wikimedia Commons/CC-BY-SA-3.0*)

*Left:* 9. Two bronze 5.5-pounder *sacres* (Madrid, Museo Naval), recovered from the wreck of the Spanish galleon *San Diego*, which was sunk off Fortune Island, the Philippines, on 14 December 1600. (*Dorieo/Wikimedia Commons/CC-BY-SA-4.0*)

10. Half-figure portrait of Sebastiano Veniero (or Venier) at Lepanto (Wien, Kunsthistorisches Museum, inv. GG_32), oil on canvas by the Venetian artist Jacopo Robusti, better known as Tintoretto (†1594), dated to 1578. (*Biddatenbank / Wikimedia Commons / Public Domain*)

11. Pen and black ink drawing (London, British Museum, inv. Pp, 1.19) of a seated janissary by Gentile Bellini (†1507), one of the earliest illustrations of a member of this élite corps, dated to 1480 when the Venetian artist was in Constantinople. (*Hohum / Wikimedia Commons / Public Domain*)

12. Two Ottoman *yatağanlar*, dated to the 19th century. (*Worldantiques / Wikimedia Commons / CC-BY-SA-3.0*)

13. *Don Quixote releases the Galley Slaves* (New York, Metropolitan Museum of Art, inv. 32.35[59]), one of six illustrations for *Don Quixote* by William Hogarth (1697–1764). (*Metropolitan Museum of Art / Wikimedia Commons / CC0-1.0 / Public Domain*)

14. Photograph taken on 2 April 2018 from the International Space Station (NASA Photo ID ISS055-E-008381) as it passed over western Turkey. (*Image courtesy of the Earth Science and Remote Scanning Unit, NASA Johnson Space Center*)

15. The town and port of Naupaktos, the Gulf of Corinth, and the Panachaiko massif in the Peloponnesos, viewed from the Venetian fortress. (*Conudrum / Wikimedia Commons / Public Domain*)

16. Polychrome panel (Bilbao, Museo Vasco) from a coffered ceiling, Casa-Torre de Arana, Bilbao. Part of a scene depicting a 16th-century naval battle, we can see two galleys about to come to grips. (© *Esther Carré*)

17. Spanish rapier (Bilbao, Museo Maritimo Ria de Bilbao, inv. 0242), with characteristic complex, sweeping hilt, second half 16th century. (© *Esther Carré*)

18. Half plate armour (Bilbao, Museo Maritimo Ria de Bilbao), consisting of a heavy corselet complete with gorget, pouldrons, vambraces, cubitières, gauntlets and short tassets, as well as a morion cabasset. (© *Esther Carré*)

19. *The Battle of Lepanto of 1571*, oil on canvas (Greenwich, National Maritime Museum, inv. BHC0261) by an unknown near-contemporary artist. (*Madame Grinderche / Wikimedia Commons / Public Domain*)

20. *The Allegory of the Battle of Lepanto* (c. 1572), oil on canvass (Venezia, Gallerie dell'Accademia) by Paolo Veronese (1528–88). (*Eugene a / Wikimedia Commons / Public Domain*)

Genoa, on the other hand, already relied heavily on *forzati* and slaves at the beginning of the century. A high number of free oarsmen not only considerably enhanced the effectiveness of the *a terzarolo* rowing system, which required the presence of a substantial percentage of professional rowers to coordinate the stroke, but it also limited the number of combatants it was profitable to keep on a galley at any time (because the *buonevoglie* could join the fight if needed), and it avoided the need for constant surveillance. In exceptional circumstances, if defeat entailed a worsening of their already miserable conditions, even *forzati* and slaves of different *nationi* or confessions could be persuaded to join the fight, generally in exchange for freedom.

## Pros and Cons

Rowing involves an oscillatory motion: the oar must be halted and reversed twice in each cycle. The greater the mass of the oar, therefore, the greater the amount of energy which must be expended simply to start it and stop it each time, which of course leaves less for the propulsion of the vessel. To a certain extent this problem can be solved by having a number of men pull a large oar together. But there is a limit to the increase in efficiency which this solution can offer simply because as the inboard length of the oar is increased, the length of the sweep is increased too. This means the inboard oarsmen must move more of their own body mass farther to keep up with the oar, which is energy wasted insofar as the propulsion of the vessel is concerned.

A contemporary of Vettor Fausto, Alessandro Zorzi was a member of a large family from Venice's aristocracy, and knew at firsthand the problems of rowing galleys, in which he had obviously had to serve. He lived in a key era in the history of this type of warship, an era in which the two types of rowing, *alla zenzile* and *a scaloccio*, still coexisted alongside each other, and in which attempts were made to make the galley faster and more powerful by increasing the number of oarsmen on each bench.

In his technical writings, Zorzi severely criticises *alla zenzile* rowing, which he considered to be 'un-stealthy' (the impact of the oars was noisy) and in which it was difficult to back the oars. 'Back water' in rowing terminology means to row the wrong way, a crucial manoeuvre for an oared fighting vessel, particularly when it came to a sea fight. To go about, the 'back water' command was given for one side only: starboard to go right and port to go left.

Zorzi took an interest in the comfort of the oarsmen because in his opinion this would help them to row better. Thus, for instance, he explains in great detail that it was of no use to try and squash a fourth rower on to a galley bench designed for three, that is, convert a *triremi alla zenzile* to a *quadriremi alla zenzile* by simply squeezing say an extra forty-eight oarsmen onboard. Speaking from experience afloat, he sensibly explains that the best way of rowing, in whichever of the two modes, was to give the oarsmen the maximum possible leverage. A fourth rower would have nothing but difficulties, and zero effect.

## Galley Navigation

The movement of fleets is inconceivable without charts. In the 16th century the art of finding one's way at sea was already divided in two parts: in the open ocean it was navigation, by compass and observation of latitude,[22] and inshore it was pilotage, which was mainly a matter of 'caping', or following the coast from cape to cape. The voyages which the Holy League and the Ottoman fleets foresaw called for almost nothing but pilotage.

Before we talk about pilotage, a word or two must be said about the compass of the period. There had been references to the nautical compass as early as the 12th century in Europe, with most crediting its 'invention' to the Italians, though it is likely that it came from China. In the *Roteiro*, the journal of the first voyage of Vasco da Gama to India (1497–9) kept by one of the crew – evidently somebody who had the ability to read and write as well as understand charts, maps and tables – it is referred to as the *genoisca* or Genoese needle.[23]

The 16th-century compass was very much like a modern compass, except that it was not filled with liquid and was more roughly made. The compass cards of the period however were vastly different from today. Given high illiteracy rates, instead of numbers and letters on these cards, the points were given in different shapes or colours radiating from the pivot point in the centre. The compass card was already divided into thirty-two points, and the north was marked by a *fleur-de-lys*, as it still is; but the east was marked by a cross, which had something to do with the Star of Bethlehem. To protect the needle from disturbance by the wind, a compass was mounted in a round wooden box inside a binnacle, or bittacle, in front of the helmsman, and was lit at night by a candle or oil lantern. The needle, stuck on the underneath of the card, was not a permanent magnet, and ships carried a lump of magnetic iron ore, a lodestone, which was used to 'feed' the compass from time to time by rubbing it on the needle. Eventually gimbals were added to keep the compass level during the pitching and rolling of the vessel. Rough though the compass was, it probably showed the course as accurately as a sailing ship or galley could be steered.

The Mediterranean Sea was already well-charted, with coastal outlines and wind roses to determine direction before the advent of the compass. When a navigator was approaching land, the most important and most ancient instrument was the lead. On long voyages, ships carried two different leads and lines. The dipsie (or deep-sea) lead weighed fourteen pounds, and it had a line with the astonishing length of 150 or even 200 fathoms – 1,200 feet or 365.76 metres.[24] But to use it one had to stop the ship or put off in a boat. For lesser depths, there was a lighter and handier lead of seven pounds with a shorter line, which a leadsman could use while the ship was under way. With a dipsie lead a navigator could tell when he had crossed the continental shelf and was entering pilotage waters. Both leads were 'armed' with a lump of tallow stuck in a hollow at the lower end, which picked up a sample of the sea bottom; and this, from previous experience, could tell the pilot roughly where he was. This kind of experience was recorded in books of sailing directions which the English called rutters, the Portuguese *roteiro*, from the French *routiers*. Rutters had existed for centuries in the Mediterranean, where they were known as *peripli* (sg. *periplus*, the Latinisation of the Greek word περίπλους, 'a sailing around').

These rutters were meant for coastal pilots 'caping' round the shores, and would contain vital information regarding soundings. Thus, as one English rutter reads in part:

When ye be at lxxx fadom ye shal fynde small blacke sande, and ye shall be at the towarde of Lezarde [i.e. in the longitude of the Lizard in Cornwall].

When ye be at lx or lxv ye shal fynd whyte sande, and whyte softe wormes, and ye shall be very nygh to Lezarde.[25]

Hitherto, coastal pilots had not used charts. The rutters gave them all they needed: the compass courses from cape to cape, the worst of the hidden dangers, the landmarks for entering harbours, the state of the tides in each port at full and new moon, and the navigational beacons and buoys, of which there were few. None of the information was exact – for example, the only distances given in rutters were not in nautical miles or leagues,[26] but in kennings, and a kenning was the range at which a seaman might expect to ken or recognise the coast.

Coastal navigation allowed galleys to avoid prevailing winds out to sea and to reach along the coasts with the diurnal cycle of moderate land and sea breezes on either beam. Particularly in the summer, when the land heats and cools much more rapidly than the sea by day and night respectively, onshore and offshore breezes override prevailing wind systems around most of the coasts up to twenty or so kilometres out to sea. These breezes were used from antiquity to the end of the days of sail by shipping attempting to make its way in any direction against prevailing winds, which were generally from the northwest. It must be said that winds in the Mediterranean basin are known to be highly unpredictable, even more so during our period of study, before the age of weather forecasts.

Navigation by coastal landmark was the order of the day therefore. In the clear Mediterranean summers, shipping navigated from promontory to promontory. *Peripli* were constructed around passages from island to island and promontory to promontory. Coasts with high profiles and clearly identifiable landmarks visible well out to sea provided the best conditions for navigation. Although other factors were involved, including the fact that southern coasts were generally dangerous lee shores and that the east-west current drift along the northern coasts assisted navigation from east to west, it was at least partly as a consequence of the high-profile land of the northern coasts that these were favoured above the southern coasts whenever political conditions permitted.

## The Hazards of Sea

Of course, promontories thrusting south from the mainland on the northern coasts created some of the worst conditions for galley navigation in the entire sea. As the geographer Strabo once wrote during the days of Augustus concerning Cape Malea (Gk. Ακρωτήριο Μαλέας), the eastern of the three southernmost promontories of the Peloponnesos:

> And just as in early times the Strait of Sicily was not easy to navigate, so also the high seas, and particularly the sea beyond Maleae, were not, on account of the contrary winds; and hence the proverb, 'But when you double Maleae, forget your home'.[27]

In fact, whole fleets could come to grief of Malea, as that of Kerkyra (Corfu) in the summer of 480 BC, when it was unable to round the cape against the Etesian winds (Meltemi) to join the Hellenic League fleet at Salamis.[28]

The cape has been notorious for its bad weather since time immemorial, most famously as recounted in the *Odyssey* where Homer describes how Menelaos, with Troy left in flames and ruins, was at last reunited with Helen and returning home to Sparta. The king is on the last leg of his long voyage, only to find himself blown off course by "waves that bulged and grew monstrous" as he rounds Malea, resulting in his lengthy wanderings abroad.[29] The same fate awaited homeward-bound Odysseus. In his own words he recounts, "as I turned the hook of Malea, the sea and current / and the North Wind beat me off course, and drove me on south past Kythera."[30]

The name of the cape derives from the Greek word *malerós* (μαλερός), which can mean terrible, vehement, raging, devouring, and it was a cape that caused fear and terror to sailors and is still considered amongst the most dangerous capes across the Mediterranean. In the words of Pìrì Re'ìs:

> Good friend, a storm is in fact a wind and thus it blows. But it is very strong, sometimes abnormally so. Rain storms are also known to have very strong gales. As the waves strike, the sea rises without limit. Those seeing this are amazed. Their vessels shake awesomely.

Listen now while I tell you what they can do. They are driven where
they would not go and God knows what things will happen there.
They may sink at sea or be driven onto rocks. Lord deliver them
from such a fate![31]

But even with such terrors at Cape Malea, the northern coasts were
infinitely preferable to the southern.

The low-lying coasts of the southern Mediterranean offered the worst
conditions for navigation that relied on visual observation. Their lee
shores, shoals, sandbanks, and lack of harbours and landmarks made
them extremely treacherous for shipping dependent on human muscle
and the wind for power, and on visual observation for navigation. For
galleys, low-lying coasts were even more dangerous than for sailing ships
because their masts were much smaller and consequently the range of
visibility of lookouts at their mastheads was much shorter.

It is to be expected that Mediterranean mariners were expert weather
watchers, dependent as they were on the whims of the heavens. There
is a Maltese proverb which puts it nicely into context: 'A wakeful moon,
sleeping sailors, and a sleeping moon, wakeful sailors'.[32] In brief, geography
and climatology are of overwhelming importance to the understanding of
navigation and maritime movements in the 16th-century Mediterranean.

## Galley Tactics

In the 16th century, naval warfare in the Mediterranean world was still
dominated by the galley. Indeed, Habsburg Spain was the galley power
*par excellence* among Mediterranean Christian states, and its prestige as a
*galley* power would remain greater than that of any other Mediterranean
state until France challenged and finally surpassed it late in the 17th
century. *Galeras, galeras y mas galeras* was the method of His Most
Catholic Majesty of Spain.

True, they often carried ordnance and routinely employed slaves,
captives or convicts for propulsion but essentially galley tactics were little
removed from that of the ancients, except the projecting three-bladed
waterline bronze-sheathed ram was now more likely to be a close-range
forward-firing salvo of cannon fire briskly followed by boarding and

entering. In reality, the ram was no ram at all, more like a sharp spur to damage the opponent's upper works thereby forming a useful boarding bridge for the attackers. On the galleys of most nations it was well above the waterline and angled upward slightly and had a reinforced iron-shod tip. If the spur, *sperone*, could be lodged forcefully in the light upper planking of an enemy galley it would ride up and over the gunwales and give the boarding party an all-important height advantage in launching their assault. Once their vessel had crashed into an enemy, they would swarm across and slaughter its crew hand to hand. Thus, it was deemed better to clear and capture vessels than to sink them. The violence was sharply concentrated.

The French-speaking chronicler Jean Froissart (†1410) wrote in an earlier age that sea-fights were always murderous. At Lepanto, as at most earlier naval encounters, the fleets met like armies. Their formation was rigid; the commands were military; and tactics were based upon experience by land. In this respect, Lepanto would be the last great battle of the mediaeval-type navies that had the character of its predecessors. In this fight at close quarters on the narrow space afforded by the galleys' decks there was no question of surrender on either side, no thought but of which could strike the hardest and kill the most. Nor could men, striving hand to hand in the confusion of the floating mêlée, know anything of what was being done beyond their limited range of view, so that even the captains became for the moment only leaders of small groups of combatants. "Sea-fights", wrote Froissart, "are always fiercer than fights on land, because retreat and flight are impossible; every man is obliged to hazard his life and hope for success, relying on his own personal bravery and skill."[33] In a sea-fight, every man faced the same danger at the same time. Gunpowder had made the biggest difference though, both from the point of view of shipboard artillery, which we will discuss in the next chapter, and that of personal firearms.

Combat tactics at sea, lacking the possibility of the broadside and therefore the notion of a stand-off slugging match with cannon, bore a recognisable resemblance to tactics on land. Indeed, even though the skilfulness of naval gunners was generally considered to be superior to that of their land colleagues, the poor accuracy and low rate of fire of 16th-century ordnance usually meant that during an engagement between two galleys there was only time for a limited exchange of volleys at a very close range, while each ship rushed forward trying to gain an angle of attack that would maximize the effects of the discharge of its own bow guns, and at the same time minimise the damage caused by the enemy's.

The accuracy and therefore the lethal effect of gunfire shot from one moving (and probably rolling or listing) ship at another are easily overestimated. To improve it and to reduce the pulsating motion of a ship at speed under oar, speeds would probably have been deliberately kept low, but sufficient for steerage. The accuracy of a volley would have been greater in direction than in range, so a target ship which is head-on to the bow guns was more likely to be hit somewhere along its length than a target lying at an angle to the line of shot. Thus galleys approaching in line abreast would be good targets.

The objective was not to sink the enemy vessel (a rare occurrence), but to gain some advantage in the boarding and ensuing violent mêlée across rolling or listing blood-soaked decks, which would eventually decide the outcome of the battle. Even when the results of these initial volleys were spectacularly devastating and bloody they were rarely decisive, and in some cases it made better sense to renounce the penetration power of iron or stone cannonballs and load the main guns *a mitraglia* (with scatter shots), because the target was not the ship itself, but the people that thronged its deck. Even the long, heavy spurs mounted on the prows of early modern galleys were designed not to pierce the hull of an enemy vessel and compromise its seaworthiness, but rather to smash the fighting and rowing structures which were built upon it, lock the two ships and provide the boarding parties with a breach and a bridge to reach it.

In his firsthand account of the life of a galley slave at the turn of the 18th century Jean Marteilhe (1684–1777), a French Protestant condemned to the galleys of Louis XIV from 1701 to 1713 for his faith, has this to say regarding boarding and entering:

> This presented a chance of boarding, for the manoeuvre of a galley to board a ship is to bring the bow of the galley against the stern of the ship (its weakest part). The whole strength of a galley is in her bows, and here she has the greatest part of her artillery. She therefore endeavours to force her bows into the enemy's stern, firing her five guns, before her crew scramble on board.[34]

The practice may have been for the boarders to spring towards the victim at the last moment just before contact was made. Making fast by grappling irons on short lengths of chain (to prevent grappling ropes from being cut immediately) must have called for much skill not only to grapple successfully but also to prevent those doing it (obvious targets in trying to defeat the action) from being shot by those defending the other galley. Downward fire from masts would have added to the casualties on the other side.

Another major consequence of the increased need to protect the highly-vulnerable sides and stern, which was the command centre of the galley, from the fire of the bow guns was the adoption of a battle array that was much more rigid and tight than was the case in the past. During engagements between squadrons, galleys laboriously formed a compact line-a-breast formation with the prows facing the enemy and advanced slowly, following a pace and a course of attack set by the *galea capitana* (the flagship, usually positioned in the middle of the line) and keeping to a minimum any adjustments and changes of direction that might easily disrupt the battle array.

Every galley protected the sides of its neighbours, and ships and squadrons caught astray in dispersed order were easy prey, while an overextended or broken formation offered the enemy the chance to slip some of its vessels through and crush the squadron, one galley after another. After two lines abreast had collided and boarding fights had begun, it was almost impossible for galleys to disengage from combat, and defeat therefore entailed the loss, by capture or sinking, of most of the force committed to battle.

In small galley actions and naval operations of relatively limited size the outcome of a possible fight was usually easy to foresee. In fact, unless the surprise was total, it was difficult to force a group of galleys to a general engagement when the odds were clearly against them. Moreover, naval combat in the Mediterranean was almost always a means and not an end. The preservation of the ships, their precious manpower and the harbour facilities was of paramount importance, whereas the advantages that could ensue from control of the sea (as we mean it today) after the destruction of an enemy fleet were negligible.

## Galleass

The galleass deserves a word. The first galleass, *galeazza* (pl. *galeazze*), was laid down in the Arsenale di Venezia in about 1550. Utilising the now redundant *galee grosse*, of which at least ten had been laid up in the Arsenale some years previously because they were economically non-viable, the deck equipment of the *galea grossa* was made over by Gian Andrea Badoer so as to make it better fitted for battle. It was fifty metres long (as against the forty-one metres of the Venetian war galley, the *galea sottile*) and nine metres wide (ditto, five to six metres), making it longer than a *galea sottile* and with a much more spacious and seaworthy hull. It was propelled by sails as well as oars, with twenty-six banks and probably six oarsmen on the same bench pulling the same heavy oar. The galleass had three masts, besides the so-called *bompresso*, or bowsprit, which jutted out of the bow; the sails were all lateen.

More importantly, the galleass was far better armed. We know for certain that the four Neapolitan galleasses that sailed with the Armada of 1588 carried an average of five whole cannon, two or three demi-cannon (not the small swivel guns which went by the same name), eight *pedreros* of indeterminate calibre, four demi-culverins, seven *sacres*, four half-*sacres* and around twenty sizable swivel pieces apiece.[35] It would seem, therefore, that the standard galleass carried in effect five times as much ordinance as a *galea sottile*, which meant it carried a load of artillery fearsome to other galleys.

There is no reason to doubt that the Venetian galleasses at Lepanto were just as well endowed with ordnance. An anonymous observer who served with the Holy League fleet in 1572 estimated that each of the Venetian galleasses at Lepanto bore thirty pieces of artillery.[36] That very same year, Cosimo I de' Medici wrote a letter discussing "how to *armare* a *galeazza* like the ones utilised by the Venetians at the battle of Lepanto", including everything from timber and sails to artillery. He estimated these mighty gunships bore forty-two artillery pieces: two 50-pounders,[37] eight 30-pounders, eight 20-pounders, fourteen 6-pounders, and eight 3-pounders.[38] Actually, as we shall see shortly, while Venice had an adequate supply of suitable cannon, the six Venetian galleasses at Lepanto did not carry a standard armament.

There is one other tactical factor to consider with regards to the galleass. Because of the greater deck space aboard a galleass and because all the heavy ship-killing ordnance was not pointed immovably forward, it could be more effectively employed in battle. The shelter which the high freeboard and protective superstructures offered the gunners allowed them to reload and continue firing even after a boarding fight had been joined in earnest. Even so, the high freeboard would have impeded boarding parties.

The galleass soon proved its worth. At Lepanto the Ottomans mistook the Venetian galleasses for merchant supply vessels and paid a heavy price for their error.[39] And as for those four galleasses from Naples that sailed with the duque de Medina Sidonia, though only one made it back to Spain, they proved formidable in action during the fire fights up the English Channel.

A single *galeazza* fully equipped for war cost Venice the princely sum of 120,000 *ducati*, while its actual upkeep for war came to 26,000 *ducati*, this sum being exclusive of the money needed for gunpowder and other ammunition.

## Galiot

Next we should look at the smaller relative of the *galea sottile*, namely the *galeotte*, galiot. The galiot was classed as a warship. It was a smaller, swifter version of the galley, usually furnished with fourteen to eighteen rowing benches on each side of the vessel and rowed two by two, *alla scaloccio*, and very similar to it structurally. The galiot was a double ended open boat, very swift, much lower in the water, having one mast rigged with a lateen sail and a decorated *carosse* or stern cabin. It normally carried one gun on the bows, larger enough to count (probably larger than a *sacre*) and it was not provided with a raised fighting platform, but the galiot would carry also heavy muskets and perriers.

This is confirmed by a Spanish report of 1561 from a Spaniard who had been captured, served as a galley slave on one of the four galiots of the paşa of Vélez in Barbary. Of the four galiots, the paşa's *capitana* of twenty-one banks carried a centreline bow gun of "thirty-eight *quintales*" (1,723.68 kg); the *patrona*, also of twenty-one banks, carried a centreline piece which was only slightly smaller; the third galiot, of eighteen banks, carried a piece of "twenty-five *quintales*" (1,134 kg); and the fourth galiot, of seventeen banks, carried no artillery at all.[40] The two largest galiots thus carried a centreline bow gun equivalent to a small whole cannon or a very large demi-culverin, while the third carried a piece as large as a demi-culverin. Evidently, one cannot be too dogmatic about the relative sizes and armament of this type of vessel.

The mast of a galiot was easily lowered and such a manoeuvre was intended to confuse the enemy when approaching. It should be mentioned that the simple but highly-efficient lateen rig permitted fast handling by few members of the crew.

It is interesting to note that a galiot was partially decked at the bows and the stern; a *corsia* or raised gangway ran all along its centre between the rowing benches. Like all other lateen rigs the galiot did not carry a figurehead. It was equipped with a *caïque* (Ottoman Turkish *qayïq*), a round hulled tender for the normal carrying of water, firewood, personnel or when approaching very shallow waters; lowering duties pertained to the *caïque* also. Each member of the crew on a galiot had to be an oarsman, a marine and a mariner as dictated by the prevailing changing exigencies. In the fighting mode, the crew relied on their composite recurve bows and harquebuses.

Most of the time a galiot moved from one destination to another under sail; the crew would man the oars when chasing or escaping from an enemy. To lessen the fatigue for the oarsmen the hull of the galiot was projected with V shape frames. Due to the restricted space on a galiot – the crew had to stay in the open without a shelter over their head for the whole duration of an operation or cruise against the enemy – a tarpaulin was provided which was only rigged up on rainy days.

The rôle of a galiot was primarily that of a corsair ship – it was an ideal vessel to wait in ambush for fat merchantmen – but it was utilised also for reconnaissance missions and to link up information between galleys at sea. Although a galiot was never posted in the vanguard in a conflict at sea because of its size and restricted firing power, it was utilised as a support ship and for small operations near enemy territory. Its shallow draught facilitated operations in shallow waters where galleys or other great ships would not dare to approach. This attribute was particularly important in what we recognise as little wars, raids upon coasts and commerce, which could directly weaken a nation economically and militarily.

Similar but smaller than the galiot was the *fusta* (the term is of Italian origin), an agile and economic vessel which had ten to fifteen rowing benches on each side and a single lateen-rigged sail on a single mast. Like galiots, a *fusta* was rowed two by two *alla scaloccio* and they carried a single centreline gun. Corsairs likewise preferred the *fusta* because its size and speed made it effective for surprise raids or attacks.

*Chapter 13*

# The Guns

[A]nd the nimble gunner / With linstock now the devilish cannon
touches.

William Shakespeare, *Henry V*, 3.0.32–3

Thec placement of the pieces on a *galea* and their calibre were
dictated by the long and narrow shape of the vessel. In fact, it
mirrored what had always been the distribution of the offensive
and defensive potential on a galley since the times of the classical triremes.
The main battery was set in the bow, where most of the galley's fighting
potential was concentrated, while the platform built upon the stern, which
housed the command, steering and signalling functions, and the long
central section (with the benches of the rowers all placed diagonally on
a single level) were the galley's vulnerable parts. Provided that it had the
chance – that is, unless it had been somehow outmanoeuvred or simply
outnumbered – a galley always attacked and faced attacks with its bow
turned towards the enemy ship. By increasing their frontal destructive
capabilities, cannons emphasised, so to speak, the traditional strengths
and weaknesses of oared war vessels. As a result of these changes, by the
fifteen-twenties the *galea grossa*, whose size had become a problem rather
than an advantage, were replaced by the smaller *galea sottile*, which lacked
the cargo hold of the former, and in so doing devoted most of its space
to the oarsmen. For almost a century, the *galea sottile* offered the optimal
combination of speed under oars, seaworthiness, agility, firepower and
manpower.

Far from being the direct cause of the decline of Mediterranean galley
warfare, as has been frequently inferred in the past, effective heavy
ordnance was integrated remarkably early and with considerable success.
It seems that by the end of the fifteen-twenties a fairly common solution
was to equip a galley with a main centreline gun flanked by at least one

pair of lighter pieces. The bow of the flagship of Filippino Doria (†1531), presumably the best equipped galley of the Doria family fleet, was armed in 1528 with a centreline *basilisco* (probably a long whole cannon of cast bronze, which threw cast-iron balls of approximately 20 kilograms), two *medios canônes* (demi-cannon, large swivel guns), two *sacres* and two *falconetti* (also swivel guns but smaller). In addition to the main battery, the stern, the sides and the bow of a war galley sometimes also housed a variable number of small calibre swivel guns like *moschiette*. This level of armament was only a short step from that of the galleys that fought at Lepanto.

A mixed Venetian-Genoese fleet was providing support to the advancing Valois army, the Genoese under Filippino Doria – he was the son of Andrea Doria – even defeating a Spanish naval force off Capo d'Orso on 28 May 1528. It was there that the Doria flagship fired what was probably one of the most famous cannon shots of the 16th century. As the *capitana* of Don Ugo de Moncada rushed towards that of Filippino Doria, the ball fired by the centreline *basilisco* of the latter's galley ran through the *rembata* or forecastle, literally clearing the gangway between the rowing benches, which was crammed with soldiers, and smashed against the *spalliera*, instantly killing the galley's second-in-command and most of the officers around him, while the other smaller pieces decimated the oarsmen. Almost forty men died immediately, smearing the survivors with blood and entrails.[1] The riposte of Moncada's ship, on the other hand, caused little damage to Filippino's *capitana*, which had altered its angle of approach immediately after discharging its main battery under cover of the resulting cloud of smoke.

## Terminology

Guns, of which the Christian fleet at Lepanto held a two-to-one advantage,[2] are even harder to compare than galleys, primarily because cannon of the 16th century inherited a mediaeval system of naming and classification. This traditional nomenclature was complex, imprecise, and often confusing, especially considering the wide range of calibres and lengths extant in the period before standardisation came about in the 18th century. Consider, for example, the fact that Henry VIII used no less than eleven different calibres at his siege of Boulogne in the summer of 1544. What is more, in the Tudor period alone there were at least twelve types of culverin (large, small, ordinary, extraordinary, bastard, special, and so forth), five types of demi-cannon, five types of saker, and a multitude of others, often with mythological or zoomorphic (usually avian or reptilian) names such as falcons, robinets, pelicans, sparrows, basilisks, lizards, fowlers, minions, murderers and double-murderers, serpentines, drakes (dragons), syrens, apostles, and even shrimps. Most of these were made of bronze.

Likewise, the Venetian classification was different from those used by the other Italian and European states: names like demi-culverin, demi-cannon, *medios canones*, *medios legitimos*, *bastardos*, *aculebrinados*, *couleuvrine extraordinaire*, *canon légère*, *couleuvrine bâtarde léger*, and so forth, were never employed by the Republic. On the contrary, the Venetians fielded (in local weight) the 1-pounder *moschetto da zuogo*, the 3-pounder *falconetto*, the 6-pounder *falcone*, the 12-pounder *aspide* and *sacro* (saker), both having a calibre of 95 to 100 millimetres, the latter being a foot longer than the former. Larger pieces were the 14- to 60-pounder *cannone* (cannon) and *colubrine* (culverin), the latter being a third longer than the former. Venetian cannon, regarded by contemporary experts as the best in the Mediterranean,[3] were markedly shorter and lighter than equivalent Spanish or Ottoman pieces, making them easier to handle under combat conditions. They were invariably functional in design and entirely devoid of the elaborate raised ornamentation characteristic of many of the best German, Spanish and Portuguese guns.

Sufficient will have been said in this rapid sketch to show that the classification of guns in the period under discussion was somewhat erratic. As Michael Lewis framed it in his *Armada Guns*, "the major subtleties of Elizabethan ordnance classification ... nothing less than a full-dress monograph could deal". This is due principally to "the careless and erratic nomenclature employed by the contemporary writers, and, probably, by the contemporary gunners, and even the gun-founders. Names are bandied about from piece to piece in a most bewildering way."[4] A classic example is when Englishmen call falcons 'minions', but in the Venetian and Italian classification, owing to their calibre, they are more properly termed 'falcons'. Likewise, when an Englishman speaks of a 'cannon' he means a type of gun a Spaniard would describe as a *cañón de batir*, that is, a battery piece throwing a 40- to 50-pound shot. But to a Spaniard the term *cañón* meant something different: it was a relatively short-barrelled gun (25 calibres or less in length) firing 28- to 35-pound shot. An Englishman would have called guns of this type 'demi-cannon'. The same could be said of any nation in our period of study.

## Classification

Despite the complex terminology and diverse range of sizes, the basic classification of muzzle-loading ordnance in the 16th century was essentially quite simple. The four main classes – the culverin, the cannon, the perrier, and the mortar – were based on the ratio of calibre to length, thus 26 calibres long equated to twenty-six times the bore diameter.[5]

The longest guns, with a 32 to 34 calibre to bore ratio (sometimes as high as 40 or more), were called culverins. The culverin class (from the Latin *colubra*, a snake, thus It. *colubrina*, Fr. *couleuvre*, Sp. *culebrina*) covered a wide range of calibres (from 1.5 to 5.5 inches) and included the culverin itself (which fired an 18-pound shot) as well as demi-culverins (9-pound shot) and their kin, the sakers (5.5- to 9-pound shot), minions (4-pound shot), falcons (2.5- to 3-pound shot), falconets (1.25- to 1.5-pound shot), and robinets (less than 1-pound shot). The long barrel of the culverin family made the culverin a high velocity weapon that could – if handled well – be very accurate and have a great range, and they were used on both ships and (the smaller types) as field artillery. It must be remembered, however, that terms like whole cannon, demi-cannon, demi-culverin, and bastard culverin were never used in Venice.

Although modern commentators argue that longer barrels did not produce longer ranges,[6] the Venetian naval commander Cristoforo Canal and his contemporaries knew better. One of these, the famous Italian metallurgist Vannoccio Biringuccio (1480–1539), explains that the length of the barrel set the limit on the amount of gunpowder, a gun loaded with more gunpowder than its barrel allowed would eject some of it unburned.[7] Thus, longer barrels used more gunpowder, which produced higher muzzle velocities and longer ranges. Canal gives the specifics: a 50-pounder culverin could shoot to 650 *passi*, (1,140 metres) and

50-pounder cannon could shoot to 550 *passi* (960 metres).[8] For the sake of brevity, the culverin family were made with barrels that were long, thin and of small calibre, and had a longer range than the cannon family, although their shot was smaller.

The next longest type, the whole cannon, or 'cannon of battery' (Sp. *cañón de batir*), were relatively short-barrelled (15 to 28 calibres long), large-bored, low velocity guns that fired heavy (up to 50-pound) shot with great force at relatively close range. Fully exploiting the power of gunpowder, what they lost in range and accuracy, they gained in destructive power. Originally intended as battering pieces to use against fortifications, they were rare on ships in the period with which we are concerned here. Subdivisions of this class included the cannon-royal, cannon-of-seven, cannon, demi-cannon, and, in the Spanish services, the thirds-of-cannon (*tercias*) and quarter-cannon.

A well-preserved example of this family is the bronze siege gun, *cañón de batir*, recovered from the Spanish Armada ship *La Trinidad Valencera* in the broad sandy bay of Kinnagoe, on the Inishowen Peninsula of North Donegal, Ireland, on 16 September 1588. Firing a 40-pound shot, it has a calibre of 183 millimetres, weighs 5,186 Castilian *libras* (2,904 kg), and is 2.90 metres in length. Intended for a land siege of London, even on a vessel of the size of *La Trinidad Valencera*, which was the refitted and refurbished (and renamed) 1,100-tonne (1,212.5 tons) Venetian armed merchantman *La Balanzara*, commandeered and pressed into service as a supply transport ship,[9] the cannon was probably unsuited to shipboard use. The fourth largest ship in the fleet, on board she carried three such siege guns, a matching set donated by Philip II and cast in 1556 by the renowned Flemish gun founder Remigy de Halut (†1568), *fondeur royale* at Mechelen (Fr. Malines) gun foundry near Antwerp in the Low Countries. These brazen monsters were emblazoned with Philip's royal arms combined with the English ones of his wife Mary Tudor, queen of England. A fourth siege gun was a huge Turkish piece, possibly a prize from Lepanto seventeen years before.

*La Trinidad Valencera* carried a listed armament of forty-two guns in all, of unspecified type and size, four of which have been recovered. These are an Italian bronze 6-pounder *sacre*, 3.45 metres in length with a calibre of 90 millimetres and cast by Giovanni (Zuane) II Alberghetti (identified by the presence of the initials Z A on its chase),[10] an Italian bronze *media culebrina* 3.25 metres in length with a calibre of 118 millimetres, a bronze *falcon pedrero* 2.92 metres in length with a calibre of 72 millimetres and cast by Niccolò di Conti II, and a bronze *petriere da braga* with an iron *braga*.[11] Unbelievably, this gun was found fully loaded with a stone shot in the barrel and a fine-grained powder charge in the *braga*; it was therefore ready for action, just as its gunner had left it in 1588. The Alberghetti and di Conti families held at the time a monopoly of bronze artillery production in Venice, and these guns must have been part of the merchantman's original armament.

The next class were the short and stubby perriers, which usually measured between six and eight calibres in length. The perrier had a relatively large bore, and fired a heavy shot at a low velocity. As the name implies (*petriera*, 'stone-thrower'), these pieces were originally intended to fire stone shots, which, contrary to perceived wisdom, did not tend to shatter on impact with a wooden hull, though by the turn of the 17th century cast-iron shot would be the norm. Some perrier were breech-loaders, such as those in Venice, which were usually of the swivel gun kind, the so-called *petriere da mascolo* and *petriere da braga*, an example of the last, as already noted, was recovered from the wreck of the *La Trinidad Valencera* (née *La Balanzara*). Venetian galleys were armed with several 6- or 12-pound *petriere*, each one provided with three chambers to enable rapid firing. Mounted on its swivel, a perrier was quicker to swab out and it could be turned around by one or two men. Firing a 24-pound shot, the cannon-perrier was the largest member of this family, a ship-smasher in fact, and smaller pieces included port-pieces, slings, and fowlers. All of the perriers would become obsolete by the mid-17th century, though similarly-stubby howitzers and carronades would take their place in the mid-18th century.

This brings us to swivel guns, which are believed to derive from the smallest of the perriers, the sling.[12] These were small, one-man, close-range, anti-personnel weapons designed either to sweep an enemy's deck immediately before a boarding action or, should the galley herself be boarded, to bring down enfilading fire across her own decks. They were commonly mounted on the bow fighting platform, the *spalliera*, and along the rails of galleys.[13] They could be packed with odd bits and pieces of iron, marble, stone and other such lethal projectiles, and when this scattershot was fired, a frightening hail would whiz along the deck of the enemy vessel. As the name implies, their trunnions rotated vertically within a swivel yoke bracket that was itself mounted to rotate horizontally. A long tiller extended from the rear of the gun by which the gunner aimed and held it.

Swivel guns were quite frequently made of wrought iron and were usually breech-loaders, using easily removable chambers (like tankards with handles) with touchholes and containing the gunpowder and closed by wooden wadding. A stone shot or scattershot was placed in the barrel. The chamber was narrower at one end to make insertion easier and so that it would not wobble when in position.[14] It was then locked in place by a wooden or metal wedge. These wedges had to be hammered in position in order to force the chamber hard up against the barrel and to prevent its sudden ejection after firing.[15] Each weapon was equipped with at least two chambers and so the firing rate was superior in comparison with similar calibre muzzle-loaders. They were known by several names, sometimes 'murder' in English, *pierrier à boîte* in French, *berços* in Portuguese, and *versos* in Spanish. Interestingly, the Japanese called the swivel gun a 'child cannon' (子砲).[16] Finally, composite (viz. wrought iron and cast bronze) swivel guns, known as *petriere da braga* in Venice and *smerigli petrieri alla veneziana* in Genoa, were seemingly manufactured only in Venice and Genoa.[17]

The final class, mortars, were the shortest of the muzzle-loaders at 1.5 to 3 calibres in length. The direct descendants of large-bore mediaeval bombards, mortars were large calibre, low velocity artillery designed to fire the largest and heaviest projectiles at the highest possible trajectories, in order to drop them on targets from above. Because of this they were most commonly used as siege weapons, though occasionally small versions were used as field artillery. They were not normally used in ship-to-ship engagements.[18]

## International Arms Trade

Depressing as it may seem, today's international arms trade and weapons technology also had a mirror image in our period of study. Buying and selling guns was an international trade, although it was sometimes contraband, *merces prohibitae*. Elizabeth of England, for instance, was to forbid the export of guns, but in 1587 disloyal merchants would illegally smuggle 140 bronze culverins out to Naples, thereby allowing Philip of Spain to dismount many larger pieces from the Naples fortifications to fortify his Armada ships.[19] By the following decade the production of cast iron artillery for use by the Elizabethan navy and for export was booming, a result of the positive publicity which the iron 18-pounder culverin and 32-pounder demi-cannon had received in the damaging defeat of the Armada. Incidentally, the Spaniards were unable to cast iron guns of equal size until well into the 17th century. Cast iron guns from Spanish foundries, if they were not heavy, blew up during testing, and, if they were heavy, proved unwieldy for shipboard use.

Already in the mid-15th century, European founders had attempted to cast iron guns but with no success. A breakthrough came in 1543 during Tudor England's preparation for war with Valois France. When Henry VIII could no longer afford bronze guns produced in the Low Countries, he supported domestic founding based upon extensive reserves of iron ore from the Weald. The cast iron guns that the English manufactured, for reasons that are still not altogether clear, were relatively reliable, though initially heavier than equivalent bronze guns. Until the end of the 16th century, the English held a virtual monopoly on the mass production of trustworthy cast iron guns. England's technological success soon led to economic success.

At the moment, war was stimulating business. By the end of the century certain English gun foundries were even selling to the Spanish, so much so that Sir Walter Raleigh was moved to protest in the House of Commons:

> "I am sure heretofore one ship of Her Majesty's was able to beat ten Spaniards, but now, by reason of our own ordnance we are hardly matched one to one".[20]

Likewise, the English created for themselves a lucrative trade with the Ottoman Turks in materials for war, especially with regards to tin, an essential but difficult to acquire ingredient for the manufacture of artillery. An English ship is mentioned as being at Livorno in 1573 with a cargo of tin, broken bells and ingots of lead, all materials that were used for the production of cannon and shot. The French ambassador to Constantinople, Jacques de Germigny, notes that in 1580 the English brought to the Sublime Porte plenty of steel, broken images, bronze and brass for the casting of cannon. The broken bells and images, of course, came from the monasteries and churches in England despoiled during the Reformation. Two years later the Spanish ambassador to London, Don Bernardino de Mendoza (1540–1604), is reported to have told Philip II that the English sent large amounts of broken bells and images, tin and lead, which the Ottomans brought "almost for its weight in gold, the tin being vitally necessary for the casting of guns and the lead for the purposes of war".[21] At a time when we talk too lightly about the international arms trade, as if it was a recent business, it may come as a surprise to say the Anglo arms trade is no new thing, for in Elizabethan England it had become a booming business.

Yet there is perhaps one glaring difference for us to think about. Today arms sales can never be apolitical. They do not just provide military support; they also send a clear endorsement and have gone hand in hand with a fawning and uncritical support for the odious regimes that can afford them. One highlight to date: arms-selling governments usually show their deadly wares at arms fairs. I am not so sure this was the case in the period with which we are concerned here. Take the Dutch for instance. In late 1588, following the Armada alarm, Elizabeth I wanted the government of the United Provinces to prohibit trade with the enemy. Yet on this particular point her envoy met with the usual tactics of the Dutch when faced with uncomfortable requests: delay and evasion. They were never eager to restrict commerce, even when it involved the enemy, for they knew their strength lay in the profits of trade, particularly in arms, and believed their gains outweighed those of the Spanish.

### Bronze versus Iron

Mediaeval names of guns were more or less the same in every European language – some even in Arabic too. One can be sure that what the Spaniards called a *culebrina*, the French a *couleuvrine* and the English a culverin, was substantially the same beast. If truth be told, as we have just alluded to, they all came from the same foundries, mainly in Italy, the Low Countries and England – the guns of Philip II of Spain, for instance, were all cast in Italy, the Low Countries or England.[22] In fact, just as it is the state of affairs at present, the international arms trade was controlled by just a few players.

The best of these guns were cast in bronze, a technique that had long been used for church bells, and the resemblance between gun and bell, both metal cylinders with hollow cores, did not escape the notice of the gun makers: molten metal was poured into a mould that was broken when the metal had cooled. The iron ones can be divided into those made of wrought iron and those realised by fusion cast. Forged wrought iron had offered a cheaper alternative to bronze casting. Wrought iron is a two-component metal consisting of high purity iron and iron silicate – an inert, non-rusting slag similar to glass. These two materials are merely mixed and not chemically joined as in an alloy. But guns wrought in iron were not so strong or accurate. Thus, the most powerful guns had to be cast, not hand-wrought, and as cast iron guns were overly heavy or dangerously unreliable, bronze (generally known by English contemporaries as 'brass') was the material of choice throughout the 16th century. Though the *Mary Rose* (built 1509–10, launched July 1511, sunk 19 July 1545, raised 11 October 1982), a 700-ton/635-tonne (after the 1536 enlargement), 96-gun, four-masted carrack-type warship of the Tudor navy of Henry VIII, displayed a marked diversity of bronze and iron ordnance,[23] by 1569 the decision was made to equip the Elizabethan navy entirely with cast bronze guns.[24] Thus, as late as September of 1595, less than twenty per cent of English naval guns (188 of 977) were cast from iron.[25]

Although cast iron guns became lighter and shorter over time and always had economic advantages, the process required years to perfect. Well into the 16th century, most European and Mediterranean naval powers continued to equip their vessels with wrought iron and cast bronze guns. Even the English fleet late in the reign of Henry VIII had far more wrought iron pieces in the inventories: the Anthony Rolls of 1546 and a manuscript account of 1548 list over 1,700 wrought iron pieces out of a total of 2,008 guns.[26]

The main disadvantage of cast bronze guns was their price, which was generally three to four times higher than iron guns. Other than expense, however, bronze guns were still superior to iron ones in almost every way. Bronze was stronger, withstood the shock of discharge better, and lasted longer at sea. Bronze also was easier to cast, could be re-cast, and guns of bronze could be easily embellished with elegant decoration such as ornament in relief and the coats of arms of their proud owners, and attachments such as dolphins. The plunging sea beasts, cast integral with the barrel, formed loops of bronze perfect for the function of serving as carrying handles. Because of this last quality, along with their hefty price tag, guns in gleaming bronze invariably served as status symbols. Yet, the care lavished on the inscribing and embellishment of large bronze pieces still bore witness to the earlier instinct that guns did not only communicate prestige but could have a mysterious personality of their own.

Despite the fact that bronze is twenty per cent heavier than iron, bronze guns were lighter than their counterparts because the stronger metal could be used to make thinner guns of the same calibre. One especially salient advantage was that bronze guns were less likely to break while firing, and when they did the barrel usually bulged or split open longitudinally at the breech rather than explode. When iron guns burst they did so without warning and with a tendency to shatter and fly to pieces, which caused much more catastrophic damage to nearby personnel.[27] Little wonder, therefore, gunners regarded iron guns with grave suspicion.

The sole disadvantage of bronze as a gun founding material was its propensity to heat up quickly, which meant that when firing a great number of shots in continuous action it was prone to becoming soft and susceptible to sagging or other bore damage. However that may be, due to the nature of 16th-century naval tactics this defect was not readily apparent.

Amusingly, since both contained large quantities of valuable bronze, bells and guns exchanged form with each other from time to time over the decades. A peace treaty, for instance, could witness obsolete battlefield cannon re-formed into church bells. In 1506 pope Julius II personally led, as overlord of the city, a papal army to Bologna to drive out its disobedient despot Giovanni II Bentivoglio. Part of the papal spoils was a great bell, which Michelangelo melted down in 1508 to cast a four-metre high portrait of the fighting pope,[28] which he placed over the portal of the Basilica di San Petronio, the main church of Bologna. Alfonso d'Este, the duca di Ferrara (r. 1505–34), a skilled artillerist nicknamed *Il Bombardiere* (he had selected a bomb as his personal emblem), got hold of the statue three years later and, heartbreakingly for the Renaissance master, had it melted down so as to cast a massive cannon that he cheekily christened *Giulia* and added it to his celebrated train of artillery.[29] Ferrara, by the way, was a papal fief.

## Composition

Copper by itself is of course too soft for use in ordnance, but the addition of the right proportion of tin produces a tenacious alloy harder than either constituent, and with a melting point somewhat lower than that of copper but considerably higher than that of tin. The great advantage of bronze ordnance was its strength; its disadvantage (besides expense) was its aforementioned tendency to heat up quickly, meaning that it could not sustain rapid firing over a long period of time.

While this study uses the technically correct term 'bronze' for the copper/tin alloy used by historic gun founders, the word 'brass' was that in general use until the eighteen-forties, when – ironically – the ordnance in question was nearing obsolescence. French terminology could be even more confusing, as contemporary manuscripts used *cuivre* interchangeably for both pure copper and for bronze. A related term was 'gun-metal', which meant a specific alloy of (usually) ninety-one per cent copper and nine per cent tin, while 'bell-metal' specified seventy to seventy-eight per cent copper and twenty-two to thirty per cent tin. Gun founders sometimes added other metals, usually brass, that is true brass, an alloy of copper and zinc, or latten, a brassy alloy with copper, zinc, and an often heavy proportion of lead.

It is well known that Venetian gun founders added ten per cent in weight of brass to the liquefied copper and tin. The brass (*laton* in Venice) was produced by melting copper and zinc ore calamine (*giallamina*): pure metallic zinc was isolated only in 1746.[30] In this way zinc and silicon was added to the alloy, resulting in a less porous, harder and more resistant metal. In a document of the 16th century we can actually read: "If you want to cast artillery you need for every thousand pounds of copper eighty pounds of tin and one hundred pounds of brass."[31] According to a manuscript written by Giulio Savorgnan del Friuli, bronze alloy was prepared with copper and eight to twelve per cent of tin, but "In Venice they add ten per cent of brass to improve the melt as the copper is not as perfect as the one used in Germany."[32] Generally speaking, high-grade bronze with a nine-to-one copper to tin ratio is most suitable for a weapon like cannon due to the alloy's high resistance to wear, high hardness, and moderate strength.

## Range

We casually speak of short-range and long-range guns, but the figures for range in this period are extremely varied. For one thing, range had to be judged – which meant guessed. Another thing, the range of a gun depended on the quality of the gunpowder (more of which below), and also on the windage – the difference between the diameters of the shot and the bore, which might be as much as half-an-inch. So every gun and every shot was different. For another thing, the range was measured in paces, and nobody knows for sure what Spanish gunners meant by a pace – and perhaps even then there was no exact definition of it.[33]

Point-blank range (from the Spanish *punto de blanco*, pointed at the target), of course, was the distance at which a gunner could point his gun at the enemy and fire without much regard for elevation. The gunner simply aligned the top of the barrel directly with the target. This system, called sighting by-the-line-of-metals (*por el raso de los metales* in Spanish), continued to be used almost exclusively by naval gunners everywhere until the second decade of the 19th century, an eloquent commentary on the intrinsic inaccuracy of smooth-bore artillery. The records of Venice's test-firing programme, for example, show that their point-blank range was 640 metres, while their maximum range, at fifteen degrees elevation, was no less than three kilometres.[34]

If the target were beyond point-blank range the gunner simply elevated his line of aim slightly above the target, judging from experience how much elevation was required and let drive. At any range where there was a reasonable expectation of hitting the target at all this system was quite accurate. The random range was the greatest distance the gun could carry when it was elevated, and 'at random' was a vivid expression for long-range gunnery; for it depended on guessing the distance, guessing the elevation and choosing the moment to fire when the ship swayed. It meant firing as many shots as possible, literally at random, in the general direction of the enemy, and hoping for an occasional hit.

Apart from such considerations, which in themselves were sufficient to ensure that the concentration by the attackers of overwhelming firepower was an unlikely event, there were the related questions of the standard of production and the inherent instability and short shelf-life of gunpowder itself. Without adequate quantities of high quality and well stored and preserved gunpowder the effectiveness of the guns was in any case negated. Achieving optimal results even from state-of-the-art weaponry was thus not just a matter of design, but highly contingent on the expertise in pyrotechnical matters and familiarity with metallurgical principles of those who were charged with their use.

## Rate of Fire

The rate of fire was, to our minds, lamentably slow. Gunners used several tools to load a muzzleloader gun, a sponge, a ladle, a ramrod and a worm, each mounted on a long staff. The barrel of a 50-pounder cannon was three metres long and that of a culverin four metres. Obviously the staves need to be longer than the barrels, four to five metres, and gunners needed that much room in front of the muzzle to manipulate their long tools. With the gun near the mainmast, however, the gunners had easy access to the muzzle of the main gun.

The gun itself was fired by applying a lighted torch to a small hole situated towards the rear top of the barrel. This ignited the powder in the barrel, causing an explosion and this in turn hurled the ball down the barrel in the general direction of the target. Because of the windage the actual flight of the shot depended on how it glanced out of the barrel, so shooting at other than close range was not accurate. Having fired, it was then necessary to clean out the barrel in order to remove the remains of the burnt powder. Fresh powder was then poured into the barrel and rammed home, both to stop the ball rolling out and also to ensure a compact mass within the tube. The touchhole was then recharged with powder, the gun was once again aimed and elevated as required and the piece was then once more ready to be fired.

Generally speaking, we tend to view Mediterranean galley tactics as a matter of small arms and cold steel, with artillery as the overture to the closer fight, that is to say, fired at zero range. There is no dispute that a shot at close range was more effective than one at long range, yet multiple cannon shots were feasible and worthwhile. Once reloaded, a 50-pounder weighing 2,400 kilograms could be on the bow again within seven seconds thanks to the oarsmen yanking on the two ropes attached to its well-greased oak sledge.[35]

Indeed, Lepanto became the prime instance of multiple cannon shots after Don Juan de Austria told his galley captains to fire whenever they thought they could do the most damage but to retain two rounds for the boarding phase.[36] Another eyewitness, the Venetian Giovanni Pietro Contarini, writes in 1572 that "in this battle (of the centre squadron) as in the wings, the artillery of the Christians fired twice, three times and even five times, mainly with the centreline guns, before the galleys joined together for boarding".[37] Contarini goes on to describe its effects: it prevented some of the enemy from discharging all their guns, several of which were found to be loaded upon capture.[38] It is also known that the guns were kept loaded at all times, which meant that whenever battle was joined one salvo was therefore available for immediate use.

## Types

As we have unquestionably gathered by now, everything in 16th-century gunnery was inexact: the names of the guns, their calibres, their range, the quality of their powder, and above all their aim – in practice most pieces are in the main remarkable for their individuality and profusion of forms. Another problem to consider, a major one in fact, was that a galley as a gun platform was always in motion, even at the best of times and in the kindest weather, so that unless guns were so close that their shot could not miss, the chance of inflicting serious damage on the enemy was uncertain. But roughly speaking there were eight kinds of guns that could have done some damage to a light-framed craft such as a galley. As most naval gunners employed straight-trajectory firing, with regard to ranges the chart below restricts itself to this method alone:

| | Calibre (in/cm) | Weight of shot (lbs/kg) | Point-blank range (paces) | Range at random (paces) |
|---|---|---|---|---|
| Cannon royal | 8½/21.6 | 60/27.2 | 450 | 2,400 |
| Whole cannon | 7¼/18.4 | 50/22.7 | 360 | 2,100 |
| Demi-cannon | 6–6½/15.2–16.5 | 24–36/10.9–16.3 | 270 | 1,500 |
| Cannon-perrier | 8/20.3 | 24½/11.1 | 320 | 960 |
| Culverin | 5¼–5½/13.3–14 | 15–19/6.8–8.6 | 500 | 4,000 |
| Demi-culverin | 4¼–4½/10.8–11.4 | 10/4.5 | 400 | 3,000 |
| Saker | 3½/8.9 | 5½–9/2.5–4.1 | 300 | 2,400 |
| Minion | 3¼/8.2 | 4½–6/2–2.7 | 270 | 2,100 |

We should also add the following types of guns that could be used effectively against crews and rigging:

| | | | | |
|---|---|---|---|---|
| Falcon | 2½/6.4 | 3/1.4 | 240 | 1,500 |
| Falconet | 2/5.1 | 1–2/0.45–0.91 | 180 | 900 |
| Robinet | 1¼/3.2 | 1/0.45 | 120 | ———— |

All the big guns fired a cast-iron ball except the cannon-perrier, which fired a ball of stone. It is doubtful whether this stone shot could have done much damage to a ship, except the rigging, because if it broke up on impact, or sometimes even in flight, and so formed a kind of shrapnel, lacerating splinters that whizzed at invisible speed. Because they could be produced using moulds, cast-iron balls obviated the large amount of highly skilled labour required to cut a smooth, perfectly spherical shot. They could also be reused. Furthermore, being perfectly spherical they fitted into the gun barrel with a smaller gap, making more efficient use of the kinetic force of the gunpowder. Little wonder, therefore, cast-iron overtook the frangible stone of cannon shot.

Yet it is important to understand that Lepanto was not only the largest galley battle of the modern era, it also represented a collision between two different fighting traditions; one based more on impetuosity and courage, the other on the technological superiority of their offensive and defensive armament. As a rule, the Ottoman galleys were assault and boarding crafts, and, as such, at least according to western sources, they were equipped with limited quantities of artillery: normally three pieces, the largest of which was the centreline *corsiere* or chaser. This was usually of the *petriero* type, capable of launching a large ball of stone with a relatively limited range and at a somewhat reduced velocity. This befitted the Ottoman tactic of firing at close range, just before boarding and entering the enemy vessel. At short range, stone balls were much more destructive than cast iron ones, which, if the gun was well handled, had a greater range and were much more accurate.

## Placement

Cannon themselves locked up large quantities of capital. They were used less frequently than their civilian counterparts, church bells. Indeed, navies required more guns in relation to seamen than did armies in relation to soldiers. Thus artillery was a significant item on the shopping list of a galley; its cost was proportional to its weight. In 1558 it was ninety-eight *ducati* per *migliara* (1,000 *libbre grosse*, 477 kilograms) without the gun-mount; by 1586 the price had escalated to 140 *ducati per migliara*.[39] At this price, the cost of just one 50-pounder cannon was almost twenty-five per cent of the cost of the entire hull of a galley, including masts and oars. But cannon lasted. In 1605 the Spanish *San Agustín* sailed from Panama with one dated 1522 and two founded in 1500.

Christian galleys, and in particular those of Venice, focused not only on their offensive firepower, but on defensive firepower too. A few small swivel guns might be mounted along the bulwarks and the poop; they could do considerable damage among enemy oarsmen and fighting crew. Though there was never any such thing as standard galley armament, that of the galley of Giacomo Celsi in 1568 provides a good example: one 60-pound culverin, two 16-pound cannon, three 6-pound *falcones* (English minions), two 3-pound *falconetti* (English falcons), two *moschetti da zuogo* (muskets), two 6-pound *petriera*, fourteen 3-pound perriers, eight 1-pound robinets (*moschetti da braga*, breech loaders with bronze barrel and iron breech).[40] Another good example is *La Real*, the flagship of Don Juan: this vessel carried a bow battery of five guns – a *cañón* (cannon), two *media culebrinas* (demi-culverins) and two *sacres* (sakers).

This was typical of the powerful suite of ordnance carried in the larger Christian galleys and outgunned substantially the batteries fitted in the bows of their Ottoman counterparts. The battery was supported by a selection of smaller *versos* (breech-loading swivel guns) mounted on the raised fighting platform above the guns. Here it is convenient to note that Spanish galleys sported a permanent raised structure above the bow artillery, the *arrumbada*. Occupying the space just forward of the two foremost rowing benches and just behind the most sharply tapered forward portion of the bow, the *arrumbada* spanned the full width of the hull and was no more than three metres long.

The primary function of the *arrumbada* was to serve as a platform from which covering fire could be directed to cover an assault of infantry onto an enemy galley. It was highly effective tactically, but it also added weight, and added weight was the antithesis of speed under oars. Instead of the *arrumbada* (It. *arrembata*), Venetian galleys had an elevated fighting platform over their bow artillery which was lighter in construction and removable, the emphasis being on the efficient use of artillery. Though this structure did have temporary ramparts of timber and cordage to protect the soldiers and sailors stationed there, it was lower and less easy to defend than the Spanish *arrumbada*. Ottoman galleys, on the other hand, seem to have had a low, permanent fighting platform which covered only the forward portion of the bow artillery, leaving the breeches exposed. Moreover, they usually did not reinforce their bows with movable ramparts of reinforced timber, leaving the men stationed there exposed to ball and bullet.

The artillery was under these raised fighting platforms, permanent or not, the main gun in the centre, inside the *corsia*, or raised gangway, with lesser calibres on each side. Thick wooden parapets protected the gunners on both sides and in the front.[41] Though the space beneath these structures must have been cramped and poorly ventilated, the gunners therein were certainly better protected than the soldiers above them. Of course, they would be exposed to enemy fire if they stepped outside of their protected enclosure to reload the guns. On the other hand, they did not have to do so to reload the centreline gun, snug inside the *corsia* and mounted on a solidly constructed sledge with no wheels. The centreline gun could be aimed, rather like those of a modern fighter aircraft, by correctly positioning the whole vessel, and the massive recoil was absorbed by its sledge, which was allowed to slide back to a stout pad of ropes just short of the mainmast, some eleven metres to the rear. Gunners thus reloaded the gun in that position. The gunners of the main gun at least were as safe from enemy fire as anyone could be on a galley.

## Small Arms

We come now to the consideration of handheld gunpowder weapons, which were designed to injure men, not ships. The deployment of small gunpowder weapons on early modern European battlefields followed a far more discontinuous path. Thanks to progress in metalworking and in corning black powder, a first generation of handheld weapons, known collectively as 'handgonnes', was created in the early 15th century. At its simplest, the handgun consisted of little more than a thick metal tube, with a vent hole bored through the top at the chamber end, attached to a wooden stock. Firing this new 'weapon of fire' was a fiery, clumsy process. Powder and ball were rammed into the chamber using a ramrod, and a small amount of powder was poured down in the vent hole. It was then levelled in the direction of the enemy, and the vent hole powder ignited by a hot wire or a length of smouldering match cord held in a linstock, either by the gunner himself or by a third party. Since this was a two-handed operation, without the help of a third party the wooden stock had to be gripped under the arm of the gunner, making it impossible to do more than simply point the weapon in the vague direction of the target. Nonetheless, the handgun marks the transition from the mechanically thrown missile to the bullet. The tube was to direct the projectile, and the bow and string were replaced by a powder chamber and ignition device.

By the middle of the century, large numbers of handgunners had become an important feature of European warfare. A further step forward came in the second half of the 15th century, with the spread of the matchlock harquebus, in which the lighted extremity of a slow burning match cord – made of linen or hemp, soaked in a saltpetre solution and then allowed to dry – was applied to the primer by a trigger mechanism ('lock', from a rudimentary resemblance to the mechanism of a door lock) and not by hand (as with the handgun), allowing the gunner to fire with both hands on the gun. The tip of the match cord was grasped in a pair of adjustable jaws atop a pivoted arm, which was connected to the trigger. Pulling on the trigger released an internal spring causing the jaws to rotate downward, bringing the end of the smouldering match cord into contact with the priming powder in the flash pan to set off the main charge in the barrel. The new firearm was still a muzzle loader, powder being poured down the barrel and rammed home, followed by the shot and a plug.

Primitive but effective, this invention was simple, but revolutionary. Two important things stand out with regards to this early firearm. The barrel consisted of a simple tube of wrought iron plugged at one end and provided with a touch hole. To permit aiming, a flash pan beside the touch hole replaced the former vent hole, and a matchlock, operated by an internal spring and trigger mechanism, was mounted inside the stock. The result – the harquebus (or arquebus, from the Spanish *arcabuz*) – was an innovation that enabled a gunner to maintain a steady aim on the target while firing the gun. By the fifteen-twenties the matchlock harquebus had become by far the most common type of portable gunpowder weapon. It was still inaccurate, dirty, and heavy and in terms of performance it was still outclassed by bows and crossbows on many levels. Yet the matchlock harquebus was simple to operate and it was relatively easy to train somebody in its use.

The harquebus was a smoothbore weapon, weighing about 4.5 to 5.5 kilograms, with a barrel about a metre long. It fired a lead ball weighing around fifteen grams of about .66-calibre (viz. sixty-six hundredths of an inch) up to an effective range of around fifty metres. However, in the 16th century many combatants on the battlefield wore armour, so a commander had to think not only of hitting the enemy, but also of penetrating the enemy's carapace. The duque de Alba recommended to his harquebusiers an effective distance "of a little more than two pike lengths" – around eleven metres.[42]

The weapon derived its name from the German *hackenbusche*, 'hook gun', an early defensive gun that apparently included a hook beneath the barrel to fit over a wall or branch for steadying the weapon and dampening the recoil. Alternatively, the term 'hook gun' came from the hooked shape of the butt, since these developments were contemporary with the name, while the hook beneath was present on many pre-harquebus guns and absent on the majority of harquebuses.

In addition to the harquebus itself, there was all the ancillary equipment: a flask of ordinary 'corned' powder carried at the waist, which provided the main charge; a box of finer priming powder, suspended on a piece of cord long enough to reach the gun for priming; a canvas or leather bag for bullets; three or four metres of match cord, which smouldered steadily when lit (in action it was lit at both ends and looped on the third finger of the left hand); paper or tow for wadding; and finally a flint and steel to rekindle the match cord if it went out (the harquebusier blew upon one end until it glowed before using it to ignite his priming powder).

In a similar process to the handgun, the harquebus was loaded by pouring the right amount of powder into the barrel: too little would produce a feeble shot; too much would burst the barrel in the harquebusier's face. It was then primed with the priming powder. Finally, the bullet was rammed down the barrel with the ramrod, followed ideally by a tow or paper wadding, although it was quicker to wedge the bullet with a few grains of powder dropped down the barrel. The weapon was now ready to fire.

There were disadvantages of course, especially under battle conditions. It had to be accurately aimed. Seven or eight shots could overheat the weapon and make it as dangerous to the person firing it as to the one aimed at. It was heavy to carry, and easily damaged. The match cord, priming powder, and main charge all had to be perfectly dry. Then there was the need to take constant care of the burning match cord, which could accidentally ignite all gunpowder and turn the harquebusier into a live Roman candle. The match cord itself had to be kept smouldering all the time, so blowing on it every so often and adjusting its length in time was another concern. Strong winds also impeded the use of the match cord. Loading and firing was a slow process. Both priming powder and the main charge needed to be measured properly. If the wadding were forgotten, the bullets would roll from the barrel before the weapon was fired. The butt of the weapon needed to be pressed firmly against the shoulder when firing. On top of this, the performance of the weapon deteriorated and the rate of misfires increased as its barrel fouled up with combustion residues.

The apparent feebleness of their fire caused Michel de Montaigne (1533–92) to say, certainly on military authority, "The arms have so little effect, except on the ears, that their use will be discontinued".[43] The Gascon was proved to be wrong of course, but there again, he is most famously known for his skeptical remark: "*Que sçay-je?*", "What know I" (or "What do I know,") in Middle French (*Que sais-je?* in Modern French).[44]

As we have discussed earlier, especially with regards to Gonzalo Fernández de Córdoba, and his military reforms, it was the Spanish who first appreciated the power and value of a weapon which – although invented several decades earlier – was still regarded with suspicion. Yet there is another small arm for us to consider, namely the musket. It was the aforementioned duque de Alba who replaced the harquebus, which still faced competition from the crossbow, with a bigger, heavier, longer-barrelled firearm. This innovation was the Spanish *mosquete* – the original musket, first used at the siege of Parma in 1521.[45] The Spanish *mosquete* was essentially a much larger harquebus; with a barrel about 1.8 metres long and weighing about eight to twelve kilograms. Because of this weight the musketeer had to use a forked pole rest to support the barrel when firing.

The weapon was fired with the musketeer's left foot forward, his left hand steadying the rest, and his right hand encircling the small of the butt, pulling it in toward his shoulder to absorb as much of the recoil as possible. When the trigger was activated, the serpentine lowered the smouldering match cord into the priming pan.

This larger gun had a calibre of between .70 and .85, and its fifty- to seventy-gram ball could reach further – it was used at sixty to eighty metres – and smash through body armour, flesh and bone as never before. Thus the obvious advantage of this weapon was its increased killing power (the massive musket balls weighted ten or twelve to the pound, harquebus balls half this), but the disadvantage was its weight. The musket needed a strong man to carry it, tolerate its recoil and fire it, and even by the mid-17th century, harquebuses were still being used in greater numbers than muskets, perhaps in a ratio of two to one.[46]

## Gunpowder

The most fundamental leaps in weapons technology have been the harnessing of new forms of energy. The harnessing of fire made metal weapons possible, while the discovery of gunpowder was the harnessing of chemical energy as a propellant and explosive.

By the end of the 16th century, those who continued to scorn gunpowder weapons were seen as out of touch or two-faced, the deserving butt of humour. Shakespeare has the Northumbrian paladin Sir Henry Percy – probably better known to us as Harry Hotspur – express droll contempt for a gun-shy courtier, attributing the man the sentiment:

> Of guns, and drums, and wounds, and wounds, God save the mark!
> And telling me the sovereign'st thing on earth
> Was parmacity[47] for an inward bruise,
> And that it was a great pity, so it was,
> This villainous saltpetre should be digged
> Out of the bowels of the harmless earth,
> Which many a good tall fellow had destroyed
> So cowardly; and but for these vile guns
> He would himself have been a soldier.[48]

The "neat and trimly dressed" courtier had confronted the very masculine and aggressive Hotspur immediately after a pitched battle and the latter had found the former so simpering and effeminate that it disgusted him. It might be worth mentioning that our humorous Hotspur, having rebelled against his anoited king, would meet his untimely death at the battle of Shrewsbury (21 July 1403), struck down by an arrow as he led a rash and reckless charge against Henry IV. The legend that he was slain by the Prince of Wales, the future Henry V, was given currency by Shakespeare.[49]

Bear with me on the chemistry, but I shall be brief. Things 'burn' or are oxidised when a material (fuel) is raised to the ignition point in the presence of oxygen so that combustion occurs, releasing heat, gas, particles, and light. Substances vary in their combustibility, the temperature at which the reaction becomes self-sustaining as the heat being released adequately warms the contiguous material. Substances that burn extremely rapidly but without exploding when unconfined, often with sparking, hissing, and the evolution of large quantities of gas, are said to deflagrate rather than detonate. Because of the rapidity of the pressure wave front and high temperatures generated, such substances provide ideal materials for incendiary warfare. Now, all incendiary materials require an oxidizing agent, a chemical that emits oxygen when heated. Saltpetre, otherwise known as potassium nitrate ($KNO_3$) or nitre, is one such chemical, for as it burns it releases virgin oxygen. The oxygen accelerates the process of deflagration. In the nitrate radical that is the crux of saltpetre, three oxygen atoms are fastened to one of nitrogen. When exposed to heat of 335° centigrade, the normally stable salt breaks down, letting loose the three oxygen atoms that had been bound up with the single nitrogen atom. This property makes saltpetre the key ingredient of gunpowder.

The remarkable mixture known as gunpowder deflagrates when all the components are present in less than the proper portions, seventy-five parts saltpetre (oxidizer) to fifteen parts sulphur (fuel) to ten parts charcoal (fuel), with the type of charcoal surprisingly affecting the burn rate (willow or alder being preferred). Sulphur, while also serving as a fuel, lowers the temperature required to ignite the mixture, thereby increasing the rate of combustion. Even when perfectly balanced, only weak explosive effects will be achieved unless the mixture has undergone such a thorough process of pre-grinding, sifting, premixing, mixing, wetting, pressing or rolling, and finally grinding that a uniform, fine powder with high surface area results whose combustion properties are said to approach those of a compound rather than a composite mixture. Centuries of painful experience and experimentation were required to evolve the craft knowledge and production techniques necessary to maximise gunpowder's explosiveness, enabling it to provide the required force for cannon and handguns.

The recipes for gunpowder varied from place to place, but the ingredients were always the same. Saltpetre, sulphur, and wood charcoal were combined 6:1:1 and then the mixing operation would take twenty-four, thirty, and even thirty-six hours. So long as the mixture remained damp there was little danger of an explosion. The gunpowder was then laid out to dry. It was then reduced to powder and graded according to fineness.

The only raw material exploited for war was saltpetre, or nitre, the chief (and most precious) ingredient of gunpowder (even sulphur, the second ingredient, was used for medical as well as incendiary purposes). Saltpetre (from the Latin *sal petrae*, 'salt of stones') was found naturally in the soil in certain parts of Europe, notably in France and Lombardy, but locations were patchy and laborious to prospect, so greater reliance was placed on earth that had become saturated with urine and faeces, animal or human: sheepfolds, cattle yards, stables, dovecots, earth closets, and other domestic areas that had, in the course of time, become saturated with nitrate–laden night soil. The metamorphosis of the droppings and stools of animals and humans into the stuff of war was one of the weird ironies of the gunpowder trade.

*Chapter 14*

# The Men

We pulled for you when the wind was against us and the sails were low / *Will you ever let us go?* / We ate bread and onions when you took towns, or ran aboard quickly when you were beaten back by the foe.

Rudyard Kipling, 'Song of the Galley-Slaves',
*Contemporary Review* (July 1891)

The very word *galley* conjures up a grim picture of men covered with copious sweat and loaded with weighty chains, forced to work in appalling circumstances; some of the worst horrors of life afloat are associated with galley history. Galleys are now notorious, whether French or Spanish, Venetian or Genoese, papal or Tuscan, Maltese, Ottoman or Barbary. In the past, 'To labour like a galley slave' was a familiar proverb, and when faced with hardship, the French will often exclaim "*Quelle galère!*" or in English, "What misery!" Just conjure up William Wiley's epic extravaganza *Ben-Hur* (1959) where the hero is enslaved and condemned to work as a galley slave, while chained to his fellow oarsmen who sit two-by-two down either side of a narrow gangway. Admittedly, this is one of the film's (and the book's) biggest blunders, not the least because Roman warships were manned by skilled oarsmen. For it was nigh impossible to create the desired *ésprit de corps* with the broken spirits of pitiable slaves or condemned criminals. Without a well-drilled professional rowing gang you could never hope to attain the speed and agility required for ramming manoeuvres, the most lethal of all naval tactics in ancient oared battles. Chained convicts enslaved as oarsmen is a phenomenon belonging to the early modern Mediterranean, first reliably recorded in 1443, when Charles VII of France licensed a shipping magnate to press-gang vagabonds into his private fleet to ply its oars.

Thus we can rapidly dismiss the Hollywood image of Roman galley slaves kept in appalling conditions and flogged until they dropped. Even so, academic pedantry aside, *Ben-Hur*, whether on the page or on the big screen, provides a gripping first-person experience aboard a galley, that is to say, from the perspective of a chained oarsman, in this case galley slave number Forty-One, rather than the conventional viewpoint of omniscient battle tactician.

## The Mariner

The rest of the basic crew of a galley was made up of sailors (at least some thirty to forty of them), the commander and his staff – generally supplemented by a band of young *nobili* who were at the same time apprentice officers and élite fighters – and a relatively small but essential group of technical experts (pilot, gunners, carpenters, surgeons, et cetera) and their attendants. The size and composition of the specialised fighting complement embarked on a galley was the crew's main variable, since it was almost always (except when a battle or landing operation was expected) linked to the quantity – and quality – of the other combatants of the ship, a category that included practically all those who were not actually chained to a rowing bench, from the *buonevoglie* to the sailors and the *nobili*.

According to Joseph Furttenbach each Genoese galley, with which he was well acquainted, had a captain, a priest, a scribe, a helmsman, a pilot, a carpenter, a cooper, two caulkers, two cooks, two ship's boys, a barber/surgeon, four gunners, three overseers, forty seamen, 270 oarsmen (half Muslim slaves and half Christian convicts, with five men per oar), between fifty to one hundred marines, and between ten to fifteen young gentlemen volunteers.[1]

The helmsman could have been protected below the poop house or on a small gallery above the rudder, where he would have been relatively safe. However that maybe, Andrea Vicentino's fresco of the battle of Lepanto in the Palazzo Ducale, Venice, clearly shows helmsmen on some Venetian and Ottoman galleys balancing precariously on the *triganto*, the stern beam, outside the *castello da pupa*: "And indeed our helmsman, who is the target of every attack, in contrast to the western and Turkish helmsmen, who are safe under the after house."[2]

## The Marine

Besides artillery, the fighting capability of a galley was provided by its complement of soldiers. A *galea sottile* normally had the capacity to carry between 100 to 150 soldiers serving as marines, up to 400 in the case of *galee bastarde*. Still, as we shall see anon, at Lepanto these numbers were not hard and fast. With the exception of Venice, Genoa and the Knights Hospitaller, at Lepanto the allies did not have soldiers specifically assigned for naval service.

Spain, for instance, had lost the cream of its experienced naval fighters at Djerba, and from then onwards deputed regular infantry from the *tercios* and their mercenary German and Italian comrades in arms to serve temporarily as marines on it galleys. It needs to be said that Spanish loses were primarily in quality and experience, not numbers. Though infantrymen of the *tercios* were a good deal easier to come by than the marines of the pre-Djerba days, many of the Spanish soldiers were green (the best were slogging it out in the Low Countries). Don García Álvarez de Toledo Osorio commented that they hardly knew how to fire their harquebuses, and that if he had to fight the seasoned Ottoman soldiers he would much prefer to have some battle-hardened veterans from Flanders.

Much of the fighting value of the galley, its effectiveness as an instrument of war, depended on veteran soldiers. They yearned for action; they dreaded action. Then the action came. Most land battles of the period occupied at most a day of intense conflict, interspersed with intervals and pauses. War at sea was more intense and more visceral. Ships battered each other with gunfire, and then fighting crews boarded a crippled enemy. There was nowhere to run in a ship-to-ship fight, so men would grip like bulldogs and never let go, hacking and stabbing at each other on deck until one or the other side went down, hacked and stabbed and dying.

As we can well appreciate, galley fights meant close quarter combat, which made soldiers as valuable as the galleys themselves. In a boarding action seamen and soldiers with specific training in naval combat were far more effective than embarked land troops, but the latter were generally easier to find in large numbers at short notice and more easily replaced in case of loss or defeat. In his advice to Charles V, the Habsburg emperor, written in 1539 in the aftermath of the catastrophic Christian defeat of Préveza, Antonio Doria (1495–1577), a relative of the more famous Andrea Doria (1469–1560) and a reputable *condottiere* of the sea in his own right, considered as "well provided for combat [*ben provista da combattere*]" a galley that carried sixty sailors and at least one hundred naval soldiers (mostly harquebusiers),[3] though their number could be even higher. On the eve of the bloody naval battle of Capo d'Orso (1528), for instance, the six Spanish and Italian galleys, two *fuste*, three *brigantini* and an unspecified number of *barche armate*, or armed skiffs, which made up the squadron of Naples embarked some 700 handpicked Spanish and German veteran foot soldiers – these were the plunderers of Rome (1527), the victors of Bicocca (1522) and of Pavia (1525).[4]

As in skirmishes and assaults on land, in boarding fights men did not fight as part of rigid formations; the required qualities were agility, aggressiveness and familiarity with the vessel itself. A shipboard fight took place on a swaying and uneven battlefield that combined insurmountable (that is, unless one fell overboard) obstacles and the space restrictions imposed by a very narrow deck with a very high density of combatants. The long and cumbersome pike was practically impossible to wield in a shipboard fight, so sailors and soldiers had to rely on various types of shorter *arme in asta*, such as half pikes (a more versatile 2.4- to 3-metre version of the full pike), halberds (usually carried by sergeants) and partisans (usually carried by corporals), and on the swords that most of them carried, either as a backup weapon or as a main one in combination with a *rotella*. Even though the crossbow remained in active service well into the 16th century, by the end of the fifteen-twenties the matchlock harquebus had in fact already replaced it as the main individual shipboard missile weapon – at least on Christian galleys. The Genoese and Spanish galleys that fought off Capo d'Orso literally bristled with harquebusiers.

The list of individual missile weapons commonly used in Mediterranean naval warfare was completed by a variety of rudimentary explosive and incendiary devices, by different kinds of short throwing pole arms, and last but not least, by the heavy stones that were dropped with deadly effect on enemies who thronged the deck below by seamen positioned, during the battle, on a galley's maintop and lateen yards.

As far as the *arme defensive*, defensive equipment, was concerned, on Christian war galleys it was possible to observe an almost complete range of possibilities, from their total absence in the case of the average seaman, commonly known as *homini di bragessa*, men in breeches, who fought wearing only his shirt, breeches and a *berretta*, beret, to *da piede* corselets worn by commanding officers and the teams of assault marines that spearheaded and supported the action of the boarding and counter-boarding parties. The Spanish in particular seem to have made a fairly generous use of various types of 'white' armour (It. *in arme bianche*) for their embarked troops, including the harquebusiers. In 1535, during the campaign of Charles V against Tunis, a galley of Spain had carried about sixty-five *gente de cabo* (officers and mariners) and *gente de guerra* (marines), in addition to its *gente de remo* (oarsmen),[5] with the latter group obviously forming the largest complement on any given galley. The following year, the *capitana* of Don Álvaro de Bazán el Viejo (1506–58), *capitán general de las Galeras de España*, carried the usual complement of *gente de remo* plus three *oficiales* (viz. *patrón*, *sotapatrón* and *comitre*)[6] and 120 *gente de cabo* and *gente de guerra*, the latter group being composed of a hundred harquebusiers.[7] By Lepanto the level of manning had increased remarkably. A galley of Spain carried a normal complement of about eighty *gente de cabo* who were reinforced with infantry from the *tercios*.[8] In addition to their 200 *gente de remo*, Spanish galleys at Lepanto carried an average of 112 *gente de cabo* plus *aventureros*, hot-blooded young noblemen, and about 150 attached soldiers from a *tercio*.[9] Obviously, as presently we shall see, *lanterne* and *capitane* carried considerably larger complements.

The fighting complements of the galleys of Venice and Genoa, on the other hand, were both principally composed of lightly armoured specialists recruited in large quantities usually but not invariably from Venice's *impero da mar*, that is, the coastal areas of eastern Italy, Dalmatia, Albania and Greece, and in the Ligurian *riviere*. These were genuine marines intended to serve exclusively at sea, and those employed by Venice were known as *scapoli* or *uomini da spada*, swordsmen.[10] Contemporary chroniclers were intrigued by the stark contrast of the struggle between the *armati* (armoured) Spanish embarked soldiers and the *desarmati* (unarmoured) agile Ligurian fighting men of the private galleys of Andrea Doria, who fought almost naked but, as the Genoese historian Giovanni Battista Salvago put it, were "skilled in maritime operations [*pratichi ne lo esercitio maritimo*]".[11]

## The Gunner

The gunner's tale: sponge out the gun to stop it getting too hot; load the chamber by a ladle of copper on a long staff, a measure of powder in fact; add the shot and ram it down with a long-staffed ramrod; lay the trail of powder to the touchhole; run the gun forward to its firing position; sometimes turn it to left or right with crowbars to aim at a visible enemy; drive the wedges in or out to change the elevation; stand clear of the recoil. When it was done, the gunner was itching to put the glowing end of his slow match to it, and often did not wait for an order but let fly as soon as he saw a target, although it was sometimes hopelessly out of range. It is illogical but human to think one's shots are hitting and hurting, while the enemy's are wasted.

The naval gunner's life depended on speed. Accidents were frequent – after all, this was a job that punished slackness by the loss of the entire vessel in one great thundering roar. If the vessel did not blow up, then there was always the risk of loss through fire. How terrible a monster was fire afloat, landsmen in their ignorance may wonder how a ship can burn in the midst of endless water, but not seamen. They knew the reality. A galley was made of seasoned timbers, pitch and tar and canvas and rope, which made her a virtual tinderbox.

It is true that gunpowder weapons, because of the force of their bullets or balls, owed nothing to the muscle power that tensed a bow stave, wound the string of a crossbow into its notch, or racked back the arm of a trebuchet, were looked on by some as supernatural. And there were times when a selective hindsight that imagined wars of the past to have been all hand strokes caused writers to revile the 'coward's weapon'. In his epic poem *Orlando Furioso* (1516), Ludovico Ariosto, Machiavelli's contemporary and Italian compatriot, narrates how Orlando (the Christian paladin known in French, and subsequently English, as Roland), his hero and the embodiment of all knightly virtues, was forced to face an enemy wielding a firearm:

> He, where 'tis closed behind, in the iron round,
> Touches with fire a vent, discerned with pain;
> In guise that skilful surgeon tries his ground,
> Where need requires that he should breathe a vein.

> Whence flies the bullet with such deafening sound,
> That bolt and lightning from the hollow cane
> Appear to dart and like the passing thunder,
> Burn what they smite, beat-down or render asunder.[12]

The poem is clearly about war and love and the romantic ideal of chivalry, no longer alive in the 16th century. Beyond that, however, it is also a polemic against gunpowder and firearms. Blaise de Monluc, who as a young man almost lost an arm through a gunshot wound, roundly condemned the development of firearms:

> Would to God that this unhappy weapon [viz. the harquebus] had never been devised, and that so many brave and valiant men had never died by the hands of those who are often cowards and shirkers, who would never dare to look in the face those whom they lay low with their wretched bullets. They are tools invented by the devil to make it easier for us to kill each other.[13]

Worse was to come, for at the age of seventy he was disfigured by a bullet from a harquebus and obilged to wear a mask for the remainder of his embittered years.

Correspondingly, speaking through the character of the knightly Don Quixote, we have the gunshot maimed Cervantes' own indictment on gunpowder:

> "Happy were those blessed times that lacked the horrifying fury of the diabolical instruments of artillery, whose inventor, in my opinion, is in hell, receiving the reward for his accursed invention, which allows an ignoble and cowardly hand to take the life of a valiant knight …".[14]

The black soot, the scorched stench, the swirling sulphurous smoke, the obvious association with witchcraft, all of these attributes gave credence to gunpowder's diabolical connection. The swaggering soldier turned political playwright Ben Jonson (†1637), a near contemporary of Shakespeare, scurrilously refers to a mythical inventor "Who from the Divels-Arse did Guns beget".[15] Early in his literary career Jonson liked to remind his English audiences of his own service in the court of Mars so as to give authority to his criticisms of the military profession. In 1616 the author had served, though briefly, in the Low Countries and had seen firsthand guns vomiting death, fire and smoke.

Weapons development is only one corner of a triangle, of which the other two are a tactical doctrine for using the weapon, and the training of the combatants, individually and collectively to use it. What at first sight may seem to be a technological superiority is often more a result of technique, and may even result from using a simpler or more robust technology.

By the 16th century professional gunners, now known as bombardiers, derived from the Latin word *bombus* (Gk. Βόμβος, *bómbos*, 'booming', 'rumbling'), with their high knowledge of skills and knowledge had become a valued commodity. In Venice, for instance, potential salaried (*provisionati*) gunners, given the cash value of the weapons they served, were not only required to have had two years of experience at sea or in the army (a requirement dropped as the years of peace rolled by) but were given firing tests for accuracy on light pieces – the government grudging the expense of issuing gunpowder save in small quantities – and a *viva voce* examination of their knowledge of the manufacture, types, charge and ball of other artillery, and of the making of gunpowder and artificial fire.[16] Venice also trained its gunners to shoot not only at fixed marks on land but also on sea targets bobbing 400 paces off the Lido.

From its beginnings in 1500, the number of gunners had risen by 1600 to 4,700, shared between nineteen mainland towns. Unlike the Spaniards (whose gunners tended to be Flemish or Germans anyway) or Ottomans, the Venetians had an elaborate training régime for their gunners, who formed the real élite in Venice. Graded in three ranks (master gunner, gunner, apprentice) they were trained in the Scuola di Santa Barbara in Venice ('school' not only in the training sense, but that of a craft guild with religious and charitable roles), or in other artillery companies around the *terraferma* and overseas territories. They enjoyed numerous tax concessions, had the right to bear arms (earlier than the normal militia), and were responsible not only for the artillery but also for the signal rockets and other incendiary devices. Yet even in Venice gunnery was more an art than a science. The gunner with the right knack was more likely to get good results than the gunner who relied on handbook and instruments. In other words, experience, basic intelligence, and a feel for the business paid off more surely than precision in following a rigid set of procedures.

It is not surprising, then, that the best 16th-century gunnery surpassed that of the 18th and early 19th centuries. Fully trained gunners, however, were few in Venice. For instance, there were only twenty-one gunners among a galleass' complement of 572, so other members of the crew had to help load, shift and even fire the guns. In addition, for all its innovations, the galleass carried an excessive variety of ordnance among the forty plus guns aboard, including a pair of 60- or 50-pounder culverins weighing over 10,000 pounds each, which were supplemented by a variety of cannon, falcons (It. *falcones*), falconets (It. *falconetti*), and small bronze pivot guns.

## The Oarsman

With the introduction in the Mediterranean of the rowing system known as *a scaloccio*, galleys could be rowed effectively with a small number of skilled oarsmen, each directing the other men who rowed the same oar. With this new system, therefore, most of the additional muscle power necessary to operate the galleys would be supplied by virtually anyone who could be forced or coerced into pulling an oar. Since the *Réale* flagship of the galley fleet of Louis XIV had eight men to an oar, that number may represent the practical upper limit.

Which brings us finally to the galley slaves, most of them from Muslim lands, by and large prisoners of war taken in the perennial but sporadically intensified warfare between Christian and Muslim states in the Mediterranean, some of them renegades or pagans, and all of them infidels from the Christian point of view; as such, they could be enslaved and put to the oar. The Church of Rome encouraged the practice of enslaving infidels, non-Catholics; it set the example itself by using Muslim slaves on papal galleys, and on the galleys of the Knights Hospitaller at Malta, by capturing thousands of Muslim and other 'infidels' in crusading campaigns on land and sea, and by making a lucrative market at Malta in Muslim slaves, selling to the Mediterranean powers of Christendom.

It is notable that the Hospitallers made confessional identity a zero-sum game: all non-Catholics – Orthodox Christians, Muslims and Jews alike – found aboard Muslim ships could be seized and sent to the slave auctions on Malta. And even smaller states got in on the act, such as Medici Tuscany.

As a merchant state seeking to preserve its autonomy in the face of French and Spanish Habsburg territorial pretensions on the Italian peninsula, Florence established the Order of Saint Stephen (Latin: *Sacro Militare Ordine di Santo Stefano Papa e Martire*), pope and martyr (†2 August AD 257), in 1561, with Cosimo I de' Medici serving as its first grand master. The parvenu Cosimo had worked hard to revive Tuscany's maritime power, which had atrophied since the mediaeval decline of Pisa's naval republic. From as early as 1547, Cosimo vigorously sought slaves to man his galleys, then under construction in the new Arsenale di Pisa. There were soon five galleys, manned by 554 convicts (mainly from Tuscan prisons), 243 slaves and 144 volunteer oarsmen. Two more galleys were then built in 1559 by shipwrights from Messina and Venice, and high salaries were offered to attract competent seamen. Soldiers and gentlemen adventurers who fought on board drew their pay from the Duca di Firenze. Tuscany had no active maritime population of its own from which to draw seamen. The officers and seamen were Genoese, Venetian, Corsican, Greeks, renegades and other *rifiuto*, riff-raff. Cosimo decided to establish a proper seaborne militia on the model of the Knights Hospitaller.[17]

With the broadcast goal of defending Christendom from Muslim predatory raids in the Tyrrhenian Sea, by means of the Order of Saint Stephen the Medici state reaped both religious, political and economic rewards: its raids and skirmishes with the 'infidel' yielded not only booty in the shape of money and merchandise, but also thousands of men for the oars of its newly-established fleet and a steady stream of human beings for sale to other Catholic states.[18] Revealing enough, the Tuscan galleys were called 'the corsairs of Leghorn' in Ottoman archival documents.[19]

Let us picture the living space given to a bench crew condemned to what was a floating hell: five shackled men had to work, eat, sleep and perform their ablutions when they could in a rectangular space no bigger than 2.30 metres long by 1.25 metres wide.[20] This gave each man a space of forty-five centimetres in which to sit, a level of crowding you and I would experience today only on public transport during a rush hour. Each of the five was barefoot with their heads shaven – although Muslim slaves had a distinctive small knot of hair in the middle of the shaved skull – so as to prevent the accumulation of lice, which was responsible for typhus epidemics in all navies, and to make identification easier in case of escape. With little more than a ragged set of garments, they lived in the open, subject to the fierce heat of the Mediterranean sun by day and the chill and damp by night. The stinging salt water and rubbing shackles gave the oarsmen sores and blisters on their legs; the rowing broke their backs or tore their abdominal muscles.

The involuntary and oppressive nature of galley slavery is difficult to overemphasise. Each man was given a station according to his relative strength; often Ottoman slaves held the most onerous positions. Each bench was a little over fifteen centimetres wide, with a slanted back and foot planks on the back for the oarsmen on the bench behind. The five oarsmen moved shoulder to shoulder, completing one stroke every three seconds, their oar measuring at least twelve metres in length and weighing over 130 kilograms. In calm seas and providing the hull was in reasonable condition, the oarsmen could normally sustain a cruising speed of three to three-and-a-half nautical miles per hour, occasionally managing the considerable speed of five nautical miles per hour. Short bursts of up to seven to seven-and-a-half nautical miles per hour were possible for around twenty minutes, but only at the risk of exhausting the oarsmen.[21] Only cutting sugar cane or mining were remotely comparable in the expenditure of human energy. The exhausting régime was prey to the petty tyrannies of the overseers, who were free with the lash and open to corruption.

Nothing more lay ahead for our five slaves than the sea, battles with the vessels of their (probably) Ottoman or Barbary compatriots, and the very real possibility of ending up at the bottom of the Mediterranean, trapped in their reeking and rocking wooden prison. The chances of being freed were minimal: only if their master won a naval engagement or if they were lucky enough to win the lottery of a prisoner exchange. We must, of course, point out that inhuman living conditions were not a prerogative of Muslim slaves but were also inflicted on Christian slaves too. While

Muslims endured captivity in places including Messina, Genoa, Venice, Marseilles, Naples, Ancona, Malta, and Livorno, Christians likewise suffered in the slave pens of Constantinople, Algiers, Tunisia, and Tripoli. Though all three monotheistic religions condoned human slavery, all early modern polities sought to regulate it to suit cultural, economic and political ends.

Some of the Christians found serving as galley slaves on the Ottoman vessels taken at Lepanto had been in captivity for thirty years or more. They were exceptional. Most slaves found release from their rowing benches only through death at the oar, and few could survive more than a few years of that backbreaking toil and privation. Lines from a ballad penned by the lyric poet Luis de Góngora y Argote (1561–1627) in 1583 throw an uncompromising light upon the gruesome existence of galley slaves:

Chained to a bench of a Turkish galley, with both hands on his oar and both eyes fixed on the land, one of Dragut's [viz. Turgut Re'īs] prisoners off the coast of Marbella groaned to the harsh noise the oar and chain. Oh, sacred seas of Spain... bring me news of my wife, and tell me if the tears and sighs she expresses in her letters have been sincere... since I've lived ten years without freedom and without her... At this six ships of our navy were sighted and the commander of the slaves ordered the prisoners to pull harder.[22]

The overseer's lash was not the only terror the galley slave had to suffer. Giacomo Bosio, for instance, describes the horrible scene that occurred on the evening of 23 September 1555 when four galleys of the Knights Hospitaller capsized in the Grand Harbour of Malta after they were hit by a sudden hurricane. The four galleys turned turtle with only their keels visible above the water, which meant hundreds of galley slaves, still shackled to their rowing benches, were drowned.[23]

Like the forced labour of later centuries, on the galleys a fine balance was maintained between punishment and the need to preserve sufficient strength to pull an oar. But the way the chained humanity was treated depended on the individual captains, and only very foolish ones would unnecessarily overwork or maltreat their oarsmen: forced oarsmen did not come cheap, costing anything from forty *Real de a ocho* upward in the mid-16th century.[24]

Upon disembarkation at the Christian port of destination, and before entering quarantine, secretaries and interpreters would meticulously record the personal name, place of origin, age, father's name and distinguishing features of each new captive. The level of specificity in describing a slave's origin ranged from cities including Bursa, Susa, Rhodes, Algiers, Tripoli, Bône, Bizerte, and Fez, to more general geographic identifiers such as 'the Black Sea' or 'Anatolia'. The following are two sample entries from a list of seventy-eight slaves taken at sea from a Barbary galiot near Sapienza by the Knights Hospitaller:

20. Caramemet, son of Bubarca from Tripoli, aged twenty, a Negro having a great wound and seven small ones on his right arm.
21. Musa Caradinghis, who does not know his father's name, aged thirty-one circa, with various crescent shaped cuts on his left arm.[25]

On a list of galley slaves drawn up in Sevilla in 1583 we have the physical descriptions of twenty galley slaves. Eleven of them were of North African origins, including eight specifically labelled as 'Moors'. Another six from Anatolia, Rumeli, Rhodes, and the Black Sea were each described as 'Turks'. Among the North Africans, the youngest man was twenty-four years old; four others ranged in age from thirty to forty-five, men hardly in the prime of their lives. The rest were fifty years old or more, with two men said to be fifty-eight, and another listed as only *viejo*, 'old'. Of the 'Turks', one did not know his age, and the remaining five were between twenty-five and forty-six years old. Several carried wounds or scars testifying to previous experiences of combat, illness, or violence inflicted on them in captivity. Some were missing hands or thumbs, and one fifty-year-old from Djerba had the upper parts of his ears cut off. One identified as Abrahen [Abraham], son of Gotun, from Bursa, also had his ears mutilated, a punishment commonly meted out for attempted mutiny.[26]

One final, but important, point needs to be made: not all galley slaves on Christian vessels were Muslims of course, or even slaves for that matter. On Spanish galleys the *gente de remo* was divided into three categories, with convicts (*forzados*) usually outnumbering all other oarsmen, namely free skilled oarsmen and galley slaves, the latter generally comprised only about one-fifth of the oarsmen.[27] Most *forzados* served limited sentences, typically ranging from two to ten years. Still, least we forget, condemnation to the galleys remained a dreaded form of punishment and the direct precedent for the totalising institution of the prison. For many convicts, what was supposed to be a short term at sea became a death sentence.

Occasionally, former convict oarsmen chose to remain on the galleys after the completion of their sentences, drawing a daily wage as volunteer oarsmen or *buenas boyas* (an adaptation of the Italian term *buonavoglia*), though we can believe that some convicts were forced to continue to ply the oar as *buenas boyas* after their sentences had expired.

For unrepentant Protestants as for obstinately pious Jews, for immoral monks, clerical embezzlers, captured bandits, defeated *moriscos*, sexual deviants and devilish sodomites (sodomy was known as *el pecado nefando*, or 'the abominable sin'), and men so poor that they had to sell themselves to eat, the war galleys that Philip II of Spain would launch year after year were the great repository of human misery. This was a society which treated crimes related to money, beliefs and sexual practices more harshly than murder. And so into the galleys of His Most Catholic Majesty went all the rebels and misfits and dissenters of Catholic Christendom, the criminal, the nonconformist, the unlucky.

It was a very similar story within the later galleys of Louis XIV of France (r. 1643–1715) and his great-grandson Louis XV (r. 1715–74). Their galley fleet was an aesthetic marvel. Even before its restoration, 17th-century voyagers described intricate carvings, gilded bows, multicoloured flags and the rhythmic sweep of oars. Some also saw fit to mention the stench and misery within. While twenty per cent of the royal fleet's *chiourme*, rowing force, were *esclaves turcs*, Ottoman and Moroccan slaves, the other eighty per cent were *forçats*, French convicts.[28] Between 1680 and 1748, some 60,000 men were condemned to row. During the numerous wars of Louis XIV between 1685 and 1715, about 17,000 deserters, after capture, were given a life sentence on the galleys of *le Roi-Soleil*. We have already made mention of Jean Marteilhe, a Protestant condemned to the galleys of France for his religious beliefs. In 1685

Louis XIV revoked the Edict of Nantes (1598) – a law passed by his grandfather Henri IV (r. 1589–1610) that had ensured the freedom of Protestant worship in France – and issued the Edict of Fontainebleau and thus Protestantism was outlawed in France. However, many of Marteilhe's fellow convicts of the galleys' servile labour force were guilty of pitifully minor crimes – the theft of silver spoons and forks, or of a mulch cow. In addition about five per cent were, like him, *forçats pour la foi*, convicts for the faith, Huguenots in other words. Followers of the *Religion Prétendue Réformée*, or so-called Reformed Religion, were to remain enslaved until they recanted.

An earlier victim of this savage penal system was of course John Knox (†1572), former Catholic priest and the founder of the Presbyterian Church of Scotland. After the siege of Saint Andrews Castle, Knox spent nineteen months (1547–9) of his prime years shackled to a bench and pulling an oar in a French galley, which perhaps not only put iron in his wrists but in his soul too.

In one of his harebrained escapades Don Quixote liberates a chain of convicts sentenced to the king's galleys. As mentioned before, Cervantes himself had been captured in 1575 and served me as a slave in Algiers for five years before he was ransomed. When the author describes his knight-errant coming across "approximately twelve men on foot strung together by their necks, like beads on a great iron chain and all of them wearing manacles",[29] he clearly knew what he was talking about. He clearly knew what was waiting for these men too, a hellish existence shackled to a hard bench and living amid their own ordure. The galleys created another hell, a parallel hell – a hell on earth. Still, the other hell awaited them, for in battle or if the hull foundered upon shoals, chained to their benches, they and not the captain, went down with the ship.

## The Surgeon

By the 15th century gunpowder weapons had spread all over Europe, with large guns being deployed for sieges, smaller weapons used in battle and on ships, and towards the last decades of the century handheld gunpowder weapons were being carried by foot soldiers as a more powerful, although less accurate, replacement for archery. Despite these technical developments, however, military surgeons had no idea how to treat gunshot wounds. Ambroise Paré, born in 1510 (1509 in some sources) of humble parents, saw the effects of gunpowder weapons at firsthand. Apprenticed to a country barber he had become a military surgeon to four French kings (Henri II, François II, Charles IX, Henri III) and accompanied the royal armies of France on more than seventeen military campaigns, that is to say, during the last three Italian wars (1536–8, 1542–6, 1551–9) and during the Religious wars in France (1562–98), so he experienced firsthand the urgent need to find a way to treat the wounds made by gunpowder weapon.

'The father of modern surgery', Paré is best known for developing techniques for improving the battlefield amputation of limbs, increasingly necessary as gunshot wounds became more frequent and killed more men. Paré noticed that many of the patients who had the stumps of their amputated limbs cauterised with a red-hot iron, or the pouring of boiling elder oil into those wounds that did not require amputation, died of shock. He therefore revived the ancient technique of tying off veins and arteries – first used by Galen (b. AD 129) treating gladiator wounds – to control haemorrhage rather than cauterising them.

Fresh from his early training in Paris and still unsure of himself and his capabilities, it was on his first campaign, the siege of Turin in 1536, that by chance or Providence – the reader will choose – Paré ran out of boiling elder oil. Treating a deluge of casualties following a recent assault, he had to resort to treating gunshot wounds with, as he says in his own words, "a digestive made of the yolke of an egge, oyle of Roses, and Turpentine",[30] which, to his astonishment, reduced inflammation and enhanced patient comfort, at least compared with seething oil. This discovery prompted him to apply similar poultices to gunshot wounds. Paré concluded that these wounds were not, as commonly believed by medical practitioners at the time, inherently poisonous. According to this theory, the common symptoms of gunshot wounds such as fever, physical debility, a blue hue to skin, vomiting and mental confusion, were all explained as the effects of 'poison matter' penetrating the body together with the bullet and gunshot powder. This theory provided the rationale for cauterizing of all gunshot wounds.

The most influential and popular medical treatise at the time was that of Giovanni da Vigo (1450–1525), an Italian surgeon whose medical manual

*Practica in arte chirurgica copiosa* was first published in 1514, printed in more than forty editions, and was translated into French (1525), Italian (1540), English (1543), Spanish (1557), and into German and Portuguese in the 17th century. Da Vigo himself had performed frontline military surgery during the siege of Saluzzo (1485–6) and as personal physician and surgeon to Cardinal Giuliano della Rovere, later the warrior pope Julius II. During these and perhaps other military engagements da Vigo undoubtedly saw frequent and numerous gunshot victims, far more than those seen by earlier surgeons, and it has been suggested by Kelly DeVries that because of the number so wounded da Vigo required a quicker, less painstaking method of treatment than the careful removal of debris, flushing out of the wound, and suturing traditionally employed by military surgeons.[31]

In his work da Vigo devoted an entire chapter to the treatment "of wounds made by hacquebuttes, gunnes, and lyke instruments". In this chapter, the eighth, da Vigo prescribes that, after determining the size of the weapon which caused the wound and whether debris remained in the body, the surgeon was to treat it by cauterization with a red-hot iron or by pouring boiling sambucene oil into it. This was to eliminate the poisonous residue of gunpowder, described by da Vigo as "the most dangerous thinge" to treat in gunshot wounds.[32] Da Vigo emphasizes that the extensive damage caused by bullets was because the gunpowder left a residue of poison on the projectile that made the flesh deteriorate rapidly. For this reason, therefore, gunshot wounds needed to be treated with cauterization. Once the wound was cauterized, it was to be cured by using either melted butter or, in the case of wounds in the sinews, by melted butter, barley water with earthworms, hollyhock, and red sugar. Finally, the wound was to be bandaged with a *digestiva* of turpentine, oil of roses, and egg yolks under a plaster. Although some attempt should be made to remove bullets that remain in the wound, there was to be no effort made to remove hard-to-find fragments or bullets.

On the other hand, the arguments of Paré against the extremely painful practice of cauterisation were as follows: gunpowder consists of a mixture of sulphur, charcoal and saltpetre. None of these ingredients on their own are poisonous and so they cannot be poisonous as a blend. He adds that during the Italian wars he saw German prisoners-of-war put a pinch of gunshot powder into their wine to make it stronger and were not poisoned as a result.[33] Instead, he argues that the infection was carried into gunshot wounds from the outside. To cure such wounds Paré recommended *débridement* (opening and cleaning of the wound) to assist the process of healing, which was not without risks as little was understood at the time about the need for antiseptic surgery and the ligatures were often a source of infection. However, it was better than the standard procedure of sealing the wound with a red hot iron which could result, as already mentioned, in the patient dying of shock.

The technique is of further interest because *débridement* was revived with spectacular success during the Falklands/Malvinas War of 1982,[34] where the majority of wounds sustained by soldiers were of the limbs. Often the soldiers (both British and Argentinian) had sustained multiple wounds caused by high-energy-transfer fragments, with gunshot wounds as the second most common.[35] In the Falklands/Malvinas *débridement* involved dead and damaged tissue, grossly contaminated with bacteria and debris, being completely cut away. The removal of the nonviable tissue left an area of healthy tissue with a good blood supply and capable of combating residual surface contamination, provided the wound was not closed. By way of background, it has to be remembered that as recently as the Second World War, cauterisation was still used to treat gunshot wounds in the German army – the practice is mentioned in the memoirs of Hans Franz Edmund Killian (1892–1982), who was a military surgeon in the Wehrmacht on the Eastern Front.[36] Of course, German surgeons used this method in the absence of other medicines in the extreme environment of battle, and the procedure often caused gangrene and mortification of tissues.

Few armies of our period of study had men as widely competent surgeon as was Paré. On one occasion, Paré saved a wounded soldier who needed a bullet removed. The surgeon in attendance could not find the bullet, so Paré suggested asking the soldier to stand exactly as he was when he received the bullet. He was then able to surmise the likely position of the bullet. It was found and removed. Although simple, it was typical of his scientific and logical approach to battlefield surgery.

Unquestionably, Paré was an inspiration to those he served and saved. Sent by Henri II (r. 1547–59) at the beginning of December 1552 to assist the half-starved garrison of Metz, then besieged by the Habsburg forces under the personal command of Charles V, he was introduced into the beleaguered city during the night by an Italian captain. The following morning, when he was spotted by the French soldiers, he was received with cries of recognition. It is said that the soldiers exclaimed "We shall not die even though wounded; Paré is among us."[37] Whether or not this celebrated surgeon was the sole cause, Charles V was finally forced to lift the siege and depart with his army minus the sick and the wounded. Interestingly enough, though Charles V is noted for praising the abilities of his soldiers on the battlefield, Paré notes that the emperor cared little for the soldiers who died during the siege, saying that:

> [I]t was no matter if they did die, comparing them to caterpillars, grasshoppers and cockchafers which eat the buds and other good things of the earth, and that if they were men of worth they would not be in his camp for six *livres* a month, and therefore there was no harm if they died.[38]

This is not to imply that those who fell sick or were wounded while serving the Habsburg cause at the sharp end did not receive any medical attention. Gerat Barry, the Irish captain in Spanish service we have previously met, writes that a captain:

> [I]s of necessite to have a barber in his Company, and if possible of goode skill in this arte, for being a verie necessarie instrumente in war; for when a Souldier is hurte the greateste comforte he can have is a goode barber, that shall cure him wekk, and with speede".[39]

Obviously through firsthand experience our Irish captain understood the worth of a surgeon's skill and speediness in performing his duties on or near to the battlefield.

England's most enlightened military doctor, William Clowes, wrote in 1591 that incompetent surgeons caused more deaths than the enemy.[40] And, of course he was right. Three years later the hazards of military medicine claimed the life of Sir Martin Frobisher (1535–94). The renowned English seaman and privateer received a gunshot wound to his thigh during the siege of Fort Crozon, a Spanish-held *presidio* near Brest in Brittany. A careless surgeon who extracted the ball left the wadding behind, which allowed the wound to become infected. Frobisher had just enough time to return to Plymouth and compile his will before expiring of gangrene.

It would be an understatement to say that early modern surgery and its practitioners have a negative reputation. This is nothing new. Thomas Gale (†1586) had seen active service as a military surgeon in the French campaigns of 1544 and 1557, and afterwards became an eminent London practitioner. But outside the craft quacks and their like continued to flourish. Gale describes them as:

> The rabble of rude empiricks (and drosse of the earth, which when they cannot otherwise live, chop straight waies into the art of chirurgerie) be no chirurgions, but manquillers, murtherers, and robbers of the people: such are some hosiers, tailours, fletchers, minstrels, souters, horseleeches, jugglers, witches, sorcerers, bawds, and a rabble of that sect, which would by lawes be driven from so divine an art, the exercise of which, for want of knowledge bringeth sometime losse of member, sometime of life, and sometime both of limb and life.[41]

The eminent Gale had no difficulty in calling a spade a spade, and many of his 'rabble of rude empiricks' unfortunately found their way into the English armies during this period. At the siege of Montreuil-sur-mer in 1544, the standard of surgery was so low that the commander of the English forces, Thomas Howard, 3rd Duke of Norfolk (1473–1554), was compelled to order an enquiry into the matter. It transpired that many of those acting as surgeons were totally unqualified for their positions, and were incapable of performing the duties of that office. Some of them were treating wounds with grease, normally used for dressing horses' hooves; others cobbler's wax mixed with rust from old tins, which more than hints that some treatments were probably more deadly than the ailment they sought to cure. The duke had these ignorant quacks rounded up and thrown out of the camp, informing them that should they ever return he would have them hanged from the nearest tree.[42]

Contemporary theory of the army medical service was of course well ahead of practice. According to Thomas Styward:

> Needefull it is that euerie companie haue one Surgeon, a man
> honest, sober, and of good counsaile, skilfull in that science, able
> to heale and cure all kindes of sores, woundes and griefes, to take a
> pellet [viz. bullet] out of the flesh and bone and to slake the fire of
> the same.

He then adds that the surgeon's field equipment was expected to include
a full set of tools and instruments, "with other necessairie stuffe, as oyles,
balmes, salues, stepres, roulers, boulsters, splenters, and al other things
to the science belonging, which also ought to haue courage for his patient
and allowed stuffe".[43] In theory, every English captain was supposed to
employ a surgeon for his company (about a hundred men) to treat the
battle wounded. Multiple complaints in dispatches, however, make clear
the lack of surgeons in English armies and the inadequate medical skills
possessed by those that were in the field.

In 1585 Clowes, when with Leicester in the Low Countries, found he
was up against the same problem. Most Elizabethan army surgeons were
meant to be sent from what was officially recognised as the Company
of Barber Surgeons of London, a price for its charter's privileges, yet
Clowes found that in Leicester's army there was a "sort of stragglers that
did thrust themselves in to the captaines bands, for principal masters in
Surgerie".[44] It was on the basis of his surgical experience gained during
service in the Elizabethan army and navy that Clowes published his
*Prooved Practice for all young Chirugians.* Interestingly, in it he advocates,
like Paré before him, the technique of *débridement* and the avoidance of
cauterisation in treating gunshot wounds. Strangely enough, however,
Clowes contributed to the 'gunpowder as poison' debate by stating that
a gunshot wound was not necessarily poisoned, but the bullet could be
smeared with poison.

Returning once again to our French surgeon. Paré was one of the first
to note a common deleterious effect of the "great thunderous noise, large
bells and artillery", and noticed that:

> One often sees gunners losing their hearing whilst drawing the
> machinery because of the great agitation of the air inside the ear
> which breaks the aforementioned membrane.[45]

The delicate mechanism of the inner ear could not withstand the repeated concussions of cannon fire. Noise-induced hearing loss was an all too common consequence of the gunner's trade. But the demands of the profession came before personal comfort. Interestingly enough, the detrimental effects of constant cannon detonations to hearing is a recurrent theme in one of the poems composed in Latin immediately after Lepanto in response to the news of the great battle.[46] Likewise, in *Don Quixote* Cervantes provides a brief insight that hints at the noise of this particular battle, where "the hard thunder of terrifying artillery sounded; there infinite muskets being fired; the voices of the combatants cried out close by; the Muslim *leleíes* were repeated in the distance".[47] Nonetheless, the morale boosting value of such loud weapons could outweigh their detrimental effects. The formidable booming of their own guns greatly bolstered the courage of the soldiery, an asset in the bloody hand-to-hand combat which invariably followed.

## Ship's Provisions

Rations were minimally adequate. On the galleys of Habsburg Spain slaves received a daily ration of hardtack or sea biscuit called *bizcocho*, a stew of beans moderately flavoured with olive oil and sea salt, and a measure of fetid water. On the galleys of the Knights Hospitaller the stew for the *ciurma* could be a "*minestre di riso, pasta, fave, fagioli, ceci, lente, amandoli, passoli, taria*".[48]

As for specifics, we can look at two years, 1538 and 1580. For the year 1538, the rations for the *ciurma* serving in the galleys of Sicily were as follows: twenty-six ounces of *bizcocho* per day; four ounces of meat three days a week; a stew of vegetables four days a week served in two-ounce portions.[49] For the year 1580, the rations for the *ciurma* serving in the galleys of Spain were as follows: twenty-six ounces of *bizcocho* per day; eight ounces of meat five days a year; around one-eighth of a cup of *garbanzos* per day.[50] What we witness here, with virtual disappearance of meat from the diet of the *ciurma* serving Spanish galleys, is the deterioration of an oarsman's diet. Presumably the five meat rations were doled out at the Christian feasts such as Christmas, Easter, Whitsuntide, and so forth.

Clearly some form of cooking was done on a galley because the daily bowl of stew served to the *ciurma* would have been hot. Though fires onboard ships have always been a concern, there is evidence that the primary method of cooking was with firewood. On some galleys it is known that the ninth rearmost rowing bench on the port side was missing, its place being taken up by the cook and his firewood stove.

Hot or not, their everyday food was monotonous, coarse, unwholesome and insufficient in quantity; we can be pretty sure that today's topflight rowers do not live on a régime of beans and biscuits, the last article perhaps being the most reviled by soldiers and sailors since time immemorial: made from plain flour, water and sometimes salt, hardtack had fed armies and navies from the beginning of recorded history – and was the butt of many jokes. A staple of sea voyages and military campaigns for millennia, hardtack is exceptionally dry, solid, and designed to be nonperishable; it is not edible until soaked in liquid, and – if sailors' jokes are any indication – not even then.[51]

While we are on the subject, hardtack was exactly that, *bizcocho* (It. *biscoctus*), from the mediaeval Latin meaning 'twice-cooked', so that it was hard but light and easily preserved (loaf bread tended to go mouldy), though if insufficiently baked or packed too soon after baking it was prone to turn mouldy.[52] Baking cereal grains into a dense biscuit made for easy transportation and reduced the risk of spoilage, although maggot and weevil infestation was a different story. More importantly, it was relatively cheap and had a very long shelf life.[53]

Hardtack is frequently referred to as being a very basic type of provision, and that the biscuit used in war time were made "twise baked, and without leauen or salt: because it should not vinewe or mowell in short time".[54] The hard, dry biscuit was often broken up and mixed with water or sour wine to create a form of bread potage. The teeth (or lack thereof) of our forefathers would have been ill equipped for chewing through what was essentially a tile made of soft rock.

Water was an important munition of war on a galley, for each oarsman would need at least eight litres of water a day, especially when rowing in hot weather – an average individual requires about two litres of fluid per day. For the oarsmen, therefore, it was essential to drink water, and lots of it. It was like fuel, indispensable for the survival of the *ciurma* and the working of the galley. Even moderate dehydration would have severely reduced a galley's oarsmen's ability to pull efficiently. Modern studies have shown that dehydration sufficient to cause a loss of three per cent of body weight leads to observable decline in performance, including approximately a thirty per cent decrease in endurance.[55] In an individual weighing seventy kilograms (154 lbs), the standard widely used in nutrition studies, this level of water loss would be 2.1 litres. Extended heavy exertion can lead to a water loss of up to 6.6 litres per day.[56]

Galleys could carry over 5,000 litres of water in barrels, which spoiled easily and had to be purified and flavoured with sour wine or vinegar. The water barrels, which were small enough to be carried by one man, were stored near the rowing benches.[57] Supplies needed to be replenished, and, as in antiquity, frequent landfalls were the solution. But while water was probably the most critical consumable required by the galley crew, food – and enough of it to enable the oarsmen to maintain a high level of exertion – was also important. Least we forget, without the wheat, biscuit and wine from Naples and Sicily Lepanto could not have taken place.

It would appear that things had changed little since the times of the Greek soldier poet Archilochos,[58] even if they had to consume their basic rations leaning on pikes rather than spears. Bread and wine were the basis of the soldiers' nutritional régime, and *capitano* Imperiale Cinuzzi (†1592), a Tuscan veteran of the Spanish Army of Flanders, considered one-and-a-half to two pounds of either bread or biscuit and a *boccale* of wine or beer the minimum daily ration needed to keep a foot soldier operational while on campaign.[59] However, with or without the maggots and weevils, these were short rations, serving the demands of tactical mobility. Without the addition of expensive protein food such as meat and of oil, salt, vinegar, assorted vegetables, cheese and so on, it could not sustain a soldier for long periods without damaging his morale and health.

Accordingly, for a contemporary Elizabethan soldier at least, the staple diet was bread or biscuit, butter, cheese and beer, water being too risky to drink. This was leavened out with oatmeal, peas, beans, pork, bacon, fresh and salt beef, dried codfish, ling and herring. The beer that was issued was weak, but salt meat and hard biscuit had to be washed down with something. In a typical example (of 1598) the daily allowance was one pound of bread or biscuit, three ounces of butter, six ounces of cheese, and three-quarters of a pint of oatmeal. Naturally the daily ration varied according to circumstances. Another version of 1598 was one pound of biscuit, or one pound and a half of bread. Every seventh day the bread ration was accompanied by two pounds of salt beef, or two-and-a-half pounds of fresh beef.[60] The relatively small allocation of meat was not unusual, flesh not being a daily component of the diet of the lower orders at the time. By way of comparison, the janissary at war during the mid-18th century was expected to need a daily intake of a double loaf of bread (roughly 320 grams), or a 50-*dirhem* biscuit (160 grams), and was allowed half an *okka* of meat (641 grams).[61]

The food provided for Martin Frobisher's second voyage to Arctic Canada in 1577 may be of interest too: one pound of hardtack per man per day; one gallon of beer per man per day; one pound of salt beef or pork per man on meat days, plus one dried or salted codfish for every four men on fast days; oatmeal and rice as backup in case the fish supply ran out; one-quarter-pound of butter and one-half-pound of cheese per man per day. Beer was the primary beverage on board an English ship because it stored longer than water without being contaminated. Frobisher's sailors ate and drank well.

Modern studies have indicated that diets that are high in carbohydrates such as bread, pasta – or ship biscuits – are much more efficient for prolonged heavy work, and even increased endurance over those that obtain most of their calories from fats. The diet of hard, dry biscuit, the primary carbohydrate, a soup of beans and a little salted meat, accompanied by beer per day, while not appealing to a gourmand was well suited to the physiological needs of a soldier.[62] All in all, throughout our period of study a soldier's rations were sufficient to keep a man reasonably well fed, provided he received them.

We have already made mention of the bean stew served to the *ciurma* of a Hospitaller galley. The knights themselves fared much better to say the very least. When a galley of the Order put to sea, it took on board about 220 *cantari* (9,009 kg) of hardtack and 5,000 small loaves as well as four heads of cattle and other meat on the hoof. It loaded about forty Sicilian rams, 150 hens, and 150 pigeons. Hardly surprising, therefore, the knights dined on fresh meat four times a week, and not boiled either, but roasted, grilled or fried. The galley also carried quantities of wine, vinegar, olive oil, salted tuna, sardines, cheese, lard, salted beef, 5,000 eggs, dried fish, caviar, cocoa, rice, butter, peas, and flour.[63]

For the Lepanto campaign the eleven Genoese galleys personally owned by Gianandrea Doria received from the Spanish crown 40,000 *libras* of biscuit, 9,000 litres of wine, 3,100 *libras* of salted meat, 1,535 *libras* of dried herrings, 2,940 *libras* of cheese, 4,600 *libras* of (olive?) oil, 810 litres of vinegar, 2,400 *libras* of fava beans and 240 *libras* of salt, supplies sufficient for just a fortnight.[64] The galley's strength in manpower was also its chief drawback. It consumed provisions at a rate commensurate with the number of people wedged into it.

Without a doubt, keeping the men of a war fleet fed was a major undertaking. Gathering rations for such was never going to be an easy task, as Miguel de Cervantes would later discover to his own detriment. After attempting and failing to make a living as a playwright (only two of his plays survive), he took a job as a roving royal purveyor in Andalusia, requisitioning supplies (barley, wheat and olive oil) for the Armada before it set sail for England in the summer of 1588. This led to his incarceration for a few months in the royal prison of Seville – apparently a living hell of noise, confusion, violence and stench in those days – after a banker with whom he deposited a considerable sum of Crown money went bankrupt and absconded.[65]

This is not to say corruption did not happen. Ruses and tricks can be discovered at all levels. It is known that French convict oarsmen in the time of Louis XIV were indulged when royal officials came to measure how much bread each *galérien* needed, clever captains conducted tests using *les plus grand mangeurs*, the biggest eaters. The large surpluses were later sold on the open market.[66]

## Life aboard

"I know the taste of the hardtack and the overseer's whip", explains Cervantes' galley slave, Ginés de Pasamonte. Serving "God and the king", the picaroon Ginés had "already spent four years on the galleys".[67] On a galley those who grafted the most were the most undernourished and the most ill-treated. They were also the most exposed. When a galley was fully laden, the benches were only a metre from the surface of a flat calm sea and about seventy centimetres from the scupper holes, situated thirty centimetres above the waterline where the deck water flowed out. Little wonder, therefore, the slaves were permanently wet, their skin blistered and ulcerated from the salty sea spray. When the Mediterranean was less kind, they no doubt plied the oars with their feet in water.

Witness the fate of the Spanish Carmelite Fra' Jerónimo Gracián de la Madre de Dios (1545–1614), confessor and close collaborator of the religious reformer Santa Teresa d'Ávila (1515–82), who was a captive in Tunis for two years (1593–5). He recalls his first days as a slave aboard a corsair galiot:

> We had run out of biscuits (*bizcocho*), the water was very fetid, the heat and the smell of that place, great, and thus, the confusion, the thirst, the heat, the narrow confinement and the complaints and moans of the captives, everything caused grief (…).[68]

Fra' Gracián's vivid description of his first days of captivity in a Tunisian galiot, in the midst of horrendous heat and the fetid conditions of the crammed, narrow vessel of war, speaks for itself. The Knights Hospitaller – who had a sense of hygiene acute for those days – would clean out their galleys at every chance that came their way, by sinking them in shallow water. Galley commanders of other nations tended to ignore the perpetual stench more stoically. Six months before Lepanto, on 7 April 1571, the Venetian Senate would write to Agostino Barbarigo, the *provveditore generale da mar*, accusing the commanders of the previous year's expedition of having kept the galleys in totally unhygienic conditions:

> From which it may be understood the disease and deaths that hit our fleet … causing an offence to God our Lord and great damage and misfortune to the public good.[69]

They may have looked elegant gliding across the water, but it was sometimes said that you could recognise a slave galley by the stench that preceded it. As a French galley commander wrote during the reign of Louis XIV:

The evil smells being so strong that one cannot get away from them
in spite of the tobacco with which one is obliged to plug up one's
nostrils from morning to night.[70]

Often the human faeces and the like was left were it was, and the whole
mess was simply cleared away by a storm or downpour.

Generally speaking, a galley was extremely crowded, carrying more
men per tonne of displacement than any other vessel afloat. There were,
in the words of our French galley commander, "an infinite number of
villages that are far from having as large a number of inhabitants" as
a single galley. "When every man is at his post, only heads can be seen
from prow to stern."[71] Sanitation, a constant problem aboard any ship,
was aggravated by the crowding. To say that a fully-manned galley was
crowded is to understate the case. Taking a twenty-four-bench *galea
sottile* or ordinary galley as our example, on campaign it would have been
swarming – between 350 and 500 men were confined to an area about
forty-one metres (134.5 feet) long and five metres (16.5 feet) wide.

A galley was provided with one deck and all activities look place on it.
Below deck there was the captain's room at the stern and next to it there
was space enough for a small group of officers. Moving forwards to the
bows there were the bread store, the great room for victuals, a tavern where
wine would be sold from time to time, the powder magazine, the sail and
rope store and the space in the bows where coal and brushwood were kept.
In an emergency the sail room was utilised for the sick and wounded. In the
*corsia* or the raised passageway between the rowing benches, were stored all
the spare sails, ropes and awnings together with the clothing of the *ciurma*.
Access to the hold below deck was gained by a companion way on the port
side of the *spalliera* and through six hatches located beneath the removable
rowing benches. Lead ballast was located on the flat timbers of the galley.

As we can see, life aboard a galley was appallingly uncomfortable even
for the free men. The oars and rowing benches took up most of the ship's
space, leaving little room for much else. Besides this, hundreds of soldiers
were always crowded on the narrow *corsia*, the only available surface, and
whenever the sails were hoisted or furled, chaos reigned in a tangled mess
of rigging, scrambling sailors and shoving soldiers. On a fighting galley,
space was at a premium.

No amount of discomfort suffered by slaves, sailors and soldiers alike on board galleys could compare with the cruelty of the disease that constantly assaulted them without warning and carried away thousands of men at one blow. Stalking the galley like a shadow, the epidemic usually started among its undernourished slaves, who lived in the filthiest conditions, but since all were squeezed together in such close quarters, the pestilence spread quickly to soldiers, sailors and even to the officers, turning the galley into a ghost ship of the dead and the dying. Although surgeons served at sea, there was little they could do in the face of major epidemics. Epidemic diseases were the unrecognised but most deadly weapon of early modern warfare, and the two worst kind of plagues in the Mediterranean fleets were cholera and typhus, neither of which had any cure at that time: take for instance the plague of 1720–1, which carried off one fifth of France's rowing force.[72] Indeed, typhus, a malady that thrives in environments where overcrowding and unwashed humanity congregates, would take more lives at sea than the hottest action or the wildest weather.

*Part III*

# The Contest

*Chapter 15*

# The Approach

There was a man sent from God whose name was John.

Pius V, quoting John 1:6[1]

As September drew to a close, both sides were still unsure of each other's strength. The Holy League fleet was believed to number no more than 164 galleys. A daring corsair captain, Kara Hodja, had painted a longboat pitch black (a ruse borrowed from the Knights Hospitaller for raiding at night) and actually floated among the Christian fleet at anchor near Grava (It. *Gomenniza*, today Igoumenista), north-western Greece, to obtain what he believed was an accurate tally. His tally was short by some forty galleys, while he took the Venetian galleasses for nothing more than six round merchant ships.

## The Ottomans

Müezzinzāde Ali Paşa, *kapudan-ı deryā* of the sultan's naval forces, and Pertev Paşa, the commander of the land forces aboard the galleys, were to combine their commands during the Ottoman operations on Cyprus and moved to Rhodes, and then attacked Crete. The Ottoman fleet, misinformed of the whereabouts of the Christian fleet, had opted to confront it at Crete where they were joined by the Barbary contingent of Uluç Ali Re'īs, *beylerbeyi* of Algiers, who had twenty ships under his command. Together they attacked the island of Kephalonia and seized three Venetian-held fortresses; at the time of which they were still uninformed about the activities of the enemy fleet.

Since it was nearing October, most of the timariot horsemen on Ottoman ships asked for permission to return home, which they were granted: they would serve as a rule only during the campaign season, that is to say, from spring to autumn. Some oarsmen and fighting men also took advantage of the opportunity to leave their ships when the fleet anchored at the port of Naupaktos. There the news arrived about the coming of the enemy fleet to confront the Ottoman fleet. The Ottoman fleet had sailed into the harbour of Naupaktos in September and wasted no time in mounting raids against a couple of Venetian-held fortresses (Dulcigno and Antivari in Albania) in the neighbouring regions. But a question of self-preservation at once occurred to the Ottoman rank and file. As we learn from Ottoman chroniclers, many of the combatants who had landed to fight ashore deserted and never returned to their ships.[2]

For a number of weeks the Ottoman fleet had been anchored under the fortress guns of Naupaktos, and, on 5 October, it began to sail slowly westward, passing the dividing headlands that separated the Gulf of Corinth from the shorter Gulf of Patras (part of the Ionian Sea). Still uncertain of the enemy's position, Müezzinzāde Ali order the fleet to drop anchor for the night in a sheltered bay some twenty-four kilometres from the entrance of the gulf, where it remained all the following day awaiting the return of the fleet's scouting vessels. Around midnight the intrepid Kara Hodja reached the anchorage with the news that the Christian fleet was then at Kephalonia.

With the first light of dawn the following morning, 7 October, lookouts stationed on the northern shore at the mouth of the Gulf of Patras signalled to Kara Hodja that the enemy was rounding the headland into the gulf itself. The signal was relayed to Müezzinzāde Ali, who gave the order to weigh anchor and prepare for battle. Only some twenty-four kilometres of open water separated the forces of Islam from those of Christendom.

Müezzinzāde Ali Paşa in some ways resembled Don Juan de Austria: closely connected to princely blood and extremely young for such an important command, yet brave and intelligent. He too had subordinate officers who were very much his senior in years and naval experience. As the 17th-century Ottoman chronicler Kātib Çelebi put it, "the grand admiral of the Ottoman navy had not commanded a single rowing boat in his life".[3] This is true, for Müezzinzāde Ali came from a janissary background and had no knowledge of matters nautical, let alone naval warfare. True, janissaries could and did serve aboard galleys, as they would that day at Lepanto, but according to another 17th-century

Ottoman chronicler, Solakzade Mehmed (1592–1658), Müezzinzāde Ali "has not seen a naval battle nor was he informed of the science of piracy".[4]

Under him indeed were Uluç Ali Re'īs, the chief of the Barbary corsairs, and Şuluk Mehmed Paşa (better known to Europeans as Mehmed Sirocco)[5] and Amuret Turgut Re'īs, both of whom were regional governors of important Ottoman provinces in Egypt and Greece, as well as skilled naval commanders. Although these men served the same master, the Ottoman sultan, and, unlike the Christian commanders, were not jealous confederates, Müezzinzāde Ali also had to cope with conflicting opinions on strategy among his subordinates. In fact, it was he alone who was happy regarding Selīm's command to seek out and destroy "the fleet of the Infidels, fully trusting in God and the name of the Prophet".[6] Besides, his head was at stake.

The objections of Uluç Ali are worth noting at this point, for they emanated from his knowledge of the conditions of the ships in the Ottoman fleet. In his view the ships were worn out owing to the six-month campaign that they had been involved in. Also, many of the fighting men of the fleet had returned to their homes, with or without permission. In his opinion the fleet should adopt a defensive positon, nestled under the fortifications of Naupaktos, and let the infidels come to them. The Ottoman fleet would then be protected by a stout fortress armed with long-range *balyemez* cannon, which fired shots weighing between thirty-one and seventy-four kilograms, what Europeans would consider as siege guns.[7] Naupaktos was not only singularly difficult to attack, but could easily be supplied, since the Gulf of Patras communicates with the Aegean via the narrow Isthmus of Corinth. In the Aegean was another Ottoman naval base, at Negroponte (Chalkis or Chalkida), on the island of Euboia (Gk. Εὔβοια).[8] Without a doubt, the corsair chief was the most experienced of *all* the Ottoman commanders present that fateful day.

Once everyone had given his opinion, Müezzinzāde Ali aired his own views. He pointed out that the Christians were rent by jealousy and discord, which was true. He dismissed the galleasses as worthless, which was untrue. He admitted many of his fighting men were green, but they would be fighting alongside veterans, such as the janissaries, which was a fair point. Earlier, Pertev Paşa had raised the very important detail that the Christians were heavily armoured and equipped with harquebuses. In reply, Müezzinzāde Ali pointed out armour or no armour the Ottomans had always been victorious, a debatable point. Besides, he added, bows were better weapons than harquebuses, having a much faster rate of fire, which was true. He then reminded his commanders of Ottoman duty and honour. The war council ended with all agreeing with their *kapudan-ı deryā* "either because convinced, or in order not to be accused of cowardice".[9]

With the benefit of hindsight, it is easy for us to criticise the Ottoman grand admiral. It is possible that Müezzinzāde Ali was simply acting out of personal ambition, a human trait we underestimate at our peril when dealing with the art of venal self-preservation necessary to survive the sordid sport of pendulum politics. Much as in today's affairs of state, the *status quo* will always prevail. No one wins; at best they carry on.

The son of a müezzin in Edirne, hence his epithet *Müezzinzāde* ('son of a *müezzin*), Ali had entered the *bevvab*, the corps of gatekeepers, apparently thanks to the patronage of Hürrem Sultan, who admired his deep, melodious voice. From there he advanced by merit to become a *çasnigir*, a taster, *kapıcılar*, steward of the gatekeepers, *ağa çırağı*, commander of the janissary corps, *beylerbeyi* of Alexandria, and finally *kapudan-ı deryā*. Not bad for the son of a prayer caller. And that was his problem. For in the bear pit of Porte politics, Müezzinzāde Ali was looked down upon as an outsider by those grandees who had trained in the inner palace service, for not having been recruited through the *devişrme*. In fact, the allegation of inexperience made by Kātib Çelebi was unwarranted, for the chronicler clearly downplayed Müezzinzāde Ali's achievements on the high seas. Indeed, the subordinate officers who agreed to back his decision to attack knew full well that their commander in chief had participated in the Djerba and Malta enterprises, had acted as the deputy of Piyale Paşa, and had held the position of *kapudan-ı deryā* since 1567. Obviously Müezzinzāde Ali had some understanding of naval affairs. The forthcoming showdown with the Christian fleet was a golden opportunity to silence his critics.

## The Christians

Don Juan de Austria arrived in Genoa on 26 July 1571, departing five days later. On 9 August he arrived in Naples where he was to solemnly receive the banner of the Holy League from the hands of Cardinal Antoine Perrenot de Granvelle. At this juncture Don Juan headed forty-seven galleys that included the *tercios* of Don Lope de Figueroa and Don Miguel de Moncada. Moncada had added two companies to his *tercio* in Naples; Cervantes, as well as his brother Rodrigo, were among the recruits. The Spanish contingent moved south to the Sicilian port of Messina to join the waiting papal and Venetian contingent led by the seventy-five-year-old *capitano generale da mar* Sebastiano Veniero, arriving there on 23 August. "*De las mejores que jamas se han visto* [among the best galleys that were ever seen]", says Don Juan of his contingent, in a letter from Messina to Don García Álvarez de Toledo Osorio.[10]

The papacy's bantam contingent consisted of twelve galleys that the pope had hired from Cosimo I de' Medici (not from the Venetians), but they were in excellent order. It was commanded by the courteous and courageous but nautically inexperienced Roman noble, Marc'Antonio Colonna. He had, however, commanded troops in the Italian campaigns of the fifteen-fifties on behalf of Charles V, the Habsburg emperor, and Cosimo I de' Medici (Cosimo was married to Leonor Álvarez de Toledo y Pimentel-Osorio, the daughter of Don Pedro Álvarez de Toledo y Zúñiga). On aboard the papal galleys were 1,600 Italian foot soldiers, divided into eight companies. They had been recruited by a noble related by marriage to the Colonna clan, Onorato Caetani (1542–92), duca di Sermoneta and *capitán generale delle fanterie pontifcie*. The Tuscan crusading Order of Saint Stephen manned five of these galleys themselves, with about a hundred knights aboard.

En route to Messina Colonna was met by his son-in-law Antonio Carafa (†1578), duca di Rocca Mondragone, who had decided to join him in the coming venture, apparently with two galleys from Naples. He was then joined by three galleys of the Knights Hospitaller, who had volunteered to go with the Christian armada "as adventurers and without stipend". In fact, these Maltese galleys contained the highest proportion of knights and the largest number of gentlemen adventurers. They were under the command of the prior of Messina, Fra' Pietro Giustiniani, a Venetian by birth.

On 1 September Gianandrea Doria entered Messina harbour with eleven galleys of the Doria family fleet, along with fifteen others furnished by other Genoese patrician families, like the Grimaldi, the Centurione and the Sauli,[11] while sixty Venetian galleys from Crete turned up the

next day, in good shape and well equipped with oarsmen. Some had a few
of the famed Cretan archers, and most had the standard complement of
fifty *scapoli* but no other soldiers. Prospero Colonna had also arrived from
Naples with infantrymen he had managed to recruit in that kingdom.
But even with these troops and the 1,200 'bellicose Calabrian soldiers'
recruited for Sebastiano Veniero by Gaspare Toraldo, barone di Badolato,
the Venetian galleys were still short of fighting men. Thirty galleys led
by Don Álvaro de Bazán, marqués de Santa Cruz and *capitán general
de Napoli*, made their way into Messina on 6 September, bringing the
Christian fleet to its full fighting strength.

The streets and taverns of the Sicilian port were thronged with a violent
and volatile bunch of Spaniards, Italians and Germans. The professional
marines of *la Serenissima* and the soldiers in the pay of Habsburg Spain
looked sideways at each other and occasionally came to blows, because old
grudges and differences, real or imagined, never fade away. Meanwhile,
their commanders were suspicious of each other, sarcasm rather than
swords being their weapon of choice. To make matters worse, wages were
in arrears and the season was advancing, the weather was unsettled and
the sea choppy.

On 14 September, an early storm blew over the Holy League as it lay
at anchor in the crowded harbour of Messina – a bad omen for some
who doubted of the wisdom of sailing so late in the season. It was an old
Mediterranean nautical rule of thumb to postpone putting to sea with the
coming of the stormy autumn weather. Nevertheless, it was time for the
Christian soldiers to quit Messina to start their campaign in the eastern
Mediterranean, fighting the people they were supposed to fight. At dawn
on 16 September, the Holy League fleet weighed anchor and eased out
of the harbour of Messina, with Don Juan's flagship *La Real* leading the
way. *La Real* was a splendid ship built of Catalan pine at the Atarazanas
Reales de Barcelona for the Viceroy of Catalonia three years before. She
had seventy oars pulled by 420 oarsmen, five bow guns, and another
gun on her high poop, pointing over her stern, which was adorned with
elaborate wood carvings depicting a mixture of motifs borrowed from
both pagan and Christian traditions, the work of Juan Bautista Vázquez el
Viejo (†1588), one of the most famous sculptors of the day. The interior of
the stern was furnished in a style of luxury that seemed to be designed for

pleasure rather than for the rough duties of war. She led the largest naval armament the Christians were ever to assemble in the 16th century.[12]

Standing on the end of the jetty, the papal nuncio, Odescalchi, bishop of Penna, dressed in his pontifical robes, blessed each ship as it passed and headed out to sea. All the fleet's forces had already been granted the same special indulgences (remission of punishment for sins) enjoyed by the original Holy Land crusaders centuries before. This would be the last time the papacy was able to direct organise violence against a rival of Christianity before the wars of religion between Catholics and Protestants divided Europe. In short, Lepanto was to be the Last Crusade.

By mid-morning, the Strait of Messina was filled with a flamboyant array of fluttering pennants and white sails, the canvas snapping and billowing in the sea breeze, as the Christian armada ploughed towards the southern Italian coast. Three days later, while the armada sheltered from a storm in the lee of Capo Colonna at the entrance to the Gulfo di Taranto, its commanders received some disquieting news. It seemed that the Ottoman fleet they sought was reportedly dispersing and might never confront them. But that night, a brilliant meteor flashed across the sky, lighting up the sea. To the watchful Christian fleet, it seemed to portend a momentous event. On 19 September the fleet put into the harbour of Crotone (Cotrone), where Don John embarked 600 soldiers, who had been waiting for him. He generously offered them to Sebastiano Veniero, whose galleys badly needed them, but the Venetian *capitano generale da mar* insisted that he did not. On 24 September, after rounding Capo Santa Maria di Leuca on the heel of Italy, the Christian armada steered eastward for Greece across the stormy mouth of the Adriatic Sea.

Fra' Gil d'Andrada, captain of *La Real* and a veteran Castilian Knight Hospitaller who had fought eleven years earlier at Djerba, was sent ahead of the fleet with four first-rate galleys, each with a double complement of oarsmen, to seek out the Ottomans and send back word. And so it was that new reports came to Don Juan and his commanders that the Ottoman fleet had, in fact, not dispersed, but had raided the Greek island of Corfu, at the mouth of the Adriatic, two weeks before and was now making its way southward for the Gulf of Patras. More stormy weather forced the Christian fleet to take shelter amid the reefs and islands off north-western Greece. When the skies cleared on 26 September, Don Juan's ships sailed into Corfu harbour.[13] His soldiers went ashore to forage for food and water and found that the Ottoman raiders had bypassed Corfu's fortress but had gutted the villages and farms for miles around of all the available victuals. At Corfu, the Holy League fleet commanders gathered in formal council for the last time. Don Juan listened to his commanders, weighed the opinions (many were contrary), and finally he announced his decision to go and meet the enemy in battle.

On 29 September, about 4,000 troops from the island garrison were embarked and trained for two days. Don Juan reviewed their gunnery exercises. At the same time Don Juan personally inspected the fleet, condemning four Venetian galleys that were unfit for active service. A month earlier, while still in Messina, in his correspondence with his trusted advice-giver Don García Álvarez de Toledo Osorio, Don Juan speaks with high disgust of the negligence shown in equipping the Venetian galleys:

> You cannot imagine what bad conditions I found aboard the Venetian galleys. They have weapons, but these do not fire by themselves, and what few men they have are either sick or too old to fight.[14]

Not only were the Venetian galleys in poor trim and undermanned, but also they were manned by soldiers who were under prepared, in other words, not properly accustomed to the hardships of the service at sea. As a result, he tried to redistribute his available soldiers throughout the fleet, and in the process almost caused the collapse of the alliance. Most of the Venetian galleys were chronically undermanned and 1,500 Spanish and 2,500 Italian veterans from Spain's well-manned contingent were used to augment the Venetian soldiers on board the galleys.[15]

Friction between the two groups soon caused a fracas on one Venetian galley from Crete, the *Uomo Armato* of Retimo. One Muzio da Cortona, a subject of the king of Spain and a truculent turbulent fellow, let fall some insulting remarks about the Venetians. A quarrel at once arose, warmly espoused by some Spanish harquebusiers on the one side and some Venetian sailors on the other. It soon became serious. From words they came to blows, which led again to a free-for-all, and the deck was littered with dead and wounded men. The Venetian naval commander-in-chief,

Sebastiano Veniero, ordered the officer involved, along with his sergeant and one of his corporals, to be immediately hung from the yardarm. The order was at once carried out, and the corpses of these brawlers hanging aloft were clear evidence of the Venetian commander's *modus operandi*.

Yet, as these men were in the service of Spain, Veniero's arbitrary actions sparked a major incident; Spanish soldiers and Venetian crews prepared to fight each other. Troops were armed, guns were loaded, and the two contingents squared off for a fight. Only the intervention of the papal admiral Marc'Antonio Colonna prevented the fleet from tearing itself apart in an orgy of internecine fighting. Of his eleven councillors, eight advised the furious Don Juan immediately to send twenty galleys against the Venetian fleet, seize Veniero from its midst, and straightway hang him on a yardarm. However, the more sagacious counsel of Colonna prevailed. The Roman softened the Spaniard's fury with the suggestion, which was accepted, that the choleric Venetian should no longer take part in the deliberations of the commanders in the councils of war.[16]

The following day, although a still furious Don Juan refused even to speak to the disgraced Veniero, the fragile alliance was restored. Agostino Barbarigo, the *provveditore generale da mar*, the Venetian naval second-in-command,[17] and a man of more equable temper and considerable experience both in diplomatic and seafaring matters, became the new Venetian representative, and although tensions remained high, both sides were persuaded that the real enemy was the Ottoman fleet, not each other. Besides, Don Juan felt, as so many military leaders had felt and were to feel, that God was with him. There would be no turning back.

Eventually, on 3 October, the Christian armada weighed anchor again and steered southward against strong headwinds toward the Gulf of Patras, where the Ottoman fleet had assembled. Passing by Ithaka, the ancient home of Odysseus, continuing foul winds and shifting fog forced Don Juan's armada to take refuge in the bay of Phiscardo, a large opening in the Kephalonian shore opposite the Greek mainland not far from Marcus Antonius' Actium. War galleys were a fair-weather weapon and for two days the fleet lay weather-bound in the bay. During one of these days of storm Kara Hodja, the corsair, tried again to reconnoitre the Christian fleet, but was driven off by the guard ships at the entrance of the strait. Moreover, on the evening of 5 October, a Turkish renegade

– perhaps a double agent – reported to Don Juan that the strength of the Ottoman fleet had been reduced to one hundred galleys and that a plague was afflicting its men. The Christians were anxious that the Ottomans not evade them, but, in fact, during the night of 6 October, the confident Ottoman fleet set sail westward from Lepanto in search of battle.

Don Juan's fleet weighed anchor at 0200 hours on Sunday morning, 7 October, and approached the Gulf of Patras between the Curzolaris archipelago, anciently known as the Echinades (today's Ekhinadhes), the small cluster of rocky isles in the Ionian Sea at the mouth of the Acheloüs,[18] and ragged shoals of north-western Greece, some forty nautical miles west of Naupaktos. The sea was choppy, and a south-easterly wind blew in the faces of the Christian seamen. There was a certain amount of straggling. It was difficult to keep the fleet closed up, and the Venetian galleasses especially felt the effect of the headwind, and some of the galleys had to assist them by towing. As the first light of dawn broke and the allied vanguard butted into the mouth of the gulf, Don Juan asked that Catholic mass be celebrated throughout the fleet. Almost simultaneously, observers in the flagship's maintop sighted two sails in the distance (most sightings were made at dawn). Soon, they shouted that there were four sails, and then eight silhouetted against the slanting rays of the rising sun. Within a few minutes, they had the first glimpse of the entire Ottoman fleet – hurried westward by a favourable wind after leaving its anchorage – now visible on the horizon and bearing toward the Holy League fleet in a crescent formation. The die was cast.

The first principle of naval tactics – in so far as any tactics existed – in a battle under sail had always been to get to windward of the enemy, because in that position a naval commander could choose his moment to bear down and attack. Thus, when all is said, the most important factor was always the sea itself and winds that disturb its surface. However brave and skilful the crews might be, however good the plans, a change of wind changed everything. If one believed, as everyone more or less believed in those days, that God observed human actions and decreed the wind, then clearly a battle at sea was directly subject to His will. The wind then suddenly shifted around from the east to the opposite direction and thus in the Christians' favour.[19] Having lost the fair wind, the Muslims were seen to be furling their now useless sails. As the day wore on, the sun also moved to the west, shining into the eyes of the Muslims. The advantage had shifted too.

The Venetian admiral, the quiet-spoken and popular Agostino Barbarigo, took position on the northern end of his squadron while the fifty-three galleys formed a line abreast, heading eastward. The papal admiral, Marc'Antonio Colonna, was on Don Juan's immediate right, while the septuagenarian Venetian *capitano generale da mar* Sebastiano Veniero, a scarred warrior and the most experienced officer in the Christian fleet, was on his immediate left. Two of the thirty-eight galleys of the reserve squadron led by Don Álvaro de Bazán, marqués de Santa Cruz and *capitán general de Napoli*, were directly astern. Over Don Juan's flagship, *La Real* of his Catholic Majesty, the banner of the Holy League was unfurled. Of azure damask, embroidered on the upper part of the banner was an image of Christ the Redeemer, while below were the arms of the three main allies: the Holy See, Habsburg Spain, and the Republic of Venice, united by a chain, from which were suspended the arms of Don Juan de Austria.

With the Ottoman navy in full view and the fleet poised for combat, a confident Don Juan reportedly danced a galliard with two other Spanish gentlemen on the *spalliera* of *La Real* to the music of the fifes – after offering one of the tersest pre-battle harangues in military history: "Gentlemen, this is not the time to discuss but fight."[20] Even so, as the forces readied for mortal combat, priest and friars on Christian galleys moved from stem to stern armed with crucifixes, blessing the men, hearing their final confessions, and encouraging them to be ready to shed their blood for God the Saviour.[21] The sight of the enemy seemed to bring about an era of good feeling; old animosities were quickly forgotten. Both Don Juan and Marc'Antonio Colonna took especial pains to conciliate the irascible old admiral Veniero, and the interchange of compliments, doubtless sincere, contributed to the spirit of comradeship.[22] Perhaps at no period of his short career was Don Juan more remarkable than at this moment.

Around 1100 hours, the opposing battle lines slowly rowed together until they were about 500 metres apart. Until that time, the Christians had underestimated the Ottoman fleet, and the Ottomans the Christian fleet. Now the moment of truth had arrived, the Ottomans burst forward to move in for the kill. So began the last great battle to be fought between oar-powered ships.

# Chapter 16

# Battle Arrays

The one whom the two lines of battle, coming together, call upon separately, the nearer and the farther, both foes

'To Indra', *Rig Veda*

Historians can and do quibble about numbers of the two greatest galley armadas ever assembled, but agree that both fleets at Lepanto had near parity with regards to numbers of galleys. The number of soldiers on board the ships of each side was similar too: somewhere around 29,000 fighting troops, though it is possible the Ottoman soldiers had greater combat experience, which was certainly the case with the 10,000 veteran janissaries. There were more Ottoman ships than Christian ones: just 206 galleys and 6 galleasses on the Christian side, and 216 galleys and 56 galiots on the Ottoman, which the Ottoman fleet commander and sultan's brother-in-law, Müezzinzāde Ali Paşa, organised in a crescent shape in the hope of wrapping his fleet around the Christian fleet, while the centre of his line would attempt to break the enemy into digestible chunks. Christian ships, though, were built to last, whereas part of the Ottoman fleet was constructed out of 'green' wood and was regarded as disposable – suitable for a couple of seasons before replacement. The *capitana* of Malta at Lepanto, the *Santa Maria della Victoria*, was a seasoned galley of seventeen years, having been launched in 1554.[1]

The Ottoman fleet consisted mainly of light galleys that sat low in the water, increasing their vulnerability but also enabling them to handle shallower inshore waters in which they could hope to outflank the heavier Christian craft; the Venetians, famed for the excellence of their naval artillery – their good and experienced gunners could load and fire more quickly than the Spaniards – also favoured lighter and faster galleys. The Christian navy possessed about twice as many cannon as the Ottoman

Turks, but the latter had brought along very many archers; guns were devastating, but slow to load, while archers could reload in an instant. Both sides also used matchlock harquebuses, hand-held guns which were not terribly accurate, but which could be reloaded reasonably fast, and had replaced the deadly steel crossbows of more recent times. The Spanish flagship, *La Real*, had 35 rowing banks and some 420 oarsmen rowing 6 to a bench. Its fighting complement centred around 400 harquebusiers, all from the *Tercio de Sardinia* we are told. This was closely matched by her Ottoman opposite number. The *Sultana* carried 300 janissaries and 100 harquebusiers.[2]

## The Christians

As already noted, Christian galley sizes and crew allocations varied, but a typical *galea sottile* required a *ciurma* of about 200 oarsmen to operate the vessel. The larger, heavier *lanterne* required a proportionately larger crew, while the galleasses needed a minimum of 320 oarsmen and sailors. As for soldiers, the typical *galea sottile* carried 125 soldiers on board, but at Lepanto these numbers varied widely. Despite the fact that Venice had been busy recruiting troops at home and abroad, the Venetian fleet was understrength in both marines and oarsmen, prompting Don Juan to order Sebastian Veniero to take on board Spanish and Italian veterans to augment his crews. A document mentions the Venetians having a meagre forty *scapoli* per galley when they arrived off Corfu, but once Veniero was forced to take on foreign troops (5,200 Italian mercenaries under duc di Acri and Prospero Colonna), and once men were stripped from the Corfu garrison, the situation improved enough to allow about eighty-five soldiers per galley. Under pressure from the Spaniards, Veniero accepted 1,614 Spaniards and 2,489 Italian mercenaries in Spanish service were distributed throughout the still short-handed Venetian galleys (the crusty Venetian refused to have any Germans); meaning that on average each Venetian galley carried approximately 120 soldiers.[3] The average Spanish strength was 150 soldiers and gentlemen adventurers per galley, though many contingents ran well over this figure. The galleys of Naples, for instance, shipped an average of some 150 *tercio* infantry and 30 gentlemen adventurers per galley.[4] The papal and Genoese galleys, on the other hand, carried 120 to 130 soldiers each. Invariably, *lanterne* carried larger contingents of troops.

The following soldiers were reported as being available for service in the fleet before the battle: 5,000 Venetian, 1,500 papal, 5,000 German and 5,000 Italian mercenaries in Spanish pay, all good soldiers, 8,000 Spanish regular infantry of excellent quality, and 4,000 gentlemen adventurers, the latter being very blue-blooded indeed, for a total of 28,500 soldiers. The Spanish regulars were divided into four *tercios*: those of Don Lope de Figueroa, Don Miguel de Moncada, Don Diego Enriquez, and Don Pedro de Padilla. All four had served under Don Juan de Austria in the war against the *morisco* rebels in Granada, and without exception were so depleted that some companies had to be almost entriely recruited. Yet it should be mentioned that the Venetian oarsmen were mainly free citizens and were able to bear arms, thereby adding to the fighting power of their ship, whereas convicts and slaves were used to row many of the galleys in other Christian contingents. It is said that just prior to the battle all the Christian indentured and criminal galley slaves were unchained and handed short swords and promised their freedom. Given that the fleet contained about 40,000 sailors and oarsmen, the total Christian force amounted to just under 70,000 men. It should be understood, however, that during the campaign there would have been a constant wastage, weekly, even daily, from desertion, disease and death.

Don Juan and his army were fortified in spirit by the blessings of the pope and the blessed banner of the Crucified Redeemer; the ministrations of the black-cassocked Jesuits, black-robed Dominicans, grey-cowled Franciscans, and bearded Capuchins who accompanied the fleet, the prayers of the faithful; and the rosaries – more of which anon – that were pressed into the hands of every Christian oarsman. A Capuchin and a Jesuit were the chaplains aboard Don Juan's *La Real*.

It should be noted too, least we be charged with omission, that Don Juan had decided that the way to get the maximum performance from his polyglot command was to shuffle the national contingents and form new, mixed ones. Although it is not usually expedient to break up fighting units, this was a very astute political move on the part of Don Juan, for it would ensure against the defection of any one national group and also inspire the individual galleys to fight harder in order to outdo their nearby rival allies. Naturally, as this fusion was supposed to have been made to guard against treachery – and there seems little reason to doubt that this was the case – it tells a sad tale of the suspicion and distrust which reigned amongst the allies. What is more, in one of his correspondence to Don Juan, Don García Álvarez de Toledo Osorio offered some very sound tactical suggestions. Remembering Barbarossa's battle array at Préveza all those decades ago, he recommended the Christian fleet be divided into three divisions, all sailing in one line but with significant distance between them to allow room for manoeuvring.[5]

Don García would have known that it was virtually impossible to maintain a compact formation of more than sixty galleys abreast. Changing direction required superhuman efforts from the end galleys to keep up. Elsewhere an accordion effect bunched galleys up or spread them apart, opening dangerous gaps to the enemy, who was assured victory if allowed to attack from the side. A second line of reserve galleys made it possible to stop some of the gaps. Moreover, they could attach themselves to the rear of a friendly galley and feed reinforcements into the mêlée combat taking place on its deck.

The names Don Juan gave to the various divisions of the Christian fleet may be confusing if not paradoxical, but the Spanish being essentially a martial people, he used army terms throughout. On land, on the march, the army was divided, as indeed everyone else then did, into three divisions: vanguard, main battle, and rearguard. And so it was that the Christian fleet was divided (besides the small vanguard, *antiguarda*, of four Sicilian and four Venetian galleys led by the Spaniard Giovanni Antonio de Cardona) into four separate contingents, the left wing (It. *corno sinistro*, Sp. *cuerno izquierda*), the centre (It. *battaglia*, Sp. *battalla*, viz. 'main battle'), the right wing (It. *corno dextro*, Sp. *cuerno derecha*), and the reserve (It. *retroguarda*, Sp. *socorro*), each distinguished by pennants of a particular colour to be flown from each vessel. As for the six Venetian galleasses, two would be towed to the forefront of each of the three main contingents of the armada before it met the Ottoman Turks.

## The Ottomans

The Ottomans had 216 galleys (including *lanterne*) at Lepanto, giving them parity in numbers. In addition, they were supported by fifty-six galiots and sixty-four *fuste*. Although the Ottomans had a higher number of *bastarda* than the Christians, they had fewer *lanterne* (twenty-one compared to twenty-five or twenty-six). Like the ordinary galleys in the Christian fleet, each Ottoman galley needed a *ciurma* of approximately 200 men, while the galiots carried about 80 men each, and the *fuste* 60. This gives an approximate fleet total of 37,000 oarsmen, virtually all of them slaves, and 13,000 experienced sailors, generally drawn from the maritime nations of the Ottoman empire, namely Greeks, Syrians, and Egyptians. Some 27,000 soldiers were distributed throughout the fleet, including 10,000 janissaries from Greek garrisons, 2,000 dismounted *sipāhis*, and approximately 4,000 volunteers and adventurers. If we assume just over 5,000 soldiers were distributed throughout the smaller galiots and *fuste* (with an average of 55 and 25 soldiers on each craft respectively), then about a hundred to 120 Ottoman Turkish soldiers were carried on board each galley, with proportionately more on the Ottoman lanterne.

The *Sultana* of Müezzinzāde Ali Paşa carried on board the aforementioned 300 hardened janissaries who wielded their composite recurve bows with awesome efficiency. Flying from her masthead was a battle flag from Mecca made of white silk and embroidered in gold with a verse from the Qur'ān and the name of Allah inscribed upon it no less than twenty-eight thousand nine hundred times.[6]

Suffice it to say that much like the Christian fleet, the Ottoman fleet was divided into the right wing, the centre, the left wing and the reserve. On the other hand, the centre was deployed in two lines, the reserve was composed mainly of galiots, and the left wing, commanded by Uluç Ali, a master of manoeuvre, made stronger than its Christian counterpart with the evident hope of using its superior numbers and manoeuvrability to turn the enemy flank.

## Holy League Fleet[7]

### The Left Wing (Agostino Barbarigo)
(53 galleys, 2 galleasses, yellow pennant flown from each foreyard)

### Venetian galleasses (2)
Galleass of Ambrogio Bragadin: two 50-pounder culverins, two 30-pounder culverins, four 14-pounder culverins, four 30-pounder

cannon, four 20-pounder cannon, two 16-pounder cannon, two 6-pounder *falcones*, twelve 3-pounder *falconetti*, eight 1-pounders.

Galleass of Antonio Bragadin:[8] two 50-pounder culverins, two 30-pounder culverins, four 14-pounder culverins, two 30-pounder cannon, four 20-pounder cannon, one 16-pounder cannon, two 6-pounder *falcones*, six 3-pounder *falconetti*, four 3-pounder *pedreros*, six 1-pounders.

*Venetian galleys (39)*
*Capitana lanterna* of Venice (L) – Agostino Barbarigo †, *provveditore generale da mar*
*Capitana* of Venice (L) – Marco Querini, *provveditore* of the fleet
*Fortuna* of Venice – Andrea Barbarigo †
*Tre Mani* of Venice – Giorgio Barbarigo †
*Due Delfini* of Candia – Francesco Zen
*Leone e Fenice* of Candia – Francesco Mengano
*Madonna* of Candia – Fillipo Polani
*Cavallo Marino* of Candia – Antonio de Cavalli
*Due Leoni* of Candia – Niccolò Fradello
*Leone* of Candia – Francesco Bonvecchio
*Cristo* of Candia (I) – Andrea Corner
*Angelo* of Candia – Giovanni Angelo
*Piramide* of Candia – Francesco Bono †
*Cristo Risorto* of Venice (I) – Simon Guoro
*Cristo Risorto* of Venice (II) – Federico Renieri
*Cristo* of Corfu – Cristoforo Condocolli
*Cristo Risorto* of Candia (I) – Francesco Zancaruol
*Cristo* of Venice (I) – Bartolomeo Donato
*Cristo* of Candia (II) – Giovanni Corner
*Cristo Risorto* of Candia (II) – captain unknown
*Rodi* of Candia – Francesco Molini
*Sant'Eufemia* of Brescia – Orazio Fisogni
*Bravo* of Candia – Michele Viramano
*Cavallo Marino* of Venice – captain unknown
*Cristo* of Candia (III) – Danielo Calefatti
*Braccio* of Venice – Niccolò Lippomano
*Nostra Signora* of Zante – Niccolò Mondini

*Cristo Risorto* of Candia (III) – Giorgio Calergi
*Nostra Signora* of Venice (I) – Marc'Antonio Pisani
*Dio Padre e la Trinità* of Venice – Giovanni Contarini del Zaffo
*Cristo Risorto* of Venice (III) – Giovanni Battista
*Angelo* of Venice – Onfre Giustiniani
*Santa Dorotea* of Venice – Polo Nani
*Ketianana* of Retimo – Niccolò Avonali
*Lion's Head* of Istria – captain unknown
*Croce* of Cefalonia – Marco Cimera
*Vergine Santa* of Cefalonia – Cristoforo Criffa
*Cristo Risorto* of Veglia – Lodovico Cicuta
*San Niccolò* of Cherso – Colane Drascio

Some sources include:
*Dama a cavallo* of Candia – Antonio Eudomeniani
*Leone* of Capodistria – Domenico Del Taco

*Spanish & Neapolitan galleys (12)*
*Lomellina* of Naples (L) – Agostino Cancuale
*Fiamma* of Naples – Juan de las Cuevas
*San Giovanni* of Naples – García de Vergara
*Invidia* of Naples – Teribio de Accaves
*Brava* of Naples – Miguel Quesada
*San Jacopo* of Naples – Moferat Guardiola
*San Niccolò* of Naples – Cristóbal de Mongiu
*Vittoria* of Naples – Occava di Rocadi
*Fortuna* of Gianandrea Doria – Giovanni Alvig Belvi

Three other unnamed galleys, given by some sources as:
*Sagittaria* of Naples – Martino Pirola
*Idra* of Naples – Luigi Pasqualigo
*Santa Lucia* of Naples – Francesco Bono

*Papal galley (1)*
*Regina* – Fabio Valicati

*Genoese galley (1)*
*La Marchesa* of Gianandrea Doria – Francesco San Fedra

## The Centre (Don Juan de Austria)

Commanded by Don Juan himself, the main contingent, occupying the centre position in the battleline, was the largest in number, consisting of 62 galleys (almost half of these were Venetian and the rest from Naples, Spain, the Papal States, Genoa, Malta, and Savoy, and four of the eleven galleys personally owned by Gianandrea Doria) and two Venetian galleasses. Its identifying colour was a blue pennant at each masthead.

### Venetian galleasses (2)

Galleass of Jacopo Guero: two 60-pounder culverins, two 30-pounder culverins, four 14-pounder culverins, four 30-pounder cannon, six 20-pounder cannon, five 3-pounder *pedreros*.

Galleass of Francesco Duodo: two 50-pounder culverins, two 20-pounder culverins, six 14-pounder culverins, two 30-pounder cannon, six 20-pounder cannon, two 3-pounder *falcones*, eight 3-pounder *pedreros*.

### Venetian galleys (29)

*Capitana* of Venice (L) – Sebastiano Veniero, *capitano generale da mar*
*Capitana* of Lomellini (L) – Paolo Giordano Orfino
*Padrona* of Lomellini – Pietro Battista Lomellini
*Capitana* of Mari – Giorgio d'Asti
*San Giovanni* of Venice (I) – Pietro Badoaro
*Tronco* of Venice – Girolamo Canal
*Mongibello* of Venice – Bertucci Contarini
*Donzella* of Candia – Francisco Dandolo
*Nostra Donna* of Venice (II) – Giovanni Zeni
*Cristo* of Venice (II) – Girolamo Contarini
*Ruota con un serpente* – Gabrio Canal
*Piramide* of Venice – Francesco Boni
*Palma* of Venice – Girolamo Veniero †
*San Teodoro* of Venice – Teodoro Balbi
*Montagna* of Candia – Alessandro Vizzamano
*San Giovanni Battista* of Venice – Giovanni Mocenigo
*Cristo* of Venice (III) – Giorgio Pisani
*San Giovanni* of Venice (II) – Daniele Moro
*Passaro* of Venice – Niccolò Tiepolo
*Leone* of Venice – Pietro Pisani

*San Girolamo* of Venice – Gasparo Malipiero
*Giuditta* of Zante – Marino Sicuro
*San Cristoforo* of Venice – Alessandro Contarini
*Armellino* of Candia – Marco Quirini
*Mezza Luna* of Venice – Valerio Vallereno
*L'Uomo di Marino* of Vicenza – Jacopo Dreffrano
*Sant'Alessandro* of Bergamo – Giovanni Antonio Colleone
*San Girolamo* of Lesina – Giovanni Balzi

Plus one unnamed Venetian galley

*Genoese galleys (8)*
*Capitana* of Genoa (L) – Ettore Spinola, principe di Parma †
*Capitana* of Gil d'Andrada (L) – Bernardo Cinoguera
*Padrona* of Genoa (L) – Pellerano
*Padrona Imperiale* of Davide Imperiale (Sicily) – Niccolò da Luvano
*Perla* of Gianandrea Doria – Giovanni Battista Spinola
*Temperanza* of Gianandrea Doria – Cipriano di Mari
*Vittoria* of Gianandrea Doria – Filippo Doria
*Doria* of Gianandrea Doria – Jacopo di Casalo

*Spanish & Neapolitan galleys (15)*
*La Real* (L) – Don Juan de Austria, admiral of the navy
*Capitana* of Castile (L) – Luis de Requeséns y Zúñiga, *comendador mayor de Castilla*
*Capitana* of Savoy (L) – Andrea Provana di Leinì
*Patrona Real* of Spain (L) – Juan Bautista Cortés
*Capitana* of Bandinelli (Naples, L) – Bandinelli Sauli
*Capitana* of Grimaldi (Naples, L) – Giorgio Grimaldi
*Padrona* of Naples (L) – Francesco de Bonavides
*Roccaful* of Spain – Roccaful
*San Francisco* of Spain – Cristoforo Guasches
*Granada* of Spain – Paolo Bottino
*Figiera* of Spain – Diego López de Ilianos
*Luna* of Spain – Manuel de Aquilar
*Fortuna* of Naples – Diego de Medrano

*Mendozza* of Naples – Martino di Caide
*San Giorgio* of Naples – Eugenio de Vergas

Another unnamed galley, given by some sources as:
*Piramide con un cane* of Spain – Marc'Antonio Santa Uliana

*Papal galleys (6, including Tuscan contingent)*
*Capitana* of His Holiness (papal *capitana*, L) – Marc'Antonio Colonna, duca di Tagliacozzo
*La Toscana* of Tuscany – Metello Caracciolo
*La Pisana* of Tuscany – Ercole Lotta
*La Fiorenza* of Tuscany – Tommaso de' Medici
*La Pace* of His Holiness – Jacopo Antonio Pergignamo
*Vittoria* of His Holiness – Baccio da Pisa

Some sources also include:
*Grifona* of His Holiness – Alessandro Negrone[9]

*Maltese galleys (Knights Hospitaller) (3)*
*Santa Maria della Vittoria* (Maltese *capitana*, L) – Fra' Pietro Giustiniani, *priore di Messina*
*San Pietro* – Fra' Pierre La Roquelaure-Saint-Aubin
*San Giovanni* – Fra' Alonso de Texada

**The Right Wing (Gianandrea Doria)**
(53 galleys, 2 galleasses, green pennant flown at the peak of each mainyard)

*Venetian galleasses (2)*
Galleass of Andrea da Cesaro: armament unknown
   Galleass of Pietro Pisani: two 50-pounder culverins, two 30-pounder culverins, four 14-pounder culverins, four 30-pounder cannon, four 20-pounder cannon, two 16-pounder cannon, three 6-pounder *falcones*, two 3-pounder *pedreros*, twelve 1-pounders.

*Venetian galleys (25)*
*Padrona* of Mari (Parini) – Antonio Corriglia
*Forza* of Venice – Rinieri Zeni

*Regina* of Candia – Giovanni Barbarigo
*Nino* of Venice – Paulo Polani
*Cristo Risorto* of Venice (IV) – Benedetto Soranzo †
*Palma* of Candia – Jacopo di Mezzo †
*Angelo* of Corfu – Stelio Carchiopulo
*Nave* of Venice – Antonio Pasqualigo
*Nostra Signora* of Candia – Marco Foscarini
*Cristo* of Candia (IV) – Francesco Cornero
*Fuoco* of Candia – Antonio Boni
*Aquila* of Candia – Girolamo Zorzi
*San Cristoforo* of Venice – Andrea Tron
*Cristo* of Venice (IV) – Marc'Antonio Lando †
*Speranza* of Candia – Girolamo Cornaro †
*San Giuseppe* of Venice – Niccolò Donato
*Torre* of Vicenza – Lodovico da Porto
*Aquila Nero e D'Oro* of Corfu – Pietro Bua †
*Aquila* of Retimo – Pietro Pisano
*San Giovanni* of Arbe – Giovanni de Dominis
*La Donna* of Friuli/Traù – Luigi Cipoco
*Re Attila* of Padua – Pataro Buzzacarini

Plus three other unnamed galleys, given by some sources as:
*Uomo Armato* of Retimo – Andrea Calergi, signore di Candia
*San Vittorio* of Crema – Evangelista Zurla
*San Trifone* of Cataro – Girolamo Bisante

*Spanish & Neapolitan galleys (10)*
*Sicilia* – Francesco Amadei
*Piemontesa* of Savoy – Ottaviano Moretto †
*Margherita* of Savoy – Battaglino
*Cingana* of Naples – Gabriel de Medina
*Luna* of Naples – Julio Rubio
*Speranza* of Naples – Pedro de Busto
*Gusmana* of Naples – Francesco de Osedo
Plus three other unnamed galleys, given by some sources as:
*Fortuna* – Diego de Medrano
*Determinada* – Juan de Angustina Carasa
*Turca* – Simone Goto

*Genoese galleys (16)*
*Capitana* of Gianandrea Doria (L) – Gianandrea Doria
*Capitana* of Negroni (L) – Giovanni Ambrogio Negroni
*Padrona* of Grimaldi – Lorenzo Treccia
*Padrona* of Niccolò Doria – Giulio Centurione
*Padrona* of Negroni (L) – Luigi Gamba
*Padrona* of the Lomellini (L) – Giorgio Greco
*Swordsman* of Retimo[10] – captain unknown
*San Vittorio* of Crema – Evangelista Zurla
*Furia* of the Lomellini – Jacopo Chiappe
*Negrona* of Negroni – Niccolò da Costa
*Bastarda* of Negroni – Lorenzo da Torre
*San Tritone* of Cataro – Girolamo Bisante
*Monarca* of Gianandrea Doria – Niccolò Garibaldo
*La Donzella* of Gianandrea Doria – Niccolò Imperiale
*Diana* of Genoa – Giovanni Giorgio Lasagna

Another unnamed Genoese galley, given by some sources as:
*Urania* of Genoa

Other sources include:
*Capitana* of Niccolò Doria – Pandolfo Polidoro
*Padrona* of Mari (L) – Antonio Corniglia

*Papal galleys (2)*
*Santa Maria* of His Holiness – Pandolfo Strozzi
*San Giovanni* of His Holiness – Angelo Biffoli[11]

### The Reserve (Don Álvaro de Bazán)

(38 galleys, including 8 galleys of the Vanguard, white pennant flown from a flagstaff over the stern lamp)

One of the most experienced naval commanders at Lepanto, the task of Don Álvaro de Bazán was to watch developments during the engagement, and to feed reinforcements into the three main 'battles' at the points where they would have the greatest effect. This meant that although he had thirty-eight galleys under his command, this reserve was viewed more as a pool of fighting manpower rather than as a manoeuvrable naval force in its own right.

*Venetian galleys (12)*
*Cristo* of Venice – Marco da Molino
*Due Mani* of Venice – Giovanni Loredano †
*Fede* of Venice – Giovanni Battista Contarini
*Pilastro* of Venice – Caterino Malipiero †
*Maddalena* of Venice – Alvigi Balbe
*Signora* of Venice – Giovanni Bembo
*Mondo* of Venice – Filippo Leoni
*Speranza* of Cipro – Giovanni Battista Benedetti †
*San Pietro* – Marco Fiumaco
*Sibilla* of Venice – Danielo Troni
*San Giorgio* of Sebenico – Cristoforo Lucio
*San Michele* – Giorgio Cochini

*Spanish & Neapolitan galleys (13)*
*La Loba* (Spain, L) – Don Álvaro de Bazán, marqués de Santa Cruz and *capitán general de Napoli*
*Capitana* of Vaicos (Spain, L) – Juan Vásquez de Coronado
*San Giovanni* of Sicily – Davide Imperiale?
*Gru* of Spain – Luis Heredia
*Leona* of Spain – captain unknown
*Constanza* of Naples – Pietro Delagia
*La Marchesa* of Spain[12] – Juan de Machado †
*Santa Barbara* of Naples – Giovanni de Ascale
*Sant'Andrea* of Naples – captain unknown
*Santa Caterina* of Naples – Juan Rufis de Velasco
*Sant'Angelo* of Naples – captain unknown
*Terana* of Naples – Giovanni de Riva de Neillino
Another unnamed Spanish or Neapolitan galley, given by some sources as:
*Ocasión* of Spain – Pedro de Roig

*Papal galleys (3)*
*Padrona* of His Holiness (L) – Alfonso d'Appiano
*Suprema* – Antonio da Ascoli
*Serena* – captain unknown

*Genoese Galleys (2)*
*Baccana* – Giovanni Pietro di Morilo

Plus another unnamed Genoese galley, given by some sources as:
*San Bartolomeo*

**The Vanguard (Giovanni Antonio de Cardona)**
(8 galleys, attached to the Reserve)
*Capitana* of Sicily – Giovanni Antonio de Cardona
*Padrona* of Sicily – captain unknown
*San Giovanni* of Sicily – Davide Imperiale?
*San Ionica* of Sicily – captain unknown
*Santa Maria Maddalena* of Venice – Marino Contarini †[13]
*Il Sole* of Venice – Vincenzo Querini †
*Santa Caterina* of Venice – Marco Cicogna †
*Nostra Donna* of Venice – Pietro Francesco Malipiero †

## Ottoman fleet[14]

**Right Wing (Mehmed Sirocco Paşa)**
(60 galleys, 2 galiots)

*Constantinople galleys (20)*

| | | |
|---|---|---|
| Süleymān Bey (L) | Ali 'Genoese' | Drusari Pìrì |
| Kara Mustafā (L) | Hali Re'īs | Koda Ali |
| İbrāhīm Re'īs | Seydi Selīm | Sinaman Mustafā |
| Süleymān Re'īs | Kumar Iusuf | Caracoza Ali |
| Karaman İbrāhīm | Bardas Çelebi | Mustafā Alendi |
| Çender Sinān | Bardas Hasan | Marmara Re'īs |
| Hasan Nabi | Fazıl Ali Bey | |

*Tripoli galleys (5)*

| | |
|---|---|
| Ağa Paşa (L) | Süleymān Re'īs |
| Arnaut Ferhad | Fazıl Memi |
| Darnad Iusuf | |

*Anatolian galleys (13)*

| | | |
|---|---|---|
| Mehmed Bey – | Murād Mustafā | Adagi Hasan |
| *capitana* | Hyder Mehmed | Sinjji Mustafā |
| Mysor Ali | Sinān Darius | Hacı Çelebi |
| Amurat Re'īs | Mehmed Darius | Tursan Mustafā |
| Kalifi Memi | Amdjazade Sinān | |

*Alexandrian galleys (22)*

Mehmed Sirocco Paşa †(L) – Right wing commander, *beylerbeyi* of Alexandria

| | | |
|---|---|---|
| Kari Ali (L) | Osmān Occan | Yusuf Ağa |
| Herus Re'īs (L) | Darius Ağa | Yusuf Magyar |
| Karas Turbat | Drazed Sinian | Khalifa Hyder |
| Dagli Sarif | Osmān Ali | Mustafā Kemāl |
| Hasan Çelebi | Deli Ağa | Darnadi Pìrì |
| Osmān Çelebi | Dardagut Bardabey | Memi Hasan |
| Dink Kasali | Kasli Khan | Kari Ali |

*Alexandrian galiots (2)*

| | |
|---|---|
| Abdul Re'īs | Piyale Murād |

**The Centre (*Müezzinzāde Ali Paşa*)**
(87 galleys)

*First line (the newest and fittest galleys of the fleet)*
(62 galleys)

Constantinople galleys (22)
*Sultana* (L) – Müezzinzāde Ali Paşa †, *kapudan-ı deryā*

| | | |
|---|---|---|
| Osmān Re'īs (L) | Uluç Re'īs | Sinān Mustafā |
| Pertev Paşa (L) – | Pìrì Uluç Bey | Haseki Re'īs |
| commander, embarked | Dardagan Re'īs – *re'īs* | Hasan Uluç |
| troops | *Tersāne-i Āmire* | Kosem Yusuf |
| Hasan Paşa[15] (L) | Deli Osmān | Ağa Ahmed |
| Hasan Re'īs | Pìrì Osmān | Osmān Seydi |
| Kos Ali | Demir Çelebi | Darius Çelebi |
| Kılıç Re'īs | Darius Haseki | Kafar Re'īs |

Rhodes galleys (12)

| | | |
|---|---|---|
| Hasan Bey – *beylerbeyi* | Postana Uluç | Karagi Re'īs |
| of Rhodes (L) | Khalifah Uluç | Occan Re'īs |
| Deli Çender – warden | Ghazni Re'īs | Deli Ali |
| of Rhodes (L) | Dromus Re'īs | Hacı Ağa |
| Osa Re'īs | Berber Kali | |

Black Sea (Bulgarian & Bithynian) galleys (13)

| | | |
|---|---|---|
| Prauil Ağa (L) | Magyar Ali | Sinān Re'īs |
| Kara Re'īs (L) | Kali Çelebi | Kari Mustafā |
| Arnaud Re'īs | Deli Çelebi | Seydi Arnaud |
| Cami Uluç | Deli Assan | |
| Arnaud Çelebi | Kaman Ağa | |

Gallipoli galleys (4)

| | |
|---|---|
| Pìrì Hamagi | Yusuf Ali |
| Ali Re'īs | Sinān Bektaşi |

Negroponte galleys (11)

| | | |
|---|---|---|
| Osmān Re'īs (L) | Bektaşi Mustafā | Kali Çelebi |
| Mehmed Bey – | Sinān Ali | Bagdar Re'īs |
| *beylerbeyi* of Metelina | Agdagi Re'īs | Hunyadi Mustafā |
| (L) | Deli Yusuf | |
| Bektaşi Uluç | Orphan Ali | |

*Second line*
(25 galleys, 8 galiots)

| | | |
|---|---|---|
| Constantinople galleys | Deli İbrāhīm | Dardagi Ali |
| (12) | Murād Korosi | Hyder Carai |
| Tramontana Re'īs (L) | Darnad Ali | Darius Ali |
| Murād Re'īs | Kari Re'īs | Kari Ali |
| Süleymān Çelebi | Darius Sinian | |

Tripoli galleys (6)

| | | |
|---|---|---|
| Hyder Ağa | Hasan Kahlim Ali | Seydi Ali |
| Kari Hamat | Daram Uluç | Mohammed Ali |

## Gallipoli galleys (7)

| | | |
|---|---|---|
| Aziz Khalifa – | Selīm Sahi | Hasseri Ali |
| *beylerbeyi* of Gallipoli | Seydi Paşa | Hasan Deli |
| (L) | Hasan Mustafā | Yusuf Seydi |

## Left wing (Uluç Ali Re'īs)
### (61 galleys, 32 galiots)

### Constantinople galleys (14)

| | | |
|---|---|---|
| Nasur Ferhad (L) | Memi Bey | Çelebi Re'īs |
| Kasam Re'īs (L) | Pìrì Osmān | Tartar Ali |
| Osmān Re'īs (L) | Pìrì Re'īs | Kafir Hacı |
| Kiafi Hacı | Selīm Basti | Karaman Paşa |
| Ferhad Ali | Talatagi Re'īs | |

### Algerian galleys (14)

Uluç Ali Re'īs (L) – Left commander, *beylerbeyi* of Algiers

| | | |
|---|---|---|
| Kari Ali (L) | Turgut Ali | Macasir Ali |
| Karaman Ali | Seydi Ali | Ionas Osmān |
| Alemdar Paşa | Pìrì Selīm | Sālim Deli |
| Sinān Çelebi | Murād Darius | |
| Amdjazade Mustafā | Uluç Re'īs | |

### Syrian galleys (6)

| | | |
|---|---|---|
| Kara Bey (L) | Osmān Bey | Kari Alemdar |
| Dermat Bey | Yusuf Ali | Murād Hasan |

### Anatolian galleys (13)

| | | |
|---|---|---|
| Karali Re'īs (L) | Cademly Mustafā | Tursun Osmān |
| Pìrìman Re'īs (L) | Uschiufly Memi | Iosul Piyale |
| Hazuli Sinān | Kari Mora | Keduk Seydi |
| Chios Mehmed | Darius Paşa | |
| Hignau Mustafā | Piyale Osmān | |

### Negroponte galleys (14)

| | | |
|---|---|---|
| Seydi Re'īs (L) | Çendereli Mustafā | Sali Re'īs |
| Arnaud Ali (L) | Mustafā Hacı | Hamıd Ali |

| Karaman Hyder | Nasi Re'īs | Kos Memi |
| Magyar Fehrad | Kara Rhodi | Karam Bey (Albanian) |
| Nasūh Ferhad | Kos Hacı | |

*Constantinople galiots (19)*

| Uluç Pìrì Paşa (L) | Karaman Memi | Çelebi Yusuf |
| Karaman Süleymān | Guzman Ferhad | Hascedi Hasan |
| Haneshi Ahmed | Hunyadis Hasan | Sian Memi |
| Hyder Enver | Kemāl Murād | Osmān Dagli |
| Nur Memi | Sarmusal Re'īs | Karaman Re'īs |
| Karaman Re'īs | Tursun Süleymān | |

Plus two more unnamed Ottoman galiots

*Albanian galiots (8)*

| Deli Murād | Alemdar Ali | Hasan Sinān |
| Alemdar Re'īs | Hasan Omar | Cami Fazıl |
| Sian Siander | Seydi Ağa | |

*Anatolian galiots (5)*

| Kara Alemdhar | Nabi Re'īs | Hunyadi Yusuf |
| Suzi Memi | Hasan Osmān | |

**The Reserve (Amuret Turgut Re'īs)[16]**
(8 galleys, 22 galiots)[17]

*Negroponte galleys (4)*

| Amuret Turgut Re'īs | Deli Dori |
| Kaidar Memi | Hasan Sinān |

*Anatolian galleys (4)*

| Deli Süleymān | Kiafar Bey |
| Deli Bey | Kasım Sinān |

*Mixed squadron of galiots (22)[18]*

| Ali Uluç | Ferhad Kara Ali | Kasım Kara |
| Kara Deli | Dardagud Re'īs | Hasan Re'īs |

| | | |
|---|---|---|
| Alemdar Hasan | Hyder Ali | Kari Ali Re'īs |
| Kos Ali | Hyder Deli | Murād Ali |
| Hacı Ali | Armad Memi | Iumez Ali |
| Köprülü Çelebi | Hasan Re'īs | Haneschi Murād |
| Setagi Meni | Cami Naser | |
| Setagi Osmān | Nur Ali | |

*Chapter 17*

# Sunday Seventh

"My sons, we have come here to die, or to conquer, if the heavens so provide."

Don Juan de Austria on the eve of Lepanto

The combined Christian fleet – with nautical oddments deriving from Tuscany, Genoa, Savoy, the Papal States and the Knights Hospitaller, as well as the ships of Spain and Venice – were destined to meet the Ottoman Turkish fleet in the Gulf of Patras. The battle of Lepanto would be fought on Sunday, 7 October, when 206 Christian galleys faced 216 Ottoman galleys, and while the apparent difference in numbers would be miniscule, it would be the body armour of the 28,500 soldiers packed on board the Christian fleet and the guns carried by the six Venetian galleasses that would play an important part in the bloody events of that day.

A word of warning: the original accounts of the fights which started that morning west of Naupaktos are brief and vague and sometimes plainly wrong. It is not surprising. Before the end, some 250 fighting vessels were involved, all moving, though very slowly, and scattered over many kilometres of sea, and nobody on board any one of them could possibly watch them all and comprehend what all of them were doing. So everyone who wrote about it at all wrote only what he had done himself, and what he thought he had seen – they might all be accounts of different battles. Moreover, men who survived this battle, men such as the young Miguel de Cervantes, had a good story to tell for the rest of their lives – making perhaps a good story even better – so of course their imaginations flourished and rumours grew.

## In the Name of All That is Good and Holy

The Christian commander-in-chief Don Juan de Austria had ordered one cannon to be fired, so that the Ottoman commander could identify the Christian flagship. An answering shot had come from the flagship of Müezzinzāde Ali Paşa. This gentlemanly exchange identifying the two fleet flagships marked the civilised portion of the battle. Once the two fleets clashed, both sides would abandon all chivalric niceties in their fight with the 'infidel'. In these circumstances, it is no surprise that the battle resulted in both sides absorbing horrific casualties. The fleet of the Holy League was convinced that the crucial moment in the struggle against the Ottoman Turks had come, and impressive acts of bravery under Turkish fire led to many deaths.

To cite just a couple of cases to give us an idea of the recklessness of Christian commanders at Lepanto, the Venetian *provveditore generale da mar*, Agostino Barbarigo, showed almost complete disregard for his vessel's safety when he directed the *capitana lanterna* of the Most Serene Republic towards the advancing Ottoman galleys, and tried to stand in their way. As a consequence of his actions, one Venetian captain after another fell dead – members of the noblest houses of Venice such as the Querini and the Contarini, the latter actually one of the oldest families of Italian nobility. Barbarigo pressed on regardless, though he foolishly lifted his visor as a hail of arrows descended on the *spalliera* of his ship, and he was struck in the left eye, dying down below soon afterwards.

In the meantime, on the port side of *La Real* was the white bearded, cantankerous and fiery old Sebastiano Veniero, *capitano generale da mar* of Venice, though still in disgrace with the commander-in-chief. Twenty years older than Agostino Barbarigo, Veniero stood proudly on the *arrembata* of the *capitana* of the Most Serene Republic wearing carpet slippers for comfort, but explaining to anyone who asked that they gave him a better grip on the deck. A staunch patriot who ignored protocol, he could remember the golden days of Venice before its humiliation during the war of the League of Cambrai. Wielding a wheel lock blunderbuss, he fired the first shot as the Venetian galley closed in for the kill, blasting away at the bow gunners operating on the enemy galley. Back on his own *spalliera*, Veniero took up the crossbow, a weapon he had known all about in his own youth, when the harquebus was still a newfangled contraption.

A seaman stood by Veniero's side so he could wind the crank for him, a task beyond his strength. But the old man could still aim. Strange as it may seem to us, in civilian life Veniero had been a successful lawyer but, like ancient Rome, Venice often sent its most accomplished civilians out as war leaders. Furthermore, military commands in Venice, with all their physical demands, were *not* reserved for younger men. Veniero proved to be a thoroughly competent servant of the Republic.

## Into Action

First blood was drawn by the Venetian galleasses stationed forward of the Christian battleline. Their combined ordnance, heavier than anything the Ottomans possessed, were used with such effect that no enemy vessel could close with them. Heavy gunfire from the bows of the "turreted ships of the Venetians, those six [in fact, four engaged initially] castles of the sea [viz. galleasses]"[1] tore Ottoman ships and men apart, and the galley slaves shackled to their positions were dragged down to the bottom of the sea with the splintered ruins of their galley. The Venetian heavy ordnance roared and rolled in swirling smoke, so much so that the acrid cloud of blue-grey powder smoke from the constant cannonade impeded the foremost Ottoman galleys of the right wing and the centre, confusing their battle array at the crucial moment of contact. The slaughter was relentless, hideous and fanatical, marked by the silent dead and howling wounded. The Christian fleet began slowly to advance towards the now wrecked battleline of the enemy. The reckoning had begun.

## The North Wing

The first to meet in close conflict were the Christian left or north wing led by Agostino Barbarigo and the Ottoman contingent led by Mehmed Sirocco Paşa, which was opposed to it on the Ottoman right wing. With his own galley at the northern end of the Christian battleline, Barbarigo sailed as close as he dared to the inshore rocks and shoals with the hope that his flank could not be turned. However, better acquainted with the depths of the waters here, the governor of Alexandria brought his own galley into action on the extreme flank bow to bow with the *capitana lanterna* of Venice.

Fortunately, four Venetian galleys of the vanguard under Giovanni Antonio de Cardona had just reached the Christian left and had positioned themselves to the rear of Barbarigo, who immediately ordered them to stop the Ottoman outflanking movement. It was a timely decision. As the Ottomans rounded the promontory of Malcantone, as it was called by the Venetians, they found their route blocked by the first of these galleys, the *Santa Maria Maddalena* under Marino Contarini. Counting on superior numbers, the Ottomans attacked it immediately, and very soon Contarini and his men were fighting for their lives. It did not take long for the *Santa Maria Maddalena* to resemble a charnel house. Marino Contarini himself was mortally wounded by a harquebus shot, while Paolo Orsini, in command of the Venetian marines on board, received a ball in the right shoulder and burns all over his body from a fire pot. Then *Il Sole*, also from the vanguard and captained by Vincenzo Querini, came to the rescue, crashing into the Ottoman ships and relieving the pressure on the *Santa Maria Maddalena*. Blasting away at point blank range the Venetians managed to keep the enemy at bay, but *Il Sole* in turn suffered serious losses from Ottoman harquebusiers, archers and swordsmen, including the gallant Querini. Nevertheless, with their reckless courage the marines of Contarini and Querini brought precious time for the Christian left.

Some of the lighter Ottoman galleys, by working through the shallows between Barbarigo and the mainland, were able to fall on the rear of the extreme left of the Christian battleline, while the larger galleys pressed the attack in front. The *capitana lanterna* of Venice found herself in the thick of the fray, hit as it was by the withering fire of eight Ottoman galleys. Barbarigo's vessel was rushed by a boarding party of janissaries, who poured over the gunwales and forward platform, clearing her decks as far as the mainmast. Barbarigo rallied his men and led them in one counterattack after another. More Venetian galleys came up alongside and their marines allowed Barbarigo to push back the tormentors on his ship. But Mehmed Sirocco was not yet willing to surrender the initiative, redoubling his efforts to clear and capture Barbarigo's flagship with the hope of demoralising the Venetians.

Meanwhile, off Malcantone, the *Santa Maria Maddalena* and *Il Sole* had prevailed over their enemies. Locked together side by side, the two stricken vessels provided mutual support for each other, and with the aid of the galleys *Santa Caterina* and *Nostra Donna*, all originally part of the vanguard, repulsed attack after attack. Paolo Orsini of the *Santa Maria Maddalena*, exploiting a momentary lull in the fighting, managed to organise a counterattack with his surviving men. Taken by surprise, the Ottomans attempted to resist, but suddenly, having somehow managed to break their chains and grab the weapons of the fallen, the Christian galley slaves attacked their former masters. Overwhelmed on all sides, the Ottoman fighting men were quickly dealt with and the Ottoman galleys near Malcantone fell one by one to the Venetians. The *Santa Caterina* and *Nostra Donna* now turned to join the hard pressed Barbarigo, but immediately their captains, Marco Cicogna and Pier Francesco Malipiero, were struck down.

As mentioned previously, Barbarigo, fighting with his visor open, was mortally wounded when an arrow pierced his left eye, and he was hastily carried below *hors de combat*. Confusion followed, and the Ottomans seized the moment to hack their way up to the mainmast. But Barbarigo's deputy, Federigo Nani, took command and with Silvio da Porcia attempted to stem the tide. Luckily for the Venetians relief was close at hand. With all guns blazing, the galley *Dio Padre e la Trinità* under Giovanni Contarini del Zaffo, struck the *capitana* of Mehmed Sirocco at the stern, carrying away her rudder. At the same time another Venetian vessel ploughed into her amidships. A rush of Venetians and Neapolitan Spaniards poured towards the *capitana*, whose decks were swept by the fire of the harquebusiers before the charge of swords and half pikes burst over her bows. The onset was irresistible. The surviving Ottomans were cut down, stabbed, and hurled overboard, including Mehmed Sirocco himself. Although by then badly wounded, he was pulled from the water, but only to be beheaded on the spot by the sword of another member of the Contarini clan, Giovanni Pietro, or so runs one of the many versions of his premature death.

Nonetheless, whether the *beylerbeyi* of Alexandria fell in battle, died by drowning, or was summarily executed, when his standard was hauled down by the victorious Venetians, and the Christian oarsmen suddenly ceased to be slaves and fraternized with the conquerors, some of the captains on the Ottoman right lost heart and drove their galleys aground in the shallows, deserting them for the shore where they hoped to find refuge among friends. On the Christian left, though the fighting continued in a fierce mêlée of vessels locked tightly together, and with mariners and marines doing wild work with harquebus and sword, the battle here was practically won. Barbarigo lived long enough to hear of the victory, and expressed himself as well content to die.

## In the Centre

Let us now turn our attention to the centre. Müezzinzāde Ali, who had been heading towards the Venetian *lanterna* of Sebastiano Veniero, flying the Lion-flag of San Marco, promptly altered course and, accompanied by a group of *lanterne*, his flagship steered straight towards the *La Real* of Don Juan. On that particular prize one hundred attendants were aboard, including thirty-eight Spanish nobles and Don Juan's personal confessor priest Francisco, who had been especially appointed by Philip II. More importantly, there were 400 carefully selected harquebusiers from the *Tercio de Sardinia* in steel corselet and headpieces, "as well as many other lords and gentlemen".[2] And so the oarsmen of the *Sultana* sliced through the sea swell. At the same time the *lanterna* of Pertev Paşa headed for that of Veniero. Giovanni Pietro Contarini has left us a dramatic, first-hand account of the fierce fighting here in the centre of the two battling fleets:

> There happened a mortal storm of harquebus shots and arrows, and it seemed that the sea was aflame from the flashes and continuous fires lit by fire trumpets [Greek fire siphons?], fire pots and other weapons. Three galleys would be pitted against four, four against six, and six against one, enemy of Christian alike, everyone fighting in the cruellest manner to take each other's lives. And already many Turks and Christians had boarded their opponents' galleys fighting at close quarters with short weapons, few being left alive. And death came endlessly from two-handed swords, scimitars, iron maces, daggers, axes, swords, arrows, harquebuses and fire weapons. And besides those killed in various ways, others escaping from the weapons would drown by throwing themselves into the sea, thick and red with blood.[3]

Consequently, the combat soon became too general for the two opposing divisions of the centre armaments to preserve their respective battle arrays. Contarini's eyewitness report is a good reminder that galley fights were not one-on-one duels; they involved multiple galleys on each side, typically in dense, jostling clusters.

And another point. There are many places in this history where one has to make a guess, as well-informed as possible; and at this point the most plausible guess lies in the supply of ammunition. By the end of the battle, both sides had shot off all they had, or very nearly all. In the early stages, the Christians were certainly using artillery, and in the later stages they were not. But a ship does not suddenly run out of shot; it does not blaze away until the very last is gone. There must be a period when the shortage is growing acute and the gunners are warned not to waste a shot until they have a perfect target. The Ottoman Turks, on the other hand, may have reached this stage very early in the battle. They may have fought all day with this threat hanging over them: that unless the Christians ran out before they did, they would be utterly destroyed.

Yet in each galley the moment when they ceased to fire may have come suddenly and unexpectedly, because shots which penetrated the gun platforms were appallingly destructive of life and morale: not so much the shots themselves as the splinters of wood that flew in all directions. Guns could also burst. Every gun, of course, was proof tested when it was made, but that was normally done in ideal conditions. A gun that burst on a gun platform would have been devastating, not only to the gun crews but to the galley too, tending to blow out the caulking and start the planks, or lift fixtures and fitting with its concussion.

Meanwhile, manoeuvring around the stern of the *Sultana* with the intention of bringing aid to the *kapudan-ı deryā*, Pertev Paşa was to lose heavily under the devastating fire from the *capitana lanterna* of Veniero and would fail in his efforts to board her. He cut his *lanterna* adrift. Veniero let her go, and turned to attack other enemies. His rudder gone, Pertev's stricken ship drifted down on two Christian galleys, the *capitana* of the Lomellini under Paolo Giordano Orsini (son-in-law of Cosimo I de' Medici) and the *San Giorgio* of Sebenico commanded by Cristoforo Lucio, and was promptly boarded. Still, it took some time for the Christians to subdue their adversaries, Orsini suffering a leg wound from a spent arrow. In the end Pertev, having lost most of his men and badly burnt in the shoulder, abandoned ship together with his son. Slipping aboard a small craft rowed by a Bolognese turned Muslim, he reached the safety of another ship, the Italian renegade shouting "Don't shoot. We also are Christian."[4] Giving up all hope of victory, Pertev fled from the fight and would make his way back to Constantinople. In the meantime, Veniero had taken out two other Ottoman galleys. He was wounded with a bullet in the leg, but he had the wound bandaged and remained defiant on his *spalliera*.

The two corsairs, Kara Hodja and Kara Deli, attacked the *Grifona* of His Holiness, captained by Alessandro Negrone. On board also was Onorato Caetani di Sermoneta, *capitano generale delle fanterie pontifcie*, who later would write a detailed account of the ensuing fight he had witnessed firsthand. As the two corsairs fell upon their prey, the papal soldiers poured harquebus lead and cannon shot into the waiting Barbary fighting men, whose ranks were already depleted since they had already fought two Venetian galleys. True to his deserved reputation, Kara Hodja led his men over the gunwales of the *Grifona*, falling to a leaden shot fired by an Italian harquebusier. The arrival of a Venetian galley from the reserve, the *Due Mani* captained by Giovanni Loredano, put an end to the matter, allowing the capture of the two Barbary vessels. Caetani paid tribute to the fighting spirit of his opponents, noting that between the two galleys "no more than six Turks remained alive".[5]

The hottest fighting in the centre raged between the opposing flagships as Müezzinzāde Ali's *Sultana* carrying a hundred archers and thrice as many harquebusiers bore down on the *La Real*. Point-blank cannon fire crashed into the Christian flagship, and Ottoman fighting men scrambled aboard it twice. Storming an enemy galley was no easy task, yet it would have been at this crucial point that the janissaries would have been at their best. It has to be understood that to board was not simply a matter of overhauling an enemy galley, run up alongside and grapple. The assaulter had to place his galley in firm contact with his victim, preferably at some weakly defended point, and hold there long enough for his men to enter. He had to get a good many of his fighting men over the enemy railing in the initial rush to maximise his chances of overwhelming the resistance at the point of contact. Then he had to hold his position for as long as needed to support them with covering fire and reinforcements while they fought for control of the enemy decks. In the light of this, therefore, boarding and entering for the janissaries implied a level playing field, when firepower was irrelevant and sheer courage and close-quarter combat weapons were at a premium on the bloody, slippery decks of an enemy galley.

Don Bernardino de Cárdenas brought up a reserve from the waist of the flagship and rushed the Ottoman boarders, who had now cleared the forecastle. He was struck by a leaden ball fired from a swivel gun. It dinted his steel helmet, but failed to penetrate. Cárdenas fell, stunned by the shock of the blow, and died next day, though he showed no visible mark of a head wound. A deadly seesaw struggle continued for some time, the boarders being finally driven back with loss when Marc'Antonio Colonna manoeuvred to grapple the *Sultana*. The *capitana* of His Holiness, flying the ensign of the Papal Keys, was jam packed with numerous Roman nobles and volunteer knights from France – it should be remembered that France respected its open or sometimes secret alliances with the Sublime Porte – as well as twenty-five Swiss papal guards accompanying Colonna as a personal guard, and 180 other foot soldiers. Also, the *La Loba* of Don Álvaro de Bazán, marqués de Santa Cruz, who had been given complete freedom of action, arrived at the crucial moment with 200 additional soldiers. Then, other Christian galleys moved alongside the Ottoman flagship and raked its deck with harquebus volleys. Allied gunfire effectively stopped men from aiding the *Sultana* by boat, and those who tried to do so were picked off as they attempted to climb up the ship's sides.

For the embattled *Sultana* the finale was approaching fast. Italian and Neapolitan Spanish soldiers, including Don Juan himself resplendent in his mirror-polished half-armour and wielding a two-handed sword,[6] scrambled aboard the *Sultana* and, jabbing at the Ottoman defenders with half pikes and swords, firing harquebuses and pistols, managed to push the defenders back towards the *spalliera*. There the remaining janissaries threw up a makeshift barricade made of mattresses, from behind which they shot arrows at the Christian boarders. It was then that Filippo Veniero loaded one of the *petriere* aboard the *capitana lanterna* of Venice and blasted the barricade of the resisting janissaries, allowing the Christians to clear the *spalliera* of the *Sultana*.

This was the turning-point of the fight in the centre. Müezzinzāde Ali, struck in the forehead by a harquebus shot, had died fighting manfully; renowned as an archer, when battle was joined he had picked up his composite recurve bow and, regardless of his exalted rank, fought alongside his shipboard archers to the very end. It was said that it was an arrow shot by Müezzinzāde Ali that pierced both the breastplate and the back-plate of a soldier on the *La Real*.

Anyway, a convict who had been freed and armed by Don Juan swiftly severed the Ottoman admiral's head and hoisted it on a pike to the great benefit of Christian morale (other sources have the bodiless head tossed into the sea). Christians could acknowledge the bravery of their foes, and the Ottomans frequently did the same; yet each also regarded the other as damned and accursed infidels. The Christian boarders killed the remaining *Sultana* crewmen. It was 1400 hours, and the battle in the centre had been won by Don Juan.

## The South Wing

This did not end the fighting, for other Barbary ships entered the fray also. In the south, off-shore flank, Gianandrea Doria was engaged in a mêlée with his old acquaintance Uluç Ali, taking the worse part. When the battle began at noon, first on the Christian left wing, then in the centre, Doria was not yet in position. His orders were to mark with his flagship the extreme right of the line of battle so that the rest of his contingent could form on this point. But it was soon seen that he was keeping away, steering southward into the open sea, with his command trailing after him in a long line, the two galleasses that should have been out in front coming slowly up behind. Uluç Ali with the left wing of the Ottoman fleet had also altered his course, and was steering on a parallel line to that taken by the Genoese. Some of the Christian captains who watched these movements from the right centre thought that Doria was deserting the Christian armada, and even that he was in flight, pursued by Uluç Ali. Perhaps they were recalling that eleven years earlier Doria had run from Uluç Ali, at Djerba.

As the Christian armada had sailed eastward grave misgivings about Gianandrea Doria had been raised among the other Christian commanders, for it was being said in Rome that having sold his galleys to Philip II, the current patron of the Doria family, he had just repurchased them. Not only was Doria well paid for his trouble on a galley-per-month basis (each of his eleven galley's cost Philip ten per cent more than an equivalent Spanish one), he was raking in an annual interest rate of fourteen per cent (with inflation running at four per cent) on the money that the king had borrowed from him to hire his services. It was also a means of realising hidden profits, such as having access to jealously-guarded currency export licences, or the right to purchase Sicilian grain free of taxes and duties, for resale elsewhere at a profit.[7] At a later date, Doria would point out to Philip that it would have been much cheaper to pay the contractors the money due to them on time and in full rather than to allow the interest and late-payment penalty fines to accrue.[8] This wise counsel of course did not prevent Doria himself from earning an enormous income from the king's extreme indebtedness.

For Gianandrea Doria, a very experienced seafarer, but also a ship owner, even a battle was a matter of profit and loss.[9] After the defeat he had suffered at Djerba it was said – and perhaps rightly – that he had fled in order to preserve intact the galleys he personally owned. His actions on 7 October did little to dispel such suspicions, and in the opinion of some, suspicion quickly became a clear certainty. Doria afterwards explained that, as he steered out from behind the centre to take up his position in the battleline, he saw that Uluç Ali, instead of forming on the left flank of the Ottoman centre, was working out to seaward, and he therefore believed that the *beylerbeyi* of Algiers was trying to get upon the flank of the Christian line, in order to envelop it and attack from both front and rear, so as to crush the extreme Christian right with a local superiority of force. His plan was, therefore, to confine himself to observing Uluç Ali's movements, steering on a parallel course in the hope of eventually closing and meeting him fairly ship to ship.

More like a corsair than a Genoese gentleman, Gianandrea Doria was a shrewd sailor, perhaps the most experienced naval commander in the Christian fleet except the veteran Veniero. He was also cold, cautious, self-centred, clever, and not afraid to cut his losses. If he had been less of a tactician, perhaps he would have come into action sooner. And it is strange that, while playing for position against Uluç Ali, he did not realise that if, instead of continually increasing his own distance from the centre, he had at any moment turned back towards it, he could thus have forced the *beylerbeyi* either to close with him or leave him free to overwhelm the Ottoman centre by enveloping its left flank.

It was Uluç Ali, not Gianandrea Doria, who suddenly doubled back and venture on a stroke like this. Outmanoeuvring the over-clever Genoese, the *beylerbeyi* of Algiers himself commanded sixteen galleys in a fast attack on the Christian centre, taking six galleys – amongst them the *capitana* of Malta, killing all but three of the thirty knights and sixty sergeants-at-arms on board. Its commander, Fra' Pietro Giustiniani, the prior of Messina and a personal enemy of Uluç Ali, was severely wounded by five arrows, but was found alive propped against the main mast.[10] Two other knights were so severely wounded as to seem dead. Around them were their dead comrades surrounded by over 300 dead and dying corsairs.

It was all going well for Uluç Ali; until it was not. The manoeuvre was brilliant, but the Barbary corsair was not allowed to gobble up the Christians ship by ship. With the intervention of the Spaniards Álvaro de Bazán and Giovanni Antonio de Cardona with the galleys of the reserve turned the battle, both in the centre and on the south wing. In the words of the Captive, a character in *Don Quixote* who "took part in that glorious battle":

Uchalí, the king of Algiers, a daring and successful corsair, attacked and defeated the Maltese flagship, leaving only three knights alive, and they were badly wounded: the flagship of Juan Andrea [Gianandrea Doria], on which I and my company were sailing, came to her assistance, and doing what needed to be done on such an occasion, I jumped onto the enemy galley that then disengaged from our ship, which had grappled her, preventing my soldiers from following me; and so I found my self alone, surrounded by my enemies., who were so numerous I could not successfully resist them; finally, when I was covered with wounds, they took me prisoner. And, Señores, as you have probably heard, Uchalí escaped with his entire squadron, and I was his captive ...[11]

Despite the obvious misfortune of our loquacious friend the Captive (he was a captain of infantry), once more superior ordnance and harquebusiers proved crucial, even if the corsairs managed to board Cardona's *capitana* of Sicily and clear it to the mainmast. Uluç Ali was forced to disengage and flee with thirteen galleys, along with twenty-four galiots, abandoning all of his prizes – the Venetian galley *Aquila Nero e D'Oro* under the slain Pietro Bua had already been towed back to Naupaktos – bar the huge ensign of the *capitana* of Malta, with its distinctive white cross, or so he thought. It was Francesco de Osedo, captain of the Napolese galley *Gusmana*, who recaptured the battered, blood-soaked wreck which had been the *capitana* of Malta, and in recognition thereof, the Knights Hospitaller apparently pensioned him for life. According to the Order's own records, the grievously wounded Fra' Pietro Giustiniani, who believed his end was nigh, had ordered one of his officers to hide the ensign of the Order in a safe place and hoist in its place "one of those flags which were usually hoisted on the galleys on the occasion of some celebration".[12]

However, no less than five of Doria's galleys had been stricken. The *San Giovanni* of His Holiness and the *La Piemontesa* of Savoy were ships of the dead, the latter with its eighteen rowing benches more a galiot than a galley. The *La Donzella*, personally owned by Doria, was not in much better shape, while in the *La Fiorenza* of Tuscany only the captain, Tommaso de' Medici, a kinsman of Cosimo I, and fourteen of his men survived out of a complement of 200.[13] The *Cristo Risorto* of Venice, captained by Benedetto Soranzo, had been boarded by the Algerians, and was in sore distress. Soranzo himself had died fighting gallantly, and his *scrivano*, or secretary, had assumed the command. Seeing that all hope of rescue was in vain, he judged it would be more to the honour of Venice to destroy himself and his comrades, together with their foes, than to live in slavery or face a death of ignominy and torture. He accordingly set a lighted fuse to the powder magazine on board the *Cristo Risorto*, and the whole mass, friends and foes alike, "in one wild roar expired".[14] It was now 1600 hours.

### The Butcher's Bill

As dusk fell that autumnal evening the battered but victorious fleet of the Holy League quickly pulled away from the corpse-littered, blood-tainted waters and took shelter from an approaching thunderstorm in the port of Petalas, the largest islet of the Curzolaris archipelago, and the inlets just north of the islet of Oxeia. Here the ships' surgeons took care of the sick and wounded, and the Christians were able to contemplate their good fortune.[15] For it is a certainty that fortune is fluctuating, fickle and capricious, for does not Machiavelli infamously claim that "Fortune is a woman" in *il Principe*, "and if you wish to keep her under it is necessary to beat and ill use her."[16]

The next morning it became apparent from the sheer evidence of death and destruction that the Holy League had not just won a massive victory, but that the number of Ottoman dead was almost beyond counting. Broken and sinking ships lay "scattered over about eight miles of water. The sea was entirely covered, not just with masts, spars, oars and broken wood, but with an innumerable quantity of corpses which turned the water red as blood."[17] Other eyewitness accounts mention that the smoke obscured the sun; ships burned gold and crimson against the night sky.

In an encounter that depended on close ship-to-ship battles and men fighting at close range with harquebus and bows and arrows, the casualties were appalling. Nevertheless, the tactics set down by Don Juan to maintain the closest possible formation of his galleys and his measures to ensure his fleet could not be outflanked by the more manoeuvrable Ottoman galleys earned him an overwhelming victory.

The Ottoman fleet was decimated, losing all but fifty of their ships; 117 galleys, ten galiots and three *fuste* were prizes – some ready for scuttling once stripped – and sixty burned to water level or sent to the bottom along with many of the galiots. In the proportion settled by the terms of the Holy League accord, the prizes were formally divided as follows: nineteen galleys and two galiots went to the pope; fifty-eight and a half galleys and six and a half galiots went to Spain; thirty-nine and a half galleys and four and a half galiots went to Venice. Of the capture ordnance, the pope, Spain and Venice received as many centreline pieces (Sp. *canõnes de crujia*) as galleys, and proportional shares of the remaining 256 small calibre guns and seventeen *pedreros* (It. *petrieri*).[18] The pope got 881 prisoners, Spain 1,742 and Venice 1,162. Of course, such numbers are open to debate.[19] There was complaint, for instance, from Don Luis de Requeséns y Zúñiga that the Venetians had managed to fraudulently lift at least eleven large and medium-sized guns, despite the papal ban of excommunication on anyone who illegally held on to the spoils of war. Excommunication was (and remains) a serious matter, but 16th-century Catholic leaders saw it as a risk intrinsic to their job.

Of the Ottoman crews, maybe 25,000 or even 35,000 had perished, including not just galley slaves – between 12,000 and 15,000 Christians found on board the Ottoman galleys were liberated – but veteran galley commanders, gunners, timariots, janissaries, and of course Barbary corsairs. Of the 3,486 prisoners captured,[20] the Venetian galley commanders were officially instructed to liquidate "in whatever secret and discreet manner you see fit to use" anyone who showed any level of skill, thereby reducing the Ottoman pool of skilled naval personnel even further.[21] *La Serenissima* was perfectly aware that while the Ottoman empire could rapidly replace any quantity of lost ships, sea personnel and janissaries were a very different story. Marc'Antonio Barbaro, in his report to the doge and Senate, had this to say:

And we have seen that when they (the Ottomans) were dealt the great defeat, they rebuilt their fleet in six months: one hundred and twenty galleys, in addition to those that remained. When this fact was forecast and reported in writing by me, it was judged unbelievable, and even more so after these new galleys were armed. Although the Turks do not lack new galleys, this is not true as sailors, officers, gunners, and similar people are concerned. Because of the route that your serenity gave them, they are deprived of almost all maritime militia, which can not be so easily reorganised, as that needs much time and experience, and also, the Turks generally perform quite inadequately in this activity. You should therefore attribute hardly any importance to the number of their galleys, the cause of more confusion than of benefit, especially now that by the grace the Lord God has not only removed from the Turks that superb impression that Christians would not dare fight against them, but that on the contrary, they have their spirits so oppressed by fear, who dare not to cope with ours, and admitting themselves that their galleys are in every detail inferior in respect to ours, this being also true for fighting people, artillery, and all the other things relevant to navigation.[22]

All this may seem a little exaggerated. Yet two facts remain: first, that the galley commanders, officers and fighting men were almost entirely exterminated without mercy by the Venetians; second, for a number of years, the Ottoman fleet was short of well-trained crews.

Christian losses were much lighter, though still very considerable: between twelve and sixteen galleys captured, sunk or scuttled; an approximate count gives 7,650 killed and a further 7,800 wounded (including Miguel de Cervantes),[23] of who a further 4,000 soon died. About two-thirds of the casualties were Venetian, a blow to its skilled manpower the Republic cannot have found easy to bear. The eyewitness Giovanni Pietro Contarini reckons the Christian total at 7,656, out of this the Venetians lost one captain of a flagship (viz. Agostino Barbarigo), seventeen galley commanders, eight nobles, five chaplains, six counts, five *patroni* (from the Arsenale), six scribes, seven pilots, 113 bombardiers, thirty-two skilled workers, 124 mates, 925 seamen, 2,274 galley slaves, and 1,333 soldiers. [24] On the vessels of His Holiness 800 died and some one thousand were wounded, which is a high percentage when you consider there were only twelve papal galleys, and on the vessels of Habsburg Spain, 2,000 and 2,000 respectively, with the total casualties of *Tercio de Sicilia* amounting to 600 men.[25] At least forty Hospitallers lost their lives, the majority on the *capitana* of Malta.[26] These were grievous losses for the order that counted 300 or 400 knights on active service.[27] All in all, the battle proved that war is a horribly expensive, bloody business.

*Chapter 18*

# Barren Victory

Toward the land that gave them birth / Turn they now the ships
about, / As they seek their native earth.

Friedrich von Schiller, 'Feast of Victory',
*Poems of the Third Period*

Even if the larger historical significance of the Ottoman defeat at
Lepanto is still hotly debated, from a military point of view the
technological innovations should not be overlooked in explaining
the result of the battle. The sharp, heavy spurs of the Christian galleys
were removed for the battle so that their bow artillery was more effective.
It had been observed that the slightly upturned spur would not allow the
main centreline gun to be depressed at very close range, that is to say
'cloth burning' range, thereby precluding shots aimed at the waterline of
an attacking vessel. The bulk of Ottoman galleys were lower in the water
than at least the galleys of Spain and its dependencies, and probably
those of Venice too. In addition, the fact that Spanish and Venetian galleys
mounted five bow guns in contrast to the three on Ottoman galleys – a
main centreline gun (*baş topu*) flanked by two deck pieces (*sayka topu*) –
was a definite plus in the Christians' favour too.

What is more, Spanish soldiers were armed with harquebuses in far
greater numbers, and half armour and morion cabasset made them nearly
invulnerable to Ottoman archery. As previously discussed, harquebusiers
were easy to train and their weapons were effective at short ranges, though
they were so slow to reload that each carried secondary weapons in the
form of a sword and a dagger. The Turkish composite recurve bow was
still a redoubtable weapon and remained in service throughout the 17th
century and even after. Such bows were accurate, powerful and rapid, but
it took years to train an effective archer, and in a long battle they would
tire.

However that may be, the greatest technological advantage that fateful day was surely supplied by the six Venetian galleasses. Filippo Bragadin, *provveditore generale del Golfo*, wrote to the doge on 18 November 1571 from Corfu, urging that the heavily-gunned galleasses should not be decommissioned. It was thanks to their firepower "that it was clear from the start that the victory was to be ours". What Venice needed in future was more gunners and fewer soldiers, and, indeed, a general lesson to be learned from the battle was that ships' crews, armed and armoured, fought more bravely and terrified the enemy more than could soldiers "of the sort we get nowadays".[1] The considerable disorder and loss four of these six behemoths caused to the opposition *prior* to the general engagement certainly gave the Christians the upper hand. This was unquestionably understood by one of the captains of the Venetian galleasses, Francesco Duodo, who mentioned after the battle their valuable cannonade at the battle's onset.[2] When Don Juan de Austria greeted Duodo, he confessed that the Holy League was indebted to the galleasses for their victory.[3]

Ultimately, the battle was indecisive. While Lepanto was the greatest disaster for the Ottoman empire since that of 1402, when the Ottoman Turks were crushed by the central Asian empire-builder Timur, there were no permanent adjustments to power in the Mediterranean world in 1571. Lepanto consolidated a position that had already come into being: the Mediterranean was now divided between two naval powers, the Ottoman Turks in the eastern basin, holding all major coasts and islands apart from Venetian Crete (with Cyprus digested, this became the prime object for Turkish appetite), which, situated as it was in the midst of their possessions, close to the sea lanes between Alexandria and Constantinople, served as a thorn in the side of the Ottoman Turks, as Rhodes had earlier been; the Spaniards in the western basin, with the support of fleets from Malta and Italy. No territory changed in the wake of the battle.

While all were ready to render homage to the talent and bravery which had won the greatest naval battle of the time, men, as they grew cooler and could criticise events more carefully, were disposed to ask, where were the fruits of this great victory? It was said, had Charles V gained such a victory he would not have quitted the field so quickly. On the contrary, before the enemy could recover from the blow, he would have followed it up by another. Many expressed the conviction that the young generalissimo should at once have led his Christian armada against the very heart and brain of the Ottoman empire, Constantinople itself, which would have led to nothing less than the swift and utter defeat and dismemberment of the empire itself. Yet it should not be forgotten that Don Juan de Austria, unlike his father before him, did not possess absolute power over the forces under his command, forces led by men so nearly equal in rank that they each claimed a right to be consulted on all matters of importance. There was also a feeling of jealousy between the Spaniards and the Venetians which was, as we have seen, so great in the early part of the campaign as nearly to bring ruin on it.

Furthermore, Uluç Ali Re'īs had succeeded in bringing the remnants of the shattered fleet safely back to the still waters of the Golden Horn. Many in Constantinople were convinced that having survived the defeat, the *beylerbeyi* of Algiers would now face the block for his share in the débâcle. But the wily corsair not only had fifty vessels with him, but also the so-called banner of the Knights Hospitaller, which was soon put on display in the imperial mosque of Hagia Sophia (Tk. *Camii Ayasofya kiber*). For these two gallant achievements, Uluç Ali was promoted to the rank of grand admiral or *kapudan-ı deryā*, and the soubriquet *kılıç* 'scimitar', was added to his name to signify the bravery that he had demonstrated in the battle. Malicious observers in the Ottoman court would comment that the Calabrian renegade's lofty elevation had less to do with his abilities than to the simple fact that nobody else was on call for the job.

Now officially known as Kılıç Ali Paşa, he appeared the following July at the head of a fleet of 200 new galleys (the Ottomans could draw on timber-rich Black Sea sources). Greatly impressed by the fighting qualities of the Venetian galleasses encountered at Lepanto, the new fleet included five galleasses too. Built in record time – thanks to the energy of the grand vizier Sokollu Mehmed Paşa – the cost of this new fleet was paid from the treasury without imposing any emergency taxes (*akçe-i imdadiye*) on the subject populations and without asking private individuals to provide ships. Moreover, to man this new fleet with oarsmen and mariners, the bulk of the old galley crews, the rowing gangs in particular, having been lost at Lepanto, judges (*kadıs*) from every part of the empire, from as far west as Buda to as far east as Van and Erzurum, received imperial commands to send to the new galleys in Constantinople all the prisoners in their districts, and all criminals arrested after the receipt of the command.[4]

There was one major problem however, and that was finding the fighting men for naval service in the new fleet. Those *sipāhis* who had survived Lepanto were exhausted, dispirited and naturally less than willing to serve at sea again. Eventually the Porte scraped together 4,396 *sipāhis* and 3,000 janissaries to serve at sea, far short of the 20,000 or so fighting men required by the fleet. The only alternative was to enlist volunteers, which was not an innovation as it had been done before. What was an innovation, however, was the post-Lepanto novelty to raise as many men as possible armed with harquebuses. Firearms were distributed to the *sipāhis*, but it appears the traditionally-minded timariots were more than reluctant to accept the 'new fangled' weapons. This would explain the increase in the number of volunteers in the years ahead. Indeed, the number of fighting men of the fleet now bearing firearms struck European observers. On 10 June 1572, François de Noailles (1519–85), évêque de Dax and current French ambassador to Constantinople, wrote to Charles IX that the Ottomans were putting 20,000 harquebusiers aboard their fleet – obviously an exaggeration but an indication of the shift in the Porte's naval tactics.[5]

Kılıç Ali Paşa would remain *kapudan-ı deryā* until his death. Under his energetic leadership by 1576 the Ottoman fleet was completely back to its pre-Lepanto strength, while the pool of experienced naval personnel had been replenished thanks to the arrival of the grand admiral's former corsair compadres from the Barbary Coast. Lessons learnt from Lepanto meant that Ottoman galleys now had more firepower by way of artillery and firearms. In 1582 Kılıç Ali sailed to the Tartar Khanate of the Crimea to install the Porte-appointed khan of this vassal state before going into semi-retirement. He died in July 1587, the last of the great Ottoman seafarers from the school of Barbarossa and Turgut.

*Part IV*

# The Myth

*Chapter 19*

# War Stories

A true war story in never moral and does not instruct …
Tim O'Brien, 'How to Tell a True War Story',
*The Things They Carried* (1990)

The battle of Lepanto, known among the Turks as *İnebahtı Deniz Muharebesi*, was a single historical event. It left many human traces behind. Tales of heroism, sacrifice, cowardice, captivity and homecoming made the rounds in Europe and the Ottoman lands. It was to inspire poets such as G.K. Chesterton, painters such as Tintoretto, and novelists such as Miguel de Cervantes.

## A Ship of Beauty

The *Sultana* was apparently a vessel of surpassing beauty. The deck, says Richard Knolles, was of black walnut wood, dark as ebony, "checkered, and wrought marveilous fair fine with divers lively Colours and variety of Histories", while the admiral's cabin "glittered in every place with rich Hangings wrought with Gold Twist, and set with divers sort of precious Stones with ornaments of gold, rich hangings and precious gems, with certain small Counterseits most cunningly wrought".[1] Apparently Müezzinzāde Ali had brought his entire personal wealth to sea with him – 150,000 gold *sequins*, no less – rather than leave this hoard behind in Constantinople, and risk having it confiscated should he earn the displeasure of the sultan.

## Fighting Farnese

The *capitana* of Genoa was carrying the young Alessandro Farnese, the future duca di Parma e Piacenza, Don Juan's half-nephew and boyhood friend, and future Habsburg general, who had brought with him 202 personal followers to the fight, including thirty-two noblemen and gentlemen adventurers, and 152 Italian soldiers in his pay. He enthusiastically led his men onto a corsair galley and quickly cleared its decks. It is recorded that in the midst of the action Farnese, with his good broadsword, hewed down all who opposed him, opening a path into which his comrades poured one after another, and, after a short but murderous contest, succeeded in carrying the vessel. At this point of the battle the galley carrying Farnese and his men laid just astern of the *La Real*. Don Juan thus witnessed the achievement of his nephew, which he acknowledged in the first letter which he wrote to Philip II while lying off Petalas after the action.[2]

Another youth was in the fight that day. Humble and unheard of as yet, no more than a common soldier serving on the Spanish galley *La Marchesa* in the company of *capitán* Diego de Urbina, *Tercio de Moncada* (most of them veterans of the fighting in the Alpujarras). This was of course our future world-famous writer, Miguel de Cervantes.

## Gentlemen Adventurers

We have already made mention of the non-appearance of Catholic France as a nation at Lepanto, but this is not the whole story. Despite their king's disapproval, several individual Frenchmen of distinction had volunteered, including the celebrated Louis des Balbes de Berton de Crillon (1541–1615), known as the man without fear; in 1589 Henri IV would call him *le Brave Crillon*.

There were at least two English gentlemen adventurers present at Lepanto. One was Sir Thomas Stucley (also written Stukley or Stukeley), the consummate soldier of fortune who had a lively career spanning piracy, being a double agent, a forger, and a womaniser. He was a man constant only in his inconstancy. Having served every English monarch since the time of his alleged father, Henry VIII,[3] whether they were Catholic or Protestant, and several foreign kings too, Stucley had now put his Catholic sword arm at the service of Philip II. Seven years later – 1578 – the pope, Gregory XIII, outfitted the English swashbuckler with ships and an army of 2,000 men to land in Ireland to aid the Irish

Catholics against the Protestant plantations. He also made him marquis of Leinster. To his holiness' dismay, Stucley, having landed, on his way, in Lisbon, was invited to join his forces with those of the king of Portugal, Dom Sebastiano, in his ill-fated invasion of Morocco (an ally of England against Spain). Stucley thus abandoned the Irish venture, only to meet his untimely death when a cannonball (apparently of English fabrication; England had exported munitions to Morocco) took away his legs at the battle of al-Qasr al-Kabir. An alternative account (doubtless the product of balladeers and dramatists) of his untimely end has Stucley, wounded and a fugitive, killed by the remainder of his own Italian soldiers, because he had brought them to the slaughter of al-Qasr al-Kabir.[4]

The second known Englishman present that day was the notorious Sir Richard Bingham (1528–99). He knew the Spanish well and spoke their language too, and served under Don Juan de Austria on that fateful day at Lepanto.[5] A tough, pragmatic career soldier, he had previously fought with the Spanish against the French at Saint-Quentin (1557), and then against the Spanish with the Dutch in the Low Countries. He attempted peace negotiations with Don Juan on behalf of the States-General of the Netherlands (1576), and when the negotiation broke down, fought for his employers at Rijmenan (1578). He took part in the notorious cold-blooded massacre at Smerwick (now known as *Ard na Caithne*, County Kerry) of hundreds of papal, Spanish and Irish soldiers who had surrendered to the English (1580).[6] In a letter he wrote to Sir Robert Dudley, 1st Earl of Leicester, dated 11 November 1580, he claims the butchery was perpetrated by the English sailors and not the English soldiers.[7] Later in his life, as governor of Connaught (Connacht), his name would become one to which much infamy clings. He was appointed to the post in 1584, and his philosophy of governorship is probably best summed up in his own words: "The Irish were never tamed with words but with swords." He has passed into Irish folklore as a cross between Genghis Khan and Bluebeard.

## The War Dancer

An unusual occurrence was the presence at Lepanto of María *la Bailadora* – 'the Dancer' – the lover of one of the Spanish soldiers aboard the *La*

*Real*, who disguised herself as a man in war gear and willingly served in Don Lope de Figueroa's *Tercio de Sicilia*. She had vowed to avenge all women violated by the 'terrible Turk', so proving that sometimes the best man for the job is a woman. A trained harquebusier, she was one of the first wave of soldiers to swarm the bloody decks of the *Sultana*, engaging the enemy in hand to hand combat and dispatching one of her antagonists with one well-placed thrust of her two-edged sword. The latter was likely the Spanish double-edged *espada* with a metre-long, straight blade with a sharp point suitable for both cutting and thrusting, with a complex, swept hilt – that is, curved back to protect the hand wielding the sword. A large pear-shaped pommel secured the grip, which was usually wood wrapped with cord, to the weapon and provided some weight to balance the long blade. Being a soldier's woman during the time the Spanish empire was at its military height, María evidently lived her daily life immersed in the martial culture of the time, which stressed skill both with firearms and edged weapons. Apparently, after the battle, Don Juan, despite his prohibition of women (God forbid) with the fleet, gave orders that María, for her brave exploits in cross-dressing and for killing her man, should be borne on the books of her *tercio* and draw regular pay.[8]

## Deliverance

Lepanto for some was also a day of redemption for past transgressions. Remember the ne'er-do-well nephew of Pius V, Paolo Ghislieri, ransomed by the pope from captivity only to be run out of Rome. Well, he was the first man from his ship to board an Ottoman galley. There he found himself face to face with one Karabaĭvel, well known to him, said Ghislieri, when he was dragging a chain in Algiers. With certain regret, so Ghislieri explained afterwards, since in Algiers the corsair had treated him well, when Karabaĭvel lunged at him with his sabre, he was obliged to level his harquebus and to shoot him in the chest.[9]

## New Tricks

One of the Swiss involved in the fighting, Hans Nölly of Kriens, canton of Lucerne, captured two Ottoman standards and sent them to the government in Lucerne, for which he received fifteen crowns in recognition of bravery and honorary citizenship for himself and his family. Jost Segesser von Brunegg, who commanded the Pontifical Swiss Guard between 1566 and 1592, wrote a detailed after-action report for the Swiss authorities in Lucerne on how the twenty-five men from his command had fared in the battle:

> They all acquitted themselves with honour and only one of my people, my scribe, died, God bless him; several, however, suffered light injuries because they were not very familiar with the weapons, although their injuries could have been much worse. Also, one of our men from Kriens – his name is Hans Nölly – captured two banners from the Turks' main galley [viz. the *Sultana*] ... We recommend him to you.[10]

It is an interesting observation made by the *oberst* regarding unfamiliarity "with the weapons". Did this imply the guardsmen were using the half-pike, or was it the harquebus? In their familiar rôle of protecting the pope they were obviously very handy with the pike proper as well as other long and heavy two-handed weapons, such as the halberd and two-handed sword.

With regards to the latter weapon, the papal *capitano generale* Pantero Pantera, when discussing two-handed swords and their efficacy "in the hands of those who know how to use them on board ship", cites the case of the Venetian *provveditore* Antonio Canal at Lepanto:

> He, though old and stricken in years [he was fifty-years of age], having donned a pair of string shoes in order to stand more stoutly, and having put on a jerkin or short coat all wadded with cotton, with a similar bonnet on his head to protect him from the arrows, mounted an armed Turkish vessel with spirit, and jumping from one galley to another with a big sword in his hand, wrought marvellous prowess in his own person on the foe, and rescued a galley which was already in the hands of the Turks.[11]

## No Surrender!

Another body of élite warriors were apparently employing unfamiliar weapons. Even in the thick of it, a group of janissaries was seen to fight on long after their defeat and demise was clearly on the cards:

> [A]nd when they had no more weapons with which to attack us, [they] collected up oranges and lemons and started to throw them … the mêlée reached such a point that, in many places, one saw men laugh as often as cry.[12]

Obviously, having their backs to the wall just made the janissaries fight that much harder. However, let us try to imagine the psychological effect of close quarter combat. No doubt they were horribly shocked and utterly exhausted by five hours of battle that had gone so badly for them; horribly shocked too by the ghastly aftermath, the wreckage and the blood, the wounded groaning or screaming for help, and practically nobody with the skill to help them, the corpses to be thrown overboard with what little ceremony the imams could mutter.

## A Note on Scurvy

The mention above of those citrus fruits reminds us of that age-old scourge of sailors around the world, scurvy. We do know that the contemporary English surgeon William Clowes was using plentiful berries, vegetables, and scurvy-grass (*Cochlearia officinalis*), a member of the cabbage family and now known to contain as much ascorbic acid, vitamin C, as orange juice, in his cures for scurvy among English soldiers and sailors. He describes what these men suffered:

> Their gums were rotten even to the very roots of their teeth, and their cheeks hard and swollen, the teeth were loose neere ready to fall out … their breath a filthy savour. The legs were feeble and so weak, that they were not scare able to carrie their bodies. Moreover they were full of aches and paines, with many bluish and reddish staines or spots, some broad and some small like flea-biting.[13]

He was probably aware too of those major outbreaks of the disease which had occurred after long sea voyages, such as Vasco da Gama's in 1497 with relief by citrus fruits, or Jacques Cartier's in 1535 with relief by a concoction made from spruce bark and leaves. However, it seems that Clowes was unusual in this respect among northern European surgeons and physicians, because in 1593 Sir Richard Hawkins (†1622) bought hundreds of oranges and lemons in Brazil for his men to cure the scurvy they were currently suffering from. As for the cure itself, he writes "that which I have seene most fruitful is sower oranges and lemons". He continues with an appeal:

> I wish that some learned man would write of it, for it is the plague of the sea, and the spoyle of mariners. Doubtless, it would be a meritorious worke with God and man, and most benificiall for our countrie; for in twenty years, since that I have used the sea, I dare take upon me to give accoumpt often thousand consumed with the disease.[14]

Hawkins' appeal was perhaps based on his later experience as a prisoner-of-war in Spain (1597–1602). It is known that the Spanish acquired their knowledge for curing scurvy from Nueva España, where members of the indigenous population had cured their sailors with scurvy (*escorbuto*) with lemons (*limon*), oranges (*naranja*), and limes (*lima*).[15] Apparently, it seems, not all European sailors were aware of the value of antiscorbutic remedies, or if they were, they simply did not bother to use them. Hardtack and salted meat was the standard.

### An 'Infidel' in an 'Infidel' Land

One Ottoman whose fortune the battle shaped was Hindī Mahmūd, courtier, poet and historian. The story of this *İnebahtı* veteran, much like that of his fellow literary luminary Miguel de Cervantes, is one of captivity and homecoming, resulting in a remarkable poetic opus of 8,000 verses, *Sergüzeştnāme-i Hindī Mahmūd*, 'Memoirs of Hindī Mahmūd'. Born in Afyonkarahisar in western Anatolia into a family of local standing, Hindī Mahmūd rose through the ranks of the Ottoman government, serving as a court official, treasurer, and ambassador. His nickname 'Hindī' (Dark) was given to him by the then crown prince Selīm, in whose household he served. Steadily advancing in the prince's service, his career took a leap when Selīm became sultan. Like all administrators, Hindī Mahmūd had military duties, and in this capacity was on board one of the Ottoman ships at Lepanto. Later he would write, "While fighting for the faith, I was taken prisoner on the sea – I fought hard but I was overcome."[16] Almost certainly his words serve as a fitting tribute to many of his comrades that fateful day.

Taken prisoner by the victors, Hindī Mahmūd was brought first to Messina, then to Naples and finally to Rome, where he was incarcerated in the dungeon of Castel Sant'Angelo, the impregnable fortress tomb by the Tiber. It was here, in his dank cell, that he composed his poetically-written diary, large parts of which are extant (1,113 verses remain missing). In it he praises Don Juan de Austria for his caring and chivalric attitude to the Ottoman prisoners of war. On the other hand, he criticises Vatican politics and papal vanities. From his prison cell, he was able to follow the death of Pius V (1 May 1572) and the succession of Gregory XIII (13 May 1572), and the extraordinary thanksgiving for the mass killings of the Huguenots in Paris on the night of 24 August 1572, the massacre of Saint Bartholomew's Day. He makes colourful observations on Europeans, their mores and their habits. He also talks about prison conditions and the religious practices of his fellow prisoners. His work is very remarkable for the simple reason that Muslim slaves did not typically participate in the literary genre of captivity narratives. In contrast, the availability of early modern sources abounds in polemical Christian captivity narratives published in European languages.

When Hindī Mahmūd was released in 1575 as part of a prisoner exchange, he was sixty-four years old. He spent the rest of his days in Constantinople and in 1579 wrote his famous work *Kīsas-ı Enbiyā*, 'Stories of the Prophets'. He dedicated both works to Murād III, the sultan who gave back his freedom. For Hindī Mahmūd, as it would be for Miguel de Cervantes, the homecoming was a resurrection and a cause for joy and gratitude. Although they were from different worlds and of different faiths, what kept them going in their years of captivity was more or less the same: faith, hope and persistence. Both men were strong in their respective faiths. In war, fighting is not the only form of heroism: sometimes simply surviving is equally heroic.

Consider Cervantes' case. The rigours of work and life aboard the galley, the treatment at port, and the hopelessness of a future without the comforts of a familiar culture or family – drove a very high percentage of Catholics and Protestants in the *bagnios* of North Africa toward conversion.[17] The rewards due a Catholic or Protestant slave after his conversion to Islam might include a pass to release him permanently from the prison, new clothes, and even a stipend from the treasury. By contrast, in Catholic lands, the real and anticipated benefits for converts, particularly galley slaves, were modest indeed and rarely involved manumission. In Tuscany, for example, converts could shed their shackles and sleep outside the *bagnio* but they were still considered prisoners of war and hence property of the Order of Saint Stephen.[18]

## Slave of Saint Stephen

Not all the chattel properties of the Order of Saint Stephen were Muslim of course. One Christian in particular was Aurelio Scetti, a musician condemned to row in the Tuscan galley *La Pisana* who recorded his impressions of his small wooden world in a vivid journal he kept during twelve years of servitude. In Scetti's journal, as in Shakespeare's play *The Tragedy of Othello*, the troubles of the outside world are reflected in the personal world. Like Othello, Scetti murdered his wife for what he claimed was "her bad behaviour",[19] but the resemblance ends there. There is no subtle "put out the light, and put out the light",[20] here. On the contrary, on the night of 20 August 1565, Scetti aroused his sleeping wife, Caterina, by delivering two hefty blows to her head with a candlestick; then, as she dazed on the edge of the marital bed, he slashed her throat with a razor, punched her in the mouth, and continued to slash and strike until the poor woman finally expired. Nor is there any feeling of regret or overpowering guilt, which will result in the dashing, if volatile, Moor of Venice committing a violent suicide with "a sword of Spain, the ice-brook's temper".[21]

Scetti, in an attempt to escape justice, leapt from the walls of Arezzo, broke his right thigh in the fall, and was promptly arrested. He was tried, found guilty, and brought to the common block in the main square of Arezzo. He was allowed to suffer all the horrible pangs of the approach of death; but at the last minute Cosimo I de' Medici, who was struggling to man the galleys of the Order of Saint Stephen, commuted Scetti's penance to penal service at sea, and even promised Scetti's father, privately, that his son would eventually be released. It was with this hope that Scetti lived out his agonising days as a *forzato*.

And Scetti wanted his freedom badly. Once, after he petitioned the Granducato di Toscana for a pardon and was denied, he fell quite ill. "This hardship", he writes in his journal, "caused a terrible sickness that brought Aurelio close to rendering his spirit to God and his body to the earth."[22] Scetti nearly always writes about himself in the third person, a sad instance of flipping roles whereby the perpetrator becomes the victim. After Cosimo's death, it was to his son and successor to the title, Francesco I (r. 1574–87), that Scetti had to appeal once again for his freedom. In 1577, then, Scetti dedicated his journal to the second Granducato di Toscana. The man, who had brutally murdered his wife twelve years before, however, seems never to have regained his freedom, and the wound to his leg seems never to have healed properly. The latter surely acted as a permanent, agonising reminder of the violent manifestation of the paranoid neurosis of Scetti's masculinity.

What redeems his tragic life of course is the journal itself, the climatic moment of which is the battle of Lepanto. Among the dead that fateful day, says Scetti, were 5,000 Christians and 40,000 Muslims. He continues:

> The galleys could barely sail through the site of the naval battle … because of the countless corpses floating on the sea. It was extraordinary to see that one could recognize the Christians from the Turks, for the former were looking upwards, while the latter were facing down, toward the sea.[23]

Such exaggeration is not out of place, of course, but much like the sea fight in *Ben-Hur*, it does provide a gripping first-person experience aboard a fighting galley during a sea battle.

### Maltese Miracles

One of the three survivors from the corpse laden shell that was the *Santa Maria della Vittoria*, the *capitana* of Malta, was the Aragonese knight Fra'

Martin de Ferrara, who was the standard bearer. Left for dead, he had his left arm, half his shoulder and part of his neck and temple slashed by a Barbary scimitar. In after years he was appointed castellan d'Emposta and lived to a ripe old age in spite of his horrible disfigurement.

The other survivor was the Sicilian knight Fra' Angelo Martellini, who was registered as dead by the Order ("... *ebbe tante ferite, che vi fu lasciato per morto* ... "). Though he was cured of his battle wounds by his family, he remained blind in one eye and weak in his shoulder and leg. Poor and advanced in years, he petitioned for a grant from the Hospitaller treasury for his food and lodging even though he was no longer residing in the Convent (i.e. Malta). The Order agreed to give Fra' Angelo a small annual pension, payable on the feast of Saint John the Baptist.[24]

## The Captain-General's Gifts

And here is a charming tale with which to finish this brief anthology of Lepanto war stories. On 13 June 1571, Marc'Antonio Colonna sailed to Civitavecchia on his way to the Sicilian seaport of Messina, appointed as the rendezvous for the Holy League fleet. He was received at Civitavecchia with every demonstration of joy and respect by the inhabitants of that town, who, to do honour to the *capitano generale* of the papal contingent, presented him with the following curious offerings: twelve boxes of white sugarplums; eighteen packets of white wax torches; eighteen packets of large white wax candles; twenty-four loaves of fine sugar; twenty-five capons; twenty-five chickens; one hundred cocks; twenty-four ducks; twelve geese; five Guinea fowls and one Maltese hen; six peacocks, three males and three females; two *genchi* (?); six *crastati* (?); two barrels of wine; three coffers of white bread; four coffers of fruit; and one portion of *nivi* (?). These gifts, somewhat resonant of the Twelve Days of Christmas, were made with noticeable ostentation: a procession of numerous serving men dressed in livery carried the gifts publicly on trays or cars, covered with cloths, flowers, placards, and banners, preceded by trumpeters who proclaimed on high the magnificence of the donors and the dignity of the guest whom they wished to honour.[25] The gift, it is said, blesses the giver.

*Chapter 20*

# Mary's Victory

"With this [the Rosary], one wins battles!"
Padre Pio of Pietrelcina to<br>Fr. Onorato Marcuccli

S ea battles are almost invariably wrapped in a cloak of glory. Lepanto was indeed decisive, but only in the psychological sense. Although we have claimed that this was a victory that led nowhere, in the opinion of the Captive, a character in *Don Quixote* we have already met, a critical objective was accomplished:

> And that day, which was so fortunate for Christendom because that was when the world and all the nations realized their error in thinking the Turks were invincible at sea, on that day, I say, when Ottoman pride and arrogance were shattered, among all the fortunate men who were there (for the Christians who died there were more fortunate than those left alive and victorious), I alone was unfortunate, for, contrary to what I might have expected in Roman times, instead of a naval crown[1] I found myself on that night following so famous a day with chains on my feet and shackles on my hands.[2]

Fernand Braudel, who studies the problem from a number of different angles, agrees with the Captive. According to the French historian, by turning:

> [O]ur attention to what had gone before, the victory can be seen as the end of a period of profound depression, the end of a genuine inferiority complex on the part of Christendom and a no less real Turkish supremacy. The Christian victory had halted progress towards a future which promised to be very bleak indeed.[3]

Even though Ottoman naval power was not destroyed, it is the myth of Ottoman invincibility – concludes Braudel – that collapsed at Lepanto.[4] From then on, Christians felt free to show their galleys everywhere on the sea, as bands of soldiers and adventurers of every nation began flocking to the south in search of employment on the Mediterranean battlefield.

A battle won or lost is what Braudel and his *Annales* School look down upon as a glaring example of the very limitations of *l'histoire evenementielle*, in contrast to the *longue duree* built upon demography, climatology and *mentalite*. Braudel devotes sixty pages to the formation of the Holy League across five years, two pages to the battle itself and three to whether the victory was as fleeting as sceptics have insinuated.[5] Others concur with Braudel on the psychological effects of this victory over the Ottomans. John Lynch posits that after Lepanto, even if Cyprus remained under Ottoman rule, even if the sultan replaced the lost Ottoman ships, sailors and soldiers with astonishing rapidity and the Barbary corsairs were still at large, the spell of Ottoman power was broken; Christendom finally gained a moral victory and freed itself from an old sense of insecurity. After Lepanto, Christendom breathed a collective sigh of relief.

## Papal Piety and Paint

Still, we may debate and quibble today about the historical significance of Lepanto, yet the importance of the victory of Christian forces over those of Islam at Lepanto did not escape Cervantes' writings or Titian's paintings. Nor even the Roman Catholic Church, which still celebrates the victory of the Holy League on the feast day of the Holy Rosary. It was, in fact as in name, a league drawn from most of Catholic Europe, France excepted, and the victory itself was attributed to the intercession of the Virgin Mary, specifically through the Rosary.[6] From Rome Pius V, the very same pope who had not just bankrolled part of this military endeavour but had gone and excommunicated Elizabeth I of England for schism too, believing that the Holy League fleet was a poor match for the Ottoman armada, had asked all of Catholic Europe to pray for a Christian victory at sea, and it was a beautiful banner bearing the Crucified Redeemer that had led the bickering Catholics during the battle to victory against the Ottoman fleet. Catholic Christendom had finally turned the tables on Mehmed II *Fatih*.

The success of the Christian coalition forces at Lepanto – attributed by Pius V to the passionate prayers of the rosary confraternity in Rome – helped reinvigorate the notion (already present in mediaeval thought) that the Blessed Virgin's militant advocacy would guarantee Catholicism's ultimate triumph over the infidels (more specifically, over Islam and the Ottoman empire). Those of you who are atheists will be generally sceptical of marvellous explanations for less-than-marvellous circumstances. Yet beneath the large mural celebrating the victory in the Salla dello Scrutinio of the Palazzo Dogale, the Venetian Senate inscribed: "Not our power and arms, nor our leaders; but the Madonna of the Rosary helped us to victory." Incidentally, the greatest living painter, Titian (†1576), who was ninety, declined the task as being too much for him. An up and coming artist, Jacopo Robusti (1518–94) – called Tintoretto – offered to complete a large wall painting on the theme of Lepanto in a year, and for no fee, and to remove it if a better painting should turn up within the next two years. The commission made Tintoretto's name.

The best painters were employed to perpetuate the memory of the glorious event. We have just made mention of the nonagenarian Titian, who in the time of Charles V had passed two years in Spain, and who now executed for Philip II the oil on canvas *Allegory of the Battle of Lepanto*, now in the Museo Nacional del Prado, Madrid. The painting not only commemorates the event that took place on 7 October, but also the birth of the Infante Fernando, heir to the throne, on 5 December 1571. The proximity of these two events led them to be viewed repeatedly as gifts from Heaven in circles close to the king.

## Protestant Poems and Plays

Lepanto fever spread even as far as Protestant England, where the English celebrated the Ottoman defeat with bonfires and banqueting and great rejoicing not so much as the victory of the Venetians and the Spanish but as a triumph of all Christendom. To show exactly what she thought, Elizabeth of England ordered the Church of England, which she had established by law, to hold services of thanksgiving. England's interest in the Ottoman defeat continued to develop despite the personal resentment of certain kings such as James VI of Scotland (later James I of England, r. 1603–25).

James was the unlikely product of the union between Mary Stuart, queen of Scots, and Henry Stuart, Lord Darnley (1545–67). His unhappy, turbulent upbringing amid the blood-splattered power struggles of the Scottish nobility (his father was butchered in cold blood less than a year after his birth) had endowed James with plentiful opportunities for observing the inner workings of men's minds. James, in the Scottish phrase, was canny. Mary Stuart on the other hand was definitely not canny. The mini-epic poem *Lepanto*, a battle "Betwixt the babtiz'd race, / And circumcised Turband Turkes",[7] was written by a bookish twelve-year-old James in 1583 and published in 1591. The poem was republished in 1603 when James was transferred to alien England at the age of thirty-six. In it the *Protestant* prince – he had never known his mother's influence and, besides, the Scottish historian and humanist scholar George Buchanan was currently making sure Calvinism was being drummed into his royal head – tells of the famous naval victory over the Ottomans by a *Catholic* coalition led by Don Juan de Austria. In other words, James was writing a heroic poem about someone else's victory under someone else's religion in someone else's war. As we well know it was a signal military victory for Catholicism, but in 'heretical' Scotland it was not the attractive subject for artists and writers that it was in Spain and Italy, where it was treated by Miguel de Cervantes, Lope de Verga, Cambiaso, Titian, Tintoretto, and Veronese, among others. Naturally, of course, news of the victory incited celebrations across Catholic Europe, fomenting hopes of a renewed crusade against Islam and even Protestantism.

In any case, James does admit at the outset of his 11,000-line poem that he understands that its hero is a "foreign Papist bastard" but that his reason for dealing with the sensitive subject at all (Don Juan was also known to the English as a hammer of their Protestant allies in the Low Countries) is that the defiance of the Turks by the Holy League is analogous to the defiance of Catholic persecutors by the forces of Protestantism. The story of the great Catholic victory becomes a suitable subject for English and Scottish readers only when it is manipulated to fit to the proper political frame, even if that fit is a Procrustean one in which Don Juan, of all warrior princes, becomes a *Protestant* hero. Accordingly, and despite his pronounced Catholic sympathies, the royal author would not have his readers suppose that the story of the battle of Lepanto was simply a record of the event, for the event cannot be recorded without activating its connotations as a rallying cry for Catholic Europe.[8]

The battle and the poem were at the back of Shakespeare's imagination when he penned *The Tragedy of Othello* for the 1 November 1604 performance at the court of the new-crowned monarch. Shakespeare seems also to have been influenced by *The generall historie of the Turkes* of Richard Knolles, which was first published in London in 1603 and dedicated to James VI, particularly his dramatic details of Lepanto. Knolles writes:

> It was a right horrible spectacle to see, how in the Battell the Sea stained with blood, and covered with dead Bodies, Weapons, and the Fragments of the broken Gallies; besides the great number of them that were slain, and beaten into the Sea; many of the Turks blinded with fear, casting away their Weapons, to escape the fury of the Enemy, threw themselves headlong into the Sea ...[9]

Thought Lepanto was the only major Catholic victory over the Ottoman Turks in the 16th century, it was interpreted by Knolles as a victory for Christendom as a whole. It is a reasonable assumption that Shakespeare drew upon Knolles for some of the military background to Othello.

Shakespeare's primary source for his play – about a soldier who is betrayed by his ensign into thinking his wife is unfaithful, and then kills her – was the novella *Un Capitano Moro*, 'A Moorish Captain', by the Italian novelist and poet Giovan Battista Giraldi Cinzio (1504–73), commonly referred to as Cinthio, and first published in 1565. What we should note here is that in Cinthio's story, Cyprus is a peaceful island, threatened by nothing more than fair weather and calm seas.

In fact, Cinthio mentioned nothing about Turks or Mediterranean sea-battles and sieges: his story described a domestic affair concerning a Moor and his Desdemona. Only in the first lines of his tale did he mention the service of the Moor to the state. In *Othello*, Shakespeare retained the domestic tragedy but moved it into the vast and confrontational world of the Mediterranean, where Catholic Venetians employed Muslim Moors to fight the Ottoman Turks. As a consequence, and for dramatic intensity, Shakespeare set parts of *Othello* in war-torn Cyprus,[10] giving the play a strong political resonance for its first audience. Given also that Othello was a Muslim soldier of fortune who had fought on behalf of Venice,[11] Knolles' description gives a sense of the kind of war stories he would be able to recount. Knolles actually describes the celebrations of the Christian victory in England,[12] so we can assume the events would have been known in Shakespeare's London.

## The Miracle of Mary

Not only was Lepanto memorialised in dozens of popular early baroque paintings throughout Europe; it also led to the creation of a new liturgical feast, that of the Holy Rosary, which came to be celebrated (and is still observed) by Roman Catholics worldwide. Christians in the 16th century inhabited a world in which a divine intervention was nothing out of the ordinary but one more expression of a world sustained by omnipotent, omniscient and ever-present personal tripartite Deity who, surrounded by choirs of angels and galleries of saints, was looking down on earth as the pinnacle and purpose of his works. The story of the battle is filled out with legends and stories of miraculous events which inevitably undermine the modern reader's confidence in the story of Lepanto as a whole. At the very least, however, accepting that mentalities differ across the centuries is one crucial step in understanding 16th-century convictions concerning the efficacy of the Rosary. To do otherwise would mean making judgements formed upon our own intellectual and moral standards.

We strive to understand the past, not to shape and instrumentalise it in the service of the present. Our backward gaze leaves us in history's majestic haze, and rewards us with many misconceptions. But more than one step is required of us if we are to fully appreciate the heavenly power of Mary and her Holy Rosary. The image of Mary, Queen of Heaven, in the Apocalypse: "A great and wondrous sign appeared in heaven: a woman clothed with the sun, with the moon under her feet and a crown of twelve stars on her head."[13] This perception of the Virgin, adorned with gold, pearls, and priceless gems, was especially popular in the Spain of the Counter-Reformation, where a new form of veneration for Mary's Immaculate Conception emerged. Works by painters in early modern

Spain, such as Velázquez, El Greco, Zurbarán, and Murillo, attest to the efforts to depict Mary as the heavenly apparition that transcends death, as illustrated by Velázquez's painting *La inmaculada concepción*.

Like Pallas Athena, the Virgin also presided over peace and war. From the 6th century on, her image was often paraded in battles against the heathens, Turks and Calvinists alike.[14] The fact that Pius V instituted the feast of Our Lady of Victory to celebrate the Christian defeat of the Turks at the battle of Lepanto illustrates these notions about Mary's powers. The associations between the cult of the Virgin and the victory of Lepanto by the Christian armies bring to mind the numerous references to the Virgin that traverse both *La historia del cautivo* and *El trato de Argel*, among other literary works of Cervantes.

The Christian coalition's victory at Lepanto is also one of the principal reasons why the rosary became so prominent in an early modern Catholic reform programme that sought to unite all human persons in 'peace and solidarity' (guided and governed, of course, by the Roman Church). Prelates like Pius V were quick to assert that Christian military success at Lepanto had resulted from direct intervention by the Blessed Virgin Mary, because during the battle, members of the rosary confraternity in Rome had gathered at the basilica of Santa Maria sopra Minerva "to pray for victory".

A fateful link was thereby forged between the political and military fortunes of Christian armies and Mary's powerful intercession. Not only was she Christ's gentle mother and mistress of heaven (popular mediaeval images), Mary was also a fiercely aggressive warrior queen who guaranteed an emboldened, militant Christianity victory over 'alien others' (especially Islam). The liturgical feast of Our Lady of the Rosary (still celebrated annually on 7 October) has its origin not, as it would seem at first glance, in simply a prayer, but in a battle, namely the Christian military victory at Lepanto.[15]

Even after generations, churches in Catholic Europe were being consecrated to Maria della Victoria. Lepanto, which is the earliest naval battle of the western world to be celebrated by artists of renown, remains a subject for art today. See especially the extraordinary suite of twelve large-format canvases in acrylic, wax crayon and graphite, *Lepanto, a painting in twelve parts*, created by the American abstract painter Edwin

Parker 'Cy' Twombly, Jr. (1928–2011) for the 49th Biennale di Venezia in the summer of 2001, and since the autumn of 2008 on permanent display at the Museum Brandhorst, München. The Biennale di Venezia is the art world's most prominent international gathering.

Yet we should not lose sight of the fact that the emblem that the victors had continually before their eyes on that fateful day was not the Virgin but her son, Crucified Christ. In the mind of the architect of the Holy League, Pius V, the enterprise was wholly a religious one, a war for the defence of Catholic Christendom against the followers of Muhammad. On each Christian vessel, large and small, Jesuit, Dominican, Franciscan, and Capuchin friars, crucifixes clutched firmly in hand, urged on the combatants, chanting the mass and offering eternal hope. Don Juan toured his fleet holding aloft the ivory crucifix he had seized during his recent repression of the rebellious *moriscos* in the Kingdom of Grenada. His flagship, the *La Real*, displayed the papal gift of a life-sized crucifix atop its mainmast. He also flew a banner blessed by the pope, one of blue damask upon which was embroidered the insignia of the parties of the Holy League. Christ Crucified was at the top, and beneath, the papal coat of arms; below on either side, were the arms of Spain and Venice, on the right and the left; pendant from a chain which united them, the arms of Don Juan de Austria.

And the losers were not without faith either. On one hand, God and the Virgin were invoked, on the other hand, Allah and the Prophet. Muslim expectations that prayer would deliver a miracle were less than in Christianity. Islam recognises three primary acts of devotion: the *salāh* five times a day; *dhikr*, a ritual not unlike the Rosary, for remembering the Divine Name; and *du'ā'* as a personal plea. Every day, all Müezzinzāde Ali's men would have performed the *salāh*. On the day of the battle, most would have been able to do so safely only at dawn – and the survivors perhaps before sleep. However, throughout the hours of 'fear', all could ceaselessly recite any of the ninety-nine names of Allah; *dhikr* a devotion which the Prophet had declared would secure greater esteem on the Day of Resurrection than a man who "wielded his sword against unbelievers and idolaters until it is broken".[16]

# Lepanto Finale

> Now a battle can be won or lost. It was destined to happen this way
> according to the will of Allah.
>
> Ottoman decree, issued on 28 October 1571[1]

On 1 May 1572 the crusading pope, Pius V, died after a brief
illness. With him went the driving force that had kept the Holy
League in being; the new pope Gregory XIII, while committed
to the Catholic alliance against the Ottomans, did not possess his
predecessor's charisma and austerity. Yet its death knell was the separate
peace the Serene Republic negotiated with the Sublime Porte signed on
Saturday, 7 March 1573. Gregory XIII was dumbstruck and threatened
to excommunicate the whole republic.

The upshot was that by this treaty the Venetians agreed to cede all the
fortresses they had recently conquered in Albania and Dalmatia, return
all Ottoman prisoners without ransom, limit their active fleet to sixty
galleys and pay an indemnity of 300,000 *ducati* by instalments over three
years. While the annual tribute of 8,000 *ducati* for Cyprus previously
paid by Venice was cancelled, the Venetian tribute of 500 *ducati* for the
possession of Zante was raised threefold.[2] From the harsh terms of this
peace, as Voltaire was to remark years later, one might well suppose
that at Lepanto the Venetians had lost: "*Il semblait que les Turcs eussent
gagné la bataille de Lépante.*"[3] Even if Voltaire was one of those annoying
polymaths who never surrendered an opportunity to exercise their all-
embracing wit and cynicism, it would not be wrong of us to argue that
the victory at Lepanto bore no fruit nor served any purpose whatsoever
for the Serene Republic.

Lepanto and its aftermath had re-confirmed Venice's status as a major
power in the Mediterranean. From a peacetime force of 9,000 men
spread across the empire in garrisons, *la Serenissima* in 1570 raised an

army of 36,000 men, hired partly on the international manpower market. In 1573 Venice had put 130 galleys to sea, with 23,000 infantry on board.[4] It maintained a fleet half the size of the Ottoman one and garrisoned the *impero da mar*, the *terraferma* and the lagoon too, all with the most modern *matériel*.

All the same, the doge and the Senate had always wanted a short war and a quick peace. War with the Porte had severed Venice's commercial monopoly of low bulk, high value merchandise out of the Levant. In addition, its fleet mobilisation had scooped up its labour force of fishermen, merchant seamen and farm hands to serve as oarsmen, sailors or soldiers. Least we forget, just over half of the galleys in the Holy League fleet that fought at Lepanto were Venetian, some 108 out of 206, or roughly fifty-two per cent, and that is not including the six cannon-laden galleasses. Habsburg Spain may have considered peace with the 'infidel' as downright treasonable, but it, along with its viceroyalties of Naples and Sicily, had only contributed forty-nine galleys, about twenty-four per cent of the whole. Besides, Mediterranean commerce meant little to Spain; its commanders saw themselves as Christ's soldiers in an unrelenting holy war with the Ottomans and their Barbary satellites.

In a private conversation with his lifelong friend, the Venetian *bailo* in Constantinople Marc'Antonio Barbaro, the Ottoman grand vizier Sokollu Mehmed Paşa supposedly said the following concerning the débâcle at Lepanto:

> As you have been observing, our courage has not faded away after the battle of Lepanto; there is a discrepancy between your losses and ours. We ceded from you a land [referring to Cyprus] where you can build a kingdom, thus cut off one of your arms. [Whereas] you defeated our fleet which meant nothing more than shaving our beard. A missing arm can not be replaced but a shaved beard grows thicker.[5]

Humble occasions are no enemies of wisdom. Admittedly the conquest of Cyprus and destruction of the Ottoman fleet at Lepanto were brought about by the scheming of his enemies, led by his main rival in the Ottoman court, Lala Kara Mustafā Paşa – the grand vizier had strongly advised his master against the entire Cyprus campaign. Even so, Sokollu Mehmed was a man with whom one should not trifle, a man who had successfully served three sultans without interruptions for fourteen years, effectively ruling the empire from his appointment as grand vizier by the elderly Süleymān I in 1565 until his murder by a petitioner dressed as a dervish in 1579. In a court where vigilance was a duty, dexterity a talent, and shrewdness a must, Sokollu Mehmed did not lack any one. It was he who had taken the trouble to hoist Süleymān's winebibbing son, Selīm, to the throne.

This was no proud empty boast on Sokollu Mehmed's part. At the end of the day the Venetians had no hope of recovering Cyprus, and resigned themselves to letting it go, in consideration of securing the safety of Crete and their other outlying possessions. It seemed obvious to the Sublime Porte, if not to the Serene Republic, that the conquest of Cyprus was much more important than the battle of Lepanto. The island would remain in Ottoman hands for the next three centuries. The loss of Cyprus was a disaster for Venetian sovereign interests and reputation and the treaty of 1573 meant *la Serenissima* and the Porte refrained from serious hostility for a full seventy years, until in 1645 the Ottomans embarked upon the conquest of the Venetian-held island of Crete in the War of Candia.

The Venetian defection killed the Holy League, but the Spanish still had a substantial Mediterranean armada in being. Philip II could now transfer the war to the quarter he had preferred. He resolved, accordingly, to send an expedition to the Barbary Coast. Tunis was selected as the place of attack, a thriving seaport and the home of many a corsair who preyed on the commerce of the western Mediterranean. It had been taken by Charles V in the memorable campaign of 1535, but had since been recovered by the Muslims. The Spaniards, however, still retained possession of the strong fortress of La Goleta. Situated in the inlet of that name, La Goleta was the stronghold that overlooked the approaches to Tunis, considered inexpugnable once Charles took the city four decades earlier.

In October 1573 a fleet under Don Juan de Austria took Tunis and Bizerte practically unopposed, effectively blocking Ottoman access to the western Mediterranean, something the Porte could not ignore for long. Sure enough, in July of the following year, an Ottoman armada issued from Constantinople and appeared before the port of Tunis and the *presidio* of La Goleta with a force between 250 and 300 ships, carrying around 75,000 troops. The Ottomans, commanded by Ciğalzade Yusuf Sinān Paşa and Kilç Ali Paşa, joined the contingents of troops led overland by the corsair governors of Algiers, Tripoli, and Tunis. The impressive Ottoman armada, constituted by a force perhaps as large as 100,000, launched simultaneous attacks on Tunis and La Goleta, from both land and sea, taking the *presidio* of La Goleta, fiercely defended by 7,000 Spanish and Italian soldiers, on 23 August after a five-week siege in which thousands of men died or were taken captive by the Ottomans. After repeated assaults, the remaining Christian soldiers in the small fortress opposite Tunis surrendered on 13 September.

Awaiting the arrival of reinforcements from Italy and Sicily, the besieged Christian soldiers had fought valiantly yet in vain. In spite of Don Juan's insistent requests for assistance from the cardinal-statesman Antoine Perrenot de Granvelle, the king was in no condition to grant this help, owing not only to the financial crisis affecting Spain but also to the current troubles in the Low Countries. Notwithstanding, Don Juan attempted to come to the rescue of La Goleta with a contingent of galleys and troops from Naples and Sicily, but his fleet was repeatedly diverted from the coasts of Africa by furious storms that forced him to return to the port of Trapani, in Sicily. However, as Don Juan sailed for the third time for Tunis, determined to succour the besieged at all costs, La Goleta had already fallen and had been razed to the ground. Thus ended the campaign, in which Habsburg Spain, besides its recent conquests, saw itself stripped of the *presidio* which had defied every assault of the Muslims since the time of Charles V.

From the naval point of view, the reconstruction of the Ottoman fleet over a period of five months demonstrates the resilience of the Ottoman state in relation to such a disastrous incident. The launching of new amphibious expeditions to La Goleta and Tunis and the successful conquests of these places testify to the quick recovery of Ottoman sea power from the effects of such a tragic event. Yet the Sublime Porte had lost its taste for naval warfare on a grand scale, and was content to leave Habsburg Spain to its own devices, while pursuing its traditional rivalry with the Shi'a shahs of Persia. As a matter of fact, with relative peace on the European front, the Ottomans embarked on some twelve years of costly, exhausting warfare with Safavid Persia (1578–90), from which the Porte appeared to emerge victorious, having established a semblance of authority over Kurdistan, Georgia, Azerbaijan, Shirvan, and Dagestan. All this was extremely convenient, since Spanish Habsburg preoccupations also now turned away from the Mediterranean; Philip's great ambition was to stamp out the new type of infidel who was crawling all over northern Europe: the Protestants. Nine years after Lepanto Philip, like the Venetians before him, came to terms with the Sublime Porte.

In fact, Philip's tepid response to this new challenge from Barbary is explained by the war in the Low Countries against his rebellious subjects, which had utterly drained the Spanish treasury, and by the enormous cost of maintaining a Mediterranean navy, factors that would plunge the Spanish state into bankruptcy a year later, on 1 September 1575. In 1574, however, because Tunis was too far from Spain, the Ottoman forces decimated the imperial garrisons and even, as Cervantes' captive tells us, "ordered the Goleta to be dismantled".[6] In his 1590 *Memorial* to the Spanish crown, Miguel de Cervantes clearly states that after the failed enterprise before the town of Navarino (1572), he was present at Tunis and La Goleta.[7] It is in *La historia del cautivo*, however, that the soldier author shows himself at his most eloquent, telling us what happened between Don Juan's October 1573 expedition to Tunis and the catastrophe of August and September 1574. Even more, Cervantes devotes two sonnets to the fall of the fortresses at Tunis and La Goleta, mourning the heavy losses suffered by the soldiers who defended the *presidios*.

From the Captive's detailed narration of these episodes, we can surmise that Cervantes the soldier probably disembarked with the Christian troops in La Goleta in October 1573, when Don Juan took the island fortress and the city of Tunis, placing a puppet ruler, Muley Muhammad VI, the brother of Muley Ahmad, in charge of the Moorish and Berber population. Since Charles' conquest of Tunis in 1535, the fortress of La Goleta had remained under Spanish Habsburg control. Fortunately, Cervantes did not remain behind with the garrison in La Goleta after Don Juan's 1573 offensive. Instead, he would embark with Don Lope de Figueroa's *tercio, el Tercio Nuevo de la Mar de Napoles*, and would probably spend part of the winter in Sardinia. Escaping misfortune, he missed this encounter with the grim reaper.

Through the Captive's words, Cervantes praises the stout defence of Tunis and La Goleta by its soldiers, even while implicitly denouncing the Spanish crown for not coming to the aid of the besieged. Alluding to the criticisms that arose in Spain in response to this shocking defeat, the Captive points out:

> "It was the general opinion that our forces should not have closed themselves inside the Goleta but waited for the landing in open country, and those who say this speak from a distance and with little experience of this kind of warfare, because inside the Goleta and the fort there were barely seven thousand soldiers, and how could so small a number, no matter how brave, have gone into open country and defended the forts at the same time against the far larger numbers of the enemy? And how is it possible not to lose a fort when there is no relief, and it is surrounded by so many resolute enemies fighting on their own land?"[8]

Highlighting the intrepid resistance of the soldiers who guarded these North African *presidios*, Cervantes claims that in the twenty-two Ottoman assaults against the fortress of Tunis, its small contingent of Spanish and Italian soldiers managed to kill 25,000 attackers; in the words of the Captive only "three hundred of our soldiers survived, every one of them wounded when he was taken prisoner".[9] Cervantes was among the troops of Don Juan which tried to arrive in vain to help the assailed men of La Goleta. Against the backdrop of the Mediterranean wars with the Ottomans, the Captive's reminiscences are rigorously historical.

Virtually excluded from the commercial routes of the Maghrib, the *presidios* were inhospitable strongholds surrounded by enemy territories, where men could hope at best to stay alive. Braudel reminds us that life was utterly miserable in these garrisons:

> So near the water, rations rotted and men died of fever. The soldiers were hungry all year round. For a long time, the only supplies came by sea.[10]

Worse, when the supplies came, if at all, it was usually in winter, when the corsairs were presumably at bay. Braudel goes on to explain that

Orán was an exception to this rule, because it obtained meat and grain from the countryside around the citadel. The fate of La Goleta was no different from that of the other *presidios*, despite its apparently favourable location near the abundant supplies of bread, wine, cheese, and chickpeas of Naples and Sicily. According to Braudel, when Don Alonso Pimentel "took command of La Goleta in 1569, the garrison was living off its reserves of cheese – without either bread or wine".[11]

Soldiers in these garrisons were supplied with rations by the storekeepers at the price fixed on the shipping labels, and often on credit, through which the soldiers could amass frightful debts, as they bought food, on credit also, from passing merchants. The problem was aggravated by the fact that pay was lower in the *presidios* than service in Italy – one more reason, when troops were being embarked for the *presidios*, not to let them know beforehand of their destination, and, once they were there, never to repatriate them. Diego Suárez spent twenty-seven years in Orán, in spite of several attempts to flee as a stowaway on galleys. Only the sick were able to escape the horror of the *presidios* – and then, not always – by being sent to the hospitals of Sicily and Spain. In sum, the dry, desolate and dirty "*presidios* then were virtually places of deportation".[12]

Yet as far as Philip II was concerned, the Mediterranean looked quite small within the massive conglomeration of lands he ruled in the Old World and the New. The Italian priest and anti-Machiavellian political theorist, Giovanni Botero, published a work on *Della Ragion di Stato*, 'Reason of State', in 1589 that was to prove especially popular in Spain. Translated into Spanish in 1609 by Spain's great historiographer-royal, Antonio de Herrera, the text proved to be enormously influential amongst courtiers and nobles, standing alongside *Utopia* (1516) of Thomas More. Botero argued that dispersed states are inherently weak, but that the Spaniards had managed to overcome this through the flexible use of their fleet. Within the Spanish empire, "no state is so distant that it cannot be aided by naval forces", making it possible for Catalan, Basque and Portuguese sailors to join together Iberia, Philip's Italian states and even the Low Countries in a single unit: "the empire, which might otherwise appear scattered and unwieldy, must be accounted united and compact with its naval forces in the hands of such men."[13]

# The Gunpowder Reformation

Fixed fortifications are a monument to the stupidity of man. If mountain ranges and oceans can be overcome, anything made by man can be overcome.

George S. Patton

Charles VIII of France (r. 1483–98), finding himself at the head of a great army experienced in the art of war,[1] looked for fresh fields to conqueror. As a representative of the House of Anjou, Charles had a certain meagre and generally dormant claim to the throne of the Kingdom of Naples, which was currently under the dominion of the House of Aragón. And so it was, in the winter of 1494/5, that the malformed and ambitious young monarch of the House of Valois rode south, ponderous lance on knee, to make good his convoluted claim to Naples.

His father, the hothead and belligerent Louis XI (r. 1461–83), had died when Charles was only thirteen. The young king had left the administration of his kingdom in the hands of his elder sister Anne de Beaujeu (1461–1522), and had spent his time reading novels of chivalry. He developed what we would now call a quixotic fascination with the glories of war. On grasping the reins of power in 1491, Charles realised that he had the means to turn his flamboyant dreams into reality. Like all vain and little men, he was anxious to cut a romantic and considerable figure on the world stage. Thus it was that his high ambition did not terminate at Naples, for he planned to embark from there, retake Constantinople, turn back the Ottomans, and establish himself as emperor in the east.

For the history books, however, the significance of Charles' invasion of the Italian peninsula was that it swiftly demonstrated that the old mediaeval fortifications of Christendom were now largely redundant. With astonishing speed and power Charles had taken, one after another, castles and fortified cities, all of which had crumbled before the pounding of his thirty-six cannon, fashioned from gleaming bronze and firing compact iron balls. Francesco Guicciardini (1483–1540), a Florentine historian, courtier and diplomat, and friend and critic of Niccolò Machiavelli, wrote in his masterpiece *Storia d' Italia* that the cannon were:

> Planted against the walls of a town with such speed, the space between shots was so brief, and the balls flew so speedily, and were driven with such force, that as much execution was inflicted in a few hours as used to be done in Italy over the same number of days.[2]

This was no exaggeration.[3] In February 1495 the French attacked the Neapolitan border stronghold Castello di Monte San Giovanni Campano, a fortress that had earlier reputedly withstood a siege of seven years. The French cannon quickly opened a breach in its walls through which the French soldiers surged and slaughtered its garrison, all within a mere eight hours. By the middle of March of that year, the conquest of Naples was accomplished, and the French rested upon their victory, took their ease, and enjoyed the sensual delights of the capital of the vanquished kingdom.

Hitherto the strength of a fortress had derived principally from the height of its walls; the higher the curtain wall the more difficult for the storming-party to scale the crest, while the thickness entailed by height rendered attack by siege engines less effective. By the latter half of the 15th century, however, dominance in the centuries-old competition between those who built fortresses and those who sought to knock them down had swung dramatically in the favour of the latter. According to Niccolò Machiavelli, writing in 1519, from 1494 onwards "the force of artillery is such that no wall can stand it, not even the thickest, for more than a few days".[4] Charles' invasion led to the swift realisation that the Italian cities and petty princedoms could only last a half-day under his cannon bombardment.

Opposed-weight engines threw projectiles that struck only blows that glanced at such walls, while torsion-machines, though working with a flat trajectory, were intrinsically under-powered. Even stone-firing bombards had made little impression upon the art of siege warfare. The only certain means of bringing down a wall was to attack it at its base by mining, a laborious task that ditches and moats readily defeated, and that was also open to the riposte of counter-mining. The new cannon, because they could be brought rapidly into action close to a wall, and then handled to fire accurately in a predictable arc of impact, transferred the effect of mining to artillery. Iron cannonballs, directed at the base of a wall in a horizontal pattern of attack that did not vary in height, rapidly cut a channel in the stonework. The cumulative effect was to use the physics of the wall against itself: the higher the wall, the more quickly it would become unstable and the wider the breach it left when it toppled.

With relative ease Charles' cannon had knocked down walls that had stood stoutly for many centuries, thereby making good his claim to the Kingdom of Naples. *Col gesso*, 'With chalk in hand', was the *bon mot* of the current pope in Rome, Alexander VI,[5] and implies that it was only necessary for the French king to despatch his quartermasters to chalk up the billets for his soldiers to conquer the peninsula.

Italy, as a consequence, became the new school of not only experienced master masons, but also experts in mathematics and engineering. It was Giuliano da Sangallo, with his brother Antonio, who founded the first and most important of the Italian fortification 'families', an extremely competitive group of Mafia-like bands that were contained by ties of blood, companionship and patronage. These not only included the Sanmicheli, Savorgnano, Peruzzi, Genga and Antonelli, but also unlikely practitioners. In fact, the phenomenon of war has fascinated cultured men of genius, many of whom trained in military engineering.

Renaissance giant Leonardo da Vinci (1452–1519) is perhaps best known as a master artist but he was also an engineer, inventor and freethinker. In the rôle of military engineer,[6] da Vinci served for a time as *Architecto e Ingegnero Generale* for Cesare Borgia. He was also commissioned by Cesare to design a series of great hydraulic constructions to canalise the river from Cesena to the sea. The drawings have survived but the work was never carried out.

In a similar capacity, there was da Vinci's younger contemporary and acquaintance, Michelangelo Buonarroti (1475–1564), who, as *Governatore generale sopra le fortificazioni*, equipped his native Florence with new defences between 1527 and 1529.[7] Michelangelo, who is now remembered chiefly for his titanic struggles with blocks of marble and the ceiling of the Cappella Sistina, was also renowned in his own day as a military engineer (he was also a poet and an architect). In 1545, in the course of a heated argument with his fellow Florentine Antonio da Sangallo il Giovane (1484–1546), the Renaissance genius gave vent to the astonishing statement that "I do not know very much about painting and sculpture, but I have gained a great experience of fortifications, and I have already proved that I know more about them than you and the whole tribe of the Sangallos."[8] Michelangelo it seems had a habit of unrestrainedly speaking with perfect frankness. In 1508 Julius II ordered Michelangelo to paint the ceiling of the Cappella Sistina. Michelangelo wanted to practice sculpture: whereupon he was told to paint a ceiling. "I'm not a painter! (*Nè io pittore!* )" he roared at the pope, who fulminated and thundered in reply. They both were equally *terribile*.

As cannon fire did its worse against high walls, new walls to resist it must therefore stand low. However, a fortress so built was open to escalade, the rush-forward of a storming-party with ladders to sweep over the crest and into the fortress' interior by surprise attack. The new system of fortification had to incorporate features that resisted bombardment and, at the same time, held the enemy's infantry at bay. The solution to this problem of surrendering height while acquiring depth was the wall-height, angular bastion. This structure stood forward of the curtain walls, dominated the ditch or moat, served as a solid fire platform for both cannon and firearms, and was strong enough not to be battered shapeless by a concentration of enemy fire.

The most suitable design proved to have four faces. Two of these faces formed a wedge that pointed out toward the surrounding countryside so as to present a glancing surface to enemy fire, and where attacking artillery could be mounted. The other two faces, those that joined the wedge to the wall at right angles, allowed the defenders to use cannon and small arms from atop the ramparts to sweep the ditch and stretches of the curtain wall between bastions. The bastions should be built of stone, though brick was an acceptable substitute, backed and filled with rammed earth, the whole constituting a structure of immense solidity so as to provide both a solid cannon platform and an outer face on which impacting shot would make the least possible impression.

Before we leave this topic it should be remembered that the most impressive fortified network of the time, the Hospitaller fortifications of the island of Rhodes, were built or improved between 1480 and 1520. The main forts have a clearly experimental nature and some of the works carried out in the 15th century are closer to a regular angular outline: this is the case of the bastion of Auvergne (c. 1496), protecting the tower of Saint George, and of the bastion protecting the tower of Spain (after 1481). The latter, in spite of its irregular design, seems to be well protected with artillery gun ports on its faces and flanks. One of the last fortifications to be erected, perhaps the most impressive out of all of Rhodes' main circuit, is the bastion del Carretto (1515–17). It has nothing to do with the angular design, being instead a perfect example of the circular typology: a semi-circular bastion with a diameter of over fifty metres and of three storeys that protects the tower of Italy, which stands as a circular *cavalier*.

Influenced by the theoretical designs of Albrecht Dürer (1471–1528), the circular design also prevailed during the extensive (and expensive) scheme to improve the fortifications of the English coast, ordered by Henry VIII and carried out between 1539 and 1543. Characteristically, these gun-forts are centrally planned, compact in form, and feature a cylindrical central tower containing guns mounted in tiers of casemates and on the roof. The central gun tower is protected by lower semi-circular bastions mounting guns in casemates, firing through open embrasures or mounted barbette platforms to fire over the top of the parapet. The forts – set in ditches – are all built of stone with thick walls, sloping parapets to deflect cannon shots and chimney flues in casemates to remove gun smoke. Deal castle on the Kent coast, one of the largest and most impressive of Henry's coastal defences, could mount up to 145 guns.

# Bull Against Elizabeth I

Lord, what fools these mortals be!
William Shakespeare, *A Midsummer's
Night Dream*, 3.2.117

Mention Elizabethan England to most people, and they usually think of the following: Good Queen Bess and her many disappointed suitors; Mary queen of Scots, the lovely unfortunate; William Shakespeare and the Globe Theatre; Sir Frances Drake and the Spanish Armada; Sir Walter Raleigh and his gallantry with a cloak. A papal bull against Elizabeth of England is probably the last thing to come to mind.

Elizabeth I was a convinced Protestant. You may recall that it was her father, the schismatic Henry VIII (he had been excommunicated on 11 July 1533), who dissolved the monasteries in his kingdom and made himself head of the church as well as head of the state. Of course, there were many Catholics left in England still devoted to the Holy Mother Church. In October, 1569, a group of English nobles led by the powerful earls of Westmoreland and Northumberland raised an army against their anointed monarch in the Catholic north of England, which had not yet been fully integrated either politically or in the matter of religion. Though Elizabeth's government suppressed the northern uprising, the incident, known as the Northern Rebellion, contributed to a growing fear and distrust of Roman Catholics. After all, the aim of the rebellion had been to oust Protestant Elizabeth from her throne, replacing her with the Catholic Mary queen of Scots. It appears régime change is no new phenomenon.

To support the Northern Rebellion, the crusading pope – and future Saint – Pius V issued a papal bull (25 February 1570) that excommunicated Elizabeth for Protestant heresy and wicked persecution of English Catholics during her reign (thus far she had actually tolerated Catholic worship in private), and absolved her Catholic subjects from any requirement to obey her. Philip II of Spain was a man of long views: despite commenting that England and Spain were "nearly in a state of war",[1] the king was trying not to alienate the English to the point of throwing them into the arms of the Valois. There was also the fact that Philip, as was Elizabeth too in her own way, was a prudent, frugal soul who hated unnecessary risk and, still more perhaps, unnecessary expense. If there was any nation whom Philip might be excused for hating at that time it was the English; those insular upstarts, pirates and heretics of the cold north who were perpetually swooping down on the coastal towns and waters of Spain and its empire, destroying its galleons, and devastating its homeland and colonial possessions. On the other hand, Pius V had correctly perceived that by then the queen was committed to the Protestant cause.

The bull commanded English Catholics to resist the queen's rule, and it stated that those who remained loyal to Elizabeth would also be excommunicated. The early years of Elizabeth's reign had seen relative leniency towards Catholics since it was believed that Catholicism would gradually lose its attraction; but the bull made every Catholic a potential traitor and this, combined with high-profile conversions such as that of Edmund Campion (1540–81) – now Saint Edmund Campion – and regular plots, led to renewed fear and repressive action against Catholics. But as well as subjects being absolved from their oath of allegiance to the excommunicant, her throne was declared vacant; kings and princes of Christendom were invited to invade her realm, to take her crown and sceptre, to expel her a homeless friendless outcast in a world that shunned her like a pestilence.

But events had moved swiftly, for the papal bull did not arrive in England until after the rebellion had been suppressed. Entitled *Regnans in Excelsis* ('Reigning on High'), the bull ran as follows:

Pius Bishop, servant of the servants of God, in lasting memory of the matter. He that reigneth on high, to who is given all power in heaven and earth, has committed one holy Catholic and apostolic Church, outside of which there is no salvation, to one alone upon earth, namely to Peter, the first of the apostles, and to Peter's successor, the pope of Rome, to be by him governed in fullness of power. Him alone He has made ruler over all peoples and kingdoms, to pull up, destroy, scatter, disperse, plant and build, so that he may preserve His faithful people (knit together with the girdle of charity) in the unity of the Spirit and present them safe and spotless to their Saviour.

1. In obedience to which duty, we (who by God's goodness are called to the aforesaid government of the Church) spare no pains and labour with all our might that unity and the catholic religion (which their Author, for the trial of His children's faith and our correction, has suffered to be afflicted with such great troubles) may be preserved entire. But the number of the ungodly has so much grown in power that there is no place left in the world which they have not tried to corrupt with their most wicked doctrines; and among others, Elizabeth, the pretended queen of England and the servant of crime, has assisted in this, with whom as in a sanctuary the most pernicious of all have found refuge. This very woman, having seized the crown and monstrously usurped the place of supreme head of the Church in all England together with the chief authority and jurisdiction belonging to it, has once again reduced this same kingdom—which had already been restored to the Catholic faith and to good fruits—to a miserable ruin.

2. Prohibiting with a strong hand the use of the true religion, which after its earlier overthrow by Henry VIII (a deserter there from) Mary, the lawful queen of famous memory, had with the help of this See restored, she has followed and embraced the errors of the heretics. She has removed the royal Council, composed of the nobility of England, and has filled it with obscure men, being heretics; oppressed the followers of the Catholic faith; instituted false preachers and ministers of impiety; abolished the sacrifice of the mass, prayers, fasts, choice of meats, celibacy, and Catholic ceremonies; and has ordered that books of manifestly heretical content be propounded to the whole realm and that impious rites

and institutions after the rule of Calvin, entertained and observed by herself, be also observed by her subjects. She has dared to eject bishops, rectors of churches and other Catholic priests from their churches and benefices, to bestow these and other things ecclesiastical upon heretics, and to determine spiritual causes; has forbidden the prelates, clergy and people to acknowledge the Church of Rome or obey its precepts and canonical sanctions; has forced most of them to come to terms with her wicked laws, to abjure the authority and obedience of the pope of Rome, and to accept her, on oath, as their only lady in matters temporal and spiritual; has imposed penalties and punishments on those who would not agree to his and has exacted then of those who preserved in the unity of the faith and the aforesaid obedience; has thrown the Catholic prelates and parsons into prison where many, worn out by long languishing and sorrow, have miserably ended their lives. All these matter and manifest and notorious among all the nations; they are so well proven by the weighty witness of many men that there remains no place for excuse, defence or evasion.

3. We, seeing impieties and crimes multiplied one upon another the persecution of the faithful and afflictions of religion daily growing more severe under the guidance and by the activity of the said Elizabeth—and recognising that her mind is so fixed and set that she has not only despised the pious prayers and admonitions with which Catholic princes have tried to cure and convert her but has not even permitted the nuncios sent to her in this matter by this See to cross into England, are compelled by necessity to take up against her the weapons of justice, though we cannot forbear to regret that we should be forced to turn upon one whose ancestors have so well deserved of the Christian community. Therefore, resting upon the authority of Him whose pleasure it was to place us (though unequal to such a burden) upon this supreme justice-seat, we do out of the fullness of our apostolic power declare the foresaid Elizabeth to be a heretic and favourer of heretics, and her adherents in the matters aforesaid to have incurred the sentence of excommunication and to be cut off from the unity of the body of Christ.

4. And moreover (we declare) her to be deprived of her pretended title to the aforesaid crown and of all lordship, dignity and privilege whatsoever.

5. And also (declare) the nobles, subjects and people of the said realm and all others who have in any way sworn oaths to her, to be forever absolved from such an oath and from any duty arising from lordship, fealty and obedience; and we do, by authority of these presents, so absolve them and so deprive the same Elizabeth of her pretended title to the crown and all other the above said matters. We charge and command all and singular the nobles, subject peoples and others afore said that they do not dare obey her orders, mandates and laws. Those who shall act to the contrary we include in the like sentence of excommunication.

6. Because in truth it may prove too difficult to take these presents wheresoever it shall be necessary, we will that copies made under the hand of a notary public and sealed with the seal of a prelate of the Church or of his court shall have such force and trust in and out of judicial proceedings, in all places among the nations, as these presents would themselves have if they were exhibited or shown.

Given at St. Peter's at Rome, on 25 February 1570 of the Incarnation; in the fifth year of our pontificate.

Pius PP.[2]

# A Town Called Naupaktos

The Corsican ruled countries / But the Briton ruled hearts.
Verse dedicated to Lord Byron by Kostis Palamas

Ancient Naupaktos (Gk. Ναύπακτος) was taken in 455 BC by the Athenians. Here they established a colony of rebel Messenians following their defeat by Sparta in the Third Messenian War.[1] Unsurprisingly, they were staunchly loyal to Athens. Ideally sited on a small and well-protected bay just inside the Gulf of Corinth on its north shore, it was to serve as an Athenian outpost and naval station.

At the start of the Peloponnesian War (431–404 BC) the Athenian admiral Phormio made Naupaktos his base for a blockade of Sparta's ally, Corinth.[2] In 429 BC it was the scene of a small naval engagement. Twenty Athenian triremes were bounced by a fleet of seventy-seven Peloponnesian triremes, resulting in nine of them being driven ashore, and but for the presence of Messenian soldiers from Naupaktos, all nine would have been lost.[3] Meanwhile, the remaining eleven Athenian triremes had dashed for the safety of Naupaktos with twenty triremes from the Peloponnesian fleet in hot pursuit. Ten of the Athenians made it safely into harbour, and took station near a temple of Apollo, with prows facing outwards, ready to fight. But the last Athenian trireme, finding itself closely followed by a Leukadian trireme, rounded a merchantman anchored off shore and rammed the Leukadian amidships. This caused panic among the remaining pursuing ships, and some dropped oars to let the rest catch up – as Thucydides says,[4] a foolish thing to do with the enemy so close – while others ran aground in ignorance of the coast. Encouraged by this, the other Athenian triremes swept out to re-engage, and after a brief resistance, the Peloponnesians fled, losing six triremes in the process.

Because of its strategic location, Naupaktos was to change hands many times following the dissolution of the Byzantine empire after the Fourth Crusade (1202–04), with the Angevins, the Catalans and the Hospitallers, to name but a few, ruling in their turn. The town was to suffer the same fate during the various wars between the Venetians and the Ottomans.

Called *Lepanto* by the Venetians, the now strongly fortified town had come under their rule in 1407. Although Mehmed II *Fatih* had attempted in vain in 1483 to capture Naupaktos (Tk. *İnebahtı*), it was his son and successor Bāyezīd II (r. 1481–1512) who finally succeeded in taking the Venetian fortress on 28 August 1499 through the efforts of the freelance corsair Kemāl Re'īs.[5] It was during this operation that Hacı Ahmed Muhyiddin Pìrì, the nephew of Kemāl Re'īs, was given command of his own ship. He was to become the famed cartographer and corsair Pìrì Re'īs.

Naupaktos was turned into one of the eleven districts, *liva*, in the province of Cezayir, *Eyalet-i Cezayir*, within the Ottoman administrative system. The conquest of Naupaktos, together with those other Venetian fortified footholds on the south-western corner of the Peloponnesos (Morea), namely the twin ports of Modon (Gk. Μεθώνη) and Corone (Gk. Κορώνη) in 1500, Venice's 'two eyes' in the Morea, along with nearby Navarino (Gk. Παλαιό Ναυαρίνο) in 1501 – again the work of Kemāl Re'īs – gave the Ottomans not only a new frontier well to the west, but also near control of the whole eastern half,[6] except Crete, of the Mediterranean Sea, which was the fundamental basis of fortune and power of Venice, the only important Christian power in the region.

By the end of the Second Ottoman-Venetian War in 1502, the Ottoman fleet led by Kemāl Re'īs had reversed centuries of Venetian (and Genoese) dominated waters and with the treaty of the following year – 1503 – the Venetians reconciled to the stark reality that their hold over the eastern Mediterranean was over. Venice had to pay ten thousand *ducati* annually to Bāyezīd as tribute, and captured Venetian galleys were absorbed into the growing Ottoman navy. However, the treaty also allowed Venetian merchants to trade freely in Ottoman territory. It is pertinent to remind ourselves that fighting against your principal trading partner was (and still is), indeed, a risky business. Except for a brief period of Venetian control in 1687–99, Lepanto remained under the Ottomans, serving as an important naval station for their fleet, until Greek independence in March 1829.

## Byron in Greece

George Gordon Noël Byron (1788–1824), 6th Baron Byron, had been given the task of a land-based assault "against Lepanto [Naupaktos], with two thousand men",[7] the Ottoman-held fortress some thirty kilometres east of Mesolóngi, in order to pressurize Ottoman shipping on the north coast of the Gulf of Corinth. It appears the Albanian garrison stationed there were discontented due to pay arrears and consequently offered to put up only a token resistance if Byron was willing to bribe them into surrender.

The venture, however, was delayed and eventually abandoned. In part because Byron's heroic Souliotes refused to fight "against Stone walls",[8] and in part because of the atrocious weather in what Byron called "this mud-basket": "The dykes of Holland when broken down are the Deserts of Arabia for dryness, in comparison", he wrote on 5 February 1824.[9] Nothing during his stay at Mesolóngi frustrated him more than the conduct of his band of three-hundred Souliotes. According to George Finlay (1799–1875), an eyewitness to the Byronic events at Mesolóngi, Byron "saw that he had degraded himself into a chief of a band of personal followers, who thought of nothing but extorting money from their foreign leader".[10] The fellow Scotsman and philhellene also adds that upwards of a third of them "demanded double pay and triple rations, pretending to be officers, whose dignity would not allow them to lounge about the coffee-houses of Mesolonhgi [sic] unless they were attended by a henchman or pipebearer".[11] The Souliotes were a military caste – ne'er-do-wells, in truth – from the Albanian badlands, which Byron had visited back in 1809. Byron still had his moments of silliness: he was drawn to the Souliotes by their perceived likeness to a Scottish clan and by their magnificent regalia. Byron had obviously engaged them out of nostalgia and an ill-considered sense of their efficacy.

## The Flawed (Homeric) Hero

But all that was in the future as Byron, accused in England of marital abuse, sodomy and incest, fled to the continent, vowing to model himself on Napoléon and become a pan-European traveller and warrior. He was self-aware, though, and admitted that "With me there is, as Napoléon said, but one step between the sublime and the ridiculous."[12] Byron eventually reached Waterloo, and hired a Cossack horse to tour the battlefield. This was only one year after the battle and the atmosphere must have been eerie to say the least. The third canto of Byron's youthful epic *Childe Harold's Pilgrimage*,[13] written the same year, was partly inspired by the visit. He opens with a stark anti-British, anti-royalist, line inspired by arriving at the battlefield: "Stop! – for thy tread is on Empire's dust!"[14]

Byron was horrified at the number of deaths caused by Britain and its allies in their determination to do away with the 'Corsican ogre' and reinstate the royalists on the French throne. The poet, who was a supporter of Napoléon and a harsh critic of the war effort, regarded Waterloo not as a victory but as a calamity. He had lost one of his cousins at Waterloo, Major Frederick Howard. Thus, standing on the battlefield of Waterloo Byron's hero Harold regrets the bloody human cost of war: "… curb the lust for war / nor learn that tempted Fate will leave the loftiest star".[15] When Byron visited the battlefield, there must have been human remains in open view. No one could have collected, buried or ploughed over all those human fragments. The following year, in 1817, the artist, J.M.W. Turner, appended Byron's description of the carnage at Waterloo to a large-scale canvas called *The Field of Waterloo*. Like Byron, who was well aware that his views on the battle were at odds with those of the majority of his countrymen, Turner was appalled by the violence of battle, and to this end his painting focuses not on the romance of war, but on its ghastly consequences. His picture shows a group of grieving women, searching a pile of dead and dying bodies in the hope of finding their partners.

By denouncing Waterloo as a "king-making Victory",[16] Byron makes clear his belief that the defeat of the French empire and the restoration, in his view, of the detestable Bourbon monarchy was not worth the deaths of nearly 50,000 soldiers. That Byron himself had been raised a Scotsman and a Calvinist (his first ten years had been spent in Aberdeen) placed him from birth slightly askew from the ruling English élite (it is easy to forget that his hereditary title conferred on him membership of the House of Lords). That he was also bisexual and deformed by a clubfoot further made his life one of varying accommodations and rebellions. Moreover, in the words of Finlay:

> He regarded politics as the art of cheating the people, by concealing one-half of the truth and misrepresenting the other; and whatever abstract enthusiasm he might feel for military glory was joined to an innate detestation of the trade of war.[17]

This was a shrewd observation from one who was sharing the uncertain hazards of Mesolóngi too.

Of course the poet was not a pacifist: he famously paraded himself as the champion of Greece and Greek freedom. For Byron the only battles worth fighting were battles for freedom, as evinced by the poet's enlisting in the Greek war of independence. His dedication to Greek freedom however was overturned by fate: he would die (Easter Monday, 19 April 1824), soon after his thirty-sixth birthday from rheumatic fever rather than cannon fire, at Mesolóngi (or Missolonghi) on the flyblown, fever-ridden coast of Akarnania. Byron's life had been such an extraordinary rollercoaster adventurer that, dazzled by it, people have constantly underrated his poetry. In fact, no one was more eager to ridicule his romantic Byronic image than Byron himself; his lordship was even, in some moods, prepared to take the mickey out of his own work and call it 'poeshy'. In a letter just before his death Byron had written: "If I do outlive the campaign, I shall write two poems on the subject – one an epic, and the other a burlesque, in which none shall be spared, and myself least of all."[18] For one, and we may be oddly struck when we realise the obviousness of this, Byron never actually engaged directly in any battle (he died before the beginning of the final siege of Mesolóngi).[19]

"Mad, bad and dangerous to know", at least according to his dumped mistress Lady Caroline Lamb,[20] the glamorous swashbuckling poet may well have been. In this respect, he certainly had the misfortune to attract more than his fair share of dysfunctional and humourless admirers. Yet Byron was also an interventionist, a cunning diplomat, and a surprisingly shrewd wartime administrator who drew a following of capable men. Having sung in his youth of the glory of Greek independence from Ottoman rule, and having been humbled and wised-up by decidedly less romantic personal experiences in his own life, Byron went off to a war zone to partake of the dirty business of nation-building at a time when isolationism was running high in Europe.

At the time, the Ottoman empire was not only an important ally of Britain but also of the Holy Alliance, consisting of Russia, Prussia and Austria, which together formed the three most reactionary governments on the European continent. These were committed to ensuring a new order founded on the realpolitik of the Congress of Vienna (November 1814 – June 1815), which aimed to restore stability to Europe after the ravages of the Napoleonic wars. At the Congress of Vienna was born the Conservative Order, the principle that the legitimate monarchies of Europe should be inviolable, in both their constitution and territory. The new order was to be defended against all by the Great Powers acting in concert, after negotiations at periodic conferences. Its arch strategist was Prince Klemens von Metternich, the Austrian foreign minister and bane of the Romantics.

Yet Greece was both inspiration and disillusionment for the poet. Byron had been fully exposed to the classical past a decade earlier, while he was engaged on a Grand Tour that encompassed much of the northern Mediterranean – Italy, Albania, and Greece. Yet it would be hard to argue that his interest in Greece was motivated by a profound attachment to its classical past, rather than a romantic belief in liberty. Bear in mind *Childe Harold's Pilgrimage*, a poetic product of his peripatetics, holds modern Greece to the impossible standards of antiquity and finds it a "sad relic of departed worth! / Immortal, though no more; though fallen, great!"[21] Contemporary Greeks were sorry disciples of their mythic forebears: slaves awaiting emancipation, or, as Byron cruelly recorded in prose form in 1810, "plausible rascals, – with all the Turkish vices, without their courage".[22]

The Greece he had wanted to see emerge finally got its chance in March 1821 when Greek rebels revolted in Wallachia and Moldavia (now Romania), then both principalities of Ottoman-occupied Europe guarded by Russia as a special dispensation for Christian Orthodox inhabitants in the region. Fighting spread southward a month later to the Morea, and Greek battlefield successes were marred by atrocities against Turkish civilians. Around 15,000 out of the 40,000 Turkish inhabitants of the Morea were slaughtered. In retaliation, the Ottomans burned Orthodox churches to the ground and slew Greeks in Constantinople and Smyrna, a spate of sectarian massacres that culminated in the Easter hanging of the eighty-year-old patriarch of Constantinople, Grigorios V, by janissaries. His corpse, which was subsequently flung in the Bosporus, had a *fatwa* pinned to it. These are just a sample of the horrific stories that had been reaching Europe about extreme violence on both sides.

For all these barbarities, the Ottoman empire was still deemed a necessary evil by Viscount Castlereagh, Britain's foreign secretary from 1812 to 1822 and Metternich's Anglo counterpart,[23] who saw in the Greek cause nothing that would further Britain's national interests but much that would harm them. To Castlereagh, a quixotic war would lead to regional or continental turmoil; he was by no means sanguine about Russia's own designs on Greece, particularly as Tsar Alexander I (r. 1801–25) – Holy Alliance or no – now thought war inviting and popular at home. Moreover, Russia contended that the Conservative Order did not apply to the non-Christian 'Asiatic' Ottoman empire. Not for the last time, then, would arguments for intervention veer wildly between, on the one hand, the democratic and humanitarian and, on the other, the revanchist and imperialist. Castlereagh consequently advocated a meek and unenforceable political solution to the conflict consisting of Ottoman troop withdrawal from Wallachia and Moldavia, amnesty for Greek rebels, and reparations for destroyed property. For these and other reasons, the Tory "intellectual eunuch" was flayed by Byron in the introduction to *Don Juan*, the epic masterpiece he stopped writing when he left to join the obscure, savage pageant of the Greek war in 1823. And so moving from words to action in Greece, he had uniforms – and even neoclassical helmets – made for himself and his two aides-de-camp: his Homeric helmet flaunted the old Byron crest, with the old motto: *Crede Byron*, 'trust Byron'.

He alighted at Mesolóngi on 5 January 1824. One of his first acts was to call for badly needed supplies: "[T]he principal material wanted by the Greeks appears to be – 1stly. a pack of field Artillery – light – and fit for Mountain service – 2dly. Gunpowder – 3dly. hospital or Medical Stores." Byron also understood that the Greeks needed foreign military advisors. "Raw British soldiers", Byron wrote back to London, "[would be] unruly and not very serviceable – in irregular warfare – by the side of foreigners. It would be wiser to send élite officers who spoke Italian, the second tongue of Greece, and who had proficiency with artillery and were familiar with the amphibious terrain of the Mediterranean."

## Freedom's Poet

Byron may have been the first and best-known philhellene, yet Λόρδος Βύρωας, as he is still called by the Greeks, was not alone in fighting for the freedom of a homeland that was not even his own. Other foreign volunteer adventurers, filibusters and idealists – commonly veterans of the Napoleonic wars and liberals (nationalism was inextricably linked to liberalism) sympathetic to the cause – supported the Greeks in their struggle for national independence from the Ottoman empire (1821–32), usually through Greek associations and societies. Yet these European philhellenes, such as Byron, were neither so numerous nor significant as their self-advertisements tend to suggest. The reality was rather different. In truth, it was an adventure as quixotic as could be imagined by the maddest Spaniard.

As Byron facetiously confessed in a letter written in Mesolóngi, "between Suliote chiefs, German barons, English volunteers, and adventurers of all nations, we are likely to form as goodly an allied army as ever quarrelled beneath the same banner".[24] An army, composed of assorted races naturally antagonistic, could only be welded together by the magic of military success or of the personal influence of a popular leader. Such a bond is but a weak one. A cause, which rests upon a single man, will stand no strain. Indeed, the European philhellenes' military rôle in this Balkan conflict was the most extraordinary piece of knight-errantry on record – at least since the days of Don Quixote.

After Byron's death, John Cam Hobhouse suggested that if his good friend had lived to see the battle of Navarino, which would be fought on 20 October 1827, he would have stood a decent chance of being "at the head of Greece". The notion was not so terribly far-fetched. Prior to the sinking of the Turco-Egyptian fleet in the bay of Navarino, the still-ailing Greek government would beseech George Canning, who had succeeded Castlereagh as foreign secretary after the latter's death by suicide in August 1822, to make Greece a British protectorate with an English-born monarch – an offer Canning turned down. Canning was a liberal Tory, and hostile to the conservative faction led by the Duke of Wellington. He had even fought a duel with Castlereagh in 1809 over policy disagreements. He detested Metternich's intrigues and was more sympathetic to the Greeks, having joined the London Philhellenic Committee. Nevertheless, until 1826 his policy remained the same as Castlereagh's: non-intervention.

But when Greece did finally attain formal independence, in 1832, the first king of the Hellenes, Otho I (r. 1832–62, †1867), was not a native Athenian at all but a Bavarian Wittelsbach prince. To mark the centenary of its subject's death, the British diplomat and author Sir Harold Nicolson (1886–1968) wrote a marvellous essay mapping out what might have been had Byron lived and taken Otto's place at the throne.[25]

# Notes

**Lepanto Prelude**

1. Voltaire, *Histoire des voyages de Scarmentado*, in F. Deloffre et J. Van den Heuvel (eds.), *Voltaire: romans et contes* (Paris, 1979), pp. 136–7. For a decent English translation, Votaire, *The Best Known Works of Voltaire: Eight Volumes in One* (New York 1927) pp. 293–5.
2. Lord Raglan, *How Came Civilization?* (London, 1939), p. 170.
3. Ibid. 179.
4. W.T. Stead (ed.), *The Last Will and Testament of Cecil J. Rhodes* (London, 1902), pp. 96, 98.
5. Ibid. 84.
6. Antony Beevor, 'Why did Ukraine ban my book?', *The Guardian*, 3 February 2018.
7. Miguel de Cervantes, *Don Quixote*, part 1, ch. 49, p. 427 Grossman. Bernardo del Carpio is a legendary hero of the mediaeval Kingdom of Asturias; in constrast to El Cid, he was not based on a real person, and thus could be whatever the creator wanted him to be. So, in the opening to *Don Quixote*, Cervantes has Don Quixote admire Bernardo because at the battle of Roncesvalles (Fr. Roncevaux) "he had killed the enchanted Roland by availing himself of the tactic of Hercules when he crushed Antaeus, the son of Earth, in his arms" (part 1, ch. 1, p. 21 Grossman). As for the historical encounter, on 15 August, 778, a large force of Basques ambush the rearguard of Charlemagne's army in the Roncesvalles Pass, a high mountain passage (elev. 1,057 m) in the western Pyrenees. The Basques succeeded in capturing considerable amounts of booty, while among those slain that day was a relatively obscure Frankish commmander, Roland (OF *Hrōþiland*) – the incident is related in Einhard's *Vita Karoli Magni*, who refers to Roland as *Hruodlandus Brittannici limitiis praefectus*, "Roland, prefect of the borders of Brittany" (cap. 9) – whose death elevated him into legend. The first and most famous of these epic treatments was the Old French *Chanson de Roland* of the 11th century (transferred to Italian romance as Orlando). What is more, the mountain ambush was romanticised by oral tadition into a heroic battle between the Christians and the Muslims, the Basques rudely replaced by a Saracen host numbering 400,000 warriors of the faith.
8. H.G. Wells, *The New World Order* (London, 1940), 'Socialism unavoidable', ch. 6, p. 54.
9. John Shirley, *The History of the Wars in Hungary* (London, 1685), p. 95: "the grand vizier (i.e. Kara Mustafā Paşa) broke ground running his trenches with incredible speed [...] so that in six days 13,000 men were entrenched". Western fortifications may have been superior, but few armies in Christendom could equal the skill and resourcefulness of the Ottoman engineers.
10. According to calculations recorded by the Ottoman polymath Kātib Çelebi (1609–57) in his history of Ottoman maritime warfare, a typical Ottoman fleet in the mid-17th century consisted of only forty-six vessels (forty galleys and six *maonas*), whose crew complement was 15,800 men, of whom roughly two-thirds (10,500) were oarsmen, and the remainder (5,300) fighters (*Tuhfetü'l-kibār fi esfāri'l-bihār* ['Book of the Maritime Wars of the Turks'], Darü't Tıbaati'l Mamureti's Su [İstanbul, 1141/1729], p. 92).

11. Like Iustinianus I (r. 527–65), one thousand years earlier, one of the sultan's greatest achievements was the codification of laws. Many of these laws dealt with taxation and use of land. The laws also included issues that were decided by religious judges.

12. Imber 2002: 118–20.

13. These campaigns were Belgrade (1521), Rhodes (1522), Mohács (1526), Vienna (1529), Güns (1532), Baghdad (1533), Corfu (1537), Moldavia (1538), Buda (1541), Gran (1543), Tabriz (1548), Erivan (1552), and Szigetvár (1566), where the great Süleymān was to breath his last, in his tent, on the night of 5–6 September.

14. Richard Knolles, *The generall historie of the Turkes, from the first beginning of that nation to the rising of the Othoman familie*, 3 vols. (London, 1687–1700 [7th edn.]), vol. 1, p. 559.

15. Ibid., 'To the Christian Reader unto the Historie following'.

16. The Venetian diplomatic mission was the longest-serving one in the Ottoman capital and the *baili* were expert diplomatic negotiators and keen observers of political and military developments in Constantinople. See Dursteler 2001.

17. Quoted in Capponi 2007 [2006]: 99–100.

18. Wotton had actually written, in Latin, this epigram in the album of his friend Fleckamore as he was passing through Augsburg on his way to Venice, where he was the ambassador for James VI/I. The original Latin, *Legatus est vir bonus peregre missus ad mentiendum rei publicae causa*, does not admit of the double meaning, that is, he intended a pun in the use of the word 'lie', the other sense being, to live out of his country "for his country's good".

19. Süleymān's beloved legal wife Hürrem Sultan (†1558), known in the west as Roxelane, was almost certainly of Slavic origin (Ruthenia, now parts of Ukraine and Belarus), and some maintain that her birth name was Aleksandra Lisowska and she was the daughter of an Orthodox priest. However, in Italy there is the tradition that she was the daughter of Nanni Marsili, a Sienese gentleman, and was kidnapped by Muslim corsairs when a child and sold in the slave market at Constantinople. She is the subject of a portrait painting by Titian titled *La Sultana Rossa* (c. 1550). The name she was given, 'Hürrem', means 'the cheerful one' in Middle Persian.

20. However, it did not originate with him. Charles Haddon Spurgeon (1834–92) attributed it to an old proverb delivered on Sunday morning 1 April, 1855. Spurgeon was a celebrated English fundamentalist Baptist preacher. His words were: "A lie will go round the world while truth is pulling its boots on." Even earlier, in 1710 Jonathan Swift (1667–1745) wrote on the same subject in *The Examiner* (No. 14 Thursday, 9/11/1710), a Tory broadsheet edited by the satirist from 2 November 1710 to 14 June 1714. In his words, "Falsehood flies, and truth comes limping after it, so that when men come to be undeceived, it is too late" (*The Examiner* No. 14, Thursday, 9/11/1710).

21. Riyad-us-Saliheen, Hadīth 1393.

22. The term Sublime Porte is a translation of the Ottoman Turkish *dergah-ı-ali*, which originally indicated the place where the sultan heard legal suits and engaged in lawmaking activities. The term eventually became the common way in diplomatic circles to describe the Ottoman government.

23. Giovanni Baptista Arcucci, *Victoria Naupactiaca*, ll. 17–24, apud Wright-Spence-Lemons 2014: 195.

24. John 11:1–44.

25. Antonmaria Graziani, *De Bello Cyprio* (Roma, 1624), p. 41.

26. Jacques Le Saige, *Voyage de Jacques Le Saige de Douai à Rome, Notre-Dame-de-Lorette, Venise, Jérusalem et autres Saints lieux*, apud Cobham 1908: 57. Jacques Le Saige started on the journey to Jerusalem 19 March 1518, and reached his home on Christmas Day of the same year. His autograph, scratched on a wall of the church of Saint Francis at Famagusta, was found in 1901 by Camille Enlart.

27. Fra' Angelo Calepio, 'Conquest and Defence of Famagosta', apud C. D. Cobham (ed. & trans.), *Excerpta Cypria* (Cambridge, 1908), p. 157.
28. Quoted in Guilmartin 2003 [1974]: 226.
29. The catch phrase repeated in closely parallel form in the diplomas of appointment for all commanders was: "… you are to treat his every word as if it had issued forth in personal audience from my own (i.e., the sultan's) pearl-dispensing tongue forming part of our own auspicious utterances" (quoted in Murphy 1999: 136).
30. Archivo di Stato di Venezia, *Annali*, s.a. 1571, fol. 460r (25 January 1571).
31. Bragadin's 'martyrdom' is believed to have provided the inspiration for Titian's painting the *Flaying of Marsyas* (1573). Marsyas was a satyr who rashly challenged the god Apollo to a musical contest, and Titian follows the account of Ovid's *Metamorphoses* (bk. 6, ll. 382–400), which covers the contest very quickly. In a bizarre twist, nine years later Girolamo Polidoro, a Venetian seaman who survived the siege of Famagusta, stole the skin of Bragadin from the Tersāne-i Āmire, the arsenal in Constantinople, and returned it to Venice where it was buried with full military honours. To this day, it is buried in a niche in the Basilica di Santi Giovanni e Paolo in Venice; the niche was opened in 1961 and it was found to contain several pieces of human skin.
32. *The Prophecies and Revelations of Saint Briget (Birgitta) of Sweden*, bk. 1, ch. 19, § 9.)

### Chapter 1: The Veteran

1. In 2002 a group of one hundred top international writers voted *Don Quixote* "the most meaningful book of all time" in a poll organised by editors at the Norwegian Book Club in Ósló.
2. In Castilian: *Perdiste el movimento de la mano / Izquierda, para gloria de la diestra* (Miguel de Cervantes, *Viaje del Parnaso*, 24:8–9).
3. The English proverb comes from the 1701 translation of *Don Quixote* by Pierre Antoine Motteux; in the original Spanish the proverb reads: *al freír de los huevos lo verá*, 'you will see it when the eggs are fried'. Do please note where Sancho says to his master: "if you don't believe me, *the proof is in the pudding* [emphasise mine], I mean, you'll have your proof when his grace the innkeeper asks you to pay damages for everything" (Miguel de Cervantes, *Don Quixote*, part 1, ch. 37, p. 325 Grossman). The longer English version, as oppose to this the American version of the proverb, makes more sense, especially when you know that 'proof' here is the verb meaning 'test' as oppose to the noun meaning 'verification'. The pudding we are discussing here, of course, is not the sweet sticky steamed variety, but that savoury mishmash of oatmeal and offal gracelessly stuffed into a sheep's stomach, none other than the "Great chieftain o' the puddin'-race!", celebrated with much aplomb by Robert Burns in his perennial 'Address to a Haggis' (1786).
4. Yet many people besides Don Quixote accepted these romantic war fictions as true history. For centuries before the Renaissance, chivalric romances were the most widely read secular literary works, and after the publication of *Amadís de Gaula* in Zaragoza in 1508 it became a craze with few parallels in history. Even such unlikely figures as Ignatius Loyola, Santa Teresa d'Ávila, and Philip II of Spain were at one time or another hooked on the genre. There were those, however, who would agree with Cervantes, one being the Huguenot captain François de la Noüe (1531–91), who argued that the books of Amadís corrupted and harmed their readers, in particular young noblemen of his early days, through the promotion of unchristian habits and values such as *amours déshonnêtes* (*Discours politiques et militaires*, 160–76). Our critic, of course, was a determined Calvinist, who also complained that the elder generation read too much Machiavelli.
5. 1 Samuel 9, cf. 10, 11.

6. Miguel de Cervantes, *Don Quixote*, part 1, ch. 9, p. 68 Grossman.

7. Francesco Balbi di Correggio, *La verdadera relacion de lo que en el año 1565 ha sucedito en la isla de Malta, de antes que llegase la armada sobre de ella de Soliman Gran Turco* (Barcelona, 1568), p. 2.

8. This was the year those two larger-than-life Renaissance monarchs, Henry VIII and François I, died. It was also the year Ivan IV (the Terrible) of Muscovy assumed the title of Tsar of Russia. With regards to Habsburg Spain, it was the year Charles V defeated the Lutherans at Mühlberg (Martin Luther had died the previous year) and, on a more local note, it was the year Philip II, at the time only a prince, spent Christmas in Alcalá de Henares.

9. Archivo General de Simancas, *Registro General del Sello*, IX – 1569. Simancas Castle, near Valladolid, is where Philip II created Europe's first public record office.

10. A dedication appearing in the pastoral romance *La Galatea* (1585) states that Cervantes was chamberlain to Cardinal Giulio Acquaviva in Rome.

11. Miguel de Cervantes, *El coloquio de los perros*, apud *Three Exemplary Novels*, p. 145.

12. This *tercio* was raised to replace the *Tercio de Nápoles* – one of the first three *tercios* raised by Charles V in 1534 – which had been disbanded in disgrace by Philip II sometime after 1567 for a series of mutinies.

13. Don Diego de Urbina hailed from Guadalajara, a city near Alcalá de Henares, Cervantes' birthplace.

14. Testimony delivered by *alferez* Mateo de Santistebán, a *compadre* of Cervantes at Lepanto, Madrid, March 20, 1578, apud Sliwa 1999: 50–1.

15. Quoted in Notario López and Notario López: 2012: 15.

16. Testimony delivered by *alferez* Mateo de Santistebán, a *compadre* of Cervantes at Lepanto, Madrid, March 20, 1578, apud Sliwa 1999: 50–1.

17. William Shakespeare, *All's Well that Ends Well*, 3.2.92–3.

18. Blaise de Monluc, *Commentaires de messire Blaise de Monluc, mareschal de France*, 3 vols. ed. Paul Courteault (Paris, 1911–25), vol. 1, pp. 78–9. The *Commentaires* were written between 1570 and 1576 and published posthumously in 1592. Monluc was born in Gascony, a region reputed to be fertile in soldiers; it has provided French literature with a type, *le cadet de Gascogne*, an improvised young adventurer, ambitious, brave and boastful. The best known examples are d'Artagnan and Cyrano de Bergerac. Monluc was such a man: an extraordinary soldier and self-made man, talented, ruthlessly ambitious, and a courageous braggart. He began his military career in 1521 as a common militiaman, *franc-archer*, in Italy; fifty years on he was rubbing shoulders with dukes and kings as well as a celebrated captain of war who would be elevated by Henri III in 1574 to the illustrious rank of *maréchal de France*.

19. William Clowes, *A Prooved Practice for all young Chirugians concerning Burnings with Gunpowder, and Woundes made with Gunshot, Sword, Halbard, Pike, Launce, or such other* (London, 1591), pp. 25–7.

20. William Clowes had a son who was Serjeant Surgeon to king Charles I.

21. William Shakespeare, *I Henry IV*, 4.2.51–2.

22. Quoted in Parker 2004: 168.

23. Miguel de Cervantes, *Don Quixote*, part 1, ch. 38, p. 332 Grossman.

24. Luis Cabrera de Córdoba, *Filipe Segundo, Rey de España*, 4 vols. (Madrid, 1876–7), vol. 2, p. 113.

25. Miguel de Cervantes, 'From Miguel de Cervantes, captive: to my lord, M. Vazquez', apud J.Y. Gibson (ed. & trans.), *Journey to Parnassus* (London, 1883), p. 319.

26. Miguel de Cervantes, *Don Quixote*, part 2, prologue, p. 455 Grossman.

27. Astrana Marín 1948–58: II, 347.
28. A document in the Archivo General de Simancas, dated 30 June 1572, records the monthly salary of three *escudos* paid to Miguel de Cervantes.
29. Cervantes' promotion to *soldado aventajado* is first mentioned in the pay order of 15 November 1574, signed at Palermo, Sicily, by Gonzalo II Fernández de Córdoba (his grandfather was *El gran* capitán), III duque de Sessa, assigning the soldier pay of twenty-five *escudos* (Sliwa 1999: 44). An *escudo* was a gold coin worth about 400 *maravedíes*, approximately the same worth as. a *ducato*. The *maravedí* was the most basic unit of Spanish coinage, and by the time of Cervantes it was being produced in copper (in 1605, when the first part of *Don Quixote* was published, 127 *maravedíes* would have brought you a hen). The terms *ducato* and *escudo* were often used interchangeably, even though their value was not exactly the same. The *ducato* was a coin, typically of gold, which originated in Sicily but was used throughout Europe, including Venice, Holland, Austria, the Low Countries and, of course, Spain. Though the value of the *ducato* varied from region to region, in 16th-century Spain, it was worth about 375 *maravedis*. The *escudo* (from the Latin *scutum*, shield, because it carried the king's crest on the obverse) was introduced in 1523 by Charles V to replace the *ducato*.
30. Miguel de Cervantes, *La Galatea*, 5.484–5.
31. Ibid. 5.493.
32. Archivo General de Simancas, *Comisaría de Cruzada*, leg. 221.
33. The term *baños*, which in Spanish simply means 'bath' (in Italian *bagno*), was derived from the Ottoman Turkish word *banyol*, meaning 'royal prison'. Some scholars suggest that the term harkens to the North African practice of using bathhouses as a site to house slaves (Garcés 2002: 270).
34. Fra' Diego da Haedo, *Topografía e historia general de Argel*, 3 vols. (Madrid, 1927–9), vol. 2, p. 102.
35. Op. cit.
36. Ibid. vol. 2, pp. 164–5.
37. Davis 2003: 3–25, 116.
38. Bono 1997: 193.
39. Sliwa 1999: 63. The Order of the Holy Trinity and Captives (Latin: *Ordo Sanctissimae Trinitatis et captivorum*) was founded by Jean de Matha (1154–1213) after his vision of Christ with two captives around 1193. Jean de Matha – now Saint Jean de Matha – was a native of Provence and a doctor of the University of Paris. Innocent III (r. 1198–1216), though little in favour of new religious orders, granted his approbation to the Trinitarians in his letter *Operante divine dispositionis clementia*, issued on 17 December 1198. The order's guiding rule enacted that each house should comprise seven brothers, one of whom should be superior, and that the revenue of the house should be divided into three parts: one for the monks, one for the support of the poor, and one for the ransom of Christian captives.
40. Miguel de Cervantes, *Don Quixote*, part 2, ch. 58, p. 832 Grossman.
41. Miguel de Cervantes, *Don Quixote*, part 1, chs. 39–41.
42. The Castilian word *trato* means 'way of life'. Yet this term also applies to a commercial deal, specifically, to the negotiation itself; in this case, to the appalling commerce in human beings, bought and sold as slaves in Algiers. Cervantes alluded twice in *El trato de Argel* to this *trato*, called "*trato mísero intratable* [miserable, untreatable treatment/ dealings]" (1.15), and "*trato feo* [ugly dealings]" (4.2535). Even today, in Spanish, the term *trato* refers to commerce in animals, and *tratante*, to the person who engages in this business.

43. William Shakespeare, *Timon of Athens*, 4.3.161.
44. Pierre de Bourdeilles, abbé et seigneur de Brantôme, *Œuvres complètes*, 11 vols. (Paris, 1864–82), vol. 7, p. 53.
45. Miguel de Cervantes, *El trato de Argel*, 1.5–6.
46. In one of those coincidences of history, Shakespeare died on 23 April 1616 according to the Julian calendar (the old style dating system, still then followed in England) *but* on 3 May 1616 according to the Gregorian calendar (new style dating system, adopted by Catholic kingdoms but not recognised by Protestant churches). So Cervantes in fact died ten days ahead of Shakespeare. Extent medical records support the view that Cervantes died from an advanced state of diabetes, an untreatable disease at that time.
47. Fyodor Dostoyevsky, *A Writer's Diary*, vol. 1 (1873–1876).
48. Ellis 1905: 678.
49. T.S. Eliot, 'Dante', *Selected Essays* (London, 1932), p. 265.

## Chapter 2: The Corsair

1. This rock-fortress is still under Spanish sovereignty and only inhabited by a handful of military personnel.
2. Pedro's place of birth was the Navarrese valley of Roncal. He had started his career as a groom to Cardinal Juan de Aragón and then risen to become one of the best known and most highly esteemed soldiers of his time. His mastery of defensive-offensive tactics that resorted to the combined use of gunpowder weapons and earthworks and also of siegecraft – thanks to the explosive mines he had helped to perfect – made him an extremely useful factor in any battle or siege. Navarro would be captured by the French after the Spanish defeat at Ravenna (1512) and, having waited in vain to be ransomed for what he considered a reasonable period of time, he decided to offer his services to the king of France, where the *maestro di campo* would end his days, dying of the effects of an illness contracted during the ill-fated siege of Naples.
3. In Osmānlı Turkish Khizr was known as Hızır. For his part, Oruç was known as Arûj in Spanish and Italian, and Oruç Re'īs (*ra'īs* or *re'īs*, a commander of a corsair vessel) in Osmānlı Turkish. Osmānlı Turkish was a fusion of Arabic, Persian and Turkish words.
4. Unlike the Arabs, the Ottoman Turks reserved the name of 'Mohammad' exclusively for the Prophet of Islam and used 'Mehmed' as a proper name for Muslims, but the spelling is the same and only the pronunciation is different.
5. *Odyssey* 9.82–97, Herodotos *Historiē* 4.177, Strabo *Geographia* 1.2.17.
6. Braudel 1973 [1966]: II, 866.
7. The slayer of Oruç, *alferez* García Fernández de la Plaza, was rewarded for this feat by Charles V with a coat of arms bearing the head and crown of the elder Barbarossa. It is said that Garcia Fernandez was wounded in the finger by Oruç in the course of the fight, and that for the rest of his life he proudly exhibited the resulting scar as a sign that it was none other than he who felled the remarkable and ruthless corsair.
8. Başbakanlık Osmanlı Arşivi (İstanbul), Kamil Kepeci, 1863, p. 68.
9. The title of *kapudan paşa* itself is only attested from 1567 onwards. The holder was also known as *kapudan-ı deryā*, Captain of the Sea. Earlier designations for the grand admiral of the Ottoman navy included *deryā bey*, Bey of the Sea, and *re'īs kapudan*, Head Captain. For this, see Özbaran 1978.
10. Archivo General de Simancas, *Secretería de Estado*, leg. 1027, fol. 13, legajo 1031, fols. 26, 58, 98–9, leg. 1033, fol. 160, leg. 1372, fols. 57, 60, 64, 66, 73, 84, (anno 1539); Archivo General de Simancas, *Secretería de Estado*, leg. 1373, fols. 15, 18–20, 28, 30, 41–2, 85, 88, 117–19, 151, 156, 160, 165, 176, 178, 181, 187, 226 (anno 1540); Archivo General de Simancas, *Secretería de Estado*, leg. 1376, fol. 34 (anno 1543–4).

11. In her nocturnal flight Giulia Gonzaga (1513–66) was accompanied by a single knight of her household; she subsequently had him killed because, being somewhat underdressed, the poor unfortunate man had seen too much.

## Chapter 3: The Emperor

1. The same Maximilian who, in a portrait by Albrecht Dürer in the British Museum, modestly styles himself *Imperator Cæsar Maximilianus Pius Felix Augustus*; and, in another, on vellum in the same collection, bears, after the imperial titles, the styles of all the sovereigns of Europe, including *Rex Anglia*, in spite of Henry VII then happily reigning, the first Tudor king who had been a renegade and a refugee all his informative years until he fought his way to an unlikely throne.

2. Dante Alighieri, *Divina Commedia*, 'Pugatorio', canto VII.91-6 Digital Dante.

3. The violent death of Charles *le Téméraire*, duc de Bourgogne, in 1477 at the hands of a Swiss halberdier, placed that imposing edifice in danger of collapse. Louis XI of France annexed Burgundy and made no secret of his intentions with regard to the remaining territories. To counter this threat, Mary, the only heir of Charles, was quickly married to Maximilian von Österreich, a Habsburg and head of the house of Austria and future Holy Roman Emperor.

4. Although English speakers generally first hear this phrase in their native tongue, with reference of course to the British empire of the 19th century, it had been, in fact, first employed to describe the Spanish empire; opinions vary on whether it was first said to Charles V by one of his courtiers or whether it is a quote from his son Philip II. But it does not really matter who in the Spanish court first uttered it because if you read Herodotos, the first historian, a man of inquisitive mind with the gift of the gab, you will find the story recounting how Xerxes explains to the council of Persian nobles his reasons for invading Greece. At one point in his monologue the Great King says, according to Herodotos: "No land that the sun beholds will border ours, but I will make all into one country, when I pass over the whole of Europe" (*Historiē* 7.8c.2 Godley). A similar concept in the Old Testament might predate Herodotos where Psalm 72 speaks of the Messianic King: "He will endure as long as the sun… He will rule from sea to sea and from the River [viz. the Euphrates] to the ends of the earth" (verses 5, 8 NIV). Even pre-Old Testament there is *The Tale of Sinuhe*, set in the aftermath of the assassination of Amenemhat I, the founder of the Twelfth Dynasty (1991–1778 BC), which announces that the Egyptian king has "subdued all the circuit of the sun" (B 213 Gardiner); while a Mesopotamian text contemporary to Sargon of Akkad (c. 2334–2284 BC [Middle Chronology]) proclaims that this king extended his conquests from the "upper sea [viz. Mediterranean]" to the "lower sea [viz. Persian Gulf]", thereby ruling "all the lands from sunrise to sunset".

5. Palacio 1999: 5–7. The Virgilian phrase *solis ad occasum* is to be found in *Georgics* 3.335. On the ornamental version of the royal coat of arms of the kings of Spain from Carlos III (r. 1759–88) to Alfonso XIII (r. 1886–1931, †1941) the motto *A solis ortu usque ad occasum* can be seen above the crest.

6. Psalm 113:3 NIV.

7. It was not until 1561 that Philip II chose Madrid as the capital of Spain. By this action he was simply following the express wishes of his father who, once his wars in Europe were over, intended the capital to lie at the geographical centre of the Iberian peninsula. In 1544 Charles had awarded Madrid the right to carry the emblem of the crown on its coat of arms.

8. Contemporary poets were fond of comparing the emperor to the god of war, praising him even as the greater: "Had there been two Mars, he would be the first, / And Mars

the second of the two". Of course no one could seriously believe Charles V was a second Mars. A comparison with Hercules, by contrast, was much more convincing; he, too, was the embodiment of strength and power, and as the son of a mortal he was closer to men than the to the gods.

9. Charles V had his court painter/war artist, Jan Cornelisz Vermeyen (1500–59), with him on the military expedition to Tunis. The Flemish artist had shared the whole expedition from start to finish and painted to order and the events of the siege he reproduced eventually became the magnificent series of twelve large tapestries. *The Conquest of Tunis* measure in all some 600 square metres, the weaving taking years of work – from 1546 to 1554. The ten that survive are housed in the Kunsthistorisches Museum, Wien.

10. In his *Mémoires*, Charles V lists each time he suffered a gout attack. With pedantic obession, the emperor therefore enumerates seventeen different gout attacks (*Mémoires de Charles-Quint*, apud Alfred Morel-Fatio [ed.], *Histriographie de Charles-Quint* [Paris, 1913], pp. 170–1).

11. The kingdom of Bohemia included, besides Bohemia, the territories of Moravia, Silesia and Lusatia, while that of Hungary was in truth just the north-western perimeter of the mediaeval kingdom, for the rest was under the sway of either the Ottoman sultan or his Christian vassal, the prince of Transylvania.

12. Though Charles' Holy Roman imperial title passed to his brother Ferdinand, not his son Philip, his legacy enhanced Spain's own sense of empire and Spanish warships and *tercios* continued to carry flags with the imperial black double eagle into the 17th century.

## Chapter 4: The King

1. Henry Neville, *Plato Redivivus* (London, 1681), 'The Third Dialogue'.
2. Mary Tudor was England's last Catholic ruler. English law still bars Catholics from ascending to the throne and requires that the monarch, who is the official head of the Church of England, be a Protestant. Mary had refused to accept the new Protestant religion and immediately restored Catholicism as England's official religion. She outlawed Protestantism and persecuted its supporters, her government burning at the stake some 300 Protestant men, women, and children – many of them ordinary people who had no political power – for having religious opinions that conflict with the doctrines of the Roman Catholic Church. Though other European monarchs (Catholic and Protestant) had put heretics to death by means of steel and faggot, Mary's persecution reached unprecedented levels and soon caused her subjects to hate her. England's first female monarch soon came to be despised as a cruel tyrant. However, it should be noted that her younger half-sister after her had more Catholics put to death for their faith, the caveat being that Mary reigned only a few years while Elizabeth reigned for a much longer period of time. In fact, the records show Mary was the least of all of her dynasty in having people executed, Protestant, Catholic or otherwise.
3. Philip and Mary were married in Winchester cathedral on 25 July 1554. By this marriage Philip became *jure uxoris* of England and Ireland. Philip did not like her very much personally – she was eleven years his senior – and cared even less for her countrymen.
4. Couplet based on *Iliad* 5.428–30, and Ovid *Heroides* 13.84; attributed to Matthias Corvinus, king of Hungary, on hearing of the marriage of Maximilian von Österreich with Mary of Burgundy in 1477. The degree of inbreeding is stunning. Mary of Burgundy had only six great-grandparents instead of eight, while her son Philip married his third cousin Joanna, daughter of Ferdinand and Isabella, themselves the product of numerous intermarriages among the various branches of the House of Trastámara.

5. Miguel de Cervantes first picked up the pen in 1568 when he contributed four poems to a voluminous memorial work (published the following year) dedicated to the recently deceased Elisabeth de Valois.

6. Catherine of Lancaster, the daughter of John of Gaunt, duke of Lancaster (†1399) and sister of Henry Bolingbroke, duke of Hereford (later Henry IV, r. 1399–1413), had married Henry III of Castile (†1406).

7. Philip's cousin, the young Dom Sebastiano, had died with the flower of Portuguese nobility – among them many members of the Hospitallers – in the disaster of al-Qasr al-Kabir in Morocco on 4 August 1578, extinguishing the House of Aviz that had ruled since 1385. Philip's forcible annexation of Portugal to Spain was made with the excuse of a family claim to its throne which he (amongst others) had disinterred. Sebastiano was imbued with fanatical religious fervour, and considered himself another Christian knight with dreams of winning glory crusading against the Muslim 'infidels' of North Africa. Small wonder, therefore, his army, because of the reluctance of his own subjects to serve, was heavily padded with German, Flemish, Italian and Spanish contingents (there was even a contingent of English soldiers) serving for loot and lucre. Sebastiano was succeeded by his aged great-uncle, Cardinal Henrique, whose brief reign ended with his death on 31 January 1580.

8. The Latin title *Rex Catholicissimus* was first used by the Borgia pope, Alexander VI, in a Papal bull, *Inter caetera*, he issued on 4 May 1493. The bull granted to the Catholic Majesties of Ferdinand and Isabella (as sovereigns of Castile) "all islands and mainlands found and to be found, discovered and to be discovered towards the west and south, by drawing and establishing" a pole-to-pole line "to be distant one hundred leagues west and south from any of the islands commonly known as the Azores and Cape Verde".

9. It was no easy matter to reject Catholicism. Those who challenged official church doctrines, as Protestants did, were considered heretics, and heresy (viz. an opinion that conflicts with the Roman Church's doctrines) was one of the most serious crimes imaginable because it threatened both the moral and the social order. Its punishment was death, most often by burning at the stake. The Inquisition, however, in theory judged but did not punish. The guilty were handed over to be dealt with by the civil power. They became figures in an *auto-da-fé*, a jostling spectacle acted out in public, which culminated with the guiltier victims being burned alive, and all the others publicly humiliated.

10. Biblioteca del Real Monasterio de San Lorenzo de El Escorial, MS I. III. 30/122v, *Raggionamento* of Philip II for his son Philip.

11. E. Poullet et C. Piot (eds.), *Correspondance du Cardinal de Granvelle 1565–1586*, 12 vols. (Brussels, 1877–96), vol. 4, p. 558, Granvelle to Morillon, 11 May 1573, quoting with approval Don Pedro Álvarez de Toledo y Zúñiga, viceroy of Naples 1532–53.

12. L. Firpo (ed.), *Relazioni di ambasciatori veneti al Senato, tratte dalle migliori edizioni disponibili e ordinate cronologicamente*, 14 vols. (Turin, 1965–96), vol. 8, p. 670.

13. Alba was the overseer of brutal repression in the Netherlands from 1567 to 1573. The papacy had passed the first judicial act of genocide of modern times, and on 16 February 1568 the entire population of the Provinces – three million – were condemned to death as heretics apart from a few named exceptions. Ten days later Philip II, implacable as Jehovah, ordered Alba to carry out the sentence. In the terror that followed, the wealth of the prosperous merchants made them a particular target, and axe, rope, and fire consumed the natural leaders of Dutch society. Alba wrote to his royal master coolly estimating the number executed after Holy Week of that year "at eight hundred heads". Alba is said to have admitted to personal responsibility for 18,600 executions during his six-year tenure – a plausible figure, but the additional number massacred with increasing

barbarity by his soldiers can never be known. We can quote from a letter of 1573 to Philip from Alba: "It is not the Turks who are troubling Christendom but the heretics, and these are already within our gates."

14. Quoted in Maltby 1983: 82.

15. E. Poullet et C. Piot (eds.), *Correspondance du Cardinal de Granvelle 1565–1586*, 12 vols. (Brussels, 1877–96), vol. 11, p. 272, Granvelle to Margaret of Parma, 21 September 1584.

16. Previously for Spain Ferdinand had served as a young man, while Charles V led his Tunis campaign (1535) and left sealed instructions to be opened only in case of his death or capture during his invasion of northern France (1544). His predecessor as the Holy Roman Emperor, Maximilian I, was nearly killed leading a cavalry charge (1504), and went on to earn the soubriquet 'heart of steel'. The French monarchs Charles VIII and Louis XII personally led their respective invasions of Italy (1494, 1498), while François I owed his life at the battle of Marignano (1515) to the soundness of his armour before being taken captive ten years later while fighting at Pavia. True, Philip II had seen active service in the campaigns of 1557 and 1558, but he remained essentially an armchair strategist. In fact, he was the last of the Habsburgs to be present on the field of battle – at Saint-Quentin in 1557 – and from then on comparisons with Mars or Hercules were no longer appropriate; the rupture with the martial ways of Charles V was complete.

17. G.K. Chesterton, 'Lepanto', stanza 6, ll. 1–9.

18. Marchesa de Pidal y Míguel Salvá (eds.), *Colección de documentos inéditos para la historia de España*, 112 vols. (Madrid, 1842–95), vol. 35, p. 61, letter of Philip II to Alba, 2 August 1580, holograph postscript; Archivo General de Simancas, *Secretería de Estado*, leg. K 1448/197, letter of Philip to Don Bernardino de Mendoza, 28 July 1588.

19. For example, in 1559, the monarchy's debt totalled 25 million *ducati*, and at Philip's death in 1598 it had climbed to 85 million (a far more considerable sum then than today in any currency), or ten times ordinary revenue.

20. The fifty-eight French ships and eleven English privateers were fighting under the flag of Dom Antonio, prior of Crato and claimant to the crown of Portugal. Elizabeth I had refused her ships, but France had been lured by the offer of Brazil and the Azores. Incidentally, Miguel de Cervantes' brother Rodrigo was serving in Santa Cruz's fleet.

21. Santa Cruz's Estimate of March, 1586, survives: he demanded 556 ships and an army of 94,222 men, 1,280 artillery pieces, twenty *fregatas*, twenty *faluas*, and 200 flat-bottomed boats, all to be carried in the larger ships, bringing the total of floatable craft up to 796, of which 196 were ships built exclusively for fighting (150 galleons, forty galleys, six galleasses). His list of wants – reckoned on a basis of eight months – is likewise staggering: ship's biscuit, 373,337 *quintales*; bacon, 22,800 *quintales*; cheese, 21,500 *quintales*; tunny fish, 23,200 barrels; salt beef, 16,040 *quintales*; pease, beans and rice, 66,000 bushels; strings of garlic, 50,000; vinegar, 50,916 litres; water, 20,000 pipes; wine, 46,800 pipes. Total cost, 1,526,425,798 *maravedies*, or about four million *ducati*! Doubtless, it was to this figure that Philip II directed his first glance. A *quintal* (Gr. κεντηάριον, Ar. *qintār*) was equivalent to a hundredweight, thus in Spain it would have been defined as 100 *libras* (32.90 kg). A pipe was a large cask holding 500 litres. The *maravedí* was the smallest Spanish unit of account, the thirty-fourth part of a *real*. Note well, eight *reales* was the famous Spanish silver dollar bearing the numeral 8 or piece of eight; the original United States dollar was based on it. For Santa Cruz's Estimate, see Lewis 1960: 57, Martin and Parker 1999: 92–3.

22. Archivo General de Simancas, *Secretería de Estado*, leg. 165/2–3, letter of Philip II to Archduke Albert, viceroy of Portugal, 14 September 1587 (message for Santa Cruz).

23. Guilmartin 2003 [1974]: 143.

24. The shortened form of boatswain is bo'sun and referred to the man responsible for checking the state of the galley daily and reporting his findings to the vessel's commander.

25. Quoted in Martin and Parker 1999: 68.

26. Quoted in van Herwaarden 2012: 91–2.

27. Public Records Office, *Calendar of State Papers Relating to English Affairs in the Archives of Venice 1558–1580*, vol. VII, no. 267, letter of Paulo Tiepolo to the Senate and the Doge of Venice, 21 July 1561.

28. Marchesa de Pidal y Míguel Salvá (eds.), *Colección de documentos inéditos para la historia de España*, 112 vols. (Madrid, 1842–95), vol. 29, pp. 482–4, letter of García de Toledo to Francisco de Eraso, 7 September 1565.

29. Ibid. vol. 29, pp. 311–12.

30. Vargas-Hidalgo 2002: 684.

31. See Martin and Parker 1999: 124–5.

32. England was a latecomer to the transatlantic trade that had vastly enriched Spain (and Portugal). Still, Elizabeth I wanted to weaken Spain's power and claim some of the riches of the New World for her kingdom. Yet she could not risk openly provoking Philip II. She gave permission to English sea captains to sail to the Caribbean and attack Spanish ships and ports. Soon seafarers were returning to England with wealth from Spanish ships. The queen secretly welcomed them, but she publicly maintained that they had acted on their own. Francis Drake (1540–96) in particular became notorious for his ruthless piracy – under one pretext or another and always with a Protestant tincture – against either the king of France or the king of Spain. In 1577 Elizabeth had sent Drake on a secret mission to circumnavigate the globe, with the intention that he would attack vulnerable Spanish outposts on the unguarded Pacific coast of South America. The success of his mission caused Spain considerable worry, increasing hostilities between the two nations.

33. In our own lifetime the Falklands/Malvinas War completely altered what it was possible for Margaret Thatcher to achieve as prime minister. Without Argentina's invasion of April 1982, over which she had no control, her premiership would have been very different to say the least.

34. Public Records Office, Calendar of *State Papers* 11/6/26, 'Memoria', August/September 1555. See also Parker 1996A: 91.

35. These dates are adjusted to conform to the new (Gregorian) calendar (NS), which the Spaniards, but not the English, used in 1588.

36. Archivo General de Simancas, *Secretería de Estado*, leg. 165, fols. 104–14 (1 April 1588).

37. On 2 August (NS) a shift of wind favoured the Spaniards for the first time, who then seized the chance to maul Martin Frobisher's 60-gun *Triumph* (1,110 tons and a crew of 500), the greatest and largest of the royal ships, and *bigger* than any comparable galleon in the Armada. The following day Frobisher would be knighted for valour by Lord Howard aboard his flagship 55-gun *Ark Royal* (800 tons and a crew of 250).

38. Quoted in Graham 1972: 106. By following Spanish accounts, which are usually quite objective regarding their own loses, by nightfall of 8 August (NS), at the close of the battle of Gravelines, the Armada had lost eleven ships: eight already accounted for as lost by other causes, and *only* now, a certain three lost by English gunfire, two of which were royal galleons of Portugal and the other the Biscayan María Juan, which sank.

39. See Martin and Parker 1999: 188.

## Chapter 5: Spanish Steel

1. Quoted in Oman 1937: 54.

2. Francesco Guicciardini, *Storia d'Italia*, bk. 14, ch. 14, ed. Silvana Seidel Menchi (Torino, 1971), p. 1406.

3. Blaise de Monluc, *Commentaires de messire Blaise de Monluc, mareschal de France*, 3 vols. ed. Paul Courteault (Paris 1911–25), vol. 1, p. 2.

4. The sword of François I would be kept in Madrid until it was returned to France by order of Napoléon Bonaparte. Others taken captive that day included the young Blaise de Monluc, then a plain man-at-arms; being too poor to warrant a ransom, the Gascon adventurer was soon released. As he politely explained to his captors, "*n'ayant pas grande finance*" (Blaise de Monluc, *Commentaires de messire Blaise de Monluc, mareschal de France*, 3 vols. ed. Paul Courteault [Paris, 1911–25], vol. 1, p. 53).

5. Quoted in Notario López and Notario López: 2012: 7.

6. Quoted in Colonel Ardant du Picq, *Études sur le combat [Battle Studies]* (New York, 1920), p. 207.

7. The slaughter of France's nobility in this battle was only equalled by that of Agincourt 110 years before. Ironically enough, amongst the fallen in the French ranks was Richard de la Pole, last remaining grandson of Richard duke of York, rightful heir in Yorkist eyes to the crown of England: White Rose – or variants thereof, including *Blanche Rose* and *la Rosa Blanca* – as he called himself. A talented and brave captain of war, he had distinguished himself on many a battlefield, fighting the complex and bloody wars that raged in the unstable kingdoms and principalities of northern Italy, southern France and the Iberian peninsula. At Pavia the Black Bands of Giovanni, *Bande Nere*, were under his overall command, along with the *Landsknechte* serving the French crown. And so it was that this unexpected outcome of a battle fought halfway across Europe would bring the security the upstart Tudor dynasty so badly craved. The shock and scale of the French defeat stunned many in Europe: but it absolutely delighted Henry VIII and his right-hand man Cardinal Wolsey.

8. Quoted in Fernández Álvarez 1979: 167.

9. We get the word 'swashbuckler' from the Elizabethan proclivity for the sword and buckler – fencing thugs were the bullies of city life and their swaggering manner led them to be called 'swashbucklers', from the clattering sound they made bashing their bucklers. 'Swashbuckler' is a compound of 'swash' (archaic: to swagger with a drawn sword) and 'buckler'. The first known use of the term dates to 1560, yet this weapon combination had been in use across Europe since the 12th century. The oldest fencing manual in existence, the anonymous 13th-century German manuscript I.33 in the collection of the Royal Armouries Museum (British Museum No. 14 E iii, No. 20 D vi), is entirely devoted to the sword and buckler. In Germany swashbucklers were called *Schwertzucher*, *Eisenfresser* (ironeaters), or *Raufdegen* (brawling sword).

10. A Spanish *palmo* was a little less than twenty-one centimetres. Generally, it was the length of the hand used as a unit of measurement.

11. Niccolò Machiavelli, *Arte della guerra*, bk. 2, p. 51 Farneworth/Wood.

12. Though these mercenary contingents were actually not as homogeneous as is usually supposed and the geographical origins of 'German" or 'Swiss' units could be quite diverse at times. The Swiss were occasionally referred to as *Allemans*, and *Landsknechte* could be recruited in Guelders, the Vaud, and Savoy.

13. *Ein schoens neuwes Lied von der Schlacht newlich vor Pavia geschehen* ('A Beautiful New Song about the Battle of Pavia').

14. The *Landsknechte* serving the French, known as the Black Band, *Schwarze Bande* (probably from the colour of their armour), were regarded as 'traitors to the Fatherland' by their fellow *Landsknechte* (viz. those led by Georg von Frundsberg – 'Father of the *Landsknechte*' – and Max Sittich von Ems) for having gone over to the French side, despite a decree by the Holy Roman Emperor that it was a capital crime for any *Landsknecht* band to serve his enemies. When the two *Landsknechte* units met in battle, it was mutually

understood that no quarter would be given; struck in both flanks and hacked to ribbons, the *Schwarze Bande* was wiped out almost to the last man and ceased to exist thereafter. Confusingly for us, there was another Black Band involved in the bloodletting at Pavia, headed by Ludovico di Giovanni de' Medici (1498–1526), also known as Giovanni *delle Bande Nere*, son of one of the most famous women of the Italian Renaissance, Caterina Sforza. The *Bande Nere* consisted primarily of Italian mercenary harquebusiers who had just entered French service after a pay dispute with the pope. At the time they were considered the finest Italian troops available.

15. Erhard Schön, *Der Schneider als Landsknecht und die Näherin* (1535), Nürnberg, Germanisches Nationalmuseum. Schön was noted for his contemporary woodcuts that portray common soldiers and camp followers, who each tell of their previous occupation and how they left it behind.

16. The adage 'War is sweet to those who have no experience of it', a quote from Pindar (†438BC): γλυκὺ δὲ πόλεμος ἀπείροισιν, "Sweet is war to the untried" (frs. 110–109 Snell-Maehler), is Erasmus' most celebrated statement on war. By the edition of 1515 it was the longest entry in the *Adagia*, a collection of thousands of popular sayings, epigrams, proverbs and anecdotes that Erasmus gathered from Greek and Latin sources and commented on.

17. Desiderius Erasmus, *Adagia* (Basel, 1515), 4.1.1.

18. As depicted in the engraving *Vom Hosen Teuffel* serving as the front piece of a treatise published in 1555 by the German Gnesio-Lutheran theologian, Andreas Musculus (1514–81), in which he is critical of the current transgression in fashion. In other words, the devout Musculus and his ilk were quite simply the fashion police. In the engraving we are treated to a *Landsknecht* in voluminous pantaloons. A demon sits on his left shoulder and the devil lurks at his feet. The apparel of the *Landsknecht* reveals that its wearer is steeped in sin and entirely in the service of Lucifer.

19. In England, James I would abolish sumptuary laws in 1604 but continued to control dress by other means.

20. Quoted in Gush 1983 [1982]: 69.

21. Op. cit.

22. Allegedly, this war cry's first usage was during the battle of Las Navas de Tolosa (16 July 1212), an important turning point in the *La Reconquista*. Miguel de Cervantes quotes it when Don Quixote and Sancho Panza are discussing *Santiago Matamoros*, Saint James the Moor-slayer (*Don Quixote*, part 2, ch. 58, p. 835 Grossman).

23. Used not to keep the troops in step, save on parade, but to provide diversion on the march, drummers and fifers were primarily engaged to transmit the sound orders (move off, assume battle order, charge, halt, retire, etc., etc.) that supplemented the mimed commands semaphored by sergeants' manipulation of their halberds.

24. It is unlikely that many Spanish soldiers were treated by an expert surgeon, or that they went to hospital. The army sent to Algeria in 1572, for instance, comprised 30,000 foot and 600 horse, four doctors, four apothecaries and twenty-five surgeons, an average of one surgeon for every 1,200 men and one doctor for 7,650. See White 2002: 26.

25. Each squadron was composed of two equal sections known as a *camarada* (pl. *camaradas*), 'comradeship', under the command of a *cabo de camarada*. The *camarada* was a vital component of the *tercio*, being as it was a group of eight to ten soldiers who lived and ate together, helping and supporting one another, even sharing their money and possessions in times of need, and strong bonds of comradeship were naturally forged. The Huguenot captain La Noüe notes that the members of a *camarada* lived very closely, *comme s'ils estoient freres*, "as if they were brothers" (*Discours politiques et militaires*, 345). By way of

a comparison, the Elizabethan ideal was a lieutenant assisted by an ensign-bearer, two sergeants and about six corporals for every company of 150 men (Cruickshank 1966: 57). But no army achieved a full complement of corporals because of the reluctance of captains (who were, of course, responsible for doling out pay) to pass on the extra cash from their bonus funds that would have made their extra duties worthwhile (in terms of base pay, corporals were meant to receive double). Indeed, their real profits from war were made illegally. Two chief devices were employed: falsifying company numbers in order to receive money for non-existent men and, as already alluded to, manipulating the company bonus fund. The captains looked upon their companies as little gold mines, out of which they could make money quickly and easily. It mattered little to them whether this money came from cheating the state or robbing their soldiers.

26. Quoted in Roberts 2010: 28.

27. Raimondo Montecuccoli, 'Vom Krieg mit den Türken in Ungarn (Della guerra col Turco in Ungheria)', in A. Veltzé (ed.), *Ausgewähte Schriften des Raimund Fürsten Montecuccoli, General-lieutenant und Feldmarschall*, 4. vols. (Wien und Leipzig, 1899–1900), vol. 2, p. 221.

28. By way of contrast Elizabethan England failed to provide a permanent paid army, though by Elizabeth's reign war had become a profession in the truest sense of the term. Even one of the queen's favourites, Robert Devereux, 2nd Earl of Essex (1565–1601), argued in favour of a small efficient army: "Monstrous unwieldy bodies cannot be governed properly, and nothing can last that cannot be governed" (*The Hulton Manuscripts: Papers of the 2nd Earl of Essex*, fol. 160b = B.M. Loan 23). English nobles like Essex, having experienced the type of warfare being played out on the much wider state of the continent, acquired valuable knowledge of contemporary military practice which they could never have gained in Elizabethan England. That nation was slow in accepting the transition from the bows and bills of the late mediaeval period to the disciplined formations of pike and shot which constituted modern 16th century armies on the continent. Even with the threat of the Parma's professionals arriving on the kingdom's doorstep during the summer of 1588, the realm could mobilise 130,000 men, of which only 44,000 were in the trained bands, armed and drilled for modern warfare, with the rest men of the general muster still being armed with archaic bills and bows. The best of the trained bands was that levied by the city of London, numbering some 6,000 men. All things being equal, Parma could have landed in Kent on 9 August with 27,000 men with horses, artillery, and a siege train (Nolan 1997: 108, 113, 121).

29. During the battle of Kinsale (24 December 1601, OS) in County Cork, the invading Spaniards – 3,184 veterans led by Don Juan del Águila (1545–1602), an experienced commander – held the town of Kinsale, the gates of which had been opened by the governor of the town's fort, David Barry, the father of Gerat Barry, the prominent Irish soldier who fought for the Spanish crown during the Thirty Years' War. Though outnumbered, the English under Charles Blount, Lord Mountjoy, overcame the Irish led by Hugh O'Neill of Tir Eoghain, 2nd Earl of Tyrone and chief of the most Gaelic clan. The Spanish in the town neutralised themselves by sitting tight when the battle was on and refusing to catch the English between two fires. The Spanish truly describe the battle of Kinsale as *una derrota*, a rout.

30. Spain's foreign troops in the Netherlands, though speaking a diversity of tongues (French, Italian, German), were, it is true, in the main Habsburg subjects. Indeed, the only true exception to the Noah's ark rule as regards to European armies was Elizabethan England, where, denuded of Reformation spoils, the crown's restricted income forced a

revived reliance on subjects with the ability to recruit locally for volunteers willing to serve abroad on a short-term basis.

31. The Protestant provinces of the Netherlands entered a treaty with Spain in 1609, the terms of which granted them independence and also imposed a twelve-year armistice. The war in the Low Countries would resume with Spanish attacks on Dutch strongholds in 1622.

32. Sir Roger Williams, *A Briefe Discourse of Warre* (London, 1590), pp. 7, 11.

33. Quoted in Deleito y Piñuela 1947: 177–8.

34. Parker 2004: 47, n. 1.

35. Claudio Sánchez-Albornoz y Menduiña, *España: un enigma histórico*, 2 vols. (Buenos Aires, 1957), quoted in Notario López and Notario López: 2012: 3.

## Chapter 6: The Bastard

1. Quoted in Drane 1858: 201.

2. Don Carlos was the son of Philip II by his first wife María de Portugal, both of whom were grandchildren of Juana *la Loca*. Such inbreeding was not uncommon among the Habsburgs; but this time the results had been spectacularly bad. Don Carlos turned out to be a kind of monster in a frail shell, with an enormous head, a permanent stammer, a cruel disposition, and a tendency to madness. Added to this was a deep hatred for his father, and an unmeasured ambition which may have led him into making sympathetic overtures to the Dutch rebels. His father finally incarcerated the twenty-three-year-old *infante* in the Alcázar, wherein he was to die under mysterious circumstances. Did his father have Carlos murdered because of his inclination towards Protestantism or because of his guilty passion for his beautiful young stepmother, Elisabeth de Valois? Such were the speculative questions that began to circulate and that finally made their way into imaginative literature and music, notably Schiller's dramatic play *Don Carlos, Infant von Spanien* and Verdi's grand opera based upon it.

3. Archivo General de Simancas, *Varios/Galeras*, leg. 1, fols. 33–5.

4. The Order of the Golden Fleece, *l'ordre de la Toison d'or*, is the second oldest order of knighthood in the world – the oldest is the Order of the Garter – and was instituted by Philippe III de Bourgogne (r. 1419–67), better known as Philippe *le Bon*, on 10 February 1430 to celebrate his marriage to Isabella, the Portuguese *infanta* of the House of Aviz, the only surviving daughter of João I de Portugal (r. 1385–1433) and Philippa of Lancaster. At the time of Don Juan's acceptance, Philip II was the Grand Master of the Order. Arthur Wellesley, 1st Duke of Wellington, was to receive the order in 1812, thus becoming the first Protestant to be honoured with the Golden Fleece.

5. Although comprising around four per cent of the population, the *moricos* provided around seven per cent of the galley slaves, their lack of religious orthodoxy providing the king's authorities with valid excuses to sentence them to life on the king's galleys. Gallery service was not officially abolished in Spain until 1748.

6. Miguel de Cervantes, *Viaje del Parnaso*, Appendix. In the self-portrait he provides his readership in the *Novelas ejemplares* prologue, the aged Cervantes describes himself as having *cisne en los canos*, "hair as white as a swan". Not only does the song of the swan improve with age, but the melodious swan, dedicated to Apollo and the Muses, represents the 'good' poet (Mercury salutes Cervantes as 'O Adam of the bards') and "a white and elegant swan" (*Voyage to Parnassus*, 7.40 Gyll) is the insignia of those who fight alongside Apollo in the major showdown between the 'good' and the 'bad' poets. The soul of Orpheus himself migrated into a swan (Plato *Republic* 10.620a), Orpheus being of

course the master singer and muscian and the son of Apollo and Kalliopê, the Muse who presides over eloquence and epic poetry.

7. Quoted in Marx 1966: 79.

8. At the onset of the rebellion in 1566, the Spanish Netherlands consisted of seventeen provinces with about three million inhabitants. The Rhine, Maas, and Scheldt river systems divided the ten southern provinces, open prosperous farming country that also included the major towns, from the poorer, more sparsely inhabited north. However, it was the north, the *Vesting Holland* as the Dutch would call it, which was the crucial asset to the rebels. Protected north and west by the North Sea and the Zuider Zee, in the south by the rivers, and in the east by the Ijsel and marshlands, it consisted mainly of low-lying terrain, cut up by canals, dikes, estuaries, and bogs and studded with small fortified towns.

9. Owen Feltham, *A Brief Character of the Low Countries under the States*, 2 vols. (London, 1652), vol. 1, p. 5.

10. Though it was possible to buy exemption, service in the local burgher militia became a matter of pride, associated with republican values, masculine sociability and solidarity, though we should not forget such picturesque units as the ferocious corps of women, armed with sword, dagger and firearm, raised by the wood merchant Kenau Simonsdochter Hasselaer (1526–88) to help defend Haarlem against the Spanish in 1572–3. Militia companies commissioned leading artists to paint their group portraits, of which Rembrandt's *The Militia Company of District II under the Command of Captain Frans Banninck Cocq* (1642), better known (erroneously) as *De Nachtwacht* or *The Night Watch* (in fact, the scene is set during daytime), became the most famous example. Amsterdam's answer to Dad's Army, in this colossal painting (the figures are almost life-size) the citizen militia company of District II gather for their official group portrait. Behind the brightly illuminated figure of their captain Frans Banninck Cocq and his lieutenant William van Ruytenburch, the militia crowd into the picture, get their hands in the way of each other's faces, even fire off a musket by accident. Others look off in all directions, wave banners clumsily and get their pikes in a twist. Is this Rembrandt's anti-war poster? Well, people do not argue about a Rembrandt painting being old or new. They just say it is eternal. At the time of writing, this magnificent tableau is undergoing restoration.

11. Pierre de Bourdeilles, abbe et seigneur de Brantôme, *Œuvres complètes*, 11 vols. (Paris, 1864–82), vol. 7, p. 141. As well as giving dukes to Parma, the House of Farnese would reach the throne of Spain in the person of Elisabetta Farnese (Sp. *Isabel de Farnesio*) before becoming extinct in 1731 when the last Farnese duke, Antonio Farnese, died without direct heirs. However, his niece Elisabetta, now queen of Spain, passed a successful claim to her sons, Don Carlos (later Carlos III of Spain) and Filippo, who established the House of Bourbon-Parma. The fortunes of the Farnese all started in the Consistory of September 1493 when the Borgia pope, Alexander VI (r. 1492–1503), granted the red hat of a cardinal to Alessandro Farnese (later Paul III), the brother of Madonna Giulia Orsini *nato* Farnese, known as *la bella*, the pope's mistress.

12. The German Protestant princes of the Holy Roman Empire provided soldiers for the Dutch rebels, but the Catholics were equally active, supplying Spain with 57,200 men between 1567 and 1575 alone. For this, see Wilson 2009: 153.

13. Geoffrey Parker (2004: 336) gives the Spanish, Italian, German, Burgundian and Walloon contributions to the 1601 Army of Flanders: the Spaniards numbered 6,001 men out of 22,453, some 37.4 per cent of the total.

14. In 1564 Johann Casimir put himself forward as a bridegroom for Elizabeth I and sent her his portrait via the Scottish courtier Sir James Melville. The queen, however, showed no interest in him.
15. Quoted in Hale 1998 [1985]: 188.
16. Miguel de Cervantes, *Don Quixote*, part 1, ch. 38, pp. 330–1 Grossman
17. Desiderius Erasmus, *Ultilissima consultatio de bello Turcico inferendo* (Antwerp, 1530), quoted in Rupp 2001: 382.
18. Quoted in Rieman 2020: 6.
19. Mention should be made in passing of the notorious 'Day of the *Landsknechte*' at Caen in 1513 when soldiers ransacked the town after having not been paid for months (Pierre de Bourdeilles, abbé et seigneur de Brantôme, *Œuvres complètes*, 11 vols. [Paris, 1864–82], vol. 4, pp. 220–7).
20. There were five major mutinies in 1572–6 and a further thirty-seven in 1589–1607, the most spectacular that of 1576, leading to the terrible sack of Antwerp, or 'Spanish Fury' – *la furia española* – as the Dutch rebels chose to call it, which left some 8,000 dead in its wake. See Parker 2004: 157–76, 253–6.
21. Quoted in Parker 1987 [1984]: 200.
22. On 28 March 1581, Philip II had issued a proclamation in which he put a price on William's head. Because William had disturbed the religious peace in the Low Countries, "every one is authorized, to hurt him and kill him", stated the document. Whoever succeeded could claim the reward of 25,000 gold crowns, along with land and titles. The following year, on Sunday, 18 March, the first attempt was made upon William's life.
23. As the Dutch had embraced Calvinism, a form of Protestantism shared with Scotland, it is easy to understand why Scots should be drawn to this part of Europe, where many joined the armed struggle in the Netherlands. The fall of Haarlem to the Spanish in 1573 had aroused an unknown but sizeable number of Lowland Scots to volunteer in the Dutch cause, and the Privy Council in Edinburgh noted the issue of a recruiting licence to captain Thomas Robesoun to be in the "defence of Goddis trew religioun" (*Records of the Parliaments of Scotland to 1707*, vol. 2, p. 237).
24. Jean Dumont (baron de Carlscroon), *Corps universal diplomatique du droit des gens*, 8 vols. (Amsterdam, 1726), vol. 1, nos. cc, cciii–cciv, pp. 446, 454–7, documents dated 6 lune and 10 August 1585 and 6 February 1586, which pact was nullified by the 'perpetual alliance' which James I of England signed in August in 1604 with Philip III of Spain and the Archduke Albrecht de Austria and the Infanta Isabel Clara Eugenia, who co-ruled southern (Belgian) Netherlands (ibid. vol. 2, no. xvii, pp. 32–6). Importantly for Spain the Treaty of London, as the peace accord was known, brought a complete halt to the actions of privateers and pirates (both of which James truly detested) against Spanish shipping, an end to English support of the Dutch rebels, a restoration of trade with Spain, and an acceptance of Spain's monopoly over the Americas.
25. Miguel de Cervantes, *El trato de Argel*, 3.1517–19.

### Chapter 7: La Serenissima

1. The Most Serene Republic of Venice was extinguished by Napoléon Bonaparte in 1797, and he passed control to the Austrian Habsburgs later the same year. Composed in 1802, Wordsworth's poem was published in 1807.
2. In the words of Gasparo Contarini, "the rôle of the young is to obey, that of the old to command" (*La Republica e i magistrati di Venezia* [Venezia, 1564], p. 32).
3. Braudel 1973 [1966]: II, 1088.
4. Lane 1973: 407.

5. Glete 2000: 1.
6. Crowley 2008: 71.
7. Lane 1973: 369.
8. Dante Alighieri, *Divina Commedia*, 'Inferno', canto XXI.7–18 Digital Dante. In 1289, at age twenty-four, Dante served as a *feditore*, 'wound giver' or 'striker', a militia horseman fighting in the vanguard of the Florentine *cavallata* in the upper Arno valley at Campaldino. It was here, on Saturday, 11 June, the Feast Day of Saint Barnabas, that the Florentine Guelphs (loyal to the Holy See) slogged it out with their hated Ghibelline foes from Arezzo (ostensibly loyal to the Holy Roman Emperor: currently Rudolf von Habsburg). Though outnumbered that summer day, one chronicler tells us that the Ghibelines scorned the Florentine communal militia as worthless men who "adorned themselves like women, and combed their tresses" (Giovanni Villani, *Nuova Cronica*, bk. VII, § 131). Still, on the day the goddess Fortuna was to smile upon the Florentine 'girly men' of Ghibelline fantasy. As for our young soldier poet, one of the survivors that warm and muggy noontime, the brutal bloodletting he had just witnessed beforehand was to feed his uncanny vision of Hell for *Divina Commedia* (see especially, 'Pugatorio', canto V.88–129 Digital Dante), which was begun within a decade of the battle. He was to confess later to have been smitten with *timenza molta*, 'great fear'.
9. Archivo di Stato di Venezia, *Senato Mar*, registro 23, filza 85, 44.
10. The pound generally used for artillery nomenclature was equal to 0.320 kilograms, even in places where the local pound was different. For instance, Venetian pounds were either 0.477 kilograms (*libbra grossa*) or 0.302 kilograms (*libbra sottile*) but a 50-pound Venetian cannonball weighed 16 kilograms or 35.2 English pounds.
11. Guilmartin 1981: 50.
12. Pantero Pantera, *L'Armata navale* (Roma, 1614), quoted in Grima 2001: 120.
13. Marin Sanudo, *I diarii* (Venezia, 1897), vol. 46, coll. 457.
14. Capponi 2007 [2006]: 201–02, 217.
15. Guilmartin 2003 [1974]: 255.
16. The *terraferma* (in what is now Lombardy, the Veneto and Friuli) was taken partly as a buffer against predatory neighbours, partly to guarantee safe passage to the Alpine passes, and partly because Venice relied on mainland wheat for its survival. Venice's first serious involvement on the *terraferma* dated from 1338, with its defeat of Padua and the destruction of the family of the Carrara, and the seizure of Treviso.
17. Niccolò Machiavelli wrote of Agnadello that in one day, the Venetians "lost that which in eight hundred years they had acquired with so much trouble" (*il Principe*, ch. 12, p. 59 Marriott).
18. Gjergj Kastrioti (1405–68), known as Skanderbeg (from Ottoman Turkish İskender Beǧ), was an Albanian nobleman and military commander who led a national rebellion against Ottoman rule in what is today Albania. He always signed himself *Dominus Albaniae*, and claimed no other titles but that in documents.
19. Angelo Beolco, *Parlemento de Ruzante che iera vegnú de campo. Due dialoghi*, ed. L. Zorzi (Turin, 1968), p. 24.
20. William Shakespeare, *Pericles*, 23.147–9.
21. E. Salaris (ed.), *Relazione di Giulio Savorgnan d' Osoppo capitano delle milizie venete sulla difesa di Zara* (Venezia, 1909).
22. Francesco Guicciardini, *Storia d'Italia*, 5 vols. ed. Costantino Panigada (Bari, 1929), vol. 1, pp. 71–2. The cause of conflict was disagreement over access to the Black Sea (and thence to the grain lands of the Crimea) from the Aegean, hence the alternative name of the War of Tenedos/Chioggia. When the war broke out in 1377, attention focused initially on the

small island of Tenedos, dominion over which was thought to guarantee mastery over the route through the Dardanelles. A couple of years earlier a Byzantine usurper had donated the island to the Genoese, in return for their aid, but Venice secured promises from one of his rivals that it could take control of the island. Historians of Venice would like to classify the War of Chioggia as a Venetian victory, but the arrival of the Genoese in 1379 on the sandbanks of the Lido was an enormous humiliation. By the terms of the Treaty of Turin (1381) Venice lost Tenedos, failed to recover Dalmatia, had to recognize Genoese rights in Cyprus (and therefore the Genoese rôle in the lucrative sugar trade), and even had to hand its mainland dependency of Treviso to the Austrian duke, thereby losing such grain lands as it possessed in north-eastern Italy – a Habsburg shadow would fall over parts of north-eastern Italy until the end of the First World War. Thus, Trieste, with its mixed population of German-speakers, Italian-speakers and Slav-speakers, of Christians and Jews, gave the Austro-Hungarian empire access to the Mediterranean. Moreover, since the fleets of both maritime republics were virtually ruined in the bruising encounters in the lagoons of Chioggia, neither Venice nor Genoa was thereafter in any fit shape to blunt the rising ambition and enterprise of the Ottoman Turks.

23. Luigi Colliado, *Practica Manuale di Arteglieria* (Venezia, 1586), p. 16.
24. Ágoston 2005: 167.
25. Archivo di Stato di Venezia, *Consiglio dei Dieci, Parti Comuni*, registri 45V, 46 (21 July 1526).

**Chapter 8: The Hospitallers**

1. In England there is the Saint John Ambulance Association, founded in 1878, and the Saint John Ambulance Brigade, which was established in 1888. Today, the logo of the Saint John Ambulance, emblazoned on the sides of ambulances and on the uniforms of its volunteers, is easily recognised, namely a white eight-pointed cross on a black background. It has remained unaltered through nine centuries.
2. Engel 1968: 15, 16.
3. The simple but noble *modus operandi* of the hospital was probably based on Galatians 4:14: "Even though my illness was a trial to you, you did not treat me with contempt or scorn. Instead, you welcomed me as if I were an angel of God, as if I were Christ Jesus himself" (NIV).
4. Engel 1968: 25.
5. Quoted in Carr 2016: 23.
6. The other two were the Poor-Fellow Soldiers of Christ and of the Temple of Solomon (Knights Templar) and the Order of Brothers of the German House of Saint Mary in Jerusalem (Teutonic Order).
7. During the later part of the crusader period the Latins gave currency to a tradition that Qurūn Hattīn was the Mountain of the Beatitudes, or scene of the Sermon on the Mount, and also the place where the thousands were fed. For the Druze and Sunni Muslims the shrine of Nabi Shu'ayb is located here, Jethro/Reuel of the Hebrew Bible (Exodus 2:16–21).
8. France 2015: 120. Apparently Master of the Temple Gérard de Ridefort (r. 1184–9) was spared for profitable ransom, but having lost some 230 of his knights that day, the Order was on its knees.
9. Ibn al-Athīr, *Al-Kāmil fī al-tārīkh* ('The Complete History') 12 vols. ed. C.J. Tornberg (Leiden and Uppsala, 1851–76), vol. 12, p. 304.
10. 'Imād al-Dīn al-Isfāhanī, *Kitab al-Fath al-qussī fī l-fath al-Qudsī* ('The Eloquent Exposition of the Conquest of Jerusalem'), apud Henri Massé (trans.), *Conquête de la Syrie et la Palestine par Saladin* (Paris, 1972), pp. 30–1.

11. D.S. Richards, 'A consideration of two sources for the life of Saladin', *Journal of Semitic Studies* 25/1 (1980), 46–65.
12. Quoted in Riley-Smith 2010: 61.
13. Amir Timur, popularly known as Timur the Lame (Persian, *Temūr-i Lang*) or Tamerlane (1336–1405) was a distant relation of Genghis Khan through the female line. He was not a Mongol himself, being of Turkic extraction: his name, predictably perhaps, means 'iron' in the Turkic tongue (*temür*). Two years previously – in 1400 – Timur had met the Arab historian Ibn Khaldūn (1332–1406) outside Damascus, in what must be one of the most interesting interviews ever recorded. Ibn Khaldūn quickly realised that Timur's oblique questioning was intended to divine as much strategic intelligence as possible about Egypt and the dominions further west. The Asiatic conqueror then asked the Arab chronicler to write a detailed description of the west, "in such a manner that when the conqueror read it, it would be as if he were seeing the region". There can be few more graphic descriptions of the effect of good and complete intelligence, compiled by an expert and presented to a military genius. Ibn Khaldun completed the assignment in a few days. Timur's reputed lameness was authoritatively confirmed in 1941 by a Soviet medical team that examined his skeleton and reported that it showed signs of tuberculosis in the bone. According to tradition, however, Timur's disability arose from numerous wounds to his right hand and leg in a succession of battles.
14. National Library of Malta, Valletta, MS 53 (iii), fol. 217 *et seq.*
15. The buildings in Clerkenwell were put to different uses. In the reign of Elizabeth, they were used as the offices of the Master of Revels. Thirty of Shakespeare's plays were licensed here. In the 18th century the former priory was used as a coffee house, run by the father of the artist William Hogarth, and then as a pub, *The Old Jerusalem Tavern*, where artists and writers, including Charles Dickens, used to meet. Today, Clerkenwell Priory serves as the Museum of the Order of Saint John.
16. Latin chroniclers of the First Crusade mention the presence of contingents called *Turcopoli* (Gk. Τουρκόπουλοι/ *Tourkópouloi*, 'sons of Turks') in the army of Alexios I Komnenos (r. 1081–1118). As we would expect, *Tourkópouloi* were mounted on swift mettlesome horses. Without the caparison of the 'heavy' cavalryman, they were equipped with only a mail shirt, a helmet, and a diverse array of offensive weapons, with the composite recurve bow being prominent. Talking of Frankish *Turcopoli*, Guillaume de Tyr, the Latin archbishop of Tyre (r. 1175–86), describes them as *"levis armature"* (*Historia rerum in paribus transmarinis gestarum* 19.25, 22.18 [17]), the same term he uses to describe Turkish mounted archers, *"armature levis equitibus"*, and *"levioris armature milites"* (ibid. 4.7, 21.27 [28]), and at least on one occasion Guillaume makes it clear that *levis armatura* means bows, since he claims that the strength of the Seljuq Turks lay in their swift horses *"et armorum levitate, arcuum videlicet et pharetrarum"* (ibid. 16.22). At Qurūn Hattīn the *Historia Regni Hierosolymitani* records 4,000 *Turcopoli* as being part of the defeated Latin army, and those captured were executed on the orders of Salāh al-Dīn as having betrayed Islam.
17. The admiral of the Hospitaller fleet is first mentioned in 1299 when the Order was operating out of Limassol, Cyprus (Riley-Smith 2012: 93).
18. During the siege of Malta, Francesco Balbi di Correggio reports in his war journal that the *pilier* of the tongue of England was the Order's turcopolier: *"El de Ingalaterra, es Turcpiller, sobre intendiéte de las guardas q[ue] se hazen, y puede mádara a todos los vassallos de la religion"* (Francesco Balbi di Correggio, *La verdadera relacion de lo que en el año 1565 ha sucedito en la isla de Malta, de antes que llegase la armada sobre de ella de Soliman Gran Turco* [Barcelona, 1568], p. 14). Among the Hospitallers defending Malta at the time

we find but one Englishman, to represent a tongue formerly the foremost in the list; he was Fra' Oliver Starkey (†1588). In the crypt of Saint John's Co-Cathedral in Valetta is a plaque bearing a Latin epitaph composed by him for Grand Master Jean Parisot de la Valette (r. 1557–68); he finishes the epitaph thus: "Fra' Oliver Starkey, Pro-Turcopolier, wrote [this] epitaph" (Hannibal P. Scicluna, *The Church of St. John in Valetta* [Rome, 1955], pl. cxxx). As well as holding the office of turcopolier, Starkey was also the Latin secretary to la Valette.

19. Abbé Rene de Vertot, *Histoire des chevaliers de Saint-Jean de Jerusalem appelés depuis chevaliers de Rhode at aujourd'hui chevaliers de Malte* (Paris, 1761), vol. 5, p. 301.

20. Fra' Bartolemeo dal Pozzo, *Historia della sacra religione militare di S. Giovanni Gerosolimitano detta di Malte*, 2 vols. (Verona, 1703–15), vol. 1, p. 494.

21. Archives of the Order in Malta, MS 1759, fol. 115.

22. Fra' Bartolemeo dal Pozzo, *Historia della sacra religione militare di S. Giovanni Gerosolimitano detta di Malte*, 2 vols. (Verona, 1703–15), vol. 1, p. 791.

23. Archives of the Order in Malta, MS 92, fol. 67v.

24. Ibid. MS 92, fol. 71v.

25. The English term *carrack* (via Old French *caraque*) is unclear, perhaps derived from the Arabic *qarāqīr*, meaning 'merchant ship' itself perhaps from the Latin *carricare* 'to load a car' or Greek καραϰίς 'load of timber'. The three galleys were the *Santa Croce*, *San Filippo* and *San Giovanni* (Giacomo Bosio, *Historia della sacra religione e illusirissima militia di San Giovanni Gerosolimitano* [Venezia, 1695], vol. 3, p. 88).

26. Ibid. vol. 3, p. 150.

27. Ibid. vol. 3, p. 114. For a full description of the *Sant' Anna*, see Muscat-Cuschieri 2002: 17–20.

28. Grand Master Juan d'Homedes y Coscon had other plans, however, and decreed that the *Sant' Anna* was too massive and her maintenance costs too prohibitive (the Order having recently lost its properties and holding in England). He ordered two galleons to be built to replace her; the smaller, faster galleon was currently replacing the carrack in Habsburg Spain and Tudor England, for instance. The *Sant' Anna* was stripped and decommissioned in 1540 and she was left to rot away in the Grand Harbour (Giacomo Bosio, *Historia della sacra religione e illusirissima militia di San Giovanni Gerosolimitano* [Venezia, 1695] vol. 3, pp.197, 254).

29. The three galleys were the *Santa Maria della Vittoria*, *San Pietro*, and *San Giovanni* (Giacomo Bosio, *Historia della sacra religione e illusirissima militia di San Giovanni Gerosolimitano* [Venezia, 1695], vol. 3, p. 893). Apparently, the three galleys had on board fifteen cannon, 600 soldiers, 200 sailors, 900 oarsmen, plus the usual complement of knights and gentlemen volunteers (Fra' Bartolemeo dal Pozzo, *Historia della sacra religione militare di S. Giovanni Gerosolimitano detta di Malte*, 2 vols. [Verona, 1703–15], vol. 1, p. 11).

30. Abbé Rene de Vertot, *Histoire des chevaliers de Saint-Jean de Jerusalem appelés depuis chevaliers de Rhode at aujourd'hui chevaliers de Malte*, (Paris, 1761), vol. 7, p. 54.

31. For the compulsory two-year caravan, see National Library of Malta, Valletta, MS 223, s.v. *Caravana*.

32. Braudel 1973 [1966]: II, 875–6.

33. Richard Knolles, *The generall historie of the Turkes, from the first beginning of that nation to the rising of the Othoman familie*, 3 vols. (London, 1687–1700 [7th edn.]), vol. 1, p. 535.

34. Voltaire, *Annale de l'Empire*, s.v. Maximilien II, 1565.

35. Fra' Bartolemeo dal Pozzo, *Historia della sacra religione militare di S. Giovanni Gerosolimitano detta di Malte*, 2 vols. (Verona, 1703–15), vol. 1, p. 11. In the years following Lepanto Romegas was appointed prior of Ireland, and captain general of the

Order's galleys from 1575 to 1577, an onerous and yet prestigious post conferred only for two years on the best maritime captain of the Order. Elected lieutenant to the grand master in 1577, Romegas would get embroiled in the internal politics of the Knights Hospitaller, in 1581 heading a revolt against the then grand master, the doddering Jean l'Evesque de la Cassière (r. 1572–81). Called to Rome to answer before Gregory XIII for his actions, the most celebrated and daring seafarer of the Order died there on 4 November of the same year.

36. Fra' Bartolemeo dal Pozzo, *Historia della sacra religione militare di S. Giovanni Gerosolimitano detta di Malte*, 2 vols. (Verona, 1703–15), vol. 1, p. 13.

37. It was not until 1625 that the Maltese *capitana* would be distinctively painted black. See, National Library of Malta, Valletta, MS 223, s.v. *Capitana*.

**Chapter 9: His Holiness**

1. William Tyndale, *The Obedience of a Christian Man*, ed. Henry Walter (Cambridge, 1848), p. 186.

2. William Tyndale, *Practice of Prelates*, ed. Henry Walter (Cambridge, 1849), p. 299.

3. This was the same Church council where Henry V of England (r. 1413–22) attempted to cement an anti-French alliance with the Holy Roman Empire.

4. It should be recalled that between 1309 and 1378 a total of seven popes reigned in Avignon; all were French, and they increasingly fell under the influence of the French crown. The absence from Rome is sometimes referred to as the Babylonian Captivity of the Papacy. Finally, or so it must have seemed at the time, the dispute was over, for on 13 September 1376 Gregory XI (r. 1370–8) abandoned Avignon and moved his court to Rome. He is the most recent French pope.

5. The Reformation, which brought about a condition of war in Europe which lasted till 1648 and indeed for some time afterwards, was the movement initiated by Martin Luther to reform Catholicism. His actions led to the eventual development of Protestantism in its various guises, chiefly Lutheran and Calvinism, and the Council of Trent (1545–63) convened in response to the Reformation to clarify Catholic faith and doctrine in the 16th century. It was on the eve of All Saints, 31 October 1517, when Luther nailed to the door of the cathedral of Wittenberg the ninety-five page thesis by which he challenged the authority of the pope. Luther had visited Rome in 1511, had made his pilgrimage round the seven basilicas, and had climbed the Sacred Staircases on his knees. He would write, "Is there nothing more corrupt, more pestilential, more offensive than the Roma Curia? It surpasses beyond all comparison the godlessness of the Turks" (Martin Luther, apud Dillenberger 1961: 47). Leo X (r. 1513–21) condemned the thesis of Luther on 15 June 1520, and he excommunicated the rebellious friar the following January.

6. Matthias Gerung, 'Die Türken töten Christen; der Papst verfolgt die Armen', woodcut dated circa 1548, Kunstammlungen der Veste Coburg, inv. I.349.13.

7. Quoted in Hale 1998 [1985]: 15.

8. While still a cardinal, Rodrigo Borgia had at least nine children whom he acknowledged and legitimised. The identity of the mother, or mothers, of the first three (Pere Lluís, Jerònima and Elisabet) is unknown. For the eldest, Pere Lluís (c. 1468–88), he set up the duca di Gandia, the Borgias' chief possession in the Crown of Aragón. He had four more children by Vannozza dei Cattanei, a very enterprising and discrete Roman matron: Cesare (1475–1507), who was destined to a church career from infancy, Giovanni (c. 1478–97), who became II duca di Gandia on the death of his half-brother Pere Lluís, Lucrezia (1480–1519), a vital pawn in the pope's political strategies in Italy, and Gioffre (born in 1481 or 1482), who became principe di Squillace through his marriage to Sancia d'Aragona, an illegitimate daughter of Alfonso II of Naples. Two more sons are known to

have been born during Alexander's pontificate: Giovanni (1498–1546), duca di Nepi and di Camerino, known as the *Infans Romanus* and rumoured to be the fruit of an incestuous relationship with Lucrezia, and Rodrigo (c. 1503–27), who became a priest.

9. Niccolò Machiavelli, *Legazione e commissarie XI*, doc. 81.

10. "I have seen," says Blaise de Monluc, "the perversity of these people cause us (French) the loss of many a town, and wreck the King's campaigns. It is true that they are veritable soldiers, and form the backbone of an army, but you must never be short of money if you want them – and they will never take promises in lieu of cash" (Blaise de Monluc, *Commentaires de messire Blaise de Monluc, mareschal de France*, 3 vols. ed Paul Courteault [Paris, 1911–25], vol. 1, p. 24). Obviously the young Monluc was referring to Biccoca, the defeat already named, in 1522, when the Swiss *reisläufer* complained, through their captains, that money was owing to them and so offered the unfortunated French commander, Odet de Foix, vicomte de Lautrec, one of three choices: to pay their wages; to give them leave to return home; or to attack the enemy without a moment's delay. The 'perversity' of the Swiss compelled him, against his better judgement, to engage in battle.

11. Blaise de Monluc once raised two companies of Gascons for French service beyond the Alps. En route to Italy, the Gascons took advantage of their captain's momentary absence to storm and sack a French town. Laden with plunder, they then dispersed back to their hoes. For why should these soldiers go to Italy if they already secured their booty (Blaise de Monluc, *Commentaires de messire Blaise de Monluc, mareschal de France*, 3 vols. ed Paul Courteault [Paris, 1911–25], vol. 1, pp. 125–6.

12. Francesco Guicciardini, a friend of Machiavelli's, in narrating the life of Cesare Borgia relied upon the Cain and Abel narrative, casting him as fratricidal Cain in his younger brother's murder and using that reading to impart meaning to his history (Niccolò Machiavelli, *Lettere di Niccolò Machiavelli*, vol. 2, pp. 60–1).

13. *Il Principe* was a treatise compiled to serve as a guide in government to Giuliano de' Medici, the feeble son of the famed Lorenzo *il Magnifico*, who had ruled Florence in all but name, and the older brother of the newly elected pope, Leo X (r. 1513–21), a treatise inspired by Cesare Borgia, who is the model prince held up by the acknowledged inventor of statecraft, Niccolò Machiavelli, for emulation. The astute Florentine daily saw and spoke with Cesare for some three months, from October 1502 to January 1503, and sent his republican government, the Signoria of Florence, the results of his analyses (Dispatch from Cesena, 14 December 1502), and was inspired by them to later write *il Principe* (1513). He was present at Sinigaglia when Cesare had persuaded a number of treacherous and rebellious *condottieri* to meet with him and then ordered his men to slay them. Machiavelli was the only man who ever knew the real Cesare Borgia naked face to naked face, naked soul to naked soul, which is why he is the most captivating character in the author's *il Principe*.

14. Quoted in Browning 1895: 185.

15. Maximilian married first Mary of Burgundy (1457–82), daughter of Charles *le Téméraire* (r. 1467–77); after her death, Bianca Maria Sforza (1472–1510), eldest daughter of Galeazzo Maria Sforza (r. 1466–76), and thus became involved in Italian politics. Her elder half-sister was of course the magnificent and alarming Caterina Sforza (1463–1509), the illegitimate daughter of Galeazzo by his mistress Lucrezia Landriani. Her life, to say the least, was colourful; well worth further reading. Caterina, as signora di Imola e contessa di Forlì, held various posts of a political and military nature; with many, many murders to her credit (poison and torture seem to be her favourite means of disposal). Caterina is one of the handful of women discussed by Niccolò Machiavelli at length, the wily Florentine even gracing her with the title *la Madonna di Forlì* (he came to Forlì in

1499 on his first diplomatic mission for the Republic of Florence mainly to negotiate her son Ottaviani's military contract). The incident of having lifted her skirts to bare her genitalia during a standoff over the rule of Forlì in 1488 is recounted at length by him in *Discorsi* (3.6) and *Istoria fiorentine* (8.7), while being only mentioned in *il Principe* (ch. 20). Apparently, during the siege of the Rocca di Ravaldino, the fortress of Forlì, where her children were captured and threatened with death, she lifted her skirts, grabbed her crotch, and proudly declared that she possessed the instruments to make more.

16. The National Archives (United Kingdom), Special Oyer and Terminer Roll Principal Defendants and Charges: John Felton, high treason.
17. George Buchanan, *A Detection of the Douings of Marie, Queen of Scots* (London, 1721), p. 57.
18. Ibid. p. 27.
19. John Lesley, *A Defence of the Honor of Marie, Queene of Scotland* (London, 1569), p. 6.
20. *Vide* Appendix 2.
21. Cardinal Tolomeo Gallio, letter to William Parry (12 December 1580).
22. Cuts and economies brought the overall cost to be shared between Spain and Venice down to about two million *escudos*. See Parker and Thompson 1978: 13–14.
23. The Latin text of the treaty of 25 May 1571, is given in Luciano Serrano (ed.), *Correspondencia diplomatics entre España y la Santa Sede durante el pontificado de S. Pio V*, 4 vols. (Madrid, 1914), vol. 4, no. 136, pp. 299–309. See also Setton 1986: 1015–16.

## Chapter 10: The Porte

1. After the inhabitants of Otranto refused to surrender, the Ottoman *kapudan paşa*, Gedik Ahmed Paşa (†1482), made clear what would happen to the survivors and pressed on with his assault; the city possessed poor defences and no cannon, and the outcome was predictable. Otranto was besieged on 28 July, and fell on 11 August. On capturing the city Ahmed Paşa slaughtered the entire male population, leaving 10,000 people alive out of about 22,000; 8,000 slaves were sent across the Adriatic to Albania. The elderly archbishop was struck down at the high altar of Otranto cathedral. The Ottomans then began to ravage the lands of Lucca and Brindisi.
2. Barkey 2008: 294.
3. G.K. Chesterton, 'Lepanto', stanza 1, line 12.
4. Charles IX, although emotionally disturbed (and would be increasingly so after the massacre of Saint Bartholomew's Day), was an intelligent man. His education had been entrusted to the humanist Jacques Amyot (1513–93), who helped him to develop a sincere love of literature. Indeed, Charles himself practised poetry and a treatise on hunting (*Traité de la chasse royale*) and was a patron of *La Pléiade*, a literary group dedicated to the advancement of French literature.
5. See Graf 2017: 59. In early modern English, the phrase 'to turn Turk' also had a sexual meaning which was absent from its continental equivalents. In English drama, for example, renegades were frequently shown to have converted because they had succumbed to the wiles of a Muslim woman.
6. In the Ottoman empire, the most dynamic of Muslim states, of the forty-eight grand viziers who held power in Constantinople between 1453 and 1623, at least thirty-three are known to have been of Christian origin.
7. Public Records Office, *Calendar of State Papers, Domestic* 1603–10, 8 August 1606. Sir Walter Raleigh, who, as *a privateer*, was looked on as a heroic figure who served the national interest (and, of course, the royal coffers), recorded the "Renegedoes, that turn'd Turke, are impaled", and this appears to be the usual punishment for such apostate pirates.

8. E.g. Talha İnanç, 'Jack Sparrow might be inspired by a Muslim captain', *Daily Sabah* (in English), 20 March 2017.
9. Johannes Wild, *Neue Reysbeschreibung eines Gefangenen Christen* (Nürnberg, 1623), sigs. Xv–Ii ivr.
10. Ibid. sigs. G iiiv, Uv.
11. Niccolò Machiavelli, *il Principe*, ch. 4, p. 18 Marriott.
12. Káldy-Nagy: 1977.
13. Padre Alberto Gugliemotti, *Storia delta marina pontificia: vol. VII: La squadra permanente, 1573–1644* (Roma: 1892), p. 136. See, also, Archivo General de Simancas, *Secretería de Estado*, leg. 1158, fol. 186 (1 October 1598), fol. 187 (fifteen letters between the *kapudan-ı deryā*, his family and Habsburg authorities dated September 1598).
14. Fra' Bartolemeo dal Pozzo, *Historia della sacra religione militare di S. Giovanni Gerosolimitano detta di Malte*, 2 vols. (Verona, 1703–15), vol. 1, p. 407.
15. Monchicourt 1913: 139.
16. Pierre de Bourdeilles, abbé et seigneur de Brantôme, *Œuvres complètes*, 11 vols. (Paris, 1864–82), vol. 5, p. 153.
17. National Library of Malta, Valletta, MS 53 (iii), fol. 164.
18. Miguel de Cervantes, *Don Quixote*, part 1, ch. 40, p. 342 Grossman.
19. Ibid. p. 343 Grossman.
20. In 1574 Zahara married Abu Marwan Abd al-Malik, who was proclaimed sultan of Morocco in 1576 and died (from natural causes) during the battle of al-Qasr al-Kabir (Alcazarquivir) against the Portuguese in 1578. She was remarried to Uluç Hasan Paşa, and after 1580 resided in Constantinople. Hacı Murād Re'īs (†1609), her father, was an Albanian renegade who had renounced Christianity. In other words, some of the characters in *La historia del cautivo*, 'The Captive's Tale', of Cervantes are historical, though the action is fictional.
21. Miguel de Cervantes, *Don Quixote*, part 1, chs. 40–1, pp. 343–68 Grossman.
22. Ibid. 171–8.
23. Ibid. 189.
24. Archivio di Stato di Venezia, *Consiglio dei Dieci, Parti Comuni*, registro 30, fol. 156v (28 November 1572).

## Chapter 11: Invincible Infantry

1. Kafadar 1995: 111–13, 138–50, Finkel 2006: 75.
2. Bertrandon de la Broquière, *Le Voyage d'outremer*, pp. 182–5, 268.
3. Quoted in Imber 2002: 260.
4. On this, see Káldy-Nagy 1977: 165–6.
5. Quoted in Imber 2002: 134–5.
6. Lowry 2003: 139.
7. Imber 2002: 134.
8. As slaves of the sultan, they had been able to do so only if the sultan had granted their individual requests. Since it was feared that family life would interfere with the janissaries' training, discipline, and mobility, however, marriages had, in general, been discouraged. However, under Selīm II the janissaries obtained blanket permission to marry. See Imber 2002: 140–1.
9. The final structure of the janissary *ocak* consisted of 196 *ortas* divided into three unequal divisions: 101 of *cemaat* (or *yaya*), 61 (or 62) of *ağa bölükleri*, and 34 (or 33) of *sekban*.
10. Ágoston 2014: 113, cf. Murphy 1999: 43–9, Imber 2002: 257–8.
11. Busbecq, 'The First Letter', apud Foster 2005 [1927]: 8.
12. Ibid. 9.

13. Busbecq, 'The Third Letter', apud Foster 2005 [1927]: 146.
14. Ibid. 147.
15. Mustafā Çelebi Celālzade, *Geschichte Sultan Süleymān Ḳānūnīs von 1520 bis 1557, oder, Tabakāt ül-Memālik ve Derecāt ül-Mesālik* (Wiesbaden, 1981), fols. 146b-147a.
16. This particular tactic dates back to the successful tactical system employed by the Hussites during the uprisings of Jan Žižka in Bohemia (1419–34), the one-eyed leader who never lost a battle. It involved the use of especially built wagons with protecting panels, behind which soldiers fired with every sort of missile weapon existing at the time, including portable fire-weapons and artillery used massively for the first time. These Hussite war wagons were deployed in strong defensive positions that were, in fact, carefully-built hill fortifications that could even be protected by ditches. The Hussites, all but forgotten today, were the followers of the martyred Czech theologian, Jan Hus: condemned by the Roman Catholic Church, he was burned at the stake on 6 July 1415. A sect of religious reformers, they were the forerunners of the Protestant Reformation that was to come a century later.
17. Fethullah Ārif Çelebi, *Süleymān-nāme*, MS Hazine Ktp. 1517, fol. 219b-220a, Topkapı Sarayı Müzesi Kütüp; fol. 220a, depicting the janissaries, is published in Artemel 1988: 79.
18. Quoted in Imber 2002: 277–8.
19. Busbecq, 'The Third Letter', apud Foster 2005 [1927]: 146.
20. Gerat Barry, *A Discourse of Military Discipline* (Bruxelles, 1634), preface.
21. Ibid. bk. 1, ch. 1, p. 9.
22. Barnabe Rich, *Allarme to England* (London, 1578), Sig. G iv. Incidentally, Barnabe's short story 'Of Apollonius and Silla' in *Farewell to Militarie Profession* (London, 1581) was the source for Shakespeare's *Twelfth Night*.
23. Evliya Çelebi, *Seyāhatnāme*, vol. 1, p. 620. Çelebi had been present at the battle of Saint Gotthard (1 August 1664), where he witnessed Raimondo Montecuccoli, commanding a combined Austrian, Imperial and French army, inflicting a shock defeat upon a superior Ottoman army.
24. Matrakçı Nasûh, *Süleymān-nāme*, MS Revan Ktp. 1286, fol. 30b, Topkapı Sarayı Müzesi Kütüp.
25. See Karl Signell, 'Mozart and the mehter', *The Consort* 24 (1967), pp. 310–22.
26. It has been generally accepted that the invention and diffusion of firearm volley fire among early modern armies were highly significant and had far-reaching consequences. The invention of this tactic came about in response to a deficiency in muzzle-loading firearms, which were slow to reload. Under ideal conditions, an experienced harquebusier or musketeer in the 16th century could fire one round of shot only every two minutes; the reloading time between shots was long enough to allow the advance of enemy forces – motivated troops could cover up to forty metres a minute. The only effective solution to this problem was to arrange the harquebusiers or musketeers in ranks and to 'program' them to shoot in sequence (viz. by rotation of the ranks) so that a constant barrage of fire could be maintained, keeping the enemy at bay (Parker 1996A: 18–20). It should be emphasised, however, no western army used volley fire *in action* until the sixteen-twenties, with the possible exception of the Dutch at the battle of Nieuwpoort in 1600. Ottoman sources, on the other hand, prove that the janissaries were already using volley fire by 1605, and possibly as early as the fifteen-twenties (Börekçi 2006).
27. Stephen Brodaric, p. 1193.
28. Ottoman chroniclers differentiated between *darbzens* and *top*, cannons proper. Thus, Çelebi Celālzade, in his account of Mohács, refers to *darbzens* as *saff-şiken*, '[battle]line-

breaker,' and *merad-efgen*, 'neck-destroyer, and called cannons *kale-ken*, 'castle-destroyer' (Mustafā Çelebi Celālzade, *Geschichte Sultan Süleymān Ḳānūnīs von 1520 bis 1557, oder, Tabakāt ül-Memālik ve Derecāt ül-Mesālik* [Wiesbaden, 1981], fol. 139a).

29. İstanbul, TSMA D 9633.

30. Jehan de Wavrin, *Recueil des chroniques etanchiennes Histories de la Grant Bretaigne, à present nommé Engleterre*, apud Imber 2006: 130. Composing his chronicle at the court of Philippe *le Bon*, duc de Bourgogne, Jehan de Wavrin based this account of the Varna crusade largely on the memoirs of his nephew Waleran de Wavrin, who commanded the Burgundian fleet operating on the Bosporus, the Black Sea and the lower Danube in 1444–5. Jehan himself was no armchair warrior, for as a young man aged fifteen he had fought in the mud of Picardy with the French army at that fearsome engagement we know as Agincourt (Friday, 25 October 1415), but which the lamenting French called *l'affaire de Picardie*, the Picardy affair.

31. Busbecq, 'The Third Letter', apud Foster 2005 [1927]: 133–4.

32. The composite bow constructed from sinew, horn and wood with stiffeners (ear- and grip-laths) of bone was the standard type of bow in the east and had been so for many centuries. Certainly, clear representations of composite bows appear in Mesopotamia as early as the middle of the third millennium BC in Early Dynastic III and Akkadian art, such as the Victory Stele from Susa showing Naram-Sin (r. c. 2291–2255 BC) triumphing over a tribe of the Zagros (south-east Kurdistan) called the Lullubi. The warrior king is depicted armed with a composite bow of a double-concave form, which fell out of use after the fall of the Akkadian empire. The ancient Egyptians, for instance, used angular composite bows, as would the Persians. These bows can be recognised as composite by the recurve ends standing above the bowstring when the bow is braced. Despite its prehistoric origins, however, the composite bow was no simple stick and string. Technically it is one of the most complicated and most advanced artefacts among those of perishable materials.

33. The kingdom of Hungary covered present-day Slovakia and parts of Austria on it northern border, a long slice of Romania to the south, and a whole stretch of present-day Serbia and Croatia to the west. It was an enormous realm, rich in pasture and arable land.

34. Recently-discovered sources show a mixed Hungarian army consisting of 16,000 horsemen and 10,000 footmen, armed with handguns, pikes, and pavises and supported by eighty-five cannon, 600 harquebuses, and 5,000 wagons that could be used as *wagenburg*.

35. Ágoston 2005: 24.

36. Ibid. 2014: 98.

37. On the peculiar characteristics of smoothbore ballistics and the more technical side of the development of small firearms, see Hall 1999: 134–51.

38. Busbecq, 'The Third Letter', apud Foster 2005 [1927]: 132.

39. Busbecq, 'The First Letter', apud Foster 2005 [1927]: 50.

40. Murphy 1999: 134–5.

41. Fra' Diego da Haedo, *Topografia e historia general de Argel*, 3 vols. (Madrid, 1927–9), vol. 1, p. 77.

42. On Thursday, 15 June 1826 the janissaries would revolt for the very last time. Mahmūd II (r. 1808–39), whose rule had so often been threatened by the janissaries (by 1826 the sultan was giving rations and wages to 135,000 of them each month), acted with ruthless efficiency and sealed off the *Et Meydanı* with loyal troops who had been trained *à la occidente*. The janissaries refused to listen to reason and the gates of their barracks were blasted away by round shot and 4,000 of them slain. Many more were rounded up in the capital and in the provinces. All janissary leaders were hunted down and executed, while the ordinary janissaries were either exiled or imprisoned. The power of the centuries-old, conservative janissary corps was thus broken forever (along with the Bektaşi order).

This was known, in Constantinople at least, as *Vaka-i Hayriyye*, the Auspicious Event, removing as it did the last serious barrier to military modernity.

43. The telling of jokes and humorous tales was an important part of Bektaşi culture and teaching. Frequently these poke fun at conventional religious wisdom by counterpoising the Bektaşi dervish as an iconoclastic figure. For example: A Bektaşi was a passenger in a rowing boat crossing the Bosporos from Eminönü in the heart of Constantinople to Üsküdar on the Asiatic shore. When a storm blew up, the boatman tried to reassure him by saying "Fear not, God is great!" the Bektaşi replied, "Yes, God is great, but the boat is small". Üsküdar was formerly known as Scutari (Gk. Σκουτάριον / Scutàrion), and in classical antiquity as Chrysopolis (Gk. Χρυσόπολις, 'Golden City').

## Chapter 12: The Galleys

1. Archivo General de Simancas, *Secretería de Estado*, leg. 1389, fol. 71. The Genoese Doria clan was famous as maritime mercenaries who hired out ships, sailors and soldiers.
2. The lateen (or Latin, *latino*) sail was so called, says Luigi Fincati, from *alla trina* to distinguish it from the quadrangular, or *alla quadra* sail (*Le Triremi* [Roma, 1881], p. 41).
3. Guilmartin 2003 [1974]: 219.
4. Ibid. 73–100.
5. Alfred Thayer Mahan (1840–1914), the influential American oracle of sea power.
6. Juan Latino, *Austrias Carmen*, ll. 387–8, apud Wright-Spence-Lemons 2014: 313. Born Juan de Sessa (1518–96), the remarkable Juan Latino was a black African former slave (Gonzalo II Fernández de Córdoba, III duque de Sessa, was his one-time master) who gained fame as a professor of Latin in Granada. One of the most intriguing figures in the history of Renaissance Latinity, his two-book neo-Latin epic, *Austrias Carmen* ('The Song of Juan de Austria'), chronicles the battle of Lepanto and asserts himself as a worthy heir of Virgil. Though the poem focuses on Lepanto, he presents the battle as the culmination of a conflict that began with Granada's *morisco* revolt, or Second Revolt of the Alpujarras (1568–71), which Don Juan repressed.
7. Lane 1992 [1934]: 236.
8. Bartolemeo Crescentio, *Nautica Mediterranea* (Roma, 1607), p. 15.
9. The palm was based on the width of the human palm and then variously standardised. In Italy the palm (It. *palmo*) varied regionally. The Neapolitan *palmo* could vary between 20.31 and 21.80 centimetres, whereas a Genovese *palmo* measured about 24.76 to 24.85 centimetres. On Sicily and Malta, it was 24.61 centimetres.
10. Joseph Furttenbach, *Architectura navalis: Das ist von dem Schiffgebäw, auff dem Meer und Seekusten zugebrauchen* (Ulm, 1629), pp. 19–20.
11. Morrison-Coates-Rankov 2000: 138–41, Fields 2007: 7, 13, 38.
12. Vettor Fausto, *Aristotelis Mechanica, Victoris Fausti industria in pristinum habitum restituta ac latinitate donate* (Paris, 1517).
13. Pseudo-Aristotle, *Mechanica* 4.850b10 Hett.
14. Morrison-Coates-Rankov 2000: 137–8, Fields 2007: 6–7.
15. Marin Sanudo, *I diarii* [Venezia, 1897], vol. 50, col. 347, Marin Sanudo (1466–1536) wrote the history of the Republic of Venice from 1496 to 1533 in fifty-six folio volumes. The learned *patrizio* of Venice cited the state archives, despatches of the leading men etc., and his work is marvellously well put together.
16. Capponi 2007 [2006]: 147, 152.
17. Morrison-Coates-Rankov 2000: 226, cf. Rogers 1937: 231–2.
18. Archivo General de Simancas, *Colección Fernandez de Navarrete*, vol. 12, dto. 83, fol. 309.
19. Archivo General de Simancas, *Colección Don Juan Sanz de Barutell*, Articulo 4, vol. 2, dto. 323, fols. 424–6.

20. Marteilhe 2010 [1758]: 119.
21. "Bastardly things were never any good [*Cosa bastarda non fu mai bona*]", *provveditore* Giovanni Moro on the 'bastard' galleys of his squadron. According to him, the *bastarde* under his command simply absorbed more resources than the others, while at the same time slowing down the whole squadron by forcing the *sottili* to wait for them or even tow them (Marin Sanudo, *I diarii* [Venezia, 1897], vol. 46, coll. 289, 446).
22. The astrolabe (in Arabic *al-Asturlāb* or 'to take a star') had proven of great value to the Portuguese on their oceanic voyages during the so-called age of discovery. This instrument was essentially a flat wooden or brass circle etched along the edges in degrees and minutes with two sights for reading celestial bodies. Used in conjunction with tables of declination provided in works like Zacuto's *Almanach Perpetuum Celestium*, the astrolabe could provide fairly accurate readings of latitude.
23. Ames 2009: 53.
24. The fathom (6 feet, 1.83 metres) was a unit of measurement of depth and for ropes.
25. Pierre Garcie-Ferrande, *Le Grant routtier et pilotage de la mer*, trans. by Robart Copland (London, 1528), p. 15.
26. A variable unit anyway: a Spanish league was three nautical miles, a Dutch league four and an English league three.
27. Strabo, *Geographia* 8.6.20 Jones.
28. Herodotos, *Historiē* 7.168.4.
29. *Odyssey* 3.287–90 Lattimore. The gods always get their dues: Menelaos loses his wife so he stirs up an army to bring her back to him, costing countless lives and creating countless widows, orphans and slaves.
30. *Odyssey* 9.80–1 Lattimore.
31. Pirì Re'īs, *Kitab-ı Bahriye* ('Book of Navigation'), vol. 1, p. 71.
32. Quoted in Muscat-Cuschieri 2002: 121.
33. Froissart, *Chroniques*, 1.50.
34. Marteilhe 2010 [1758]: 107.
35. Lewis 1961: 138, cf. Morin 1975: 57.
36. Archivo di Stato di Venezia, *Materie Miste Notabili*, busta 28–31.
37. The figure mentioned in connection with an artillery piece refers to the weight of the shot it could fire.
38. Archivo di Stato di Firenze, *Mediceo del Principato*, registro 238, fols. 66v – 68r: Cosimo I de' Medici to Concino, 27 February 1572.
39. Capponi 2007 [2006]: 260.
40. Archivo General de Simancas, *Colección Don Juan Sanz de Barutell*, Articulo 6, dto. 45, fols. 117–18.

**Chapter 13: The Guns**
1. This story is in a letter from Paulo Giovio to the pope, Clement VII, in Marin Sanudo, *I diarii* (Venezia, 1897), vol. 46, coll. 666–7.
2. Archival evidence disputes Padre Alberto Gugliemotti's (1862: 211–12) neat estimate of the guns present at Lepanto, namely 1,815 for the Christians and 750 for the Ottomans. See Capponi 2007 [2006]: 259, cf. Lesure 1971: 115–16.
3. Luis Collado, *Platica Manual de Artilleria* (Milano, 1592), fol. 8. Luis Collado was an experienced and informed Spanish artillerist, the 16th-century counterpart of Sébastien le Prestre de Vauban (1633–1707), the Director of Military Engineering under Louis XIV. When effective artillery appeared, a new form of fortification was devised in Renaissance Italy, based on the bastion, facilitating enfilade fire along all curtain walls (*vide* Appendix

1). The complex geometry, with its associated recondite vocabulary, which reached its peak in the designs of Vauban, was necessary because one cannot fire through one's own walls.

4. Lewis 1961: 15.

5. This straightforward basis for classification was first adopted by Robert Norton in *The Gunner* (London, 1628).

6. For this, see especially Guilmartin 2003 [1974]: 295–303.

7. Vannoccio Biringuccio, *De la pirotechnica* (Venezia, 1540), 172v – 173r.

8. Cristoforo Canal, *Della milizia maritima*, 66.

9. Martin and Parker 1999: 23–4. Discovered on 20 February 1971 by members of the City of Derry Sub Aqua Club, *La Trinidad Valencera* was excavated in 1979 with the aid of the marine archaeologist Colin Martin of Saint Andrews University. See Martin 1975: 203–1979, Atherton 2013.

10. Giovanni Alberghetti marked the guns he produced for the private market with his name and surname in Italian – *Zuane Alberghetto* (Z A), while using the Latin *Iohannes Albergetus* (I A) for pieces cast for the Venetian Republic. As a young man at the beginning of his career in 1573, he was in charge of the public foundry in the Arsenale, together with his elder brother Alberghetto III. Later he moved to Florence, where, working in gun and statue founding, he was active between 1591 and 1594.

11. Martin and Parker 1999: 272–4.

12. Lavery 1987: 103.

13. Guilmartin 2003 [1974]: 171, Morin 2011: 2.

14. National Library of Malta, Valletta, MS 223, s.v. *Mascolo del Petriere*.

15. Ibid, s.v. *Chiavetta del Petriere*.

16. In Japan, the Christian *daimyō* Ōtomo Sōrin Yoshishige (1530–87) seems to have been the first recipient of the swivel gun, possibly as early as 1551 when it appears he was presented two of them by the Portuguese. Yoshishige embraced European trade, culture, weaponry and (ultimately) its religion with an enthusiasm that was unparalleled among his warring contemporaries. His conversion to Christianity made him the darling of the Jesuits.

17. Scordato 2011: 28, 30.

18. Mortars were put into seagoing vessels by the French in the sixteen-eighties and sea-service mortars were bigger than those used on land since they were usually further away from their targets.

19. Lewis 1961: 137.

20. Quoted in Hale 1998 [1985]: 223.

21. Parry 1970: 226.

22. Henry VIII (r. 1509–47), a monarch better known for his acquisitive attitude to monasteries and wives, loved guns and the *Mary Rose* was his favourite warship. The Tudor king hired continental gun casters to set up operations in England, as well as foreign naval architects to improve his warships. Pictured in an illustrated catalogue of the king's navy known as the Anthony Roll (Cambridge, Magdalene College, Pepys Library MS 2991), we see the *Mary Rose* in full sail, after the extensive refit of 1536. A veritable floating fortress, she carries a large number of guns both in the enormous 'castles' at the ship's bow and stern and on the lower decks, proving that the importance of guns at sea had been fully appreciated in England by this time. Unfortunately, however, the importance of keeping the lower gun ports closed in rough seas was not: while moving down the Solent to thwart a French attack on the Isle of Wight, the *Mary Rose* heeled over, flooded, and sank like a stone. Out of a crew of at least 400, more than ninety per cent perished, including Vice-

admiral George Carew. Henry had used the ship as a weapon that, over thirty-three years, had brought terror to ordinary folk living on the coast, mostly in Brittany.

23. Guilmartin 1994: 148. When the *Mary Rose* sank it had thirty-nine wrought iron and cast bronze carriage guns, fifty-two wrought iron swivel guns, fifty handguns, 250 yew longbows, 300 staff weapons such as pikes and halberds, and almost 500 darts for hurling from the fighting tops (Hildred 2005: 147–72).

24. Lavery 1987: 84.

25. Parker 1996B: 294 n. 17.

26. At the end of Henry's reign his navy list enumerated "gonnes of brasse, shotte of yron and shotte of stoen and leade", and among the king's men were "souldiers, marriners and gonners' in proportion" (quoted in Munday 1998 [1987]: 4).

27. Guilmartin 1983: 563.

28. Apparently, when Michelangelo asked Julius II whether he wanted a book placed in the figure's hand, signifying scholarship and intellect, the pope responded, "Give me a sword; I am not a man of letters."

29. The only remaining trace of this Michelangelo bronze is a rough sketch in the Rothschild Codex of the façade of the Basilica di San Petronio, complete with its pugnacious pope.

30. Calamine is actually two distinct minerals, zinc silicate ($Zn_4Si_2O_7[OH]_2.H_2O$) or hemimorphite, and zinc carbonate ($ZnCO_3$) or smithsonite.

31. Quoted in Morin 2011: 9.

32. Archivo di Stato di Venezia Secreta, *Materie Miste Notabili*, busta 18bis.

33. Venetian shipbuilders of the period, for instance, worked with the following dimensional units: 1 *passo* = 5 *piedi* = 7 *palmi* = 80 *dedi* (1 pace = 5 feet = 7 spans = 80 inches). Alternatively, the Spanish span, *palmo*, was equivalent to 8 inches (cf. Venetian *palmo* of 11.43 inches).

34. Morin 1975.

35. Eliav 2013B: 404.

36. Sereno, *Commentari della Guerra di Cipro*, 154.

37. Giovanni Pietro Contarini, *Historia delle cose successe dal principio della guerra mossa da Selim Ottomano a' Venetiani, fino al di della gran giornata vittoriosa contra Turchi* (Venezia, 1572), fol. 52r.

38. Eliav 2013B: 406.

39. Ibid. 398.

40. Archivo di Stato di Venezia, *Consiglio dei Dieci, Parti Comuni*, registri 28, 133r (31 August 1568). See also Morin 2014: 256. A *moschetto da mascolo* or *da braga* was a light swivel gun having a bore diameter of about 45 millimetres firing a 1-*libra* lead shot.

41. Eliav 2013A: 262–74.

42. Quoted in White 2002: 15. Spanish 'full' pike had to be around twenty-seven Castilian 'palms' long (about 18ft/ 5.5m), and never less than twenty-five palms (16.4ft/ 5m).

43. Quoted in Colonel Ardant du Picq, *Études sur le combat* [*Battle Studies*] (New York, 1920), p. 206.

44. Michel de Montaigne, *Essais* (Bordeaux, 1595), bk. 2, ch. 12.

45. Martin du Bellay, *Mémoires* (Paris, 1585), bk. 2, p. 189. The memoirs, spanning the years 1513 to 1547 and focusing mainly on the Valois-Habsburg wars, were actually started by Martin's brother Guillaume du Bellay, seigneur de Langey, who had served François I as soldier, diplomat and administrator. His work was incomplete at his death in 1543; it was continued by Martin (†1559), who was foremost a soldier.

46. White 2002: 14.

47. 'Parmacity', *spermaceti*, a waxy substance found in the head cavities of the sperm whale used as ointment.
48. William Shakespeare, *I Henry IV*, 1.3.55–63.
49. Ibid. 5.4.58–85.

## Chapter 14: The Men

1. Joseph Furttenbach, *Architectura navalis: Das ist von dem Schiffgebäw, auff dem Meer und Seekusten zugebrauchen* (Ulm, 1629), pp. 13–14.
2. Luigi Fincati (Contr' Ammiraglio), *Le Triremi* (Roma, 1881), p.16.
3. Antonio Doria, *Discorso sopra le cose turchesche per via di mare* (Genova, 1539).
4. A galley always carried a *caïque* and a *fregatina*. The *caïque* was utilised for heavy duties such as the transportation of the crew to or from land, carrying of water and other supplies and towing duties; sometimes it was armed to attack enemy land fortifications. The smaller *fregatina* was mostly reserved for the service of the captain and his officers and to carry messages at sea.
5. Archivo General de Simancas, *Colección Don Juan Sanz de Barutell*, Articulo 5, vol. 2, dto. 323, fols. 43–4.
6. The *patrón* was the sailing master; the *sotapatrón* and *comitre* were roughly equivalent to first and second mates.
7. Archivo General de Simancas, *Colección Don Juan Sanz de Barutell*, Articulo 4, vol. 1, dto. 41, fols. 121–7.
8. Ibid. Articulo 4, vol. 2, dto. 323, fols. 424–6.
9. Ibid. Articulo 4, vol. 2, dto. 322, fols. 420–2.
10. Hale 1983: 312–13.
11. Giovanni Battista Salvago, *Storia di Genova*, MS in Archivio Doria, at the Faculty of Economics and Commerce of the University of Genoa, scat. 417, n. 1912, fol. 34r.
12. Ludovico Ariosto, *Orlando Furioso*, canto 9, stanza 29 Stewart Rose.
13. Blaise de Monluc, *Commentaires de messire Blaise de Monluc, mareschal de France*, 3 vols. ed. Paul Courteault (Paris, 1911–25), vol. 1, p. 2. However, his judgement on artillery is more balanced than that of many 16th-century commentators. In his view, *bien souvent fait plus peur que de mal*, "very frequently cause more fear than harm" (ibid. vol. 1, p. 102).
14. Miguel de Cervantes, *Don Quixote*, part 1, ch. 38, pp. 332–3 Grossman.
15. Ben Jonson, *An Execration upon Vulcan*, line 201.
16. Archivio di Stato di Venezia, *Consiglio dei Dieci, Parti Comuni*, registri 13, 13V (19 April 1539).
17. At the outset there were about sixty knights, but that number expanded quickly to several hundred, attracting virtually as many Italians as the Knights Hospitallers in Malta. The peak came early in the 17th century when there were about 600 knights of all nations, who were supported by personnel of noble volunteers, soldiers, seamen and oarsmen totalling some 2,000 men (Hanlon 1998: 38).
18. Despite the sporadic victories of the Order of Saint Stephen, the Tuscan galleys were never profitable, which led the *Granducato di Toscana* to sell part of the naval fleet 1647, thereby reducing it to three galleys. Following the death of the last Medici *Granducato* Gian Gastone in 1737 (he was childless, and the state of Tuscany now belonged to the House of Lorraine), the Order of Saint Stephen was disarmed.
19. See the decree, dated 12 Zilhicce 1023 (13 January 1615), Başbakanlık Osmanlı Arşivi (İstanbul), *Mühimme Defterleri*, vol. 80, p. 425/1025.
20. National Library of Malta, Valletta, MS 413, fols. 178, 185.

21. The nautical mile, or knot, is a nautical measure of speed (one sea mile per hour) and formerly measured by a logline divided by knots at equal distances of 1/120 of a geographical mile (every 14.7 yards). The number of knots travelled in half-a-minute corresponded to the number of sea miles travelled per hour. One sea mile equals one and one-fifth statue miles. Time was kept by an hour glass. The logline first appeared in 1574.

22. Antonio Carreño (ed.), *Los Romances de Góngora* (Madrid, 1985), sonnet 11, p. 123.

23. Giacomo Bosio, *Historia della sacra religione e illusirissima militia di San Giovanni Gerosolimitano* [Venezia, 1695], vol. 3, p. 367. See also, National Library of Malta, Valletta, MS 53 (iii), fol. 252.

24. Archivo di Stato di Firenze, *Mediceo del Principato*, registro 638, fol. 199r-v: Cosimo I de' Medici to Pier Francesco del Riccio, 3 March 1548.

25. Archives Order in Malta, MS 1770, fol. 305.

26. Archivo General de Simancas, *Colección Vargas Ponce*, serie 2, tomo 10-B, doc. 1, 'Testimonio', fols. 3v, 5v, 9r-v, 12v-13r.

27. Archivo General de Simancas, *Colección Don Juan Sanz de Barutell*, MS 389, fol. 220r-v.

28. Weiss 2014: 37.

29. Miguel de Cervantes, *Don Quixote*, part 1, ch. 22, p. 163 Grossman.

30. Quoted in DeVries 1990: 132.

31. Ibid. 142.

32. Ibid. 140–1.

33. Ambroise Paré, *Les Œuvres d'Ambroise Paré ... divisées en vingt huict livres avec les figures et portraicts, tant de l'anatomie que des instruments de chirurgie, et de plusieurs monstres, reveuës et augmentées par l'autheur* (Paris: 1585), pp. 454–5.

34. Jackson 1984. The procedure seems to be as old as Homer: thus the first possible record of *débridement* and soft tissue management comes from the *Iliad*. In the eleventh book Achilles' war buddy, Patroklos, extracts an arrow from the right thigh of Eurypylos of Thessaly by taking "a knife [to] cut the sharp tearing arrow out of his thigh, and washed the black blood running from it with warm water and, pounding it up in his hands, laid on a bitter root to make the pain disappear, one which stayed all kinds of pain. And the wound dried, and the flow of blood stopped" (*Iliad* 11.843–7 Lattimore). The unnamed root may have been onion, or *Achillea millefolium* (soldier's woundwort) or *Aristolochia clematitis* (European birthwort), a plant used for the relief of birth pangs. Homer tells of the centaur Chiron who taught Achilles to use "kind medicines" in the treatment of wounds (ibid. 11.829–30 Lattimore). Western medicine has a historical pedigree that reaches back to the epoch of the Homeric epic, in which disease and war wounds are described and treated by divine will or magical incantations, or *with* surgery and drugs. And here we should remember that the *Iliad*, one of the wellsprings of western literature, is still the saddest, most troubling treatment of warfare. Though Homer was mainly concerned with describing the wrath of Achilles and its awful consequences, the bard took for granted that his audience at the close of the 8th century BC (the period when scholars generally agree Homer composed his epic poem) knew a war had been fought for what was alternatively called Ilios or Troy.

35. Batty 1999: 337.

36. Hans Killian, *Der Kälte-Unfall: Allgemeine Unterkühlung* (München, 1966).

37. Quoted in Gross 1861: 20.

38. Packard 1921: 203.

39. Gerat Barry, *A Discourse of Military Discipline* (Bruxelles, 1634), bk. 1, ch. 5, p. 26.

40. William Clowes, *A Prooved Practice for all young Chirugians concerning Burnings with Gunpowder, and Woundes made with Gunshot, Sword, Halbard, Pike, Launce, or such other* (London, 1591), quoted in Cruickshank 1966: 177.

41. Quoted in Stewart 1947: 236.
42. Thomas Gale, *Office of a Chirurgerie* (London, 1566), pp. 26–7. Gale's treatise on surgery was the first to be written in English as oppose to Latin.
43. Thomas Styward, *Martiall Discipline* (London, 1581), p. 40.
44. William Clowes, *A Profitable and Necessarie Booke of Observations* (London, 1596), p. 111. This was a new edition of his *A Prooved Practice for all young Chirugians*.
45. Ambroise Paré, *La Méthode de traicter les playes faictes par hacquebutes et aultres bastons à feu et de celles qui sont faictes par flèches, dardz et semblables, aussy des combustions spécialement faictes par la pouldre à canon, composée par Ambroyse Paré* (Paris, 1545), quoted in A. Mudry 'Contribution of Ambroise Paré (1510–1590) to otology'. *American Journal of Otology* (1999) 20/6: 809–13.
46. Guglielmo Moizio, *De victoria Christianae Classis Carmen*, ll. 606, 647, 669, apud Wright-Spence-Lemons 2014: 263, 267.
47. Miguel de Cervantes, *Don Quixote*, part 2, ch. 34, p. 688 Grossman.
48. Archives of the Order in Malta, MSS 1759, fol. 519, 1845, fol. 233.
49. Archivo General de Simancas, *Colección Don Juan Sanz de Barutell*, Articulo 5, dto. 16.
50. Archivo General de Simancas, *Colección Fernandez de Navarrete*, vol. 12, dto. 100.
51. The first recorded mention of a type of hardtack is from the time Rameses II (r. 1279–1213 BC) when sailors in the pharaoh's navy carried with them a flat, hard loaf of millet bread called *dhourra* cake (probably a pancake).
52. When Herman Melville's Tommo rapidly becomes disillusioned with whaling life at the beginning of *Typee*, one of his complaints is about the rations aboard, especially the ship's "store of sea-bread, previously reduced to a state of petrifaction, with a view to preserve it either from decay or consumption in the ordinary mode" (Herman Melville, *Typee: A Peep at Polynesian Life* [Evanston, 1968], p. 21).
53. In Spanish service the price of hardtack, the single largest expense in the operation of a galley, quadrupled between 1529 and 1587. See Guilmartin 2003 [1974]: 236, fig. 11.
54. Robert Crowley, *The Subtyle Sophistrie of Thomas Watson* (London, 1569), p. 169.
55. Torranin-Smith-Byrd 1979.
56. Guyton 1981: 392.
57. Fra' Bartolemeo dal Pozzo, *Historia della sacra religione militare di S. Giovanni Gerosolimitano detta di Malte*, 2 vols. (Verona, 1703–15), vol. 2, p. 81.
58. For Archilochos, like any other hoplite mercenary, the spear not only brought death but also provided the soldier with his daily bread: "On my spear's my daily bread, / on my spear my wine / from Ismaros, and drinking it, / it's on my spear I recline" (Archilochos fr. 2 West).
59. Imperiale Cinuzzi, *La Vera militar disciplina antica e moderna* (Siena, 1604), vol. 1, p. 106.
60. Cruickshank 1966: 88.
61. Aksan 1998: 32.
62. The British army, based on their experiences during the Falklands/Malvinas War of 1982, revised upwards their estimates of the caloric needs of combat soldiers from 3,700 kilocalories per day to 4,200 kilocalories and have increased the carbohydrate content of the twenty-four-hour ration pack (*The Times* [London], 6 August 1988, p. 3).
63. National Library of Malta, Valletta, MS 413 fol. 186.
64. Capponi 2007 [2006]: 217. The metric equivalent of the *libra* is 0.329 kg.
65. Astrana Marín 1948–58: V, 230–8.
66. Zysberg 1984: 248.
67. Miguel de Cervantes, *Don Quixote*, part 1, ch. 22, p. 169 Grossman.
68. Fra' Jerónimo Gracián, *Escritos de Santa Teresa*, vol. 2, p. 457.
69. Archivo di Stato di Venezia, *Senato Mar*, registro 40, fol. 21r.

70. The words of Jean Barras de La Penne (1650–1730), quoted in Zysberg 1984: 96.
71. Op. cit. 96.
72. Bamford 1973: 246.

## Chapter 15: The Approach

1. Fra' Antonio de Lorea, *Vida de Pio Quinio* (Madrid, 1673), cap. 24, § 2.
2. E.g. Kātib Çelebi, *Tuhfetü'l-kibār fi esfāri'l-bihār*, Darü't Tıbaati'l Mamureti's Su, (İstanbul, 1141/1729), p. 92.
3. Op. cit.
4. Solakzade Mehmed, *Tarih-i Solakzade* ('History of Solakzade'), Mahmūd Bey Matbaası, (İstanbul, 1297/1879), p. 593.
5. Both European and Ottoman Turkish nicknames were derived from the name of hot stifling wind blowing from North Africa into southern Europe, the Sirocco, from Greek σιρόκος and hence derived Levantine Arabic *shlūq* respectively. The nickname thus denoted his primary occupation of corsair.
6. İnalcık 1974: 188–9.
7. The term *balyemez* means 'that eats no honey', and is in all probability a jesting and popular corruption of the German *Faule Metze* ('Lazy Metze'), the name of the famous bronze bombard cast in the city of Brunswick in 1411 which, together with the *Faule Grete* ('Lazy Grete'), cast in Marienburg two years earlier, altered the entire conduct of warfare, as it stood at that time.
8. The phrase στὸν Εὔριπον (to Evripos), corrupted as στὸ Νεὔριπον (to Nevripos), eventually became *Negroponte* (Black Bridge) in Italian by folk etymology, the *ponte* being interpreted as the bridge of Chalkis, which crossed the Evripos straits and connected the island with the mainland. This name was most relevant when the island was under Venetian rule (1390–1470). See, Edward Gibbon, *Decline and Fall of the Roman Empire*, 6 vols. (London, 1898), vol. 6, ch. 60, p. 390, n. 69.
9. Kātib Çelebi, *Tuhfetü'l-kibār fi esfāri'l-bihār*, Darü't Tıbaati'l Mamureti's Su, (İstanbul, 1141/1729), p. 93.
10. Marchesa de Pidal y Míguel Salvá (eds.), *Colección de documentos inéditos para la historia de España*, 112 vols. (Madrid, 1842–95), vol. 3, p. 15, letter of Don Juan to García de Toledo. The earlier part of the third volume of the *Colección de documentos inéditos* is taken up with the correspondence between Don Juan and Don García de Toledo, in which the former asks information and advice in respect to the best mode of conducting the forthcoming war.
11. Unlike its great rival Venice, Genoa never had its own state fleet. The participation in the crusades, the colonisation in the eastern Mediterranean and the Black Sea and the wars against Pisa and Venice, were always carried out with ships placed at the Republic's disposal by private citizens remunerated by hire or profit sharing. In 1559, however, the Republic did fit out a little squadron of state galleys (at first four ships) in order to oppose the North African piracy along the Ligurian and Corsican coasts and to escort the silver shipments coming from Spain as reimbursements for the loans of the Genoese financiers to the Spanish Habsburg crown (Lo Basso 2004: 206–07).
12. I will make no apologies for referring to a ship by the feminine third singular personal pronoun, despite current trends to do otherwise. Mariners and marines of the seven seas are like men produced by one single thing, born from the belly of one woman, one mother, one goddess: the ship. She gives her 'children', security and sustenance.
13. Corfu had originally fallen to Venice during the carving-up of the Byzantine empire following the Fourth Crusade. It was, however, soon lost to the Kingdom of Naples and had to be purchased back in 1386.

14. Marchesa de Pidal y Míguel Salvá (eds.), *Colección de documentos inéditos para la historia de España*, 112 vols. (Madrid, 1842–95), vol. 3, p. 18, letter of Don Juan to García de Toledo, 30 August 1571.
15. Ibid. 3.20, letter of Don Juan to García de Toledo, 29 September 1571.
16. Ibid. 3.365, Orta Relacion.
17. The *provveditore generale da mar* (Superintendent General of the Sea) was the supreme commander of the Venetian fleet in peacetime, but in wartime he was replaced by the *capitano generale da mar* (Captain General of the Sea) with more ample powers.
18. The silt of the Acheloüs, Greece's largest river, has extended the shoreline some three nautical miles to the south, turning the Ekhinadhes into hills a short distance inland from the coast, with Oxeia being the only isle left of the original archipelago. The Athenian soldier historian Thucydides describes clearly the silting of the river of his own day, the islands being "so close to the mouths of the Acheloüs that the powerful stream is constantly forming deposits agaianst them, and has already joined some of the islands to the continent, and seems likely in no long while to do the same with the rest" (2.102.3 Strassler). For the possible coastline of 1571, see Throckmorton-Edgerton-Yalouris 1973.
19. Marchesa de Pidal y Míguel Salvá (eds.), *Colección de documentos inéditos para la historia de España*, 112 vols. (Madrid, 1842–95), vol. 11, p. 368, Relacion escrita por Fr' Miguel Servia, confesor de Don Juan.
20. Capponi 2007 [2006]: 265–6.
21. Fra' Bartolemeo dal Pozzo, *Historia della sacra religione militare di S. Giovanni Gerosolimitano detta di Malte*, 2 vols. (Verona, 1703–15), vol. 1, p. 21.
22. Marchesa de Pidal y Míguel Salvá (eds.), *Colección de documentos inéditos para la historia de España*, 112 vols. (Madrid, 1842–95), vol. 3, pp. 242, 246, Ortas Relaciones.

## Chapter 16: Battle Arrays

1. Giacomo Bosio, *Historia della sacra religione e illusirissima militia di San Giovanni Gerosolimitano* [Venezia, 1695], vol. 3, p. 353.
2. Guilmartin 2003 [1974]: 241.
3. Archivo di Stato di Venezia, *opusculo* 3000, report of Sebastiano Veniero to the doge (29 December 1572). Also, MS 1693, *Documentos de Lepanto*, dto. 14, fols. 73ff., a detailed listing of the total Spanish contribution to the Holy League fleet.
4. MS 1693, *Documentos de Lepanto*, dto. 14, fol. 73.
5. Marchesa de Pidal y Míguel Salvá (eds.), *Colección de documentos inéditos para la historia de España*, 112 vols. (Madrid, 1842–95), vol. 3, pp. 8–10, 11–15.
6. Ibid. 3.270, manuscript of Luis del Marmol. The Qur'ānic verse on the battle flag read: "Allah rewards believers who perform good works for him and His prophet Mohammed". This verse is from Sūrah 48 al-Fath (Victory, Triumph), āyah 29. Taken as a trophy, the flag hung near the tomb of Saint Pius V in Santa Maria Maggiore. In 1965 pope Paul VI made a gesture of goodwill by returning it to the Turks. The flag now hangs in İstanbul Deniz Müzesi, the Istanbul Naval Museum in Beşiktaş.
7. Several vessels among the fleet of the Holy League bore the same name. Whilst this is not unheard of among ships belonging to different nationalities, some of the said ships belonged to the same nation. These did not seem to be of great importance to Christian commanders at that time. In order to avoid confusion, those vessels bearing the same name were suffixed with ordinal number according to nationality (i.e. *Cristo* of Candia (I), *Cristo* of Candia (II); *Cristo* of Venice (I), *Cristo* of Venice (II), etc.). In Italian use, various flagships were called by the rank of their commander. A *reale* ('royal') was personally commanded by a king or his agent; a *capitana* ('captainess', viz. flagship) by a *capitano*

*generale*; a *padrona* ('master', viz. deputy flagship) by a *padrone*. A *capitana* (pl. *capitane*) and a *padrona* (pl. *padrone*) were usually but not invariably a *bastarda* and a *lanterna* (Venetian *fanò*). Finally, the symbol †denotes the commander was killed in action. For a full list of the Christian fleet at Lepanto, with the name of each vessel, its commander and its battle position, see National Library of Malta, Valletta, MS 53 (iv), fols. 313–19.

8. The brothers were kinsmen of the Marc'Antonio Bragadin who had been tortured and killed by the Ottoman Turks at Famagusta. They had vowed to revenge to his hideous death.

9. One of the galleys leased by Cosimo I de' Medici to Pius V, *la Grifona* was a vessel that had been given to the grand duke by Uglino Grifoni, a rich and powerful Medici partisan.

10. It is possible that this vessel is actually the Venetian galley *Umo Armato* of Retimo, captained by Andrea Calergi, signore di Candia.

11. Receiving two bullets in the throat, Angelo Biffoli is usually included among the fallen. However, he was certainly still alive and kicking in 1576 (Archivo di Stato di Firenze, *Mediceo del Principato*, registro 695, fol. 341r: Piero Tiragallo to Francesco I de' Medici, 12 May 1576).

12. This was the galley that Cervantes served on.

13. Marino Contarini was the nephew of the *provveditore generale* Agostino Barbarigo.

14. Contemporary Ottoman records referred to individual galleys by the name of their commander rather than by the name of the ship itself. Therefore, unlike the Christian fleet, no individual ship names are known or, at least, have been unearthed. Rather, the relevant galley was listed by its commander, and then grouped according to its squadron. For the sake of simplicity, the term *lanterna* has been used to refer to large flagship galleys and *Sultana* for the fleet flagship of Müezzinzāde Ali Paşa.

15. The son of Hayreddin Barbarossa.

16. Amuret Dragut Re'īs was the son of the celebrated corsair Turgut Re'īs, who met his death at the siege of Malta in 1565.

17. In addition, sixty-four *fuste* were attached to the reserve. These small oared vessels were used to transfer reinforcements from one portion of the line to the other. It is unclear whether they were concentrated behind the centre or not, but it is likely they were apportioned throughout the fleet, supporting the galleys of the left and right as well as the centre.

18. The Ottoman reserve included also 18 *fuste*.

## Chapter 17: Sunday Seventh

1. Giovanni Baptista Arcucci, *Victoria Naupactiaca*, l. 235, apud Wright-Spence-Lemons 2014: 209.

2. Giovanni Pietro Contarini, *Historia delle cose successe dal principio della guerra mossa da Selim Ottomano a' Venetiani, fino al di della gran giornata vittoriosa contra Turchi* (Venezia, 1572), fols. 5v – 52v.

3. Ibid. fol. 51v.

4. Ferrante Caracciolo, *I commentarii della guerre fatte co' turchi da D. Giouanni d'Austria, dopo che venne in Italia, scritti da Ferrante Caracciolo conte di Biccari* (Firenze, 1581), p. 38.

5. Onorato Caetani e Girolamo Diedo, *La battaglia di Lepanto, 1571* (Palermo, 1995), p. 135.

6. This two-handed sword, some 1.8 metres in length, can be seen on display in the Museo Naval, Madrid.

7. Guilmartin 2003 [1974]: 40–4.

8. Archivo General de Simancas, *Secretería de Estado*, leg. 1423, fol. 60, letter of Gianandrea Doria to Philip II, 2 February 1591.

9. It has been calculated that the galleys of Genoa were involved in some 338 missions between the years 1559 and 1607. Of these 250 were for the transport of personnel, diplomats and eminent persons. Ninety-one times they rode out to save damaged or endangered vessels; only eight-eight sailings had a pronounced military character, including the transport of troops (Kirk 2005: 61–2). In other words, Genoa's oared warships were mainly employed for the ferrying of men, *matériel* and provisions.

10. Seventy years later the Ottoman polymath Kātib Çelebi would write that Uluç Ali had personally decapitated Giustiniani (*Tuhfetü'l-kibār fi esfāri'l-bihār*, Darü't Tıbaati'l Mamureti's Su, [İstanbul, 1141/1729], p. 43). The eyewitness Giovanni Pietro Contarini, on the contrary, writes that he was "so badly wounded that he was all but killed" (*Historia delle cose successe dal principio della guerra mossa da Selim Ottomano a' Venetiani, fino al di della gran giornata vittoriosa contra Turchi* [Venezia, 1572], fol. 53v).

11. Miguel de Cervantes, *Don Quixote*, part 1, ch. 39, p. 337 Grossman.

12. National Library of Malta, Valletta, MS 53 (iv), fol. 328v.

13. And thus was fulfilled the prophecy that in this year the Medici would lose Florence.

14. Pantero Pantera, *L'Armata navale* (Roma, 1614), bk. 1, p. 327.

15. Giovanni Pietro Contarini, *Historia delle cose successe dal principio della guerra mossa da Selim Ottomano a' Venetiani, fino al di della gran giornata vittoriosa contra Turchi* (Venezia, 1572), fols. 53v – 54v.

16. Niccolò Machiavelli, *il Principe*, ch. 25, p. 1 17 Marriott. For Renaissance historians like Machiavelli and his good friend Francesco Guicciardini history was a process controlled by Fortuna, and therefore beyond human control. So it goes, as 'America's Voltaire' Kurt Vonnegut said not once but many times.

17. Quotation from the eyewitness account of Girolamo Diedo in Lesure 1972: 142.

18. Archivo General de Simancas, *Colección Don Juan Sanz de Barutell*, Articulo 4, vol. 2, dto. 317, fols. 406–07.

19. Capponi 2007 [2006]: 288.

20. The number is mentioned in communiqués detailing the distribution of booty among the victors (ibid. 145).

21. The order of the Council of Ten, *consiglio dei dieci*, to execute all prisoners with naval experience – *oficiales*, 'experts', as they are called – is printed in Lesure 1972: 151–2.

22. *Relazioni degli Ambasciatori Veneti al Senato*, series III, vol. I.

23. Capponi 2007 [2006]: 289.

24. Giovanni Pietro Contarini, *Historia delle cose successe dal principio della guerra mossa da Selim Ottomano a' Venetiani, fino al di della gran giornata vittoriosa contra Turchi* (Venezia, 1572), fols. 54r – 56 r.

25. A Spanish document drawn up in May 1571 credits the *Tercio de Sicilia* with 2,125 men (Gárate Córdoba 1971: 112–13).

26. Capponi 2007 [2006]: 289–90.

27. Fra' Bartolemeo dal Pozzo, *Historia della sacra religione militare di S. Giovanni Gerosolimitano detta di Malte*, 2 vols. (Verona, 1703–15), vol. 1, p. 12.

### Chapter 18: Barren Victory

1. *Annali*, s.a. 1571, 267v-268. On firepower, see Morin 1975.

2. Archivo di Stato di Venezia Secreta – *serie diverse* – *Annali*, s.a. 1571, 'Adi, 8, Ottobre Seriemme Franc. o Duodo capitano delle galee grosse'.

3. Morin 1975: 52.

4. Imber 1996.

5. Ernest Charrière, *Négociations de la France dans le Levant*, 4 vols. (Paris, 1848–60), vol. 3, pp. 271–3.

**Chapter 19: War Stories**

1. Richard Knolles, *The generall historie of the Turkes, from the first beginning of that nation to the rising of the Othoman familie*, 3 vols. (London, 1687–1700 [7th edn.]), vol. 1, p. 599.
2. *Documentos inéditos relativos á la Batalla de Lepanto*, p. 26, letter of Don Juan to Philip II, 10 October 1571.
3. The Irish soldier writer Philip O'Sullivan Beare (†1660), alludes to the rumour and opinion that Stucley "by some was said to be an illegitimate son of Henry VIII, King of England; by others, son of an English Knight and an Irish lady; by others, Irish by both parents, who either from anger at the English, or from religious motives, or desiring war and revolution in hopes of gain, or aspiring to reign, being perhaps a man of royal blood, was supplicating in the name of the Irish for succour against the English" (*Historiae Catholicae Iberniae Compendium* [Madrid, 1621], bk. 4, ch. 15, p. 112).
4. Tazón 2003: 222–35.
5. In the south choir aisle of Westminster Abbey is a wall tablet of black alabaster, bearing his shield of arms, for Sir Richard Bingham. The inscription it carries lists his many and varied soldierly exploits, including "In the Isle of Candy [Crete] under the Venetians, At Cabo Chrio [?] and the famous battaile of Lepanto against the Turks ...".
6. Three decades later, when Sir Walter Raleigh had fallen from royal favour, his involvement with this massacre was brought against him as a criminal charge in one of his trials. Raleigh argued that as a mere captain he was obliged to obey the commands of his superior officer (viz. Lord Arthur Grey de Wilton) but he was unable to exonerate himself.
7. Thomas Wright (ed.), *Queen Elizabeth and Her Times: A Series of Original Letters*, 2 vols. (London, 1838), vol. 2, pp. 120–2.
8. Astrana Marín 1948–58: II, 336.
9. De la Gravière 1888: 186–7.
10. Paul M. Krieg, *Die Schweizergarde in Rom* (Luzern, 1960), p. 104, who quotes from Segesser's dispatches.
11. Pantero Pantera, *L'Armata navale* (Roma, 1614), bk. 1, p. 84.
12. Quotation from the eyewitness account of Girolamo Diedo (*La Battaglia di Lepanto descritta da Girolamo Diedo*) in Lesure 1972: 141.
13. William Clowes, *A Prooved Practice for all young Chirugians concerning Burnings with Gunpowder, and Woundes made with Gunshot, Sword, Halbard, Pike, Launce, or such other* (London, 1591), pp. 40–3, 119–22.
14. Richard Hawkins, *Observations of Sir Richard Hawkins, Knight, in his Voyage into the South Sea Anno Domini 1593* (London, 1622), pp. 16–17.
15. Fr' Agustín Farfán, *Tractado breve de anothomia y chirugia y de algunas enfer medades, que mas comunmente suelen haver en esta Nueva España* (México City, 1579).
16. Quoted in Capponi 2007 [2006]: 289.
17. Weiss 2011: 77–8.
18. Bono 1999: 255.
19. Scetti 2004: 4.
20. William Shakespeare, *The Tragedy of Othello*, 5.2.7.
21. Ibid. 5.2.250.
22. Scetti 2004: 106.
23. Ibid. 122.
24. Sebastiano Pauli, *Codice Diplomantico del Sacro Militare Ordine Gerosolimitano, oggi di Malta* (Lucca, 1737), vol. 2, p. 240.
25. Wiel 1910: 256.

**Chapter 20: Mary's Victory**

1. The naval crown, *corona navalis*, was made of gold and awarded to the first man to board an enemy vessel; the Captive had done just this, only to be marooned alone when the enemy crew disengaged from his galley.
2. Miguel de Cervantes, *Don Quixote*, part 1, ch. 39, p. 337 Grossman.
3. Braudel 1973 [1966]: II, 1103.
4. Ibid. 1103–05.
5. Ibid. 1027–1106.
6. The name derives from the Latin *rosarium* (literally, 'rose garden'), which in Catholic Europe had also come to signify a collection of devotional texts ('roses') offered in praise and petition to Jesus Christ and/or the Virgin Mary. In the 16th century, the rosary was developed to its present form – with the three sets of five mysteries; joyful, sorrowful and glorious. In 2002, John Paul II added a fourth set of five mysteries, the Mysteries of Light to this devotion. Muslims, especially Sūfīs, use rosaries to tell the ninety-nine attributes of God, or certain expressions from the Qur'ān, such as God is great, Praise be to God, etc. The threefold division of the rosary corresponds to the usual division of the ninety-nine names, i.e. referring to God's power, His wisdom, and His Mercy. On reaching the final, elongated bead, the worshipper says the name of God, Allah. In the Qur'ān, the holy name of the Blessed Virgin Mary is mentioned no less than thirty times. No other woman's name is even mentioned, not even that of Muhammad's beloved daughter Fātima. Remember, when his daughter died, Muhammad expressed in his grief: "She has the highest place in heaven after the Virgin Mary." Among men, only Abraham, Moses, and Noah are mentioned more times than Mary, who is described as "Virgin, ever Virgin". Make no mistake about it; there is a very special relationship between the Blessed Virgin Mary and the Muslims.
7. King James I, *Lepanto*, stanza 1, ll. 10–11.
8. One of the serious divisions between the Protestants and Catholics at that time was the Protestant belief that individuals should study the Bible directly as the word of God; Catholics believed it was the rôle of the Roman Catholic Church to interpret the truth for the people.
9. Richard Knolles, *The generall historie of the Turkes, from the first beginning of that nation to the rising of the Othoman familie*, 3 vols. (London, 1687–1700 [7th edn.]), vol. 1, p. 598.
10. It is important to note that Shakespeare never specifically mentions Famagusta, only 'A Seaport in Cyprus' (*The Tragedy of Othello*, 2.1.0).
11. For the argument whether Othello was a Muslim or Christian Moor, see especially Matar 2005: 29–32.
12. Richard Knolles, *The generall historie of the Turkes, from the first beginning of that nation to the rising of the Othoman familie*, 3 vols. (London, 1687–1700 [7th edn.]), vol. 1, p. 885.
13. Revelations 12:1 NIV.
14. Warner 1976: 236–57.
15. Pius V had originally declared 7 October to be the feast of Our Lady of Victory (Νικἠ, Poliziano would have said); it was changed by Pius' less bellicose successor, Gregory XIII (r. 1572–85), to the feast of Our Lady of the Rosary, and extended throughout the Universal Church by Clement XI (r. 1700–21) in 1716 (who canonised Pius V in 1712).
16 Quoted in C. Glasse, *The Concise Encyclopedia of Islam* (London, 2008), p. 130.

**Lepanto Finale**

1. This decree is cited in İnalcık 1974: 190–1.
2. Setton 1986: 1091.

3. Voltaire, *Essai sur l'histoire générale et sur les mœurs et l'esprite des nations, dupuis Charlemagne jusqu' à nos jours* (Paris, 1756), ch. 160.
4. Hale 1974.
5. The conversation is quoted by I.H. Uzunçarşılı, *Osmānlı Tarihi, II. Selim'ın Tahta Çıkışından 1699 Karlofça Andlas,masına Kadar* (Ankara, 1983), vol. III, part I.
6. Miguel de Cervantes, *Don Quixote*, part 1, ch. 40, p. 342 Grossman.
7. Sliwa 1999: 225–6. Likewise, in the same year, Cervantes' Captive says "I found myself at Navarino" (*Don Quixote*, part 1, ch. 39, p. 337 Grossman).
8. Miguel de Cervantes, *Don Quixote*, part 1, ch. 39, p. 339 Grossman.
9. Op. cit.
10. Braudel 1973 [1966]: II, 860.
11. Ibid. II, 861.
12. Ibid. II, 862.
13. Giovanni Botero, *Reason of State*, trans. D. and P. Waley (London, 1956), p. 12.

**Appendix I**

1. There is a long-standing argument about whether war is an art or a science. Clausewitz (1780–1831) considers it to be one of the social sciences and that more than anything it "closely resembles a game of cards" (*Vom Krieg*, bk. 1, ch. 1, sec. 21 Howard and Paret). In cards, probability is the key, not algebra. By contrast, Baron de Jomini (1779–1869) considers "war, far from being an exact science, is a terrible and impassioned drama … dependent for its results upon a number of moral and physical complications' (*Précis de l'Art de la Guerre, 2ème* annexe Messenger). This is underlined by the fact that there are no universally agreed principles of war.
2. Quoted in Parker 1996A: 10.
3. Guicciardini was, unfortunately, prone to the occasional exaggeration. One instance will suffice to explain this. His portrayal of bloodless campaigns of Italy's *condottieri* still holds sway among the *literati*. In the view of that remarkable historian, Italians were content for many years with the images of war, but not its substance, and at the critical moment they lacked the resolve to confront the *furore francese*. His portrayal of mercenary pseudo-war and bellicose posturing, 'explains' the collapse of Italian armies when confronted with the French invasion of 1494. See Francesco Guicciardini, *Storia d'Italia*, in Vittorio de Caprariis (ed.), *Opere* (Milano, 1961), p. 434.
4. Niccolò Machiavelli, *Discorsi*, 2.17.
5. Niccolò Machiavelli, *il Principe*, ch. 12, p. 56 Marriott.
6. At some point in 1482, Leonardo da Vinci wrote a letter to Ludovico Maria Sforza *il Moro* (1452–1508), the then *de facto* ruler of Milan (1480–1500) – the legitimate ruler being under lock and key – boasting of his prowess as a military engineer, including such lines as "Should the need arise, I will make cannon, mortar and light ordnance of very beautiful and functional design that are quite out of the ordinary." His abilities as a painter came bottom of the epistle in what appears to be a throwaway line. A decade later, it was Sforza who commissioned him to paint *The Last Supper* for the convent of Santa Maria delle Grazie. Leonardo was unusual in being not just a jack of all trades, but master of many. Of relevance here is the fact that he published a treatise on gunnery (Codex Atlanticus, Biblioteca Ambrosiana, Milano).
7. Though born in Caprese, a small town near Arezzo, Tuscany, several months after his birth Michelangelo's family returned to Florence, where he was raised.
8. Quoted in Gustave Clausse, *Les San Gallo: architectes, peintres, sculpteurs, medailleurs XVe et XVIe siècles, vol. 2, Antonio da san Gallo le Jeune* (Paris, 1901), p. 351.

## Appendix II
1. Quoted in Capponi 2007 [2006]: 166.
2. Reprinted in Shostak-Benson 2007: 82–5.

## Appendix III
1. Thucydides 1.103.1–3.
2. Ibid. 2.69.1.
3. Ibid. 2.90.4–6.
4. Ibid. 2.91.4.
5. Marin Sanudo is a rich source for the activities of Kemāl Re'īs (1440–1511). He is the first 'Turk' mentioned in *I diarii*. Sanudo's first reports concern Bāyezīd's recruitment of Kemāl Reis in 1496, referring to him as "*Camali turcho corsaro*". Since Sanudo refers to Bāyezīd as "*Signor turcho*" it is not surprising that he refers to Kemāl as a Turk (*I diarii* [Venezia, 1897], vol. 1, col. 10. The corsair's family actually originated from Karaman in Anatolia, and it was not until 1474 that final resistance in Karaman was virtually eliminated and its lands and inhabitants became definitively part of the possessions of the Ottoman sultan.
6. Bāyezīd publicly rewarded the achievements of Kemāl Re'īs and his nephew Pìrì after the victory at Navarino in 1501; he invited them to a meeting of the imperial divan where Kemāl kissed the sultan's hand and received 3,000 *akçes* (pieces of silver) and a sable robe of honour (Pìrì Re'īs, *Kitab-ı Bahriye* [İstanbul, 1988], 2.660).
7. Letter to the Hon. Douglas Kinnaird (?), Mesolóngi, 21 February 1824 (quoted in R.G. Howarth, *The Letters of George Gordon, 6th Lord Byron* [London: J.M. Dent & Son, 1933], p. 452).
8. Letter to the Hon. Douglas Kinnaird, Mesolóngi, 30 March 1824 (quoted in R.G. Howarth, *The Letters of George Gordon, 6th Lord Byron* [London: J.M. Dent & Son, 1933], p. 460).
9. Letter to Charles Hancock, Mesolóngi, 5 February 1824 (quoted in R.G. Howarth, *The Letters of George Gordon, 6th Lord Byron* [London: J.M. Dent & Son, 1933], p. 448).
10. Finlay 1861: 24. Note here Finlay puts their number at 300 men, whereas Stephen Minta says Byron "took five hundred into his pay, agreeing to maintain them for a year" (1998: 254). The eyewitness testimony of Finlay is to be preferred.
11. Finlay 1861: 24–5.
12. This phrase is one of Napoléon's inventions. He once said that "*du sublime au ridicule, il n'y a qu'un pas* [there is only one step]" (*Maximes de guerre et pensées de Napoléon 1er*, 382).
13. The poem is ostensibly a fictionalised Grand Tour through mainland Europe, through Spain and Portugal, Greece, Italy, Switzerland and Belgium. Each location provides Byron with the opportunity to deliver, through his eponymous hero, political opinions and social comment. The sombre poem was immediately and wildly popular: on the day after the publication of the first two cantos (20 March 1812), the poet later wrote, "I awoke one morning, and found myself famous" (quoted in Thomas Moore, *Letters and Journals of Lord Byron: with Notices of his Life* [London: John Murray, 1830], vol. 1, ch. 14).
14. Byron, *Childe Harold's Pilgrimage*, III xvii 1.
15. Ibid. III xxxviii 8–9.
16. Ibid. III xvii 9.
17. Finlay 1861: 22.
18. Quoted in R.G. Howarth, *The Letters of George Gordon, 6th Lord Byron* (London: J.M. Dent & Son, 1933), Introduction, p. vii.

19. On 27 April 1825 Reşid Mehmed Paşa (1780–1836) of Ioannina appeared before the walls of Mesolóngi. His force then consisted of 6,000 men and three guns, while the defence consisted of 4,000 soldiers and armed peasants, and forty-eight guns and four mortars (Finlay 1861: 85). At the beginning of June, the besiegers obtained reinforcements from Patras, which increased their artillery to eight guns and four mortars (ibid. 86). Hampered by vigorous sorties by land and sea and by a lack of supplies, Reşid Paşa could make no headway for six months. Then İbrāhīm Paşa (1789–1848) of Egypt, with 10,000 Egyptians, advanced to his aid from the Peloponnese. After fluctuating struggles for the small islands dotting the shallow lagoon, the Ottomans closed round the town. At the end of their resources after twelve months of siege, almost the whole population determined to break out. Their attempt (ἡ ἔξοδος/the *Exodos*) was made on the night of 22/23 April 1826. Though they managed to get clear of the besieged town, they were frustrated by the treachery of a deserter, who had forewarned the Ottomans. The fugitives, imagining themselves safe, were ambushed by a thousand Albanians on the slopes of Mount Zygos. Out of 9,000 who left Mesolóngi – combatants and civilians – only about 2,000 made good their escape to the town of Salona (modern Amphissa), near Delphi (Finlay 1861: 110). Meanwhile those who had stayed behind fired their powder magazines, overwhelming themselves and their enemies in a common destruction. In 1829 the Ottomans surrendered Mesolóngi without firing a shot.

20. The statement comes from her after their first meeting, when the publication of *Childe Harold's Pilgrimage* (1812) made Byron the literary and social lion of London at the age of twenty-four. However, the married Lady Caroline was notoriously worse than he on all three accounts, and when she threw herself at Byron, her irrationality and sexual excesses so appalled him that he terminated the affair after six months. Not that he was a saint. It was his one sincere attachment (1813–16), to his half-sister Augusta Leigh (who seemingly bore him a daughter), which led to his own downfall in London society.

21. Byron, *Childe Harold's Pilgrimage*, II lxxiii 1–2

22. Letter to Henry Drury, *Salsette* frigate, 3 May 1810 (quoted in R.G. Howarth, *The Letters of George Gordon, 6th Lord Byron* [London: J.M. Dent & Son, 1933], p. 31)

23. Metternich, though he described himself as a man of prose, not of poetry, enjoyed reading Byron's *Childe Harold's Pilgrimage*. He also recognized better than Castlereagh the importance of public opinion. "Public opinion", wrote Metternich in 1808, "is one of the most powerful weapons, which like religion, penetrates the most hidden corners where administrative measures lose their influence; to despise public opinion is like despising moral principles ... Public opinion requires a cult all its own ... Posterity will hardly believe that we regarded silence as an effective weapon in this, the century of words" (quoted in Henry Kissinger, *A World Restored: Metternich, Castlereagh and the Problems of Peace, 1812–1822* [Boston, MA: Houghton Mifflin Company, 1957], pp. 16–17).

24. Letter to Charles Hancock, Mesolóngi, 7 February 1824 (quoted in R.G. Howarth, *The Letters of George Gordon, 6th Lord Byron* [London: J.M. Dent & Son, 1933], p. 449).

25. H.G. Nicolson, *Byron: The Last Journey, April 1823–April 1824* (London, 1924).

# Bibliography

Abulafia, D., 2011. *The Great Sea: A Human History of the Mediterranean*. Oxford: Oxford University Press

Ágoston, G., 2005. *Guns for the Sultan: Military Power and the Weapons Industry in the Ottoman Empire*. Cambridge: Cambridge University Press

Ágoston, G., 2013. 'War winning-weapons? On the decisiveness of Ottoman firearms from the siege of Constantinople (1453) to the battle of Mohács (1526)'. *Journal of Turkish Studies* 39: 129–43

Ágoston, G., 2014. 'Firearms and military adaptation: the Ottomans and the European Military Revolution, 1450–1800'. *Journal of World History* 25/1: 85–124

Ágoston, G., 2017. *Firearms in the Ottoman Empire and the Military Revolution Debate*. Istanbul: İş Bankası Yayınları.

Aksan, V.H., 1998. 'Whatever happened to the janissaries? Mobilization for the 1768–1774 Russo-Ottoman War'. *War in History* 5/1: 23–36

Aksan, V.H., 2002. 'Ottoman military matters'. *Journal of Early Modern History* 6/1: 52–62

Alföldi, L.M., 1982. 'The battle of Mohács, 1526', in J.M. Bak and B.K. Király (eds.), *From Hunyadi to Rákóczi: War and Society in Late Medieval and Early Modern Hungary*. New York, NY: Brooklyn College Press, 189–202

Almond, I., 2011 [2009]. *Two Faiths, One Banner: When Muslims Marched with Christians across Europe's Battlegrounds*. Cambridge, MA: Harvard University Press

Ames, G.J. (trans. & ed.), 2009. "Em nome de Deus": *The Journal of the First Voyage of Vasco da Gama to India, 1497–1499*. Leiden: E.J. Brill

Anderson, R.C., 1952. *Naval wars in the Levant 1559–1853*. Liverpool: University of Liverpool Press

Angiolini, F., 1996. *I cavalieri e il principe: L'Ordine di Santo Stefano e la società Toscana in età moderna*. Firenze: Edifir

Arbel, B., 2017. 'Daily life on board Venetian ships: the evidence of Renaissance travelogues and diaries', in G. Ortalli e A. Sopracasa (eds.), *Rapporti Mediterranei, Pratiche Documentarie, Presenze Veneziane: Le Reti Economiche e Culturali (XIV – XVI Secolo)*. Venezia: Estratto, 183–219

Arfaioli, M., 2005. *The Black Bands of Giovanni: Infantry and Diplomacy during the Italian Wars (1526–1528)*. Pisa: Edizioni Plus – Pisa University Press

Arnold, T.F., 2001. *Renaissance at War*. London: Cassell & Co

Artemel, S. (trans.), 1988. *Ottoman Empire in Miniature*. İstanbul: İstanbul Research Center

Astrana Marín, L., 1948–58. *Vida ejemplar y heroica de Miguel de Cervantes Saavedra*. Madrid: Instituto Editorial Reus

Atherton, D., 2013. *La Trinidad Valencera*. Portstewart: Great Sea

Bamford, P.W., 1973. *Fighting Ships and Prisons: the Mediterranean Galleys of France in the Age of Louis XIV*. Minneapolis, MN: Minnesota University Press

Barkey, K., 2008. *Empire of Difference: the Ottomans in Comparative Perspective*. Cambridge: Cambridge University Press

Batty, C.G., 1999. 'Changes in the care of the battle casualty: lessons learned from the Falklands campaign'. *Military Medicine* 164/5: 336–40

Beaton, R., 2013. *Byron's War: Romantic Rebellion, Greek Revolution*. Cambridge: Cambridge University Press

Beeching, J., 1982. *The Galleys at Lepanto*. London: Hutchinson

Beltrame, C. and Ridella, R.G. (eds.) 2011. *Ships & Guns: the Sea Ordnance in Venice and Europe between the 15th and the 17th centuries*. Oxford: Oxbow Books

Berger, E. and Glyantsev, S., 2019. '*Wounded*: "They had no fever…" Ambroise Paré (1510–1590) and his method of gunshot wounds management'. *Science Museum Group Journal* 11: http://dx.doi.org/10.15180/191105

Bicheno, H., 2003. *Crescent and Cross: the Battle of Lepanto 1571*. London

Black, J., 1991. *A Military Revolution? Military Change and European Society, 1550–1800*. London: Macmillan

Bono, S., 1997. *Corsari nel Mediterraneo: cristiani e musulmani fra guerra, schiavitù e commercio*. Milano: Mondadori

Bono, S., 1999. *Schiavi Musulmani nell'Italia moderna: galeotti, vu' cumpra', domesticiv*. Perugia: Universitá degli Studii

Börekçi, G., 2006. 'A contribution to the military revolution debate: the Janissaries' use of volley fire during the Long Ottoman-Habsburg War of 1593–1606 and the problem of origins'. *Acta Orientalia Academiae Scientiarum Hungaricae* 59/4: 407–38

Braudel, F., 1966 (2nd edn. trans. S. Reynolds 1972 and 1973). *The Mediterranean and the Mediterranean World in the Age of Philip II*, 2 vols. New York, NY: Harper & Row Publishers

Browning, O., 1895. *The Age of the Condottieri: A Short History of Mediæval Italy from 1409–1530*. London: Methuen & Co.

Byles, J.M., 1996. 'Shakespeare and the Cyprus setting', in *Chypre hier et aujourd'hui entre Orient et Occident: Actes du colloque tenu à Nicosie, 1994, Université de Chypre et Université Lumière-Lyon* 2. Lyon: Maison de l'Orient et de la Méditerranée Jean Pouilloux, 155–60 (Travaux de la Maison de l'Orient méditerranéen 25)

Byles, J.M., 2000. '"The Cyprus wars": psychoanalysis and race in Shakespeare's *Othello*', in *Chypre et la Méditerranée orientale. Formations identitaires: perspectives historiques et enjeux contemporains. Actes du colloque tenu à Lyon, 1997, Université Lumière-Lyon 2, Université de Chypre*. Lyon: Maison de l'Orient et de la Méditerranée Jean Pouilloux, 139–46 (Travaux de la Maison de l'Orient méditerranéen 31)

Campbell, C., Chong, A., Howard, D. and Rogers, M., 2006. *Bellini and the East*. London: National Gallery Publications

Capasso, C., 1932. 'Barbarossa e Carlo V'. *Rivista Storica Italiana* 49: 169–209

Capponi, N., 2007 [2006]. *Victory of the West: the Great Christian-Muslim Clash at the Battle of Lepanto*. Cambridge, MA: Da Capo Press

Carr, J.C., 2016. *The Knights Hospitaller: A Military History of the Knights of St John*. Barnsley: Pen and Sword Military

de Castro Vicente, M., 2013 [1900]. *Vida del soldado español Miguel de Castro (1593–1611)*. Sevilla: Ediciones Espuela de Plata (Biblioteca de historia, serie *Vidas pinorescas*, 10)

Chase, K., 2003, *Firearms: A Global History to 1700*. Cambridge: Cambridge University Press

Clissola, S., 1977. *The Barbary Slaves*. London: Paul Eiek

Close, A., 2007. 'The liberation of the galley slaves and the ethos of *Don Quijote* Part I'. *Bulletin of the Cervantes Society of America* 27/1: 11–30

Cobham, C. D. (trans. & ed.), 1908. *Exerpta Cypria: Materials for a History of Cyprus*. Cambridge: Cambridge University Press

Cohen, R., 1920. *Knights of Malta, 1523 – 1798*. London: Macmillan & Co. (Society for Promoting Christian Knowledge)

Couto, D., Günergun, F. and Pia Pedani, M. (eds.), 2014. *Seapower, Technology and Trade: Studies in Turkish Maritime History*. İstanbul: Piri Reis University Publications/Denziler kitabevi

Concina, E., 1984. *L'Arsenale della Repubblica di Venezia*. Milano: Electa

Crowley, R., 2008. *Empires of the Sea: the Final Battle for the Mediterranean, 1521–1580*. London: Faber & Faber

Cruickshank, C.G., 1966 (2nd edn.). *Elizabeth's Army*. Oxford: Oxford University Press

Dakin, D., 1973. *The Greek Struggle for Independence*. Berkeley, CA: University of California Press

Davis, R.C., 2003. *Christian Slaves, Muslim Masters: White Slavery in the Mediterranean, the Barbary Coast, and Italy, 1500–1800*. Basingstoke: Palgrave Macmillan

Deleito y Piñuela, J.,1947 (2nd edn.). *El declinar de la monarquía española*. Madrid: Espasa-Calpe

DeVries, K.R., 1990. 'Military surgical practice and the advent of gunpowder weaponry'. *Canadian Bulletin of Medical History / Bulletin canadien d'histoire de la médecine* 7: 131–46

Dillenberger, J. (ed.), 1961. *Martin Luther: Selections from his Writings*. Chicago, IL: Quadrangle Books

Drane, E.H.T, 1858. *The Knights of St. John: With the Battle of Lepanto and the Siege of Vienna*. London: Burns & Lambert

Dursteler, E.R., 2001. 'The bailo in Constantinople: crisis and career in Venice's early modern diplomatic corps'. *Mediterranean Historical Review* 16/2: 1–30

Dursteler, E.R., 2006. *Venetians in Constantinople: Nation, Identity, and Coexistence in the Early Modern Mediterranean*, Baltimore, MD: Johns Hopkins University Press

Earle, P., 1970. *Corsairs of Malta and Barbary*. London: Sidgwick & Jackson

Eliav, J., 2013A. 'The gun and *corsia* of early modern Mediterranean galleys'. *Mariner's Mirror* 99/3: 262–74

Eliav, J., 2013B. 'Tactics of sixteenth-century galley artillery'. *Mariner's Mirror* 99/4: 398–409

Elliott, J.H., 2002 (rev. edn.). *Imperial Spain, 1469–1716*. London: Penguin Books

Ellis, H., 1905. 'The tercentenary of "Don Quixote"'. *The North American Review* 180: 670–80

Eltis, D., 1995. *The Military Revolution in Sixteenth-century Europe*. London: I.B. Tauris

Engel, C. E., 1968. *Histoire de l'Ordre de Malte*. Genève: Nagel

Eppicha, R., Pittasb, M. and Zubiaga de la Calc, M., 2018. 'Conservation of Martinengo Bastion, Famagusta, Cyprus'. *Defensive Architecture of the Mediterranean* 9: 1209–16

Ercole, G., 2010. *Galeazze: Un sogno veneziano*. Trento: Gruppo Modellistico Trentino

Fabris, A., 1997. 'Hasan "il Veneziano" tra Algeria e Costantinopoli'. *Quaderni di Studi Arabi* 5: 51–66

Faroqhi, S., 2006. *The Ottoman Empire and the World around it*. London: I.B. Tauris

Fernández Álvarez, M., 1979. *España y los españoles en los tiempos modernos*. Salamanca: Universidad de Salamanca

Ferreiro, L.D., 2010. 'The Aristotelian heritage in early naval architecture: from the Venice Arsenal to the French navy, 1500–1700'. *Theoria* 68: 227–41

Fields, N., 2007. *Ancient Greek Warship, 500–322 BC*. Oxford: Osprey Publishing (New Vanguard 132)

Fields, N., 2017. *God's City: Byzantine Constantinople*. Barnsley: Pen & Sword Books

Finkel, C.F., 1988. *The Administration of Warfare: the Ottoman Military Campaigns in Hungary, 1593–1606*. Vienna: Verband der wissenschaftlichen Gesellschaften Österreichs

Finkel, C.F., 2006. *Osman's Dream: the Story of the Ottoman Empire, 1300–1923*. New York, NY

Finlay, G., 1861. *History of the Greek Revolution*, vol. II. Edinburgh/London: William Blackwood and Sons

Forster, C.T. and Daniell, F.H.B. (eds.), 1881. *The Life and Letters of Ogier Ghislain de Busbecq, seigneur of Bousbecque, knight, Imperial ambassador*, 2 vols. London: Kegan, Paul & Co.

Forster, E.S. (ed.), 2005 [1927]. *The Turkish Letters of Ogier de Busbecq*. Baton Rouge, LO: Louisiana State University Press

France, J., 2015. *Hattin: Great Battle Series*. Oxford: Oxford University Press

Friedman, E.G., 1983. *Spanish Captives in North Africa in the Early Modern Age*. Madison, WI: University of Wisconsin Press

Friel, I., 2010. 'Guns, gales and God: Elizabeth I's "merchant navy"'. *History Today* 60/1: 45–51

Gárate Córdoba, J-M., 171. *Los tercios de España en la ocasión de Lepanto*. Madrid: Servico Histórico Militar

Garcés, M.A., 2002. *Cervantes in Algiers: A Captive's Tale*. Nashville, TN: Vanderbilt University Press

Glete, J., 2000. *Warfare at Sea, 1500–1600: Maritime Conflicts and the Transformation of Europe*. London: Routledge

Graf, T.P., 2017. *The Sultan's Renegades: Christian-European Converts to Islam and the Making of the Ottoman Elite, 1575–1610*. Oxford: Oxford University Press

Graham, W., 1972. *The Spanish Armadas*. London: Collins

Gravière, de la, J., 1888. *La guerre de Chypre et la bataille de Lépante*. Paris: Libraire Plon

Grima, J.F., 2001. 'The rowers on the Order's galleys (c. 1600–1650)'. *Melita Historica* 13/2: 113–26

Grima, J.F., 2018. 'Malta and the battle of Lepanto – October 7, 1571'. *Times of Malta*, 14 October 2018

Gross, S.D., 1861. *A Manual of Military Surgery: on Hints on the Emergencies of Field, Camp and Hospital Practice*. Philadelphia, PA: J.B. Lippincott & Co.

Guarnieri, G., 1960. *I Cavalieri di Santo Stefano nella storia della Marina Italiana (1562–1859)*. Pisa: Nistri-Lischi

Gugliemotti, A., 1862. *Marcantonio Colonna alla battaglia di Lepanto, 1570–1573*. Firenze: Felice Le Monnier

Guilmartin, J.F., Jr., 1981. 'The tactics of the battle of Lepanto clarified: the impact of social, economic, and political factors on sixteenth century galley warfare', in C.L. Symonds (ed.), *New Aspects of Naval History: Selected Papers Presented at the Fourth Naval History Symposium, United States Naval Academy 25–26 October 1979*. Annapolis, MD: Naval Institute Press, 41–65

Guilmartin, J.F., Jr., 1983. 'The guns of the *Santíssimo Sacramento*'. *Technology and Culture* 24/4: 559–600

Guilmartin, J.F., Jr., 1994. 'Guns and gunnery', in R.W. Unger (ed.), *Cogs, Caravels, and Galleons: the Sailing Ship 1000–1650*. London: Conway Maritime Press, 139–50

Guilmartin, J.F., Jr., 1997. 'The galley in combat'. *Quarterly Journal of Military History* 9/2: 20–1

Guilmartin, J.F., Jr., 2003 [1974]. *Gunpowder & Galleys: Changing Technology & Mediterranean Warfare at Sea in the 16th Century*. London: Conway Maritime Press

Guilmartin, J.F., Jr., 2007. 'The earliest shipboard gunpowder ordnance: an analysis of its technical parameters and tactical capabilities'. *The Journal of Military History* 71/3: 649–69

Gürkan, E.S., (MA thesis) 2006. *Ottoman corsairs in the western Mediterranean and their place in the Ottoman-Habsburg rivalry (1505–1535)* . Ankara: Bilkent University

Gürkan, E.S., 2010. 'The centre and the frontier: Ottoman cooperation with the North African corsairs in the sixteenth century'. *Turkish Historical Review* 1: 125–63

Gürkan, E.S., 2014. 'My money or your life: Habsburg hunt for Uluç Ali'. *Historia Moderna* 36: 121–45

Gürkan, E.S., 2016. 'His bailo's kapudan: conversion, tangled loyalties and Hasan *Veneziano* between Istanbul and Venice (1588–1591)'. *Osmanlı Araştırmaları / Journal of Ottoman Studies* 277–319

Gürkan, E.S., 2018. *Sultanın Korsanları: Osmanlı Akdenizi'nde Gazâ, Yağma ve Esaret 1500– 1700*. İstanbul: Kronik Kitap

Gush, G., 1983 [1982] (2nd edn.). *Renaissance Armies, 1480–1650*. Cambridge: Patrick Stephens

Guthrie, H.C., Clasper, J.C., Kay, A.R. and Parker, P.J., 2011. 'Initial extremity war wound debridement: a multidisciplinary consensus'. *Journal of the Royal Army Medical Corps* 157/2: http://dx.doi.org/10.1136/jramc-157-02-09

Guyton, A.C., 1981 (6th edn.). *Textbook of Medical Physiology*. Philadelphia, PA: W.B. Saunders Co.

Hale, J.R., 1974. 'From peacetime establishment to fighting machine: the Venetian army and the war of Cyprus and Lepanto' in G. Benzoni (ed.), *Il Mediterraneo Nella Seconda Meta Del'500 Alla Luce Di Lepanto*. Firenze: Leo S. Olschki Editore, 163–84

Hale, J.R., 1975. 'Men and weapons: the fighting potential of sixteenth-century Venetian galleys', in B. Bond and I. Roy (eds.), *War and Society: A Yearbook of Military History*. London: Croom Helm, 1–23

Hale, J.R., 1983. *Renaissance War Studies*. London: Hambledon Press

Hale, J.R., 1998 [1985]. *War and Society in Renaissance Europe, 1450–1620*. Stroud: Sutton Publishing

Hall, B.S., 1997. *Gunpowder, Technology and Tactics: Weapons and Warfare in Renaissance Europe*. Baltimore, MD: Johns Hopkins University Press

Hamilton Currey, E., 1910. *Sea-wolves of the Mediterranean the Grand Period of Moslem Corsairs*. London: John Murray

Hanlon, G., 1998. *The Twilight of a Military Tradition: Italian Aristocrats and European Conflicts, 1560–1800*. London: University College Press

Hanß, S., 2017. *Lepanto als Ereignis. Dezentrierende Geschichte(n) der Seschlacht von Lepanto (1571)*. Göttingen: V&R Unipress (Berliner Mittelalter- und Frühneuzeitforschung 21)

Harari, Y.N., 2004. *Renaissance Military Memoirs: War, History, and Identity, 1450–1600*. Woodbridge: The Boydell Press (Warfare in History)

Heers, J., 2001. *Barbaresques: La course et la guerre en Méditerranée, XIV–XVI siècle*. Paris: Editions Perrin

Hémardinquer, J.J., 1963. 'Vie matérielle et comportements biologiques, bulletin no. 11: A propos de l'alimentation des marins, sur les galères de Toscane au XVIᵉ siècle'. *Annales: Economies, Sociétes, Civilisations*: 1141–9

Herwaarden, J., van, 2012. 'The emperor Charles V as Santiago Matamoros'. *Peregrinations: Journal of Medieval Art and Architecture* 3/3: 83–106

Hess, A.C., 1972. 'The battle of Lepanto and its place in Mediterranean history'. *Past & Present* 57/1: 53–73

Hess, A.C., 1978. *The Forgotten Frontier: A History of the Sixteenth Century Ibero-African Frontier*. Chicago, IL: University of Chicago Press

Hildred, A., 2005. 'The *Mary Rose*: a tale of two centuries', in B; Steele B and T. Darland (eds.), *The Heirs of Archimedes: Science and the Art of War through the Age of Enlightenment*. Cambridge, MA: Massachusetts Institute of Technology Press, 137–80

Hillenbrand, C., 1999. *The Crusades: Islamic Perspectives*. Edinburgh: Edinburgh University Press

Howarth, D., 1982 [1981]. *The Voyage of the Armada: the Spanish Story*. London: Penguin Books

Hull, M.D., 2011. 'Lepanto – Triumph of Faith'. *Latin Mass Magazine* 19/1:10–15

Imber, C., 1996. 'The reconstruction of the Ottoman fleet after the battle of Lepanto, 1571– 1572', in C. Imber (ed.), *Studies in Ottoman History and Law*. İstanbul: Isis Press, 85–101

Imber, C., 2006. *The Crusade of Varna, 1443–45*. Aldershot: Ashgate Publishing (Crusader Texts in Translation 14)

Imber, C., 2009 (2nd edn.). *The Ottoman Empire, 1300–1650: the Structure of Power*. New York, NY: Palgrave Macmillan

İnalcık, H., 1973 (trans. N. Itzkowitz and C. Imber). *The Ottoman Empire: the Classical Age, 1300–1600*. London: Weidenfeld and Nicolson

İnalcık, H., 1974: 'Lepanto in the Ottoman documents', in G. Benzoni (ed.), *Il Mediterraneo nella seconda metà del '500 alla luce di Lepanto*. Firenze: Leo S. Olschki, 185–92

İnalcık, H., 1994. *An Economic and Social History of the Ottoman Empire*. Cambridge: Cambridge University Press

Isom-Verhaaren, C., 2011. *Allies with the Infidel: the Ottoman and French Alliance in the Sixteenth Century*. London: I.B. Tauris

Isom-Verhaaren, C., 2014. 'Was there room in Rum for corsairs?: Who was an Ottoman in the naval forces of the Ottoman empire in the 15th and 16th centuries?' *Osmanlı Araştırmaları / Journal of Ottoman Studies* 44: 235–64

Jackson, D.S., 1983. 'Sepsis of soft tissue limb wounds in soldiers injured during the Falklands campaign 1982'. *Journal of the Royal Army Medical Corps* 130: 97–9

Jackson, D.S., Batty, C.G., Ryan, J.M. and McGregor, W.S.P., 1983. 'The Falklands war: army field surgical experience'. *Annals of the Royal College of Surgeons* 65/5: 281–5

Jennings, J.C., 1993. *Christians and Muslims in Ottoman Cyprus and the Mediterranean World, 1571–1640*. New York, NY: New York University Press

Jones, E., 1968. '"Othello", "Lepanto", and the Cyprus Wars'. *Shakespeare Survey* 21: 47–52

Kafadar, C., 1995. *Between Two Worlds: the Construction of the Ottoman State*. Berkeley, CA: University of California Press

Káldy-Nagy, Gy., 1977. 'The first centuries of Ottoman military organization'. *Acta Orientalia Academiae Scientiarum Hungarica* 31/2: 147–83

Kamen, H., 2005 (2nd edn.). *Golden Age Spain*. Basingstoke: Palgrave Macmillan (Studies in European History)

Karataş, A., 2011. 'Bir İnebahtı Gâzisinin Esâret Hâtıraları: Sergüzeştnâme-i Hindî Mahmûd'. *Osmanlı Araştırmaları / Journal of Ottoman Studies* 37: 17–48

Kelly, J., 2004. *Gunpowder: A History of the Explosive that Changed the World*. London: Atlantic Books

Kirk, T.A., 2005. *Genoa and the Sea. Policy and Power in an Early Modern Maritime Republic, 1559–1684*, Baltimore, MD: Johns Hopkins University Press

Konstam, R.A., 1988. '16th century naval tactics and gunnery'. *The International Journal of Nautical Archaeology* 17/1: 17–23

Konstam, R.A., 2002. *Renaissance War Galley, 1470–1590*. Oxford: Osprey Publishing (New Vanguard 62)

Konstam, R.A., 2003. *Lepanto 1571: The Greatest Naval Battle of the Renaissance*. Oxford: Osprey Publishing (Campaign 114)

Konstam, R.A., 2016. *The Barbary Pirates, 15th–17th Centuries*. Oxford: Osprey Publishing (Elite 213)

Lane, F.C., 1973. *Venice: A Maritime Republic*. Baltimore, MD: Johns Hopkins University Press

Lane, F.C., 1992 [1934]. *Venetian Ships and Shipbuilders of the Renaissance*. Baltimore, MD: Johns Hopkins University Press

Lavery, B., 1987. *The Arming and Fitting of English Ships of War, 1600–1815*. London: Conway Maritime Press

de León, F. G., 2004. 'Spanish military power and the Military Revolution', in G. Mortimer (ed.), *Early Modern Military History, 1450–1815*. New York, NY: Palgrave Macmillan, 25–42

Lesure, M., 1971. *Lépante: la crise de l'empire Ottomane*. Paris: Julliard

Lewis, M.A., 1960. *The Spanish Armada*. London: B.T. Batsford

Lewis, M.A., 1961. *Armada Guns: A Comparative Study of English and Spanish Armaments*. London: Allen & Unwin

Loades, M., 2016. *The Composite Bow*. Oxford: Osprey Publishing (Weapon 43)

Lo Basso, L., 2004. *Uomini da remo. Galee e galeotti del Mediterraneo in età moderna*. Milano: Selene Edizioni

Lowry, H., 2003. *The Nature of the Early Ottoman State*. New York, NY: State University of New York Press

McCrory, D.P., 2014. *No Ordinary Man: the Life and Times of Miguel de Cervantes*. London: Peter Owen Publishers

McKeown, A.N., 2009. *English Mercuries: Soldier Poets in the Age of Shakespeare*. Nashville, TN: Vanderbilt University Press

Mallett, M.E. and Hale, J.R., 2006 [1984]. *The Military Organization of a Renaissance State: Venice c. 1400 to 1617*. Cambridge: Cambridge University Press

Maltby, W.S., 1983. *Alba: A Biography of Fernando Alvarez de Toledo, Third Duke of Alva, 1507–1582*. Cambridge: Cambridge University Press

Manning, M.M., Hawk, A., Calhoun, J.H. and Andersen, R.C., 2009. 'Treatment of war wounds: a historical review'. *Clinical Orthopaedics and Related Research* 467/8: 2168–91

Mantran, R., 1973. 'L'écho de la bataille de Lépante à Constantinople'. *Annales Historie Sciences Sociales* 28/2: 396–405

Marsden, P., 2019. *1545: Who Sank the Mary Rose?* Barnsley: Pen & Sword Books

Marteilhe, J., 1758 (ed. V. McInerney, 2010). *Galley Slave*. Barnsley: Seaford Publishing (Seafarers' Voices 1)

Martin, C.J.M., 1975. *Full Five Fathom: Wrecks of the Spanish Armada*. London: Chatto & Windus

Martin, C.J.M, 1979. '*La Trinidad Valencera*: an Armada invasion transport lost off Donegal Interim site report, 1971–76. *International Journal of Nautical Archaeology* 8/1: 13–38

Martin, C.J.M and Parker, G., 1999 (rev. edn.). *The Spanish Armada*. Manchester: Manchester University Press

Marx, R.F., 1966. *The Battle of Lepanto, 1571*. Cleveland, OH: World Publishing

Matar, N., 2005. *Britain and Barbary, 1589–1689*. Gainesville, FL: University Press of Florida

de Mesa Gallego, E., 2015. 'Gerat Barry: swordsman, military theorist, entrepreneur and servitor of the Spanish monarchy'. *The Irish Sword* 120: 151–6

Mihailovic, K., (trans. B. Stolz, 1975). *Memoirs of a Janissary*. Ann Arbor, MI: University of Michigan Press

Minta, S.M.J., 1998. *On a Voiceless Shore: Byron in Greece*. New York, NY: Henry Holt and Company

Mitchell, N.D., 2009. *The Mystery of the Rosary: Marian Devotion and the Reinvention of Catholicism*. New York, NY: New York University Press

Monchicourt, C., 1913. *L'expédition espagnole de 1560 contre l'île de Djerba (essai bibliographique, récit de l'epédition, documents orignaux)*. Paris: E. Leroux

Morin, M.F., 1975. 'La battaglia di Lepanto: il determinante apporto dell' artiglieria veneziana'. *Diana Armi* 9/1: 54–61

Morin, M.F., 2006. 'Artiglierie navali in ambito veneziano: tipologia e tecniche di realizzazione'. *Quaderni di Oplologia* 23/2: 3–28

Morin, M.F., 2011. 'Morphology and constructive techniques of Venetian artilleries in the 16th and 17th centuries: some notes', in C. Beltrame and R. Gianni Ridella (eds.), *Ships & Guns: the sea ordnance in Venice and Europe between the 15th and the 17th centuries*. Oxford: Oxbow Books, 1–11

Morin, M.F., 2012. *'Le galeazze a Lepanto'. Oltre Lepanto: dallo scontro di ieri all'intesa di oggi*. Milan: Centro Studi Vox Populi di Pergine Valsugana

Morin, M.F., 2014. 'Lepanto: fearlessness was not enough', in *Uluslararası Piri Reis ve Türk Denizcilik Tarihi Sempozyumu* (6 Cilt Takım) Ankara: Türk Tarih Kurumu Yayınları, 251–60

Morrison, J.S., Coates, J.F. and Rankov, N.B., 2000 (2nd edn.). *The Athenian Trireme: the History and Reconstruction of an Ancient Greek Warship*. Cambridge: Cambridge University Press

Morrison, J.S. and Gardiner, R. (eds.), 2000 [1995]. *The Age of the Galley: Mediterranean Oared Vessels since pre-Classical Times*. London: Conway Maritime Press

Munday, J., 1998 [1987]. *Naval Cannon*. Princes Risborough: Shire Publications (Shire Album 186)

Murphy, R., 1999. *Ottoman Warfare, 1500–1700*. London: University College London Press

Muscat, J., 1996. 'The warships of the Order of St John, 1530–1798', in *Proceedings of History Week 1994*, Floriana, Malta: Malta Historical Society, 77–113

Muscat, J., 2002. *Food and Drink on Maltese Galleys*. Pietà, Malta: Publikazzjonijiet Independenza

Muscat, J. and Cuschieri, A., 2002. *Naval Activities of the Knights of St John*. Sta Venera, Malta: Midsea Books

Nicholson, H.J., 2001. *The Knights Hospitaller*. Woodbridge: Boydell & Brewer

Nicolle, D., 1995 [1987]. *The Venetian Empire 1200–1700*. Oxford: Osprey Publishing (Men-at-Arms 210)

Nicolle, D., 1997 [1995]. *The Janissaries*. Oxford: Osprey Publishing (Elite 58)

Nicolle, D., 2009 [2001]. *Knight Hospitaller (2) 1306–1565*. Oxford: Osprey Publishing (Warrior 41)

Nolan, J.S., 1997. *Sir John Norreys and the Elizabethan Military World*. Exeter: University of Exeter Press

Notario López, I. and Notario López, I., 2012. *The Spanish Tercios 1536–1704*. Oxford: Osprey Publishing (Men-at-Arms 481)

Oman, C.W.C., 1885. *The Art of War in the Middle Ages AD 378–1515*. Oxford: B.H. Blackwell

Oman, C.W.C, 1937. *A History of the Art of War in the Sixteenth Century*. London: Methuen & Co.

Özbaran, S., 1978. 'Kapudan Pasha'. *EI²* IV: 571–2

Packard, F.R., 1921. *Life and Times of Ambroise Paré (1510–1590)* . New York, NY: Paul B. Hoeber

Palacio, P.N. (ed.), 1999. *Carolus V Imperator*. Barcelona: Lunwerg

Pálffy, G., 2008. 'Scorched-earth tactics in Ottoman Hungary: on a controversy in military theory and practice on the Habsburg-Ottoman frontier'. *Acta Orientalia Academiae Scientiarum Hungaricae* 61/1–2: 181–200

Palmer, J.A.B., 1953. 'The origins of the Janissaries'. *Bulletin of the John Rylands Library* 35/2: 448–81

Parker, B.K. and Parker, D.F., 2003. *Miguel de Cervantes*. Philadelphia, PA: Chelsea House Publications

Parker, G., 1979. *Spain and the Netherlands, 1559–1659: Ten Studies*. Glasgow: Fontana Collins

Parker, G., 1987 [1984]. *The Thirty Years' War*. London: Routledge & Kegan Paul

Parker, G., 1996A (2nd edn.). *The Military Revolution: Military Innovation and the Rise of the West, 1500–1800*. Cambridge: Cambridge University Press

Parker, G, 1996B. 'The Dreadnought revolution of Tudor England'. *Mariner's Mirror* 82: 269–300

Parker, G., 2000 [1998]. *The Grand Strategy of Philip II*. New Haven, CT: Yale University Press

Parker, G., 2004 (2nd edn.). *The Army of Flanders and the Spanish Road, 1567–1659: the Logistics of Spanish Victory and Defeat in the Low Countries' Wars*. Cambridge: Cambridge University Press

Parker, G., 2019. *Emperor: A New Life of Charles V*. New Haven, CT: Yale University Press

Parker, G. and Thompson, I.A.A., 1978. 'The battle of Lepanto, 1571: the cost of victory'. *The Mariner's Mirror* 64/1: 13–21

Parry, V.J., 1970. 'Materials of war in the Ottoman empire', in M.A. Cook (ed.), *Studies in the Economic History of the Middle East from the Rise of Islam to the Present Day*. Oxford: Oxford University Press, 220–7

Perjés, G. (trans. M.D. Fenyó, 1989). *The Fall of the Medieval Kingdom of Hungary: Mohács 1526 – Buda 1541*. Highland Lakes, NJ: Atlantic Research and Publications

Petrie, C., 1967. *Don John of Austria*. London: Eyre & Spottiswoode

Pezzolo, L., 2006. 'The rise and decline of a great power: Venice 1250–1650'. *Working Paper* 27: 1–32

Predmore, R.L., 1973. *Cervantes*. New York, NY: Dodd, Mead & Company

Prescott, W.H., 1882 (rev. edn.). *History of the Reign of Philip the Second, King of Spain*, 3 vols. Philadelphia, PA: J.B. Lippincott & Co.

Pruitt, B.A., Jr., 2006. 'Combat casualty care and surgical progress'. *Annals of Surgery* 243/6: 715–29

Pryor, J.H., 1988. *Geography, Technology, and War: Studies in the Maritime History of the Mediterranean, 649–1571*. Cambridge: Cambridge University Press

Riemann, M., 2020. '"As Old as War Itself"? Historicizing the universal mercenary'. *Journal of Global Security* 0/0: 1–16

Ridella, R. G., 2014. 'L'evoluzione strutturale nelle artiglierie di bronzo in Italia tra XV e XVII secolo', in C. Beltrame and M. Morin (eds.), *I Cannoni di Venezia. Artiglierie della Serenissima da fortezze e relitti*. Venezia, 13–28

Ridella, R.G., Galili, G., Cvikel, D. and Rosen, B., 2016. 'A late 16th-to early 17th-century European shipwreck carrying Venetian ordnance discovered off the Carmel coast, Israel'. *International Journal of Nautical Archaeology* 45/1: 180–91

Riley-Smith, J.S.C., 1999. *Hospitallers: the History of the Order of St John*. London: Hambledon

Riley-Smith, J.S.C., 2010 [2008]. *Templars and Hospitallers: as Professed Religious in the Holy Land*. Notre Dame IN: University of Notre Dame Press

Riley-Smith, J.S.C., 2012. *The Knights Hospitaller in the Levant, c. 1070–1309*. Basingstoke: Palgrave Macmillan

Roberts, K., 2002. *Matchlock Musketeer, 1588–1688*. Oxford: Osprey Publishing (Warrior 43)

Roberts, K., 2010. *Pike and Shot Tactics, 1590–1660*. Oxford: Osprey Publishing (Elite 179)

Rogers, C. J. (ed.), 1995. *The Military Revolution Debate*. Boulder, CO: Westview Press

Rogers, L., 1937. *Greek and Roman Naval Warfare*. Annapolis, MD: Naval Institute Press

Rossi, E., 1926. *Storia della Marina dell' Ordine di S. Giovanni di Gemsalemme di Rhodie e di Malta*. Roma: Società editrice d'arte illustrata

Royal, R., 2006. *The Pope's Army: 500 Years of the Papal Swiss Guard*. New York, NY: The Crossroads Publishing Company

Salzmann, A., 2013. 'Migrants in chains: on the enslavement of Muslims in Renaissance and Enlightenment Europe'. *Religions* 4: 391–411

Scetti, A., (trans. & ed. L. Monga, 2004). *The Journal of Aurelio Scetti: a Florentine Galley Slave at Lepanto (1565–1577)* . Bingham, NY: State University of New York (Medieval and Renaissance Texts and Studies, vol. 266)

Schmidt, H., 2015. *The Book of the Buckler*. Derby: Wyvern Media

Scordato, R., 2011. 'Two Venetian swivel guns from Messina Strait, Sicily', in C. Beltrame and R. G. Ridella (eds.), *Ships & Guns: the Sea Ordnance in Venice and in Europe between the 15th and the 17th Centuries*. Oxford: Oxbow Books, 28–34

Setton, K.M., 1984. *The Papacy and the Levant (1204–1571). Volume III: the Sixteenth Century to the Reign of Julius III*. Philadelphia, PA: The American Philosophical Society

Setton, K.M., 1986. *The Papacy and the Levant (1204–1571). Volume IV: the Sixteenth Century from Julius III to Pius V*. Philadelphia, PA: The American Philosophical Society

Setton, K.M., 1991. *Venice, Austria, and the Turks in the Seventeenth Century*. Philadelphia, PA: The American Philosophical Society

Shaw, C., 1996 [1993]. *Julius II: the Warrior Pope*. Oxford: Blackwell Publishers

Shostak, E. and Benson, S.E., 2007. *Elizabethan World: Primary Sources*. Detroit, MI: Thomas Gale

Sire, H.J.A., 1994. *The Knights of Malta*. New Haven, CT: Yale University Press

Sliwa, K. (ed.), 1999. *Documentos de Miguel de Cervantes Saavedra*. Pamplona: Ediciones Universidad de Navarra

Slocombe, G., 1935. *Don Juan of Austria, the Victor of Lepanto (1547–1578)*. London: Nicholson & Watson

Soto y Abbach, S.M., Conde de Clonarde, 1851–62. *Historia orgánica de las Armas de Infantería y Caballería españolas desde la creación del ejército permanente hasta el día*, 10 vols. Madrid: Boletin de Jurisprudencia

Spiteri, S.C., 2001. *Fortresses of the Knights*. San Ġwann, Malta: Book Distributors Limited

Stewart, D., 1947. 'The English army surgeon in the sixteenth century'. *Journal of the Royal Army Medical Corps* 88/6: 231–47

Stewart, D., 1949. 'Military surgery in the sixteenth century'. *Journal of the Royal Army Medical Corps* 92/5: 229–37

Sünnetçioğlu, H.E., (MA thesis) 2013. "Audi alteram partem" (*Hear the other side too*): *The meaning of the battle of Lepanto (1571) among late sixteenth-century Ottoman historians*. Budapest: Central European University

Taylor, F.L., 1921. *The Art of War in Italy, 1494–1529*. Cambridge: Cambridge University Press

Tazón, J.E., 2003. *The Life and Times of Thomas Stukeley (c. 1525–78)*. Aldershot: Ashgate Publishing

Testa, C., 2002. *Romegas*. Sta Venera, Malta: Midsea Books

Throckmorton P., Edgerton, H.E. and Yalouris, E., 1973. 'The battle of Lepanto, Search and Survey Mission (Greece) 1971–72'. *The International Journal of Nautical Archaeology and Underwater Exploration*: 2/1: 121–30

Torranin, C., Smith, D.P. and Byrd, R.J., 1979. 'The effect of acute thermal dehydration and rapid rehydration on isometric and isotonic endurance'. *The Journal of Sports Medicine and Physical Fitness* 19: 1–9

Tracy, L. and DeVries, K. (eds.), 2015. *Wounds and Wound Repair in Medieval Culture*. Leiden: E.J. Brill (Explorations in Medieval Culture 1)

Twombly, C., Howard, R. and Varnedoe, K., 2002. *Lepanto: a painting in twelve parts*. New York, NY: Gagosian Gallery

Upton-Ward, J. (ed.), 2008. *The Military Orders, Volume 4: On Land and by Sea*. Aldershot: Ashgate Publishing

Uyar, M. and Erickson, E.J., 2009. *A Military History of the Ottomans: from Osman to Atatürk*. Santa Barbara, CA: ABC-CLIO

Vargas-Hidalgo, R., 2002. *Guerra y diplomacia en el Mediterráneo: Correpondencia inédita de Felipe II con Andrea Doria y Juan Andrea Doria*. Madrid: Ediciones Polifemo

Veinstein, G., 2013. 'On the Ottoman janissaries (fourteenth-nineteenth centuries)', in E-J. Zürcher (ed.), *Fighting for a Living: a Comparative History of Military Labour 1500–2000*. Amsterdam: Amsterdam University Press, 115–34 (Work Around the Globe, vol. I)

Warner, M., 1976. *Alone of All Her Sex: the Myth and Cult of the Virgin Mary*. New York, NY: Knopf

Warner, O., 1972 [1963]. *Great Sea Battles*. London: Spring Books

Webb, H.J., 1944. 'English military surgery during the age of Elizabeth'. *Bulletin of the History of Medicine* 15: 261–75

Weiss, G., 2011. *Captives and Corsairs: France and Slavery in the Early Modern Mediterranean*. Stanford, CA: Stanford University Press

Weiss, G., 2011. 'Infidels at the oar: a Mediterranean exception to France's free soil principle'. *Slavery & Abolition* 32/3: 397–412

Weiss, G., 2014. 'Ransoming "Turks" from France's royal galleys'. *African Economic History* 42: 37–57

Wheat, D., 2010. 'Mediterranean slavery, New World transformations: galley slaves in the Spanish Caribbean, 1578–1635'. *Slavery & Abolition* 31/3: 327–44

White, L., 2002. 'The experience of Spain's early modern soldiers: combat, welfare and violence'. *War in History* 9/1: 1–38

Wiel, A., 1910. *The Navy of Venice*. London: John Murray

Williams, P., 'The strategy of galley warfare in the Mediterranean (1560–1620)', in D. Maffi y E. García (eds.), *Guerra y Sociedad Política, strategia y cultura en la Europa moderna (1500–1700)*, 2 vols. Madrid: Laberinto, 891–920

Williams, P., 2015 [2014]. *Empire and Holy War in the Mediterranean: the Galley and Maritime Conflict between the Habsburgs and Ottomans*. London: Bloomsbury Academic

Wilson, P.H., 2009. *Europe's Tragedy: A History of the Thirty Years War*. London: Allen Lane

Wismayer, J.M., 1997. *The Fleet of the Order of St John, 1530–1798*. Sta Venera, Malta: Midsea Books

Woodhouse, C.M., 1965. *The Battle of Navarino*. London: Hodder & Stoughton

Wright, E.R., 2016. *The Epic of Juan Latino: Dilemmas of Race and Religion in Renaissance Spain*. Toronto: University of Toronto Press

Wright, E.R., Spence, S. and Lemons A. (trans. & ed.), 2014. *The Battle of Lepanto*. Cambridge, MA: Harvard University Press (The I Tatti Renaissance Library 61)

Yeo, M., 1934. *Don John of Austria*. New York, NY: Sheed & Ward

Yıldırım, O., 2007. 'The battle of Lepanto and its impact on Ottoman history and historiography'. *Mediterraneo in armi (secc. XV-XVIII) (Supplement of the Journal Mediterranea)* 2: 533–56

Yilmaz, G., 2017. 'Change in manpower in the early modern janissary army and its impact on the *devshirme* system'. *Rivista di Studi Militari* 6: 181–8

Zysberg, A., 1984. 'Galley and hard labor convicts in France (1550–1850). From galleys to hard labor camps: essay on a long lasting penal institution', in P.C. Spierenburg (ed.), *The Emergence of Carceral Institutions: Prisons, Galleys, and Lunatic Asylums, 1550–1900.* Rotterdam: Erasmus Universiteit (Centrum voor Maatschappijgeschiedenis, vol. 12)

Zysberg, A., 1987. *Les Galériens du roi – vies et destines de 60,000 forçats sur les galères de France: 1680–1748.* Paris: Seuil – l'Univers historique

# Index

Cabrera de Córdoba, Luis, Spanish
    historian, 14
Caetani, Onorato, duca di Sermoneta,
    *capitán generale delle fanterie pontifcie*,
    261, 294
*caïque*, 198, 385 n.4
Calabria/Calabrian(s), 25, 113, 143–5,
    262, 305
Çaldıran, battle of (23 August 1514), 168
Callistus III, pope (r. 1455–8), 121
Campaldino, battle of (11 June 1289), 371
    n.8
Campion, Edmund (Saint), English
    Catholic martyr, 341
Canal, Antonio, Venetian *provveditore*, 313
Canal, Cristoforo, Venetian naval
    commander, 203
Canning, George, British foreign
    secretary (in office 1822–7), 352
Capo d'Orso, naval battle of (28 May
    1528), 201, 228
Carafa, Antonio, duca di Rocca
    Mondragone, 261
Cárdenas, Don Bernardino de, 295
Cardona, Giovanni Antonio de, 271, 281,
    290, 298
Carpio, Bernardo del, legendary hero of
    Asturias, xxiii, 354 n.7
Carlos III of Spain (r. 1759-88), 360 n.5,
    369 n.11
Carlos, Don (Carlos de Austria), 75, 368
    n.2
carrack(s), 176, 374 n.25
    *Sant' Anna* (Hospitaller), 114, 374 n.28
Casimir, Johann, von Pfalz-Simmern, 81,
    370 n.17
Cassière, Jean l'Evesque de la, grand
    master of the Hospitallers (r. 1572–81),
    374–5 n.35
Castlereagh, Viscount, British foreign
    secretary (in office 1812–22), 351–2,
    396 n.23
Castiglione, Baldassare, 122
Cervantes Saavedra, Miguel de, *passim*
    and
    captive in Algiers, xiii, 11, 15, 18–21,
        23, 145, 147, 239, 358 n.42

his death and (re)burial, 22–3
flees Spain, 8–9
soldier at Lepanto, ix, 10–11, 13–16,
    82
suffers PTSD, 19–22
his works,
    *Don Quixote* (1605, 1615), *passim* and
        *La historia del cautivo*, 20–1, 326,
        332, 378 n.20
    *El trato de Argel* (1582), 20–1, 85,
        326, 358 n.42
    *La Galatea* (1585), 17, 21, 357 n.10
    *Los baños de Argel* (1615), 20–1
    *Los trabajos de Persiles y Sigismunda*
        (1617), 8, 21
    *Novelas ejemplares* (1613), 22–3,
        368–9 n.6
        *El amante liberal*, 8
        *El coloquio de los perros*, 8–9
        *La gitanilla*, 8
    *Viaje del Parnaso* (1614), 4, 16, 76,
        368–9 n.6
his wounds, ix, 11, 15–16, 23
Cervantes, Rodrigo de, father of
    Cervantes, 7
Cervantes, Rodrigo de, brother of
    Cervantes, 17, 18, 261, 363 n.20
Charles V, king of Spain (r. 1516–56),
    Holy Roman Emperor (r. 1519–56,
    †1558), xi, 4, 30, 32, 49, 56, 60, 67, 75,
    89, 105, 227, 243, 304, 357 n.12, 358
    n.29, 360–1 n.8
his abdication, 39
his empire, 35–7, 68, 360 n.4
suffers gout, 39, 41, 361 n.10
and Tunis campaign (1535), 36–8, 114,
    229, 330, 332, 361 n.9, 363 n.16
Charles VII of France, 225
Charles VIII of France (r. 1483–98),
    335–7, 363 n.16
Charles IX of France (r. 1560–74), ix,
    135, 240, 306, 377 n.4
Charles *Téméraire*, duc de Bourgogne
    (r. 1467–77), 70, 360 n.3, 376–7 n.15
Chesterton, G.K. (Gilbert Keith), 134,
    135, 309
    'Lepanto', x, 44–5, 56